ANDREA SACCHI

I. *The Annunciation to Zacharias*. 1641–9. Rome, Lateran Palace. (Cat. No. 54)

ANN SUTHERLAND HARRIS

Andrea Sacchi

Complete edition of the paintings
with a critical catalogue

PRINCETON UNIVERSITY PRESS
PRINCETON, NEW JERSEY

Publication of this book has been aided by a grant from

 The Millard Meiss Publication Fund
of the College Art Association of America

Princeton University Press
Princeton, New Jersey

© 1977 by Phaidon Press Limited, Oxford

ISBN 0–691–03117–7
LCC 77–6101

Printed in Great Britain
Text printed by Western Printing Services Ltd, Bristol
Monochrome plates printed by The Cavendish Press Ltd, Leicester
Colour plates printed by Well Hall Press, Kent

CONTENTS

ACKNOWLEDGEMENTS   vii

PREFACE   ix

INTRODUCTION

  I. Andrea Sacchi's Career and Artistic Development   1

    Early Career and the Patronage of Cardinal del Monte   1

    Early Maturity and the 'Divina Sapienza' Ceiling: 1627–1631   5

    Barberini Patronage and the Journey to North Italy: 1631–1635   13

    *Major Commissions from 1635 to 1640 and Minor Commissions
of the 1630s*   17

    The Decoration of S. Giovanni in Fonte: 1639–1649   19

    Sacchi's Last Works: 1649–1655   22

  II. Andrea Sacchi and his Contemporaries   26

    Sacchi, Bernini and Duquesnoy   30

    Sacchi, Cortona and the Academy of St. Luke   33

  Notes   38

CATALOGUE

  Autograph Works   49

  Lost Works   104

  Rejected Attributions   108

APPENDIXES

  Preface   113

  Appendix I: *Transcript of Sacchi's Will and Codicils*   115

  Appendix II: *Transcript of the Inventory of Contents of Sacchi's
House in June 1661*   119

  Appendix III: *Transcript of the List of Books from the Inventory*   123

  Index of Names and Places in the Will, Codicils and
Inventory   126

BIBLIOGRAPHY   129

SOURCES OF PHOTOGRAPHS   134

PLATES   135

INDEX   257

To my parents

ACKNOWLEDGEMENTS

This book began as a doctoral dissertation presented to the Courtauld Institute of the University of London in January, 1965. Professor Sir Anthony Blunt directed my research. He caught many errors, helped to solve many problems, took endless pains to insure that the material was presented as clearly as possible and was generous with his time and his ideas. My greatest debt is to him. Michael Kitson, who first aroused my interest in Italian seventeenth-century painting, and Ellis K. Waterhouse, who in a brief conversation at the beginning of my researches dropped all the hints that led to the discovery of the documents published here, also deserve special thanks. Marchese Giovanni Incisa della Rocchetta, whose article of 1924 was the most important contribution to the subject apart from Posse's book, has shown sympathetic and helpful interest in the progress of this new study. I am also much indebted to Mrs Marilyn Aronberg Lavin for access to her unpublished material in seventeenth-century Barberini archives, and to Dr Frances Vivian for the use of her unpublished research on all later Barberini archive material. When references are made to Barberini archive material (principally inventories) without any reference to a publication, it can be assumed that the material came from Mrs Lavin or Dr Vivian. As a graduate student I was assisted by a three-year State Studentship and by grants for travel and photographs from the Central Research Fund of the University of London. Subsequent study trips were aided by three grants from the Council for Research in the Humanities of Columbia University; to all these institutions I am extremely grateful.

With one exception, all private owners of works by Sacchi have been not only helpful but extremely hospitable. The staffs of the various museums, print rooms, libraries, photographic collections and archives that I used often went to considerable lengths to assist me. Many colleagues passed on tips and were of practical assistance. Though I hope that all ideas and suggestions have been properly noted in the text, the following deserve special mention: Roseline Bacou, Jacob Bean, Ilaria Toesca Bertelli, Evelina Borea, Gino Corti, Italo Faldi, Hellmuth Hager, Howard Hibbard, Myron Laskin, Denis Mahon, Donald Posner, Philip Pouncey, Eckhard Schaar, Walter Vichi, the late Walter Vitzthum and the late Rudolf Wittkower. My publishers have patiently accepted a stream of additions, subtractions and corrections to the original manuscript completed in December 1970. My aunt, Marjorie M. Sutherland, not only supervised the typing of the dissertation. She also helped with the preparation of the final manuscript. Her conscientious checking caught many errors and was invaluable towards the end, when my patience began to give out.

In addition to the grant from The Millard Meiss Publication Fund of the College Art Association of America, acknowledged on the reverse of the title-page, I also wish to acknowledge gratefully a further grant from The Dr M. Aylwin Cotton Foundation.

A.S.H.

New York, November, 1972

Marilyn Aronberg Lavin's researches and findings have now been published in her book, *Seventeenth-Century Barberini Documents and Inventories of Art*, New York (New York University Press), 1975.

I am very grateful to Dr I. Grafe for pointing out a number of errors and suggesting some welcome improvements to the text, both at manuscript and at proof stage.

New York, January, 1977

PREFACE

This book is the first complete study of Andrea Sacchi since Hans Posse's monograph on the artist appeared in 1925. Much new material has emerged since then. The single most important discovery was the life of Sacchi by G. P. Bellori, published by Piacentini in 1942 from the manuscript in Rouen. Bellori records works not mentioned in any other *seicento* source, some of which it has been possible to trace; he also had access to personal information about the artist through Carlo Maratta, Sacchi's pupil and close friend. Though not totally reliable, Bellori's *vita* of Sacchi is far more informative than either of the biographies known to Posse, namely those of Passeri and Pascoli. Its discovery alone would have justified a new book on the artist.

Posse did not have the benefit of Pollak's extensive publication of documents for the art patronage of the Barberini, which appeared in 1928 and 1931, nor of Jacob Hess' scholarly edition of the lives of G. B. Passeri. Other documents establishing Sacchi's place of residence in the late 1620s and early 1630s and then from the mid-1640s until the artist's death in 1661 were published by Hoogewerff in 1947, along with the artist's death certificate. To his documents I add here the artist's will and the inventory made of his household possessions at the time of his death.

Twenty-six paintings, two prints and three architectural projects have been added to Sacchi's oeuvre since 1925, some of these additions being attributions advanced here for the first time. Five of Posse's attributions have been rejected, as have a number of other attributions made in publications subsequent to Posse's monograph. Posse knew a small number of drawings by Sacchi, but not all of his attributions are acceptable today, for in this field our knowledge of Sacchi has been enormously expanded in the last ten years. To the over eighty autograph drawings published by Blunt and Cooke in 1960 I added over a hundred in the Kunstmuseum, Düsseldorf, in 1967. A few more new drawings in other collections related to known works are published here in the catalogue. Other drawings not related to known works have been published in my article, 'Drawings by Andrea Sacchi: Additions and Problems', *Master Drawings*, Vol. 9, no. 4, 1971, pp. 384–91.

All this new material concerning Sacchi, and the burgeoning researches into Roman *seicento* art in general, inevitably render Posse's monograph out of date. His book remains nevertheless a sound introduction because Posse was a careful scholar and much of his essay depends on documented material. I have not attempted to incorporate all of his observations about particular works into my introductory essay or into the catalogue entries because I think that his book deserves to be and will still be read. In particular I have given little space to Sacchi as a court artist; Posse and Incisa della Rocchetta, followed more recently by Haskell, provide the reader with a much fuller picture of the Barberini court and of Sacchi's role in it than I have given here. I have preferred to concentrate on those areas most affected by the new evidence, namely the development of Sacchi's career, his relations with contemporaries such as Pietro da Cortona, Gian Lorenzo Bernini, Nicolas Poussin and Francesco Duquesnoy, and, to a lesser extent, the iconography of his paintings and prints. There is room for further research into these and other aspects of his career, in particular his architecture, but I plan to leave this field to others. Nothing would please me more than to learn that this book has provoked others to reconsider Sacchi's personality and achievements.

INTRODUCTION

I. Andrea Sacchi's Career and Artistic Development

Early Career and the Patronage of Cardinal del Monte

The early formation of Andrea Sacchi's artistic personality cannot be studied in detail. Only five original paintings and a handful of drawings made before 1627 have come down to us; documentary evidence before this date is also slight. His two chief biographers, G. P. Bellori and G. B. Passeri, record another five works painted in these years including one major commission, the decoration of the Casino of Cardinal del Monte, none of which survive. An additional handicap is the unreliability of these writers' accounts of Sacchi's origins and training. Both writers were misinformed on a number of points. Information in their accounts for which no corroborating evidence is available must therefore be used with caution.

Sacchi's father was not Benedetto Sacchi, as both Bellori and Passeri state, but a certain Nicola Pellegrini from Fermo. Benedetto was probably Andrea's first teacher, however, and may have adopted his young apprentice. The question of Sacchi's paternity raises another issue, namely his place of birth. Although always called 'romano' in seventeenth-century documents and sources, it has been accepted since Bottari proposed the idea in his notes to the 1772 edition of Passeri's *Vite* that Sacchi was born in Nettuno, a small town on the coast south of Rome. The existence of an early altarpiece in S. Francesco in Nettuno (Plate 5) was the only evidence cited by Bottari, though Brovelli-Soffredini claimed to have more. If Sacchi was not born in Rome, he was probably born in his father's home town, Fermo. That he was born around 1599/1600 is not in doubt. Since he was clearly living in Rome from an early age and received much of his training there, the issue of his actual birth place seems academic.[1]

What influence, if any, Benedetto Sacchi had on Sacchi's early style we do not know. Both Bellori and Passeri dismiss Benedetto as a man of mediocre talents who was soon outdistanced by his pupil. According to Passeri, Benedetto realized this and sent Andrea to study with Francesco Albani, who taught him to paint. Bellori provides a different and fuller account of Sacchi's training. Having been sent by Benedetto to study with Cesare d'Arpino, Sacchi spent his time instead drawing the house façades of Polidoro da Caravaggio, the frescoes of Raphael and classical statuary. Sacchi looked at the work of his new teacher as well, however, for Cesare's influence is detectable in the St. Isidore altarpiece and in some later works as well.

When Sacchi was ten, he won a prize at the Academy of St. Luke with a drawing of Adam and Eve.[2] Shortly after this event, Bellori reports that Cardinal Francesco Maria del Monte, happening to see Sacchi drawing, decided that this promising young artist deserved support and took him into his household, thus permitting him to pursue his studies undistracted by practical problems. Sacchi meanwhile had been attracted by the work of the Carracci and decided to introduce himself to Annibale's pupil and follower, Francesco Albani. Albani was delighted, says Bellori, to have such a talented student and encouraged Andrea to study works by the Carracci and their studio, such as the Herrera Chapel in S. Giacomo degli Spagnuoli and the Gallery in the Palazzo Farnese. Bellori agrees with Passeri that it was Albani who first encouraged Sacchi to start painting. This careful apprenticeship soon qualified him to undertake his first public commissions. Both Bellori and Passeri emphasize that these were given to him by Cardinal del Monte.

The stylistic evidence of Sacchi's early works belies Bellori's emphasis on those stylistic sources and models of which he particularly approved—Raphael, Polidoro, the Carracci and their school and classical antiquity. Bellori and Passeri also omit all reference to a trip to Bologna by Sacchi during his apprenticeship, most probably in or after 1618 when Albani returned to Bologna from Rome.[3] It is Malvasia who states that Sacchi, during his visit to Bologna in the mid-1630s, remarked that he wished he had studied the works of Francesco Brizio in Bologna when he was there earlier as a student of Albani.[4] The statement indicates that part of Sacchi's apprenticeship with Albani took place in Bologna. Malvasia's authority for this statement may have been Albani, who died in 1660 only a year before Sacchi and who was in contact with both Malvasia and Sacchi during his last years.[5] Although it is tempting to dismiss Malvasia's statement as yet another manifestation of his well-known *campanilismo*, borrowings in Sacchi's work of the 1620s and early 1630s of both a specific and a general kind from Bolognese works bear out Malvasia. It is odd that Bellori at least did not report this early trip to Bologna. Perhaps he knew about it but suppressed the information, preferring to stress the Roman sources of Sacchi's art. Perhaps Sacchi himself attached less import-ance in later life to his early Bolognese experiences than to his Roman training and later journey to Lombardy and Venice, and therefore failed to tell Maratta about it.

With the possible exception of the fresco overdoor in the convent attached to S. Giuseppe a Capo le Case, all of Sacchi's recorded works before 1627 were paid for by Cardinal Francesco Maria del Monte. Quite apart from the advantages of such steady patronage, Sacchi's contacts with the Cardinal gave him certain opportunities.[6] Sacchi must have met the other artists patronized by Cardinal del Monte in the 1620s, namely Simon Vouet, Antiveduto Grammatica and Filippo d'Angeli. Sacchi could also have studied the Cardinal's art collection, which contained besides the well-known group of early paintings by Caravaggio, pictures by Agostino and Annibale Carracci, Guido Reni, Caracciolo, Scipione Pulzone, Giovanni Baglione, Ribera, Guercino, Saraceni, Alessandro Turchi, Girolamo Muziano and Cesare d'Arpino as well as works attributed to older masters such as Dürer, Leonardo, Raphael, Michelangelo, Andrea del Sarto, Titian and Bassano.[7] Other artists whom Cardinal del Monte is known to have patronized were not represented in his collection, for example Ludovico Cigoli, but Sacchi, who admired Cigoli, may nevertheless have been introduced to his work by the Cardinal.[8] Vouet's influence can also be traced in several of Sacchi's early altarpieces and portraits. Caravaggio did not leave his mark on Sacchi's work in any obvious formal sense, but Sacchi perhaps learned to appreciate Caravaggio's power to communicate psychological states of feeling to a wide audience. Sacchi's active participation in the affairs of the Academy of St. Luke in the early 1620s can also probably be attributed to del Monte, who had been the official protector of the Academy since the late 1590s.[9] There Sacchi must by 1628 have met— if he did not already know them—artists as varied in outlook as Vouet, Pietro da Cortona, Ottavio Leoni, Agostino Ciampelli, Alessandro Algardi, Gian Lorenzo Bernini, Giovanni Baglione, Antonio Tempesta, Nicolas Poussin, Lanfranco and Jacques Stella.[10]

The Nettuno altarpiece (Plate 5) may be Sacchi's earliest surviving work, but the documentary evidence for a date before 1623 is firmer for *The Vision of St. Isidore* (Plate 4). Despite obvious imma-turities, it is an impressive picture. Posse emphasized its Bolognese sources—Ludovico Carracci for the pose and earthy peasant type of the saint, Giacomo Cavedone for the colour and Francesco Albani for the poses and types of the Virgin, Child and attendant angels. Ludovico's St. Roch in S. Giacomo Maggiore in Bologna is indeed close in pose and type to St. Isidore; the relationship of both saints to their picture format is also close. Cavedone's fondness for reds and blues, for example in his *Madonna of Sts. Petronius and Alò* of 1614 (Pinacoteca, Bologna), recalls Sacchi's colour scheme in the *St. Isidore*. Sacchi may equally well have been inspired by the saturated primaries in Titian's

Bacchanals, by Barocci's rich palette or even by the bright tones preferred by Florentine *seicento* painters. Albani was certainly the source for the angels above St. Isidore, who come straight from his frescoed apse in S. Maria della Pace,[11] but the Madonna is a Cesare d'Arpino type.[12] The compositional framework with the air-borne Madonna and the earth-bound saint arranged on a surface diagonal was well established by 1620.[13] Lanfranco had also used it for his first public commission, *The Virgin with St. Joseph appearing to St. Teresa,* which was then in the nearby church of S. Giuseppe a Capo le Case, where Sacchi also painted one of his first commissions. The chalky lapis-lazuli blue of the Virgin's robe and the warm crimson of St. Isidore's tunic are colours that appear in all of Sacchi's oil paintings of the 1620s. Indeed the colour and the simple composition, which stresses the deeply felt spiritual contact between the protagonists, are the most personal aspects of the *St. Isidore* and already mark it as a characteristic work by Sacchi.

The Nettuno picture is a less impressive work than the *St. Isidore* but it is a valuable source of information about Sacchi's early years. The damaged upper half derives from the Carracci school picture of the same subject in S. Onofrio in Rome. The lower half depends on Raphael's *St. Cecilia* altarpiece in Bologna.[14] Sacchi evidently found it difficult to relate the Virgin seated on the Holy House in the sky to the standing figures of the four saints below and to accommodate the four saints in poses that were not repetitive.[15] The doll-like Virgin is too small. The saints lack the forceful individual characterization of male figures in Sacchi's later work. A date after 1623 is indicated if Cardinal del Monte was the patron, as seems likely, although the awkwardness of the design when compared with the *St. Isidore* may suggest that the former preceded the latter. Perhaps the *St. Isidore* is a more successful composition because Sacchi did not have to cope with as many figures as in the Nettuno picture.

Sacchi's public reputation was established in 1626 by *The Miracle of St. Gregory the Great* (Plate 8), which he painted for St. Peter's, his most prestigious commission to date. Bellori tells an odd story about the awarding of this commission to Sacchi. He says that Cardinal del Monte's enthusiasm for the young Sacchi was such that in 1620 he obtained for him the commission to paint *The Burial of St. Petronilla,* one of the largest altarpieces in St. Peter's, a commission subsequently carried out by Guercino. Sacchi turned down the commission, saying that he was not yet ready for such a task. Cardinal del Monte therefore obtained for Sacchi instead the commission for one of the small altarpieces, the *St. Gregory,* but even this more modest challenge Sacchi did not attempt for another six years. As is known from published documents, Guercino finished the *St. Petronilla* in 1623, Sacchi the *St. Gregory* three years later.[16] Bellori rarely reports gossip and the gist of this story may be true. On the other hand, Bellori may simply be reporting a garbled version of the story of the unfinished *Pasce Oves Meas* fresco, which was to occupy the space to the left of Guercino's huge oil painting. At face value the story illustrates both Cardinal del Monte's tremendous faith in Sacchi and that lack of self-confidence which was eventually to prove such a handicap to the artist.

The Miracle of St. Gregory the Great is an ambitious work, which Passeri justly singles out for special praise. Two composition studies in Windsor and Paris record the evolution of the composition from a roughly symmetrical design with the saint at the altar in the centre turning awkwardly to face the pilgrims behind him to an asymmetrical design that allows us to see the facial expressions of both St. Gregory and those witnessing the miracle. In addition Sacchi has skilfully related the architectural setting in the picture to the picture's position in the church. The altar for which the *St. Gregory* was designed is situated in the central body of St. Peter's behind the main piers of the crossing. Standing in front of the *St. Gregory,* the spectator is dimly aware of the vast transept to his right. It is just such an interior that Sacchi has shown in the painting, although the architecture differs in detail from that in St. Peter's. The position of the altar in St. Peter's means that the visitor approaches the picture either from the right or from the front but not from the left. The viewpoint of the setting in the painting takes these approaches into account. This careful planning gives the picture an organic unity with its setting which is stressed when a priest says Mass at the altar to a small crowd of pilgrims, repeating the scene in the painting.

Titian's *Pesaro Madonna* in S. Maria dei Frari in Venice is the ultimate source of all subsequent *sacra conversazione* altarpieces with asymmetrical figure arrangements and large architectural elements set at an angle to the picture surface and cut off by the frame, hinting at even greater architectural spaces outside the picture's boundaries. Derivations from Titian's famous altarpiece by Annibale and Ludovico Carracci also show the setting as a kind of open portico.[17] A closed architectural setting of this type is less common, but Rubens, inspired by Giovanni Balducci, used such a background for *The Miracles of St. Ignatius of Loyola* in 1620.[18] Simon Vouet, who may have seen Rubens' altarpiece when he visited Genoa in 1621, used a similar arrangement in his *Circumcision* altarpiece, painted in Rome in 1622 for S. Arcangelo a Segno in Naples.[19] Sacchi's and Vouet's connection through their mutual patron, Cardinal del Monte, would ensure that Sacchi knew Vouet's picture even if it was not displayed in public before being sent south.

Posse stressed the importance of Barocci as a source for the saturated colours, the exquisite rendering of special fabrics and varied textures and the *sfumato* treatment of atmospheric space in the *St. Gregory*.[20] Barocci's drapery forms are also recalled by the blue robes of the man in the left foreground. The subject inevitably recalls Raphael's *Mass of Bolsena*, but there are no direct quotations from that fresco although, as Posse noted, Sacchi understood and repeated in essence Raphael's presentation of the psychological reactions to such an event, contrasting the calm of the believers with the amazement of the converts. Sacchi now disposes his figure masses with greater skill than in his previous works, stressing major figures and subordinating accessory figures. He had clearly been studying Lanfranco's works to good effect, but, as with Raphael, the lesson has been absorbed and no direct quotations from Lanfranco's paintings are evident. Sacchi's own style is emerging, a style distinguished from that of his contemporaries by greater realism and greater subtlety in the portrayal of human emotions. His later work will display greater depth of characterization and more sophisticated compositions and colour schemes but few of them can rival the freshness, the colour orchestration and the emotional impact of this early masterpiece.[21]

The most important of the lost works from Sacchi's early period was in the Casino that he decorated for Cardinal del Monte (Cat. no. 11). Bellori's long and careful description and a few drawings in the British Museum (Plate 10) provide us with some idea of the appearance of Sacchi's work. The central scene of Annibale's Farnese Gallery was the source for Sacchi's lost *Bacchanal* fresco;[22] whether the layout of Annibale's complex ceiling was also adapted by Sacchi to the smaller garden house of del Monte cannot be determined from Bellori's text. Sacchi did use reclining *ignudi*, who were shown supporting the vaults, but they could have been inspired by many other earlier ceiling decorations. Bellori's description does suggest that Sacchi's scheme was a simple one, closer probably to Albani's ceiling in the Palazzo Verospi than to Annibale's Gallery. Albani's *Allegory of the Four Seasons* on the Palazzo Verospi ceiling was used by Sacchi as the basis of his fresco of this subject at Castelfusano (Plate 15). The same subject appeared in the Casino; perhaps Albani was again the source. Unlike the Gallery at Castelfusano, where Sacchi worked within a scheme provided by Pietro da Cortona, the Casino was his own project and so would have reflected far more of his artistic personality than do his few small, damaged scenes in the Sacchetti villa. The mythological subjects that Bellori records in the Casino were more likely to reflect the impact of Titian's Aldobrandini *Bacchanals* than the religious paintings that have survived from this early period. It must be admitted however that there are no quotations from Titian in the Castelfusano frescoes by Sacchi, and indeed no quotations from the *Bacchanals* at all until the *Divina Sapienza* of 1629–31.

Sacchi's contribution to Cortona's Gallery at Castelfusano has been carefully analysed and discussed by Incisa della Rocchetta, Briganti and Vitzthum. It is significant that at this point in their careers Sacchi and Cortona could work together, Sacchi being given the central and some of the adjacent scenes to execute, with preliminary working sketches provided by Cortona. In the case of the *Sacrifice to Pan* (Plate 19), for which Cortona's sketch survives, Sacchi reworked the suggested composition radically. He modified and clarified it further in the early 1630s in an easel painting of the same subject, the design of which is now known only from an engraving (Plate 18) and a preparatory composition study (Plate 16). Possibly, as with the Casino, Sacchi had to work faster than he wished and carried out the easel painting partly in order to perfect the design. It was the first of his compositions to be copied and imitated—by Castiglione,[23] by Filippo Lauri[24] and perhaps by Duquesnoy.[25] Sacchi's source in turn may have been the fresco in the Palazzo Fava in Bologna showing *The Sacrifice of Aeneas*, attributed by Ottani to Ludovico and Agostino Carracci.[26]

Early Maturity and the 'Divina Sapienza' Ceiling: 1627–1631

When Cardinal del Monte died in late August, 1626, Sacchi's career had been successfully launched and he was recognized as one of the most promising new young painters in Rome. He was the first of his generation to be given the chance to paint an altarpiece in St. Peter's and his talents were on display in several other churches. He received no major commissions from the Barberini family, however, before 1629,[27] and until 1633, when Cardinal Antonio Barberini began to patronize him regularly, he had to depend on commissions from other members of the Barberini family and their immediate circle.[28] His only recorded patron outside this privileged group of papal favourites was the diamond merchant Valguarnera, who ended his strange career trading stolen jewels for works by Sacchi, Poussin, Guido Reni and others.[29]

Sacchi's work to date has shown early independence from the styles of his known teachers, Cesare d'Arpino and Albani, and from the styles of the two Carracci pupils, Domenichino and Lanfranco, whose rivalries and divergent styles constitute an important part of artistic developments in Rome in the second decade of the century.[30] We have noted Sacchi borrowing from Albani on several occasions. Apart from the head of the *St. Isidore* Madonna, Cesare's influence is hardly detectable. There is not a trace of his crisp, linear rhythms or elegant *maniera* in Sacchi's surviving work of any date. Only the delicacy of some of Sacchi's early red chalk composition studies suggests a technical, if not a formal, debt to Cesare. Lanfranco's impact is not fully felt by Sacchi until the late 1620s and early 1630s. Guido Reni and Guercino have no effect on Sacchi's early work.

Although Sacchi certainly studied Raphael[31] and Annibale Carracci during his early career, in general classical influences such as Raphael, Annibale, Domenichino and ancient sculpture are more evident in his work after 1640. Before 1630 it was Barocci, Cigoli, Ludovico Carracci and Titian who had the greatest impact on Sacchi's work. Bellori's portrait of the young Sacchi as a dutiful follower of the ideals of the classical school was the result of wishful thinking rather than of objective analysis of the works themselves. Nevertheless later writers tend to follow Bellori and Passeri in emphasizing Sacchi's apprenticeship with Albani above all other factors in the formation of his artistic personality. His style in 1626 is an idiosyncratic blend of motifs and ideas taken from a wide variety of sources, both Roman and Bolognese, and suggests no well-defined theoretical position but shows more instinctive sympathy for *colore* than for *disegno*. With the exception of the Nettuno picture, Sacchi prefers asymmetrical to symmetrical compositions. With the exception of the Berninesque *St. Francis and St. Anthony* (Plate 6), he prefers strong, rich colours and a medium-light palette. All of his work displays a high degree of interest in human reactions to an event, an interest that may have found encouragement, if not formal assistance, in the work of Barocci, Raphael, Caravaggio, Domenichino, Poussin, Guercino and Titian.

The importance to Sacchi of the *affetti*—the range of human emotions experienced by the participants in the subjects that he painted—is one of two important differences between his artistic persona and that of Cortona. The other is the speed and ease with which Cortona produced his work compared with the slower, more deliberate working methods of Sacchi.[32] Cortona's facial expressions are bland, his gestures trite and conventional whereas Sacchi's are always carefully observed and subtly differentiated. Although their different rates of production will be more apparent later, Cortona still produced a far greater body of work than did Sacchi even in the 1620s. To what extent either artist was aware in 1628, when they worked together at Castelfusano, of the directions in which their fundamentally different talents would take them, we cannot tell.[33]

In the 1620s the Roman art world watched conflicts that had been brewing during the previous decade between Lanfranco and Domenichino break out into the open. Lanfranco's work was better received by his contemporaries than that of Domenichino, most of whose public commissions between 1615 and 1625 were not executed for Roman patrons. There is evidence for this not only in the reactions to Lanfranco's Buongiovanni chapel in S. Agostino reported by Passeri, but also in the impact that Lanfranco had on Roman painting in the 1620s and early 1630s before his departure for Naples in 1634. Even Domenichino tried to modify his style to accommodate the more dynamic character of Lanfranco's work. Sacchi, Vouet and Poussin all show far more interest in Lanfranco than in Domenichino in the 1620s. Cortona, perhaps because of his Tuscan origins, was less affected, preferring Polidoro's house façades and Roman battle sarcophagi to the work of his contemporaries.[34] To what extent the disputes between Lanfranco and Domenichino were seen not merely as personal rivalry between two gifted but very different artists but also as an ideological battle between supporters of *colore* and *disegno* is less clear. The only young artist in Rome in the 1620s who preferred Domenichino to Lanfranco was Camassei.[35] Pietro Testa, who quarrelled with Cortona and moved to Domenichino's studio before getting caught up in Cassiano dal Pozzo's entourage, makes little use of Domenichino in his early etchings,[36] and significantly the works from which he does borrow are those of Domenichino's 'classical' period of 1608–14 and not those of his 'false-baroque' phase which followed. In other words, even those artists who would later be counted by Bellori and other writers as admirers of Domenichino's work took little heed of it at this stage, preferring the work of Domenichino's chief rival and also preferring Titian to Raphael. It is worth recalling here that even Bellori admired Lanfranco to some extent; his life of the artist, while short, is appreciative of Lanfranco's special gifts.[37]

The years 1628 to 1635 are the best documented of Sacchi's career. There are major dated works for every year; there are drawings related to most of these works and there are even oil sketches for three of them. A few small, private commissions can on stylistic grounds also be assigned to these years, giving us altogether a good idea of Sacchi's range as an artist as well as of his development during this period. For the years 1628 to 1630–31, however, we have only five variously documented works: the frescoes at Castelfusano (Cat. No. 13), *The Birth of the Virgin* in the Prado (Cat. No. 14), the *Pasce Oves Meas* overdoor for St. Peter's (Cat. No. 15), the *Madonna and Child with Four Saints* in the Old Pharmacy of the Collegio Romano (Cat. No. 16), and the *Divina Sapienza* ceiling (Cat. No. 17). Sacchi never carried out the *Pasce Oves Meas*, although he finished a *modello*, which Bellori admired and which was in the Barberini collections until the eighteenth century. The Castelfusano frescoes are not in good condition. The Collegio Romano fresco is both dirty and damaged by paint loss and crude restoration so that its true character is difficult to judge; the two sketches related to it are necessarily very different from it in tone and handling. There are thus few works in which we can study Sacchi's development during these three crucial years.

The most visible change that takes place in Sacchi's work after 1626/7 occurs in his drawings. Some of his early studies, especially those for the Casino of Cardinal del Monte, are almost excessively refined, but delicacy and a tentative quality characterize all his early drawings. Those made around 1628–30 have a new boldness and vigour (see Plates 22, 25, 32). Sacchi now prefers black to red chalk and works freely on a larger scale than previously. It is not surprising that his drawings of this period have been assigned to both Lanfranco and Bernini, although they are never as schematic and toneless as those of Lanfranco and rarely as bold as those of Bernini.[38] Sacchi must have been familiar with the drawings of both these artists, and at this date there is nothing surprising about such contacts. Not all of his drawings, however, are in this roughly confident manner. Some are more precisely handled although they lack the elegance of the more finished studies he made in the early 1630s. The only *bozzetti* of Sacchi that survive also belong to roughly the same period (1629–33), but sketches of subjects that he executed later are recorded in his studio inventory and the erratic survival of his sketches seems to be an historical accident and is not proof that he made them only in these years.

Despite the uneven condition and varied physical character of this group of works, some stylistic trends can be detected. Sacchi's ability to handle rich colours is seen in both the Prado picture and in the two Collegio Romano sketches, the latter being his only works to show some possible debt to Poussin's dark, Neo-Venetian phase. The Prado picture (Plate 20) is a spectacular piece of painting. Were it on display regularly, it would surely be one of Sacchi's most famous works. It seems to be painted without black—only hues of gold, apricot, malachite green, lapis-lazuli blue and rose pink. The colour schemes in his frescoes are necessarily lighter. In them we can observe Sacchi developing another facet of his gifts as a painter, his ability to control a carefully modulated range of light colours. There are hints of these abilities in better preserved passages at Castelfusano. Soft mauve, cream and pale olive green are used for Sts. Cosmas and Damian in the oil sketches for the Collegio Romano fresco (Col. Plate IV), but the fresco itself is too dirty and damaged to see if the same colours occur there. The rich raspberry red of St. Ignatius' chasuble has been carried over from the sketches to the fresco insofar as this is possible in the latter medium. Perhaps restoration will show that the tonal contrasts are stronger and the colours richer in this fresco than in the *Divina Sapienza,* where Sacchi used golden yellow, peach pink, pale and dark grey, soft olive green, a muted brick red, a chalky blue, dark and light malachite greens, browns and violets, each shade modulated and repeated with variations throughout the ceiling.

Denis Mahon has argued that Sacchi's subtle, light palette inspired Poussin to move away from his dark, Neo-Venetian phase to his lighter, more refined manner of the 1630s.[39] Poussin may have admired Sacchi's work at this time, and there are occasions when Poussin seems to have affected Sacchi, but their closeness has been overemphasized.[40] Though often linked in scholars' minds as two 'classical' artists working in Rome, personal contacts between them are not recorded—with one exception mentioned below—nor is either artist ever said to be an admirer of the other. It is often assumed that they had a mutual friend, Duquesnoy, but his documented contacts with Poussin occur in the 1620s, his friendship with Sacchi developed in the 1630s, and by 1640 Duquesnoy was no longer on close terms with Poussin.[41] Sacchi was not patronized regularly by Cardinal Francesco Barberini, who did patronize Poussin, and never seems to have been taken up by the Cardinal's secretary, Cassiano dal Pozzo, and his circle of artists, which included Poussin and Testa.[42] Poussin was not active in the Academy of St. Luke[43] and Sacchi was only active in it during the mid 1620s and 1630s. When Poussin attended Sacchi's drawing academy after Domenichino moved his studio to Naples in 1630, it was, says Passeri, in order to draw a model called Corporal Leone, who struck particularly lively poses.[44]

Obviously Sacchi and Poussin must have known each other. The Roman art world was not large and both were establishing their reputations in Barberini circles at the same time, but they seem to have kept their distance. By the 1640s, there is evidence that suggests Poussin had scant respect for Sacchi's work, despite the admiration that they shared by then for Raphael and Domenichino.[45] When and how Poussin came to regard Sacchi in this way is not known. In the late 1620s and early 1630s, both artists were still experimenting, although basic differences of approach are already evident. Poussin was already a Domenichino follower and had since his arrival in Rome devoted a great deal of time to the study of antiquity and Raphael. Sacchi only turned to Domenichino in the 1640s and never used the ancient world as the intellectual and formal touchstone of his art, as Poussin did. Poussin may well have regarded Sacchi as an artist whose *colore* was insufficiently tempered by *disegno*. As Poussin's artistic personality developed, he found less and less to admire in Sacchi, while Sacchi, ironically, was moving in a direction of which Poussin should have approved. Duquesnoy's role in this story of changing artistic relationships and allegiances also needs to be explained. Bellori's lukewarm *Vita* of Duquesnoy may express a disappointment, shared by Poussin, in Duquesnoy's failure to become a more versatile and ambitious sculptor. Duquesnoy's friendship with Sacchi, which is well documented in the 1630s and early 1640s,[46] seems to have developed as his contacts with Poussin ceased. Perhaps Poussin detected the flaw in Duquesnoy's character that would prevent his achieving greatness as a sculptor or perhaps they were never such good friends as has been assumed in the past. Perhaps Duquesnoy simply felt more comfortable with Sacchi, whose rate of production was closer to his own than to that of Poussin. Together Sacchi and Duquesnoy could commiserate about the lot of artists like themselves whose ideas only matured slowly. They could also complain to each other about Bernini, whom both artists had reason to dislike.[47] The full story of this triangular relationship cannot be reconstructed without better documentation, but what little evidence there is proves that the three artists were not always close friends or natural allies in the classical camp, as is generally assumed, although there were times when they admired each other's work and used each others' ideas.

Because the chronology of Poussin's work between 1625 and 1635 is so uncertain, it is difficult to know who is influencing whom when Poussin's work resembles Sacchi's, or vice versa. If an early date for Poussin's *Inspiration of the Poet* is accepted (1628–9), then perhaps the figure of Nobility in Sacchi's *Divina Sapienza* ceiling was inspired by Poussin's muse. If a later date (1631–2) is preferred for Poussin's picture, then Sacchi may have influenced Poussin.[48] After 1630 their paths diverged. Sacchi may have ignored Poussin because he was French, for Italian artists, while glad to have foreigners come to Rome to learn how to be good artists, did not entirely welcome those who settled and competed with them for prestigious public and private commissions. Generally speaking, Poussin had remarkably little impact on the Roman art world, considering how quickly and how profoundly his influence was felt in France. Only Pietro Testa came permanently under Poussin's spell and can be called a follower, if a highly individual one.[49]

This analysis of the artistic and personal relationships between Sacchi and Poussin makes a long introduction to a discussion of Sacchi's *Divnia Sapienza* ceiling fresco in the Palazzo Barberini (Plate 28), but it is necessary because the *Divina Sapienza* is always seen as the answer of the *disegno* party to the flamboyant extravaganzas of the *colore* school led by Pietro da Cortona. It does not seem to matter that the *Divina Sapienza* was finished, even by old and erroneous calculations, before Cortona's ceiling was under way, or that Sacchi's fresco presents an illusion of a room open to the sky and was clearly seen in this way by *seicento* writers.[50] On the other hand neither Cortona's life-long involvement with the Academy of St. Luke nor his extensive use of classical sculpture in his work prevent his being labelled 'baroque'. When Sacchi started the *Divina Sapienza* in 1629, there was nothing by Cortona with which Sacchi might expect his ceiling to be compared, all Cortona's existing ceiling decorations being smaller or made up of smaller, individual units. If Sacchi thought that he was competing with anyone, it must have been with Lanfranco, who had finished both the dome of S. Andrea della Valle and the ceiling fresco of the gods of Olympus in the Villa Borghese in the 1620s and who was the acknowledged expert at this kind of work. The reason why Sacchi's fresco is seen in this way is the subsequent addition to the decoration of the Palazzo Barberini of Cortona's huge ceiling fresco of *Divine Providence* in the Gran Salone, executed between 1633 and 1639, which was regarded by Cortona and his supporters as a challenge to Sacchi's slightly earlier fresco. The two works are not strictly comparable, however, even though both are ceiling frescoes depicting allego-

II. *The Preaching of the Baptist.* 1641–9. Rome, Lateran Palace. (Cat. No. 60)

ries eulogizing the Barberini. Their iconography and the rooms in which they are painted are very different, and to a far greater extent than is appreciated by the authors of brief discussions of these two works, discussions that concentrate on artistic ideologies, these physical and iconographical differences affected the final results.

Sacchi's *Divina Sapienza* (Plates 28–31, 33) was painted in the largest of the rooms in the wing of the Sforza palace that the Barberini incorporated into their own.[51] The room is about thirty feet square but the ceiling at its highest point is only about twenty feet from the floor. Although Cortona's ceiling is much larger, it is so far above the viewer's head that he is able to see it as a whole. This is difficult with Sacchi's ceiling, which is low and broad. Artists who had decorated neighbouring rooms all used *quadri riportati,* as did Camassei for his *God Dividing the Angel Hierarchies* in the room next to that assigned to Sacchi,[52] but these rooms are smaller than Sacchi's and are all rectangular. It is often maintained, despite the lack of a frame and despite the *di sotto in su* viewpoint made explicit by the throne of Divine Wisdom, that Sacchi's ceiling is nevertheless a *quadro riportato*.[53] Certainly the angle of vision is not extreme and the figures are not strongly foreshortened, but it is a mistake to assume that the painted illusion of Divine Wisdom and her attributes is to be thought of as existing above our heads. What Sacchi has done is to imagine the room opened up with the vision appearing ahead of the spectator above the small private chapel to which the room gives access.[54] Sacchi did not refuse to paint a Correggesque illusion with figures in extreme *iscorcio* because he opposed paintings of this kind on ideological grounds. A glance at his later small ceiling fresco in the sacristy of S. Maria sopra Minerva (Plate 78) is sufficient to show that this was not the case. He avoided an extreme illusionistic approach because it was unsuitable for a low, broad ceiling. The figures would be too close to the spectator for the illusion to be believable and *quadratura* architecture would be out of line from almost every point in the room.[55]

Since he reduced the sky area by painting a grisaille and gold frieze on the curved edge of the ceiling above the elaborate gilded stucco cornice that serves as a frame, it can be assumed that Sacchi thought the existing ceiling was too large for his purposes. Further, since all known versions, painted or engraved, have a rectangular and not a square format, it can be assumed that Sacchi did not find the square shape of the ceiling ideal either.[56] The simplest way to reduce the painted surface would have been to make a *quadro riportato* frame in the centre of the ceiling and either to have left the surrounding area bare or to have filled it with a decorative motif. An oblong frame in the centre of a square ceiling would have looked odd. A square frame in the centre of a square ceiling would only make the problem of painting a square composition more acute. The solution adopted—to use the whole ceiling keeping the principal elements within a broad, horizontal band and extending the composition to the edges by means of cloud banks—was both flexible and aesthetically sensible.[57]

The large composition drawing in the Cooper-Hewitt Museum in New York (Plate 27) and the six figure and drapery studies in Düsseldorf (e.g. Plate 32) are all that survive of Sacchi's preparations for the design. The compact, asymmetrical arrangement in the New York drawing suggests that Sacchi did not immediately appreciate the width of the ceiling that he was to paint, although he apparently settled on the basic elements of his design quickly. The figures in the drawing fit together neatly, especially on the left side, while those in the fresco are more spread out.[58] In the drawing, a strong diagonal thrust into space is very marked, moving from the left foreground to the right background. In the fresco, this spatial progression is still apparent but the diagonal movement has been controlled and counterbalanced by several changes, especially on the right side. Most of the figures in the drawing reappear in the fresco in almost the same positions, but the group of Justice and Fortitude has been rearranged to cover more ground horizontally. Fortitude's raised arm resting on her club makes her attribute more visible and bridges the space made between Eternity and Suavity. Beneficence has been moved away from the foot of the throne to a spot below Divinity previously occupied by another woman, almost certainly Perspicacity.[59] Perspicacity has been moved to the right and placed beside Beauty. Their horizontal grouping extends the composition to the right and anchors the huge spherical form of the globe. Symmetry is further stressed by the addition of the figure of Fear, who balances Love on the left; as Purity is made more important formally by her sweep of drapery,[60] so Fear is supported by a magnificent conformation of grey clouds and peach-pink sky. The throne of Divine Wisdom in the centre is the only architecturally solid element in the composition. The spectator finds himself continually referring to it as a point of orientation for the whole fresco.

The final composition has been described recently as one 'of almost archaic simplicity',[61] yet when it is compared with its sixteenth-century antecedents such as Raphael's Chigi chapel mosaics or his Psyche tapestries in the Farnesina, Sacchi's composition seems anything but archaic. Compared even with such recent ceilings as Lanfranco's *Gods of Olympus* in the Villa Borghese, Sacchi's figure grouping has an easy informality that looks forward to the baroque illusions of Gaulli rather than back to the more inhibited, additive designs of the sixteenth century. The ingenuity and originality of Sacchi's ceiling has not been appreciated, partly because it is better known from photographs, which distort the balance of the design, than in the original, and partly because it has been overshadowed by Cortona's far more spectacular production nearby. Forced to represent the classical side to Cortona's baroque, Sacchi's creation has not been studied for its own sake. Unless the *Divina Sapienza* is seen as an illusion, its meaning and its place in the history of ceiling decoration will be misunderstood. This vision of sunlight and cloud-borne figures is in some ways closer to Gaulli's vault of the Gesù than is Cortona's *Divina Providenza*, where the possibilities of a unified vision in infinite space have been deliberately avoided. Cortona's composition could teach Gaulli little about coordinating groups of figures in space without using obvious architectural arrangements of semi-circles and rows, both evident in Cortona's and in Lanfranco's ceilings and vaults. Lanfranco's figure groupings are also less varied than Sacchi's.[62] In the *Divina Sapienza,* he manages to link larger, more scattered units with fluid ease. It is Sacchi's flexible figure groupings and the feeling of circulating air and space achieved without dissolving the composition into an uncoordinated pattern of disjointed units[63] which Gaulli surely appreciated and which led to the illusionistic ceiling decorations of the later seventeenth and eighteenth centuries.[64]

A number of sources can be cited for individual figures in the fresco. Domenichino's *Fortezza* in S. Carlo ai Catinari perhaps inspired the figure of Love astride a lion.[65] Raphael's Galatea provided the pose of Divine Wisdom.[66] A woman in the left foreground of Titian's *Bacchanal of the Andrians* was the model for Beneficence. The whole composition shows that Sacchi had studied Raphael's Stanze frescoes, the *Parnassus* and the *Disputà* in particular. Cigoli's Psyche ceiling fresco, then in the Palazzo Bentivoglio (now Rospigliosi-Pallavicini), suggested a number of poses and groupings.[67] There are classical sources for Perspicacity, Beauty, Nobility and Holiness. All the borrowings, whether of common or unusual poses, have been restudied and reinterpreted. Classical figures, for example, do not meditate with their hands beneath their chins with the palm upwards, the fingers curled against the face, as Perspicacity does. Other revealing details are the hand of Beneficence holding an ear of wheat, the light and shade round the bent head of Justice and the hands of Suavity. The subtle variety of facial types and expressions also repay careful study. Several figures turn to each other as if to speak, others look out at us or up at Divine Wisdom. The mood is one of quiet but alert meditation.

Those who find the ceiling a failure must make clear that they appreciate and take into account the nature of the commission and the physical handicaps with which Sacchi had to cope. It is partly failure to do this which has resulted in so much half-hearted praise.[68] Perhaps a genius could have turned the handicaps into more positive virtues, as Raphael did the eccentrically placed windows in the Vatican Stanze. Ideally the ceiling in the Sala della Divina Sapienza should have been raised or the floor lowered some ten feet.[69] This would give the spectator a clear view of the whole composition and would have reduced the necessity to plan for distortions to the further parts of the ceiling due to the increased degree of foreshortening. At present it is perhaps more rewarding to study details in the room itself and the whole composition in photographs, always remembering the distortions this produces in both the globe and the cloud-bank on the left, which are too prominent in reproductions.

A *seicento* document in the Barberini archives published by Incisa della Rocchetta in 1924 provides the programme of the *Divina Sapienza* ceiling. This document gives Wisdom VII and VIII as the text for the ceiling and identifies each of the figures briefly. The choice of subject is appropriate to the Barberini family because '. . . si felice fameglia è nata et eletta in luogo d'Iddio, per li prima (sic) governi della Chiesa, così con divina Sapienza parimente amata e riverita, la governa'. Before 1924 scholars followed the identifications of the various figures provided by Teti in his *Aedes Barberinae*, published only eleven years after the completion of the ceiling, and by Passeri, first published in 1772. Bellori's description only became available in 1942, when his life of Sacchi was published from the then recently discovered manuscript. None of these three authors is in complete agreement with the others or with the Barberini document, but their confusion is understandable, for reasons that will be discussed.

Reading from left to right and omitting the airborne figures of Love and Fear for the moment, the identifications offered by the Barberini text are as follows: Nobility with the crown of Ariadne; Eternity with the snake; Justice with the scales; Strength with the club; Suavity with the lyre; Divinity with the triangle; Beneficence with the ear of wheat and a breast swollen with milk; Divine Wisdom herself;[70] Holiness with the flaming altar; Purity with the swan; Perspicacity with the eagle; and Beauty with the lock of Berenice. Passeri omits Nobility and partly conflates her with Eternity, calls Suavity Harmony, identifies Divinity with Godliness, Beneficence with Fecundity and misses the significance of Beauty's attribute. Apart from the confusion over the first two figures, Passeri followed Teti's text. Bellori calls Suavity Beatitude, Beneficence Fecund Charity, Holiness Religion and Purity 'Soavità della Parola di Dio'. He also with Passeri and Teti misses the meaning of Beauty's locks of hair, calling them simply the tresses with which beautiful women attract men.

Teti, Passeri and Bellori might have found the task of identifying the personifications easier had they noticed that the attributes of each of the figures are decorated with a constellation. The Barberini manuscript says that symbols of the constellations have been used 'essendo quelli cosa divina e rappresentandosi in cielo' (as they are divine and are found in the sky). The idea must have come from Wisdom VII, 29–30:

> For she (Wisdom) is more beautiful than the sun, and above all the order of stars: being compared with the light, she is found before it. For after this cometh night: but vice shall not prevail against Wisdom.

A visitor who looks up at the ceiling after leaving Cortona's chapel sees little of the figures, which are upside-down and against the light, but the gold stars placed on all the attributes then become visible and catch the eye. The author of the programme deliberately selected attributes for the figures accompanying Divine Wisdom which were also constellations—the crown of Ariadne for Nobility, the scales for Justice, and so on. The probable source is Hyginus' *Poetica Astronomica,* for he is the only classical author writing about stars who identifies a constellation with the lock of Berenice, the attribute used here for Beauty.[71] The author's desire to match each attribute of Divine Wisdom with a constellation meant, however, that in many cases the chief attribute of the figure was not the one normally associated with it. Purity is shown holding a swan, normally the attribute of Beauty or Poetry, Purity's usual attribute being a white dove. The triangle appears in Ripa's *Iconologia* only once, as a possible attribute for Scienza, and even then it is inverted. Religion, not Holiness, holds an altar, which explains why Bellori identified this figure as Religion. The crown of Ariadne does not help to identify Nobility, the nearest equivalent in Ripa being a middle-aged woman dressed in black with a gold and silver crown at her feet. Only in the case of Beauty is the new attribute relevant.[72] It adds nothing to Divinity to learn that her constellation is identified with the mouth of the Nile. In the cases of Purity, Fear and Suavity, the new attributes are misleading.[73] The virtues selected are also very similar: Divinity is a concept close to Holiness, Suavity is close to Beauty and easily confused with Harmony, there is no good reason why Beneficence should not be interpreted as Fecundity. Confusion could have been avoided by giving each figure more attributes or by choosing more clearly differentiated qualities in the first place.[74]

The constellations were evidently chosen for their suitability to the concepts with which they were to be associated. Their positions in the fresco bear no relationship to their actual positions in the sky and the few attributes that have more than one star are not arranged as they are in the constellation itself, except the crown of Ariadne and the lock of Berenice. There are nevertheless possible allusions to recent astronomical studies. Though Hyginus included the lock of Berenice in his collection of astronomical fables, Ptolemy relegated it to the category of 'unformed' constellation. Tycho Brahe and Johann Kepler in 1601 and 1627 respectively accepted it however as a proper constellation, along with over a thousand others. Then one of Galileo's recent discoveries, announced in the *Sidereus Nuncius* of 1610, concerned the Milky Way. His observations proved that it was not a cloudy substance exuded by the stars, as was thought, but that it was composed of many small stars. Thus before 1610, the Milky Way would not have been recognized as a constellation at all. Less certain is the selection of the snake constellation, for the snake is a standard attribute of eternity, and Eternity would seem to be an essential attribute of Divine Wisdom. At all events, a new star was detected in this constellation in 1610, a discovery published by both Kepler and Galileo, and some visitors to the room may have been reminded of this phenomenon when they saw the snake. Perhaps visitors also recalled the theories of Copernicus and Galileo concerning the relative positions of the sun and the earth, for in the fresco the sun is prominently centered and the earth is as obviously placed to one side. Sacchi's earlier association with Cardinal del Monte, who was a good friend and supporter of Galileo, makes it probable that he was aware of current astronomical debates and hence was aware of these possible interpretations of his fresco.

The author of the ceiling's programme is not known. In view of the confusing similarity of the characteristics of Divine Wisdom selected for illustration and of the additional confusion caused by using unfamiliar attributes for the personifications in order to accommodate the conceit of constellations, it seems probable that the author lacked experience with such intellectual exercises. The choice of only a few of the many attributes of Wisdom named in the Biblical text had already prompted Incisa della Rocchetta to suggest that Sacchi himself planned the programme.[75] Sacchi's predilection for compositions with a small number of figures suggests that he played a part in the planning of the iconography, even if he was not entirely responsible for the programme. The Cooper Hewitt Museum composition study, which shows the figure of Love without the lion and omits the figure of Fear on the hare altogether proves at the very least that artist and author must have worked in close collaboration at the early stages of the preparation of the ceiling. Sacchi's contacts with the household of Cardinal del Monte may have given him enough literary education to plan the programme alone, but he never shows much interest in iconographical complexities on other occasions, and it seems more likely that he had some help at least when devising a theme for the largest room in Don Taddeo's wing of the Palazzo Barberini. Haskell thought that some Roman theologian gave Sacchi this 'far-fetched idea'.[76] One such possibility is Clemente Merlini (Plate 49), the patron of the *St. Peter* in Forlì (Plate 48) and the probable author of that picture's programme, but St. Peter is shown with every one of his possible attributes, an approach which seems too pedantically literal and unselective for its author to be connected with the planning of the *Divina Sapienza*. Perhaps Merlini's friend, Sforza Pallavicino (1607–1667) was consulted. He was a member of the Accademia degli Umoristi, the most famous literary and scientific circle of scholars in Rome, and an intimate of the

Barberini court, rising quickly to responsible positions in their service after leaving the Collegio Romano in 1628.[77] More important, he was the author of a treatise which advocated a purer, simpler style of Italian prose and which stated that brevity was one of the three essential qualities of good style.[78] In short, his attitude to the writing of prose is the literary parallel to Sacchi's approach to painting, although to what extent either man had developed his theories by 1629 we do not know.

The subject of Divine Wisdom was not chosen simply as an elaborate piece of Barberini flattery. The room in which it is painted leads to the Barberini's private chapel and the subject, if correctly understood, should inspire the spectator to enter the chapel. The last verse of Wisdom VIII reads:

> . . . when I perceived that I could not otherwise obtain her, except that God gave her me; and that it
> was a point of wisdom also to know whose gift she was; I prayed unto the Lord . . .

There is no iconographical connection between Sacchi's ceiling and the chapel, which was decorated by Cortona and his assistants, other than that implied by the text of Wisdom. Indeed it is difficult to see how one could be made except perhaps by emphasizing the Holy Ghost, the New Testament equivalent of the figures of Love and Fear, who act as the agents of Divine Wisdom outside the chapel. Another aspect of the function of this room that is relevant to the iconography but has been overlooked is that, though large by the standards of that wing of the palace, the room must always have been used for private or semi-private purposes. Cortona's Gran Salone with its elaborate disquisition on the theme of Divine Providence was only used for public occasions—receptions and entertainments. It makes sense therefore for the programme of the Cortona ceiling to stress the achievements of the Barberini and the benefits of their reign. Sacchi's ceiling is intended not only to stress the divine right of the Barberini to rule but also to inspire them to seek Divine Wisdom in prayer in order to rule wisely. The two commissions as assigned certainly suited the artistic abilities and temperaments of the two artists concerned; they also heighten our awareness of the differences between Sacchi and Cortona, differences that remain even when the very different character of these two commissions is taken into account.

Barberini Patronage and the Journey to North Italy: 1631–1635

From August, 1631 when Cardinal Antonio Barberini is first documented interceding on Sacchi's behalf for a particular commission, Sacchi again enjoyed the regular support of a steady and sympathetic patron, support which he had lacked since the death of Cardinal del Monte in 1626. His production in these years, while not copious, was steady and little troubled apparently by the psychological handicaps that interfered with his creative processes in the next decade. On completing the *Divina Sapienza* early in 1631, he was free to accept other commissions again. He started with the *St. Thomas Aquinas with SS. Peter and Paul* (Plate 34), the first of the four cartoons for mosaic pendentives that he designed in this decade. His most famous altarpiece, *The Vision of St. Romuald* (Plate 41), followed shortly afterwards. The two *St. Peters*, now in Forlì and Rome (Plates 48 and 52), were probably painted in 1632. In 1633 he finished the *Three Magdalenes* now in Florence (Plate 55) and the *Miracle of St. Anthony of Padua* for the Capuchins' new church in Rome (Plate 61). He also started the four altarpieces for the crypt chapels in St. Peter's, three of which were ready before his trip to North Italy in 1635–6. Before leaving he also made drawings for Mascardi's publication recording the Festa del Saraceno in Piazza Navona and frescoed a small chapel, since destroyed, in the Quirinale.

The two most immediately noticeable changes in his style from 1631 onwards are the increased scale of his figures in relation to the format that contains them and a preference for the quieter colour schemes that he started developing in the late 1620s. He also stops making the dashing figure studies of the late 1620s. Instead he seems to have followed composition studies with rough life studies of poses and drapery and then to have reworked the poses and details more carefully, often repeating a pose several times on one sheet. These studies show subtle technical variations[79] but all of them are more precisely handled than the majority of his earlier studies, except the most delicate of his early chalk drawings. His new-found ability to work comfortably on a large scale, as he was required to do by the mosaic cartoons and by large altarpieces such as the *St. Romuald* and the Forlì *St. Peter*, is not reflected in a change in drawing style that emphasizes increased size. Rather he seems to have suppressed those tendencies which had appeared around 1629 in his studies for the Collegio Romano ceiling, the *Pasce Oves Meas* overdoor and the *Divina Sapienza*, and which seem in retrospect to symbolize his short-lived confidence in his own abilities.

The *St. Thomas Aquinas* (Plate 34) is the only one of the four mosaic cartoons to be described by Bellori, who called it 'opera degnissima, e di gran Maniera'. It is the first of Sacchi's works to have the massive proportions and restrained dignity associated with the *St. Romuald*, whose mood of alert, intense meditation it also shares. The restrained colour of the *St. Thomas* is also markedly different from the colour schemes of the other mosaic pendentives by Lanfranco, Romanelli and Muziano, although the black and white robes of the principal figure dictated the overall colour scheme to some extent. The design is the most successful of Sacchi's four pendentives. This may be because he had three figures and not just one to occupy the huge and awkwardly shaped space. The quiet, psychological dialogue between the two apostles and the Dominican saint fills the broad upper half of the triangle while the flowing robes of St. Thomas spread into the lower section. In the three other pendentives (Plates 36–39) there is a sense of strain as the saints fling out their arms, more to occupy the space than to express genuine emotion.

There is an interesting difference between the treatment of the space in which the figures are situated in the mosaics designed by Sacchi and those planned by Lanfranco.[80] Sacchi extends the space behind the niche while Lanfranco and the others limit the space behind the figures. This can be seen from the shadows cast by the figures, which in Lanfranco's pendentives are flush with the frame but which in Sacchi's break on the frame and continue on a different plane. This means that Lanfranco's figures project into our space while Sacchi's remain behind the wall surface. Their respective solutions might be described as 'baroque' and 'classical' although the differences are slight and the spectator is hardly less aware of Sacchi's than of Lanfranco's saints.

The composition of the *St. Romuald* (Plate 41) must have followed closely that of the *St. Thomas*. The scale and concentrated simplicity of the latter undoubtedly helped Sacchi to develop the 'gran Maniera' noted by Bellori in the cartoon and which from now on is a permanent part of Sacchi's artistic persona. The composition study in Stockholm for the *St. Romuald* (Plate 40) shows a different iconography as well as a different composition from those of the painting. In the former St. Romuald is shown attended by angels while having his vision. In the painting he is describing his vision to a small group of his fellow monks. The iconography and to some extent the composition of the first design were probably inspired by Antiveduto Grammatica's altarpiece of the same subject at Frascati, probably painted around 1620.[81] Sacchi had good reason to know this work and the artist responsible, for Antiveduto was another of Cardinal del Monte's protégés and was much in evidence in the early 1620s because of his disastrous tenure of office as Principe of the Academy of St. Luke.[82] Antiveduto's picture was an obvious model anyway because it was the most recent treatment of the subject available in Rome, but it was not Sacchi's only source. Posse noted that Sacchi also used Girolamo Muziano's *St. Jerome Preaching in the Wilderness* (S. Maria degli Angeli, Rome), Muziano's picture providing the main compositional framework of Sacchi's final design. He may even have recalled Cavedone's frescoes in S. Michele in Bosco from his stay in Bologna.[83] But Sacchi has gone far beyond his sources in order to create this memorable image of monks seated in a landscape.

The skill with which Sacchi handled the limited colour scheme imposed by the subject matter has been admired since the seventeenth century. Indeed this adulation creates the impression that the

St. Romuald is a cream and gold monochrome, but the sky is painted with rich lapis-lazuli blues and there are strong ochres, golds and greens in the background landscape and stronger greens and browns in the foreground. At present the colour and tonal balance are dimmed by a thin layer of yellow varnish; without it the picture would be cooler and less uniform in tone and colour. Sacchi also limited the colours in the *St. Anthony* altarpiece to a range of cream and light brown tones, perhaps because the patrons were Capuchin monks who took vows of poverty as did the subject, St. Anthony, who was a Franciscan. Other works contemporary with these such as the Forlì *St. Peter* (Plate 48), the *St. Veronica* (Plate 63) and the *St. Andrew* (Plate 64) make considerable use of rich, warm local colours. In other words, Sacchi's tendency to use lighter, blonder colours after 1630 was not a stylistic change affecting all his work equally. Subject matter and the location of the work dictated the choice of colours to some extent, but Sacchi never exploited the mood potential of dark or light colour schemes as Poussin did.

The commission from the Confraternità dei Battutì of Forlì for a banner of their patron saint, St. Peter, presented the artist with the same problem that he faced with three of the four mosaic cartoons, namely that of arranging one figure with no particular narrative or psychological context on a large scale in such a way as to engage the interest of the spectator and impress him. In the Forlì picture (Plate 48) Sacchi provided a majestic piece of supporting architecture for the saint, the portico serving as a symbol of the Church founded by St. Peter as well as being a useful formal device for increasing the impact of the single figure without giving it overbearing proportions. The landscape background relieves the severity of this austere image, unlike the artist's later landscape backgrounds, which are little more than schematic symbols of an exterior setting and make no appeal to the viewer's memories of particular locations.

During the early 1630s, Sacchi turned to an unexpected source of ideas, unexpected that is to those taught to believe that after 1600 mannerist art and artists were rejected. The heavy, domed skulls and deep brows of Sacchi's male figures during this period, which are among his most characteristic types, are remarkably close to those of his old teacher, Cesare d'Arpino.[84] Nor were the heads of his older male saints the only borrowing that Sacchi made from Cesare. The heavier proportions and basic drapery forms of some of Cesare's larger and less mannered figures only needed to have their edges softened and their anatomical structure drawn more naturally for Sacchi's new figure style to emerge. Sacchi also studied some of Cesare's compositions. The design proposed for the *St. Anthony* in the early study in the British Museum recalls Cesare's *Raising of Lazarus* of 1591–2 (Galleria Nazionale d'Arte Antica, Rome). The *St. Longinus* (Plate 65) is partly based on Cesare's *Martyrdom of St. Barbara* in the vault of a chapel in S. Maria in Transpontina. The Prado *Birth of the Virgin* of 1628 (Plate 20) reflects Sacchi's knowledge of Cesare's treatment of this subject in his picture for S. Maria di Loreto. Sacchi was evidently able to see beneath the surface elegance of his teacher's work to the foundations of a 'gran Maniera' style fully acceptable to Bellori and other adherents of the classical doctrine.

The *Miracle of St. Anthony of Padua* (Plate 61), probably finished in the late spring of 1633, is a work of special interest for several reasons. The appearance in the background of Duquesnoy's *St. Susanna* is the first datable evidence of Sacchi's friendship with the Flemish sculptor. The version of the altarpiece now in the Mahon collection is one of the few certainly autograph replicas of Sacchi's work that survive and is without doubt the finest of these. That it was made for Cardinal Antonio Barberini, whose name saint the altarpiece honours and who commissioned the altarpiece itself, cannot be doubted. The composition can be studied in its early stages thanks to the survival of several composition studies. The final design quotes openly from earlier treatments of similar themes, providing us with significant clues to Sacchi's tastes at this time. The most obvious source, noted already by Posse, is Cigoli's *St. Peter Healing the Lame* in St. Peter's, a work known to be one of Sacchi's favourites. From it Sacchi took the pose of St. Anthony and the man revived, although it must be remembered that similar poses can be found in earlier treatments of similar themes.[85] Cesare d'Arpino, as noted above, provided the framework for Sacchi's crowd arrangements at an early stage, but as the composition developed, Sacchi shifted the emphasis away from the crowd, who are reduced in number and pushed behind the few fully visible spectators and participants. In the altarpiece one spectator is reduced to an anxious pair of eyes peering over the shoulder of a better-placed spectator. Sacchi's methods here contrast sharply with those of Poussin, who prefers to arrange his figures in a row parallel to the picture plane, allowing almost equal formal emphasis to the principal and subsidiary figures. The accurate portrayal of human emotions was of paramount importance to both artists, but where Poussin thought that it was essential to show the position of the whole body of each participant as well as their gestures and facial expressions, Sacchi thought that the essence of the reactions of subsidiary figures could be conveyed more succinctly. As both artists developed and became more conscious of their particular artistic philosophies, they may have come to disapprove of each other, Poussin in particular never being one to mince his words where the work of other arists was concerned.

The iconography of the *Three Magdalenes* (Plate 55) is unique but the formal problem it presented is that common to all symbolic confrontations of personages or personifications. There is no narrative context but a discreet suggestion of one must be conveyed. The two saints named after the Magdalene must have prayed to their namesake on occasion and have contemplated her life; it is these activities that Sacchi has used to give his composition some restrained, psychological drama. The Magdalene's position above the other two saints and in the centre of the canvas indicates her higher theological status. Mary Magdalene Pazzi is shown as if interceding with the Magdalene, an action appropriate for a picture commissioned for an order that she founded. St. Mary Magdalene of Japan was included chiefly for political reasons. Urban VIII was keen to publicize the proselytizing successes of the Catholic Church abroad; the presence of his sisters at the Florentine convent for which the picture was made allowed him to do so. Appropriately perhaps she is shown withdrawn from her companions, lost in contemplative meditation, although she can also be seen as an example to the nuns who spent much of their time in prayer. The arrangement of the three figures has an easy counter-clockwise flow, to which the poses of the putti contribute. The design is one of almost austere simplicity which nevertheless fulfils all the iconographical requirements of the patrons. The loss of the Barberini's own version is regrettable. We know from a drawn copy that the putti were not draped; it is possible that the colours and surface treatment of the nuns' picture were kept deliberately plain and that the Barberini's version had a richer, more colourful surface, since it was commissioned primarily as a work of art and not as a functional religious image.

The four altarpieces for St. Peter's (Plates 63–66) were the next major public commission undertaken by Sacchi. In his recent study of the crossing of St. Peter's, Irving Lavin makes the point that the two male saints, Andrew and Longinus, were on theological grounds ranked above the two female saints, Veronica and Helen.[86] He suggests that the presentation of these four saints in the sculptures by Duquesnoy, Bernini, Mochi and Bolgi takes this difference in status into account. That Sacchi also had to consider this iconographical requirement when designing his crypt altarpieces is probable. It may explain, for example, why Veronica is formally so much less prominent in her composition than are Longinus and Andrew in theirs, although it could be argued that Christ on the way to Calvary could hardly be moved into the background in the way the executioners and spectators have been in the scenes with the two male saints. It is also obvious that, since Sacchi prefers to stress principal figures, he may have done so in the case of Andrew and Longinus without any prompting from his patrons. The design of the altarpiece for St. Helen gave the artist difficulty, however, and here the special iconographical requirement may supply an explanation. Sacchi started the picture with an asymmetrical design, the saint on the right dominating the figures on the left, but finished with the saint in the centre surrounded on both sides by figures who reduce her immediate visual impact. Sacchi's desire to produce a composition which emphasized the main figure may have conflicted with the theological requirements of his patrons and led to the delay of sixteen years that elapsed before this picture was completed.

Both Passeri and Bellori say that Sacchi made a journey to North Italy after working on these four pictures but before completing the *Vision of St. Bonaventure* for the Capuchins. He is not recorded in Rome between June, 1635 and November, 1636; the trip must have taken place during this interval. He is said to have visited Bologna, Parma, Modena, Piacenza, Milan, Mantua, Ferrara and Venice. Bellori and Passeri say that the journey was prompted by Sacchi's desire to study works of art in these towns, above all the works of Correggio, whose colours Passeri says Sacchi particularly admired.[87] We know from the artist's will and death inventory that he made drawings after Correggio's dome in Parma cathedral and after the work of Veronese. Bellori adds that he made a small copy of Agostino Carracci's *Last Communion of St. Jerome*, 'avendo l'altra del Domenichino sempre sotto gl'occhj a Roma' (the other one by Domenichino always being available in Rome). He visited his teacher, Albani, and made the portrait of him now in the Prado (Plate 74). It was unusual for an artist to undertake a study tour of this kind so late in his career. Passeri baldly states that he thinks Sacchi was unwise to do so and furthermore records the disappointment felt in Rome when he unveiled the first work he completed after his return, the *St. Bonaventure* for the Capuchins (Plate 76). Bellori, always the more tactful critic, simply omits to praise the *St. Bonaventure*, although he pointedly notes that its unveiling was eagerly awaited.

The reasons for Sacchi's journey were more complex than either Passeri or Bellori appreciated. It was not just Correggio's colour that Sacchi admired. He made careful copies not of Correggio's altarpieces but of his most spectacular example of illusionistic ceiling painting, the dome that had inspired Lanfranco's recent successes. It cannot be without significance that the other artist after whose work he made a sufficient number of drawings for the fact to be worth recording was Veronese, known primarily in the seventeenth century as a decorative painter. It would appear that, with Cortona hard at work on the *Divina Providenza* ceiling, Sacchi became anxious about his ability to compete with Cortona as a ceiling painter and set out to improve his skills in this area. If this hypothesis is correct, the small ceiling fresco in the sacristy of S. Maria sopra Minerva (Plate 78) is a better work to examine for signs of these new experiences than an altarpiece such as the *St. Bonaventure*.[88] This small fresco is in fact the most illusionistic work of Sacchi's career. It also uses a child as opposed to a baby angel, a type that Sacchi first adopted in the *St. Bonaventure* and which seems to come from the adolescent angels in Correggio's dome. Moreover, it cannot be argued that there is any marked change in Sacchi's palette after 1635, at least as far as one can detect at present: most of the work that he produced between 1635 and 1640 is too dirty or damaged to permit proper stylistic analysis.

Major Commissions from 1635 to 1640 and Minor Commissions of the 1630s

Unlike the ceiling fresco, the commission to design an exterior for the room of St. Catherine in its new installation behind the altar in the sacristy of S. Maria sopra Minerva (Plate 81 gave Sacchi no scope to demonstrate what he had learnt about decorative painting in Parma and Venice. That opportunity came a couple of years later with the commission to decorate the Lateran Baptistry. The architecture that Sacchi fitted round St. Catherine's room is almost aggressively classical. It recalls the setting of St. Anthony's miracle (Plate 61) and of St. Bonaventure's vision (Plate 76) in the two Capuchin altarpieces and looks forward to the even more austerely simple settings used for the life of the Baptist in S. Giovanni in Fonte. The contrast with Cortona's richly complex approach to architecture could not be greater. Sacchi evidently believed that such Grecian purity was appropriate to the exterior of a building, although decoration composed of more imaginative elements had its place. Thus the frame of the inscription opposite the entrance to the saint's room (Plate 79) and the carvings on the cupboards in the altar recess (Plate 82) show that Sacchi was willing and able to work in a baroque decorative idiom, a talent that he had already demonstrated with the plaster and grisaille frame of the *Divina Sapienza* ceiling. The main source for the room of St. Catherine was the Holy House of Loreto stripped of its accretions of sculpture and reduced to its essential architectural elements. Similarities between Sacchi's design and Domenichino's architectural designs are probably fortuitous.[89] Domenichino was then in Naples and Sacchi is not known to have had any contacts that would have given him access to Domenichino's studio.[90]

The *Crucifixion* altarpiece in the sacristy of the Minerva (Plates 75, 77) does not strike the visitor immediately as a work of much originality. In its present state, indeed, it is difficult to appreciate at all. The symmetrical composition, with the four male Dominican saints standing at the foot of the cross in the places usually associated with John and Mary, and with Catherine embracing the foot of the cross in the pose of Mary Magdalene, differs from traditional treatments of the Crucifixion in one important detail. Christ on the cross is usually far removed from those on the ground below lamenting his death. Sacchi however places Christ only a few feet off the ground. St. Catherine can touch his feet; the other saints could feel the wound in his side or embrace him. Sacchi was not commissioned to paint Christ's crucifixion but rather to symbolize the importance of that event to the Dominican Order. This he does by stressing the physical presence of the crucified Christ to the saints contemplating his death. The image was intended to help the devout Dominican who in his contemplations would attempt to relive this event and to imagine Christ's sufferings, as the Jesuits encouraged all believers to do with the aid of their Spiritual Exercises.

During the 1630s Sacchi produced a number of small works, most of them for members of the Barberini family. He may not have had as much control as Poussin did over the subject matter of his private commissions, but the iconography of most of these pictures is unusual and must reflect Sacchi's own ideas to some extent. When Cardinal Francesco proposed, as he probably did, that Sacchi paint a picture of his name saint, it was probably Sacchi who suggested that the picture should represent the rare scene of St. Francis marrying Poverty (Plate 57) rather than the scenes of his stigmatization or ecstatic meditation usual in the seventeenth century. Cain slaying Abel is a common *seicento* subject. Adam discovering the dead body of his son Abel is less common, but nearly all other recorded treatments include Eve as well.[91] Sacchi (Plates 68–69) shows Adam alone with the corpse of Abel, the fleeing figure of Cain and the two altars in the background spelling out the narrative to those familiar with the Biblical text. The tragedy has just occurred and we are left with Adam to try to comprehend the consequences of the first murder in the Biblical history of mankind. According to two preparatory studies (Plates 72–73), the lost fresco of Christ crowned with thorns in the Quirinale showed not Christ mocked but Christ being prepared for this humiliation, a less dramatic but psychologically more subtle moment. The two men who hand him the sceptre and crown him are not depicted as brutish louts as was customary. They even seem to treat Christ with nervous respect. The *Daedalus and Icarus* in Genoa is another iconographical rarity (Plate 87). Icarus is not shown falling from the sky but instead so entranced by the wings his father is tying on him that he daydreams of escape instead of listening to his father's advice. The formal arrangement of the two contrasting figure types supports the narrative with masterly simplicity, the curving caesura between the two men symbolizing their fatal lack of communication. Dido's suicide is usually shown as a public melodrama. In the picture at Caen (Plate 58), Sacchi emphasizes instead the personal tragedy by showing the abandoned queen alone on her funeral pyre, the armour of Aeneas beside her, hesitating to look once more over her shoulder at the departing fleet before plunging the sword through her body.

Unlike Poussin, who selects dramatic events witnessed by a number of people whose reactions can be studied and compared in detail with those of the protagonists, Sacchi prefers significant moments of psychological tension affecting only one or two people. The moment chosen may be one of sudden perception or one of calm meditation, but the subject in essence is the response of an individual to an event or an idea rather than the event itself, in which individual participation will inevitably be overshadowed by the action. Thus Dido is shown considering her suicide instead of in the act of killing herself, Icarus is shown not falling to his death but ignoring the advice that would have prevented that tragedy, and we see not the murder of Abel but the discovery and perception of that event by his father Adam. It is less obvious why Sacchi should have preferred the scene of St. Francis marrying Poverty to his stigmatization or ecstatic meditation. Perhaps the saint's quieter, less emotional response to Poverty appealed to Sacchi, or perhaps it was the rarity of the subject, for the subjects of most of Sacchi's private commissions are unusual, while the *St. Francis* is unique in the seventeenth century. Unless the pictures of the Madonna and Child and the Holy Family recorded in his death inventory were his own, he never painted these common themes.[92] Sacchi's preference for new or uncommon subjects may also explain why he never apparently painted a *Noli Me Tangere,* a subject that would seem to have been designed for his particular talents and artistic philosophy.[93] These private commissions of the 1630s are among Sacchi's most personal and individual creations. In them the narrative is reduced to its essential elements. By focusing the audience's attention on them, Sacchi forces it to consider the wider implications of the event shown. These pictures contain no irrelevant displays of artistic skill. They can only be appreciated by those who approach them intellectually as well as visually and who are familiar with the texts selected. The disciplined economy of his mature style as displayed in these works is not immediately appealing and was not meant to be, but, as Sacchi himself reportedly stated during his debate with Cortona, 'the eye (grows) weary among a multitude of figures and (has) difficulty in finding that calm and peace which alone give lasting satisfaction'.[94]

The Decoration of S. Giovanni in Fonte: 1639–1649

Sacchi had another opportunity to show what he had learnt about decorative painting in North Italy when he received in 1639 the commission to decorate the Lateran Baptistry (Plates 90–91). The ceilings did not need painting, for they had just been covered with gilded carvings during the restoration of the main structure supervised by Bernini. The areas left to Sacchi were the eight walls, all of which contain small windows (or false windows) and five of which are pierced by doors of varying sizes, and the interior of the octagonal lantern above the font. Bellori and Passeri both state that Sacchi was commissioned to carry out the entire decorative programme on his own but either out of laziness or inability to complete the work on his own before the Jubilee Year of 1650 handed over the execution of the main wall frescoes to others. Only three of these frescoes were assigned to artists not in Sacchi's studio, however, and Sacchi designed the entire layout, painted most of the friezes and prepared the cartoons for two of the large narrative frescoes. The delay in executing these large frescoes suggests nevertheless that the psychological problems that were to handicap his last years so severely were now affecting his work. He had no single project as important as the Baptistry in the 1630s. In the light of his biographers' explanations for his declining rate of production, explanations that stress Sacchi's feelings of inadequacy before the greatest achievements of Raphael and Annibale, it is significant that it was a major commission that would be studied with particular care by posterity which made Sacchi procrastinate to a degree that his patrons could not tolerate. In the 1650s, a commission of comparable importance, the decoration of the ceiling of S. Luigi dei Francesi, hardly progressed beyond the preparatory stage.

Domenichino played only a small part in Sacchi's earlier work, Raphael only a slightly more important role, but Domenichino's frescoes at Grottaferrata and Raphael's in the Vatican were Sacchi's main sources for his frescoes in the Lateran Baptistry. Before concluding that the choice of these models indicates a significant change in artistic policy from that which made Sacchi study Correggio and Veronese so assiduously in North Italy, it is necessary to remember that the architecture of the Baptistry did not permit illusionistic decoration like Correggio's dome decorations in Parma or Veronese's ceiling paintings in S. Sebastiano in Venice. Even if the ceiling areas had been available for decoration by Sacchi, they were small and were broken up into irregular shapes by the inner octagon supporting the lantern. The scheme that Sacchi devised was tailored to fit the architectural eccentricities of the Baptistry. It minimizes the asymmetries of the various wall spaces and harmonizes with the divisions of the walls indicated by pilasters and horizontal strip mouldings. It could even be argued that decorative projects of comparable clarity can be found in the work of Correggio and Veronese. Correggio's Camera di San Paolo is impeccably laid out; Veronese's frescoes at Maser respect and enhance the proportions of Palladio's architecture. The arrangement at Grottaferrata with the frieze of saints above the narrative scenes is nevertheless the basic source, as Posse noted, of Sacchi's layout in the Baptistry, with Raphael's frescoes providing the basic compositions of all the large narrative frescoes. Those in the Sala di Costantino by Giulio Romano and other assistants of Raphael were the models for the scenes in the Baptistry of Constantine's vision before the battle of the Milvian Bridge (Plate 94), his victory in that battle (Plate 97) and his victorious entry into Rome after the battle (Plate 100). The two narrative frescoes designed by Sacchi and executed by Magnone and Maratta (Plates 112, 115) are less obviously indebted to particular Raphael models.[95] Perhaps the patrons thought that a restrained approach using accepted earlier models was appropriate to a building with such a long and venerable history. Certainly the recherché, allusive iconography of—say—Cortona's *Divina Providenza* ceiling would not have been appropriate. The Baptistry was one of the major pilgrimage sites in Rome and few of its visitors had had an education comparable with that of the cardinals and diplomats who frequented the Palazzo Barberini. The story of Constantine's life and the accomplishments of Urban VIII had to be portrayed with the utmost clarity. To those versed in such matters the decoration is recognizably a work in the High Renaissance tradition, but the average visitor in the seventeenth century, if he studied the frescoes at all, was probably more impressed by the *trompe l'oeil* medallions with putti playing around them than by the Raphael quotations in the main scenes below.

Sacchi's eight canvases illustrating the life of the Baptist (Plates 116–123) also had to be comprehensible to pilgrims with little formal education; they also had to be legible from a greater distance than the wall frescoes. Much has been made of the awkwardness of the site that Sacchi reserved for himself.[96] In fact the paintings are easily seen from the ground, although they have often been obscured by dust and by stains from rain-water leaking through the lantern roof.[97] It cannot therefore be argued seriously that Sacchi's main reason for choosing that site was to keep his works away from the critical eyes of his contemporaries. Two other factors are of greater significance. The cupola decoration was carried out in oils, not fresco, and while Sacchi's technical mastery of that difficult medium is amply demonstrated by his few frescoes, he must have preferred oil, which allowed him to work slowly and deliberately and to change his mind with relative ease.[98] By 1640 also Sacchi must have been conscious of his preference for static subjects that concerned the reactions of one or two individuals to a crisis. The narrative frescoes of the Lateran Baptistry have diffuse, dramatic subjects, three of them with most of the figures in motion. It may be a measure of the limitations of Sacchi's artistic intellect that he could not respond more fully to the challenge of these compositions, although it should be noted that the *Destruction of Pagan Idols*, the more active of the two compositions that he prepared for his assistants to execute, is also the most successful. On the other hand, his decision not to design or paint the other walls can be interpreted as an indication of his awareness of the particular character of his own talents. According to the traditional hierarchies of artistic prestige, the large narrative frescoes were the most challenging and important part of the commission; Sacchi's contemporaries did not respect Sacchi for failing to carry them all out himself. Bellori spends some time analysing the two scenes executed by Magnone and Maratta; he merely lists the subjects of the eight canvases in the lantern. Only modern scholars have appreciated their austere beauty.[99]

The simplicity of the compositions in these eight pictures, the increased scale of the figures in relation to the picture format and the almost total exclusion of descriptive details such as foliage, flowers, embroidery, textures or architectural details are all partially explained by their site high up in the lantern of the Baptistry. The figures are slightly foreshortened by the distance from which they are seen, while fine detail would not be appreciated some twenty feet from the picture surface. But the execution is not totally bereft of illusionistic description of surfaces and textures. In the two best preserved scenes, the *Annunciation* and the *Beheading* (Plates 116, 123; Col. Plate 1), there are beautifully executed passages on the costumes of the high priest and on the soldier's armour. The plain surfaces of the other six scenes are partly due to their condition.[100] Few of Sacchi's pictures have suffered as much as these eight pictures, but with none of his other works from this decade in mint condition, there is little with which to compare them. Nevertheless the surface of the *Death of St. Anne* (Plate 150), a picture which seems to be in good shape beneath a heavy layer of yellowed varnish, is more carefully worked than those of the Fonte series, with much impasto visible in good detail photographs. The surfaces of the Fonte pictures, on the other hand, are often flat, a fact that also indicates wear and paint loss. Still, it is unwise to compare them with the late work of Guido Reni;[101] if the *Naming of the Baptist* reminded visitors to the Ideale Classico exhibition in Bologna of Guido's sketchy late canvases, it was an illusion caused by the loss of surface detail from this canvas, one of the palest and most damaged of the entire series, and not an effect deliberately sought by the artist. The elaborate and painstaking finish of Sacchi's final preparatory studies for the Fonte series also provides us with a measure of their loss of surface finish.

Since their recent cleaning, the colours of all eight works have proved to be of surprising brilliance with strong lapis blue throughout accompanied by crimson, plum, burnt orange, gold, grey and a rich, dark green. The *St. Anne* gives every indication of having a similarly warm, rich palette beneath its veil of dust and varnish. While Sacchi's compositions become simpler with more emphasis on the figures, his colours move away from the restrained and subtle pastels that he had favoured in the 1630s and return to the saturated hues characteristic of his work in the 1620s. Possibly he was inspired to change his colours after studying Poussin's latest work, in particular the set of *Sacraments* painted for Cassiano dal Pozzo. None of Sacchi's other contemporaries in Rome had a palette as rich or as varied as that of Poussin, and if Sacchi had any opportunities to study it, it is difficult to imagine that his painterly instincts would not have responded to their splendid colour schemes.

Keeping both condition and situation in mind, one may add some further stylistic points about the Fonte series. Although the figures are large in proportion to the picture format, they lack the bulk of earlier figures such as the monks listening to St. Romuald. This seems to be an effect brought about deliberately by reducing the chiaroscuro contrasts because Sacchi wanted the figures to dominate the compositions without overwhelming them. Condition could explain the lack of tonal contrast, but the final preparatory studies are also more even in tone than similar studies of the 1630s. The Fonte compositions also place less emphasis on forms at an angle to the picture plane and on diagonals and asymmetries than do his previous works, but the end result is still a long way from the classical relief formula favoured by Poussin, Cortona and Giacinto Gimignani. In general the drapery forms in the Fonte series are simpler than those in his earlier work, with more fold forms recalling the even pleated flow of classical draperies although, judging by the detail in final preparatory studies, this simplicity may also be due partly to damage. The settings are all of an austerity unparalleled in his earlier work. In the *Visitation* (Plate 117), an arched gate, a wall and a door indicate that the travellers have reached home. The complete absence of a landscape vista in the scene where the Baptist is blessed prior to his departure for the wilderness (Plate 120) is especially striking, for a view of the country into which he was about to go would seem to be essential to the narrative. The Baptist preaching was often used as a pretext for landscape painting in the *seicento*. In Sacchi's version (Plate 122; Col. Plate II), there is no landscape vista beyond that implied by the tree tops seen above the heads of the listening crowd. His other works of the 1640s and his few works of the 1650s have similarly plain settings. That of the *Death of St. Anne* (Plate 150) is only slightly more elaborate than those of the Fonte series with indoor backgrounds, while those of the Perugia *Presentation* and the *Dream of St. Joseph* (Plates 154, 156) consist of the barest possible indications of particular locations.

Sacchi's growing lack of confidence in his own abilities is reflected in the more frequent direct borrowings of both whole compositions and individual poses in his work of the 1640s. One of the Fonte compositions, that of the *Birth of the Baptist* (Plate 118), is virtually copied from his own earlier design for the *Birth of the Virgin* (Plate 20). The putti distributing roses disappear, one extra attendant is provided in the middle distance to help bridge the gap between background and foreground and the setting is plainer, as befits the supposedly more modest circumstances of the Baptist's family. The *Visitation* is modelled on Domenichino's fresco of this subject at Fano. The *Baptism* is close to Albani's *Baptism of Christ* for S. Giorgio in Bologna. The *Preaching of the Baptist* comes from Annibale's design for Saint Diego preaching formerly in the Cappella di S. Diego in S. Giacomo degli Spagnuoli. If the *Naming, Blessing* and *Beheading* scenes have no obvious immediate prototypes, it is probably because there was no obvious model for Sacchi to use for these less frequently painted subjects. The Raphael models for the two frescoes that Sacchi designed are less obvious than those for the five canvases cited above, but this is because the subjects did not appear in the Raphael Stanze and Sacchi had to adapt the compositions of similar subjects instead to his own purposes.

Sacchi's Last Works: 1649–1655

Whether out of his growing respect for the work of his most respected predecessors—and his admiration for Raphael was almost obsessive by the mid-1650s[102]—or whether for lack of his own ideas, Sacchi's work was in some respects less original and independent towards the end of his career. There was no decline in his abilities as a draughtsman, however, nor in his ability to portray human beings in states of heightened emotional awareness. The Perugia *Presentation* (Plate 154) has been irreparably damaged by long neglect and is now too fragile to be cleaned properly, but it is still an impressive and dignified portrayal of intense religious devotion. The network of communicating gazes that unites the participants in the drama even recalls similar effects in Poussin's late works. In another respect, Sacchi's late work should have been sympathetic to Poussin, although there is no evidence that he appreciated it. One of Poussin's professed aims was to create pictures whose paint surfaces did not distract the viewer's attention from the subject matter, but even Poussin's last works are so beautiful simply as objects of form and colour that it is extremely difficult not to be aware of Poussin the painter before one is aware of Poussin the philosopher. The disciplined austerity of Sacchi's late works conforms more completely with Poussin's intentions than do Poussin's own works. As with the Fonte series, it must be remembered that lack of surface appeal is partly due to condition. The *Death of St. Anne* is obscured by a thick layer of old varnish. Both the Fabriano and Ferrara *Baptists* (Plate 152) are damaged and very dirty. The precarious condition of the Perugia picture has been noted. The *Dream of St. Joseph* (Plate 157) is now only a palimpsest of restorations and no longer even records the outlines of Sacchi's composition accurately.[103] All these compositions concentrate on the principal figures to the exclusion of all irrelevant incident and do so to a greater degree than Sacchi's work before 1640, with the exception of the *Daedalus and Icarus*. His contemporaries did not admire or understand the almost puritanical restraint of these last creations. Even Bellori did not appreciate the originality of Sacchi's approach to history painting, but then his analysis of the dramatic content of the work of Domenichino and Poussin also fails to reveal the profound differences between their approaches to narrative painting.

The masterpiece of Sacchi's last years is *The Death of St. Anne* in San Carlo ai Catinari (Plate 150). Seen in full morning light, it comes alive with glowing reds and ochre golds. It would be even more impressive clean. Sacchi was a child when Caravaggio's *Death of the Virgin* (Paris, Louvre) left Rome for Mantua in 1607, but its composition provides so many striking formal parallels with Sacchi's painting that we must assume he knew its design. In both works we find the bed or bier set at a similar angle to the picture plane in the right centre ground with the spectators carefully grouped around it so that they do not block our view of the dead or dying woman. In both the figures express a wide range of emotional reactions to the event. In both the light falls from the left. In both a large, red curtain occupies the upper right third of the picture field. Both employ a setting that combines domestic intimacy with a ceremonial dignity. The grieving Magdalene in the right foreground of Caravaggio's picture is echoed by the woman in the right corner of Sacchi's picture, who wipes her tears on a cloth, as well as by the seated figure of Joachim. The contrasts are also significant. The reds, ochres and browns of Caravaggio's painting have been modified with lapis blues, pink, cream, soft browns, copper reds and dull greens. Caravaggio places an apostle who weeps energetically in the centre of the picture. Sacchi avoids giving such prominence to obvious gestures of grief, placing the only person who weeps openly in shadow in the lower, right corner. And while he has preserved Caravaggio's formal device of a falling line of heads leading the eye from left to right to the head of the dying woman, the difference in subject dictates changes in the narrative. Sacchi shows the Virgin and Child with St. Joseph bidding farewell to St. Anne. Servants who have come into the room with refreshments maintain a respectful distance, watching Jesus bless his dying grandmother. St. Anne looks past him to the blue sky of heaven that we glimpse through the arched doorway. Sacchi must have been sincerely impressed by Caravaggio's gifts as a designer, but he understood also in what ways Caravaggio had offended his contemporaries. The decorum of Sacchi's painting is faultless.

When Alexander VII, shortly after his election, invited Sacchi to send him some samples of his work, Sacchi sent the new Pope small copies of the *Divina Sapienza* and the *Vision of St. Romuald*. Passeri reports that the Pope was delighted until he learnt that the compositions were not new but were copies of works made almost twenty-five years earlier. It is unlikely that Alexander VII did not recognize two of Sacchi's best known works or that Sacchi intended to deceive the Pope into thinking that the designs were new ones, but Passeri's anecdote may well record the reactions of the art world to Sacchi's gesture. The choice of these two particular works by Sacchi suggests that he himself thought that they were his finest achievements, but it is significant that he went so far back in his career when selecting something with which to recommend himself to a new patron. The fact that he did not present the Pope with a new work is also evidence of his declining confidence in his own creative talents. The only work he is known to have completed for Alexander VII is the design of the Acqua Acetosa.[104] None of the large commissions that Cardinal Antonio Barberini gave Sacchi on his return to Rome in 1653 were completed.[105] Some were taken over by Maratta, others were abandoned. It was a disappointing finish to a career that had started so brilliantly and on the whole so confidently.

Sacchi's last known works are the drawings he made for the project to decorate the vault of San Luigi dei Francesi (Plates 158–164). His procrastinating perfectionism made him redraw the same poses many times with only slight variations. The whole series of drawings is a reverent homage to Annibale Carracci, whose *ignudi* on the ceiling of the Galleria Farnese were Sacchi's main source of inspiration. One of the anecdotes reported by both Bellori and Passeri concerned a conversation that took place in the chapel frescoed by Domenichino in S. Luigi, which Sacchi visited from time to time after the ceiling decoration had been commissioned from him. After discussing Raphael and Domenichino, Sacchi reportedly urged Maratta to study hard, and not to lose heart. 'If you don't do as well as you would wish, at least you won't do so badly as you feared. Not everyone can reach the same level of achievement.' It is unfortunate that Sacchi himself was unable to take this sensible advice.

Sacchi did not apparently spend much time working on the various commissions assigned to him in the 1650s, but he seems to have continued his teaching activities. By 1650 Maratta was an independent artist who needed no formal supervision. Sacchi's will shows nevertheless that a small number of students and followers frequented his house even in the late 1650s, and there are intermittent references to a studio and drawing academy in the 1630s and 1640s. Poussin attended Sacchi's drawing academy when Domenichino moved his studio to Naples in 1630. Tommaso Luini came to Sacchi after quarrelling with Lanfranco, and subsequently left Sacchi's studio for the same reason in the early 1630s. Jan Miel worked with Sacchi on the Gesù Centenary picture in 1640, but is said by Baldinucci to have been dismissed by Sacchi, who told Miel that he was too old to learn to draw properly.[106] Further evidence of an active teaching studio is provided by the persistent tradition attributing red chalk academy studies of male nudes to Sacchi. Only one of the hundred odd drawings of this kind ascribed to him is autograph, but some are copies of Sacchi types.[107] The courtyard of Sacchi's house was full of casts mainly after ancient sculpture, presumably for the benefit of his students since classical models rarely play a prominent part in Sacchi's own work.[108] There would moreover be no reason for Pascoli to attach the anecdote about Francesco Lauri's lesson to Sacchi's name if Sacchi had not had a reputation as a teacher.[109] His teaching was probably mainly practical and pragmatic. The contents of his library at least indicate little or no interest in philosophy or art theory, while anecdotes that stress Sacchi's passionate admiration for artists like Raphael, Domenichino and Annibale Carracci all date from his last years, when these artists began to affect his own work to a marked degree.[110]

As Sacchi painted less and theorized more about the most suitable models for young artists to emulate, he evidently found it more and more difficult to commit his own ideas to paint, and eventually even to paper. Teaching may have provided some relief, as did conversations with a few sympathetic friends such as Maratta. He did not suffer a nervous breakdown, as Annibale did, nor did he commit suicide, as Testa did after his career had suffered a couple of serious reversals.[111] His insecurities with regard to his own work did not make his relations with other people as difficult as were those of Domenichino and Duquesnoy. Sacchi was never apparently jealous of Maratta's success; rather he regarded him as his artistic heir and took pleasure in watching Maratta translate his ideas and precepts into paint. In the later part of the decade, Sacchi could reasonably plead that his health was too poor for him to paint.[112] Throughout this difficult decade, the continual, patient, undemanding and largely unrewarded support of Cardinal Antonio Barberini must have meant a great deal. Sacchi's desire to leave the Cardinal a valuable silver cup in his will was certainly intended as an attempt to repay some of the Cardinal's generosity, while the Cardinal's preference for a picture instead shows that his support was maintained until the artist's death.

Sacchi's career is of obvious interest to those concerned with the psychology of artistic temperament, but efforts to understand him will be severely handicapped by the shortage of primary documentation. To say that Sacchi suffered in the last twenty years of his life from an inferiority complex which eventually became so severe that it crippled his creative abilities almost entirely is merely to state the obvious. To some extent we can trace the progress of this mental handicap as Sacchi's rate of production decreases and the proportion of obvious borrowings increases. Beyond that we can only hypothesize in a general way. His late drawings are beautiful and vigorous. His late works are as powerful psychologically as his earlier works; the best preserved are also as beautiful as anything he had painted in the 1620s and 1630s. He could in theory have continued to produce private commissions such as those of the 1630s and 1640s—*Daedalus and Icarus, Dido, St. Francis and Poverty, Noah*

III. *Hagar and Ishmael in the Wilderness*. Cardiff, National Museum of Wales. (Cat. No. 22)

Fig. 1. Sacchi's tomb. Rome, St. John Lateran

—and judging from his inventory he did produce other such works, most of them now lost. He was also a superb portraitist (e.g. Plates 46, 47, 49, 134, 137), creating the impression that he has given us a record of the sitter's appearance that is both objective and sympathetic. Few portraitists have managed to subordinate their own artistic personality to the degree that Sacchi did without depriving the portrait of vitality but such self-effacement was not fashionable in the seventeenth century. Sacchi assessed the standards of his contemporaries correctly in thinking that his reputation would depend on the completion of larger commissions, such as the decoration of S. Giovanni in Fonte. Having failed to some extent in the eyes of critics such as Bellori and Passeri with the Lateran Baptistry, Sacchi knew that his treatment of the ceiling of S. Luigi dei Francesi would be examined with even more critical attention. This made it more difficult for him to start work and ultimately prevented the work being carried out at all, even though plans had reached an advanced stage. It is regrettable that he was unable to ignore those traditional measures of achievement that were irrelevant to his particular talents, although it is easy to understand why to reject those criteria would have seemed to him a rejection of much more than the significance of sheer size in relation to artistic achievement.

Sacchi was respected by his contemporaries and by later generations of Italian artists, but his influence was felt mainly at second hand through the transmutations of his style propagated by Maratta and his school. Prior to Maratta, the artist who paid most attention to Sacchi was Pier Francesco Mola, who used the *St. Romuald* for his *St. Bruno,* and the *Hagar and Ishmael* and the Fonte *Baptist Preaching* for his own treatments of these themes.[113] Bernini admired the *St. Romuald* and based his frontispiece for Padre Oliva's sermons on it,[114] and Gaulli, perhaps at Bernini's suggestion, studied the *Divina Sapienza* before designing the nave fresco of the Gesù. Sacchi's most frequently copied works are the *St. Romuald* and the *Drunkenness of Noah* but neither spawned a series of derivations. In brief Sacchi was admired but little imitated. Apart from his well documented Roman altarpieces, most of his works were after the seventeenth century neglected, forgotten and in some cases destroyed. The major portion of his surviving drawings owe their survival to Maratta; Sacchi studies outside the two large groups at Windsor and Düsseldorf, which came from Maratta ultimately, are few and far between. Many have until recently remained unrecognized among the un-mounted, unattributed sheets of the print rooms to which they belong. Even Mariette had a vague notion of Sacchi's drawing style.[115] Undocumented paintings by Sacchi have been ascribed to artists as different as Ribera, Strozzi, Gaulli and Van Dyck, while works by mediocre or even unknown painters have been given to Sacchi.[116] Such errors are indicative of both the quality of Sacchi's own work and of the low level of achievement anticipated by those unfamiliar with it.

Sacchi was an artist of great integrity whose own work never falls below a very high standard. He never wastes our time with trivia. He was one of the most sensitive and accomplished draughtsmen of his century. He was an outstanding portraitist on the rare occasions that he turned his mind to that genre. He was a perceptive and sympathetic observer of mankind, his approach to history painting was original and in some respects unique. The dignified simplicity of his finest works links him with two Italian predecessors of whom Sacchi himself was probably hardly aware, namely Giotto and Masaccio. Like Masaccio, Sacchi preferred a style that was 'puro, sanza ornato', but despite the advocacy of Bellori, these qualities were less appreciated in the *seicento* than the dynamism, brilliance, fluidity and energy of Bernini and Cortona. Sacchi lacked the confidence either to compete with Cortona and his school, as Maratta was able to later, or to refuse to compete at all, which was Poussin's solution. Sacchi did not attempt a stylistic compromise, however, as Domenichino did.

Sacchi's contemporaries regarded him as an artist who failed to fulfil his early promise; as a result, they failed to appreciate what he did achieve. Later writers have echoed this half-hearted praise. A few of his best works have regularly found their way into surveys of the period, starting with Lanzi at the end of the eighteenth century, but even if Sacchi is acknowledged to be one of the major figures in Roman *seicento* painting, the statement is made without enthusiasm. He is clearly not one of the artistic giants of the seventeenth century; he is nevertheless an artist of the first rank and should be better known. Appreciation of his work may never extend much beyond serious students of Italian *seicento* painting. Few of his major works can be seen in important public collections outside Rome; nor will this situation change, there being no major works left in private hands. Thus he will never have the public exposure of his more productive contemporaries such as Reni, Cortona or Guercino. Nevertheless Sacchi's public, while small, will be knowledgeable and able to appreciate his work on its own terms.

II. Andrea Sacchi and his Contemporaries

Accounts of seventeenth-century painting in Rome emphasize the changing fortunes of two opposing schools of artistic thought, the baroque and the classical. Cesare d'Arpino and other late exponents of *maniera* are said to have been superseded by Annibale Carracci, who revived the classical aesthetic ideals of Raphael. Annibale's art in turn is set against the proto-baroque realism of Caravaggio and his followers. As Caravaggio's influence moves north and south in the second decade of the century, leaving behind in Rome only the low-life genre of the Bamboccianti, the emphasis shifts to Annibale's students and successors. Francesco Albani and, to a greater degree, Domenichino are seen as the artistic heirs of Annibale and the opponents of the developing baroque style of Lanfranco. Guercino comes to Rome during the brief reign of the Bolognese Pope Gregory XV (1621–3), his style by then formed in the North Italian tradition of 'colore', which is linked with the baroque. On his return to Cento, he gradually modifies his style in accordance with the classically-oriented tenets of 'disegno'.[1] In the 1630s, after the brief, unifying interlude of Neo-Venetianism, Nicolas Poussin and Andrea Sacchi are seen as representing the classical ideals of Raphael, Annibale and Domenichino and challenging the new baroque styles of Lanfranco and Pietro da Cortona. At the same time Francesco Duquesnoy and Alessandro Algardi are characterized as the classical opposition to that supreme exponent of the baroque style in sculpture, Gian Lorenzo Bernini. No major architect emerged in the *seicento* in Rome to reincarnate Brunelleschi, Leon Battista Alberti and Palladio and to offer an alternative to the baroque architecture of Bernini, Cortona and Francesco Borromini. Their opposition was largely confined to a few hints later in the century in the writings of Giovanni Pietro Bellori.

In the 1640s circumstances made representatives of the classical position more prominent than their baroque rivals. Cortona moved to Florence but Poussin and Sacchi remained in Rome. With the fall of the Barberini after the death of Urban VIII in 1644, some of the baroque artists that they had preferred, including Bernini, were out of favour. Urban's successor, Innocent X Pamphili, made Algardi his principal sculptor, although Bernini soon returned to prominence after the scandal which resulted from the destruction of his bell tower for St. Peter's. In the absence of Cortona and his chief follower, Francesco Romanelli, who had joined the Barberini in Paris, the Pamphili employed Giacinto Gimignani, Andrea Camassei and Sassoferrato, artists whose work is clearly indebted to Raphael, Domenichino and Poussin. Then in the 1650s and 1660s, the baroque style is said to have revived. Duquesnoy died in 1643, Algardi in 1654; they had no significant successors who could compete with Bernini. Sacchi produced no public work of importance after 1652. The flood of baroque art grew meanwhile with the return to Rome of Cortona in 1647, the growth of his school and the sustained activity of Bernini and his enormous studio. Bernini even extended his influence to the field of painting through G. B. Gaulli, who translated Bernini's ideas into frescoes as well as easel paintings and altarpieces. The classical camp had only one spokesman during these years, namely Carlo Maratta, but he was prolific and influential. He was eventually so successful that he is said to have dominated and tamed the baroque style in Rome by the end of the century.

Sacchi's role in this fluctuating artistic debate has always been somewhat ambiguous. His natural gifts as a painter ally him with 'colore' and the baroque, but while acknowledging this, his earliest biographers and all later writers have stressed his contacts with the classical school and the aesthetics of 'disegno'. Sacchi's training with Albani is emphasized because it permits his artistic pedigree to be traced back to impeccable classical sources—to Annibale Carracci, whom he was known to admire, and to Raphael, whom he reputedly worshipped. Poussin is said by Passeri to have attended Sacchi's drawing academy and Duquesnoy is supposed to have been their mutual friend. Sacchi's biography was written by Bellori, the chief *seicento* spokesman for the classical viewpoint, who selected his few subjects for favourable treatment with great care. In addition there is evidence that Sacchi despised the Bamboccianti, opposed Pietro da Cortona in a public debate and openly criticized Bernini.

The dichotomy in Sacchi's artistic personality was appreciated by Hans Posse, who noted that, while Sacchi's gifts as a painter place him among the greatest baroque painters of his century, his mental approach to his work was that of a classical artist. Denis Mahon made the same point more succinctly, calling Sacchi 'the least obviously baroque of the leading painters of his time in Rome'.[2] Other recent attempts to define Sacchi's position in *seicento* Rome have stressed his apparent opposition to the full baroque style of Cortona and Bernini. Recognizing the *seicento* character of classical art in the seventeenth century, Rudolf Wittkower coined the phrase 'High Baroque Classicism' and called Sacchi 'the Italian leader of this movement'.[3] Ellis Waterhouse has described Sacchi as Cortona's 'greatest rival on the classical side' and 'the enemy of Bernini and the representative of the opposite camp'.[4] Marabottini has written that Sacchi 'assumed an openly polemical attitude towards the developing taste for grand baroque decoration, placing himself as a direct adversary to Cortona sustaining those principles of simplicity and compositional clarity which formed the aesthetic credo of Domenichino'.[5] Andrea Emiliani has described the 'years of anti-baroque polemic of Sacchi, Poussin and Duquesnoy' and characterized Sacchi's paintings in S. Giovanni in Fonte as 'a unique and grief-stricken expression of moral protest in the very midst of the baroque season'.[6] Vincenzo Golzio, while also acknowledging Sacchi's talents as a painter, still saw him primarily as 'a representative of the classical school, and as such opposed to Cortona'.[7] Enggass says that Sacchi, 'inheriting the struggle from Francesco Albani (who in turn had been one of the more doctrinaire graduates of the Academy) joyfully took up the attack against Pietro da Cortona'.[8] In a more leisurely essay on the artistic situation in *seicento* Rome than most of those cited above, Giuliano Briganti emphasized instead the relative isolation of Sacchi and the depth of religious feeling, particularly in his later work.[9]

Although it is easy to understand why Sacchi's classical rather than his baroque side has received so much attention, the typical description of him as an opponent or even an enemy of baroque art and baroque artists is erroneous. A more critical examination of the evidence cited in support of the portrait of Sacchi as a polemical opponent of Cortona and Bernini indicates, as does new evidence published here, that Sacchi's relations with his contemporaries have been misunderstood. For example, Bellori tells us that Sacchi was trained by Cesare d'Arpino as well as by Albani. Contrary to expectation, for a classical artist is presumed to reject mannerism as well as the baroque, Sacchi clearly felt a strong sense of attachment to Cesare at the end of his life, for he asked in his will to be buried next to Cesare in S. Giovanni in Laterano.[10] The will also reveals that his attitude to Bernini cannot have been entirely negative, for besides requesting burial next to an artist now commonly dismissed as a sterile exponent of late academic mannerism, he also asked to have his tomb designed by Bernini, the arch-exponent of the baroque style.[11] As an active opponent of Cortona, Sacchi might be expected to have taken over the Academy of St. Luke in the 1640s during Cortona's absence in Florence, but he never apparently tried to use the Academy to publicize his own aesthetic viewpoint after the famous debate with Cortona in 1636.[12] Sacchi may have written the letter, attributed to him by Malvasia, in which the Bamboccianti are severely criticized, but this attitude did not prevent him from owning a picture by the founding member of that school, Pieter van Laer.[13] He owned more than sixty books at the time of his death.[14] Remembering his debate with Cortona and his reputation as an artist who neglected his work in order to talk about art, we would expect him to own a few of the standard texts of classical art theory, but there were no books in his house directly connected with his profession. Those who see Sacchi as a leading exponent of the classical ideals favoured also by Bellori and Poussin often assume that the three men were friends and that Sacchi and Poussin admired each other's work. Direct contacts between these three men were rare, however, and Poussin at least seems to have had a low opinion of Sacchi's work.[15]

Denis Mahon has suggested that these changing artistic allegiances and rivalries are best understood in the context of an infinitely flexible, open artistic situation with artists conscious of the contrasting yet complementary concepts of *colore* and *disegno* and reacting to them in different ways during their careers.[16] These concepts could be and were interpreted in widely differing styles during the seventeenth century and none of the elements that we might consider essential to one or the other of these concepts can be assumed to be present in the work of an artist whom we associate with that concept.[17] Both depend on sixteenth-century traditions—*colore* on North Italian and Venetian painting, *disegno* on contemporary developments in Florence and Rome. Neither of these traditions was native to Rome. Indeed the city had no native artistic tradition to speak of in the fourteenth and fifteenth centuries, but *disegno* was in effect transplanted there in the sixteenth century by a succession of Florentine or Florentine-trained artists, and insofar as the experience of Rome—above all the scale and quantity of ancient monuments to be seen there—inevitably affected the work of artists who remained in Rome for any length of time, *disegno* became a Roman style but one absorbed and practised by artists born and at least partially trained elsewhere. The political and economic independence of Venice and its mainland territories in the sixteenth century largely explains the limited impact of Venetian and North Italian *colore* in Rome before 1580. With the decline of the Venetian economy in the seventeenth century and the wealth of artistic opportunities available in Rome after 1580,[18] Rome became the focal point of Italian and to some extent of European art, and the Roman style, instead of being the product largely of one Italian tradition, became a far more complex blend of different Italian styles.

Though Rome had by 1600 attracted a large, international community of artists, in retrospect it was the work carried out between 1590 and 1610 by Caravaggio and Annibale Carracci, both artists strongly rooted in the *colore* traditions of Venice and North Italy, which was to have the most profound impact on art in Rome during the rest of the century. When Caravaggio and Annibale arrived, *disegno* was established Roman practice and *colore* was regarded as an alien aesthetic.[19] In the form introduced by Annibale, however, with a heavy admixture of *disegno* elements, it was more readily acceptable than was the much purer *colore* of Caravaggio. Indeed by contrast with Caravaggio, Annibale's work seemed relatively conservative, which it was, but by demonstrating that the traditions of *colore* and *disegno* could be fused, Annibale made *colore* respectable in Rome. After his death knowledge of the works of the greatest sixteenth-century exponents of *colore*—Titian, Veronese and Correggio above all—gradually came to be accepted as a necessary part of the experience of every ambitious young painter. Some artists might prefer to associate themselves primarily with the stylistic traditions of one or other of these two concepts: to Caravaggio's *colore* can be opposed the almost equally pure interpretation of *disegno* in Domenichino's early work. Others might during their careers shift from emphasis on one to the other, as Guercino did, or, like Poussin, might experiment with both before settling on a style that emphasized one but continued to draw on the other. In brief, *disegno* ceased to dominate art and artists in Rome, and artists working there stopped thinking of *disegno* and *colore* as incompatible aesthetic philosophies. While able to conceive of them in the abstract as separate entities, artists blended both in their work, and the debate, insofar as there was any among artists in Rome between the death of Federigo Zuccaro and the publication of Bellori's *Idea* in 1672,[20] was not about the relative virtues of *colore* and *disegno* but was about the ways in which these traditions could be reinterpreted and fused.

It was not only the presence in Rome of artists of undeniable talent whose work depended on *colore* traditions that helped to break down resistance there to Venetian and North Italian sixteenth-century painting. The impact of the arrival of masterpieces by Titian and other major Venetian and North Italian artists in the Este collections, taken by Cardinal Pietro Aldobrandini from Ferrara to Rome at the very end of the sixteenth century, cannot be overestimated.[21] Their full effect was only gradually felt however. Two of Annibale's most important pupils and successors in Rome, Domenichino and Albani, emphasized the Roman and Bolognese *disegno* aspects of Annibale's mature work in theirs, while the Annibale student who did stress *colore*, namely Lanfranco, was primarily affected by the work of his Parmese compatriot Correggio. Thus it was not until the 1620s when Cortona, Poussin and Sacchi began studying the Aldobrandini collections that Titian's *Bacchanals* began to have a profound effect on Roman painting.

As the prejudices against *colore* cultivated in *cinquecento* Rome were overcome, the particular character of the works in the Este collections set the tone of Roman interpretations of *colore*. The collection was not composed primarily of works by the masters we associate with the Venetian High Renaissance—the mature Titian, Tintoretto, Veronese and the Bassani. The court for whom the elaborate intellectual puzzles of the Schifanoia frescoes had been designed continued to appreciate extremes of technical refinement and recherché subject matter and their favourite artists catered to these tastes.[22] Titian's *Bacchanals* are no exception. They are by Titian's standards unusually precisely drawn and carefully finished, even for their relatively early date. The controlled surface treatment may have been a surprise to artists familiar with the legendary reputation of the mature Titian, whose brush work was loose and free. To Roman eyes therefore the *colore* elements in the *Bacchanals* must have appeared refined by *disegno* qualities. This partly explains their extraordinary impact in Rome, in particular their power to affect artists with affinities for both *colore* and *disegno*. Inspired by Cardinal Aldobrandini's example, other collectors added Venetian paintings to their collections. By 1630 the Ludovisi, the Giustiniani, the Sacchetti, Cardinal Scipione Borghese and others owned good Venetian pictures, which would have been accessible at least to the artists they patronized. Roman churches had little to offer, but S. Luigi dei Francesi had a high altarpiece by Francesco Bassano, there was a Palma Giovane in S. Maria della Scala and Girolamo Muziano's pictures of saints in landscapes could be studied in St. Peter's and elsewhere.[23]

There are several unfortunate consequences of the widespread practice of focusing on the fluctuating fortunes of 'baroque' and 'classical' when writing about Roman seventeenth-century painting. In the first place this practice creates the impression that by about 1620 artists in Rome were aware of two trends in contemporary art and that most artists consciously preferred one of these two sets of artistic values to the other, saw them as incompatible and actively opposed those artists whose preferences differed from theirs. Those artists who fit uneasily into either camp, for example Cesare d'Arpino, who is labelled 'Late Academic Mannerist', or Caravaggio, who is essentially treated as a phenomenon of limited art-historical impact, tend to be seen as fringe figures of less significance than the central debate between 'classical' and 'baroque'. Another consequence of this practice is that scholars and critics, blinded by the stereotypes suggested by the two terms, overlook or minimize those qualities in a particular work that do not fit the stereotype while overemphasizing those that do. Thus Sacchi's work has many 'baroque', Cortona's has many 'classical' qualities, yet these aspects of their artistic personalities are rarely more than mentioned, an omission that distorts our perception of their paintings. Another distortion depends on the 'classical' artists' reputed stress on tradition. By implication 'baroque' artists, whose debts to their predecessors were less conscious, seem less dependent and consequently more original.

Just as Vasari's attitudes towards the art of the fourteenth, fifteenth and sixteenth centuries still dominate all accounts of Italian art of these three centuries, so Bellori, who provides the most clearly articulated theory of 'classical' *seicento* art and the most biased and selective survey of *seicento* art in Rome, also dominates accounts of his period. Reconstructing the viewpoints of sixteenth- and seventeenth-century critics and art historians is obviously a valuable exercise for modern scholars, but it is not good historical practice to assume, as is so often done, that the theories, tastes and preferences of Vasari and Bellori have more value than those of their contemporaries whose attitudes are less effectively preserved. To do so assumes that modern scholars cannot write an objective account of the period concerned. Few modern scholars would consciously make that assumption, but few seem aware of the extent to which they write about Italian art between 1400 and 1700 as if they did. Thus the concept of 'classical' art is legitimized by associating it with Bellori, and 'baroque' becomes what Bellori disapproved of or failed to discuss. In order to understand Sacchi, whose art has affinities with both stereotypical 'classical' and 'baroque' art, it is necessary to break away from this approach. The next sections of this essay will therefore look at Sacchi's relations with the artists and artistic institutions generally associated with current definitions of 'baroque' and 'classical'.

Sacchi, Bernini and Duquesnoy

Sacchi was a painter who occasionally worked as an architect. Bernini was a sculptor and architect who never executed a public commission as a painter. The two men were not therefore in direct competition with each other. If relations between them were poor—and several pieces of evidence have suggested to previous scholars that they were[24]—the reason would not seem to be professional jealousies. It has been assumed that Sacchi, the 'classical' artist, found Bernini's exuberant 'baroque' art antipathetic. Now that we know, however, that Sacchi wanted his tomb to be designed by Bernini, it is clear that the situation was more complicated and other explanations must be sought.

The first possible evidence of contact between Sacchi and Bernini is a pair of pictures in the National Gallery in London.[25] Both depict two half-length male figures—in Bernini's case, two apostles, in Sacchi's, two saints. The canvases are the same size; they have hung together since 1738 at least. It is not certain, however, that both were commissioned at the same time or even that both belonged to the Barberini in 1627, when the Bernini is recorded in their possession and when Sacchi was paid by them for a picture of two apostles. Sacchi's lost picture of two apostles may have been part of a series that included Bernini's *St. Thomas and St. Andrew*, while Sacchi's two saints, even if not painted to accompany Bernini's canvas, may have been modelled on it. However interpreted, the evidence suggests at the very least that Sacchi admired Bernini in the early 1620s; he may even have cooperated with him on one project.

The next evidence of contacts between them is more complicated. In 1628–9, Sacchi received a commission for an overdoor fresco in St. Peter's of the subject *Christ's command to Peter, 'Feed My Sheep'*.[26] After being paid a quarter of the total fee and after completing a *modello*, Sacchi ceased working on the commission, which was never carried out. It was one of six overdoors commissioned between 1628 and 1630 for spaces surrounding the crossing of St. Peter's. Four were completed; all are lost. Bellori, who knew the *modello* was for a commission in St. Peter's, offers no explanation for Sacchi's failure to carry out what was clearly an important commission.[27]

The circumstances surrounding these six commissions are complicated. In 1627 neither the ecclesiastics in charge of St. Peter's nor Bernini had decided what was to go on the important site in the centre of the rear wall of the apse. Various names were put forward for an altarpiece. Then it was said that either Guido Reni would paint a picture or Bernini would cast or carve a relief for this spot showing Christ giving the keys to St. Peter. This, however, was the subject given to Antonio Pomarancio a few months later for his overdoor fresco, by which time Guido Reni had been switched to another site, namely that now occupied by Algardi's relief of Leo I and Attila.[28] One more detail from these documents is relevant. On February 4, 1628, eleven days before Sacchi, Allegrini, Ciampelli or Baglione received their commissions,[29] Bernini was given 'one of the overdoors to be painted, which he may dispose of as he wishes'.[30] It is probable that Bernini chose Sacchi. The other three artists were older men whose styles must have seemed dry and academic next to Sacchi's most recent works, their colours enriched by Sacchi's admiration for Titian and Barocci. And if Sacchi was Bernini's personal choice, this fact would help to explain how Bernini could later take this commission away from Sacchi, which is apparently what happened.

Sacchi's overdoor commission must have been cancelled before 1643 when two new artists, Gian Domenico Cerrini and Mattia Preti, were given down payments for overdoors, presumably to fill the two spaces left empty by Sacchi and Allegrini.[31] One possible explanation for Sacchi's loss of this commission is that he delayed finishing it and finally had it taken away from him. All other evidence of Sacchi's slowness belongs to the later 1640s, however, and even more to the 1650s. Other commissions of the late 1620s and 1630s were carried out within a year of being requested. Moreover, Sacchi had no difficulty in designing the *modello* in a few months. Another possible explanation is that Bernini wished to reserve the subject for his overdoor relief in the portico of St. Peter's.[32] This cannot be the explanation either, however, because Ambrogio Bonvicino's relief above the main door of the portico showing Christ giving the keys to St. Peter was in place when this subject was assigned to Pomarancio for his overdoor.[33] Indeed the original plans for the overdoors of Sacchi and Pomarancio paralleled those for the reliefs of Bernini and Bonvicino. The two subjects are crucial to the central church of Roman Catholicism: one establishes Peter's divine appointment as the first Pope, the other the Pope's earthly responsibilities. The carved versions were back-to-back above the central doorway of the portico while the two paintings would have been in pendant positions across the choir in the apse.[34] When Sacchi's commission was cancelled, it must have been assumed that the subject would still be introduced into St. Peter's itself. It eventually was in the most prominent relief decorating the back of Bernini's *Cathedra Petri*. Bernini certainly did not know in 1629, when he became architect of St. Peter's, or in 1633, when he started the *Pasce Oves Meas* relief, or in 1643, when the two new *sopraporte* of unknown subjects were commissioned, exactly what was to go on the site of the Cathedra Petri, but it is highly probable that Bernini, the Fabbrica di San Pietro and the Congregazione dei Riti all thought it necessary to reserve an important subject for that site. I think that the subject reserved was the *Pasce Oves Meas,* and that Bernini wanted the site when the time came to use it, and that that is why Sacchi had to stand down.

Sacchi's *Miracle of St. Anthony of Padua,* which was installed in the Capuchins' new church in the late spring of 1633, included in the background a discreet portrait of Duquesnoy's recently completed *Santa Susanna*. Passeri says that Sacchi did this only partially to draw attention to Duquesnoy's statue. Sacchi's main motive was his desire to hurt someone—Passeri names no names—who had offended Sacchi and earned his hatred at this time. Hess[35] assumed that the object of Sacchi's hatred was Bernini, though he was unaware of the *Pasce Oves Meas* commission. Quite how the inclusion of the *Susanna* was to hurt Bernini is unclear though its appearance in Sacchi's painting does amount to a public declaration of support for Duquesnoy. It is the earliest evidence of Sacchi's admiration for and friendship with Duquesnoy.[36] That relationship almost inevitably entailed opposition to Bernini during Duquesnoy's lifetime.[37]

If the incident with the *Susanna* was inspired by Bernini's cancellation of Sacchi's *Pasce Oves Meas* commission, then the cancellation occurred late in 1632 or early in 1633.[38] It was in 1633 that Sacchi was asked to paint altarpieces for all four crypt chapels beneath the crossing piers in St. Peter's.[39]

In 1627, before Bernini was made architect of St. Peter's or assigned the task of decorating the four piers, two of the crypt chapels were declared unsuitable sites for altars because they were dark and small.[40] Bernini assumed responsibility for the piers in May, 1628. The chapels were enlarged and a combination grille-skylight was designed which enables the altarpieces to be seen, although not well, from the main body of the church.[41] Bernini certainly had control of all the commissions connected with this project. It seems that he tried to make up to Sacchi for the loss of the overdoor commission by giving him these four altarpieces instead. Sacchi probably felt cheated anyway. The overdoor was a large and prominently sited work; the crypt altars could easily be overlooked. Sacchi was not to know that the extreme dampness of the crypt chapels would mean that his were to be among the first of the paintings in St. Peter's to be removed to drier locations and to be replaced in the church by mosaic copies, and that his four altarpieces would survive, whereas all the overdoors would be lost, either because of damp or as a result of the poor technique for transferring frescoes in the eighteenth and nineteenth centuries. It is worth noting at this point that only professional jealousies have been involved and that Bernini apparently had a high opinion of Sacchi's work.

In 1639, when Sacchi designed the decoration of the Gesù for the Jesuits' centenary celebrations, an agent of the Este wrote to Modena that as a result of this commission rivalry between Sacchi and Bernini was increasing.[42] When Urban VIII died in July, 1644, it was Sacchi and not Bernini who was commissioned to design the Pope's funeral catafalque.[43] Bernini's reputation was still at a peak. He can hardly have felt that his career was threatened by these incidents, but Sacchi may well have felt that they were feathers in his cap, especially as he had recently been working on other architectural projects that invited comparisons with the work of Bernini.[44] The agent's remark implies that Bernini and Sacchi were seen as rivals before the Gesù celebrations, whether in connection with other architectural projects or Sacchi's earlier disappointment over the *Pasce Oves Meas* fresco nourished by his association with Duquesnoy we cannot tell. Professional jealousies remain the most obvious explanation for Sacchi's poor relations with Bernini, however, even if these were rationalized by Sacchi and Duquesnoy with critical judgements of Bernini's work.

After Duquesnoy's death in 1643, it might be anticipated that Sacchi's attitude towards Bernini would change. There is evidence that it did. In the late 1630s Sacchi had a pupil, Pietro Paolo Naldini, who decided to become a sculptor instead. He wanted to study with Bernini, but as Sacchi opposed this, Naldini studied with Algardi.[45] By the late 1640s, Naldini was launched on an independent career.[46] By 1655, he was working for Bernini in S. Maria del Popolo.[47] When Sacchi died in 1661, however, Naldini was remembered in the will with a bequest of two drawings. Moreover, Naldini witnessed one of the codicils and helped Maratta to prepare the inventory of Sacchi's possessions.[48] Clearly working for Bernini in the 1650s had not affected Naldini's close friendship with Sacchi. The request that Sacchi made for a tomb designed by Bernini and executed by Naldini also suggests that relations between Bernini and Sacchi had improved.

Sacchi's tomb survives in a corridor near the sacristy in St. John Lateran (Fig. 1), though comparison with Bombelli's engraving of 1769 (Fig. 2) shows that it has lost some of its decorative trimmings. It is doubtful that Bernini had anything to do with the design. Even projects carried out entirely by his studio assistants betray some originality in the design; that of Sacchi's tomb is pedestrian. More to the point, it looks like other tombs by Naldini, a little more elegant than his tomb for Prior Filippini of 1657,[49] but less exciting, and far less Berninesque, than his much later tombs for the Marcaccioni family in S. Maria del Suffragio.[50] Sacchi's motives in asking for a tomb by Bernini were probably not just simple admiration for Bernini's work. A tomb by Bernini was a prestigious memorial to have, and Sacchi, who left only 200 scudi for the purpose, may have hoped that his old patron, Cardinal Antonio Barberini, would take the hint and foot the bill. Nevertheless, if Sacchi had had strong reservations about Bernini's work, he would not have made the request in the first place.

A year before his death, Sacchi was invited by Bernini to visit St. Peter's and give his opinion of the model of the Cathedra Petri then installed at the rear of the apse.[51] Pascoli relates that Bernini sent his carriage round to Sacchi's house, but that Sacchi did not bother to change from working clothes and slippers before getting in, a deliberate gesture of disrespect in an age far more formal than our own. At St. Peter's, Bernini met him and escorted him down the nave. Half way along, Sacchi stopped. 'This is the place from which it must be judged', he told Bernini, who urged him to move a little closer. 'All right', said Bernini, 'what do you think of it?' 'The figures are too small', replied Sacchi, and walked out.

Pascoli says that Bernini was so mortified that, even though he secretly agreed with Sacchi, he refused to change anything. The executed figures are larger than the models, however, though probably not just because of Sacchi's apt, if ungraciously delivered, criticism. The incident suggests that relations between the two men were still awkward, and that, as in the 1630s, Bernini tried to be accommodating—after getting his way—and on this occasion at least took the initiative. The story, if true, also suggests a certain lofty insensitivity on Bernini's part, for what he also sought, if our hypothesis is correct, was Sacchi's approval of the commission which finally brought the *Pasce Oves Meas* into St. Peter's. It is not surprising that Sacchi was annoyed and refused to give the project his blessing.

Though there are many gaps in our knowledge of Sacchi's relations with Bernini, all the evidence so far available suggests that it was not differences in aesthetic philosophies but competition for important commissions and Bernini's virtual monopoly of the best sculptural and architectural opportunities—a monopoly that affected painters as well—which soured relations between him and Sacchi. Contemporary criticism of Bernini was in fact rarely directed at the quality or character of his work but rather at his supposed technical incompetence or at his role as artistic dictator of Rome.[52] Sacchi's resentment at Bernini's success, which he shared with Duquesnoy, no doubt made Bernini's work antipathetic as well, and after an initial sympathy for Bernini's work, seen in the *St. Anthony Abbot and St. Francis* (Plate 6) and in some of Sacchi's bold chalk studies of the late 1620s, Sacchi seems to have ignored it.[53] Bernini's respect for Sacchi is documented not only by his occasional support for Sacchi when he was awarding commissions, but also by occasional borrowings from Sacchi's work. Thus Bernini's first sketches for his *Pasce Oves Meas* relief show that he knew Sacchi's *modello* of this subject, while in a frontispiece design made after Sacchi's death, Bernini uses the device Sacchi had made famous in his *St. Romuald* altarpiece, that of a large tree which anchors and emphasizes the principal figure in a composition with a landscape setting.[54]

Bernini's vast reserves of creative energies, which enabled him to rise to a position of eminence rapidly and to remain there unchallenged for almost all of his career, would have made contemporary artists jealous even if he had always treated them generously. Nevertheless, the extent to which simple jealousies and not aesthetic squabbles divided Bernini from artists like Sacchi and Duquesnoy has been underestimated. Indeed Bernini and Sacchi shared one central concern as artists, namely the convincing expression of human *affetti*. Sacchi could legitimately criticize Cortona for his relative lack of interest in *affetti*, but Bernini, admittedly with theatrical trappings which Sacchi probably disliked, was deeply involved in the problem of communicating specific emotional states to his viewer. Sacchi's approach, especially in private commissions, was more cerebral than that of Bernini, but I think he recognized their shared artistic ground, and for this reason respected Bernini's work.

Sacchi, Cortona and the Academy of St. Luke

The activities of the Academy of St. Luke in Rome between 1630 and 1670 have been neglected or misrepresented by most writers who have broached the subject at all since Melchiorre Missirini published his history of the Academy in 1823.[55] His book is, for a start, inaccurate and consequently not to be relied on. His support for the Academy tends to make him exaggerate its importance even when there is evidence to show that it was almost totally inactive. His account of the years 1620 to 1670 is padded out with material from *seicento* biographies, nor is it always clear where Missirini ends and the biographies or documents begin. Later scholars have been content to use Missirini or have consulted the Academy's archives only to find references to specific artists or groups of artists. The result is a confused portrait of the Academy in recent literature with scholars attributing various degrees of significance to the Academy's activities on the basis of inadequately published evidence.

The most important piece of surviving documentation for the Academy's activities in the mid-seventeenth century is a minute-book of business meetings held between 1634 and 1674.[56] After assuring themselves that it contains no verbatim accounts of debates or prize-giving ceremonies with speeches, scholars have ignored it. But analysis of its contents reveals much about the Academy's activities during this period. In brief, when the Academy was active between 1630 and 1660, it was primarily due to the support and participation of Pietro da Cortona.[57] Towards the end of Cortona's life, Maratta began to play an active role but it was only under Maratta that the Academy functioned as it was intended to by Federico Zuccaro and its other late sixteenth-century founders. That is, the various artists who belonged to it began to pay their dues regularly and to contribute their time to enterprises like the supervision of drawing academies of posed models, the judging of students' drawings for prizes and the delivering of inspiring addresses on appropriate subjects at prize-giving ceremonies. The absence of any mention of such matters in the minutes of business meetings, when the necessary arrangements were made, held during Cortona's régime, strongly suggests that under Cortona very little of this went on. Indeed, to judge from the minutes, Cortona's primary concern was the construction of the church of SS. Martina e Luca, which was, among other things, his own mausoleum.[58]

Though membership in the Academy was in theory obligatory,[59] most artists, even those loyal to Cortona who attended business meetings regularly, failed to pay their dues in the 1630s and 1640s, and many well-known artists never attended meetings at all, even when elected *in absentia* to offices.[60] Cortona's motives for supporting the Academy seem to have been a mixture of self-glorification and respect for the methods of training young artists in the discipline of *disegno* that goes back to his own Tuscan origins.[61] He was, however, far more successful at promoting himself through the Academy than he was at promoting the Academy as a combined trade union and university for his fellow artists. Without him, on the other hand, meetings became infrequent, and in the late 1640s and early 1650s, petered out altogether.[62]

Sacchi's documented participation in the affairs of the Academy runs from 1624 to 1638, though he is only known to have attended meetings in 1625, 1628, 1631, 1633 and 1636.[63] His debate with Cortona, for which the unreliable Missirini is our only source, probably took place in 1636.[64] In 1658 Sacchi declined an invitation to become Principe.[65] His best pupil and by 1661 his close friend as well, Maratta joined the Academy only after Sacchi's death, but did so with alacrity and immediately became one of its most active members. Did Sacchi's artistic differences with Cortona, which became public at the debate and even more so after the completion of Cortona's ceiling in the Palazzo Barberini in 1637, make him avoid the Academy after this date because of its identification with Cortona, or did he share, with the numerous other artists who avoided the Academy, misgivings about the purpose of such an organization in Rome's artistic affairs? What were Sacchi's motives for agreeing to debate with Cortona in the first place? And what were his reactions when the majority sided with the Principe?

Sacchi might have been moved to defend his point of view publicly after the poor reception accorded to his *St. Bonaventure* altarpiece for the Capuchins in 1636. Perhaps the journey to North Italy in 1635 made him more conscious of his particular aesthetic philosophy and of how greatly it differed from that of Cortona. Perhaps Sacchi objected to Cortona's use of the Academy to advance his own career and hoped that a debate might encourage more use of the Academy along the lines intended by its founders. When it became clear that Cortona was unwilling or unable to make the Academy function as an educational institution, Sacchi withdrew his minimal support and concentrated on teaching his own students. He may even have disapproved of the Academy's system of rotating the task of supervising the drawing academy among members on a monthly basis because it would mean that the students would inevitably be taught by some second-rate artists. Whatever the explanation—and with so little evidence only hypotheses can be suggested—Sacchi avoided the Academy for the last twenty years of his life and seems to have encouraged Maratta to do likewise.

The debate between Sacchi and Cortona has attracted attention because it is one of the few recorded aesthetic discussions between 1625 and 1664,[66] and seems to indicate a developing rift between 'classical' and 'baroque'. Missirini's account is believable if only because, as Wittkower noted, 'both masters made the theoretical position which they defended explicit in their work'. By attacking Cortona's overpopulated compositions, Sacchi put his finger on the major weakness in Cortona's work according to the aesthetics of *disegno,* to which Cortona was more attached than his 'baroque' label suggests. He had good *disegno* precedents for working on large-scale frescoes (Raphael, Annibale, Domenichino), for organizing a large studio efficiently (Raphael, Annibale) and for extending his activities to the field of architecture (Raphael). His interest in antiquity was evident to any student of his work, his study of the correct masters in his youth well-known. He might even claim to have fulfilled more of the requirements for a great artist in the *disegno* tradition than Sacchi. But Sacchi could criticize Cortona's lack of interest in the portrayal of states of human emotion, a bias Cortona shared with Algardi,[67] and could even expect some support for doing so from the numerous artists who shared Sacchi's belief that the depiction of the *affetti* should be the artist's primary concern.

Sacchi probably suspected in 1636 that posterity would be more impressed by Cortona's showmanship than by his own more reserved creations. Later in his career, as Cortona and his followers consolidated their position, Sacchi probably identified with Annibale and Domenichino not only because he admired their work but also because they, like him, had failed to gain the degree of public acclaim accorded Raphael in the sixteenth century.[68] Success was now the reward of artists who did not, in Sacchi's opinion, fully deserve it. However, Sacchi himself was aware that his work judged by these same standards was open to criticism. His architectural and decorative commissions of the late 1630s were probably undertaken partly to prove to Cortona and others that he had a wider range and could tackle these large-scale tasks. And his fear of failing by his own standards was probably heightened by a fear that his achievements might not be appreciated anyway.

We may regret that Sacchi did not decide to limit himself to easel pictures for private patrons during the last ten or fifteen years of his life instead of crippling himself with his fears of failing at more ambitious projects, but such a decision would have been contrary to a long Italian tradition. Poussin was able to do so, but his circumstances encouraged this alternative. He was French and foreign artists living in Rome did not traditionally depend mainly on public commissions. The majority of them worked for private patrons, often for export to their own countries, and the majority of them specialized in art forms that many Italian artists professed to despise, namely genre and landscape. To the extent that Poussin was accepted in Italy as an important and serious artist, his nationality was crucial, for his career was simply not judged by the same standards as that of an Italian artist. Nor can it be said that Poussin established that a career devoted to serious private works was a viable alternative to a career of major public commissions for an ambitious Italian artist.[69] And just as patrons did not associate Poussin with public commissions, so Sacchi was rarely associated with private commissions once he had established himself as a court artist whose production was mainly reserved for the Barberini. In the late 1640s and early 1650s, when Sacchi would have welcomed a few sympathetic private patrons, they were not forthcoming. His lament to Albani in

1651 about the success of the Bambocciati was as much provoked by the ease with which they sold their works as by the vulgarity of their subject matter.[70]

Sacchi's lack of contact with Cassiano dal Pozzo is difficult to explain. In the late 1620s and early 1630s, before Sacchi became a regular Barberini protégé, he was in touch with Vouet, Cortona, Poussin, Duquesnoy and others who were friendly with Cassiano and who worked for him. Cassiano must have known Sacchi through these mutual friends but he never seems to have patronized him.[71] It may be that Sacchi, who only lacked influential patrons for a brief period in his early career, was always out of Cassiano's limited price range, or that even at this stage he confined his production to a few major works and had little to offer patrons of modest means who wanted original compositions.[72] He may also have been successful enough not to need the money that Poussin and Testa earned making drawings after antiquities for Cassiano's Museo Cartaceo, Sacchi was not uninterested in the antique—his cast collection proves that—but it did not play an important formal role in his work and he had no antiquarian interests comparable to those of Cassiano, Poussin, or even Cortona. Still, Leonardo Agostini's dedication shows that one knowledgeable Roman antiquarian found Sacchi sympathetic company.[73] His library also suggests that he could hold his own in the company of *letterati*.

He owned more than sixty books.[74] Though by no means a large collection by the standards of seventeenth-century artists,[75] its contents are unexpected—as noted earlier—in one respect. It fulfilled most of the requirements for a well-educated artist's library as set forth by Scaramuccia[76] except that it included no standard texts of art theory such as Alberti, Leonardo, Lomazzo, Vitruvius, Pliny or Aristotle. The only works of immediate practical use were two iconographical reference works—Cartari's *Imagini degli Dei* and Boccaccio's *Genealogia degli Dei*. The absence of works from Sacchi's library does not mean, of course, that he did not read them. On one occasion at least he borrowed a book by Vasari from G. F. Grimaldi[77] and he must have borrowed other books as well, but it is probably significant that he chose not to own such works himself. His library suggests that he was devout, reasonably well-educated, slightly hypochondriac[78] and fond of lyric poetry. His copy of Tasso's *Gierusalemme Liberata* was dog-eared but he never to our knowledge painted a picture based on the poem.[79] The few works of classical literature that he owned, such as Tacitus and Plutarch, were in translation. He owned a French dictionary.

Sacchi's relations with his contemporaries, when examined in detail, suggest that the popular image of a sharp division between 'baroque' and 'classical' artists which separates Bernini and Cortona from Sacchi and which links Sacchi automatically with Poussin, Duquesnoy, Algardi, Maratta, Cassiano dal Pozzo and Bellori both grossly oversimplifies the artistic situation in *seicento* Rome and overlooks a good deal of evidence which indicates that this division was neither large, constant nor predictable. Sacchi did not get along with Bernini because he never forgave Bernini for taking away an important early commission. His opposition to Cortona, such as it was, depended not on opposition to Cortona's work in its entirety but to one aspect of it. To a large extent all these artists accepted the same set of aesthetic values and standards of aesthetic judgement. Though Sacchi criticized Cortona, he felt himself open to criticism for failing to produce a sufficient number of major works in fresco, but this is a judgement that modern critics, who attach less importance than *seicento* artists and critics to sheer size and technical difficulties, may not accept. Maratta was able to combine Sacchi's aesthetic philosophy with a prodigious creative energy that enabled him to leave behind a huge body of work and a vast amount of related preparatory material as evidence of the care with which he painted. Ironically, however, the sheer quantity of Maratta's output has produced reservations among modern critics as to the quality of his artistic intellect, as if to prove what Sacchi argued during his last difficult years, namely that quantity and quality cannot be combined.

Sacchi and Maratta are both presently underestimated as artists, mainly because the achievements of Bernini and Cortona have attracted much eloquent scholarship. As Sacchi, Maratta and other major *seicento* artists working in Rome are studied and their contributions publicized, a more balanced picture will emerge and the shared ground of these artists will become more apparent. As early as 1762, Dezailler d'Argenville lamented that Sacchi's accomplishments had not been given the recognition they deserved by Italian writers. 'Ils devoient le célébrer comme un des plus habiles peintres qu'ils ayent eu', he wrote. The correctness of his judgement will only be confirmed as scholars continue to explore neglected aspects of Roman *seicento* art.

Notes

For Bibliographical abbreviations see pp. 129ff.

I. CAREER AND ARTISTIC DEVELOPMENT

1. See Appendix I, sections A, Q and AA, and Pellegrini in the index of names following the documents in Appendix III. See also Bottari, p. 445 and Brovelli-Soffredini, pp. 126–7. The latter mentioned but did not publish a letter of 1772 from a man in Nettuno whose grandfather claimed to have known Sacchi. He also stated, without citing good evidence, that Sacchi's father's name was Giacomo and that Sacchi had a brother called Giuseppe. The names seem to have been chosen in fact to fit the saints in the Nettuno altarpiece. For another Giuseppe Sacchi, said to be a son of Andrea, see note 13 in the Appendixes.

2. Bellori, 1672–96, p. 44. 'Era il soggetto . . . Adamo, et Eva nella disubbidienza del Pomo, ove Andrea in que' due nudi si avanzò assai . . . come si è potuto vedere il disegno istesso da lui conservato.' That Bellori knew the drawing is not proof that he was in personal contact with Sacchi; he could have been told about the drawing by Maratta, who seems to have been Bellori's main source for his life of Sacchi. Whether Sacchi was ten at the time may be doubted.

3. Volpe, 1962, p. 130, gives the usual date, 1616. The arguments for the later date are summarized by Posner (p. 135, note 3).

4. I, p. 381. After drawing from Brizio's frescoes in S. Michele in Bosco, Sacchi remarked that 'spiacergli non avergli osservati prima, ed allora che militato avea sotto l'Albani'.

5. Malvasia, II, pp. 192–3.

6. Although there is abundant evidence of Cardinal del Monte's generous patronage of Sacchi in the 1620s, there is no proof that Sacchi lived in the Cardinal's palace as some other artists, including Caravaggio and Cigoli, apparently did (see note 8). In 1624 at least, Sacchi was living with Benedetto Sacchi in the parish of S. Maria del Popolo (Hoogewerff, p. 124).

7. Scholars' deductions from later sources about the Caravaggio paintings owned by del Monte have recently been confirmed by Christoph Frommel and Chandler Kirwin, who have published the relevant entries from two inventories of the Cardinal's collection made in 1627 and 1628 (C. Frommel, 'Caravaggio's Frühwerk und der Kardinal Francesco Maria del Monte', *Storia dell'Arte*, no. 9/10, 1971, pp. 5–52 and W. C. Kirwin, 'Addendum to Cardinal . . . del Monte's Inventory . . .', *loc. cit.*, pp. 53–6. I am indebted to Mr. Kirwin for lending me his photocopies of these important documents. The only work attributed to Sacchi in the inventory of 1627 is 'Un quadro di una Roma di mano di Andrea Sacchi con cornice negre con un filetto d'oro di Palmi dodici in circa' (f. 576 verso). It reappears in an inventory of June 3, 1628 listing the works inherited by del Monte's second heir (the first died shortly after the Cardinal himself). There the picture is described as 'Roma figura intera con il tevere Romolo, et Remolo putti con la lupa quadro grande con cornice un poco indorate, e la negra mano di Andreuccio sacchi'. The painting is lost but its composition is probably recorded by a red chalk drawing at Windsor (Plate 9) attributed to Sacchi by Blunt & Cooke (no. 770). I have

recently attributed this drawing to Camassei (*Art Bulletin*, 1970, p. 65, note 37) but the subject is rare and the style of the drawing is not inconsistent with Sacchi's other early red chalk studies.

8. On del Monte as an art patron, see Haskell, pp. 28–9 with further references. To them should now be added the articles by Frommel and Kirwin cited in note 7 and three other studies: D. Heikamp, 'La Medusa del Caravaggio e l'armatura dello Scià 'Abbâs di Persia', *Paragone*, no. 199, 1966, pp. 62–76, esp. p. 74; D. Posner, 'Caravaggio's Homo-erotic Early Works', *Art Quarterly*, 1971, pp. 301–24 and L. Spezzaferro, 'La cultura del cardinale Del Monte e il primo tempo del Caravaggio', *Storia dell'Arte*, 9/10, 1971, pp. 57–92, esp. p. 81. Though all of these studies focus on Caravaggio, Heikamp and Spezzaferro in particular provide useful background material on del Monte's scientific and musical interests. Haskell's text needs one slight correction. Footnote 3 on page 29 should refer to Bellori (1672–96, pp. 45–6) rather than to Passeri, who implies that the *St. Gregory* was a Barberini commission. Bellori makes del Monte's responsibility clear, as do the documents. According to Passeri (p. 303), Sacchi thought that Cigoli's *Healing of the Lame Man* in St. Peter's was one of the three best pictures in Rome. See also Posse, 1925, pp. 27 and 60 f.

9. Romano Alberti, *Origine e Progresso dell'Accademia del Disegno De' Pittori, Scultori, & Architetti di Roma*, Pavia, 1604, pp. 3–4 and Missirini, pp. 69, 84 and 92–3.

10. Noehles, pp. 336 f., documents 154, 157, 158 and 160. These documents also contain additional, unpublished references to Sacchi attending meetings of the Academy between 1624 and 1633. On March 9, 1631, for example, when Lanfranco was Principe, Sacchi and Cortona were made 'essaminatori accademici' (A.S.R., 30 Notaii Capitolini, Ufficio 15, vol. 127, f. 633). See also L. Pirotta, 'Gian Lorenzo Bernini principe dell'Accademia di San Luca', *Strenna dei Romanisti*, 1968, pp. 295–305.

11. Boschetto, fig. 151. Albani's influence is most marked in the technique of the two composition studies, especially the study in Madrid (Plates 2 and 3).

12. I owe this observation to Ellis K. Waterhouse.

13. Sacchi would have seen Ludovico Carracci's *Madonna of St. Hyacinth* and his *Virgin and Child with St. Pellegrino* in the Oratory of S. Pellegrino during his first visit to Bologna, as well as Annibale Carracci's *Madonna of St. Luke*, now in the Louvre. He would have been familiar also with Guido Reni's *St. Ildefonsus receiving the habit from the Virgin* in the Cappella Paolina in S. Maria Maggiore and Lanfranco's Quirinale altarpiece in Rome.

14. Sacchi will have seen the original in Bologna and Guido Reni's copy in the St. Cecilia chapel, S. Luigi de Francesi, Rome.

15. It is worth comparing with Annibale's *Crucifixion with Five Saints* in S. Niccolò, Bologna; Sacchi seems to have had the arrangement of the saints in Annibale's picture in mind also when designing his picture. Sacchi manages this kind of

formal assignment far better in the late 1630s when he painted the *Crucifixion with Five Dominican Saints* for S. Maria sopra Minerva.

16. For the *St. Petronilla*, see Pollak, II, pp. 564 f. For the *St. Gregory*, see the catalogue entry. The final payments were made in 1627 when the work was 'fatta' and Sacchi had to petition for money still owing to him. Judging from the artist's difficulties in getting his account settled, he must have finished the picture after Cardinal del Monte's death in August, 1626, after which time Sacchi had no influential protector.

17. Ludovico's *Madonna dei Bargellini* (Pinacoteca, Bologna) and Annibale's *Madonna and Child with the Baptist and other saints* (Dresden). I do not accept the recent proposal of S. Sinding Larsen ('Titian's Madonna di Ca' Pesaro and its Historical Significance', *Institutum Romanum Norvegiae, Acta ad archaeologiam et historiam pertinentia*, I, 1962, pp. 139 ff.) and David Rosand ('Titian in the Frari', *Art Bulletin*, 1971, pp. 200–7 esp.) that the columns behind the figures in the Pesaro altar were added later, perhaps as late as 1669.

18. Milton J. Lewine, 'The Source of Rubens' *Miracles of St. Ignatius*', *Art Bulletin*, 1963, pp. 143–7.

19. The correct date was published by Benedict Nicolson in his review, 'Caravaggesques in Naples', *Burl. Mag.*, 1963, pp. 209–10. Sacchi's *Portrait of a Cardinal* in Ottawa (Plate 46) shows knowledge of Vouet's portraiture.

20. The colour and treatment of textures and fabrics may also owe something to Florentine *seicento* painting. The impact of Florentine artists in Rome, with the exception of Cigoli, is generally ignored. Other painters active in Rome before 1640 were Giovanni Balducci (in 1592), Matteo Rosselli (in about 1602), Domenico Passignano (in 1579–89, 1602, 1605, 1613 and 1629), Sigismondo Coccapani (in 1610), Giovanni da San Giovanni (in 1610 and 1623), Agostino Ciampelli (in the early 1620s), Francesco Furini (in 1623) and Stefano della Bella (from 1633 to 1639).

21. The *St. Gregory* evidently impressed Ribera, judging by his picture of the same subject (illustrated by Jean Vergnet Ruiz in his article, 'Peintres espagnoles des Musées de France', *La Revue du Louvre*, 1962, p. 250, fig. 5).

22. See Sacchi's *Bacchanal* drawing in the British Museum (details in the catalogue entry for the Casino). Spezzaferro (art. cit. above in note 8, footnote 118) suggests plausibly that the theme of the decoration of the Casino as stated by Bellori, 'Le stagioni che prendono vita dal sole', may well have been suggested to Del Monte by his contacts with Galileo, though I do not follow literally Bellori's implied date for the Casino decoration (1617–19) as Spezzaferro does. The author generously sent me the proofs of his article before it was published, enabling me to take account of his suggestions before my manuscript went to press.

23. See his painting in the National Gallery of Canada (R. H. Hubbard, *Catalogue of Paintings and Sculptures*, I, Older Schools, Ottawa, 1957, no. 3525).

24. See Voss, 1924, p. 302. Filippo's father, Baldassare, worked at Castelfusano also and Filippo's brother, Francesco, is supposed to have studied with Sacchi (Pascoli, II, p. 77).

25. The Duquesnoy borrowing is less certain. A relief attributed to him in an engraving of 1710 by Girardon (*Gallerie du Sieur Girardon*, pl. VIII) is clearly based on the Pan composition. Whether the relief is by Duquesnoy is another question. It was drawn to my attention by Jennifer Montagu, who is dubious about the attribution to Duquesnoy.

26. Anna Ottani, *Gli Affreschi dei Carracci in Palazzo Fava*, Bologna, 1966, pl. 58. The goat in Sacchi's design is quoted from Annibale's scene of Pan and Diana in the Farnese Gallery.

27. Late in that year he began to receive payments from Don Taddeo Barberini for the *Divina Sapienza* ceiling (references in the catalogue entry). Significantly Mancini's brief lives of living artists, which include Guercino, Lanfranco, Cortona, Filippo d'Angeli and Poussin, do not mention Sacchi.

28. Cardinal Francesco bought a picture from Sacchi in 1627, Don Taddeo began to patronize Sacchi two years later. Cardinal Lelio Biscia was the patron of the *St. Romuald* altarpiece, Monsignore Clemente Merlini of the Forlì *St. Peter* and of the portrait of himself in the Borghese Gallery.

29. Costello, 1950, *passim*.

30. See Posner, 1965, *passim*. Albani's career before 1620 badly needs a proper reconstruction and an analysis along the lines of Posner's study of Lanfranco and Domenichino.

31. No photograph is available of Sacchi's copy after Raphael's *Galatea* in the Palazzo Altieri.

32. In this respect, Sacchi and Cortona are exactly analogous to Domenichino and Lanfranco. Bellori's *Vite* dwell for some time on the agonizing slowness of Domenichino's methods as opposed to the ease with which Lanfranco transferred his ideas to canvas or plaster.

33. Cortona's architecture is an important element in his artistic personality. It should not be ignored when he and Sacchi are compared, but by 1630 Cortona had given little evidence of his enormous gifts in this area, although the Villa del Pigneto for the Sacchetti may have been under way (Wittkower, 1958, p. 153).

34. Already in the early 1620s Mancini (p. 262) was impressed by Cortona's interest in antiquity. On Domenichino and Lanfranco see Donald Posner's important article.

35. Sutherland Harris, 'Camassei Studies', p. 52. Romanelli began his studies with Domenichino but soon moved to Cortona's studio.

36. The right background of *Sinnorix Poisoned and Carried from the Temple of Diana* by Pietro Testa shows that he had been studying Domenichino's *Flagellation of St. Andrew* in S. Gregorio Magno, but the crowded composition and circular temple have more to do with Cortona.

37. Bellori (1672, p. 446) thought that Lanfranco's figures in his dome were 'molto bene esposte sopra li Vangelisti del Domenichino, li quali essendo più terminati, e diligenti, e più vicini all'occhio, la gloria di sopra meglio si diffonde, in lontananza nella commodulatione del tutto'. Bellori tends to be discussed in terms that make judgements of this kind seem out of character.

38. For Sacchi drawings of this period attributed to Lanfranco, see Sutherland Harris, 'Sacchi . . . at the Collegio Romano,' figs. 20 and 22 and Harris & Schaar, no. 36 (fig. 4). Harris & Schaar no. 13, a red chalk figure study for Christ in the lost *Pasce Oves Meas*, is very close in technique to Bernini's figure studies of the same period.

39. Mahon, 'Poussiniana', pp. 63 f.

40. The two sketches for the Collegio Romano fresco seem to be influenced by Poussin's Neo-Venetian phase; the strong colours of the Fonte series of the life of the Baptist may owe something to the strong primary colours in Poussin's sets of *Sacraments*. The colour schemes in all these works can however be explained without naming Poussin; no other influence of Poussin on Sacchi is apparent.

41. See below, especially note 46.

42. In 1689 De Cotte recorded a sketch of Sacchi's *St. Romuald* in the Dal Pozzo collection (Haskell & Rinehart, p. 325). When or how it was acquired is not known. If Cassiano bought it from Sacchi, it was the only occasion when he did patronize Sacchi.

43. The appearance of an artist's name on the membership lists of the Academy is no guarantee of active participation in the

affairs of the Academy, nor even of sympathy for its aims. According to a Breve of Urban VIII issued in 1633 (N. Pevsner, *Academies of Art, Past and Present*, Cambridge, 1940, p. 65), all artists resident in Rome had to belong to the Academy and pay dues. Names were listed for this purpose but, as a reading of the one surviving minute-book for the years 1633–74 will show, few artists paid regularly and fewer still attended meetings. Apart from the documents cited by Noehles for the 1620s (see note 10 above), Poussin is never recorded attending a business meeting; like most established artists outside Cortona's circle, he seems pointedly to have avoided the Academy throughout his career.

44. Mahon, 'Poussiniana', p. 46. Caporal Leone was paid for working as a model for the Academy of St. Luke in 1632 (Archivio dell' Accademia di San Luca, vol. 43a, f. 116–117).

45. In 1647 Félibien came to Rome (Y. Delaporte, 'André Félibien en Italie, 1647–49', *G.B.A.*, 1958, pp. 193–214). He stayed in the Palazzo Barberini and visited the leading figures of the French artistic community—Poussin, Claude, and the writer Alphonse Dufresnoy, who was then living with the painter Nicolas Mignard not far from Sacchi (see Sutherland Harris, 'In Honour of Walter Friedlaender', *Burl. Mag.*, 1967, pp. 37–8). Félibien also visited Italian artists, notably Lanfranco, whom he watched at work on the apse of S. Carlo ai Catinari. When many years later he wrote his *Entretiens*, he devoted several pages to Lanfranco and to Pietro da Cortona, but Sacchi is lumped into one paragraph with another Barberini artist of very different calibre, Andrea Camassei; of both Félibien said, 'Ils ont eû des talens qui pouvoient les faire considerer' (1725 ed., IX, p. 167). If Sacchi had had any contact with Poussin in the 1640s and if Poussin had respected Sacchi, Félibien would not have returned to Paris with such a vague idea of Sacchi's artistic personality. It is also possible that Poussin was thinking of Sacchi when he dismissed painters who limited the number of figures in their compositions to six or eight, and when he wrote to Chantelou on April 7, 1647 that there were no decent portrait painters then in Rome.

46. See the catalogue entry for the Capuchins' *Miracle of St. Anthony of Padua*; for Sacchi's casts after works by Duquesnoy see Appendix I, section U, Appendix II, nos. 251 and 281, and note 17. Bellori (1672–96, p. 77) reported that when Maratta joined Sacchi's studio (c. 1636/7), he met Duquesnoy there, who was 'amorevolissimo d'Andrea'. Finally, when the French court was trying to persuade Duquesnoy to come to Paris in 1640, it was proposed to invite Sacchi as well, 'qui est fort son ami', in order to make Duquesnoy more willing to come (*La Revue de l' Art Ancien et Moderne*, 1913, XXXIV, p. 223). Poussin's invitation was not apparently thought to have the same effect. A. Nava Cellini's recent discussion of the stylistic influence of Duquesnoy on Poussin (*Paragone*, 1966, no. 195, pp. 30 f.) significantly concentrates on the years before 1630.

47. See the section on Sacchi's relations with his contemporaries below.

48. The pose is not unusual but the type of woman down to the arrangement of the hair is very close. The arguments for an early and a later date with further references will be found in the catalogue volume of Blunt's monograph on Poussin (pp. 84–6). Blunt prefers the earlier date, Mahon the later.

49. I hope to devote an article to the relationship between Testa and Poussin in the future. Pietro del Po is better described as an imitator.

50. Scanelli (p. 207) described it as painted 'di sotto in su'. Bellori and Passeri both treat it as a painted illusion above their heads. Briganti (1962, pp. 88 f. and 131 f.) is the only modern writer

to appreciate the 'baroque' qualities of Sacchi's ceiling.

51. For details of the plans and construction of the Palazzo Barberini, see Blunt, 'The Palazzo Barberini', 1958, and more recently, Howard Hibbard's monograph on Carlo Maderno.

52. Sutherland Harris, 'Camassei Studies', pp. 54–5 and fig. 15.

53. Posse, 1925, p. 41; Waterhouse 1937, p. 21; Wittkower, 1958, p. 171; Haskell, 1962, p. 51.

54. There is also a small staircase leading directly to the chapel from the private apartments of the family, but the main access to the chapel is through the Sala della Divina Sapienza.

55. Guercino's *Aurora* frescoes are painted in a small room with a *quadratura* framework by Tassi that never seems to be correctly aligned. Passeri's objections to Lanfranco's Christ on the ceiling of the Sacchetti chapel in S. Giovanni dei Fiorentini are also relevant. Passeri noted that the figure of the risen Christ was painted 'in uno scorcio veramente strano, e non di molto decoro; ma secondo l'arte è mirabile' (p. 151). Correggio's frescoes in the dome of Parma cathedral provoked similar reactions when they were completed. Poussin deliberately exploited the feelings that an unusual, foreshortened view of the human figure distorts it in his ceiling painting for Richelieu, *Time sustaining Truth from Envy and Discord* (Louvre), for the figures of Envy and Discord are seen from much sharper and hence less flattering angles than Truth and Time.

56. Square formats have never been popular with artists (until Albers) and are uncommon outside decorative contexts.

57. Sacchi preferred a slight *di sotto in su* viewpoint for ceiling paintings of subjects taking place in the sky. His central fresco at Castelfusano has a viewpoint situated below the lower edge of the frame even though the surrounding frescoes are all straight *quadri riportati*. His Collegio Romano fresco has a similar low viewpoint and it is painted in a *quadro riportato* frame.

58. The composition in all the early versions that can be traced back to Sacchi's studio is also more compact than that of the ceiling they record. The Cooper-Hewitt Museum composition study is essentially an expanded version of the Collegio Romano design.

59. The woman on the far right makes the same gesture as Beauty in the fresco, so the remaining figure with her back turned towards us can be identified as Perspicacity.

60. This figure's pose and drapery may be based on Augurio Buono in the edition of Ripa's *Iconologia* published in Padua in 1611.

61. Haskell, 1962, p. 51.

62. Sacchi had also studied Raphael's *Parnassus* fresco in the Vatican before planning the *Divina Sapienza*.

63. An example of this is Cozza's ceiling in the library of the Collegio Innocenziano.

64. Robert Enggass (*The Paintings of Baciccio*, University Park, 1964) did not consider either Lanfranco's ceiling fresco in the Villa Borghese or Sacchi's *Divina Sapienza* as sources for Gaulli's nave fresco in the Gesù. Donald Posner has, however, suggested that the openness of Sacchi's design impressed Cortona considerably when he was planning his ceiling for the Salone (*Art Bulletin*, 1964, p. 415).

65. Incisa della Rocchetta, 1924, p. 65. It is also close to Ardire Magnanimo e Generoso in the 1611 Padua edition of Ripa's *Iconologia*.

66. Posse, 1925, p. 47.

67. What remains of these frescoes is now in the Museo di Roma (Palazzo Braschi) (Zeri, 1959, pp. 13–14).

68. E.g. Waterhouse, 1962, p. 57. 'In spite of admirable drawing and the great intellectual effort displayed this fresco, as decoration, is a disaster'. See also Waterhouse, 1937, p. 21; Isarlo, 1960, p. 40 and Haskell, 1962, p. 51.

D. O. M.
ANDREAS SACCHIVS ROMANVS
HIC EST
QVI CVM DIV AETERNITATI PINXERIT
VEL MORTVVS IN HOC TVMVLO FAMAE AETERNVM VIVIT
DIVINAE SAPIENTIAE MYSTERIA DIVINIS PENE COLORIBVS
IN BARBERINIS AEDIBVS EXPRESSIT
BASILICAM VATICANAM BAPTISTERIVM LATERANENSE
PICTVRIS SVIS CONDECORAVIT
INDE
VRBANI VIII PONT. MAX.
AC EMINENTISS. PRINC. CARD. ANTONII BARBERINI
BENEFICENTIAM ET GRATIAM PROMERITVS
OPERVM ET NOMINIS GLORIA APVD SVOS
EXTEROSQ. SVPERSTES
PICTVRAE AC VITAE LINEAS ABSOLVIT
DIE XXI IVNII A. MDCLXI AET. LXII

Pietro Leone Bombelli Scolse

Sepolcro di Andrea Sacchi esistente nella Basilica Lateranese

Fig. 2. Sacchi's tomb. Engraving by Pietro Leone Bombelli, 1769

IV. Sketch for the Collegio Romano fresco (Plate 24). London, Brian Sewell. (Cat. No. 16)

69. This ideal solution was suggested to me by Giovanni Incisa della Rocchetta.

70. For the iconography of Divine Wisdom, see the useful study by Hans Ost, 'Borromini's römische Universitätskirche S. Ivo alla Sapienza', *Zeitschrift für Kunstwissenschaft*, 1967, pp. 101–42, esp. p. 122 f.

71. See *The Myths of Hyginus*, translated and edited by Mary Grant, Lawrence (Kansas), 1960. I gave a paper on the programme of the ceiling, including the constellation imagery, at the annual meeting of the College Art Association in Chicago, 1972. George Lechner has recently published a more detailed analysis than that given here of the Solomonic imagery and the constellations ('Tommaso Campanella and Andrea Sacchi's Fresco of *Divina Sapienza* in the Palazzo Barberini', *Art Bulletin*, 1976, LVIII, 97–101). For further comments on this article, see note 76 below.

72. Ripa says of locks of golden hair that 'la chioma profumata, e riciuta con l'arte sono segni di delicatezza, di lascivia, e di effeminiti costumi' (*ed. cit.* pp. 423–4). Passeri echoes this, saying that the lock of Berenice represents 'la pompa più superba del vanto femminile (che) consiste nella copia, e sfarzo de suoi capelli de quale ambiscono di tenere legati per incatenere con quelli il cuore degl'amanti'. All this is a long way from the story of Berenice who, when her husband left home to fight, cut off a lock of her hair and placed it in the temple, vowing to cut off all her hair as a thank offering if he returned victorious. The story of Berenice gives Beauty a moral message appropriate to the theme of Divine Wisdom.

73. The mixed interpretations of Purity and Suavity have already been cited. The hare is often used with Venus to symbolize lust. Bellori knew this and interpreted the figures of Love and Fear as agents of Wisdom used to control two harmful appetites in man, anger and lust. Ripa does suggest one image of Fear using a hare (p. 515).

74. This would have been easy to do. As the Barberini manuscript says, 'Divine Wisdom has many attributes ... of which a few principal ones have been chosen and represented in the painting (Incisa della Rocchetta, 1924, p. 64). On the meaning of the frieze, see Hans Kauffman, *Gian Lorenzo Bernini: Die figürlichen Kompositionen*, Berlin, 1970, pp. 298–300.

75. Incisa della Rocchetta, 1924 (p. 65).

76. Haskell, 1962, p. 50. Pastor (XXIX, p. 504) thought that a poem by Sarbiewski, who was then in Rome, may have inspired the choice of this text. The poem is undated. It contains so many details close to those of the fresco that it would seem to have been inspired by it, rather than the reverse. For an interesting suggestion concerning the Barberini's use of the *Divina Sapienza* as political propaganda, see H. W. van Helsdingen, 'Aantekeningen bij Ikonografie van Poussin', *Simiolus*, III, 3, 1968, p. 178. I do not accept the hypothesis recently proposed by Lechner (see note 71) that Tommaso Campanella provided the programme for the *Divina Sapienza* ceiling (see my response to his article in *Art Bulletin*, 1977, LIX, pp. 304–7

77. For biographical details, see Cardella, VII, pp. 137–142 and the introduction by Pietro Giordano to the 1839 edition of Pallavicino's *Della Vita di Alessandro VII*.

78. 'Si cerca in che cosa consiste l'eleganza; e si distinguono di essa tre gradi.... Il terzo elemento dell'eleganza è la brevità' (*Opere del Cardinale Sforza Pallavicino*, Milan, 1834, xx).

79. See the group of studies for the *Three Magdalenes* in Düsseldorf, Harris & Schaar, nos. 39–49.

80. For the locations of the pendentive designs by Lanfranco, see Waterhouse, 1937, p. 77.

81. Alfred Moir, *The Italian Followers of Caravaggio*, Cambridge, 1967, I, p. 92.

82. Baglione, 1642, p. 194. Antiveduto was replaced by Vouet, another del Monte protégé, in 1624.

83. Emiliani (1962, p. 194) thought that the connection was a significant one but assumed that Sacchi studied the Cavedone during his travels in 1635, the *St. Romuald* being dated then around 1638–40. Cavedone's fresco was painted well before Sacchi's first visit, however, and he could have studied it then.

84. All three figures in Cesare's fresco of *S. Gregorio Taumaturgo receiving the rule of Christian life from the Madonna* in the Cappella Paolina in S. Maria Maggiore have the majestic build and handsome heads that inspired Sacchi at this time. I am grateful to Herwarth Röttgen for discussing Cesare d'Arpino with me and for letting me study his collection of photographs of Cesare's work.

85. Sebastiano del Piombo's *Raising of Lazarus* (National Gallery, London) might also seem to be a source for the *St. Anthony*, the poses of Christ and Lazarus being close to those of St. Anthony and the man revived. Sebastiano's picture was then in Narbonne cathedral, however, was not engraved until the eighteenth century and seems to have been little copied. The pose of Christ in Cesare's *Raising of Lazarus* is also close to that of Sebastiano's Christ and Sacchi's saint.

86. Lavin, 1968, p. 25 and p. 32, note 150.

87. The only work by Correggio that he could study in Rome was the *Noli Me Tangere*, then in the Aldobrandini collection and now in the Prado.

88. The composition of the *St. Bonaventure* is close to Lanfranco's *St. Charles Borromeo in Prayer*, then in the Giustiniani collection (illus. in *Burl. Mag.*, 1960, p. 26, fig. 34), though both may be said to derive from Ludovico Carracci's *Madonna of St. Hyacinth*.

89. See, for example, no. 1712 in Pope-Hennessy's catalogue of the Domenichino drawings at Windsor.

90. The only other architectural commission with which Sacchi may have been connected is the church of S. Maria in Via in Camerino. Santoni (p. 37) writes of the 'nuovo tempio da costruirsi colle norme e coll'opera di eccellenti artisti, diretti dal celebre Andrea Sacchi', and most subsequent writers who mention the church attribute the design to Sacchi. Bellori, however, does not. A document in the Archivio di Stato in Rome (Archivio Notarile, A.C., Iac. Simoncellus, Book 6665, July 1, 1658, p. 940 f.), which is concerned with the ecclesiastical appointments and conditions for service at the church, mentions the rebuilding and redecoration with pride but does not name the architect or the artists responsible for the interior decoration. Santoni, who appears to be a careful historian, quotes from several early sources that I have been unable to check. He even asserts that the building cost 30,000 scudi, a figure I cannot trace in any published source. Preliminary enquiries suggest that the answer may be found in the Archivio Comunale in Camerino. On stylistic grounds, the attribution is plausible, and any study of Sacchi as an architect would have to investigate this problem fully.

91. Pigler, I, pp. 19–20. In a drawing Rembrandt also includes Eve but places her in the distance, raising her arms as she senses that something terrible has happened (O. Benesch, *The Drawings of Rembrandt*, London, 1957, no. 955 recto).

92. A Madonna and Child attributed to Sacchi in Ascoli Piceno is discussed under Attributions. Unlike Sacchi, Maratta frequently painted and drew this subject throughout his career.

93. See, however, Harris & Schaar, no. 91. For drawings of this subject wrongly attributed to Sacchi, see Harris & Schaar, nos. 131 and 132.

94. Author's translation from Missirini, p. 112.

95. *The Destruction of Pagan Idols* derives from both the *Miracle at Bolsena* and *The Expulsion of Heliodorus*. *The Burning of Books at the Nicene Council* has no obvious compositional model although the rows of clerics recall *The Coronation of Charle-*

magne and two foreground figures recall Euclid and one of his pupils in the foreground of the *School of Athens*.

96. Waterhouse, 1962, p. 59.

97. See the catalogue entries for details on their condition. Since their cleaning and restoration in 1968, the paintings have been moved to the Palazzo Laterano and replaced in the Baptistry by copies.

98. The fact that fresco painting was regarded as more difficult and therefore more of a test of an artist's ability was also no doubt a factor with Sacchi as his self-confidence waned. Elsewhere I have suggested that Testa committed suicide after having one fresco commission destroyed and after failing to obtain another fresco commission with which to establish his reputation as a major artist ('Notes on the Chronology and Death of Pietro Testa', *Paragone*, 1967, no. 213, pp. 43–9).

99. Waterhouse, 1962, p. 59; Emiliani, 1962, pp. 309 and 336–7; Briganti, *Cortona*, 1962, p. 91.

100. See Cat. Nos. 54–61 for details of their condition prior to their recent restoration and afterwards.

101. Emiliani, 1962, p. 309.

102. See the anecdote told by Bellori (1672–96, p. 60) of Sacchi's angry expostulation when confronted by a student who did not worship Raphael. Passeri tells the story in almost the same words; both biographers had no doubt heard the story from Maratta.

103. The fresco should be compared with the engraving of around 1700 by Westerhout (Plate 156).

104. See Wibiral, 1955. He may have painted the Pope's portrait (see Inventory I, no. 1, Sacchi's own portrait of Alexander VII).

105. These included the decoration of the vault of S. Luigi dei Francesi, an altarpiece for S. Marco, a series of apostles for the Palazzo Barberini and, probably, illustrations to Pierre le Moyne's *St. Louis ou la Sainte Couronne Reconquise*. The S. Marco altarpiece was given to Maratta, who also painted the apostles for Cardinal Antonio. The S. Luigi commission was finally abandoned. A few engravings based on drawings by Sacchi for the Le Moyne poem were issued separately (for details, see the relevant catalogue entries). Bellori (1672–96, p. 84) mentions that Maratta's altarpiece in S. Marco was originally commissioned from Sacchi.

106. IV, p. 367. Pascoli names Luigi Garzi (II, p. 236 f.) and Agostino Scilla (II, p. 51) as pupils of Sacchi. One of his pupils was studying painting as part of his general education: on August 4, 1659, Elpidio Benedetti recommended to Mazarin a young violinist 'che savio è anco di pittura, havendo studiato sotto Andrea Sacchi, giovane quieto e tutto applicato alla virtù (H. Prunières, *L'Opéra Italien en France avant Lulli*. Paris, 1913, p. 247). According to Pernetti (*Recherches pour servir à l'histoire de Lyons ou les Lyonnais dignes de mémoire*, Lyons, 1757, II, p. 106), Horace and Thomas Blanchet, both painters, 'avoient fait connoissance à Rome chez Sacchi, Peintre renommé'. Le Blanc also studied with Lanfranco and worked with Perrier in Lyons. Titi (1763, p. 316) mentions a certain Giuseppe Sacchi, 'figliolo del famoso pittore Andrea', but no Giuseppe is named in Sacchi's will or inventory as a member of his family. See also note 109 below.

107. A characteristic selection exists at Windsor (Blunt & Cooke, nos. 821 to 851). See also Harris & Schaar, nos. 121–124 and Sutherland Harris in *Master Drawings*, Vol. 9, 1971, p. 384 f. and *Master Drawings*, Vol. 11, 1973, p. 160 and plate 26.

108. One of the rare exceptions is the *Portrait of M. A. Pasqualini*, q.v. (Plate 89; see also note 73 to the section on Sacchi's contemporaries. For an early Maratta study after the antique, see Harris & Schaar, no. 213.

109. Pascoli, II, pp. 75–90. Almost nothing is known about Francesco Lauri who lived, according to Pascoli, from 1610

to 1635. According to the Stati d'Anime of S. Lorenzo in Lucina for 1623 (p. 6 verso) he was then eleven. In 1634, when he is recorded with his family in the parish of S. Maria del Popolo (Stati d'Anime, p. 32 verso), his age is not given. In 1642, when his family are again recorded in that parish, Francesco was no longer with them. He is last recorded in the summer of 1635, when he was a witness at the trial of Tommaso Luini and G. B. Greppi (Bertolotti, 1884, pp. 179–182). It would have been relevant to that trial testimony for Francesco to state that he had been in Sacchi's studio between 1630 and 1635, when he could have witnessed the difficulties between Luini and Greppi, but Francesco does not state that he was and consequently can only have been with Sacchi before 1630, perhaps in 1628 when his father, Baldassare Lauri, was working with Sacchi under Cortona at Castelfusano. By 1635, Francesco was working independently and would have been an unlikely recipient for the kind of lecture recorded by Pascoli. Moreover, that talk mentions a *Crucifixion*, and the only picture of that subject by Sacchi was the Minerva altarpiece of 1637. The evidence is not conclusive but it suggests that Sacchi's 'lesson' was not given to Francesco Lauri at all, and consequently that its contents must be treated with circumspection as a primary source for Sacchi's ideas about art and the instruction of young artists. Even Filippo Lauri's memories of his brother's adolescence would have been dim by the time that Pascoli was collecting his material. The 'lesson' may however reflect Pascoli's conversations with later students of Sacchi such as Maratta or Garzi.

110. These anecdotes at the end of Bellori's *vita* of Sacchi were almost certainly provided by Maratta. On one occasion Sacchi was chatting with Maratta in Domenichino's chapel in S. Luigi dei Francesi, a circumstance that suggests the conversation took place after the ceiling decoration of that church was commissioned from Sacchi in 1653. The evidence linking Sacchi and Maratta with a volume of drawings by Polidoro recently mentioned by A. Marabottini (*Polidoro da Caravaggio*, Rome, 1969, pp. 237–9) is slender. Significantly, no such album is mentioned in Sacchi's inventory of 1661.

111. On Testa, see the reference in note 98. Annibale's breakdown was connected by his contemporaries with the failure of his patrons, the Farnese, to reward him adequately for his achievements in their services.

112. On April 3, 1660 Don Antonio Ruffo's agent in Rome informed him that both Sacchi and Cortona were suffering from gout (Ruffo, 1916, p. 167). On October 2 of that same year Bellori informed Malvasia that Sacchi was ill (Malvasia, II, p. 190). Bellori says in his *vita* that Sacchi was ill for some time before his death and had been bedridden for some time at the end.

113. The best version of the *St. Bruno* is that in the Incisa della Rocchetta collection in Rome. The *Hagar and Ishmael* is in the Colonna Gallery. Mola painted the Baptist preaching to the crowd a number of times; the version in the Ojetti collection in Florence uses Sacchi's crowd arrangement to some extent. Albani seems to have known Sacchi's painting of *St. Andrew Adoring the Cross* and to have used its design when planning his fresco of this subject in the Gozzadini chapel in S. Maria dei Servi in Bologna (1639–41). Giacinto Brandi's *Daedalus and Icarus* in Dresden (Posse catalogue, 1929, p. 192, no. 435) shows knowledge of Sacchi's composition of this theme.

114. Posse, 1925, p. 65.

115. Only one of the drawings in the Louvre attributed to Sacchi by Mariette is autograph, namely the study for the engraving of *Harmonillus* (see *Le Cabinet d'un Grand Amateur P.-J. Mariette*, Musée du Louvre, no. 130). No. 131 in the same exhibition as Sacchi is in fact by Giuseppe Passeri. Both were

exhibited in 1959 with other Mariette Sacchi attributions (Bean, nos. 29–32), none of them in my opinion tenable.

116. The works attributed to Sacchi in the section on Attributions are in almost all cases well below the level of Sacchi's own work. One unusual attribution is an album of drawings with scenery designs for the opera *Le Nozze di Theti e di Peleo* (libretto by F. Buti, music by F. Caporali), which went from the collection of the Earl of Wicklow (Sotheby's, Dec. 12, 1950, lot 305) to the Houghton Library at Harvard. A companion volume remains at Shelton Abbey in Ireland. The opera was first performed on April 14, 1654, in Paris with scenery designed by Iacopo Torelli, and engraved the same year by Israel Silvestre (Alfred Loewenberg, *Annals of Opera*, London, 1943, p. 16). It is doubtful that Sacchi had anything to do with the production or these drawings, the style of which does not recall his work. Sacchi did design scenery for the comedy *Palazzo d'Atlante e de l'Arioste* given by Cardinal Antonio Barberini in 1642 (the payment was published by Incisa della Rocchetta, 1924, p. 69) but the opera was not a success (Henry Prunières, *L'Opéra Italien en France avant Lulli* Paris, 1913, pp. 26–7).

II. ANDREA SACCHI AND HIS CONTEMPORARIES

1. Mahon, 1946. Many of the ideas in this section were stimulated by Mahon's study of the relationship between theory and practice in *seicento* Italian painting, a study that goes far beyond the career of Guercino. Though often praised, the significance of Mahon's study has not always been appreciated by the authors of later studies of this subject.

2. Mahon, 1946, pp. 196–7.

3. Wittkower, 1958, p. 169.

4. Waterhouse, 1963, p. 55 and 1937, p. 24.

5. Marabottini, 1954, p. 237.

6. Emiliani, 1962, pp. 331 and 309.

7. V. Golzio, *Il Seicento e il Settecento*, Turin, 1950, p. 411.

8. R. Enggass, *The Painting of Baciccio*, University Park, Pennsylvania, 1964, p. 7.

9. Briganti, 1962, p. 91.

10. Appendix I, C.

11. *Ibid.*

12. See discussion below of the Academy of St. Luke.

13. Appendix II, no. 164. See also the introduction to the Appendixes.

14. Appendix III lists the books and identifies the editions when possible. The last section of this discussion also touches on Sacchi's library.

15. Pascoli (II, p. 237) in his life of Luigi Garzi, who joined Sacchi's studio around 1654/5, reports that Sacchi urged Garzi to study Raphael, Domenichino and Poussin for their treatment of facial expression. This is the only recorded occasion when Sacchi mentioned Poussin; the source is late and not totally reliable but the anecdote may be substantially correct nevertheless.

16. Mahon, *Poussiniana*, pp. 134–5. See especially the passage beginning 'In my interpretation . . . one of the essential keys to the understanding of Roman art . . .' and ending '. . . midway between the two extremes'.

17. The aesthetic philosophies of *colore* and *disegno* consist of opposites depending on the *disegno* artists' emphasis on the drawn preparation of works of art. Thus *disegno* is disciplined, *colore* is spontaneous; *colore* accepts greater formal extremes (stronger contrasts of light and shade, greater variety in intensity and hue of colours) than *disegno*; *colore* is more likely to adopt unbalanced compositional schemata (asymmetries, diagonals, moving figures) whereas *disegno* prefers stable, balanced designs (symmetry, verticals and horizontals, figures at rest); *colore* artists work rapidly, often leaving their picture surfaces rough and impasted while *disegno* artists work slowly and control their brush strokes, often obliterating all signs of individual strokes; *colore* artists encourage an audience response to immediate sensations of visual pleasure whereas *disegno* artists anticipate a considered response that goes beyond the surface of the picture to consider its content and didactic message, the *colore* artist appealing to the eye, the *disegno* artist to the intellect. The *colore* artist works directly from the live model, if he uses one; the *disegno* artist filters his response to nature through his own idealized conception of form inspired by study of antiquity and the High Renaissance. The *colore* artist did not limit his subject matter to the noblest actions of mankind, the *disegno* artist did. Portrayal of such noble actions requires the close study of facial expressions and gestures and the ancient art of rhetoric, all matters which *colore* artists often ignore. It will be obvious from this brief summary of the two stereotypes that it would be difficult for any artist to subscribe entirely to one or other of them and that most artists, even in the sixteenth century, consciously or unconsciously subscribed to both.

18. See Domenico Sella, 'Venice: The Rise and Fall of the Venetian Wool Industry' in *Crisis and Change in the Venetian Economy*, ed. B. S. Pullan, London, 1970 with a good summary of the economic situation at the beginning.

19. A famous late illustration of the unfriendly reception of *colore* in Rome is Federigo Zuccaro's reaction to Caravaggio's pictures in S. Luigi dei Francesi reported by Baglione: 'What is all the fuss about? I don't see anything here but the thought (*pensiero*) of Giorgione' (translation from W. Friedlaender, *Caravaggio Studies*, New York, 1955, p. 235). Giorgione described by Vasari sounds remarkably like Caravaggio described by Baglione and even Bellori.

20. On the role of the Academy of St. Luke, see below.

21. Haskell, 1963, p. 25.

22. F. Gibbons, *Dosso and Battista Dossi, Court Painters of Ferrara*, Princeton, 1968, pp. 13–17. The Borghese Gallery in Rome, which in the mid-seventeenth century acquired some of Cardinal Aldobrandini's loot, has characteristic works by Battista and Dosso Dossi, Garofalo, Girolamo da Carpi, Mazzolino, Niccolò dell'Abbate, Ortolano and Scarsellino, many of them traceable to the Aldobrandini. The Venetian works in the Borghese collection did not come from the Aldobrandini, however (see P. della Pergola, *Galleria Borghese, I Dipinti*, Rome, 1955, I, *sub voce*).

23. The Bassano is still *in situ*. For the Palma, see Mancini, I, p. 270 and II, p. 175, n. 1292. On the popularity of Muziano's saints, see Mancini, I, p. 207.

24. As proof of their poor relations scholars have cited the Este court agent's remark about their rivalry in 1639, the anecdote in Pascoli about Sacchi's visit to see the model of Bernini's Cathedra Petri and Sacchi's friendship with Duquesnoy. Detailed references will be found below.

25. Details of this commission will be found in catalogue no. 8. Martinelli (1950, pp. 96–7) dismisses Grassi's suggestion that Bernini and Sacchi might have been working on a series of apostles on the grounds that others from such a series are not recorded in Barberini inventories. The inventories known to Grassi and Martinelli were incomplete, however, and such

a series could have been started but never completed.

26. Details and references will be found in the catalogue entry for no. 15. Noehles (1970, document 160) publishes a record of a meeting of the Academy of St. Luke attended by both Bernini and Sacchi in 1628.

27. As suggested above, Bellori's story of Sacchi's loss of the commission to paint the *Burial of St. Petronilla*, which is on the altar to the right of the site of Sacchi's lost overdoor, may be a confused version of the story of Sacchi's loss of the overdoor commission.

28. Pollak, II, p. 85. The only visual record of the appearance of any of these overdoors apart from Sacchi's drawings for his *Pasce Oves Meas* design are the drawings and sketches by Camassei for his (Sutherland Harris, 'Camassei Studies', pp. 53–4 and figs. 6, 9, 10 and 11).

29. Paolo Guidotti and Antonio Pomarancio had already received their commissions (Pollak, *loc. cit.*). Ciampelli's commission was switched to Camassei in 1630 (Pollak, *op. cit.* p. 88).

30. 'N. Sre. ordina che si dia uno dei sopraporti da dipingersi al Cav. re Bernino, che ne disponghi à sue int(entio)ni' (Pollak, II, p. 87).

31. Pollak, II, pp. 284–5. Neither Baglione (1639) nor Titi (1674 ed.) record *sopraporte* in the spaces now occupied by the door leading to the sacristy on the right of the Cappella Clementina and by the tomb of Clement X (spaces 36 and 23 on Bonanni's plan reproduced as fig. XXVII in Pollak, II).

32. Pollak, II, p. 175. Most of the work on the relief, which was largely executed by pupils, was carried out between 1639 and 1645 (Wittkower, 1955, pp. 196–7).

33. Wittkower, 1958, p. 9. Bonvicino died in 1622.

34. Bernini's relief was moved in 1649 to face the visitor entering the church (Wittkower, 1955, p. 197).

35. References will be found in the catalogue entry for no. 35. Nearly all of Passeri's digs against Bernini are made without naming him (Hess, 1934, *sub voce*, especially the notes on the *Vite* of Duquesnoy and Algardi. See also Hess' analysis of Passeri's attitude towards Bernini in 'Die Künstlerbiographien des Giovanni Battista Passeri', *Wiener Jahrbuch für Kunstgeschichte*, V, 1928, p. 43 f.).

36. See Passeri's life of Duquesnoy (Hess ed., pp. 102–16, especially pp. 110–11).

37. Duquesnoy blamed Bernini for the decision to switch the positions of the four statues in the crossing of St. Peter's after they had been commissioned for particular sites, but in fact the decision was made by the Congregazione dei Riti on theological grounds (Lavin, 1968, pp. 24–6). Duquesnoy's disappointment was widely known—Evelyn mentions it in his diary when he was in Rome in 1645 (*The Diary of John Evelyn*, ed. E. S. de Beer, Oxford, 1955, II, p. 399, 'Fiamingo [who made the *Andrea* in st. *Peters* & said to die madd, that it was plac'd in an ill light]').

38. See the catalogue entry for no. 35. Sacchi's preparatory studies for the composition do not show a niche with a statue in the left background, a fact that suggests the decision to include the St. Susanna may have been made quite late in the design of the picture.

39. For references, see the catalogue entries for nos. 36–9.

40. Pollak, II, p. 85. 'Vi sono di più li Altari del Volto Santo et S. Andrea. Ma in questi facilmente non vi si farran' dentro quadri per esservi sopra le medesime Reliquie, e per l'angustia et poco lume, che havran' dentro le cappellette di detti Altari'.

41. Wittkower, 1955, p. 192.

42. Fraschetti, p. 254, note 1, 'Di Roma 19 novembre 1639. Andrea Sacchi Pittore assai celebre del Signor Cardinale Antonio ha havuta cura di fare il Catafalco per l'esequie

secolari dei Padri Gesuiti, e tutto è riuscito pieno di tanta maestà, e vaghezza, che l'emulazione già nata col Cavaliere Bernini si farà maggiore'.

43. Posse, 1925, p. 11, note 5. The Pope died on July 29. Sacchi was paid 200 scudi on August 6 and 20. Sacchi was perhaps chosen because limited funds following the War of Castro meant that the funeral had to be a modest affair.

44. In 1639 Sacchi took over from Bernini the responsibility for restoring the Lateran Baptistry (see catalogue entry no. 53). See also catalogue nos. 46 and 62. Sacchi is first described as 'Architetto e Pittore' in print by Antonio Gherardi in his *Relatione* of 1639 describing the centenary celebrations of the Jesuits (Incisa della Rocchetta, 1924, p. 67). He is called 'architetto' in the household accounts of Cardinal Antonio Barberini from January, 1637 onwards (Posse, 1925, p. 6). The Stati d'Anime of 1644 to 1647 for the parish of S. Nicola in Arcione also describe Sacchi as the Cardinal's architect (Hoogewerff, 1947, pp. 125–6).

45. Pascoli, II, p. 459. He seems to have known Naldini. Naldini certainly worked with Algardi (see Sutherland, 'The Decoration of S. Martino ai Monti', p. 116).

46. See Sutherland, *loc. cit.*

47. Wittkower, 1955, pp. 218 and 224. He is recorded working on the Cathedra Petri as well but only after Sacchi's death.

48. Appendix I, sections C, W, GG; Appendix II, June 26. See also Naldini in the index of names in the Appendixes. According to Pascoli, Naldini was much affected by Sacchi's death.

49. Sutherland, *loc. cit.*

50. Pascoli, II, p. 461 and Titi, 1763, p. 420. Gaspar Marcaccioni died in 1674, his wife in 1703. Since Naldini died in 1693, her tomb, which matches that of her husband, was presumably also made in the 1670s. The silhouettes of white classical sarcophagi set into the walls are covered with a yellow and black marble 'skin' carrying the inscription and are surmounted by a pedestal with a bust. The design is stiff by Bernini's standards but it is a great improvement over the tombs of Sacchi and Prior Filippini.

51. Pascoli, I, p. 19 and Wittkower, 1955, p. 220.

52. The affair of the clock tower of St. Peter's, which had to be demolished when the foundations proved inadequate, called into question Bernini's engineering abilities. Hollowing out the four piers of the crossing of St. Peter's in order to accommodate the statues of Sts. Andrew, Longinus, Helen and Veronica was also said to have weakened the dome (for Baldinucci's account and his defence of Bernini, see *The Life of Bernini* by Filippo Baldinucci, Florence, 1682, pp. 24–8 and 82 f.).

53. See notes 35 to 37 above. Paolo Portoghesi (*Roma Barocca: The History of an Architectonic Culture*, London, 1970, pp. 281–2) thinks that Sacchi's design for the Acqua Acetosa of 1660–1 was much influenced by Bernini, which is possible. For drawings of the late 1620s that recall Bernini, see Harris & Schaar, nos. 9 to 23 especially. No. 83, a composition study for the *Drunkenness of Noah*, recalls Bernini's composition studies of the 1640s but the similarity may be fortuitous. A drawing by Sacchi after Bernini's tomb statue of Urban VIII (Blunt & Cooke, no. 34, as a copy after Bernini) was probably made in the early 1630s, when Sacchi was working on his own full-length portrait of the Pope (see cat. no. 18).

45. Posse, 1925, p. 65. In his review of the Harris & Schaar catalogue in *Master Drawings* (1969, pp. 171–2), Peter Dreyer suggested that some of Bernini's preparatory studies be given to Sacchi instead, a reattribution that I cannot accept.

55. Nicolas Pevsner (*Academies of Art, Past and Present*, Cambridge, 1940, pp. 64–6) devotes less than three pages to the Academy's activities in this period, a wise decision as he was

dependent on Missirini. The commonest mistake as regards the Academy is to assume that membership was by choice and that joining therefore meant support of the Academy and its traditional programmes (see note 59 below).

56. I wish to thank Dr. Luigi Pirotta for letting me consult the Academy's archives. I hope to publish several articles based on this minute book and other unpublished archival material shortly. Some of this material has been presented in a public lecture given at Brown University, Pennsylvania State University and the Institute of Fine Arts of New York University.

57. Cortona attended meetings whenever he was in Rome, and when he was not Principe (he held that office from 1634 to 1636), that office was held by friends (Romanelli, Algardi, Soria, Pietro Martire Neri, Moroni) whose elections were in a number of cases (not just Romanelli's) engineered by Cardinal Francesco Barberini. The other Academy regulars also belonged to Cortona's circle (Grimaldi, Mochi). I wish to thank Dr. Jennifer Montagu, who read the text of my Brown lecture and made a number of useful comments on the personal contacts between these artists.

58. The only business remotely connected with the Academy's academic programmes during Cortona's tenure of office was the appointment of Vincenzo della Greca as an instructor in civil and military architecture to students in April, 1636.

59. For the Breve of Urban VIII of 1633 which made membership obligatory, see Pevsner, p. 65. In December, 1651, it was decided that 'from now on and for all time no one may call himself "Accademico" until he has been declared to be such by a secret meeting or by a general meeting of the Academy'. The other artists' society, the Virtuosi al Pantheon, had always limited their membership. Sacchi was never a member according to the few documents that have been published (Orbaan, 1914).

60. Thus Sacchi, who held various offices between 1634 and 1638, only attended one meeting in this period, in November, 1636.

61. Mancini (p. 262) commented on Cortona's interest in antiquity. Early drawings by him after Trajan's column and Polidoro's house façades as well as his early copy after Raphael's *Galatea* all attest to the traditional *disegno* origins of Cortona's 'baroque' style.

62. During Soria's tenure of Office (1645 until his death in 1651), the Academy met rarely, and then only to arrange the traditional celebrations on St. Luke's feast day. From 1649 until October, 1651, the Academy did not meet at all. Cortona's absence in Florence, the exile of the Barberini and reduced financial circumstances after their fall and their replacement by the much less open-handed Pamphili may partly explain the Academy's inactivity. It might also be the case that Soria was too old and ill to run it effectively, but out of respect for an old Academy supporter (he had been treasurer practically since 1633), other members were reluctant to turn him out of office.

63. For the meetings of 1625 to 1633, see Noehles, Documents nos. 158, 160, 162 and 163. Noehles also publishes a document that shows Sacchi was appointed 'Proveditore' on October 27, 1624 (Doc. no. 154). References to Sacchi in an Academy Notebook of 1634–65 appear on pp. 10, 17, 19 verso and 23 (Vol. 166, no. 68). According to the Minute Book of 1634–74 (Vol. 43, p. 1. verso) Sacchi was put in charge of foreign artists on Jan. 8, 1634.

64. Missirini (pp. 111–13) says that the debate took place while Cortona was Principe, which means 1634–6. Mahon's arguments (1962, p. 97) for thinking that the debate took place in 1636 are convincing. It is probably significant that Sacchi attended a meeting on November 14, 1636 (Vol. 166, no. 68,

p. 17 verso). It was also one of the only two recorded occasions when Duquesnoy attended a meeting (for the other, see Noehles, document 163).

65. He was nominated in December but declined in March, 1656, his notarized statement pleading his many prior obligations as an excuse. The length of time that Sacchi took to turn down the invitation does not necessarily mean that it took him some time to make up his mind. The pace of business generally seems to have been slow. There were no meetings between October 4, 1656 and March 4, 1657, and when Poussin was elected Principe in November of that year, he did not turn down the invitation officially until January, 1658 (Vol. 166, no. 68).

66. The last public argument had been Lanfranco's attempt to discredit Domenichino by distributing an engraving of Agostino Carracci's *Last Communion of St. Jerome* as proof of Domenichino's plagiarism in his treatment of the same theme. This took place in the 1620s when Lanfranco was campaigning to get part of the commission to decorate S. Andrea della Valle (see Hess, 1934, pp. 148–9).
In 1664 Bellori's *Idea* was read to the Academy of St. Luke. The minute-books show that Bellori himself refused to deliver it in person, despite much encouragement to do so from Maratta, an incident that suggests Bellori's support of the Academy was not whole-hearted at this time. The occasion demonstrates nevertheless a new interest in such matters among artists, primarily due to Maratta.

67. See the remarks at the end of Jennifer Montagu's article on Algardi's altarpiece in S. Nicola da Tolentino (*Burl. Mag.*, 1970, p. 291).

68. Annibale did not receive official recognition in the sense that Cesare d'Arpino did—major commissions in St. Peter's and the Lateran and elsewhere, titles, and so on. The story of Annibale's miserly treatment by the Farnese was well known in Rome (see, for example, Bellori, 1672, pp. 92–3). On Domenichino's reception in the second decade of the century, see Posner, 1965. Domenichino's lack of success in Rome after Lanfranco, Poussin, Cortona and Sacchi established themselves partly explains why he left Rome for Naples in 1629. The publication of Bellori's *Vite* of Annibale, Domenichino and Poussin in 1672 had a great deal to do with the establishment of their reputations then and since.

69. 'Altri nondimeno sono di parere che Pussino, non per mancanza di genio, ò di sapere, ma per lunga consuetudine, si esercitasse in picciolo, cresciuto in questa riputatione: mentre la tavola di San Germano, e l'altra del Novitiato de' Gesuiti sono historie con figure grandi molto lodate, dimostrando ch'egli era capace d'opere maggiori'. This is Bellori's characteristically tactful summary of the critical opposition and his defence (1672, pp. 526–7).

70. Malvasia, II, p. 267. The letter is probably genuine. Malvasia was friendly with Albani and was in contact with Maratta and Bellori, both alive when the *Felsina Pittrice* was published. Sacchi's picture by Bamboccio (Appendix II, no. 164) with the picture by Cerquozzi (Appendix II, no. 36 and Appendix I, L) may have been acquired by Sacchi around 1630 when he was living in the artists' district near S. Andrea delle Fratte and shared his house with several painters, Italian and Flemish. The Cerquozzi was a still life, and he is said only to have painted these early in his career (details *sub voce* in the index of names to the Appendixes).

71. See note 42 to the first section of the Introduction.

72. The diamond merchant Valguarnera (Costello, *passim*) was content with copies from Sacchi and the other artists that he patronized to a large extent but Cassiano was a more discerning patron.

73. See the author's preface to *Le gemme antiche figurate di Leonardo*

Agostini senese, Rome, 1657, where Sacchi is described as 'mihi amicissimo'. The pose of the singer Pasqualini in his portrait (cat. no. 51) is inspired by the Apollo Belvedere and that of Noah (cat. no. 72) by the Barberini Faun but such obvious borrowings from the antique are rare in Sacchi's work.

74. Details in Appendix III.

75. Poussin owned nineteen books but their titles are not recorded in his inventory (F. Boyer in *Bulletin de la Société d'Histoire de l'Art français*, 1928, p. 147). Vouet, however, owned some two hundred (Crelly, p. 14), and Claudine Bouzonnet Stella also had an extensive collection (*Nouvelles Archives Français*, 1877, pp. 25–104), as did Velazquez and Rubens. The library of the Academy of St. Luke in the 1620s contained works on art theory, treatises and iconographical handbooks (Noehles, p. 336).

76. Scaramuccia, pp. 195–6, 'Quali i Libri più necessarii per gl'elevati Pittor' etc. The four categories, all represented by Sacchi's library, were 'Historie del Mondo' (e.g. Livy, Tacitus, Justus Lipsius), 'Historie Sacre', 'Poesie diverse' (e.g. Virgil, Ovid, Tasso, Marini) and 'Romanzi moderni' (e.g. Loredano, Biondi).

77. A drawing by Grimaldi in the Teylers Museum, Haarlem (K VI 122) has the following notes on the verso: '... ese imprestato al sig Antonio giorgietti il Libro detto Tito. / (Istor)ia de romani (all cancelled lightly) riporta / (cancelled word) e più imprestato al sud° sig Antonio Giorgietti il libro di / cassandra del biondi (all cancelled) il libro di plinio (all cancelled) un putto che dorme di ... / due altri angioli di terra cotta un angelo g ... di gesso (all cancelled) / sig(nore) Andrea Sachi libro del vasari sig Camillo ... legion ... / sig Camillo due teste di cristo con la croce al Giorgietti ... del P ferari e tito / al sig Mola il libro di paesi di penna ... la testa del angelo del algardi / al sig Girolamo una testa di putto / sig Giovanni Carbone un libro di figure (?) / con bassi rilievi con due ... con ... / a gio batt(ist)a una madonna con bambino che dorme / gambe di cera'. The drawing is undated. The inscription is interesting not only as a record of one artist's practice of lending both books and works of art to other artists and friends but also as a record of Grimaldi's contacts and intellectual interests. Moreover the Haarlem sheet confirms Jennifer Montagu's conclusions as to the importance of Algardi for the formation of Antonio Giorgetti's style ('Antonio and Gioseppe Giorgetti: Sculptors to Cardinal Francesco Barberini', *Art Bulletin*, 1970, pp. 278–280) and offers proof that Grimaldi did in fact own, as Malvasia reported (II, p. 93), an edition of Vasari, a volume of special interest for it had marginal annotations by Agostino Carracci. Very probably it was these inscriptions and not Vasari's text which interested Sacchi. The notes by Grimaldi must have been made before Sacchi's death in 1661 but cannot be much earlier than 1655; Antonio Giorgetti only emerges as an independent sculptor in 1658 (Montagu, p. 279).

78. See Appendix III, no. 62.

79. See Appendix III, no. 97.

CATALOGUE

CATALOGUE

For bibliographical abbreviations see pp. 129ff.

AUTOGRAPH WORKS

All paintings are oil on canvas unless otherwise stated; height precedes width of given measurements. Many of Sacchi's pictures are in poor condition. Some estimate of their present state is given, although this section of the catalogue should be used with caution, as his works in Rome are in the process of being cleaned and restored. Citations for authors whose names appear in catalogue entries without a footnote reference will be found in the bibliography provided for each entry. References to Barberini inventories without a published reference come from Mrs Marilyn Aronberg Lavin and Dr Frances Vivian. Mrs Lavin is publishing all seventeenth-century Barberini inventories. Dr Vivian is publishing those of the eighteenth and nineteenth centuries. This section of the catalogue includes some important lost works for which documents and/or visual material survive. Other lost works are catalogued in the next section, pp. 104 ff.

1. Copy after Raphael's 'Galatea'. Palazzo Altieri, Rome
Size unknown.
Condition: The picture needs cleaning but its state of preservation beneath the varnish appears to be good.
Versions: 1661   Two versions are recorded in Sacchi's house in 1661 (Appendix II, nos. 15 and 242), the first in the front parlour, the second stored rolled up in a back room. It is possible that the former is the picture now in the Palazzo Altieri.

A COPY by Sacchi after Raphael's *Galatea* is first recorded in print by Pinarolo in 1700 in the Palazzo Altieri. Two versions appear in the artist's inventory of 1661, however, one of them prominently displayed in the front parlour with portraits of Sacchi's patrons. This version may be the picture now in the Altieri collection, having been acquired by them from Sacchi's heirs on the advice of Maratta, who worked for the Altieri.
Briganti drew attention to the picture in his recent monograph on Pietro da Cortona. The attribution of copies to specific artists is always difficult, but the widely spaced eyes of Galatea in the copy are much closer to Sacchi than they are to Raphael. Moreover, Sacchi's admiration for Raphael is well known.[1] Posse (p. 47) noted that Sacchi based the figure of Divine Wisdom in the Barberini ceiling fresco on Raphael's *Galatea*. The borrowing in turn suggests a date for the Altieri copy before 1629, when work on the ceiling began. In addition, the awkward drawing of the torso of the triton on the left suggests that the copy is an early work, made as a student exercise, as was Cortona's copy of the same fresco.[2]

1. See Bellori, 1672–96, p. 60 and Passeri, 1679, p. 302. A copy after Raphael's *Transfiguration* attributed to Sacchi is said to have been taken to France from Italy during the Empire, but the evidence is vague (Posse, 1925, p. 47).
2. Briganti, *loc. cit.*

Bibliography: Pinarolo, 1700, p. 142 (1703, *ibid.*; 1713, II, p. 151); Briganti, 1963, p. 159.

2. Copy after Annibale Carracci's 'Christ Crowned with Thorns'. Museo del Prado, Madrid   Plate 1
50 × 67 cm.
Condition: The condition seems good although the surface needs cleaning.

THIS careful copy after Annibale Carracci's *Christ Crowned with Thorns* (Pinacoteca, Bologna) was attributed to Sacchi in 1712 when it was in Maratta's collection. It was bought from his heirs for Philip V of Spain in 1724 and has remained in those collections ever since. The attribution was changed to Ludovico Carracci in recent Prado catalogues, but Pérez Sánchez rightly connected the work with the relevant documents. Without them, however, an attribution to Sacchi would be impossible to sustain. The surface reveals none of his idiosyncrasies. This fact suggests that the work was a student exercise which should be dated before 1618, when he left Rome, where the work could be seen in the Palazzo Farnese, for a period of study in Bologna with Albani.[1]

1. See the Introduction, p. 2. For the history of Annibale's picture, see Posner, 1971, II, Cat. No. 89.

Bibliography: Pérez Sánchez, 1965, p. 325 (with further references); Posner, 1971, II, p. 39.

3. The Virgin and Child with St. Joseph. Formerly S. Chiara alla Ciambella, Rome

BOTH Bellori and Passeri say that Sacchi's first public work was a fresco of the *Holy Family* for the Casa Pia delle Mal' Maritate in Rome and that the patron was Cardinal del Monte. Bellori, who only gives the subject, may never have seen the fresco since it was moved soon after 1628 to the adjacent church of S. Chiara and kept in a part of the convent to which the public was not admitted.[1] Passeri was commissioned at an unknown date to paint additional frescoes around Sacchi's composition in its new site and was consequently certainly familiar with it.[2] If the *Holy Family* was in fact Sacchi's first public commission, then a date of 1620–1 before the *Vision of St. Isidore* of 1622 is possible.
According to Passeri, the fresco showed life-size half-length figures of the Virgin and Child with St. Joseph. The Child was shown playing with Joseph's spectacles. No drawings by Sacchi or after him record any part of the design, nor do any *Holy Family* paintings by him of any other date survive. Possibly the *Holy Family* in Sacchi's house in 1661 (Appendix II, no. 207) was based on the lost S. Chiara fresco, although only the rarity of this theme in Sacchi's work makes it worth connecting these two lost works of an ordinarily commonplace subject.[3]

1. Passeri and Hess, *loc. cit.*
2. He added 'alcuni putti a fresco con una gloria disopra d'un Padre eterno e nelle parti laterali un San Michele Arcangelo in una e nell'altra un San Pietro d'Alcantara' (*ibid.*).
3. According to Hess, Sacchi's fresco was destroyed in the mid-nineteenth century when the convent was rebuilt. A *Holy Family* in the Capitoline Museum attributed to Sacchi in the eighteenth century (*Museo Capitolino . . .*, Rome, n.d. [1769–74], p. 121) and in Tofanelli's catalogue (*Descrizione delle Sculture, e Pitture che si trovano al Campidoglio*, Rome, 1834, no. 48) cannot now be traced. The *Holy Family* in the Pinacoteca Comunale at Ascoli-Piceno may be based on a Sacchi design but is not by him.

Bibliography: Bellori, 1672–96, p. 44; Passeri, 1679, p. 292; Posse, 1925, p. 12, note 2; Hess, 1934, p. 292, note 3.

4. St. Teresa in Ecstasy. Formerly S. Giuseppe a Capo le Case, Rome

BELLORI, Passeri and Pascoli all say that Sacchi's *St. Teresa in Ecstasy,* a fresco formerly above the door leading to the Carmelite convent dedicated to that saint beside S. Giuseppe a Capo le Case, was one of the artist's earliest works.[1] The saint was shown kneeling, looking heavenwards, her hands folded in prayer. According to Bellori, it was commissioned for the convent because Sacchi had a sister who belonged to that order. A date of 1622–5 is probable.[2] The convent and church were rebuilt from 1628 onwards at the expense of Cardinal Marcello Lante,[3] but Sacchi's overdoor was preserved, and survived in fact until the nineteenth century. There is no record of its appearance.

1. Pascoli says that it was Sacchi's first public commission, but his account of Sacchi's early career is incomplete and erratic. Knowing that *The Dream of St. Joseph* on the high altar of S. Giuseppe a Capo le Case was Sacchi's last public commission, Pascoli seems to have distorted the facts slightly to make Sacchi paint his first and last public commissions for the same place.
2. Both Bellori and Passeri describe it before the *Miracle of St. Gregory the Great*, begun in 1625. She was canonized in 1622.
3. Cardella, VI, pp. 132–3.

Bibliography: Totti, 1638, p. 305; Fei, 1643, p. 105; Bellori, 1672–96, p. 46; Passeri, 1679, p. 292; Pascoli, 1730, I, p. 17; Roisecco, 1750, II, p. 224; Vasi, 1770 (1765), p. 116; Pistolesi, 1841 and 1846, p. 370; Posse, 1925, p. 12, note 2; Hess, 1934, p. 292, note 4.

5. St. Urban with St. Chiara and St. Francis. Formerly S. Urbano, Rome

ACCORDING to Passeri and Bellori, the composition of this lost fresco consisted of three full-length figures—St. Urban in the centre with St. Chiara and St. Francis on either side of him. Urban looked upwards, his hands on his breast, Chiara looked at the monstrance she held in her hand while Francis looked upwards, his hand extended as if to intercede for the spectator. Passeri reported that the fresco was in bad condition; Hess in 1934 reported that, though the buildings of S. Urbano still stood, Sacchi's fresco was not to be seen. It is not recorded in seventeenth- or eighteenth-century guide books and may therefore have disappeared by about 1700. Both Passeri and Bellori list the fresco as an early work. Cardinal del Monte restored the church and, according to Bellori, commissioned Sacchi to paint the lost fresco. There is no known record of its appearance.[1]

1. For photographs of the interior of S. Urbano before the church was deconsecrated, see C. Ceschi, 'S. Urbano ai Pantani', *Capitolium*, IX, no. 8, August, 1933, pp. 384 and 385.

Bibliography: Bellori, 1672–96, pp. 45–6; Passeri, 1679, pp. 292–3; Posse, 1925, p. 12, note 2; Hess, 1934, p. 293, note 3.

6. The Vision of St. Isidore the Farmer. S. Isidoro, Rome
344 × 190 cm. Plate 4

Condition: Parts of the sky, the shadowed areas around the angels and much of the landscape have darkened. The blue of the Virgin's robe is affected either by diseased varnish or deteriorating smalt pigment. Otherwise the condition appears to be good.

Drawings: Composition study, Düsseldorf (Harris & Schaar, no. 1; Plate 2); composition study, Biblioteca Nacional, Madrid (no. D 8079, light brown ink pen and wash on cream paper, 215 × 158 mm.; the corners have been damaged and partially trimmed. Plate 3).

ST. ISIDORE (died 1130) was an exceptionally pious Spanish peasant who frequently interrupted his work in order to pray. His employer feared that such devotion was interfering with his servant's work, spied on him one morning and discovered angels guiding the saint's teams of oxen while he knelt in prayer before a vision of the Virgin. This is the subject of Sacchi's altarpiece.[1] The seed held by the Virgin refers to the occasion when Isidore scattered part of his load of corn to feed hungry pigeons, his sacks being full again when he reached his destination. The hoe and spring of water record a third miracle, his discovery of water in barren ground with this tool.[2]

The attribution of this altarpiece to Sacchi, first made by Totti in 1638, has never been challenged. Passeri discusses it before mentioning the accession of Urban VIII (August 6, 1623) and after describing three frescoes commissioned from Sacchi by Cardinal del Monte, who died in 1626. Bellori also treats it as an early work but discusses it after the *Miracle of the Corporal* of 1625–6. All the more recent literature has assumed that the *St. Isidore* is connected in some way with the canonization of St. Isidore on March 15, 1622,[3] Posse for example dating it soon after 1622. The church for which the altarpiece was made, although begun in 1622, was not consecrated until 1626,[4] and this fact, with Bellori's implied date of 1626, raises the possibility of a later date. There are practical as well as stylistic arguments however for thinking that Sacchi finished the picture in 1622.[5] The work is very different from the *Miracle of the Corporal*, begun in 1625, and an early date and the artist's immaturity would best explain the change of style. Cardinal del Monte was one of those in charge of the arrangements made to celebrate the canonization of St. Isidore,[6] and it must have been on his recommendation that the Spanish Franciscans gave the commission to Sacchi.

1. The same scene appears in B. Gonzalez' altarpiece of 1622 in the Municipal Museum, Madrid, and in a small copper by Carlo Bonone (Hazlitts, London) and it may have been selected for emphasis during the canonization festivities.
2. For St. Isidore see Butler II, pp. 323–4.
3. Bonanni, II, p. 548. SS. Teresa, Philip Neri, Francis Xavier and Ignatius of Loyola were canonized at the same time.
4. Land for the new church and college was rented from the Ludovisi in March (Cleary, p. 159 f.) or April (Harold, p. 65) of 1622, but three years later the Spanish Franciscans were 3000 scudi in debt and building was halted (Cleary, p. 162). The church was 'a shell with unplastered walls' at this point (*ibid.*), although the 1625 edition of Panciroli's *Tesori Nascosti* (pp. 383–4; the dedication is dated January 17, 1625) mentions that the Franciscans 'qui dedicarono la presente chiesa co'l monasterio'. After negotiations Lucas Wadding took over the half-finished church and college for his Irish Franciscans, and the Spaniards moved to S. Maria in Aracoeli. The original dedication and the altarpiece commissioned for that dedication were presumably retained for reasons of economy; little more was done to the interior of S. Isidoro at any rate until the 1640s. It is also worth noting that by 1625 the architect of S. Isidoro, Antonio Casone, was busy with his next commission, S. Maria della Concezione, the foundation stone of which was laid in

1626. The completion of S. Isidoro may have been supervised by Mario Anconio, to whom Baglione (p. 328) attributes the design of the high altar.

5. The Spanish Franciscans would have needed an altar at least where their new saint could be worshipped, even if the new church was unfinished, and one seems to have been set up in S. Giacomo degli Spagnoli for this purpose (Gigli, pp. 61–2).

6. Bonanni, *loc. cit.*

Bibliography: Totti, 1638, p. 301; Franzoni, 1653, p. 88; Mola, 1663, p. 163; Bellori, 1672–96, p. 49; Silos, 1673, pp. 42–3; Titi, 1674, p. 370 (and all later editions); Passeri, 1679, p. 293; Sebastiani, 1689, p. 126; Rossi, 1719, II, p. 404; Pascoli, 1730, I, p. 16; Roisecco, 1750, II, p. 242; Vasi, 1770, p. 108; Rossini, 1776, II, p. 174; Pistolesi, 1841, p. 370 (and 1846, *ibid.*); Voss, 1924, p. 533; Posse, 1925, p. 21 f.; Hess, 1934, p. 293; Posse, 1935, p. 290; Waterhouse, 1937, p. 92; Refice, 1950, p. 218; Wittkower, 1958, p. 169.

7. The Madonna of Loreto with St. Bartholomew, St. Joseph, St. James of Compostela and St. Francis. S. Francesco, Nettuno. Approximately 200 × 100 cm.   Plate 5

Condition: The upper half of the altarpiece has been damaged and retouched and the appearance of the sky is now affected by diseased varnish. There is also some retouching along the lower edge. Most of the surface is not badly obscured by dirt and darkened varnish however.

Drawings: A drawing of this subject at Düsseldorf formerly attributed to Sacchi is a Maratta of the 1660s (Harris & Schaar, no. 460).

THE HIGH ALTARPIECE of S. Francesco in Nettuno was first attributed to Sacchi in 1772 by Giovanni Bottari in the notes to his edition of Passeri (p. 445), who stated that it was an early work for the artist's home town. The attribution has been accepted by all later writers and is reasonable on stylistic grounds even if it is unlikely that Sacchi came from Nettuno (see above p. 38 note 1 for details). The general arrangement of the saints recalls Sacchi's *Crucifixion with Five Dominican Saints* of about 1638 (No. 46). The shadowed 'profil perdu' of St. Bartholomew resembles that of the male spectator in the *Miracle of St. Gregory the Great* of 1625 (No. 9). The strongly characterized, foreshortened head of St. James recalls that of St. Isidore in the 1622 altarpiece (No. 6) and those of some of the monks in the *Miracle of St. Philip Benizzi* of 1632 (No. 29), while St. Bartholomew's pose and physique recall that of St. Peter of about 1632 (No. 26). The palette is brighter than that of the *St. Isidore*, closer in fact to the more saturated colours used in the *St. Gregory* or the Prado *Birth of the Virgin* (No. 14).

S. Francesco was rebuilt around 1600, and the apse surrounding the high altar was enlarged in the 1620s by Fabio and Francesco Segneri, but the inscription which records the completion of this work in 1627 does not mention the high altar (Soffredini, pp. 168–9). Either it was incorporated unchanged into the new apse, or the frame of the altarpiece was enlarged to suit the new proportions of the surrounding architecture. In either case Sacchi's painting must have been retained for it can hardly be dated later than 1625.[1] Comparison with all his other surviving works reveals signs of immaturity best explained by an early date. The Virgin is a doll-like figure, too small in relation to the figures below her. They in turn are clumsily arranged both in relation to each other and to the available picture space. St. James in particular has been uncomfortably fitted into the area beside St. Francis and his pose is difficult to understand. Sacchi managed this kind of composition far better in the *St. Gregory* altarpiece of 1625 and in all his subsequent works.

There is one possible explanation for the presence in a small town some sixty kilometres south of Rome of a Sacchi altarpiece painted before his reputation was established by the *St. Gregory*. Cardinal del Monte, the artist's regular patron from 1621 at least, was bishop of Ostia and Velletri between October, 1623 and his death in 1626 (Gams, p. VII). Nettuno was in this bishopric. If Cardinal del Monte did obtain this commission for Sacchi, then the picture cannot have been started before the autumn of 1623 and was most probably painted between then and the summer of 1624, for it is difficult to think of the far more accomplished *St. Gregory* altarpiece following the Nettuno picture immediately.

1. In a letter Ellis Waterhouse has suggested that Sacchi designed the frame for his altarpiece. The style of the frame is characterless early seventeenth century; it could as well be the work of a local craftsman as that of an inexperienced young painter. The eight-pointed stars in the upper corners of the frame do not appear on the *stemma* of Cardinal del Monte. I have been unable to trace that of the Segneri family or that of any other family which used these stars and had connections with Nettuno.

Bibliography: Bottari, 1772, p. 445; Hess, 1934, p. 291, note 3; Posse, 1925, p. 290; Waterhouse, 1937, p. 91; Refice, 1950, p. 218.

8. St. Anthony Abbot and St. Francis. National Gallery, London 61 × 76 cm.   Plate 6

Condition: Previously obscured by diseased varnish, the condition of this picture since its recent cleaning has proved to be good. Much of the paint has darkened and there are some minor paint losses from flaking. The measurements do not include strips of canvas added to either side during a previous restoration.

Versions: 'A picture with two heads of St. Francis and St. Anthony with a black frame carved with arabesques' was in Sacchi's house in June, 1661 (App. II, no. 218). Its later history is not known.

A PICTURE of this subject was in Sacchi's house at the time of his death. Another picture answering this description was attributed to Sacchi in the Barberini Palestrina Inventory of about 1738 (Posse, p. 109, note 2). The picture under discussion was until 1966 in the collection of Princess Henriette Barberini in Rome and is presumably identical with the picture in the Palestrina Inventory; the same entry contains the *St. Andrew and St. Thomas* by Gianlorenzo Bernini also recently acquired by the National Gallery from the same source. Bernini's canvas was painted before June 1, 1627, when it appears in a Barberini Inventory (Martinelli, p. 96, notes 1 and 2). Sacchi was paid by the Barberini for a painting of two apostles on June 16, 1627 (Incisa della Rocchetta, p. 63), but, as Martinelli pointed out, the subject does not agree with that of the National Gallery picture and cannot refer to it.

Although the Sacchi and the Bernini seem to have been hung together and treated as pendants since the 18th century, and even though in design and format they have a great deal in common, it does not follow that they were commissioned at the same time for this purpose. The Bernini could have been painted any time between about 1615 and 1627, but it is one of the most accomplished of his few surviving paintings, most of which probably date from the earlier part of his career. A date between 1623, when Maffeo Barberini became Pope, and 1627 is probable.[1] The Sacchi must be an early work. The types recall St. Isidore and some of the heads in the *St. Gregory*, but the characterization does not compare with that of mature works such as *St. Thomas Aquinas* (No. 19) or the *St. Romuald* (No. 20), both works of 1631. The stiffness of the spatial composition and the lack of formal or psychological communication between the figures in Sacchi's picture compares unfavourably with both Bernini and with Sacchi's *Miracle of the Corporal* of 1625–6 and suggests a date near the Nettuno altarpiece of 1623–4.

The formal connections between the Sacchi and the Bernini paintings would appear to be too close to be dismissed as fortuitous, particularly since they are the same size. Nevertheless, it seems that the Barberini only owned the Bernini in 1627 and that the

Sacchi was acquired later.[1] The difference in subject matter argues against the two works having been part of the same commission, although the apostles for which Sacchi was paid in 1627 might have belonged to a series of which the Bernini was also part. One possible explanation, which presupposes a date of 1623 or earlier for the Bernini, is that Sacchi knew it, admired it and based his two saints on it, but did his painting as a studio exercise. It was acquired later by the Barberini either from Sacchi's heirs after his death or from another collector. It certainly cannot be the case, as Martinelli suggested, that Bernini painted his picture under the guidance of Sacchi, since at this point Bernini could have learnt little from the younger painter.[3]

1. When he became Pope, Maffeo encouraged Bernini to study painting, which he is said to have done for a couple of years, according to both Filippo Baldinucci and Domenico Bernini.
2. Levey noted that the two saints represented are the name saints of three Barberini cardinals; perhaps Sacchi hoped the work would attract their attention and patronage.
3. Richard Spear informs me that there are old copies of both Sacchi's and Bernini's pictures in the Castelbarco-Albani collection in Milan. Pierre Rosenberg has recently drawn my attention to a picture of *Sts. Thomas, Bartholomew and Jacob* in the Landesmuseum, Oldenburg (depot, as Valentin de Boulogne). The artist responsible seems to have known Sacchi's and Bernini's canvases, the head of Bartholomew being almost an exact blend of Sacchi's St. Anthony and Bernini's St. Andrew. At present, I cannot support a firm attribution of this fascinating discovery to either Bernini or Sacchi.

Bibliography: V. Martinelli, 'Le Pitture del Bernini', *Commentari,* I, 1950, pp. 95–104, especially p. 96 and fig. 121; M. Levey, *National Gallery Catalogues: The Seventeenth and Eighteenth Century Italian Schools:* London, 1971, pp. 205–6.

9. St. Gregory and the Miracle of the Corporal. Chapter House, St. Peter's, Rome   Plate 8

285 × 207 cm.

Condition: The general condition of this canvas is good but it would benefit greatly from the removal of a thick layer of yellowed varnish. There are signs of paint loss from flaking but they are minor except along the lower edge where they have been partially retouched. Some of the flesh tints—the saint's right hand, for example—seem to have faded.

Drawings: Composition study, Windsor (Blunt and Cooke, no. 765); composition study, École des Beaux-Arts, Paris (no. 343, red chalk on cream paper, 262 × 161 mm. (Plate 7); the verso shows the middle third of a male nude study, also in red chalk, oddly tentative in handling and unrelated to any known work. Sacchi apparently reused the back of the paper when making the study for the *St. Gregory.* Though published by P. Lavallée and W. Rabaud in *Art Italien des XVIIᵉ et XVIIIᵉ siècles,* Paris, 1937, p. 27, this drawing has been overlooked in all later literature). Sacchi himself reused the composition of this altarpiece in a drawing in the Albertina of the miraculous communion of St. Paschal Baylon (Sutherland Harris, 1971, pp. 338–9).

A composition study in Berlin accepted by Posse is derived from the altarpiece by a later hand (KdK 15250, red chalk, 237 × 203 mm.), as is a drawing in Düsseldorf (see Harris & Schaar, no. 106). A drawing of this subject in the British Museum (No. 1946–7.13. 805), presently attributed to Sacchi, is a derivation of the composition by a contemporary but more conservative artist. A pen drawing in the Farnesina, Rome (No. 128404), perhaps of this subject, also must be excluded from Sacchi's oeuvre.

Versions: 1783   'Un Quadro di Palmi due per alto rappresentante il Miracolo di S. Gregorio Magno' is recorded in Palazzo Colonna in 1783 (Colonna, II, p. 67).

1937   A small version in the store rooms of the Pinacoteca

Vaticana was published by Waterhouse (1937, p. 91), who plausibly suggested that this version was made in the 18th century when the painting was replaced by a mosaic copy. There is also a decent copy of unknown date in the third chapel to the right of St. Germain l'Auxerrois, Paris.

Documents: On January 24, 1625, Sacchi was paid 40 scudi 'a conto di una tavola de pittura del Altare alla Clementina dove è reposto il corpo di S. Gregorio Magno'. On March 26, 1625, he received 20 more scudi. On May 14, 1627, Sacchi's commission to paint the altarpiece was confirmed. On July 3, he was given 100 scudi 'a bon conto della tavola fatta . . . oltre a scudi 60 hauti'. On August 11, 1627, he received 40 scudi. On September 27, 1627, Sacchi asked for the final payment of 100 scudi to be made. This was done twelve days later. Altogether he received 300 scudi (Pollak, II, pp. 294–6).

According to the Golden Legend, the Emperor Constance asked St. Gregory for a relic. When the saint handed him the *brandeum,* the cloth in which the relic had been wrapped, the Emperor returned it with disdain. The saint then said a prayer, called for a knife and pierced the cloth, which bled. The miracle was used as proof that relics were effective even indirectly.

This is the first of Sacchi's surviving works for which documents exist, but while the payments are complete, there is a puzzling break after the artist had received 60 scudi in the spring of 1625. No more payments were made until July, 1627 when the picture was said to be 'fatta', that is 'finished'. The final payment was made in October, 1627 but only after the artist had put in a request asking for his account to be settled. The break in the payments and the artist's difficulties in getting the last of the money owed to him were probably caused by the death of his patron, Cardinal del Monte, in the summer of 1626, for it was almost certainly he who obtained this commission for Sacchi (Bellori), who in 1627 was not yet enjoying the protection of the Barberini.[1] The date of the picture's completion can only be surmised, but a year would seem sufficient time, even for an important commission, all the evidence for Sacchi's slowness belonging to the later part of his career. The altarpiece may even have been ready when Cardinal del Monte died.

The painting remained in St. Peter's until the middle of the 18th century when it was replaced by a mosaic copy,[2] and the original is next recorded in Paris among Napoleon's loot.[3] Returned to Italy shortly afterwards, it was kept in the Pinacoteca Vaticana for part of the 19th century[4] but is now in the Sala Capitolare beside the sacristy.

1. They had bought a small picture from the artist in 1627 (Incisa della Rocchetta, p. 63) but gave him no major commissions until late in 1629.
2. The painting is last recorded in St. Peter's in the 1750 edition of *Il Mercurio Errante.* The mosaic is first noted in the 1770 edition of Vasi, which has a dedication dated 1765.
3. Pistolesi, *loc. cit. infra* and *BSHAF,* 1877, pp. 144–5.
4. Pistolesi, *loc. cit.*

Bibliography: Celio, 1638, p. 73; Baglione, 1639, p. 28; Mola, 1663, p. 72; Bellori, 1672–96, p. 48 f.; Titi, 1674, p. 23 (and all later editions); Scaramuccia, 1674, p. 38; Sandrart, 1675, p. 288; Passeri, 1679, pp. 293–4; Sebastiani, 1689, p. 12; Rossini, 1693, p. 140 (1700 and 1704, p. 158; 1750, p. 125; 1776, I, p. 239); Pinarolo, 1700, II, p. 274 (1703, p. 259; 1713, p. 259); Panciroli, 1719, II, p. 37; Pascoli, 1730, I, p. 16; Vasi, 1770 (1765), p. 338; Bianconi, 1772, p. 445; Pistolesi, 1841, p. 557 (1846, *ibid.*); Voss, 1924, p. 530; Weisbach, 1924, p. 45 and pl. 290; Posse, 1925, p. 22 f. and passim; Posse, 1935, p. 290; Waterhouse, 1937, p. 93; Wittkower, 1958, pp. 169–170; Waterhouse, 1963, p. 56.

10. Juno in her Peacock Chariot. Kunsthistorisches Museum, Vienna   Plate 13

Oil on canvas, 34 × 50 cm.

Condition: The condition appears to be good.

Documents: The picture is mentioned in the 1659 inventory of Prince Leopold Wilhelm, where it is attributed to Andrea Camassei (*J.K.A.K.*, 1883, p. cx, no. 437).

THIS WORK was first attributed to Andrea Camassei in 1659 and this attribution has been repeated, but not discussed, in all catalogues of the museum that mention the work. The 1659 inventory is not completely reliable, as the misattribution of the *Dying Mother of Aristides* to Sacchi shows. This particular work is not by Camassei (see Sutherland Harris, 'Camassei Studies', p. 68) but is an early work by Sacchi, contemporary with his lost frescoes in the Casino of Cardinal del Monte, which contained small mythological scenes. The brush work and drapery forms should be compared with the Miracle of St. Gregory the Great of 1625–6. Some difficulties with spatial construction—the perspective of the carriage wheels, the angle of the chariot to the picture plane—also suggest that this is an early work. That Sacchi was patronized by Leopold Wilhelm is confirmed by the artist's possession of a medal with a portrait of the Prince (Appendix II, no. 46).[1]

1. According to Graham Pollard, the medal owned by Sacchi can probably be identified with an undated struck medal attributed to Paul Zeggin (see Karl Domanig, *Die Deutsche Medaille in kunst- und kulturhistorischer Hinsicht*, Vienna, 1907, no. 270). I am extremely grateful to Graham Pollard for this useful suggestion.

Bibliography: F. Wickhoff in *J.K.A.K.*, 1898, XIX, p. 438, no. 437 and fig. 1; Catalogues of the Kunsthistorisches Museum: 1837, p. 32; 1896, p. 158, no. 537; current inventory no. CC 142.

11. Frescoes formerly in the Casino of Cardinal del Monte. Rome

Drawings: Composition study for the *Bacchanal*, British Museum (1963.11.9.26, red chalk on cream paper, 150 × 255 mm. There is a second small composition sketch for the same work on the verso; Plate 10); copy after the British Museum *Bacchanal* sheet, Ambrosiana, Milan (F. 232, no. 349, red chalk on cream paper, 175 × 250 mm.; Plate 12); Prometheus stealing fire from the sun, British Museum (1963.11.9.27, red chalk on cream paper, 153 × 260 mm.). Another drawing in the Ambrosiana (F. 232, no. 729, red chalk on cream paper, 195 × 260 mm.; Plate 11) showing Mercury, Argus and Io, is drawn by the same hand as the *Bacchanal* copy and may record a lost design for the Casino.

BELLORI gives the most complete description of this important lost early work. From his text it can be deduced that the 'Loggia di ricreazione', which Cardinal del Monte had had decorated for the pleasure of his guests invited to take summer meals there at the edge of the Tiber,[1] was rectangular in plan. It had a cross vault and one window and one door placed opposite each other, probably in the two long walls. In a rectangular fresco in the centre of the ceiling were four kneeling women symbolizing the four seasons. They were shown adoring the sun, represented by Apollo, who was accompanied by Juno and Mercury. These seven figures were slightly under life-size. The four lunettes also contained decorative garlands and medallions. Stories of Mars and Venus, Apollo and Vulcan, and Ceres and a Naiad were painted on the soffits of three lunette arches, the fourth, which framed a window, being left bare. In the four corners of the vault above the cornice the four seasons were represented again, this time by life-size figures seated on the cornice. Spring was represented by Venus with Cupid shooting an arrow at her, Summer by a woman partially draped in yellow cloth and holding the mirror of solar virtue and ears of corn. Winter was a farmer resting his arm on a plough, waiting for Spring in order to start work. Autumn was Bacchus wearing a tiger skin and holding a cup into which he was squeezing grape juice. Finally

there was a fresco above the door with life-size figures representing a bacchanal with Midas and Bacchus supporting Silenus amidst a crowd of drunken revellers.

The only part of the decoration for which any firm visual evidence survives is the *Bacchanal* over the door. A red chalk study by Sacchi in the British Museum shows Silenus on the back of a donkey and held up by Bacchus and King Midas while other figures dance and play musical instruments. The sheet can be dated 1622–25 and fits Bellori's description in all essential details.[2] Two other drawings may record unrecorded scenes or rejected designs for an earlier project. A second drawing in the British Museum by Sacchi of the same period shows Prometheus stealing fire from the sun watched by Athena.[3] No scene of this subject is recorded by Bellori, but since the sun god Apollo is concerned, such a scene might have been considered for a room whose theme according to Bellori was 'Le Stagioni che prendono vita dal sole'. A third drawing has a more tenuous connection with the Casino. It is a sheet showing Mercury, Argus and Io in the Ambrosiana, drawn on the same scale and by the same hand as the Ambrosiana copy after the British Museum *Bacchanal* drawing. The types and composition recall Sacchi while Mercury again is one of the gods shown in the central ceiling fresco. Possibly the scene was a rejected alternative for one of the soffit arch scenes, or possibly the decoration contained other small scenes not recorded by Bellori.

The frescoes must have been painted before Cardinal del Monte's death in 1626. The two drawings in the British Museum support a date in the early 1620s. Passeri simply lists the Casino as an early work but he does say that the Cardinal originally intended to offer the commission to Filippo Napoletano, who is documented in Rome only in the 1620s.[4] Only Bellori's testimony contradicts a date of about 1622–24. He says that the Casino was finished when Sacchi was eighteen, that is, in 1617. Since Bellori's account of Sacchi's early years is demonstrably wrong in a number of places and since Bellori is at pains throughout that section to stress Sacchi's precocity, it seems preferable to accept the date suggested by the other evidence, a date that fits the artist's other early works.

1. It was near Piazza del Popolo according to Passeri, but no seventeenth-century maps show the exact site (Hess, *loc. cit.*).
2. The delicate handling of small details is close to the *St. Isidore* composition study in Düsseldorf (Harris & Schaar, no. 1) and to the composition study for the *Miracle of St. Gregory the Great* in the École des Beaux Arts. The former can be dated 1622, the latter 1625.
3. A date of 1622–25 is indicated by reference to the drawings cited in note 2. When I published this drawing in *Master Drawings* (1971, 4, pl. 36), the subject was identified as Phaethon setting off in Apollo's chariot. Jennifer Montagu pointed out that Prometheus stealing fire from the sun watched by Athena is far more plausible.
4. Thieme-Becker, *sub voce*; he was dead by July 1630 (Arch Acad. S. Luca, Vol. 42a, f. 112 v.).

Bibliography: Bellori, 1672–96, p. 46; Passeri, 1679, p. 293; Posse, 1925, p. 13; Hess, 1934, p. 193, note 3; Refice, 1950, pp. 216–17; Haskell, 1963, p. 29.

12. Portrait of Cardinal Francesco Maria del Monte (1549–1626). Formerly Casa Sacchi, Rome

Version: 1661 A portrait of Cardinal Francesco del Monte hung in Sacchi's front parlour at the time of his death (Appendix II, no. 17). Its later history is not known.

CARDINAL del Monte was Sacchi's first important patron. According to Bellori, he spotted Sacchi's talents in a drawing contest at the Academy of St. Luke which Sacchi won at the age of eleven. Almost all of the artist's works made before the Cardinal's death in 1626 were commissioned by him. This extensive patronage of the young painter is a remarkable testimony to the elderly Cardinal's continuing interest in art up to the time of his death.[1] Sacchi's portrait of the Cardinal has not unfortunately survived. Indeed until a portrait drawing of the Cardinal by Ottavio Leoni emerged recently,[2] there was no known record of his appearance.

1. Sacchi's relations with Cardinal del Monte are discussed in the introduction (p. 3 f.).
2. *Burl. Mag.*, CIX, 1967, p. 375 and fig. 52. It now belongs to the Ringling Museum of Art, Sarasota. This drawing proves that it is not Cardinal del Monte who is represented in Sacchi's portrait in Ottawa (Cat. No. 21).

13. The Decoration of the Upper Gallery, Villa Chigi (formerly Sacchetti). Castelfusano, near Rome

Allegory of the Four Seasons. Central fresco, ceiling of the Upper Gallery   Plate 15
Condition: The gallery has always been damp and the frescoes have consequently deteriorated and have been restored several times, most recently in 1953 (Briganti, 1962, p. 179). The *Allegory of the Four Seasons* is better preserved than the three smaller scenes by Sacchi, for only Cybele is badly affected by repaint. Only her head and right hand are autograph.
Drawings: Studies for the figures of Spring and Summer, Düsseldorf; Plate 14 (Harris & Schaar, no. 2).
Documents: A payment of 60 scudi for two stories in the gallery of Castelfusano was made to Sacchi by the Sacchetti on April 3, 1628 (Incisa della Rocchetta, p. 60).

Sacrifice to Pan. Fresco, ceiling of the Upper Gallery Plate 19
Condition: Most of the nymph to the right of Pan and Pan's left arm have flaked off but have not been retouched. Other minor paint losses have been repaired but a good deal of the original surface remains.
Drawings: Composition study, Darmstadt (Hessisches Landesmuseum, no. AE 1761, red chalk on cream paper, 266 by 389 mm.); Plate 16. See Walter Vitzthum [*Burl. Mag.*, CV (1963), p. 214 and fig. 30]. A second red chalk composition study is in the Academia de San Fernando, Madrid (A. E. Pérez Sánchez, *Ventiseis Dibujos Boloñeses y Romanos del Siglo XVII*, Madrid, 1965, p. 14, no. 26). A drawing, almost certainly of the same subject, was hanging in a frame in Sacchi's house in 1661 (Appendix II, no. 212). It is probably to be identified with the drawing in Maratta's collection in 1712 described as 'Altro Disegno su la carta tinta di Foligne,[1] fatta da Andrea Sacchi, quale rappresenta un Sacrificio del Dio Pan', Galli, XXII, p. 236). The Madrid drawing can be traced back to Maratta's studio and is therefore probably the drawing recorded in Maratta's collection. The history of the Darmstadt drawing can be traced back to 1773 when it was in the Lempereur sale.[2] Many of Lempereur's drawings came from the Crozat collection, and Crozat acquired many of his drawings in Rome in 1714 and 1715 when Maratta, who owned a number of drawings by Sacchi, was selling some of his collection.[3]
Versions: A painting described as 'Un Sacrificio' was in Sacchi's house in 1661 (Appendix II, no. 227); its later history is not known. Another version, engraved by F. Aliamet in 1769 (Plate 18) when it belonged to the Earl of Lincoln (also the Duke of Newcastle), is not recorded among the items sold from the Newcastle collection at Clumber Park in 1937 (Christie's, 4.6.1937; 14.6.1937; 31.3.1939). and is apparently lost.

Romulus among the Shepherds. Fresco, ceiling of the Upper Gallery; Plate 17.
Condition: There seems to be more loss of detail through flaking than in the two frescoes described above. The shepherd reclining in the left foreground, however, is well preserved.

The story of Cincinnatus. Fresco, ceiling of the Upper Gallery.
Condition: Most of the surface has been clumsily repainted. The trees and cloak held by the man on the left, the legs of the man holding the *fasces* and the left leg of Cincinnatus are especially weak.
Drawings: There is a rough sketch in red chalk, probably of this subject, in the British Museum (1963-11.9.24), but the composition has little to do with the fresco. Walter Vitzthum has published two pen sketches by Cortona for the *Cincinnatus* in the Cooper-Hewitt Museum, New York (in the *Burl. Mag.*, CX, 1968, p. 362 and fig. 54).

PIETRO DA CORTONA planned the decoration of this long, rectangular ceiling and executed the majority of the small, narrative frescoes set between frames of painted foliage (Briganti, *loc. cit.* See his plate 77 for a view of the room under discussion), Sacchi being the most important of a number of assistants whose names are recorded, and the only one whose hand can be detected. None of Sacchi's biographers note that he worked at Castelfusano, but Luca Berettini, in a letter to Ciro Ferri of March 24, 1679 (Campori, *loc. cit.*), writes:

Hanno li Sig.ri Sacchetti un casaletto vicino ad Ostia luogo delizioso per le cacce e per la vista del mare. Questo volse il Sig.r Marcello che fusse nobilitato dalle pitture dei più famosi pennelli di quel tempo tra i quali perchè stimava non i inferiore quello del Sig.r Pietro, gli fece dipingere i siti più grandi e riguardevoli di molte stanze e fra gli altri pittore [*sic*] li dipinse ancora [*sic*] Andrea Sacchi, soggetto meritevole d'ogni lode.

When he published the documents for the gallery, which include one payment to Sacchi for two unspecified scenes, Incisa della Rocchetta attributed the four scenes under discussion to Sacchi on stylistic grounds. Only Refice has differed, giving Sacchi an additional fresco, the *Forge of Cyclops*, in an adjacent room, a work which Briganti reasonably dismissed as a much repainted work of Cortona's other assistants.

Since the publication of the documents in 1924, several drawings have been identified which both confirm the attributions made by Incisa della Rocchetta and throw some light on Cortona's supervision of the parts executed by Sacchi. Drawings by Sacchi have been traced for the *Allegory of the Four Seasons*, the *Sacrifice to Pan*, and possibly also for the *Cincinnatus*. No drawings have so far been traced for the *Romulus* but the formal and psychological parallels between it and accepted works such as the *St. Romuald* of 1631 are striking and the attribution is not in doubt.

The technique of the studies for Spring and Summer in the *Allegory* (cf. Plate 14) recalls other drawings made in the late 1620s and presents no problems. The *Pan* studies are more complicated. Neither of the two composition studies matches the fresco precisely, although the Madrid study is much nearer to it than the Darmstadt sheet (Plate 16). The latter, apart from minor details, follows instead the design of the lost painting of this subject, recorded in the collection of the Earl of Lincoln in 1769. The Madrid drawing is squared for transfer and would appear to be the artist's final pre-cartoon sketch for the fresco. The Darmstadt drawing was probably made after the fresco's completion when its composition was reworked and the easel painting made. Here it is worth remembering that Sacchi, according to Bellori, was dissatisfied with his frescoes in the Casino of Cardinal del Monte, which he had been forced to complete in great haste a few years earlier (No. 11). Perhaps at Castelfusano Sacchi again felt that the most complex of his four compositions could be improved and for this reason made the painting.

The most important difference between the fresco and the painting is the position of the nymph who crowns Pan. In the fresco she is placed in front of him, in the lost painting behind him. By moving Pan forward, redistributing the light and shade and removing the vase in the centre, the gap between Pan and his nymphs and the priest and his attendants is made clearer, and attention is focused on the two main protagonists. In addition Pan is made more prominent than the priest by placing the latter further back and in shadow. Judging from the quality of the Darmstadt drawing, rather than from the mediocre print, the painting 'doit avoir été un bien beau tableau' (Mariette, v, p. 151), and its loss is regrettable.

Cortona's drawing, which has a square and not a rectangular format, was probably made at an early stage when the plan of the whole ceiling was not yet settled and the amount to be executed by assistants was undecided. When this subject was assigned to Sacchi, it would appear that Cortona gave his sketch to Sacchi, allowing him to adapt it as he wished to the new, wider format. Sacchi kept Pan crowned by a nymph on the left and the altar on the right, but he balanced them by adding a priest to focus and control the revellers on the right. Sacchi's final design is much less symmetrical than that of Cortona's sketch which has a temple and foliage on the right balancing the nymphs and Pan on the left. Sacchi's division between the priest and Pan is also diagonal rather than vertical, which allows him to separate the two parties and to emphasize Pan further without destroying the unity of the surface composition.

The respective roles of Sacchi and Cortona in the *Cincinnatus* fresco (Briganti, pl. 84) are more difficult to understand. In contrast to the *Sacrifice to Pan*, it is Cortona's sketches which most closely resemble the final design, and perhaps the fresco should be attributed to him. Unfortunately the condition of the fresco does not permit any firm decision as to its authorship. The hand of Cincinnatus grasping his staff is more carefully drawn than is usual with Cortona and the powerful right to left pull of the composition, from the fields to the heavier public duties to which Cincinnatus has been summoned, is much stronger in the fresco than in the drawing. This increased concentration on the psychological drama in the fresco is more characteristic of Sacchi than of Cortona. Whoever was responsible for the *Cincinnatus*, it is significant that it is difficult to separate the work of two artists whose later careers were very different, but who at this stage were evidently able to work together and to benefit from this cooperation.

1. 'Fuligne serve ... per tigner fogli da disegnarvi sopra' (F. Baldinucci, *Vocabolario toscano dell'arte del disegno*, Florence, 1681, p. 61.
2. The drawing has the marks of Lempereur (Lugt 1740) and the Marquis de Lagoy (Lugt 1710); see also Mireur, vi, p. 388. The drawing entered the collection of the museum from that of the Dukes of Dalberg, having previously been also in the collection of Conti in 1777 and in that of Vassal de Saint Hubert in 1779 (Mireur, *loc. cit.*).
3. See Lugt no. 2951, esp. p. 545.

Bibliography: Campori, 1866, p. 507; Incisa della Rocchetta, 1924, p. 60 f.; Voss, 1924, p. 530; Posse, 1925, p. 29 f. and passim; Posse, 1935, p. 290; Waterhouse, 1937, p. 91; Refice, 1950, p. 219; Briganti, 1962, pp. 177–80.

14. The Birth of the Virgin. Museo del Prado, Madrid

262 × 171 cm.   Plate 20

Condition: The condition is excellent; there are only minor paint losses and retouchings.

Drawings: Six drapery and figure studies, Düsseldorf (Harris & Schaar, nos. 3 to 8). Studies for the women in the right foreground, Düsseldorf (FP 13779, Black chalk with white heightening on buff paper stained grey, 379 × 249 mm. There is an old attribution to Lanfranco on the verso. There are a few unidentifiable drapery studies on the verso). The pose of a male nude in a study in Berlin (Dahlem Museum, no. 15303, red chalk with some white heightening on cream paper, 392 × 240 mm.), which Posse connected with the figure of Apollo in the Portrait of M. A. Pasqualini,[1] is closer to the figure of Joachim in the Prado picture than to that of Apollo. The drawing in question looks like an unfinished academy study rather than a study for a particular figure however (the

leaves round the head suggest that it was not originally made with Joachim in mind), and in fact the pose turns up in a number of works (Nos. 15, 52, 57). The drawing should probably not therefore be connected with this work only.

It has not been possible to trace a black chalk study for Joachim which Posse (p. 93) cites in Dresden. The drawing he mentions (*ibid.*) in Vienna (Meder no. 759) is a *Birth of the Virgin* composition partly based on Sacchi's design but by a later hand, perhaps Pietro de' Pietri. A lost study for the Prado picture was in the Gaburri collection in Florence in 1722.[2] Others were in the Julienne collection in 1767 (Mireur, vi, p. 388), in the collection of Carlo Carlone in 1786,[3] and in an anonymous sale in 1797 (Mireur, *loc. cit.*).

THE RECORDED history of this painting begins in 1772 when it appears in Don Javier's wing of the Palacio Nuevo in Madrid, having recently been acquired from the Marquis de la Ensenada,[4] but the date of its arrival in Spain is not known. It is not recorded in any known Roman seventeenth-century source, printed or otherwise, and seems to have had no local influence; it may therefore have been sent to Spain shortly after its completion. Alternatively it may have been in a little-known church or collection overlooked by the guide books and biographers. The first printed reference (Ponz, 1776) records it as 'De Andrea Sachi (sic) ... un Nacimiento grande de Nuestra Senora', an attribution repeated by Cumberland in 1797. All the 19th-century Prado catalogues call it either 'Escuela Italiana', 'Ecole de Bianchi' or—from 1843— 'Escuela del Albano'. The reattribution to Sacchi, first made by Voss in 1924, has not been challenged.

The obscurity of this picture's early history is not the only problem it presents. Its composition is so close to that of the *Birth of the Baptist* in the Lateran Baptistry of about 1645 (56) that the Prado picture has been identified as a version of the same subject and date.[5] Putti scattering roses are normal in scenes of the Virgin's birth after the Council of Trent,[6] but it is unusual for the baby Virgin to be shown naked and the prominence of Joachim can only be paralleled in later works.[7] Perhaps the Prado picture was commissioned by one of the religious groups particularly devoted to the Virgin's parents who, after an attempt was made at the end of the sixteenth century to eliminate them from the calendar of important religious festivals, Joachim being expelled entirely from the Breviary in 1572, enjoyed a certain revival in the seventeenth century.[8] It might be thought that close examination of the baby would settle the problem, but unfortunately either sex may be read in the area below the baby's stomach fold. It is worth noting, however, that the baby is very much smaller than the definitely male baby of the Fonte picture, that the accessories suggest a richer family than those in the Fonte picture, and that Joachim wears red and blue, as he does in the Scrovegni Chapel in Padua.

The identification of a group of preparatory studies at Düsseldorf for both the Fonte and Prado pictures makes it possible to verify the attribution of the latter to Sacchi and to date it some ten years earlier than the former. One of these sheets (Harris & Schaar nos. 7 and 16) has studies on the verso for the Prado picture and on the recto for the *Pasce Oves Meas* on which Sacchi was working in 1628 (No. 15). Another (*op. cit.* nos. 8 and 25) has studies for the Prado picture on one side and for Tommaso Luini's S. Carlo al Corso altarpiece of 1628–32 on the other. Moreover the style of these studies, loosely drawn in black chalk on grey or buff paper with white heightening, resembles other studies made by Sacchi in the late 1620s, and differs from his style of the 1640s, when he usually works more carefully and in red chalk. This is the medium chosen for two other Düsseldorf studies (Harris & Schaar, nos. 74 and 75) for the one figure in the Fonte picture who does not appear in the Prado composition. These two drawings suggest that others similarly executed in red chalk for figures which appear in both compositions (*op. cit.* nos. 72 and 73) should be associated with the Fonte and not with the Prado picture.

Additional confirmation for a date in the 1620s for the Prado picture is provided by its colour scheme. Its richly saturated palette of malachite green, azure blue, rose pink and golden yellow is paralleled by only one other surviving work, the *St. Gregory* altarpiece of 1625–6, and contrasts strongly with the more restrained colours characteristic of Sacchi in the 1630s and 1640s.

1. p. 107. Posse knew the work only from an engraving which reverses the design.
2. Campori, pp. 533–4, no. 113.
3. Desmond Macrae, 'Another "Catalogo" of the sketches of Carlo Carlone', *Arte Lombarda*, XII (1967), p. 146. It was perhaps a copy.
4. Posse, p. 93 f.; Pérez Sánchez, p. 326.
5. 1933 catalogue of the Prado and Pérez Sánchez, *loc. cit.*
6. Jameson, pp. 146–9; Mâle, pp. 348–50; Réau, II, p. 163.
7. e.g. Francesco Trevisani, Solimena, Corrado Giaquinto and Pietro del Po. Earlier examples are the fresco of Ludovico Carracci in Piacenza (Bodmer, pl. 69) and the altarpiece by Francesco Albani now in the Capitoline Museum in Rome (Boschetto, p. 129) where Joachim also makes a gesture of thanks but is placed in the middle ground.
8. Mâle, p. 346. The small church dedicated to SS. Gioacchino ed Anna by Spanish Carmelites, built in 1607 beside the site now occupied by S. Carlo alle Quattro Fontane, would seem to be the logical place to look for a site for Sacchi's picture, but its contemporary altarpiece is much smaller than Sacchi's painting and cannot have replaced it. The Spaniards left S. Anna in 1809 and the church was taken over by the Belgians for an ecclesiastical college in 1846. For the church, see Armellini, 1897, p. 252; 1942 ed., p. 233 f.

Bibliography: Prado catalogues: Ponz, 1772, p. 530; Cumberland, 1787, p. 84; 1828, p. 169, no. 599 (and French ed., pp. 173–4, no. 599); 1843, p. 170, no. 785; 1845, p. 170, no. 785; 1885, p. 16, no. 3; 1933, p. 732, no. 3; 1945, p. 556, no. 3; 1952, p. 581, no. 3. Pedro Antonio de la Puente, *Viaje de España o Cartas*, Madrid, 1772 f. (1947 ed., p. 530); Voss, 1924, p. 532; Posse, 1925, p. 93 f.; Posse, 1935, p. 290; Pérez Sánchez, 1965, p. 326.

15. Christ's Command to St. Peter, 'Feed My Sheep!'.

Formerly Palazzo Barberini, Rome, present location unknown.
Drawings: There are thirteen autograph drawings and three copies of lost drawings in Düsseldorf, Florence and Windsor, for two *Feed My Sheep* compositions. The majority can be connected with the composition described by Bellori (see below) and are listed first as for the main design. The remainder are listed separately as for an alternative, rejected design.
Study for the main composition, Uffizi (Santarelli 9517, brown ink and brush on cream paper, 245 by 135 mm.; Plate 21); copy after a lost composition study closely related to the Uffizi drawing, Düsseldorf (Harris & Schaar, no. 107); composition study, Düsseldorf (Harris & Schaar, no. 9); five drapery and figure studies for the figure of Christ, Düsseldorf (Harris & Schaar, nos. 10 recto and verso, 11, 12 and 13; Plate 22); two drapery studies for Peter, Düsseldorf (Harris & Schaar, no. 14; Plate 23); studies for spectators in the background of the composition, Düsseldorf (Harris & Schaar, no. 15); studies for Christ in both the main and alternative design, Düsseldorf (Harris & Schaar, no. 16); copy after a lost study for the figure of Christ, Düsseldorf (Harris & Schaar, no. 108).
Copy after a lost composition study for the alternative design, Düsseldorf (Harris & Schaar, no. 109); drapery study for the figure of Christ in the alternative design, Windsor (Blunt & Cooke, no. 202 recto; for the verso, see my Cat. No. 16); drapery study for the figure of Christ, Düsseldorf (Harris & Schaar, no. 17 recto; the study on the verso is for Christ in the main design).

A study for 'Jesus Christ qui appelle Saint Pierre' was recorded in the Nourri collection in 1785 (Mireur VI, p. 388).
Versions: c. 1645 A picture described as 'Un quadretto di p(al)mi 2½ di Altezza rappresentante Christo che Dice a S. Pietro Pasce Oves Meas, et Altri Apostoli Mezzo Tondo in Cima' appears on an undated inventory of Cardinal Antonio Barberini's property, probably made shortly before or after his departure for France in 1645. This 'quadretto' appears also in the inventory of Cardinal Antonio's possessions made at his death in 1671 (p. 428; the words 'Mezzo Tondo in Cima' are not used and the picture is valued at 200 scudi), and in the 1686 inventory of Maffeo, son of Taddeo Barberini (p. 193, no. 239). This picture is probably identical with the sketch, which has since disappeared, recorded in the Barberini collections by the Palestrina inventory of about 1738/9, where it is described as 'Alto p[almi] 5, la[rgo] p[almi] 3 tondo da capo rapresentante Cristo che costituisce S. Pietro Pastore, con altri Apostoli, bozzetto' (Posse, p. 109, note 2). The same inventory includes 'Un quadro per alto con il tondo in cima rapresentante Cristo quando disse a S. Pietro pasce oves meas, copia di Andrea Sacchi' (*ibidem*), which is also lost.
1661 A large unfinished picture in Sacchi's house at the time of his death was probably related to the main design as described by Bellori, although the inventory describes the subject as 'Christ giving the keys to St. Peter' (A II, no. 244). Its later history is not known.
Documents: Sacchi was paid 50 scudi by the Fabbrica di S. Pietro on July 15, 1628, 'a bon conto della pittura che deve fare . . .', and on September 9, a further 50 scudi 'a conto delle pitture che deve fare in S. Pietro oltre à 50 Δ in altro mandato' (Pollak, II, p. 89 f.).

BELLORI describes a handsome *modello* by Sacchi in the Palazzo Barberini for a painting which was to have been made for St. Peter's, its subject being Christ's command to Peter, 'Feed my sheep!', 'figurato il Sig.re in piedi in atto di parlargli con altri Apostoli appresso, ed in lontananza, e con una apertura di mare su la barca le Reti' (p. 67). A sketch or *modello* of this subject is recorded in various Barberini inventories dating from about 1645 to 1738/9 but has since disappeared. In addition thirteen autograph drawings and three copies, based on lost drawings or the lost *modello*, show that Sacchi had at some time considered two compositions for a *Feed My Sheep* painting. The composition for which the largest number of preparatory studies survives corresponds with Bellori's description, in particular in showing the sea shore with figures gathering in fishing nets, an incident rare enough in depictions of this subject to make it almost certain that the composition recorded in the Uffizi drawing is closely related to the painting Bellori knew. Only one piece of related evidence raises some doubt. The subject sketched out on the large, unfinished canvas found in the artist's house in 1661 was said to be Christ giving the keys to St. Peter, and not Christ's charge to Peter, 'Feed my sheep!'. The two subjects are almost identical, especially in an unfinished state, and it is probable that Sacchi's canvas was a version of the abandoned project for St. Peter's.
The date of Sacchi's drawings for a *Feed My Sheep* design can be fixed with some precision. The Windsor study for Christ in the alternate design has studies on the verso for the drapery of St. Ignatius in the Collegio Romano fresco, finished by May 1629. A study at Düsseldorf for Christ has other drawings on the verso for the Prado *Birth of the Virgin*, an undocumented work for which other drawings and internal stylistic evidence suggest a date around 1627–8 (No. 14). The wash composition study in the Uffizi (Harris & Schaar, fig. 1) has obvious affinities with the Cooper Hewitt study for the *Divina Sapienza* ceiling, started late in 1629 (No. 17). The series of bold black chalk studies with white heightening at Düsseldorf for Christ in both designs is most closely paralleled by a group of similar studies, again at Düsseldorf, for various figures in the *Divina Sapienza* fresco. A date for the

Feed My Sheep drawings of around 1628 seems highly probable therefore.

Almost certainly Sacchi's *modello* was made for a fresco overdoor in the niche to the left of Guercino's *Burial of St. Petronilla* now occupied by the tomb of Clement x. This niche and five others—those now containing the tombs of Pius VIII, Alexander VII, Alexander VIII, Clement XIII and Benedict XIV—were prepared to receive fresco overdoors in 1627, and were assigned respectively to Francesco Allegrini, Paolo Guidotti, Antonio Pomarancio, Andrea Camassei and Giovanni Baglione.[1] The subjects of all the frescoes were events in the life of St. Peter, Antonio Pomarancio's *Christ Giving the Keys to St. Peter* being situated like a pendant across the aisle from Sacchi's intended site.[2] None of them survive, and for most of them there is no visual record of any kind. An explanation for Sacchi's failure to complete his overdoor is put forward in the introduction.

1. The documents are found in Pollak, II, p. 85 f. and *sub voce*. Allegrini never finished his and no substitute was commissioned. Guidotti's was replaced in the 1640s by Romanelli (Pollak, II, pp. 548-9), whose fresco in turn was replaced in the 1670s by Bernini's monument to Alexander VII. Ciampelli was originally commissioned to decorate the space given to Camassei when Ciampelli died in 1630. Fig. XXVII in Pollak reproduces the plan of St. Peter's from the 1696 edition of Bonanni. The six sites under discussion are nos. 36, 31, 27, 23, 19 and 13.
2. Four of the six overdoors were carried out, leaving a choice of two sites for Sacchi's *Feed My Sheep*, Bonanni nos. 36 and 23. The drawings are lit from the left and would thus suit only site no. 23.

Bibliography: Bellori, 1672-96, p. 67.

16. The Madonna and Child with Saints Ignatius of Loyola, Francis Xavier, Cosmas and Damian. Old Pharmacy, Collegio Romano, Rome   Plate 24

Fresco, approximately 300 × 100 cm.

Condition: Comparison of the fresco with the two sketches shows that the fresco has suffered considerable damage from flaking, some of which has occurred since a partial repaint. The only areas where some of the original surface seems to have survived are the putti in the upper left and part of St. Ignatius' chasuble on the lower left.

Drawings: Study for the drapery of St. Ignatius, Windsor (Blunt & Cooke, no. 202 verso, as Lanfranco; Plate 25); study of a Madonna and Child, Uffizi (no. 12704 F, black chalk on white paper with white heightening, 390 by 240 mm.; see Harris in *Burl. Mag.*, CX [1968], p. 250 and fig. 22). A drawing sold from the Wouters collection in 1801, which showed the Virgin and Child seated on clouds with St. Bonaventure [*sic?*] presenting a lily might have been a study for this fresco, although the altarpiece in the Casa del Vescovo of S. M. del Priorato is also a possibility (50) (Mireur, VI, p. 388). There is a drawn copy after the fresco in Copenhagen (Mag. XII, no. 3 as Carpioni).

Versions: 1631 The diamond merchant Valguarnera bought a small picture 'di S. Ignazio cola Mad.a et altri santi piccolo' from Sacchi before March, 1631 (Costello, pp. 271 and 173). The Collegio Romano fresco is the only work with which Valguarnera's picture could be identified; it was almost certainly a *bozzetto* for the fresco. The later history of this sketch is not recorded although it may be the version now in Brian Sewell's collection, see below.

1686 Version now in the collection of Roberto Longhi in Florence (oil on canvas, 63.5 × 43.5 cm.). It was in a Casa Barberini inventory of 1686 (p. 206, no. 557, 'La Vergine con il Bambino, S. Ignatio, e S. Fran.co ... e SS. Cosimo, e Damiano', about 2½ by 1½ palmi), in the Palestrina Inventory of 1738/9 (Posse, 1925, p. 110, note 1), in a Barberini inventory of 1844

(Harris in *Burl. Mag.*, CX, [1968], p. 253, note 21), and was still in the Barberini collection in 1922 when it was exhibited in Florence (Longhi, *Scritti Giovanili*, p. 509). See also Emiliani, 1962, p. 339 and *La Collezione Roberto Longhi*, ed. A. Boschetto and others, Florence, 1971, no. 87.

1770 Version now in the collection of Mr. Brian Sewell in London (oil on canvas, 60 × 40 cm.; Plate 26; Col. Plate IV). A mutilated inscription on the back says that the picture belonged to a French marshal in 1770. See *Masters of the Loaded Brush, Oil Sketches from Rubens to Tiepolo*, organized and catalogued by the Department of Art History and Archeology, Columbia University, New York, 1967, no. 7, pp. 11-13.

An undated version at Chatsworth (no. 516, 23½ × 15¾ in.) formerly attributed to Guido Reni was correctly linked with Sacchi by Oliver Millar. SS. Cosmas and Damian have been turned into two Dominican saints, a puzzling alteration. Judging only from a photograph, the paint handling seems too flat and some details too clumsy for this canvas to be attributed to Sacchi himself.

SACCHI'S ceiling fresco in the Old Pharmacy of the Collegio Romano is mentioned by only one seventeenth-century writer, namely G. P. Bellori, and since his life of Sacchi was not published until 1942, the reference was not known to scholars until recently. The Old Pharmacy was accessible to the general public in the seventeenth and eighteenth centuries, but the fresco somehow escaped the attention of all of Sacchi's other biographers, and of all the compilers of guide books and of all later scholars except Refice. She reported that the fresco had been detached and lost, but it is still *in situ* in a ground-floor room to the left of the church of S. Ignazio, a room used until recently as a storeroom by the Ufficio Meteorologico dello Stato. The room also contains ten frescoed lunettes depicting the ten founders of the art of medicine. In one, on a book beside Galen, is the following inscription:

> Qui si dipinse di m/aggio 1629 sotto P R /
> Urbano VIII / dal sig.e Andrea Sacho R /
> omano, emilio sava / nanzi Bolognese.

The inscription dates the frescoes but raises problems as to the share of both artists in the decoration. Despite some differences of style in the ten lunettes, it is probable that Emilio Savonanzi, a minor Bolognese painter, was responsible for all of them, and that Sacchi's share was limited to the more important ceiling painting.[1] The two preparatory sketches are almost identical. One was probably a replica of the other made by the artist himself for the diamond merchant Valguarnera, who around 1630 commissioned a number of copies from artists in Rome.[2]

1. See 'Andrea Sacchi and Emilio Savonanzi at the Collegio Romano', *Burl. Mag.*, CX [1968], pp. 249-57.
2. See *Masters of the Loaded Brush, loc. cit.*, and Harris, *Burl. Mag.*, CX, [1968], pp. 250-51.

Bibliography: Bellori, 1672-96, p. 58; Florence, 1922, no. 876; Refice, 1950, p. 220; Longhi, 1961, p. 509; Emiliani, 1962, p. 339; A. Sutherland Harris, 'Andrea Sacchi and Emilio Savonanzi at the Collegio Romano', *Burl. Mag.*, CX, [1968], pp. 249-57.

17. La Divina Sapienza (An Allegory of Divine Wisdom). Sala del Mappamondo, Palazzo Barberini (Galleria Nazionale d'Arte Antica), Rome   Plates 28-31, 33

Fresco, approximately 900 cm. square.[1]

Condition: There are many obvious cracks on the ceiling and signs of recent paint loss on the drapery of the figure of Beauty. The surface of the globe also looks as if 'a secco' detail has flaked off and other areas have been repainted. Large areas of sky along the upper, lower and right edge have been restored. The damaged areas do not, however, affect the chief figure area, which is relatively well preserved. Only the drapery and left foot of Holiness may be repainted.

Drawings) Composition study, Cooper-Hewitt Museum, New York (No. 1901–39–1714, black and red chalk, pen and ink with brown wash and white heightening on cream paper, 312 by 333 mm. The drawing was bought from Cavaliere Giovanni Piancastelli in 1901, and first correctly identified by Richard P. Wunder [*Burl. Mag.*, CI, 1959, p. 466]. See also Bean & Stampfle, no. 73; Plate 27; study for the drapery of Eternity, Düsseldorf (Harris & Schaar, no. 21; there are studies for the sleeve of Perspicacity on the verso); study for the figure of Divinity, Düsseldorf (Harris & Schaar, no. 22; Plate 32); study for the figure of Divine Wisdom, Düsseldorf (Harris & Schaar, no. 18); two studies for the drapery of Divine Wisdom, Düsseldorf (Harris & Schaar, no. 20); study for the drapery and throne of Divine Wisdom, Düsseldorf (Harris & Schaar, no. 19); study for the figure of Holiness, Düsseldorf (Harris & Schaar, no. 23).

A drawing in the Uffizi published by Refice (p. 217 and fig. 218) is a copy after the fresco or, more probably, after the engraving of the fresco in the *Aedes Barberinae*. A drawing in the Albertina connected with the figure of Perspicacity by Refice matches neither the pose of this figure nor the technique of authentic drawings.

Versions: 1631 Version bought by the diamond merchant Valguarnera, and mentioned in his trial of July, 1731, when he stated that it was bought 'dui o tre mesi (fa)'. It was 'di mezzana grandezza' and Sacchi was paid 70 scudi for it (Costello, p. 273 and passim). Nothing more is known of this version, although it may have been acquired by the Barberini after Valguarnera's death in 1632 and later sent by them to Richelieu or Prince von Eggenberg, for which versions see below.

1638 Version given to the Emperor's ambassador, Prince von Eggenberg, who left Rome early in January, 1639 (Posse, pp. 48–9). It is recorded in Prague in 1718, in Vienna in 1723 (Engerth, I, pp. 465 and 487), and is listed in nineteenth-century catalogues of the Kunsthistorisches Museum (e.g. 1896, no. 559, 80 × 102 cm.). It appears in the 1912 catalogue as a school work for the first time, an opinion with which Posse (p. 49) agreed. A number of small, subtle adjustments have been made to the composition to suit the new scale; the chiaroscuro contrasts are noticeably stronger than in the Leningrad or Incisa della Rocchetta versions. Despite these differences from other versions of the composition, the flat paint surface indicates that this version can only be a studio copy.

1642 Before this date, when it is mentioned in Teti's *Aedes Barberinae*, a version was sent to Richelieu as a present by the Barberini (Teti, pp. 83–4). It is almost certainly identical with the picture seen by Richardson in the Crozat collection in 1722 (p. 14, 'The Prudentia Divina, a finish'd sketch for the large one in the Palace Barberini') and which is now in Leningrad (Waagen, 1864, no. 209 and 1958 catalogue, I, p. 172, no. 132; 83 × 105.5 cm.). I have not seen the original, but the photograph shows it to be an exquisitely finished work, differing in small details from the Vienna and Incisa della Rocchetta versions. The possibility that it is autograph cannot be excluded.

1658 Version painted for Alexander VII (elected 1655), for which the artist was paid 500 scudi on December 30, 1658 (Incisa della Rocchetta, p. 74. The payment was for a small version of the *St. Romuald* as well, q.v.). Passeri's anecdote concerning these two small pictures (pp. 301–2) is discussed in the introduction. The Chigi arms appear on the base of the throne. This small version is recorded in the Palazzo Chigi by Pistolesi (1841 and 1846, p. 84; for a larger version also in a Chigi collection, see below under 1658) and is now in the collection of Marchese Giovanni Incisa della Rocchetta in Rome. Like the Vienna and Leningrad versions, from which this differs in small details, the Incisa della Rocchetta version is a carefully painted work, attractive but not impressive when compared with the original fresco. Its provenance almost certainly proves that it is autograph.

1658 Version recorded in the possession of Principe Don Agostino Chigi on November 8, 1658 ('Un quadro dipintovi la Divina Sapienza con li suoi attributi, alto palmi 5 e largo 7 incirca, con sua cornice intagliata con rami di cerque, monti e stelle e con cartoni in mezza, pure con monti e stelle tutta dorata, mano d'Andrea Sacchi', Libro Mastro di Guardaroba per l'Ecc.mo Sig.re Principe Don Agostino Chigi cominciato li 8 Novembre 1658, come per inventario posto in filza de conti diverso no. 13, no. 63'. I am indebted to Marchese Giovanni Incisa della Rocchetta for this reference). This version is much larger than any so far recorded, except possibly the Valguarnera picture. Its later history is not known.

1661 Two versions in Sacchi's house at the time of his death (Appendix II, nos. 297 and 327) were both large or average-sized compositions. Their later history is not known; one was said to be damaged ('rotta') and may have been destroyed immediately. It is interesting that no versions are recorded in Barberini inventories. *Engravings:* 1642 Engraving by Michael Natalis for *Aedes Barberinae ad Quirinalem*. The Barberini bees do not appear on the throne of Divine Wisdom.

1662 Engraving inscribed 'Io. Gerardini Sculp. Roma 1662, Gio. Iacomo Rossi le stampa in Roma alla Pace'. There is a portrait in the sky held by two putti of a member of the order of the Knights of Malta whose motto is 'Fortitudine et Sapientia'. Divinity has been given a triangular halo (No. 44654, GNDS, Rome).

1662 Engraving dated 1662 by 'Io. Gerardini', published by 'Gio. Iac. Rossi'. There is a portrait of an unknown cardinal in a circular frame in the sky.

Documents: It is generally accepted that payments to Sacchi from Don Taddeo Barberini, who occupied the part of the Palazzo Barberini containing the *Divina Sapienza* fresco, which run from December 22, 1629 through November or December 28, 1630, are connected with the fresco. The payments are incomplete and do not state how much the artist was to be paid. He had been given 300 scudi; a total of 500 to 1000 scudi might be expected (Incisa della Rocchetta, p. 63). For undated payments for the reconstruction of the Sala del Mappamondo and the stucco friezes, see Pollak (I, p. 285).

THE PAYMENTS generally connected with Sacchi's *Divina Sapienza* fresco begin in December, 1629 and run through 1630, but the account books for the following years are missing and the date of the fresco's completion must be determined from other evidence. Bellori's statement that the work took several years to complete and was finished in 1634, that is six years before 1640 when Cortona finished his *Divina Providenza* ceiling in the Gran Salone (II, p. 53), has been generally accepted as reliable evidence for the date of completion, although as the *Divina Providenza* fresco was finished in 1639, Bellori's date for Sacchi's ceiling is usually corrected to 1633. Denis Mahon (1962, pp. 63–6) recently examined the evidence in more detail in connection with Poussin's development around 1630 and came to the conclusion that the composition of the *Divina Sapienza* was settled some time in 1630 at the earliest, and that work on the ceiling may have started late that year. He thought the Valguarnera copy (see Versions, 1631) offered proof only that the composition was definitely settled by this date and did not necessarily mean that work on the ceiling was in an advanced state by April, 1631. I think that both Mahon's theories about the early stages of the work and the traditional date of completion need modifying and propose a period of eighteen months, from the autumn of 1629 to the early spring of 1631 for the execution of the work.

Mahon contended that the words 'a conto' in the first three payments to Sacchi (Dec. 22, 1629, 50 scudi; Feb. 26, 100 scudi; May 13, 50 scudi) mean that these were advance payments for work not yet carried out, and that the omission of these words in the last recorded 100 scudi payment of November or December, 1630, indicates that by this date the work had been approved and work on the ceiling begun, but the words 'a conto' or 'a bon conto' cannot be interpreted in this way. The lavish documentation published by Pollak for the art patronage of Urban VIII contains many examples of the words 'a (bon) conto' in payments for 'lavoro da farsi', 'lavori che fa' and 'lavoro fatto' (e.g. II, pp. 5 and 14–15), and the words 'a conto de' suoi lavori' in the payments to Sacchi suggest rather that work was in progress by December, 1629, and consequently that the *modello* had been approved by Don Taddeo Barberini by this date. The stylistic evidence supports this interpretation of the documents, for the composition of the *Divina Sapienza* grows naturally out of the design for the ceiling fresco in the Old Pharmacy of the Collegio Romano, finished in May, 1629 (No. 16), while Sacchi's preparatory studies resemble dated drawings of the late 1620s and not those of the early 1630s. It cannot be without significance either that from 1627 to 1635, a relatively well-documented period of Sacchi's life, the only year when the artist is not recorded working on other commissions is 1630. It is into the gap between the completion of the Collegio Romano fresco and the start of work on the *St. Thomas Aquinas* mosaic cartoon in February, 1631, that the *Divina Sapienza* fresco most logically fits. The sale of a medium-sized copy to Valguarnera in April, 1631 implies that the fresco was finished; Sacchi would not risk annoying an important patron by taking time off to produce an easel version of the same work for another patron of no political significance; nor would he wish to publicize his work until it was finished and ready to be judged.[2]

Bellori's statement that the work took a long time to complete is vague. It presumably derives from conversations with Maratta in the 1670s and 1680s, when Maratta's memories of Sacchi's studio, which he joined in 1635 at the age of ten, must have faded somewhat and would in any case have been more reliable for the later than for the earlier years of Sacchi's career. Maratta was probably told by Sacchi himself that the *Divina Sapienza* took many years to complete because his difficulties in the last fifteen years of his life, when his production slowed down and eventually ceased altogether, must have forced him to justify these delays to himself, his students, friends and patrons with stories of his earlier trials when producing masterpieces such as the *Divina Sapienza*. Bellori does say that the *Divina Sapienza* was finished at about the same time that the *St. Romuald* was painted, and this altarpiece, long dated 1638–40, can now be dated 1631. The only error in Bellori's statement concerning the date when the *Divina Sapienza* was finished is his estimate of the interval between the completion of Sacchi's ceiling and Cortona's *Divina Providenza*; Bellori says six years, in fact it was probably eight. Bellori was mistaken about the date when Cortona's ceiling was finished; his calculations based on that date should not therefore be taken too seriously. At the very latest, Sacchi must have finished work and removed the scaffolding by September, 1632, when the adjoining chapel was used for a ceremonial baptism.[3]

A detailed analysis of the style and iconography of the ceiling will be found in the introduction.

1. The room is 980 cm. wide. The height from the floor to the centre of the ceiling is 770 cm. and from the floor to the lower edge of the cornice 575 cm. The cornice is 100 cm. tall. I am indebted to Dr Italo Faldi for these measurements.
2. Mahon (Poussiniana, pp. 64–5) suggests that the position of the mason's accounts of the reconstruction undertaken in the Sala della Divina Sapienza far from the beginning of the book in which are listed the masons' expenses for work undertaken in the Palazzo Barberini between April, 1629 and December, 1639 implies a date after 1629/30 for the preliminary preparations in that room. He admits that the work in the masons' account book is not necessarily listed in chronological order. In fact the accounts are arranged according to the ground plan of the palace and by floor; no conclusions whatsoever as to the date

of particular pieces of reconstruction can be deduced therefore from this document.
3. On September 8, 1632, Don Taddeo Barberini's daughter was baptized in Cortona's recently completed chapel (Blunt, 1958, p. 285). At this time the chapel could only be approached through the Sala della Divina Sapienza because the staircase leading to the chapel from the private apartments above it was not finished until April 13, 1633 (Pollak, I, p. 329).

Bibliography: Totti, 1638, p. 61; Scanelli, 1657, p. 207; Scaramuccia, 1674, p. 38; Bellori, 1672–96, pp. 50–52; Sandrart, 1675, p. 288; Passeri, 1679, pp. 295–96; De Cotte, c. 1689, in *Actes*, 1960, II, p. 108; Rossini, 1693, p. 55 (1700 and 1704, p. 68; 1750, p. 79; 1776, p. 189 [where the adjacent chapel by Cortona is also attributed to Sacchi, an error repeated in the 1789 edition]; Pinarolo, 1700, II, p. 172 (1703 and 1713, II, p. 180 and later editions); Panciroli, 1719, II, p. 361 (where Cortona's chapel is also attributed to Sacchi); Richardson, 1722, p. 158; Pascoli, 1730, I, p. 16; Roisecco, 1750, II, p. 298 (where Cortona's chapel is also attributed to Sacchi); Titi, 1763, p. 333 (the ceiling is not mentioned in any later editions); Pistolesi, 1841 and 1846, p. 84 (the sketch in the Palazzo Chigi); Voss, 1924, p. 531; Incisa della Rocchetta, 1924, pp. 63–5 and passim; Posse, 1925, p. 37 f. and passim; Posse, 1935, p. 290; Waterhouse, 1937, p. 92; Refice, 1950, p. 219; Costello, 1950, pp. 237–84, esp. pp. 242–3 and 272–3; Wittkower, 1958, pp. 170–1; Mahon, 1963, pp. 63–6; Waterhouse, 1963, pp. 57–9.

18. Portrait of Urban VIII. Location unknown

Drawings: Study of a seated Pope, Düsseldorf (Harris & Schaar, no. 31; Plate 56).

Versions: 1644 'Un quadro con un ritratto di N. S.re Papa Urbano VIII in tela da testa di mano del Sacchi tutta dorata' appears in Cardinal Antonio Barberini's inventory of 1644 (Incisa della Rocchetta, p. 72).

1661 Three 'tela da testa' portraits of Urban VIII are recorded in Sacchi's house in 1661 (Appendix II, nos. 2, 143 and 150).

1692 'Un Ritratto di Urbano 8 a sedere' measuring 10 by 7 palmi is recorded in the 1692 inventory of Cardinal Carlo Barberini (p. 194) and again in the 1704 inventory of his collection (Posse, 1925, p. 123, note 2). It was for this portrait that the Düsseldorf drawing presumably was made.

SEVENTEENTH-CENTURY inventories record both a full-length seated portrait and several bust portraits of Urban VIII by Sacchi, but the only secure visual evidence for the appearance of any of these works is a red chalk drawing at Düsseldorf, which is almost certainly a study for the lost full-length portrait of the Pope seated formerly in the collection of Cardinal Carlo Barberini. Seventeenth- and eighteenth-century guidebooks also record portraits of the Pope by Sacchi in the Palazzo Barberini.

At least four portraits of Urban VIII, two in Barberini collections, have been attributed to Sacchi in the recent literature, none in my opinion correctly. One can be discounted immediately in grounds of quality.[1] The other three are closely connected technically and stylistically; all three should probably be attributed to Gian Lorenzo Bernini.[2]

1. Posse, 1925, p. 124 and pl. XXI. As he noted (p. 123), Incisa della Rocchetta doubted the attribution. The picture is now in the collection of Princess Henriette Barberini. Martinelli (1956) suggested an attribution to Carlo Pellegrini.
2. The first of these is a second portrait published by Posse (1925, p. 123 f. and fig. 33). It is now in the collection of Don Augusto Barberini, a piece of information that I owe to Marilyn Aronberg Lavin. The second is the picture bought by the Italian state in 1930 from Luigi Leggeri (Museo di Palazzo Venezia, no. 5380) and currently displayed in the Galleria Nazionale, Rome, as a work of Bernini. Waterhouse (1937, p. 91)

and Grassi (*Bernini Pittore*, p. 19 and fig. 5) accepted the attribution to Sacchi; Cantalmessa, Martinelli (in *Commentari*, 1950, pp. 97–9 and fig. 115) and Fagiolo dell'Arco (*Bernini, una introduzione al gran teatro del barocco*, Rome, 1967, no. 36) think it is by Bernini. Jan Miel's portrait of Urban VIII in the Rospigliosi-Pallavicini collection is based on the Leggeri portrait (for the Miel, see Zeri, 1959, pp. 180–1, no. 308). The third version given to Sacchi is the picture formerly in the Palazzo Colonna, Marino, published by Grassi (*Bernini Pittore*, p. 19 and fig. 6); the picture was destroyed in the Second World War. It had affinities with both the picture now in Don Augusto Barberini's collection and with the Leggeri portrait and may even have surpassed them both in quality.

Bibliography: Rossini, 1693, p. 56 (1700 and 1704, p. 69; 1750, p. 80; 1776, II, p. 188); Pinarolo, 1700, pp. 172–3 (1703, pp. 172–3; 1713, II, p. 181); Panciroli, 1719, II, pp. 360–2; Roisecco, 1750, p. 297; Incisa della Rocchetta, 1924, p. 72; Voss, 1924, p. 690; Posse, 1925, p. 122 f. and fig. 33 and pl. XXI; Gamba, 1927, pp. 32–3 and pl. XVII; *Mostra di Roma Seicentesca*, Rome, 1930, no. 11; Posse, 1935, p. 290; Waterhouse, 1937, p. 92; Grassi, 1945, p. 19; *Mostra di Ritratti dei Papi*, Palazzo Venezia, 1950–51, nos. 68 and 68a; V. Martinelli, *I Ritratti di Pontefici di Gian Lorenzo Bernini*, Rome, 1956, p. 30.

19. Cartoons for Mosaic Pendentives in the Cappella della Colonna and the Cappella di San Michele Arcangelo, St. Peter's, Rome

19a. St. Thomas Aquinas with St. Peter and St. Paul. Galleria Nazionale d'Arte Antica, Rome   Plate 34
Tempera on paper, size unknown.
Condition: Although it is in good shape for a work of this kind, which was not intended to be preserved after the work based on it was finished, much of the surface is worn and, to judge from the mosaic, the colours have darkened.
Drawings: Composition study, Düsseldorf (Harris & Schaar, no. 26); study for the left hand of St. Thomas, Windsor (Blunt & Cooke, no. 764); copy after the whole composition, Düsseldorf (Harris & Schaar, no. 110). The drawing published by Grassi (1945, fig. 46 and p. 39) is not autograph; a glance at the drawing of the book held by St. Thomas or at St. Peter's facial expression shows that it must be a copy based on the cartoon or mosaic. Refice (p. 219) connected a lively black chalk study in the Uffizi of a preaching Dominican with this composition but the attribution to Sacchi is not acceptable. A red chalk drawing of a monk and two apostles attributed to Sacchi in the Kaieman collection in 1889 (Mireur, VI, p. 338) may have been connected with this work.
Version: 1632   Mosaic pendentive in the Cappella della Colonna, St. Peter's, executed by G. B. Calandra between January and October, 1632; Plate 35 (Pollak, II, pp. 554–5).
Documents: Between February 1 and October 11, 1631, Sacchi was paid a total of 200 scudi for this cartoon (Pollak, II, p. 554).

19b. St. John Damascene. Present location unknown
Drawings: Study for the figure of St. John Damascene, Düsseldorf (Harris & Schaar, no. 27).
Version: 1634–6   Mosaic pendentive in the Cappella della Colonna, St. Peter's, executed by G. B. Calandra between March, 1634 and March, 1636; Plate 38 (Pollak, II, pp. 557–8).
Documents: The mosaic was commissioned from Sacchi in 1632. Payments run from December, 1632 to May 12, 1635 and total 200 scudi (Pollak, II, p. 557).

19c. St. Leo the Great. Galleria Nazionale d'Arte Antica, Rome
Tempera on paper, size unknown.   Plate 36
Condition: This cartoon seems more worn and faded than that for

the *St. Thomas Aquinas*. The putto on the right is a vague shadow and much of the saint's drapery looks very thin. His cuff and left hand seem to be in mint condition, however.
Drawings: Studies for the whole composition with detailed studies of hands, feet and drapery, Lisbon (Museo Nacional de Arte Antiga, no. 1070, red chalk on brownish-green paper, 247 × 352 mm. This drawing was brought to my attention by Walter Vitzthum).
Version: 1638–9   Mosaic pendentive in the Cappella di S. Michele Arcangelo, St. Peter's, executed by G. B. Calandra between November, 1638 and May, 1639; Plate 37 (Pollak, II, pp. 557–8).
Documents: See below under *St. Denys the Areopagite*.

19d. St. Denys the Areopagite. Present location unknown.
Version: 1639   Mosaic pendentive in the Cappella di S. Michele Arcangelo in St. Peter's, executed by G. B. Calandra from July, 1639 onwards; Plate 39 (Pollak, II, pp. 575–7).
Documents: Both the *St. Leo* and the *St. Denys* mosaic cartoons were originally commissioned from Sacchi in August, 1631; a payment of 50 scudi 'a bon conto de' Cartoni che fa' was made on September 6 of that year. The next payments, for both cartoons, were made seven years later, on October 30 and November 27, 1638. By January 28, 1640, Sacchi had been paid 300 scudi altogether, but since he and all the other artists who provided cartoons were paid 200 scudi for each of them, the payments published by Pollak are 100 scudi short of the expected total of 400 scudi. The missing payment, made over seven years later, was recently discovered and transcribed by Howard Hibbard. Dated April 13, 1647, it reads: 'Ad Andrea Sacchi Pittore scudi Cento m(one)ta oltre a scudi 300 hauti e sono per Intiero pagam(en)to delli Cartoni da lui fatti per li musaichi nella Cappella di S. Michele Archangelo scudi 100' (Archivio della R. Fabbrica di San Pietro, 276 (Vecchio Arm. IV, To. 247), fol. 131). Calandra executed the *St. Leo* mosaic between November 1638 and May 1639, but the date when he finished the *St. Denys* is not recorded by Pollak.

IN 1631 Sacchi was asked to provide cartoons for four of the eight pendentives in the Cappella della Colonna and the Cappella di S. Michele Arcangelo in St. Peter's, the other four having been assigned to Lanfranco, Carlo Pellegrini and Romanelli.[1] Documents indicate that Sacchi made the *St. Thomas Aquinas* in 1631, the *St. John Damascene* in 1632–5, the *St. Leo* between 1638 and 1640 and the *St. Denys the Areopagite* between 1638 and 1647. The cartoons of St. Thomas Aquinas and St. Leo survive[2] but those for the other two pendentives are lost. The *St. Thomas Aquinas* is easily the most impressive of the four compositions; the *St. Denys*, apparently the last to be completed, is the poorest design, confused and difficult to read from the floor of the church. The existence of autograph drawings for three of the four designs is additional proof that Sacchi was personally responsible for the execution of this commission. Certainly there is no reason to doubt, as Grassi has, that the *St. Leo* cartoon is autograph. The mosaicist Calandra died in 1644, three years before Sacchi received his final payment for the *St. Denys* cartoon,[3] which was presumably carried out by another, and perhaps less competent, artist. The overall patterning of the surface blurs the lines of the composition, which could well be by Sacchi. Maybe the mosaicist added or exaggerated the patterns in the lost cartoon.

1. Pollak, Incisa della Rocchetta and Waterhouse, *loc. cit. infra*.
2. The *St. Thomas Aquinas* cartoon first appears in Cardinal Antonio Barberini's inventory of 1644 (Incisa della Rocchetta, pp. 70–1), then in Prince Maffeo's inventory of 1672–86 (no. 68), then in the *stima* made by Carlo Maratta around 1686 (no. 8), then in a Casa Barberini inventory of 1686 (no. 478). The *St. Leo* cartoon appears in the same inventories with the following numbers: 1644, no. 1; 1672–86, no. 685; c. 1686, no. 8; 1686, no. 470). The *St. Thomas* is recorded later in a Barberini

Fidecommesso inventory of 1817 (Mariotti, p. 129, no. 95) and in a Casa Barberini inventory of 1844 (no. 8).

3. Though the payment talks of 'Cartoni', the *St. Leo* had been finished by 1638, when Calandra began work on the mosaic, leaving only the *St. Denys* incomplete.

Bibliography: Baglione, 1639, pp. 31 and 33; Bellori, 1672–96, p. 56; Rossini, 1693, p. 53 ('li undici quadri delli Cartoni di Andrea Sacchi, molto belli, e di buon disegno' in the Gran Salone of the Palazzo Barberini; 1710, p. 66; 1750, p. 77; 1776, II, p. 187, 'molti Cartoni d'Andrea Sacchi, e di Pietro da Cortona'); Pinarolo, 1700, I, p. 170 (the cartoons in the Palazzo Barberini) and pp. 266–7 (St. Peter's) and *ibid.* 1703 and 1713 ed.; Pascoli, 1730, I, p. 16; Roisecco, 1750, II, p. 296; Rossini, 1750, pp. 124–5 (1776, I, p. 238 and II, p. 200, and later editions); Vasi, 1770 (1765), pp. 337–38; Pistolesi, 1841, pp. 574–5 (*ibid.*, 1846 and 1852); Bertolotti, 1884, p. 204; Mariotti, 1892, p. 129; Incisa della Rocchetta, 1924, pp. 70–71; Voss, 1924, pp. 533 and 690; Posse, 1925, p. 49; Hess, 1934, p. 166, note 1; Posse, 1935, p. 290; Waterhouse, 1937, pp. 92–3; Refice, 1950, p. 219; *Il Seicento Europeo*, Rome, 1965, nos. 267 a and b.

20. The Vision of St. Romuald. Pinacoteca Vaticana, Rome
310 × 175 cm.   Plate 41

Condition: The painting has a layer of discoloured varnish but beneath it the picture's condition seems to be good. There is some brown copper resinate in the landscape background.

Drawings: Study for the whole composition, Stockholm (no. 1274/1863, red chalk with some wash on white paper, 380 × 258 mm. The paper is worn along both sides and in the upper part of the sky and has probably been trimmed on the left. It is inscribed 'Bricci Cabinet de Crozat' along the lower edge; Plate 40); study for the left hand of St. Romuald and for part of his drapery and for the heads of three monks on the left, Düsseldorf (Harris & Schaar, no. 28); study for the figure of St. Romuald, Windsor (Blunt & Cooke, no. 764 verso); study for the head of a monk on the left, Paris (Louvre, no. 14577, red chalk on buff paper, 221 × 167 mm.; see Harris, 'The Date of Andrea Sacchi's *Vision of St. Romuald*', p. 493 and fig. 8); drapery study for first monk in the left foreground, Düsseldorf (Harris & Schaar, no. 29); drapery study probably for St. Romuald, Düsseldorf (Harris & Schaar, no. 30); study for the second monk seated on the left, Besançon (Musée des Beaux-Arts, no. D 3037, black chalk with white heightening on grey paper, 400 × 287 mm.; see Harris, *art. cit.* p. 493 and fig. 7). The red chalk composition study at Dresden identified with the *St. Romuald* by Posse (1912, passim and 1925, p. 63 and fig. 19) is by Palma Giovane (Hans Tietze, *Drawings of the Venetian Painters*, New York, 1944, no. 855). Two drawings in the British Museum (Payne Knight, no. P.p. 4–65 and Fenwick, no. 1946, 7.13.80) are copies after the painting or other lost drawings, while a pen study in the Uffizi (no. 9523) is a copy after the whole composition.

Versions: 1653 Version recorded in the 1653 inventory of Cardinal Mazarin (no. 315, 'St. Romuald qui parle á ses moynes, en petites figures, l'ornement de bois couleur de noix et or. Andrea Sacchi'. Aumale, *ad vocem.*). Mazarin's 1661 inventory gives the size as 2′ 1″ × 1′ 4″ (Cosnac, p. 325, no. 1141). Its later history is not recorded.

1658 Version mentioned by Passeri (pp. 301–2) which was painted for Alexander VII and for which Sacchi was paid on December 30, 1658 (Incisa della Rocchetta, p. 74). It is almost certainly the same picture which appears in the 1692 inventory of Cardinal Flavio Chigi (No. 6, 'un quadro in tela, alto palmi 5, largo 2½ con S. Romualdo et altri frati, con cornice tutta dorata, mano di Andrea Sacchi'. This reference was kindly given to me by Marchese Giovanni Incisa della Rocchetta.) and again in the Palazzo Chigi in 1841 and 1846 by Pistolesi (1841, p. 82, 'S. Bernardo Tolomei [*sic*], del Sacchi'. St. Bernard of Tolomei also

had a vision of members of his order, which wore white, ascending to heaven on a ladder [Réau, III, p. 218]). It is now in the collection of Marchese Giovanni Incisa della Rocchetta, a descendant of the Chigi family.

1661 Version recorded in Sacchi's house at the time of his death (Appendix II, no. 148). Its size is not given so there is no way of telling whether it could be identical with any later recorded versions.

1689 Sketch recorded in the dal Pozzo collection by De Cotte in about 1689, no. 50, 'L'Abozzo del quadro dell'altar maggiore nella chiesa di S. Romualdo d'Andrea Sacchi' (Haskell and Rinehart, p. 325. They confuse the subject of this sketch with that of the *St. Gregory the Great* in the Pinacoteca Vaticana, *q.v.*). The later history of this sketch is not recorded.

1694 Small version of the *St. Romuald* reported to be in the collection of Conte Francesco Ramuzzi in Rome on March 24 by Franceschini in correspondence with the Duke of Liechtenstein (*Jahrbuch der Zentral-Kommission*, Beiblatt, 1911, p. 98). It was bought for the Liechtenstein collection but its later history is not known.

1722 Version recorded in the Palazzo Barberini in the Palestrina Inventory of 1738/9 (p. 33, 'Altro [quadro] alto p[almi] 3 largo p[almi] 2½ rappresentante S. Romualdo che predica alli suoi Religiosi con anime de medesimi che vanno in gloria, opera di Andrea Sacchi, sc[udi] 500'. Posse, 1925, p. 61, note 1). It was seen in the Palazzo Barberini in 1722 by Richardson (p. 156, 'A Sketch, Finish'd for the St. Romualdo'.).

1829 There was a picture of two Camaldolese monks in the Torlonia collection in 1829 (Mariotti, p. 106, no. 125). This is probably the picture of two monks copied from the *St. Romuald* now in the Galleria Nazionale d'Arte Antica (Palazzo Corsini, no. 102).

1830 Version in the Westmacott collection before 1830 and bought in Rome by Sir Richard Westmacott or his son in either 1793 or 1826. It was recently acquired by the Auckland City Art Gallery from Mrs. Barklie of Christchurch (*Auckland City Art Quarterly*, no. 22, 1962, oil on canvas, 25⅝ × 17¼ inches). Comparison of this small version with the Vatican picture and with Sacchi's autograph sketches suggests that the Auckland picture is not by Sacchi, but is an early copy of good quality.

1856 Version in the J. P. Nichols collection exhibited in Manchester (no. 915, 'St. Romualdo among the friars'). It was catalogued as the sketch for the Vatican picture. It came from the Rogers collection where it was described as 'St. Bruno and his disciples, in a landscape; with a vision of angels in the background' (See Graves, III, p. 1197). It has since disappeared.

1887 Version in the Musée de Nantes where it is catalogued as a reduced copy of the Vatican picture (*Inventaire des Richesses d'Art de la France*, Province II, Paris. 1881, p. 94).

1932 Version sold with a *Last Sacrament of St. Jerome* in the Ramsden Sale, Christie's, May 27 and 30, lot 172. A photograph in the Witt Library indicates that it was a copy. There is a nineteenth-century watercolour copy in the sacristy of the Camaldolese abbey at Fonte Avellana (wrongly described as a sketch for the Vatican painting in the Touring Club Italiano *Guida delle Marche*, Milan, 1962, p. 216) and another copy in the Los Angeles County Museum of Art (oil on canvas, 89 × 61 cm., no. A. 5880. 48–1).

Engravings: 1655–67 Engraving dedicated to Cardinal Flavio Chigi by 'D. Iustus de Blanchis Monachus Camald. D.D.D.', drawn by Pietro Locatelli and engraved by 'Io. Baronio Tolosini'. Chigi is described as the Papal nephew, which probably dates the print to the reign of Alexander VII.

18th Century Engraving by Jacob Frey, dedicated to the General of the Camaldolese Order, Rev. Clement Reginald Archibusieri (Nagler, V, p. 164 and XV, p. 541).

1810 Engraving in the 1810 *Galerie du Musée Napoléon*, III, pl. 157 and p. 3, by Bourdon, Petit & Dambrun.

19th Century   Engraving by Gianni and Metzger probably done while the picture was in Paris.

19th Century   Line engraving by C. Normand. It is not dated but resembles that of 1810 and was probably done around the same time.

19th Century   Engraving by Domenico Marchelli based on a drawing by Paolo Guglieli. This superb engraving is not dated but must be nineteenth century.

UNTIL 1631 the Camaldolese Order in Rome used the small church of S. Antonio (or S. Niccolò de Forbitoribus) near the Collegio Romano, but in the early spring of 1631[1] it was torn down to make way for an extension of the Collegio Romano, and the monks moved to new buildings in the Vicolo del Piombo, 'fabricandovi una chiesa et ospizio in honore di S. Romualdo nel 1632'.[2] Sacchi's *Vision of St. Romuald* was commissioned and painted in 1631[3] and remained in the church until 1797, when it was taken to Paris.[4] Back in Rome by 1823, it is recorded in the Pinacoteca Vaticana by 1841,[5] its place in San Romualdo having been taken by a copy. San Romualdo was torn down shortly after 1878 when the Via Nazionale was extended (Armellini, 1891, p. 61 f.).

1. March 18 according to Armellini (1942, I, pp. 376–7) quoting a manuscript in the Archivio Vaticano.
2. Armellini, *loc. cit.*
3. See Harris, 'The Date of Andrea Sacchi's *Vision of St. Romuald*', *Burlington Magazine*, CX, 1968, pp. 486–94.
4. *Galerie du Musée Napoléon*, 1810, III, p. 157 and p. 3.
5. Pistolesi, 1841, p. 636.

Bibliography: Mola, 1663, p. 184; Bellori, 1672–96, pp. 53–54; Titi, 1674, p. 349; Scaramuccia, 1674, p. 38; Bari, 1679, p. 12; Passeri, 1679, pp. 297 and 301–2; Malvasia, 1678, II, p. 240; Sebastiani, 1689, p. 119; Rossi, 1719, II, p. 383; Richardson, 1722, p. 298; Pascoli, 1730, I, p. 17; Dezalliers d'Argenville, 1745, I, p. 35; Rossini, 1750, p. 189 (1776, II, pp. 217–18); Roisecco, 1750, II, p. 267; Vasi, 1770 (1765), p. 137; Chiusole, 1781, pp. 41–2 (1782, p. 35); Moroni, 1840, VI, pp. 293–94; Pistolesi, 1841, p. 636 (1846, *ibid*.); Longhi, 1916, p. 280; Posse, 1912, p. 153 f.; Incisa della Rocchetta, 1924, pp. 63 and 71; Voss, 1924, p. 530; Weisbach, 1924, p. 45; Posse, 1925, p. 61 f. and passim; Posse, 1935, p. 290; Waterhouse, 1937, p. 93; Refice, 1950, p. 217; Wittkower, 1958, p. 170; Waterhouse, 1962, p. 59; Emiliani, 1962, p. 308; Haskell, 1963, p. 104.

21. Portrait of a Cardinal. National Gallery of Canada, Ottawa 135 × 99 cm.   Plates 46, 47

Condition: Apart from a few minor paint losses, which have been repaired quite neatly, and some repaint in the background, the condition is excellent. It has recently been cleaned.

Version: For a variant probably based on this composition, see the *Portrait of Cardinal Angelo Giori* (Cat. No. 66).

THIS PORTRAIT was first attributed to Sacchi by Voss in 1924, and, though not included in Posse's monograph of 1925, does appear in his Thieme-Becker article on Sacchi ten years later. However, the 1936 catalogue of the National Gallery ascribes it merely to 'one of the ablest' of eclectic *seicento* painters. It has been attributed to Caravaggio (1921 catalogue of the National Gallery), to Bernardo Strozzi (Otto Benesch, quoted in the 1948 catalogue of the National Gallery and followed by Mortari) and to Gaulli (Venturi in 1932, quoted by the 1948 catalogue of the National Gallery and followed by Zeri), a suggestion rejected by Enggass, who supported the attribution to Sacchi. In fact Voss's hypothesis is supported by stylistic and historical evidence, and there is even a probable connection with a known patron of the artist.

Research is handicapped by the absence of the identifying marks common to portraits of this kind, namely inscriptions on the papers held by the sitter and a coat of arms on the back of the chair, both clearly visible in Sacchi's portrait of Cardinal Angelo Giori. Their absence in the Ottawa portrait, together with the sketchy appearance of most of the surface, suggests that the picture is unfinished, as does comparison with the Merlini portrait in the Borghese Gallery, where only the background is handled with comparable bravura. Only the head of the Ottawa cardinal has the degree of finish found in Sacchi's other portraits.

A connection with Sacchi is implied by the close similarity of the composition of the Giori portrait (No. 66) to that of the Ottawa picture. The former was painted in or after 1643; stylistic parallels for the latter suggest a date around 1630. The latter seems, in fact, to have served as a *modello* for the former, and as the Ottawa picture is unfinished, it might well have remained in the artist's studio and have been available for such use. It is even possible that the Ottawa picture can be identified with a portrait of a named cardinal known to have been in the artist's house in 1661 (see below). This portrait is not described as 'abbozzato' or 'non finito', but neither is the portrait of Francesco Albano, now in the Prado, which appears on the same 1661 inventory, and of which only the head is complete.

There are striking stylistic parallels between the Ottawa picture and Sacchi's sketches for the Collegio Romano fresco in the Longhi and Sewell collections. The hand of St. Ignatius with a book and that of St. Cosmas with an ointment jar should be compared with the left and right hands respectively of the Ottawa cardinal. The ridged, textured impasto of the cardinal's left sleeve and the surplice below it, crumpled against the arm of the chair, is found again in the robes of St. Ignatius of Loyola and St. Francis in the Collegio Romano sketches, as are very similar drapery forms. The treatment of the Ottawa cardinal's head can be compared with the heads of Francesco Albano in the Prado and Clemente Merlini in the Borghese Gallery. All three have the same vivid and sympathetic presence of character, while the detailed handling of all the features, which are drawn with the minimum of fuss, is very close.

Apart from members of the Barberini family, none of whom resemble the Ottawa cardinal, there are three cardinals with whom Sacchi is known to have had contact and who were old men in the 1620s and early 1630s. One of these was Cardinal Domenico Ginnasi (1551–1631), for whom Sacchi worked briefly in 1628 (Pollak, II, p. 89). Sacchi is not known to have painted Ginnasi's portrait, however,[1] and the resemblance between the Ottawa cardinal and Algardi's bust of Ginnasi in the Borghese Gallery is not convincing. Another candidate is Cardinal Francesco Maria del Monte, Sacchi's chief patron between 1621 and 1626, when he died at the age of seventy-seven. However, his features as recorded in a recently published drawing of him by Ottavio Leoni, dated 1616,[2] do not look like a younger version of the Ottawa cardinal, and a date as early as 1625–6 for the Ottawa picture does not seem likely, the cited stylistic parallels all dating from the period 1629–1633. The remaining candidate is Cardinal Lelio Biscia (c. 1573–1638), who as Vice-Protector of the Camaldolese Order commissioned the *Vision of St. Romuald* from Sacchi in 1631.[3] Sacchi certainly painted him, for a 'ritratto con il Card.le Biscia' hung in the same room of Sacchi's house as a small version of the *St. Romuald* (Appendix II, no. 125), and was presumably painted at the same time as the altarpiece. Biscia was then fifty-eight, but he was weak politically and consequently poor.[4] Perhaps he could not afford the portrait and Sacchi kept it, unfinished, or perhaps Sacchi found the sketched-out work sufficient for his gallery of patrons' portraits. At all events, until some record of Biscia's appearance has been traced, the matter cannot be settled definitely, although the weight of available evidence suggests that the Ottawa cardinal is Biscia.[5]

1. The portrait of Ginnasi given to Sacchi in the Palazzo Braschi

is far too weak for the attribution to be tenable (see Cat. No. R 22). Perhaps Ginnasi's painter niece, Caterina, was responsible.

2. It was exhibited at Agnew's in June, 1967 (see *Burl. Mag.*, CIX, 1967, p. 375 and fig. 52) and is now in the Ringling Museum of Art, Sarasota.
3. See my article on the date of the St. Romuald (*Burl. Mag.*, CX, 1968, p. 490, note 13).
4. Barozzi & Berchet, I, pp. 278 and 276. See Malvasia (1848 ed., II, p. 26) for the story of Biscia losing a picture of the Magdalene he had ordered from Guido Reni to Cardinal Francesco Barberini.
5. See my article on the painting in the *Bulletin of the National Gallery of Canada*, no. 14, 1969, pp. 9-15, especially footnote 19.

Bibliography: Saint-Hilaire in the *Journal des Arts*, Jan. 16, 1909; Le Clerc in *Mercure de France*, March 1, 1909, p. 107; Brown in *Studio*, 1913, p. 16; Catalogue of the National Gallery of Canada, 1913, p. 19; 1915, p. 48; 1921, p. 37 (as Caravaggio); Voss, 1924, p. 532; Posse, 1935, p. 290; National Gallery of Canada Catalogue, 1936, p. 53 (as Italian 17th Century); 1948 ed., p. 23 (as Bernardo Strozzi); Zeri, F. in *Paragone*, 1955, pp. 54-5 and pl. 34 (as G. B. Gaulli); Mortari, L. in *Boll. d'Arte*, 1955, p. 331 (as Strozzi); National Gallery of Canada Catalogue, 1957, I, p. 21 (as Italian 17th Century); Robert Enggass, *The Painting of Baciccio*, University Park Pennsylvania, 1964, p. 164 (as Sacchi); Sutherland Harris, 1969, pp. 9-15.

22. Hagar and Ishmael in the Wilderness. National Museum of Wales, Cardiff Plate 42 and Col. Plate III
96 × 92 cm.
Condition: The general condition is good although there are a few areas of cracked and flaking paint and the landscape may have darkened a little. There are *pentimenti* around the figure of the angel, who seems to have been placed a little higher originally. A recent cleaning and reframing exposes the full design, formerly concealed by an oval frame but designed for an octagonal one.[1]
Drawing: Study for the figure of Ishmael, Düsseldorf (Harris and Schaar, no. 36).
Versions: 1661 Two versions are recorded in Sacchi's 1661 inventory (Appendix II, nos. 23 and 132; the frame of item no. 24 almost certainly belonged to no. 23). Nothing certain is known of their later history although the first could be identified with the version in the collection of Cardinal Omodei in 1664 (see below); the second may have been a sketch.
1664 Version recorded in the collection of Cardinal Luigi Omodei in *Nota delli Musei* (Rome, 1664, p. 35) and taken to Milan in 1686 (Bertolotti, *Artisti Lombardi*, p. 180). Posse's suggestion that Omodei's picture might be identified with the version of Count Berka (see below) is uncertain.
1692 Version which went from the collection of Count Berka (as a 'S. Agar de Andrea Sacchi') to that of the Prince of Liechtenstein with an *Aurora* some time after May 18, 1691 (*Jahrbuch der Zentral-Kommission*, Beiblatt. 1911, p. 115). It is recorded in the same collection in 1780 (*Description des Tableaux et des Pieces de Sculpture que renferme la Gallerie de Son Altesse François Joseph Chef et Prince de la Maison Liechtenstein* etc., Vienna, 1780, p. 186) but does not appear in later catalogues of the collection (e.g. 1930) and seems to have disappeared.
1729 Version which passed from the collection of the Marquis de Seignelay and M. le Dreux into that of Louis-Antoine Crozat, Baron of Thiers (*Recueil d'Estampes*, 1729, I, p. 116); see also Crozat, 1755, pp. 62-3). It was bought by Catherine the Great of Russia in 1771 and is now in the Hermitage Museum, Leningrad (Waagen, 1864, p. 81 and 1958 catalogue of the Hermitage, where the size is given as 68·5 by 92 cm.). Comparison with the Corsini version indicates that the Hermitage picture is an adaptation of it,

too weak to be by Sacchi but possibly made by a studio assistant (see Posse, 1925, p. 104, note 1).
1760-80 M. Oretti (*Le Pitture che si ammirano...*, Bologna, Archiginnasio, MS. B. 104, II, p. 79) records 'Un Agar con Cornice dorata, de Andrea Sacchi, £1000' in the 'Inventario delle Pitture riguardevole dello stato et Eredità Bonfilioli'. The valuation given is a high one. I owe this reference to the kindness of Jennifer Montagu.
1777 Version described as 'Agar portant Ismael endormi sur une de ses epaules', 15 × 12½ inches, in the collection of Prince de Conti (*Catalogue de Tableaux, Dessins, Bronzes... du Cabinet de Feu Son Altesse Serenissime Monsigneur le Prince de Conti*, Paris, 1777, p. 10, no. 26 and Mireur, VI, p. 338). The composition differs from that of Sacchi's picture and was a vertical, not horizontal, composition and may not have been by Sacchi at all.

BELLORI includes the *Hagar and Ishmael in the Wilderness* among the works which he says Sacchi painted for Cardinal Antonio Barberini, and in fact it appears in an undated inventory of Cardinal Antonio,[2] and in two later Barberini inventories[3] before the picture entered the Corsini collection in 1934.[4] There are no documents or reference to the picture before Sacchi's death, however, and it must be dated on stylistic grounds. A black chalk study at Düsseldorf for the figure of Ishmael is more controlled than most of Sacchi's figure studies of the late 1620s but bolder than most of his studies of the 1630s, factors which suggest a compromise date around 1630. The landscape background and colour scheme recall the Forlì *St. Peter* of 1631-2 and the *St. Romuald* of 1631, while the relatively loose brush strokes also support a date in the early 1630s rather than a later date.

1. References to the picture and to versions of it in Sacchi's inventory of 1661 and later Barberini inventories indicate that they had octagonal frames. Marks on the Leningrad version, which at present has a rectangular frame, indicate that it was also designed for an octagonal frame.
2. 'Un ottangolo per lungo che rapresenta Agar con Ismale Moribondo, e l'Angelo', 4 by 3 palmi. I am indebted to Dr. Frances Vivian for this reference.
3. Prince Maffeo, 1672-86, no. 15; Casa Barberini, 1686, p. 189, no. 146; 1730, p. 30, no. 3663; Palestrina Inventory, 1738-9, no. 39 (Posse, 1925, p. 104, note 1); 1812, 3rd class, no. 27; 1844, no. 159.
4. Gazzetta Ufficiale, 5 Maggio, 1934, R.D.L., 20 Aprile, 1934, 705, no. 36. I owe this reference to Prince Tommaso Corsini. The picture was acquired by the National Museum of Wales through Colnaghi in 1971.

Bibliography: Bellori, 1672-96, p. 67; Mariotti, 1892, p. 129, no. 38; Florence, 1922, no. 873; Voss, 1924, p. 532; Posse, 1925, p. 104 f.; Posse, 1935, p. 290.

23. Head of an Apostle. Rospigliosi-Pallavicini Collection, Rome
78·5 × 63·4 cm. Plate 44
Condition: The picture surface is much darkened and obscured by dirt and old varnish. There are indications of retouchings which have discoloured, particularly on the lower left. The canvas has been enlarged on all sides, the original measuring about 68 × 51 cm. according to Zeri.
Version: 1658? Version in the sacristy of S. Maria in Via in Camerino, where it hangs with six other busts of apostles or Church Fathers. The portrait of Cardinal Angelo Giori above the door (a strictly provincial product) was placed there in accordance with instructions in the cardinal's will in 1658 (Feliciangeli, p. 12) and perhaps the other pictures in the sacristy were part of the same legacy. For the cardinal's contacts with Sacchi, see Cat. No. 66.

THIS PICTURE, which Zeri reported first appears in a Rospigliosi inventory in 1856,[1] has been identified as a saint, an apostle and St.

Bartholomew, this last being possible if the object held in the figure's right hand is a flayed skin, an attribute of that saint. Identification of the subject must await the picture's cleaning, but it may be significant that Maratta's *St. Bartholomew* in the Palazzo Barberini is shown in a similar pose. It is very possible, as Zeri suggested, that this picture was one of a series of saints or apostles, and the Camerino version may even hang with copies of other lost works in the series.[2] The rounded nose and skull, heavy build and freely painted beard recall the *St. Romuald* and indicate a date in the early 1630s.[3]

1. A Rospigliosi inventory of May 1, 1833 includes '(Un) altro (quadro) da testa piccolo, rappresentante la testa di un vecchio, viene da Andrea Sacchi, esistente sopra il gabinetto' (Mariotti, p. 168).
2. The condition of all the pictures in the sacristy makes it difficult to tell whether they are by Sacchi or not. Two works—a *St. Jerome* and a *St. John the Baptist*—appear to be autograph works by Valentin.
3. Grassi (1946, pp. 31–2 and fig. 43) published a *Head of a Saint* in a Roman private collection that he attributed to Sacchi. I have not seen the original but the attribution seems possible. That work and the *Apostle* in Malaga may have been part of a series to which the lost *St. Paul* in Perugia might also have belonged.

Bibliography: Voss, 1924, p. 690; Posse, 1925, pp. 76 and 98 and pl. XIII; Posse, 1935, p. 290; Waterhouse, 1937, p. 92; Zeri, 1959, p. 238.

24. Head of an Apostle with a Book. Museo, Malaga Plate 43
64 × 48 cm.
Condition: I have not seen this picture. Judging from photographs, it badly needs cleaning, although the condition beneath the dirt and old varnish may prove to be decent.

THIS work is one of two heads of old men attributed to Sacchi acquired by Philip v of Spain from Maratta's heirs in 1724. The attribution seems probable. The picture may be compared with the *Apostle* in the Rospigliosi-Pallavicini collection.

Bibliography: Pérez Sánchez, 1965, p. 325 with further bibliography.

25. Head of an Old Man. Gemäldegalerie, Dresden Plate 45
71·5 × 57 cm.
Condition: There has been some flaking and paint loss around the edge of the canvas prior to a relining and the background has darkened; otherwise the condition is good.

THIS PAINTING is first recorded in the Dresden collections in 1722, when it was labelled 'Manier des Tintoretto'. In 1867 von Hübner tentatively attributed it to Pietro da Cortona. In 1908 Woerman catalogued it as the work of an anonymous North Italian seventeenth-century painter, while Posse in 1929 simply catalogued it as anonymous Italian seventeenth-century. Comparison with a number of works by Sacchi indicates that it should be attributed to him. The head of the Emperor Constance in the *Miracle of the Corporal* (No. 9) and the head of an apostle in the Rospigliosi collection (No. 23), the latter a work of about the same size, are similar in type and technique. The drawing of the eye, nose, ear and skull of the Dresden head are even closer, however, to the head of St. Paul the Hermit in the Prado picture (No. 32). The area just left of the beard where the wet paint has been streaked by the brush also resembles passages of unfinished drapery in the Ottawa portrait of a cardinal (No. 21). The Dresden head has no obvious attributes and is painted a little more sketchily than the Rospigliosi *Apostle*, and may be a *bozzetto* for a similar head. A number of unidentified heads of old men appear in the artist's 1661 inventory (e.g. nos. 6, 12 and 19). A date for the Dresden picture before 1635 is probable, and before 1630 possible.

Bibliography: Dresden catalogues: Von Hübner, 1867, p. 104, no. 110; Von Hübner, 1872, p. 105, no. 110; Woerman, 1908, p. 77, no. 668; Posse, 1929, pp. 326–7, no. 668 (illus.).

26. St. Peter. Pincacoteca Comunale, Forlì Plate 48
405 × 228 cm.
Condition: This picture has been carefully cleaned and restored and its condition can be praised. There are signs that earlier neglect resulted in paint loss due to flaking in some areas, while much of the modelling has disappeared from St. Peter's undergarment.
Drawings: Study for the figure of St. Peter, Ambrosiana, Milan (no. 239, red chalk on white paper, 220 × 295 mm. See F. H. Dowley, 'Some Drawings by Carlo Maratta', *Burl. Mag.*, CI, 1959, fig. 21 and pp. 62–3); studies for the figure of St. Peter, Düsseldorf (Harris and Schaar, no. 35); study of a standing figure, probably St. Peter, Düsseldorf (Harris and Schaar, no. 34). Studies of hands in the Ashmolean, Oxford, were connected with this painting by Parker (II, no. 941), but the long, tapering fingers of the hand and the fluid chalk strokes are not characteristic of Sacchi, and the attribution must be rejected, despite the closeness of the pose. A red chalk study of St. Peter at Hamburg (No. I 21487a; see Gernsheim no. 5208–1955) has no connection either with this picture or with Sacchi. The technique suggests the hand of an early seventeenth-century academic mannerist.
Versions: See below under the Palazzo Barberini *St. Peter* (No. 28).

ONLY BELLORI among Sacchi's biographers mentions the *St. Peter* in Forlì, which he said hung in the tribune of the chapel dedicated to the Madonna del Fuoco in the Duomo. It was moved from the Duomo to the Oratorio delle Orfanelle together with Francesco Albani's *Martyrdom of St. Sebastian* in 1838 (Guarini). Both pictures were moved to the Pinacoteca Comunale in 1851 (Guarini and Arfelli).
After Incisa della Rocchetta had identified the subject of Sacchi's portrait in the Borghese Gallery as Monsignore Clemente Merlini, who was a native of Forlì and a close friend of Cardinal Antonio Barberini, Posse suggested that Merlini might have commissioned the *St. Peter*. Merlini died in 1642. The Barberini version of the *St. Peter* (No. 28) was certainly painted before April, 1644. On these and stylistic grounds, Posse dated the Forlì picture to around 1640. An earlier *terminus ante quem* is, however, provided by an account of a religious festival honouring the Madonna del Fuoco on October 30, 1636, when the *St. Peter* was carried in the procession by the Confraternità di San Pietro de' Battuti Bigij.[1] Merlini was a member of this Confraternity, which makes it almost certain that he commissioned the picture from Sacchi (Bezzi, pp. 65–6). The decision to honour the Madonna del Fuoco in this way was, however, only made on September 26 (Bezzi, p. 20), which means that it is virtually certain that Sacchi's *St. Peter* was in Forlì by this date and was not commissioned and painted for the occasion.[2]
The decision to build the chapel which contained the *St. Peter* was made in 1618; the foundation stone was laid in July, 1619 (Bezzi, p. 12). The construction was almost certainly finished by November, 1631[3] although the chapel may have been in use by 1626.[4] The Confraternità de' Battuti Bigij could have commissioned their picture in 1631, or even earlier if the size of their altar was known. There was another good reason for dedicating a picture in the chapel of the Madonna del Fuoco at this time. Forlì was one of the few towns in Italy unaffected by outbreaks of the plague in 1629 and 1630 (Bonoli, p. 335) and this was thought to be yet another miracle due to the Madonna del Fuoco (Bezzi, p. 10). The chances that the Confraternità de' Bianchi di San Sebastiano commissioned their altarpiece, *The Martyrdom of St. Sebastian*, from Francesco Albani at this time are good, since their patron saint was traditionally invoked against the plague (see Bezzi, p. 97). St. Peter was not, but this is no reason to think that the Confraternity would neglect their patron saint at a difficult time.

A glance at the chronology of Sacchi's career between 1630 and 1635 shows that while he worked on some commissions simultaneously, he was not busy between the winters of 1631 and 1632. Historical evidence suggests that this gap would suit the Forlì *St. Peter*, and stylistic evidence confirms this date. The preparatory studies indicate a date after 1630 at least, for none are in that freely-handled combination of black chalk with white accents characteristic of Sacchi's detailed figure studies in the later 1620s. In addition, a study at Düsseldorf (Harris & Schaar, no. 35) has studies on the verso for the *Three Magdalenes*, a work of 1633 or earlier. The treatment of the landscape in the painting recalls the Corsini *Hagar and Ishmael* of about 1630 and the settings of the *St. Andrew* and *St. Longinus* crypt altarpieces of 1633–4. The role of the architecture behind St. Peter parallels that of the tree behind St. Romuald in the Vatican picture. The confidence and skill with which Sacchi manages the large-scale composition of the Forlì picture equals that of the *St. Thomas* mosaic cartoon of 1631. It seems that the Confraternity commissioned the *St. Peter* through Merlini in 1630 or 1631, and that Sacchi executed it after finishing the *Divina Sapienza* ceiling, the *St. Thomas* mosaic cartoon and the *St. Romuald* altarpiece. If Savonanzi based the setting of his *Hagar and Ishmael* at Holkham Hall on Sacchi's Forlì *St. Peter*—and the similarity is striking—then the composition at least must have been ready by December, 1631, when Savonanzi's picture appears in a Barberini Inventory (*Burl. Mag.*, 1968, p. 254 and fig. 24).

This iconographical presentation of St. Peter is apparently unique, though easy to interpret. He has been given all his attributes—the bunch of keys, the papal tiara, the cockerel, the fishing net and the traditional blue and yellow robes. The portico before which he stands must symbolize the Church which, with Peter as its firm foundation, rises from the ruins of the Old Testament. The inscription in the book to which he points comes from his own writings (his second Epistle, 1, 10) and was probably chosen for its relevance to a charitable group founded to honour the Madonna del Fuoco and to do good works. The Greek inscription on the base of the portico can be translated 'The mouth of the apostles, everywhere ardent', the source being St. John Chrysostom.[5] Presumably the iconography was planned with Merlini, although the Düsseldorf drawing, which shows the saint holding the keys, suggests that the artist was free to arrange the symbols.

1. Bezzi, p. 64. After describing the picture in great detail, the author ends, 'La pittura uscia dalla maestra mano d'Andrea Sacchi famoso pittore in Roma'. The relevant passage is quoted by Guarini without drawing any conclusions about the picture's date. Guarini is listed in the bibliography of Posse's entry for Sacchi in Thieme-Becker, but the date of the painting was not changed in the text.

2. See Bezzi, pp. 78–9 and 82 for remarks about some of the floats and mechanical displays which were not properly finished in time. Marchesi thought that the *St. Peter* was painted for the 1636 festival.

3. Casali, p. 13, no. XXIII. The inscription records the completion of the lead covering of the cupola.

4. Bezzi (pp. 95 and 97) published a madrigal dedicated to the Madonna del Fuoco in 1626 by the Confraternità dei Battuti.

5. Bezzi (p. 46) gives a reference (D. Io. Chris. Hom. 55); the passage is to be found in Migne, *Patrologia Graeca*, LVIII, col. 533, Ioann. Chrys. *Comm. in S. Matt. Homilia*, LIV al. LV. The Greek text in the painting reads as follows:

ΤΟ ΣΤΟΜΑ ΤΩΝ ΑΠΟΣΤΟΛΩΝ [Ο ΠΕΤΡΟΣ,]
Ο ΠΑΝΤΑΚΟΥ [*sic*] ΘΕΡΜΟΣ

Bibliography: Bezzi, 1637, p. 64; Bellori, 1672–96, p. 66; Marchesi, 1678, p. 787; Cignani, *Descrizione di Pitture . . . della Città di Forlì*, 1838, pp. 21 and 33; Guarini, 1874, pp. 102–5; Calzini and Mazzatinta, 1893, p. 88; Voss, 1924, p. 532; Posse, 1925, p. 74 f. and *passim*; Posse, 1935, p. 290; Arfelli, 1936, p. 5 and fig. 37.

27. Portrait of Monsignore Clemente Merlini. Borghese Gallery, Rome   Plate 49
150 × 137 cm.

Condition: The paint in the background is very thin, but the lively brush strokes suggest that this area was never highly finished. There is a little cracking on the lower right, and the curtain above Merlini's head, his robes, the table cloth and upholstered parts of his chair have darkened and are difficult to read. Otherwise the condition seems good.

Versions: 1642 Copy painted for Cardinal Antonio Barberini before September 1, 1642 by Carlo Magnone (Incisa della Rocchetta, p. 69). No copies of the Merlini portrait are recorded in subsequent Barberini inventories, and it is probable that the Magnone version, made a month after Merlini's death, was intended for a mutual friend. Merlini's will (see below) contains bequests to Cardinal Antonio Barberini, Fabio Chigi and Giulio Rospigliosi, and further research might turn up a connection between these men and Cardinal Lazzaro Pallavicini, who in 1679 left a copy to Prince Niccolò Pallavicini (see below).

1679 Version recorded in an inventory of pictures left to Prince Niccolò Pallavicini by Cardinal Lazzaro Pallavicini, dated October 2, 1679 (no. 131), where it is said to 'viene da Andrea Sacchi' (Zeri, 1959, p. 295). Although the sitter is not named, the careful description in the inventory leaves no doubt that it was a copy of the Merlini portrait. It is still in the Rospigliosi-Pallavicini collection and is, according to Zeri (*op. cit.*, p. 298) of mediocre quality.

BELLORI and Erithreus are the only seventeenth-century sources to mention this portrait, which Bellori describes in some detail. It was in Cardinal Antonio Barberini's collection in 1644 (Posse, 1925, p. 127, note 3) and may have been left to him by Merlini in 1642.[1] It appears again in the 1671 inventory of Cardinal Antonio, in the 1672 list of works which passed from Antonio to Cardinal Francesco, and was in Cardinal Carlo Barberini's possession in 1704.[2] It was valued at 400 scudi in the 1738–9 Palestrina Inventory (Posse, *loc. cit.*). It passed from the Barberini to the Borghese family some time before 1833 (della Pergola) and has remained in the Borghese collections ever since. The correct identity of the sitter, which was lost in the eighteenth century, was re-established by Incisa della Rocchetta (pp. 69–71).

Posse, followed by Voss and Paola della Pergola, have dated the Merlini portrait to around 1640, when the sitter was fifty.[3] The bronze bust on the monument in S. Maria Maggiore is presumably a posthumous portrait of the prelate as he appeared at the time of his death two years later, and he looks somewhat older than in the Sacchi portrait, where there is no sign of the prominent forehead ridge shown in the bust and where the wrinkles in the corners of the eyes are also less marked. Merlini looks about forty in the painting.[4] A date around 1631–2, when Sacchi was working on the *St. Peter* for Merlini's Confraternity in Forlì, is probable.

1. Merlini left 'tutti i miei quadri di pittura originale non parendomi che le copie siano degne della persona sua' to Cardinal Antonio, according to his will of July 23, 1642 (Archivio Storico Capitolino, Archivio Notarile, Vespignanus, C.C., Ufficio 25). I have not been able to trace an inventory.

2. I owe these references to Dr Frances Vivian. The picture is said to measure 6 by 5 palmi and is valued at 200 scudi in 1671.

3. His date of birth is given on the monument in S. Maria Maggiore (see Forcella, XI, no. 140 or Bonoli, p. 334).

4. Merlini looks about fifty in G. B. Zampa's engraved frontispiece for Merlini's *Decisiones S. Rotae romanae* (Venice, 1652), which is apparently based on the Sacchi portrait, but the difference in age is simply due to the crudity of the engraving, which hardens the lines and exaggerates the shadows.

Bibliography: Jani Nicii Erithraei (G. V. Rossi), *Pinacotheca imaginum illustrium*, 3 vols., Cologne, 1645, II, pp. 176–8; Bellori, 1672–96, p. 68; Mariotti, 1892, p. 84; Incisa della Rocchetta, 1924, pp. 69–71; Voss, 1924, p. 531; Posse, 1925, p. 127 f. and *passim*; Gamba, 1927, p. 32 and pl. XVII; *Mostra di Roma Seicentesca*, Rome, 1930, no. 67; Posse, 1935, p. 290; Waterhouse, 1937, p. 91; della Pergola, 1959, II, p. 138 (*q.v.* for a complete bibliography).

28. St. Peter. Galleria Nazionale d'Arte Antica (Palazzo Barberini), Rome   Plate 52

223 × 151 cm.

Condition: This picture hangs high up on the walls of the Gran Salone where its condition cannot be assessed. A photograph taken in 1934, which exaggerates the darkening of the background and drapery, shows patches of cracking and flaking paint, although the saint, apart from his drapery, seems well preserved.

Drawings: All the drawings connected with this work are equally relevant to the Forlì *St. Peter* and have been catalogued with it, since it is probably the first version.

Versions: 1661   Version possibly of this composition in Sacchi's house in 1661 (Appendix II, no. 11). It might be identifiable with the version now at Besançon, *q.v.*

1759   Version possibly of this composition sold in London at Dr Bragge's sale, January 24–5, 1759, 2nd day, lot 21, 'St. Peter . . . And. Sacchi'. It went to an unknown buyer for seventeen shillings.

1854   Version recorded in the 1929 catalogue of the Besançon museum as a work of Giuseppe Ribera (Chudant, p. 47, no. 222, 72 × 52 cm.; Plate 50) and correctly identified by Carlo Volpe as a sketch for the Palazzo Barberini *St. Peter*. It came to the museum in 1854 with the Jean Gigoux collection. Benedict Nicolson kindly informed me of Dr Volpe's unpublished discovery.

THE *St. Peter* now in the Palazzo Barberini was recorded there as early as 1664 (Incisa della Rocchetta) and again in 1671, 1672,[1] 1689 (de Cotte) and then in 1704 and 1738–9.[2] It is not mentioned in eighteenth-century guidebooks, but Barberini inventories continue to record it in the nineteenth century and in 1934, when it was acquired by the State from the family.[3]

The existence of seven full-length apostles by Maratta, six now in the Galleria Nazionale (Palazzo Barberini) in Rome and one (St. James) in the Leeds City Art Gallery, all roughly the same size and format as Sacchi's apostle, appears to confirm Bellori's statement that Cardinal Antonio Barberini ordered a series of apostles from Sacchi, who finished the *St. Peter* and then handed over the commission to Maratta. However, all Maratta's apostles were painted after 1661, while Sacchi's *St. Peter* was in the Barberini collections by 1644, and is based on, or was the prototype for, another *St. Peter* in Forlì, which was in Forlì by October, 1636, and was very probably painted in 1631–2. This means that there was an exceptional degree of procrastination on Sacchi's part, or perhaps that the Rome *St. Peter* was originally commissioned alone, and only later incorporated into a series of apostles.

Monsignore Clemente Merlini's motives for commissioning a *St. Peter* for Forlì are clear. Cardinal Antonio Barberini's interest in this subject is less obvious. As the nephew of a pope, St. Peter's successor on earth, he may be expected to have had some interest in the Prince of the Apostles, but not necessarily to have been devoted to his cult. Here it is worth noting, however, that the attribute in the Forlì picture which makes the most direct reference to St. Peter as first pope—the papal tiara—is absent from the Rome version. The most obvious explanation for the Rome *St. Peter* is that Cardinal Antonio, who was a good friend of Merlini, saw Merlini's picture, admired it and asked Sacchi to make a version of it. Only much later, after the Cardinal's return from his exile in France in 1653, were the other apostles commissioned. This hypothesis fits better with what is known of Sacchi's working methods in the early thirties and fifties than does Bellori's brief statement, which remains partially correct. Sacchi was at his most productive in the early 1630s, and was already in the practice of

making versions of commissions for other patrons, for example the copies of the Collegio Romano fresco, the *Divina Sapienza* ceiling and the *St. Romuald* altarpiece for the diamond merchant Valguarnera, not to mention the beautiful reduced version of the Capuchins' *Miracle of St. Anthony* for Cardinal Antonio now in the Mahon collection. In the 1650s, however, Sacchi's production dried up almost completely and a number of important tasks given him by Cardinal Antonio were never finished. The Besançon sketch was presumably made to show the Cardinal how the Forlì composition would be adapted, and to help the artist adjust the design to the smaller format of the Rome canvas.

Although none of the other apostles are by Sacchi, it is possible that he began at least one other, for 'Una Tela grande che vi è principiato un disegno di San Paolo' was to be seen in his house at the time of his death (Appendix II, no. 236). Drawings by Sacchi related to Maratta's apostles would offer further proof of Maratta's having continued a project Sacchi began, but so far no such drawings have been identified. It is possible that Maratta took over and used the canvas on which Sacchi had started a *St. Paul*, but a radiograph of Maratta's *St. Paul* in Florence would only reveal that this is what happened if Maratta had not followed the composition laid out by Sacchi, and even if the outlines of a variant design were revealed, it would be impossible to prove they were Sacchi's and not Maratta's. It is clear that Maratta's *St. Paul* was planned to hang with Sacchi's *St. Peter*, as would be suitable on iconographic grounds.[4] Both men appeal directly to the spectator something which is not true to such a marked extent in any of the others in the series. St. Peter's closed gesture complements the open one of St. Paul; the block of stone used by Peter to support his writings is balanced by the altar beside Paul; even the long line of drapery on Peter's left is echoed by a similar form on Paul's right. Maratta was of course capable of designing a pendant for a work by Sacchi, and even of imitating Sacchi's style to some extent in order to make the two works harmonize better. Certainly the *St. Paul* has an emotional intensity which is not typical of Maratta, but which, in a less exaggerated form, is one of Sacchi's hallmarks. Perhaps this difference of degree is alone sufficient to prove that here Maratta is imitating Sacchi, and not following a design prepared by him.

1. 'Due quadri grandi . . . con le figure degl'Apostoli SS. Pietro e Paolo. S. Pietro mano di And[a] Sacchi, e S. Paolo di Carlo Maratta', measuring 9 by 6 palmi, are recorded in the 1671 inventory of Cardinal Antonio (p. 486, value 400 scudi), and again in the 1672 'Divisione delli quadri del . . . Cardinal Antonio', when the Sacchi was valued at 250 scudi, the Maratta at 150 scudi.
2. It appears on p. 225 of the 'Eredità del Cardinale Carlo Barberini' of 1704 and in the Palestrina inventory of 1738–9 (for the latter, see Posse, p. 72).
3. Mariotti (*loc. cit.*) cites the Fidecommesso inventory of 1816. See also Mezzetti, pp. 323–4.
4. The inventories of 1671, 1672 and 1704 clearly record the two pictures hanging together.

Bibliography: Bellori, 1672–96, p. 85; De Cotte, c. 1689, p. 206; Mariotti, 1892, p. 129; Voss, 1924, p. 532; Incisa della Rocchetta, 1924, p. 73; Posse, 1925, p. 72 f. and *passim*; Messetti, 1955, pp. 323–4.

29. A Miracle of St. Philip Benizzi. S. Maria in Via, Rome

Approximately 137 × 153 cm.   Plate 51

Condition: The real condition of this picture is obscured by a heavy layer of dirt and discoloured varnish. There are no obvious signs of serious surface damage.

Drawings: Study for the head of the first monk, collection of the Earl of Leicester, Holkham Hall (Vol. IV, no. 10, black chalk with white heightening on greenish-grey paper, 153 mm. in diameter;

Plate 53. A. E. Popham tentatively connected it with the head of Joseph in the Dresden *Rest on the Flight into Egypt*, now attributed to Camassei);[1] composition study for a *Miracle of St. Philip Benizzi*, British Museum (1946.7.13.807, red chalk on foxed cream paper, 264 × 212 mm. The composition does not fit the painting under discussion, but the subject is an unusual one, and the drawing can reasonably be catalogued as a rejected design for it).

BAGLIONE (1642, p. 356) says that all the paintings in the chapel of St. Philip Benizzi in S. Maria in Via in Rome were by a short-lived and short-tempered young man named Tommaso Luini. Titi (1674, p. 383) is the only authority to state that the *Miracle of St. Philip Benizzi* on the right wall was painted by Luini using a design of Sacchi. Titi's statement has been accepted by later authorities, and is confirmed by a Sacchi drawing at Holkham for the head of one of the monks in the picture, which shows the saint healing a lame man by clothing him.

Apart from Baglione's brief biography, very little is known of Luini's career. He was probably born around 1605 and died about 1640.[2] One of the other paintings mentioned by Baglione, the former high altarpiece of S. Carlo al Corso, survives and can be dated 1627–32.[3] All our remaining information about Luini comes from the records of a trial held in 1635 (Bertolotti, 1884, p. 178 f.). From these we learn that Luini had attended Sacchi's drawing academy for two years, and was apparently on good terms with Sacchi until 1632, when Luini left the studio after some disagreement (Baglione, *loc. cit.*). Presumably, therefore, Luini was helped by Sacchi with the design of the *Miracle of St. Philip Benizzi* between 1630 and 1632.

The Holkham drawing is valuable evidence in support of Titi's statement, but even without it the stylistic differences between the left and right-hand lateral canvases in the chapel should have attracted attention, and the Sacchesque character of the right-hand canvas been noted. The types of the monks recall the *St. Romuald*, as does the large tree on the left used to anchor the composition. The anatomy of the beggar resembles that of the man revived in the Capuchins' *Miracle of St. Anthony*, or the figure of Love astride his lion on the Barberini ceiling. The style of the *Burial of St. Philip Benizzi* on the left wall, however, is essentially Caravaggesque, and is, to judge from Luini's nickname, 'il Caravaggino', in his usual style.[4] Stylistic points of contact can, nevertheless, be found in both the St. Philip Benizzi canvases and in the S. Carlo altarpiece,[5] even though the latter is at first sight very different from the former. Some of the differences—the lighter palette, the more idealized types—are probably the result of Sacchi's intervention, documented by two drawings at Düsseldorf.[6] The execution of the S. Carlo altarpiece is inferior to that of the *Miracle of St. Philip Benizzi*, which it probably preceded. It would appear that Sacchi supervised Luini's work on the later commission more closely than he did the S. Carlo picture.

The explanation for the quarrel between Luini and Sacchi is probably personal and not professional. The execution of the *Miracle of St. Philip Benizzi* is, as far as can be judged at present, competent, if far less sensitive than that of a work by Sacchi himself. Baglione says of Luini that he lacked serious dedication to his career, and had he not wasted his time 'impiegato alle smargiasserie, e fare il furioso, e'l bizzarro ammazzatore', he would have achieved more and lived longer.[7] The *Miracle of St. Benizzi* and the S. Carlo altarpiece are proof of the generous assistance and encouragement given by Sacchi to Luini. The latter apparently became jealous when Sacchi befriended Greppi, whom Luini had originally introduced to Sacchi. Luini then left Sacchi's studio and later sought revenge by attacking Greppi. The whole affair provides a revealing insight into Sacchi's relations with other artists at the time when he himself was having his first major public successes.

1. See Sutherland Harris, 'Camassei Studies', pp. 64–5.
2. See Baglione, 1642, pp. 356–7. If Luini died aged 35 in 1641,

that is, if we follow Baglione's account literally, then he was born in 1606. In the trial (see below), Luini says that he was younger and less experienced than Sacchi, who was probably born late in 1599. Since Luini's biography is not one of the last in Baglione, he presumably died a few years before 1642, the date of publication. The dates c. 1605–c. 1640 suit all these circumstances.

3. Hess, 1934, p. 226, note 4.
4. It is close to a work given by Voss to the circle of Manfredi (1924, plate 99), and can also be compared with a Caravaggesque work at Notre-Dame, currently labelled Andrea de Leone, which shows St. Bernard of Clairvaux curing a man possessed by the devil. Alfred Moir (*The Italian Followers of Caravaggio*, Cambridge, 1967, I, pp. 129–30) thinks it may have been Luini's character rather than his work which earned him his nickname. Moir does not discuss any of Luini's surviving works.
5. Luini's stiff, hard-edged drapery on God the Father is found again on the possessed woman on the left of the *Burial* scene; the more wrinkled drapery used for the angels in the S. Carlo picture is seen on the old woman on the right edge of the *Burial* scene. The opened hands of the second angel from the right in the S. Carlo altarpiece are very close to the hands of the possessed woman on the left of the *Burial* scene. The two St. Philip Benizzi canvases share a darkish palette and tight paint quality.
6. Harris & Schaar, nos. 24 and 25. Erich Schleier has drawn my attention to a black chalk drawing in the Musée Pincé, Angers, which fits the figure of God the Father in the S. Carlo altarpiece. It is squared for transfer, and since it is clearly too weak for Sacchi, must be Luini's final preparatory study. It has previously been published as a Lanfranco (A. Recouvreur, *Musée Turpin de Crissé* [*Hôtel Pincé*], *Catalogue-Guide*, Angers, 1933, p. 108, no. 165. The drawing measures 220 × 290 mm. and is squared for transfer in red chalk).
7. In the trial, Greppi also characterized Luini as an 'uomo bizzarretto' (Bertolotti, 1884, p. 183).

Bibliography: Baglione, 1642, p. 356; Titi, 1674, p. 383 (and later editions); Posse, 1925, pp. 12, note 1 and 62, note 1; Posse, 1935, p. 290; Carlo Cecchelli, *S.M. in Via* (*Le Chiese di Roma Illustrate*, no. 14), n.d., p. 241 and fig. 10.

30. The Three Magdalenes. Convent of San Salvi (on deposit from the Uffizi), Florence   Plate 55
Approximately 270 × 184 cm.
Condition: Emiliani's recent statement (*Ideale Classico:* p. 338) that this painting is in a 'precario stato di conservazione' is pessimistic. The tone and colour are light compared with most of Sacchi's canvases, but the mixed oil-gouache medium partly accounts for this, as does the fact that the canvas never seems to have been varnished, or exposed to smoking candles over a long period of time. The paint is thin in some areas, however. The technique should be compared with that of the *Virgin and Child with St. Basil* in S. Maria del Priorato in Rome. I have not seen it since the flood of 1966. The picture is now (1972) undergoing restoration.
Drawings: Composition study, Windsor (Blunt and Cooke, no. 740); studies for the figure of the Magdalene, Düsseldorf (Harris and Schaar, no. 39); eight figure and drapery studies, three with additional studies on their versos, all probably connected with the *Three Magdalenes*, Düsseldorf (Harris and Schaar, nos. 42 to 49); copy after the whole composition, Düsseldorf (Harris and Schaar, no. 110. There is an old attribution to Pompeo Batoni on the mount, which may well be correct).
Versions: 1661   A picture described as 'Un quadro senza cornice con Santa Teresa, et altre Sante' in Sacchi's house in 1661 (Appendix II, no. 126) was probably a version of the *Three Magdalenes*. St. Teresa, who was also a Carmelite, is easily confused with St. Mary

Magdalene Pazzi.[1] This may be the work recorded in Maratta's possession in 1712.

1686 'Un quadro alto, et in cima mezzo tondo, che rapresente tre Madalene, con tre putti', measuring 12 by 8 palmi, is recorded in an undated inventory of Cardinal Antonio Barberini (possibly made in the 1640s prior to his departure for France), then in the 1686 Case Barberini inventory (p. 190, no. 179), and in the 1738–9 Palestrina Inventory (no. 31), when it was valued at 1000 scudi (for the last of these references, see Posse, 1925, p. 109, note 2). It was in the Galleria Colonna di Sciarra in 1818 and in 1850 (Mariotti, p. 135, no. 153) but has subsequently disappeared.

1692 Version recorded in the 1692 Inventory of Cardinal Flavio Chigi (no. 193, 'Un quadro tela da testa, cornice dorata . . . delle tre Maddalene d'Andrea Sacchi'). It is now in the Galleria Nazionale d'Arte Antica (Palazzo Corsini) in Rome (oil on canvas, 68 × 50.5 cm. See Refice, p. 220 and Emiliani, 1962, pp. 337–8. I am indebted to Marchese Giovanni Incisa della Rocchetta for the full reference in the Chigi inventory) (Plate 54).

1712 The 'quadro con tre figure mano d'Andrea Sacchi in misura di 4 palmi incirca con cornice bianca' in Maratta's collection in 1712 (Galli, 1928, p. 65) may have been a version of the *Three Magdalenes*.

BELLORI is the only one of Sacchi's biographers to mention his painting of St. Mary Magdalene of Japan, the Magdalene and St. Mary Magdalene Pazzi. No one, prior to the publication of Bellori's life of Sacchi in 1942, had connected pictures of this unusual subject with Sacchi. The painting now kept at San Salvi was first recognized as by Sacchi by Roberto Longhi, who connected it with the Bellori description and noted a small version of the same subject in the Palazzo Corsini in Rome, previously given to Maratta (see Refice, Blunt and Cooke, and Emiliani).

Bellori describes the picture carefully, but apart from including it in a list of works made for Cardinal Antonio Barberini, he provides no clues as to its date or destination. The subject is unique, however, and the picture must have been commissioned for a particular site. The reappearance of one version in Florence provides a hint as to the picture's original location, for the Barberini had dealings with only one church in Florence in the seventeenth century, namely S. Maria Maddalena dei Pazzi. Two of Urban VIII's sisters lived in the attached convent from 1628 to 1639.[2] Richa, who seems to base his account on lost *seicento* documents,[3] records that Urban VIII favoured the nuns by beatifying St. Mary Magdalene Pazzi on May 18, 1626, and by granting them indulgences for the church in 1632 and for the high altar in 1633.[4] Then

'. . . nell'anno seguente (1634) ai 27 di Gennaio per ringraziamenti del dito avuto della Beata manda loro una Croce di argento con un pezzetto del legno della Santa Croce, la qual croce è retta da due Angioli, con la sua base di argento posta sopra un piede di ebano, vedendosi nei lati la Reliquia di Santa Maria Maddalena Penitente, e della Beata Maria Maddalena Giapponese, rimasovi un ovatino vuoto per dare comodo di porvi una Reliquia di S. Maria Maddalena dei Pazzi, siccome mandò una Tavola grande, nella quale erano dipinte le tre suddette Sante.'

(In the following year [1634] on January 27, in gratitude for the finger of the Blessed [Mary Magdalene Pazzi] he had received, the Pope sent them a silver cross with a piece of the wood of the true cross. The cross was supported by two angels and had a silver base set on an ebony base. On each side were relics of the Penitent Mary Magdalene and of St. Mary Magdalene of Japan, with a small empty oval left for a relic of St. Mary Magdalene Pazzi. He also sent them a large painting of the three above-named saints.) The chances that the picture sent to Florence by the Pope was Sacchi's *Three Magdalenes* seem excellent, principally because the subject is unique, and seems to have been inspired by the reliquary containing relics of the three saints in question.

No picture of this subject is recorded in S. Maria Maddalena dei Pazzi in the seventeenth or eighteenth centuries, but the explanation for this is probably that it was kept in the *clausura* part of the convent.[5] The fact that the putti are clothed, whereas they were not in the version owned by Cardinal Antonio, also supports this hypothesis. Probably it adorned an altar in a small chapel used by Urban VIII's sisters. There is certainly no altar in the church which could have housed the painting.[6] So far no reference to Sacchi's painting has been traced in the inventories of the church's contents made after its secularization in the nineteenth century.[7]

The existence of a large version of the same subject, recorded in Rome from about 1645 until 1850, raises other problems. It is possible that Urban VIII's sisters took the picture sent to Florence back with them when they returned to Rome in 1639, that Cardinal Antonio Barberini then added it to his collection, and that when the Sciarra di Colonna collections were dispersed, the picture somehow found its way back to Florence. The other hypothesis is that there were two full-size versions, the second, which Bellori knew, having been commissioned by Cardinal Antonio for himself after seeing the picture Sacchi made for Florence. The second hypothesis is, for many reasons, the more probable one.

There are several slight differences between the sketch, now in the Palazzo Corsini, and the S. Salvi picture, namely in the style of the right sleeve of St. Mary Magdalene of Japan, in the position of the right hand of St. Mary Magdalene Pazzi holding the lily, in the absence of drapery on the putti in the former, and in the position of the central putto. Almost all these variations are recorded in the drawn copy after the composition at Düsseldorf, which is unlikely to be based on a painting kept in *clausura*. The copy is not, however, based on the Corsini sketch. The sleeve of St. Mary Magdalene of Japan is different again in the drawing, where a classical fringe has been added at the shoulder line, while the position of the central putto agrees more closely with the S. Salvi painting than with the sketch, as do many slight variations of drapery. This suggests that the drawing was based on a third and different version, which in turn was based on the Corsini sketch. The majority of the *seicento* and *settecento* Italian drawings at Düsseldorf were made in Rome; the copy after the *Three Magdalenes* certainly looks like an eighteenth-century Roman drawing from the circle of Batoni. That the version it records was a Barberini picture is proved by the Barberini bees on the sleeve of St. Mary Magdalene of Japan. To all these factors must be added the fact that Bellori's description is clearly of a large painting, and not of a sketch or *modello*. That it was the version recorded in Barberini inventories from about 1645 onwards seems virtually certain. It was presumably made shortly after the S. Salvi version was completed. The latter must have been finished in 1633 to reach Florence by January 27, 1634.

The only iconographical problem posed by the *Three Magdalenes* is the precise identification of St. Mary Magdalene of Japan. She holds glowing coals, and was presumably roasted to death, but all the seven Mary Magdalenes martyred in Japan before 1633 were crucified or beheaded (Pagés, pp. 804–7). Further research into the early history of the Catholic Church in Japan might provide the answer.[8]

1. See, for example, the altarpieces of Greppi and Piccione in S. Martino ai Monti (Sutherland, 'The Decoration of S. Martino', part I, figs. 12 and 13).

2. Gigli, pp. 185–6; Pecchiai, 1959, pp. 153–5; Fabriczy, pp. 255 and 261 and Hess, 1934, p. 222, note 1.

3. Fabriczy published (*L'Arte*, 1906, pp. 255–62) extracts from a manuscript in the Archivio di Stato in Florence, which contained a history of the church and convent since the thirteenth century, compiled in 1650 by D. Innocenzo Signori, who was abbot of a related monastery. No extracts after page 118 of the

131-page manuscript are given by Fabriczy, at which point the removal of the body of St. Mary Magdalene Pazzi from the old convent at S. Frediano to the new church, on December 7, 1628, is mentioned. Richa's account must be based on some such diary of important events, but so far attempts to trace the manuscript published by Fabriczy to see if it contains a reference to Sacchi's painting have not been successful.

4. Richa, pp. 316 and 324–5.

5. The refectory was, according to Cinelli (p. 488) 'tutto adornato di pitture d'eccellenti maestri, le quali non occorre qui descrivere per che essendo dentro la Clausura, non sono esposte a gli occhi di tutti'.

6. The only possible site is the sixth (last) chapel on the right, which contains a simple grey stone frame with an arched top, the width of which is the same as that of the S. Salvi picture without its frame. This chapel also has a window in the left wall, which would suit the lighting in the picture. However, the chapel is only recorded as containing a wooden crucifix attributed to Buontalenti (Richa, I, p. 328 and Paatz, IV, pp. 98–9 and 102) until 1824, when it was decorated with frescoes illustrating the life of St. Joan of Arc (Biardi, p. 94).

7. Dr Luisa Becherucci kindly answered my enquiries about the provenance of the S. Salvi painting.

8. I was unable to consult copies of Cristoforo Borrus, *Relatione della nuova missione delli Padri della Compagnia di Giesù, al Regno della Cocincina*, Rome, 1631, or *Relatione a sua Santità delle cose dell'India Orientale, del Giappone, della Cina, del'Etiopia, dell'Isola di S. Lorenzo, del Regno di Monomotapa e della terra ingognita Australe,* or Didacus Colladus, *Ecclesiasticam Iaponiae ab an. 1601 ad an. 1622,* Madrid, 1632.

Bibliography: Bellori, 1672–96, p. 67; Mariotti, 1892, p. 135; Posse, 1925, p. 109; Blunt and Cooke, 1960, p. 93; Emiliani 1962, pp. 337–8.

31. The Suicide of Dido. Musée des Beaux-Arts, Caen   Plate 58

Oil on canvas, 139 × 148 cm.

Condition: When first brought to my attention, this work had suffered from paint loss due to flaking and was affected by attempts to restore these losses, especially in the sky areas. The work has now been cleaned and restored at the Louvre.

Version: 1661 'Un quadro senza Cornice con Didone con la spada in petto' was in Sacchi's house in 1661 (Appendix II, no. 180). This was probably not the Caen picture, for the latter is signed on the sword. It seems unlikely that Sacchi signed a work in his own collection.

ACCORDING to Mlle P. Debaisieux of the museum at Caen, who drew this painting to my attention, the Dido was sent to Caen by Napoleon in 1802 and came originally from the collection of the Duc de Penthièvre in March, 1794. His wife was Marie-Thérèse d'Este. Her family connections may explain how the Duke came to own a work by Sacchi. The existence of a picture of this same subject in Sacchi's collection in 1661 is evidence in favour of the attribution, though it must be admitted that the signature is unusual and that some aspects of the work are not entirely consistent with Sacchi's style. Anthony Blunt has in fact expressed doubts about the attribution. The closest parallels are offered by *The Three Magdalenes* in Florence and the *Santa Rosalia* in Madrid for the physiognomy of Dido and the unusually elaborate fold forms of her drapery. The isolation of the figure, who in most *seicento* representations is surrounded by members of her court, is also an iconographical variation consistent with Sacchi. Thus I am inclined to accept the attribution of this work to Sacchi.

Bibliography: A. F. Blunt, 'The new Musée des Beaux Arts at Caen', *Burl. Mag.,* 1972, p. 83.

32. St. Paul the Hermit and St. Anthony Abbot. Museo del Prado, Madrid   Plate 60

141 × 141 cm.

Condition: Although in need of a cleaning, the condition of this picture is better than it appears to be in photographs. There are indications of cracking, subsequent paint loss and retouchings, for example on the robe of St. Anthony.

Drawings: Studies for the hands and drapery of St. Anthony, Düsseldorf (Harris and Schaar, no. 53); study for St. Paul's left hand, Düsseldorf (Harris and Schaar, no. 50).

THIS PAINTING was in Spain by 1701, when it was catalogued in a Buen Retiro inventory as the companion to the *St. Rosalia* (No. 33), then attributed to Guido Reni. It was therefore probably one of the pictures of hermit saints commissioned from artists working in Rome by Philip IV to decorate Buen Retiro in the 1630s. A version must have remained in Rome, for Giacinto Brandi certainly knew the composition when he painted the same subject. His picture, now in the Kunsthistorisches Museum in Vienna, is not an early work and must date from after 1650 at least. No versions of Sacchi's painting are however recorded.

Two sheets of drawings at Düsseldorf help to clarify the date of the *St. Paul and St. Anthony.* They contain studies on their rectos and versos for the Prado picture, the *St. Francis Marrying Poverty* and the *Three Magdalenes.* The last named was ready by 1633 and a similar date can be assumed for the other two works. The psychological and, to a lesser extent, the formal connections between the Prado picture and the *St. Romuald* of 1631 are obvious, but the simplicity and concentration of the composition of the former indicates some development towards Sacchi's later work, and a date of 1633–5 is therefore indicated. Sacchi's source seems to have been Muziano's treatment of the same subject.[1]

1. Illustrated by Pigler, I, p. 417.

Bibliography: Fuente, 1772, p. 535; Prado catalogues: 1828, pp. 115–16 (no. 456); 1843, p. 146 (no. 692); 1845, *ibid.*; 1885, no. 360; 1910, no. 328 (it does not appear in the catalogues of 1933, 1945 and 1952); Voss, 1924, p. 532; Posse, 1925, p. 76 and fig. 21; Posse, 1935, p. 290.

33. Santa Rosalia Sinibaldi of Palermo. Museo del Prado, Madrid   Plate 59

140 × 140 cm.

Condition: The picture was cleaned in 1970 and appears to be in good condition considering its previous neglect.

Drawings: Two studies for the figure of St. Rosalia with additional studies of her head and hands, Düsseldorf (Harris and Schaar, no. 40, where it was tentatively linked with the *Three Magdalenes*); studies for the drapery of St. Rosalia, Düsseldorf (Harris and Schaar, no. 41, where it was tentatively linked with the *Three Magdalenes*).

Versions: c. 1689 De Cotte saw a 'Ste Rose d andrea Sacchi' in the Palazzo Barberini during his visit to Rome (Actes, II, p. 205). Perhaps it was a version of the Prado picture.

SACCHI'S *Santa Rosalia Sinibaldi of Palermo* has recently been identified in the museum at Murcia by Dr. Alfonso Pérez Sánchez. It was cleaned and included in the exhibition of Italian seventeenth-century painting held at the Prado in the spring of 1970.[1] The picture had been attributed to the school of Guido Reni as early as 1701 in the Buen Retiro inventory, where it was also stated to be a companion to Sacchi's *SS. Anthony Abbot and Paul the Hermit.* The two pictures are the same size, and the discovery of the *Santa Rosalia* allows the pair to be reunited. The discovery also allows two drawings hitherto tentatively connected with the *Three Magdalenes* at San Salvi to be correctly identified with the work for which they were made. One of these drawings (no. 40) has other studies on the verso for the Prado *SS. Anthony*

Abbot and Paul the Hermit and for the lost *St. Francis Marrying Poverty*, both works datable around 1633-5. A similar date is indicated for the *Santa Rosalia*.

Like the other saints depicted in the series painted for Buen Retiro, Santa Rosalia (d. *circa* 1160) was a hermit. She left her family at the age of twelve to live in a cave on Monte Coschina near Bivona in Sicily, and later moved to a stalactitic grotto on Monte Pellegrino just outside Palermo. The cave in which she reputedly lived contains an inscription carved into the wall, according to local legend, by the saint herself. The chisel and mallet that she holds in Sacchi's painting must refer to this story. Although venerated in Sicily from the thirteenth century onwards, S. Rosalia's cult only became widespread after the plague of 1624, when a citizen of Palermo claimed to have had a vision in which the saint appeared, urging him to go to her grotto. Her bones were discovered and a shrine was erected and the plague duly abated. Urban VIII added her to the Roman martyrology in 1630.[2]

1. Pérez Sánchez, 1970, pp. 365 and 367.
2. Butler, III, pp. 486-7 and *Acta Sanctorum*, September, II, p. 350.

Bibliography: Puente, 1772, p. 530 (as Sacchi); Pérez Sánchez, 1965, pp. 175-6 (as school of Guido Reni); Pérez Sánchez, 'Unfamiliar Italian Paintings of the Seventeenth Century', *Apollo*, 1970, May, pp. 365 and 367 and fig. 7.

34. St. Francis marrying Poverty. Formerly Corsini Collection, Florence; present location unknown   Plate 57
Size unknown.

Condition: The condition of this picture as recorded in a photograph of 1934 (G.F.N. E 18752) confirms Posse's judgment of 1925, '. . . in schlecht gehaltenem und sehr nachgedunkeltem Zustand' (p. 75). In some areas the paint had completely flaked off; in others diseased varnish or dirt obscures the design completely. A *pentimento* indicates that at one time the cross was further to the left.

Drawings: Studies for the figure of Poverty, Düsseldorf (Harris and Schaar, no. 50); studies for the figures of Poverty and St. Francis, Düsseldorf (Harris and Schaar, no. 51); studies for the figure of St. Francis, Düsseldorf (Harris and Schaar, no. 52).

Versions: 1661 Version recorded in Sacchi's house in 1661 (Appendix II, no. 131). Its later history is not known. Since it is not said to be a large picture, it probably cannot be identified with the version recorded in Barberini collections from 1663 onwards.
1663 Version recorded in the 1663 inventory of Cardinal Francesco Barberini, where it is described as 'un quadro con S. Fran(ces)co che sposa la Povertà di Andrea Sacchi con cornice alla fiorentina tutta dorata, alta p(al)mi 14½ e larga p(al)mi nove' (Incisa della Rocchetta, p. 75). It appears again in the 1679-80 inventory of Cardinal Francesco (p. 80), in the 1704 inventory of Cardinal Carlo Barberini (Posse, 1925, p. 75, note 1) and in the Eredità del Cardinale Carlo Barberini (p. 219). The given measurements vary a little (down to 12 by 8 palmi) but this happens with other works too and it is probable that only one picture is recorded. Only one appears in *sei-* and *settecento* guidebooks and only one version survived in 1934 when it passed to the Corsini family in Florence. Its present location is not known.

The *St. Francis Marrying Poverty* is undocumented and there is no reference to it earlier than 1661, when one version is recorded in the artist's house. That version may be identical with another recorded two years later in Cardinal Francesco Barberini's collection, but was probably a different and smaller version. The subject suggests that the commission came from Cardinal Francesco, as Pastor supposed. It was Cardinal Francesco's picture that survived in the Barberini collections until 1934 and that has subsequently disappeared. Two drawings at Düsseldorf with studies for this work and two others, one of which—the *Three Magdalenes*—can be dated around 1633, suggest a similar date for the *St. Francis*.

Bibliography: Bellori, 1672-96, p. 66; De Cotte, *c.* 1689, p. 206; Rossini, 1693, p. 52 (1700 and 1704 ed., p. 65; 1750, p. 76; 1776, II, p. 186); Pinarolo, 1700, p. 169 (1703, *ibid.*; 1713, II, p. 177); Panciroli, 1719, II, p. 358; Roisecco, 1750, II, p. 295; Mariotti, 1892, p. 128; Incisa della Rocchetta, 1924, pp. 75 and 76; Voss, 1924, p. 532; Posse, 1925, pp. 73, 75 and 98; Pastor, 1928, XXIX, p. 490.

35. St. Anthony of Padua reviving a Dead Man. S. Maria della Concezione, Rome   Plate 61
Approximately 290 × 200 cm.

Condition: The surface is obscured by old, yellowed varnish and the chapel in which it is situated is badly lit. Consequently no proper examination of the picture is possible at present. Comparison with the version in Denis Mahon's collection indicates that parts of the sky, landscape and left foreground may have been repainted, and the edges trimmed on all sides.

Drawings: Composition study, British Museum (No. F.f. 3-195, dark red chalk and red wash on buff paper, 227 × 171 mm. Philip Pouncey recognized that this drawing, previously given to Romanelli, is by Sacchi); composition study, Windsor (Blunt and Cooke, no. 761. There is a copy of this drawing in the collection of Lord Leicester at Holkham Hall); composition study, British Museum (no. 1963.11.9.25, red chalk on cream paper, 268 × 200 mm. There are studies on the verso for the figures in the crowd in the first British Museum composition study); drapery studies for the man revived and a study of an unidentified standing male figure, Düsseldorf (Harris and Schaar, no. 37); studies of spectators, Düsseldorf (Harris and Schaar, no. 38); studies probably for the young acolyte on the left, Düsseldorf (Harris and Schaar, no. 69, where it was tentatively associated with Magnone's fresco in S. Giovanni in Fonte); study for the head of a spectator, Windsor (Blunt and Cooke, no. 762); study for the feet of St. Anthony, Düsseldorf (Harris and Schaar, no. 33 verso).

There are drawn copies after the painting at Düsseldorf (Harris and Schaar, no. 113) and at Leipzig (Museum der Bildenden Kunst, book 89, pp. 80 and 82). Another drawing at Düsseldorf connected with this altarpiece by Schaar in 1964 (p. 47) has since been recognized as a study for Maratta's altarpiece in the Cybo chapel, S. Maria del Popolo (Harris and Schaar, no. 344).

Versions: 1661 Version recorded in Sacchi's house in this year (Appendix II, no. 197). Its size is not given, which makes it difficult to relate to later recorded versions.
1671 'Il Miracolo di S. Antonio che resuscita un Morto, et Angeli. Sopra il frontispizio d'Ebano mezza figura di un S. Michele', a painting 3 palmi high and valued at 350 scudi, belonged to Cardinal Antonio Barberini in 1671 (p. 481). The same work is recorded in 1692 on Cardinal Carlo Barberini's inventory (p. 205) when it is said to be 4 by 5 palmi and to have a frame 'di ebano fatto a Prospettive con un S. Michele Arcangelo in cima'. This version, which was valued highly and had an unusually elaborate frame, may be identical with the version now in Denis Mahon's collection (see below).
c. 1689 Version formerly in the Palazzo Barberini, where it was seen by De Cotte, who reported that it was on copper (Actes II, pp. 108-9). It may be identified with the version described as a sketch for the Capuchin altarpiece in the Palazzo Barberini in 1719 (Panciroli, II, p. 361).
1816 Version first recorded in the Palazzo Barberini in 1816 (Mariotti, p. 128, no. 39) and now in the collection of Don Augusto Barberini (G.F.N. E 18755). It was exhibited in Florence in 1922 (no. 874). Painted on panel (65.5 × 41 cm.), it appears to be autograph. It was brought to my attention by Marilyn Aronberg Lavin.
1885 Version from the Corsini collection, acquired by the State in 1885 and at present kept in the Palazzo Corsini in Rome (oil on canvas, 67 × 51 cm.). It differs from the altarpiece in having no

figure emerging from the tomb in the foreground and in having trees in the landscape. It is a copy. It was exhibited in Florence in 1922 (no. 870). See Posse, 1925, p. 60 and Refice, 1950, p. 220.

1925   Version mentioned by Posse (1925, p. 60) in a private collection in Rome. He gives no details, which means that it is not possible to connect this version with others.

1961   Version now in the collection of Denis Mahon in London (Plate 62), exhibited by Colnaghi's in 1961 (*Paintings by Old Masters*, P. & D. Colnaghi & Co. Ltd., May 16 to June 15, 1961, no. 2 and pl. II. See also Emiliani, 1962, p. 331). It was found in Paris, but its previous history is not known. Painted in oil on panel, it measures 110.5 × 76 cm.

I am informed by Professor Roberto Longhi that the version recorded in his collection by Refice (1950, p. 220) with a Barberini provenance is not now and never was in his possession.

Engravings: 1707   Engraving printed by Lorenzo Filippo de' Rossi and dedicated by him to 'Rev.mo D. D. Hieronymo Crispi di Ferrara'. It is not an engraving of high quality. The saint shown in the niche on the left is male and not female.

THE FOUNDATION STONE of the new Capuchin church, S. Maria della Concezione, was laid in October, 1626. In June, 1630, Lanfranco was paid for the high altarpiece, which was dedicated in September. Other altarpieces in the church can be dated by payments or other evidence to the years 1631, 1632, 1634, 1635 and 1636. The completed and decorated church was dedicated in August, 1636.[1] The chances that Sacchi's undocumented *Miracle of St. Anthony of Padua* was painted between 1631 and 1636 are therefore good. Both Passeri and Bellori say that it was painted before Sacchi went to North Italy, which means before June, 1635. The inclusion of Duquesnoy's *S. Susanna,* which was in place beside the high altar of S. Maria di Loreto in the early spring of 1633,[2] in the niche in the left background must also affect the date of Sacchi's altarpiece. Mahon and Emiliani dated it 1631–3; earlier suggested dates are less precise.

The altarpiece was commissioned by Cardinal Antonio Barberini the Younger, but since he and Sacchi were in regular contact after 1631, their relationship offers no clues as to the date of this particular undocumented commission. The seven preparatory studies are all in red chalk, except where ink and wash are used, and are handled more delicately than drawings datable 1628–31. The former are most closely paralleled by studies for works datable 1632–5, when Sacchi seldom uses black chalk and uses red chalk with more care and precision than previously. The presence of Duquesnoy's *S. Susanna* narrows the date down further. It is probable that Sacchi and Duquesnoy were good friends by now, although it is the appearance of Duquesnoy's statue in this altarpiece which provides the first firm evidence of their friendship. Sacchi may well have seen the work in progress, and known its final form long before it was set up in S. Maria di Loreto.[3] Several factors indicate that he did not, however, consider using it until a late stage in the planning of the work, which very possibly occurred after *S. Susanna* was installed. Sacchi shows the statue looking outwards and pointing inwards, the relationship between statue and spectator that Duquesnoy intended, and which would be more readily appreciated after the statue was in place.[4] Then it will be noted that none of the preparatory composition studies that show the architectural setting, and which are close to the executed design in all important details, show a niche, although there is a space for one. Finally, it is inconceivable that Sacchi would have revealed Duquesnoy's statue to the public before it had been unveiled. A completion date shortly after the spring of 1633 is, however, probable, for Sacchi signed the contract for the four altarpieces in the crypt chapels of the crossing of St. Peter's in March, and would have been busy with these and the *Three Magdalenes* during the rest of the year.

The only certain autograph version is that now in the collection of Denis Mahon (Plate 62). It differs from the altarpiece in showing trees and a range of mountains in the view through the archway, in having flag-stones in the left foreground, and in showing more of the composition on all sides, particularly the right. The view through the archway and the left foreground of the altar are both slightly damaged areas; possibly Mahon's picture records the original appearance of these areas more accurately. The altarpiece may also have been reduced in size by being tacked to a smaller stretcher when the canvas rolled over the edges of the original stretcher wore through. Only a thorough technical examination and cleaning will produce the answers to these queries.

The Mahon version has been called the *modello* for the altarpiece (Mahon and Emiliani), but is more probably an autograph repetition made for Cardinal Antonio. None of the large number of paintings in Sacchi's house in 1661, most of which were his own, are described as *modelli*. A number are called sketches, and sketches are known for several of Sacchi's works (see Nos. 16, 28 and 30). On the other hand, there are many cases of Sacchi's making copies of his own works for important clients, for example of the *St. Romuald* for Valguarnera, or of the *Drunkenness of Noah* for Marchese Antonio Ruffo, or of the Forlì *St. Peter* and the *Three Magdalenes* for Cardinal Antonio. The high quality of the Mahon version also hardly suggests that it was a stage in the preparation of the larger work. It was probably executed a year or less after the altarpiece was completed.

1. For these dates see Isnello, pp. 57–8, 88 and 94; Gnudi and Cavalli, p. 87; Briganti, 1962, p. 193 and Vitzthum in *Burlington Magazine:* CV, 1963, p. 215.
2. Mahon, 1962, p. 63 f.
3. *Ibid.*
4. At the moment, the statue looks at the altar and gestures outwards. The correct position was noted by Wittkower (1958, p. 356).

Bibliography: Totti, 1638, p. 301; Bellori, 1672–96, pp. 54–5; Titi, 1674, pp. 367–8 (and all later editions); Passeri, 1679, p. 297; Sebastiani, 1689, p. 125; De Cotte, *c.* 1689, p. 206; Rossi, 1719, II, pp. 361 and 402; Pascoli, 1730, II, p. 16; Rossini, 1750, p. 170 (1776, II, p. 176); Vasi, 1770, p. 105 (1765, II, p. 105); Pistolesi, 1841, p. 368 (1846, *ibid.*); Voss, 1924, p. 553; Posse, 1925, p. 60 and *passim*; Posse, 1935, p. 290; Waterhouse, 1937, p. 92; Refice, 1950, p. 220; Emiliani, 1962, pp. 308 and 331–2.

36. Christ Carrying the Cross, and St. Veronica. Chapter House, St. Peter's, Rome   Plate 63
210 × 140 cm.

Condition: Since it hangs in a dark room well above eye level, the condition of this picture is difficult to judge. It is dark and has not been cleaned since 1925 (Steinmann, p. 946), but seems to be in good shape beneath the dirt and varnish. There are *pentimenti* visible around the cross, the left arm of the left soldier, the head of the central soldier and the left arm of the soldier on horseback.

Drawings: Drawings attributed to Sacchi for a composition of Christ carrying the cross are recorded in the Nourri collection in 1785 and in the Silvestre collection in 1811 (Mireur, IV, p. 388). The former was on blue paper, which would be unusual for Sacchi. A drawing of a soldier at Windsor (Blunt and Cooke, no. 743) has been connected with this composition, but the pose fits none of the figures in the altarpiece, and the drawing is probably not even by Sacchi.

Versions: 1661   Version recorded in the artist's house (Appendix II, no. 137). It is described as a sketch, but there is no way of knowing with which, if any, of the later versions it could be identified.

1725   Version recorded in the collection of the Duke of Orleans, where it was engraved by Simon Vallée (see Dubois de St. Gelais, *Description des Tableaux du Palais Royal*, Paris, 1727, p. 20). It was sold in 1793 with other Italian pictures in this collection to Walthieu, and by him to Laforde de Méréville, and from him through Bryan to Henry Hope (see Buchanan, *Mémoires*, I, p. 18 f. I owe this reference to Sir Anthony Blunt). Waagen (1854, II, pp. 76 and 495) recorded it in the collection of Samuel Rogers, who exhibited it at the British Institution in 1821 (Graves, III, p. 1187). It was sold at Christie's in 1856 (May 3, lot 718), when the Orleans and Hope provenances were recorded, and has subsequently disappeared. It measured 69 × 46 cm.

1823 Version belonging to a Mrs. Trotter, exhibited in Edinburgh in 1823 (Graves IV, p. 2164).

c. 1900 Version formerly in the Cartwright collection, Aynhoe Park, Northants. (oil on canvas, 46 × 34 cm.). Its previous history is not recorded. It is autograph.

1967 Version with Hazlitt in June, 1967 and now at Vassar College Art Gallery, Poughkeepsie, N.Y. (oil on canvas, 47 × 36 cm.). Its previous history is not recorded. The brush work is too loose for Sacchi and some of the colouring and facial expressions are too crude. Guy Walton and Erich Schleier have recently proposed an attribution to Guglielmo Cortese (*Antichità Viva*, 1970, no. 1, p. 11). Another sketch, close in technique and size (it measures 46 × 34 cm.) is in the collection of Colonel Sir Joseph Weld, Lulworth Manor, Dorset.

Engravings: 1771 Engraving by Desiderio de Angelis and Angelo Campanella, dedicated to Francesco di Almada, Spanish Ambassador to the Holy See, by P. L. Bombelli. Another engraving was published by Pistolesi in 1829 (II, pl. II).

Documents: On May 14, 1627, the committee in charge of the decoration of St. Peter's declared that '... in questi [Altari del Volto Santo et S. Andrea] facilmente non si farran' dentro quadri per esservi sopra le medesime Reliquie, et per l'angustia et poco lume che haverran' dentro le cappellette di detti Altari' (Pollak, II, p. 85). However, the decision to commission altarpieces for all four altars beneath the piers of the crossing of St. Peter's had been made by January, 1633. The first payment to Sacchi is dated March 1, 1633. By August 19, 1634 he had received a total of 650 scudi (Pollak, II, pp. 516–17). He did not receive the final payment until September 5, 1650, when he was paid 150 scudi specifically for the *St. Helen* (I. Lavin, *The Crossing of St. Peter's*, New York, 1969, p. 25, note 119. This must be the document to which Fraschetti referred [1900, p. 70] when he stated that unpublished payments in the Archivio della Fabrica di S. Pietro showed that all four altarpieces were only installed in 1650). Pistolesi (II, p. 25) says that the *St. Veronica* was installed on July 15, 1634.

For a discussion of the *St. Veronica*, see below under *St. Helen* (No. 39).

Bibliography: Most of the references to the *St. Veronica* also cite the other three crypt chapel altarpieces discussed below. The bibliography below is complete for all four pictures. References that follow the other three pictures refer to them only. Baglione, 1639, pp. 39–40; De Angelis, 1646, p. 161; Bellori, 1672–96, pp. 55–6; Passeri, 1678, p. 298; Titi, 1675, p. 7 (and all later editions, incl. 1763, p. 7); Rossini, 1693, pp. 20 and 143 (1700 ed., pp. 23 and 161; 1704 ed., *ibid.*, 1750, pp. 72 and 130; 1776, I, p. 245 and II, p. 197; 1789, I, p. 245 and II, p. 197); Pinarolo, 1700, p. 270 (1703, p. 270; 1713, p. 255; 1725, II, p. 46); Panciroli, 1719, II, p. 27; Pascoli, 1730, I, p. 16 and II, p. 33; Chattard, 1762, I, pp. 186 and 198; Vasi, 1763, p. 332; Pistolesi, 1829, II, plates II, VIII and XIV and pp. 25, 61, 96 and 110; Nagler, 1835–52, XV, p. 540; Pistolesi, 1841, pp. 5, 86, 88–9 and 90 (1846, *ibid.*); Waagen, 1854, II, pp. 76 and 495; Fraschetti, 1900, p. 70; Voss, 1924, p. 531; Posse, 1925, p. 55 f.; Steinmann, 1925, p. 946; Hess, 1934, p. 298; Posse, 1935, p. 290; Waterhouse, 1937, p. 91; Salerno, 1955, pp. 216–17, no. 267; Blunt and Cooke, 1960, pp. 93 and 95; Emiliani, 1962, pp. 332–4; Waterhouse, 1963, p. 57; Lavin, 1968, p. 25, note 119.

37. St. Andrew Adoring the Cross of his Martyrdom. Chapter House, St. Peter's, Rome   Plate 64

215 × 145 cm.

Condition: Although Posse in 1925 described all four crypt chapel altarpieces as 'Ruinen', all are in fairly good shape. The *St. Andrew* was cleaned for the *Ideale Classico* exhibition in Bologna in 1962. It has more surface impasto than the *St. Longinus*, and fewer visible *pentimenti* than any of the other three. A copy (see Versions, 1963) shows the hand of the central soldier supporting the saint's right arm in a way now concealed by the saint's beard. This detail can be seen in some old photographs of the *St. Andrew* but is difficult to detect since the 1962 cleaning.

Drawings: Study for the torso of St. Andrew, Windsor (Blunt and Cooke, no. 763 recto). A pen drawing with indigo wash of St. Andrew's martyrdom in the Kaieman collection in 1859 was attributed to Sacchi, but the medium is improbable for him (Mireur, IV, p. 388).

Versions: 1661 Version recorded in Sacchi's house at his death (Appendix II, no. 136). This may be the picture recorded later in Maratta's collection, *q.v.*

1712 Version recorded in Maratta's inventory of his collection made in 1712 (no. 428, 'Un quadretto abbozzo del Sacchi con cornice, quale rappresenta Sant'Andrea condotto al martirio'. Galli, 1928, p. 75). It is not among the pictures sold by Maratta's heirs to Philip V of Spain and its later history is not known.

1759 Copy recorded in the 1759 inventory of paintings in the Palazzo Spada (no. 905. See Zeri, 1955, p. 175). It is no longer in the Spada collections and is presumably lost.

1759 Version sold by a Mr Pond to a Captain Hamilton in 1759 for thirty shillings and described as 'St. Andrew adoring the Cross ... a sketch' (Victoria and Albert Museum, London, Manuscript Sale Catalogues, 1711–59. I owe this reference to Mr. Frank Simpson).

1790 'Un abbozzetto di Andrea Sacchi del martirio di S. Andrea' was in the Palazzo Odoardi in Ascoli-Piceno in 1790 (Orsini, p. 81). Its later history is not known.

1901 Version recorded in St. Jean de Malte in Aix-en-Provence in 1901 (*Inventaire des Richesses d'Art de la France*, Province III, Paris, 1901, p. 215, where it is catalogued as Italian seventeenth century. Posse [1925, p. 55] identified it properly).

1963 Small copy owned by P. & D. Colnaghi & Co. Ltd. in 1963. It may be a studio copy since a variant pose for the right hand of the helmeted soldier in the centre is shown, and this position is visible as a *pentimento* in the altarpiece. Mr R. D. Thesiger drew my attention to this version and the variant position of the soldier's hand, first noticed by Howard Hibbard.

Engravings: 1771 Engraving by Vincenzo Antonelli dedicated to the Spanish Ambassador to the Holy See and printed by P. L. Bombelli (see also above under *St. Veronica*).

Documents: See above under *St. Veronica*.

Bibliography: See above under *St. Veronica*. See also De Angelis, 1646, p. 161; Hess, 1934, p. 298, note 3 and Emiliani, 1962, pp. 332–4.

38. The Martyrdom of St. Longinus. Chapter House, St. Peter's, Rome   Plate 65

210 × 140 cm.

Condition: The *St. Longinus* was cleaned in 1925 (Steinmann, p. 946) and again in 1962 for the Bologna *Ideale Classico* exhibition. In contrast to the *St. Andrew*, the paint surface is thin and badly worn, particularly in the right and centre foreground and on the left leg of the saint. *Pentimenti* are visible around the contours of the executioner's legs, and the top of his right shoulder.

Drawings: Study for the drapery of St. Longinus, Windsor (Blunt and Cooke, no. 763 verso. The verso also contains a study for a kneeling figure in the foreground of the *Destruction of Pagan Idols* in S. Giovanni in Fonte, *q.v.* Alternatively it may be a variant,

rejected pose for St. Longinus); two studies for the lower part of the kneeling saint's torso, Düsseldorf (Harris and Schaar, no. 54); drapery studies for St. Longinus, Düsseldorf (Harris and Schaar, no. 55); studies for the figure of St. Longinus, Düsseldorf (Harris and Schaar, no. 56); study for the drapery of St. Longinus, Düsseldorf (FP 13713 and FP 13714, black chalk with white heightening on grey-brown paper, 395 × 260 mm. The two sheets were until recently separated, but have now been reunited by Dr Dieter Graf. There is a further very careful drapery study on the verso, almost equally suitable for St. Andrew and St. Longinus, as is the study on the recto; study for the left-hand spectator in the background, British Museum (Fawkener collection, no. 5211–79, red chalk on buff paper, 255 × 287 mm. The same pose is found in a Lanfranco drawing in the Uffizi (12695 F recto) which has studies for a work of about 1616 on the verso (see Erich Schleier's study in *Arte Illustrata*, September, 1972, fig. 4). The study on the recto is not connected certainly with any known work and the similarity with the Sacchi may therefore be fortuitous. There is a copy after the altarpiece at Düsseldorf (Harris and Schaar, no. 114). A study, possibly for this composition, was in the Silvestre collection in 1811 ('Un saint religieux prêt á être décapité et huit études: 9 fr.' See Mireur, VI, p. 388).
Engravings: 1771 Engraving by Francesco Pozzi dedicated to the Spanish Ambassador to the Holy See, printed by P. L. Bombelli.
Documents: See above under *St. Veronica.*
Bibliography: Posse, 1925, p. 135; Hess, 1934, p. 298, note 6; Emiliani, 1962, pp. 332–4.

39. St. Helen and the Miracle of the True Cross. Chapter House, St. Peter's, Rome   Plate 66
210 × 140 cm.
Condition: This picture was last cleaned in 1925 (Steinmann, p. 946) but its tone is nevertheless much lighter than that of the other three crypt chapel altarpieces, even the two cleaned in 1962. The surface of the *St. Helen* is, however, badly worn in the lower quarter. There is a prominent *pentimento* visible between the head of St. Helen and the cross on the right.
Drawings: A drawing at Düsseldorf (Harris and Schaar, no. 57 verso) of a standing male figure is close to St. Helen in pose, and may be a life study made with this composition in mind.
Engravings: 1771 Engraving by P. L. Bombelli dedicated to the Spanish Ambassador to the Holy See.
1829 Line engraving in Pistolesi, 1829, II, pl. XIV.
Documents: See above under *St. Veronica* (No. 36).
Bibliography: See above under *St. Veronica.* See also Posse, 1925, p. 55, note 6 and Hess, 1934, p. 298, note 7.

THE DECISION to have paintings on the altars in the underground chapels in the crossing of St. Peter's beneath the piers containing the relics and statues of St. Veronica, St. Andrew, St. Longinus and St. Helen, which in 1627 was considered impractical for at least two of the chapels, had been taken by January, 1633 (see Documents above under *St. Veronica*). Payments to the artist began in March, 1633. By August 19, 1634, he had been paid 650 scudi, or just over 150 scudi for each one. The final payment of 150 scudi, specifically for the *St. Helen*, was only made to him in September, 1650. This means that he was paid 200 scudi for each altarpiece and, if the documents are taken at their face value, that three of them were finished and work started on the fourth when the project was interrupted by unknown circumstances.[1] Stylistic analysis confirms what the documents suggest, namely that the *St. Veronica, St. Andrew* and *St. Longinus* altarpieces are works of the early 1630s, while the *St. Helen* is a work of the 1640s.[2]
The order in which the three altarpieces painted in the 1630s were made is not specified by the documents, but the *St. Veronica* may have been the first completed. If so, it would follow the Capuchins'

St. Anthony, finished in the spring of 1633, with which it has one significant point in common. In both works, the crowd watching takes up a major part of the picture surface; in the *St. Longinus* and *St. Andrew* altarpieces, on the other hand, the crowds of spectators have been pushed to one side or placed in the background on a much smaller scale, thus making the protagonists far more prominent. Nothing inherent in the iconography of these four subjects dictated that the spectators should be either visually prominent or subordinate.[3] It seems that Sacchi's style evolved while working on these four pictures, and that he moved towards the more concentrated, simplified designs, since it is this concentration and simplicity which mark his mature style, and which will be even more marked in the 1640s.
No preparatory studies for the *Veronica* have survived. Those for the *Longinus* and *Andrew,* delicately drawn in red chalk, are close in handling to those for the *St. Anthony.* These two compositions must therefore have been planned shortly after the *St. Anthony* and —since studies for both works are found on one sheet in one case —possibly planned together. Clearly Sacchi's ideas were evolving very fast at this time.
Against the hypothesis that these three altarpieces were finished by 1634, Hess has pointed out that the *Longinus* depends on Correggio's *Martyrdom of SS. Placidus and Flavia,* which it is assumed Sacchi would not have known before his trip to Lombardy in 1635. Hess also thought that Albani's *St. Andrew Adoring his Cross* in S. Maria dei Servi in Bologna of 1639–41 lay behind Sacchi's *St. Andrew* altarpiece, and preferred a date in the 1640s for all four altarpieces. There are, in fact, several earlier Roman sources for Sacchi's *St. Andrew* (see Introduction), while the Correggio could have been known to him from copies, or even seen during his earlier apprenticeship in Bologna before 1621.[4]
The *St. Helen* altarpiece is a very different work from the other three, so different indeed that one Passeri manuscript has the later marginal comment, 'd'altro pittore, che non fa al nostro proposito'. The composition is frontal and almost symmetrical. The figures are on a different, more monumental scale and obscure completely the transition from foreground to background which is such an important feature of the *St. Andrew* and *St. Longinus* altarpieces. This emphasis on the figures at the expense of the setting, and the increased scale of the figures and the austerity of surface treatment are all found in the eight canvases for the Lateran Baptistry executed in the 1640s. The *St. Helen* seems, however, to have been started in the 1630s. A red chalk study in Düsseldorf, which is probably a life study for St. Helen, is a drawing of the 1630s. In addition, a prominent *pentimento,* clearly visible in the photograph taken after the work was restored in 1925 (Plate 66), shows that an earlier and different composition was tried out on the same canvas. Between the head of St. Helen and that of the young man on the right holding the cross can be seen the head of a woman looking upwards. This must have been a preliminary version of St. Helen, since it only makes sense for her to be aware of the divine agent behind the miracle which in the final composition engrosses the attention of all the other figures. This earlier composition was obviously less symmetrical than the final one, and showed the saint placed at an angle to and not parallel to the picture plane, in a position similar to that used for the other three saints. The drawing proves, however, that the executed design was planned, even if not carried out, in the 1630s.
Until the *St. Helen* is X-rayed, it will be impossible to know how much of the first composition was incorporated into the final work. The youth in the foreground rising from his shroud does not seem out of key with the slighter figures in the other three altarpieces. His drapery has the same long, flowing, triangular fold forms found in the other three altarpieces, and which contrasts with the more classical, fluted folds used for St. Helen. It is also possible to imagine St. Helen standing behind him on the right, gesturing towards him in a pose similar to that finally used. The

man with the cross now occupies the space of the first St. Helen and must therefore be a later figure. Perhaps a similar figure appeared on the left in the first design. The pure, classical head and 'all'antica' drapery of the young woman on the left indicate that she is part of the work executed in the 1640s. The old woman above her looks like a last-minute addition, for it is not clear where she is standing, nor what her hands are doing. Her presence creates a relief composition of almost symmetrically disposed figures, very different from the open, fluid designs of the other three altarpieces. The circumstances that delayed the completion of the *St. Helen* until 1650 are easily guessed. Sacchi was too busy before going to North Italy some time after June, 1635, to finish the *St. Bonaventure* for the Capuchins, a work possibly commissioned as early as 1631. On his return from North Italy, the completion of the *St. Bonaventure* altarpiece was followed in quick succession by the sacristy of S. Maria sopra Minerva, a major project, by paintings and architectural commissions for Cardinal Giori, by various tasks for Cardinal Antonio Barberini and by the planning, supervision and partial execution of the decoration of the Lateran Baptistry. That Sacchi was less than enthusiastic about finishing an altarpiece for a dark, underground chapel, where it would never be seen properly, and where it would soon be seriously affected by damp, is also understandable.

1. See final paragraph. Baglione describes all four pictures in place in 1639, and this would appear to be confirmed by Bonanni (II, p. 606), who records that a special Mass was celebrated on September 22, 1639, after their installation. Baglione must have included the *St. Helen*, knowing it was intended for the last crypt altar, in order to make his account complete for later readers, while Bonanni's Mass may have been to celebrate the final installation of the three, finished pictures. For other inaccuracies in contemporary accounts of the decoration of St. Peter's, see Lavin, 1968, p. 26, note 125.
2. All four pictures were removed from St. Peter's between 1681, when a committee recommended that this be done because of the damp (Posse, 1925, p. 56), and 1639, when Rossini mentions that they had been replaced by mosaics. The originals were kept first in the Sala di Concistoro (Rossini), then moved to the Quirinale (Rossini, 1704, p. 23; Pascoli) and eventually to Castelgandolfo, where they are recorded by Voss in 1924. In 1925 they were cleaned and restored (Steinmann) and moved to the Museo Petriano. They are now kept in the rooms near the sacristy where the Museo del Tesoro is installed.
3. See Lavin, 1968, p. 25 and p. 32, note 150, for some interesting remarks on the relative iconographic importance of these four saints, and on the ways this is demonstrated in their presentation by Bernini, Duquesnoy, Mocchi and Bolgi in the four statues in the crossing.
4. The first dated engraving of Correggio's *SS. Placidus and Flavia* is G. B. Vanni's of 1638. An undated engraving by Francesco Sus may well be earlier (see *Mostra del Correggio*, 1935, p. 185, nos. 11 and 12). Drawn copies may have circulated in the Bolognese studios of the Carracci and their followers.

40. The Festa del Saraceno in Piazza Navona, February 25, 1634. Museo di Roma (Palazzo Braschi), Rome   Plate 67

300 × 220 cm.

Condition: This painting was cleaned after its recent acquisition by the Museo di Roma. It is in excellent condition for a work of this kind, which might well have been neglected after memories of the occasion it commemorated had faded. Apart from some darkening of the areas in shadow on the left and along the bottom, the surface seems remarkably fresh and well preserved (see Incisa della Rocchetta, 1959, p. 26, note 8).

Drawings: An elaborate drawing on parchment in the Museo di Roma (410 × 360 mm.) is based on the engraving of this scene in the commemorative publication, *Festa Fatta in Roma alli 25 di Febraio, MDCXXXIV* of 1635. It is probably the same drawing recorded in the collection of Count Paar, Austrian Ambassador to the Holy See, in 1883. It measured 400 × 370 mm. (See Ademollo, 1883, p. 43 and Incisa della Rocchetta, 1959, p. 26, note 8.) There is a drawing in Windsor for the *Balletto* engraving in the *Festa Fatta* (Blunt and Cooke, no. 771 and fig. 76). A drawing in the Ashmolean of *A Conclave of Cardinals* (Parker, II, p. 476, no. 942) has been attributed to Sacchi because of its stylistic similarity to Windsor 771. The similarity exists but the attribution is not acceptable; the studies on the verso are definitely not by Sacchi.
Engravings: 1635   Engraving published as the last page in *Festa Fatta in Roma 25 di Febraio, MDCXXXIV*, Rome, 1635. The engraving is signed 'A S' and in the preface Sacchi is said to have provided drawings for the *Festa* or *Theatro*, the frontispiece, the *Balletto* and the *Comparse del Mantenitore*. The publisher, Vitale Mascardi, dedicated the book to Cardinal Antonio Barberini on February 5, 1635. It was reprinted without the engraved illustrations in 1654 as part of the *Raccolta di lettere scritte dal Cardinal Bentivoglio in tempo delle sue nunziature di Francia e di Fiandra*. This was the first time that the author of the account was stated to be Cardinal Bentivoglio (Ademollo, p. 157, note 9).

THE piazza is seen from the north end looking south, viewed probably from the roof of a palace. Only the façade of S. Giacomo degli Spagnuoli is immediately recognizable, as almost all the other buildings in the piazza have changed since 1634. Among the other buildings that can be made out in the distance are S. Andrea della Valle, the Palazzo della Cancelleria, the Palazzo Farnese and, on the hill in the distance on the right, S. Pietro in Montorio. Bleachers and barricades have been erected around the piazza to provide seats for the spectators for the jousting match and other celebrations which will take place in the central arena. On the lower right the boat of Fame, the culminating spectacle, is about to be pulled into the arena through a narrow opening.
Cardinal Antonio Barberini had originally planned to hold the *Festa del Saraceno* in January, 1634 to honour the Polish prince, Alexander Wasa, who left Rome, however, before preparations were complete.[1] Unwilling to waste the time and money spent on the preparations, it was decided to hold the *Festa* on the last Saturday before Lent instead, and it duly took place on February 25, 1634, in Piazza Navona. An elaborate account of the festivities was published about a year later by Vitale Mascardi, who apologized for the delay in his preface to the reader, explaining that it was in order to obtain four illustrations by Sacchi. The last of these four engravings, the *Theatro*, corresponds very closely with the painting in the Palazzo Braschi and formerly in the Barberini collection,[2] first attributed to Sacchi by Teti in 1642.[3]
The 1671 inventory for Cardinal Antonio attributes the perspective —that is, the architectural setting—to Filippo Gagliardi, a specialist who worked with Sacchi in the same capacity on several other occasions.[4] This is apparently the first time that they worked together, if the execution of the painting is contemporary with the *Festa* and Mascardi's commemorative publication, which seems probable. As with the Jesuit Centenary picture, Sacchi did very little of the work himself, but he certainly supervised it sufficiently to ensure a much higher degree of tonal unity and a much greater sense of atmospheric perspective than is found in Gagliardi's independent works,[5] or indeed in other contemporary pictures of the same kind.
None of Sacchi's preparatory studies for the *Theatro* survive, but a drawing at Windsor for the *Balletto* gives some idea of his approach to such a commission. The perspective was carefully worked out first and drawn with a straight-edge; then the figures were added. The larger, foreground figures gave the artist more

scope, yet the sketches in the margin show how much trouble he took over many of the smaller figures and suggest that Sacchi enjoyed recording an event which he had probably witnessed himself.

1. 'Viene considerato per humore bisbetico et fantastico ed in sostanza ha dato poco gusto.' Quoted by Ademollo (p. 24) from contemporary diaries.
2. Posse, 1925, p. 7, note 4 citing Incisa della Rocchetta, 1924, p. 71. See also Incisa della Rocchetta, 1959, p. 23 f. See also notes 3 and 4 below.
3. *Aedes Barberinae*, p. 164. The entry for the *Giostra* picture in Cardinal Antonio Barberini's 1644 inventory includes an elaborate frame ('. . . e nell'ornamento un quadro con una fama con l'arme del S. Prefetto sostenuta da putti di mano de Sacchi con ornam(ent)o tutto dorato con un cartellone da piedi per isscrittione con alcuni arnesi della giostra attaccata'), which by 1671 has been broken up, and the picture of Fame catalogued separately (see Lavin, 1644, no. 5; 1671, nos. 265 and 419; 1672, nos. 101 and 338. The picture of Fame is recorded also in an undated inventory of Prince Maffeo made between 1672 and 1686 [Lavin no. 170], and in an inventory of the contents of the Palazzo Barberini made in 1686 [Lavin no. 6]. It has subsequently disappeared.)
4. 'Un quadro grande . . . rappresentante la Giostra di Piazza Navona con la prospettiva di Filippo Gagliardi, Cavalli del Manciola e figurine' (Lavin, 1671, no. 265; in the 1672 inventory, Lavin no. 101, the value is increased from 300 scudi to 380 and the 'figurine' are said to be 'di Andrea Sacchi alcune'. These two inventories are almost identical, and the added phrase seems to have been omitted in error from the first description). For other occasions when Sacchi worked with Gagliardi, see Nos. 45 and 63.
5. An interior view of St. Peter's in the Prado is signed and dated 1640 (Pérez Sánchez, p. 279); in S. Martino ai Monti there are two frescoes of Old St. Peter's and S. Giovanni Laterano before its transformation by Borromini (Sutherland, I and II, *sub voce*). Most of Gagliardi's other recorded works are engravings, for example in G. B. Ferrari's *Hespérides*, published in 1646 but for which preparations were in hand by 1640 (Bean, 1959, pp. 26–7), or the architectural settings for cardinals' portraits in an appendix to the 1647 edition of Teti's *Aedes Barberinae*. He was employed in S. Martino ai Monti from 1648 until 1655, on architectural designs as well as on the frescoes named above (Sutherland, *loc. cit.*), and was President of the Academy of St. Luke, of which he first attended meetings in 1648 (Archivo dell'Accademia di S. Luca, Vol. 43, p. 66 verso and 67), from 1656–7. He died around 1659 (these last two dates from Noack in Thieme-Becker, *sub voce*).

Bibliography: Mascardi, 1635, *passim*; Teti, 1642, p. 164; Ademollo, 1883, pp. 23–58; Clementi, Filippo, *Il Carnevale Romano*, Rome, 1899, pp. 379–402; Incisa della Rocchetta, 1924, pp. 68 and 71–2; Voss, 1924, p. 532; Posse, 1925, pp. 7, 8 and pl. II; Incisa della Rocchetta, 1959, pp. 20–37; Blunt and Cooke, 1960, pp. 96–7 and fig. 76; Haskell, 1963, pp. 55–6.

41. Adam Grieving over the Dead Abel. Present location unknown.   Plate 69
Approx. 94 × 156 cm.
Drawings: Studies for the figure of Adam, Düsseldorf (Harris and Schaar, no. 57). A weak red chalk composition study in the Uffizi (no. 9518 Santarelli, 115 × 254 mm.) first published by Refice (p. 216) records some variations in the composition also found in a careful pen drawing in the Huntington Library in San Marino, California, brought to my attention by Professor Marcel Rothlisberger (Kitto Bible, fol. 551, 198 × 303 mm.). Both are studio

products, possibly by the same hand. A drawing in the British Museum attributed to Sacchi by Philip Pouncey (1956.4.14.13, red chalk with pen and ink on cream paper, 227 × 315 mm.) has a number of composition studies including one clearly based on Sacchi's *Adam and Abel*, but it is the work of a pasticheur and is far too weak to be by Sacchi himself.
Versions: 1644 'Un quadro sopraporto di Adamo, che piange Abele ucciso da Caino, di mano del Sig.r Andrea Sacchi con cornice tutta dorata' is recorded in the 1644 inventory of Cardinal Antonio Barberini (Incisa della Rocchetta, p. 73). Although a version of this subject is recorded in later Barberini inventories, it will be argued below that the 1644 version was given to Queen Christina, and the later Barberini references record the version they bought from Sacchi in 1662, since two pictures of this subject by Sacchi never appear in any Barberini inventories, and Queen Christina acquired one between 1652 and her death in 1689. It is first recorded in her possession in the inventory made of her collection after her death as 'Un altro quadro con Adamo genuflesso che piange Abel morto, in paese, d'Andrea Sacchi, in tela a giacere alta p(al)mi quattro e large p(al)mi sei e tre quarti, con cornice liscia dorata alla fiorentina' (Campori, 1870, p. 737 and Granberg, p. lxxxv). It was later bought by the Duke of Orleans and went to Paris.[1] It was sold in London at the end of the eighteenth century (see Bildt, pp. 1000–1003) and has since disappeared.[2] According to Hortemels' engraving (Plate 68) in the *Recueil d'Estampes* (no. 115), it was painted in oil on canvas and measured 94 × 157 cm.
1661 Three versions said to depict *Cain and Abel* but almost certainly of *Adam and Abel* are recorded in Sacchi's house in 1661 (Appendix II, nos. 165, 223 and 237). One of these was bought by the Barberini from Sacchi's heirs on November 28, 1662 for 80 scudi (Incisa della Rocchetta, p. 74). It will be argued below that this is the version recorded in the 1671 inventory of Cardinal Antonio ('Un quadro grande di p(al)mi 4 e 6 rappresentante Abelle morto con Adamo che lo piange, e Caino in lontananza che mostra fugire'; valued at 350 scudi, p. 524) and also in his 1672 inventory (p. 16), when it was moved to the Palazzo Barberini, and in Cardinal Antonio's undated inventory, and in the Case Barberini inventory of 1686 (p. 190, no. 168). It is noted by De Cotte in his account of the Palazzo Barberini made around 1689 (p. 205), but is not recorded again in the Palazzo Barberini until the Fidecommesso inventory of 1816 (Mariotti, p. 128). It is last recorded in the Palazzo Barberini in 1934, when it was photographed by the Gabinetto Fotografico Nazionale. It then passed to the Corsini family in Florence, who recently sold it to London. It is now in the Minneapolis Institute of Arts (oil on canvas, 113.5 × 151.7 cm.; Plate 69). The later history of the other two versions in the artist's house in 1661 is not recorded.
1746 Version bought in Rome by Matthew Brettingham for the Earl of Leicester and described as a copy after Sacchi by Carlo Maratta (Holkham MS, p. 108).
1783 Copy recorded in the Palazzo Colonna in 1783 (no. 112, 'Due Quadri sopra le Porte verso la Sala di palmi 4 e 8 per traverso, uno l'ubbriachezza di Noe, e l'altro Abelle ucciso da Caino—Copie buone di Andrea Sacchi', Colonna, 1783, p. 19). These copies are not recorded in later catalogues of or guides to the Palazzo Colonna and the present location of the *Cain and Abel* copy is not known.
1823 Version recorded in the collection of Conte Marco Merenda in Forlì as 'Un Quadro rappresentante la morte di Abele; la figura di Adamo, e Caino che fugge' (manuscript catalogue of the Merenda collection made in 1823 in the Biblioteca Comunale A. Saffi, Forlì). The Merenda collection was formed in Rome around 1730–40 (Calzini and Mazzatinta, p. 53). Posse reported that this picture was in poor condition in 1925. It is no longer traceable and may have been destroyed in the last war, according to a letter from Contessa Farnetti-Merenda. See also Voss, 1924, p. 690.
Engravings: c. 1660 Etching based on the painting formerly in the

Palazzo Barberini and inscribed 'Andrea Sachi inventor Ambrogio Coragioso skulpsit And Sachi inv (?)' along the lower edge. Mariette (*Abcedario*, v, p. 150) read the etcher's name correctly, but Nagler (xv, p. 542) attributed the print to Sacchi himself, while Posse (1925, p. 102, note 1) thought it was by Maratta. Nothing is known about Ambrogio Coraggioso except that he witnessed the first codicil to Sacchi's will on June 17, 1661, and was present when part of the inventory was prepared on June 22, 1661 (Appendix I). He was clearly a family friend. There is no way of telling whether the etching was made around 1660, when his contacts with Sacchi are documented, or at an earlier date. At all events, it was probably made before 1661. It is not a work of much quality. Possibly he was a pupil, or perhaps he was an amateur dilettante friend. Details such as the smoke on the altar near Cain, the crack in the upper layer of rocks on the altar and foreground details such as the straight shaft of the stick and the plants near Abel's right hand prove that this etching was based on the ex-Barberini version and not on Queen Christina's picture.

SACCHI'S composition, *Adam Grieving over the Dead Abel* (Genesis, IV, 1–16), existed in a number of versions, some attributed to the artist in old inventories, others recorded by engravings and etchings. The early history of the two most important versions is unclear; it is consequently difficult to establish the primacy of one. The first recorded version, and therefore presumably the prime version, was in Cardinal Antonio Barberini's collection by April, 1644. Three versions are recorded in the artist's house in 1661, one of which was bought by the Barberini from Sacchi's heirs in 1662. The next inventory of Cardinal Antonio, made in 1671, records only one version, as do all later Barberini inventories. There was one version in the Palazzo Barberini in 1934; it subsequently passed to the Corsini collection in Florence. The other version of some significance is that first recorded in the 1689 inventory of Queen Christina of Sweden. Since it does not appear on the inventory made of her collection in 1652, it was probably acquired after she came to Rome in 1655. The hypothesis that Cardinal Antonio gave her his version and acquired a second in 1662 to replace it explains both why only one version appears in Barberini inventories, and also why the version which belonged to Queen Christina appears, even in Hortemels' engraving (Plate 68), to have been of better quality than the version in the Palazzo Barberini in 1934. It also explains how Coraggioso was able to make a careful etched copy of the Barberini picture. The 1644 version was hung as a *sopraporta*, and clearly it would have been easier for Coraggioso to copy one of the versions in Sacchi's house rather than a picture hung well above eye level in the Palazzo Barberini.

Two facts argue against this theory. The picture bought by the Barberini in 1662 cost 80 scudi. The version recorded in the 1671 inventory of Cardinal Antonio was valued at 350 scudi. Either the second picture was better than the first, or the valuations were on the generous side. The other awkward fact is Bellori's failure to mention the prime version in the collection of Queen Christina, whom he served as librarian and whose pictures he must have known well. It may simply be an absent-minded omission, or he may have preferred to record its original location because in doing so he recorded the patron's name as well. At all events, he does not seem to have been very interested in either version, for he mistakenly records that the version in the Palazzo Barberini was on copper, a medium Sacchi is only known to have used once for a lost version of the *Dream of St. Joseph*. On the whole, the hypothesis proposed here solves many more problems than it raises, and will stand unless more substantial evidence to the contrary is found.

Some of the differences between Queen Christina's picture and that in the Barberini collection are discussed above in the entry on Coraggioso's etching. A close examination of Abel's head in the ex-Barberini painting, the etching and Hortemels' engraving will show that the weaknesses of drawing shared by the Barberini painting and the etching are not apparent in Hortemels' engraving. A comparison of Adam's right hand, palm held downwards, in the Düsseldorf drawing with the same hand in Hortemels' print and in the ex-Barberini picture will show that the drawing and engraving agree closely, and are of higher quality than the painting. The same applies to the rest of the figure of Adam and the drawing of those parts of Abel which seem weak in the painting. In other words, Queen Christina's version corresponds more closely to the one autograph preparatory study known than does the ex-Barberini picture. The last named is probably a studio copy, perhaps by Carlo Magnone, who is recorded working for Sacchi as a copyist in the 1640s. The Düsseldorf drawing suggests a date shortly before 1635 for the first version, as do other stylistic factors discussed in the introduction.[3]

1. Dubois du St. Gelais, *Description des Tableaux du Palais Royal*, Paris, 1727, p. 21. Granberg records it in Rome still in 1712 (*op. cit.*, p. ciii) but Posse quoted a manuscript in the Bibliothèque Nationale which mentions it in the collection sold to the Duke by the heirs of the Duke of Bracciano in 1695 (1925, p. 102, note 1). It was engraved by Frederic Hortemels (*Recueil d'Estampes*: no. 115), who died on November 5, 1738 (see Thieme-Becker, *ad vocem*).

2. Posse identified it with a *Cain and Abel* recorded in the collection of the Earl of Yarborough by Waagen (1857, p. 506) but an old photograph of this picture in the Witt Collection in London, whose mount carries the inscription 'Dr. Posse does not accept', shows that the Yarborough picture was a different composition entirely. There is no sign of Adam and both Cain and Abel are posed differently. It is not by Sacchi.

3. Abraham Collaert's engraving after Hans Bol's composition of Adam and Eve grieving over the death of Abel (illustrated in *La Revue de l'Art*, no. 11, 1970, p. 35, fig. 17) seems to have been adapted by Sacchi for his composition of Adam and Abel. Bol's Eve becomes Adam, while Bol's twisted pose for Abel is changed into a more natural, relaxed pose that still retains the main features of its source.

Bibliography: Bellori, 1672–96, p. 67; Passeri, 1678, p. 304; De Cotte, *c.* 1689, p. 205; Mariotti, 1892, p. 128; Voss, 1924, p. 532; Incisa della Rocchetta, 1924, p. 73; Posse, 1925, p. 101 f.; Hess, 1934, p. 304, note 4; Posse, 1935, p. 290; Refice, 1950, p. 216.

42. The Adoration of the Shepherds. Formerly Du Bois collection, Ghent
Drawings: There is a sheet at Düsseldorf (Harris and Schaar, no. 61) with studies for the young girl with a basket on her head. (Plate 71) A second Düsseldorf drawing recently connected with the Child (Harris and Schaar, no. 62) should rather be given to Maratta and connected with the Child in his fresco lunette, *The Adoration of the Shepherds* in S. Isidoro, Rome.
Versions: 1661 A *Nativity* in Sacchi's house in 1661 (Appendix II, no. 167) may have been a version of this composition.
Engraving: 1776 The Flemish engraver, Franz Pilsen, engraved the *Adoration of the Shepherds* in the collection of Jean Baptiste du Bois in Ghent before 1776, when the collection was sold (Lugt, 1938, no. 2586; the painting, measuring 44.5 × 35.5 cm., was painted on canvas mounted on wood). There is an example of the print in the Kunstmuseum, Düsseldorf (no. 7577, II, 20); Plate 70.

PILSEN'S ENGRAVING after a painting depicting *The Adoration of the Shepherds* and attributed to Sacchi has been ignored by all modern scholars. If Posse was aware of the print, he may have omitted it for lack of more substantial evidence in favour of the attribution, for the work as recorded by Pilsen is not obviously by Sacchi. The existence of an autograph study for one figure in the composition makes the attribution of the design to Sacchi at least plausible, and a date in the early 1630s probable.[1] The painting is last recorded in the 1781 sale of the Sollier collection in Paris (Lugt, 1938, no. 216) and may still be in a French private collection. Hopefully its publication here will lead to its rediscovery.[2]

1. The drawing is in the reverse sense of the print. There is a study on the verso for the painting in S. Maria del Priorato (Harris and Schaar, no. 58) executed probably between 1632 and 1636.
2. A weak drawing in the Louvre (no. 3832, red chalk and grey wash, 280 × 270 mm.) of an *Adoration of the Shepherds* is inscribed 'andrea sacqui olim ex collectione Dargenville—Eg. Destouches'. The composition echoes some details of the Du Bois composition but is not a copy of it. I have not been able to trace further information about the existence of any such work in the Dargenville collection.

Bibliography: Le Blanc, 1858, II, p. 30; Mireur, 1912, VI, p. 388; Harris and Schaar, 1967, p. 44.

43. Christ Crowned with Thorns and the Transfiguration.
Formerly Palazzo del Quirinale, Rome
Fresco, size unknown.
Drawings: Study for the figures of Christ and a soldier, British Museum (Fawkener collection no. 5211–79, black chalk on buff paper, 257 × 360 mm.), Plate 73; two studies for a second soldier with a faint sketch for the figure of Christ, Uffizi (no. 3545S, black chalk on buff paper, 265 × 375 mm.; Plate 72. It has an old attribution in chalk in the lower left corner to Domenichino. My attention was drawn to this sheet by Walter Vitzthum).
Documents: Sacchi was paid 200 scudi on May 7, 1635 'per intero pagamento delli lavori fatti nella Cappelletta del appartamento novo del Palazzo di Monte Cavallo'. Sacchi signed the receipt for the payment on May 10, 1635 (Achille Monti, 'Di Andrea Sacchi e della sua casa', *Il Buonarotti*, 1866, pp. 188–92. See also Posse, 1925, p. 66 and Pollak, II, pp. 516–17).

PASCOLI is virtually the only source of precise information about these lost frescoes formerly in the Pope's winter chapel in the Quirinale palace and his account is characteristically brief. He states that the frescoes consisted of 'N(ostro) S(ignore) coronato di spine con due altri figure a fresco nell'altare d'una piccola Cappella; e nella volta la di lui trasfigurazione'.[1] Sacchi is not recorded as having executed any other work in the Quirinale, so the payment made to him in May, 1635 for work in a small chapel must refer to these two frescoes. The location of the chapel, which no longer exists, is uncertain but it may have been near Mascherino's oval staircase at the west end of the main courtyard.[2]
Two drawings, one in the British Museum, the other in the Uffizi, for a *Crowning with Thorns* composition, can be associated with this commission. So far no drawings by or after Sacchi for a *Transfiguration* have been traced. The two drawings show that Sacchi was planning to paint not Christ mocked but Christ being prepared for that humiliation. Neither of the two soldiers handles Christ roughly or grimaces at him. One takes his arm in order to give him a reed to hold, the other crowns him. A robe draped over the latter soldier's arm is presumably the purple garment that will be draped round Christ's shoulders before the mocking begins. Christ is shown praying. The mood of scene suggested by these two drawings is in sharp contrast to that of the usual treatment of this theme with its brutality and crude juxtapositions of evil and goodness. Sacchi's treatment invites a different response from the viewer also than the anger and horror usually provoked by depictions of the treatment meted out to Christ by non-believers. Sacchi's quiet and thoughtful depiction of a different moment in the narrative encourages the visitor to the chapel to meditate and contemplate, a response appropriate to an altarpiece in a small, private chapel.

1. The only other source to give any details is the 1763 edition of Titi, which adds that the chapel had grotesques by G. P. Pannini but does not mention the *Transfiguration* in the vault. Totti merely says that there was work by Sacchi in the Quirinale, and Bellori only names the altar fresco in a list of works at the end of his *Vita*.
2. Briganti, 1962, p. 77. According to Moroni (1841, IX, p. 161), the chapel was destroyed during the French administration of the palace.

Bibliography: Totti, 1638, p. 278; Bellori, 1672–96, p. 65; Pascoli, 1730, I, pp. 16–17; Titi, 1763, p. 309; Posse, 1925, p. 66 f.; Posse, 1935, p. 290; Briganti, 1962, pp. 24 and 77.

44. Portrait of Francesco Albani (1578–1660). Museo del Prado, Madrid
Plate 74
73 × 54 mm.
Condition: The condition is basically good. The picture would benefit from a slight cleaning, but the flesh tones are remarkably fresh, even beneath a thin layer of yellowed varnish. The unfinished ground has darkened a little but is not so black as it appears in photographs.
Drawings: A red chalk 'portrait of Francesco Albani' attributed to Sacchi, exhibited by Colnaghi's in London in 1951 is neither connected with the Prado painting nor by Sacchi.
Versions: 1661 The version recorded in Sacchi's house at the time of his death (Appendix II, no. 210) was almost certainly the picture later in Maratta's collection and which passed from his collection into that of Philip V of Spain, and which is now in the Prado. Sacchi's portrait of Albani was hung beside Maratta's portrait of Sacchi in Maratta's house, where they were described as follows, 'Un ritratto del famoso Albano, fatto da Andrea Sacchi suo discepolo con cornice a oro' and 'Un ritratto del detto Andrea Sacchi fatto dal cav. Carlo Maratti suo discepolo, con cornice indorata' (Galli, XXII, p. 321, nos. 5 and 6; see also Maratta, 1724, p. 129, nos. 9 and 15, and cited Prado catalogues).
1664 The portrait of Albani in the Accademia di S. Luca in Rome inscribed 'Francesco Albano, pitt. 1664' is clearly based on the Prado picture, and may have been commissioned by Maratta for the Accademia since he was Principe in 1664 and owned the original at the time.
1704 An engraving of 1704 by Pietro de' Pietri in the Dahlem Museum, Berlin, includes an oval portrait of Francesco Albani said to be based on a portrait of Albani in the Palazzo Verospi. The portrait is fully finished around the bust, but otherwise follows the Prado picture closely. There is no other record of this portrait in the Palazzo Verospi, which contains frescoes by Albani, and there is no way of telling whether it was an autograph work, or a version by a pupil of Sacchi or Maratta.
Engravings: 1678 An engraving inscribed 'And. Sacchi pinxit, Stephanus Picart sculp. Romae, Franciscus Albanus Bonon. pictor. annorum 83' was used by Malvasia as the frontispiece to his life of Albani in the *Felsina Pittrice* (1678, II, p. 222).
1704 An engraving of 1704, designed by Pietro de' Pietri and cut by Girolamo Frezza, includes in an allegorical setting an oval portrait of Albani said to be in the Palazzo Verospi. Neither the portrait nor this engraving are recorded in the literature. There is a good example of it in the Dahlem Museum, Berlin (802–77).

ACCORDING to Bellori, Sacchi painted this portrait of his old teacher, Francesco Albani, when he visited him in Bologna during the trip he made to North Italy between July, 1635 and August, 1636.[1] Bellori also says that Bologna was the first town Sacchi visited, which means that the portrait can be dated 1635, when Albani was fifty-seven. The two men are not known to have met again at a later date. Since the portrait belonged to Sacchi and is clearly unfinished, it would seem to be a personal *ricordo*, although if the lost Palazzo Verospi version was by Sacchi, it would appear that he used it as a model for finished versions for other patrons. The unfinished portrait was bought by Maratta after Sacchi's death. He made the portrait of Sacchi to hang with it, thus underlining their common line of artistic descent. Bellori's description of the picture—'essendo di Color fresco, e rubicondo, come si conservava quel buon, e venerando vecchio'—is accurate and suggests that Bellori knew the original, probably when it was in Maratta's possession.[2]

Albani's *Self-Portrait* in the Uffizi[3] is close to Sacchi's portrait of Albani in composition but Albani is clearly a much younger man in the former. Maybe Sacchi used a version of it as a model. The two portraits make a telling comparison, Sacchi's being a far more penetrating psychological study, as is to be expected.

1. The dates of this visit are not certainly known, but he probably left Rome shortly after June, 1635, when he was paid 200 scudi by Cardinal Antonio Barberini (Incisa della Rocchetta, 1924, p. 65 and Posse, 1925, p. 75). He is not documented in Rome again until November 14, 1636, when he attended a meeting of the Academy of St. Luke (Arch. Acad. S. Luca, vol. 43, *s.v.*).
2. Prince Leopold de' Medici tried to obtain either the originals or copies by Maratta of Sacchi's *Albano* and Maratta's *Sacchi* for his collection of artists' self-portraits and portraits in 1666 but the negotiations must have fallen through because no versions joined the collection (Prinz, p. 176). The Prince's agent, Paolo Falconieri, described Sacchi's portrait as unfinished, 'ma la testa è meravigliosa a segno, che non pare ch'egli potessi far tanto'. His agent also wrote that 'di Andrea Sacco non vi è ritratto alcuno dipinto, nè di mano propria, nè di altri, e che solo ve ne sono due fatti con il disegno, uno de' quali l'ha lui (Maratta), e l'altro dice essere in mano di altro pittore' (Prinz, p. 120).
3. Boschetto in *Proporzioni*, 1948, p. 138 and fig. 170.

Bibliography: Bellori, 1672–96, pp. 56 and 68; Malvasia, 1678, II, pp. 192 and 222; Voss, 1924, p. 532; Posse, 1925, p. 125 f.; Posse, 1935, p. 290; Pérez Sánchez, 1965, pp. 325–6; W. Prinz, *Die Sammlung der Selbstbildnisse in den Uffizien*, Band I, Geschichte der Sammlung, Berlin, 1971, pp. 120 and 176. Prado catalogues: 1823, p. 31 (no. 360); 1828, p. 202 (no. 685); 1843, p. 129 (no. 622); 1845, p. 145 (no. 622); 1885, no. 358; 1933, p. 754 (no. 326); 1945, p. 556 (no. 326); 1952, p. 581 (no. 326).

45. The Vision of St. Bonaventure. S. Maria della Concezione, Rome   Plate 76
Approximately 290 × 200 cm.
Condition: There is insufficient natural or artificial light in the chapel in which this picture hangs for its condition to be assessed accurately. It is dirty and obscured by yellowed varnish and has certainly darkened to some extent. The only obvious damage is flaking and paint loss along the lower edge. A *pentimento* is visible to the left of the head of the angel behind St. Bonaventure.
Drawings: Study probably for the figure of St. Bonaventure, Holkham Hall, Norfolk, collection the Earl of Leicester (Portfolio IV, no. 9, black chalk with white heightening on buff paper, 368 × 250 mm.). There is a careful red chalk copy after the painting in Düsseldorf (Harris and Schaar, no. 115).
Versions: 1644 A version almost certainly of this composition is recorded in the 1644 inventory of Cardinal Antonio Barberini as 'S. Clemente Papa, che incensa la Vergine con il Bambino, del Sig.r Andrea Sacchi, con cornice tutta dorata' (Incisa della Rocchetta, 1924, pp. 72–3; Posse, 1925, p. 100, note 1; Lavin no. 186). No St. Clement appears in later Barberini inventories, but 'Un quadretto di tela di testa rappresentante S. Buonaventura che

incensa la Beat^ma Vergine assisa sopra le Nuvole' in Cardinal Antonio's 1671 inventory is surely the same picture (Lavin, no. 154). In 1672, it was transferred to the Palazzo Barberini (Lavin, no. 265), and it is recorded subsequently in an undated inventory of Prince Maffeo made between 1672 and 1686 (Lavin, no. 49) and in a 1686 inventory of the contents of the Palazzo Barberini (Lavin, no. 593). In the Palestrina inventory of 1738–9 (no. 50), it is described as 'Un Santo Papa inginocchioni avanti la Madonna con Bambino e diverse Angeli uno de quali tiene l'ancora, bozzetto di Andrea Sacchi' (Posse, *loc. cit.*). It has since disappeared.
1712 A small version possibly of this composition was in Maratta's collection in 1712 (no. 274, 'Due quadretti dove sono un Puttino nell'uno, mano d'Andrea Sacchi, e nell'altro un San Bonaventura, con sue cornici bianche'. See Galli, 1928, p. 69). The wording of the inventory is ambiguous, and the *St. Bonaventure* may not have been by Sacchi at all. Its later history is not recorded.

THE *Vision of St. Bonaventure* was, like the *Miracle of St. Anthony of Padua* of 1633, made for a chapel in the Capuchins' new church, S. Maria della Concezione, and is, again like the *St. Anthony,* undocumented. The date can be narrowed down to 1635–6, however, from various bits of circumstantial evidence.[1]
Although possibly commissioned with some of the other altarpieces in 1631 as soon as the decision to decorate the interior had been taken, the awarding of this particular commission may have been delayed until 1633, when the Capuchins moved to their new quarters from their old church, S. Bonaventura near the Trevi fountain. The relics of St. Bonaventure were moved to S. Maria della Concezione, and the Lucchese community, who took over the Capuchins' old church, dedicated it to S. Croce.[2] Then Passeri and Bellori both state that the *St. Bonaventure* altarpiece was the first work completed by Sacchi on his return from his trip to North Italy. This journey probably began shortly after June, 1635; Sacchi is not recorded in Rome again until November, 1636 (see Cat. 44, note 1). The completed and decorated church was, however, dedicated on August 31, 1636 (Isnello, p. 94). Bellori specifically states that Sacchi was away for a year. If Sacchi was back by June, 1636, he would have had two months in which to complete the *St. Bonaventure*. Bellori also states that Sacchi was under pressure from Cardinal Antonio to finish it, since the other altarpieces were ready, and in fact those which can be dated were all ready by 1635.[3] Perhaps the dedication ceremony was delayed until the late summer of 1636 in order to include the *St. Bonaventure*.
There are several indications that this picture was completed rapidly with the help of assistants. The modelling of the two putti on the left is particularly insensitive. Moreover, Bellori states that the architecture was by Filippo Gagliardi, an attribution borne out by comparison with his documented works in the Prado and S. Martino ai Monti in Rome.[4] He uses a simple box-like construction with a viewpoint slightly to left or right of centre and generally a low horizon. All Sacchi's works having perspective settings of this kind were done with Gagliardi and are views of specific places on particular occasions (see Nos. 40 and 64). Gagliardi's intervention also explains the difference in quality between this and all Sacchi's other altarpieces with interior, architectural settings. The altar shown here is in ideal elevation at right angles to the picture plane, its invisible front indicated only by the edge of the altar cloth. The tunnel perspective of the vault distracts the eye from the figures, whose relationship with the setting is uneasy. Passeri, who did not realize that two artists were involved, criticized the 'punto di vista stravagante'.
Sacchi and Gagliardi were in contact by 1635 (see No. 40). It seems possible that Sacchi planned the composition of the *St. Bonaventure* before leaving for North Italy in 1635, giving Gagliardi *carte blanche* to paint the setting during his absence. On his return, Sacchi had only to paint the main figures, the putti and accessories being the responsibility of an assistant, possibly Carlo Magnone.

The pose shown in a carefully finished drawing at Holkham for a figure who in pose and costume closely resembles St. Bonaventure differs from that executed mainly in being less frontal. The drawing suggests that a slightly different composition was originally planned, as does the *pentimento* visible beside the face of the angel behind the saint, which seems to be a frontal view of the strange cup held by the putti on the left in the final design, for in that position the cup could fit in with the pose of the saint recorded in the Holkham drawing. With the Virgin in the position she now occupies, the result would have been a very austere design with both main figures in profile and a strong diagonal division from top left to bottom right. Possibly the architecture as originally planned by Sacchi compensated for the severity of the figure design, and perhaps Gagliardi failed to carry out Sacchi's instructions precisely and spoilt the first design. Even a slight change in the angle of the barrel vault in relation to the picture plane, or in the level of the viewpoint for example, would make a great deal of difference. On his return from North Italy, Sacchi found that the planned figure composition was too stiff and left dead areas, especially in the upper right. By making St. Bonaventure's pose more open and by setting him further back and at an angle to the picture plane, and by giving him two supporting angels, Sacchi added some three-dimensional complexity to the foreground and blocked out the lower reaches of the tunnel vault. Whether or not the reconstruction of the two stages in the painting of this altarpiece proposed here is correct—and only the discovery of preparatory studies and a radiograph of the picture will provide the answer—some knowledge of the awkward circumstances of its creation is needed in order to understand the disappointing final result.

1. Posse dated it 1649 in 1925 but revised this to before 1640 in 1935, presumably influenced by Hess, who thought that Algardi's *St. Philip Neri* in the sacristy of the Chiesa Nuova was inspired by Sacchi's altarpiece. Only Waterhouse dated the *St. Bonaventure* within the period indicated by Isnello's history of the church, that is 1631–6.
2. Isnello, pp. 84–92 and Ciacconius, IV, col. 520.
3. See Isnello, pp. 57–8, 88 and 94; Gnudi and Cavalli, p. 87; Briganti, 1962, p. 193 and Vitzthum in the *Burl. Mag.*, CV, 1963, p. 215.
4. For Gagliardi, see Cat. No. 40, note 5. It is woth noting that Gagliardi, whose specialty might be called architectural portraiture, has based the setting of the *St. Bonaventure* on the interior of the Capuchins' new church, although iconographically this setting has no significance for the event depicted. Oddly enough, the altar shown is neither in the position of a side altar in the present church, nor can it be the high altar. This may be deliberate, to indicate that, although St. Bonaventure is now commemorated in S. Maria della Concezione, the miracle did not actually take place there.

Bibliography: Totti, 1638, p. 301; Titi, 1674, p. 380 (and all later editions); Passeri, 1678, p. 299; Bellori, 1672–96, p. 57; Sebastiani, 1689, p. 125; Panciroli, 1719, II, p. 402; Pascoli, 1730, I, p. 16; Rossini, 1750, p. 170 (1776, II, p. 176; 1789, II, p. 176); Roisecco, 1750, II, p. 240; Vasi, 1770 (1765), p. 105; Pistolesi, 1841, p. 369 (1846, *ibid.*); Voss, 1924, p. 531; Posse, 1925, pp. 68 f. and 99 f.; Hess, 1934, p. 299, note 1; Posse, 1935, p. 210; Waterhouse, 1937, p. 92.

46. The Decoration of the Sacristy of S. Maria sopra Minerva and the Room of St. Catherine of Siena. S. Maria sopra Minerva, Rome Plates 75, 77–84
The first part of the catalogue entry concerns the decoration of the sacristy and the designs for the altar area and the room of St. Catherine behind it. The altarpiece and fresco above it are catalogued separately below.

Drawings: There is a chalk and wash study at Windsor for a cartouche containing a Dominican emblem, a dog with a torch in its mouth (Blunt and Cooke, no. 786).
Documents: There are payments connected with the restoration and decoration of the sacristy and the room of St. Catherine from 1638 to 1644 (Incisa della Rocchetta, 1624, p. 66).

Christ Crucified with St. Dominic, St. Thomas Aquinas, St. Peter Martyr, an unidentified Dominican Saint and St. Catherine of Siena. S. Maria sopra Minerva, Rome Plates 75, 77
Approximately 300 × 175 cm.
Condition: This picture was cleaned in 1970–1. It proved to have been badly damaged by an earlier cleaning attempt during which much of the paint surface, especially on the torso of Christ, was removed. Only the lilies in front of St. Catherine have survived in good condition.
Version: 1712 'Un Christo in croce con cornice bianca, mano d'Andrea Sacchi' in Maratta's collection in 1712 (Galli, 1928, p. 64, no. 203) may have been a version of the Christ in the Minerva picture.
Documents: No payments to Sacchi specifically stated to be for this altarpiece are recorded in Cardinal Antonio Barberini's accounts, but Simone Lagi was paid 142.79 scudi on April 16, 1638 for gilding the 'Camera di S. ta Caterina e (la) Capella della Sagrestia della Minerba' (Incisa della Rocchetta, 1924, p. 66). This payment provides a probable *terminus ante quem* for the altarpiece.

Six Putti and an Angel Carrying the Attributes of five Dominican Saints. Frescoed vault in the altar recess of the sacristy, S. Maria sopra Minerva, Rome Plate 78
Fresco, approximately 91.5 × 363 cm.
Condition: Apart from small retouchings, which have darkened, the general condition of the fresco is good.
Drawings: Refice (pp. 216–17 and fig. 217) tentatively linked a drawing in the Uffizi (no. 9522) with this fresco, but there is no formal connection, and stylistically the drawing has no connection with Sacchi either.
Documents: A payment for gilding in the altar recess quoted above provides a definite *terminus ante quem* of April 16, 1638 for Sacchi's fresco.

DOCUMENTS concerning the alteration and decoration of the sacristy of S. Maria sopra Minerva between 1637 and 1644 are sparse and uninformative. The early sources are vague and contradictory. Nevertheless, it is possible, using the existing evidence, to provide a more precise account of the chronology of the work and of Sacchi's contribution to it than those hitherto attempted.
An inscription on the back of the altar wall of the sacristy (Plate 79) records that in 1637 Cardinal Antonio Barberini sponsored the removal of the room in which St. Catherine of Siena died from its original site in the attached convent to its present site behind the sacristy altar.[1] Totti (1637, p. 61) records that work on the restoration of the sacristy had already begun that year,[2] although payments are recorded only from 1638 onwards. Sacchi is never specifically named in connection with the work in the Minerva, but the unusually large sum of 965.80 scudi, which he received from Cardinal Antonio on June 11, 1639,[3] cannot be connected with any other major project with which he is known to have been involved.[4] The payment is, moreover, much too large to be associated with one altarpiece and one fresco, and indicates that Sacchi's responsibilities in the sacristy must have been greater, more in line, in fact, with the role attributed to him there by Bellori, who states that Sacchi was the author of all the architecture and pictorial decoration.
The installation of St. Catherine's room behind the sacristy altar (Plate 81) affected at least the design of the architecture now surrounding the room, of the means of access to the room and of the altar recess in front of it with its altarpiece dedicated to St.

Catherine and other Dominican saints (Plate 80). The saint's room is small—approximately 10 feet wide, 20 feet long and 15 feet high.[5] The intention was clearly to treat it like a relic, enclosing it behind the altar and making it visible to the officiating priest. To this end the room was raised some four feet above the ground and set some four feet behind the sacristy. A grille inserted in the wall of the sacristy chapel below the altarpiece and at the eye level of an officiating priest allows him to see through to the room beyond. The old walls of the saint's room are concealed by a new shell of shallow niches framed by Corinthian pilasters. A small double staircase in the space behind the altar gives access to the room; doors on either side of the altar recess allow pilgrims to pass from the sacristy to the saint's room beyond. It is the architecture and decoration of this complex that must have concerned Sacchi.

Bellori says that the convent was in a poor state of repair and was renovated by Sacchi when he did the sacristy, but Baglione (p. 181) says that the rebuilding of the convent in hand in 1642 was the responsibility of Paolo Marucelli, while some of the frescoes in the sacristy certainly predate the 1637 alterations.[6] In fact, apart from the installation of St. Catherine's room, no major structural alterations were involved, which is why previous scholars have been reluctant to credit Sacchi with any architectural duties in S. Maria sopra Minerva.[7] His role was certainly smaller than that claimed for him by Bellori, but it was an architectural commission in part, and coincides with the earliest reference to Sacchi as an architect in the Barberini archives.[8]

Stylistic analysis of the architecture and decorative motifs in that part of the sacristy affected by the installation of St. Catherine's room provides further support for an attribution to Sacchi. The design of the exterior walls of the saint's room is one of Grecian purity. Shallow niches are framed by Corinthian pilasters which meet at the two projecting angles of the room (Plate 83). Each niche is set above a plain, square panel, the whole unit being framed in a rectangular moulding with a Barberini bee in the upper corners (Plate 84). Above the pilasters is a frieze containing attributes of St. Catherine and the Barberini family. The architecture is clearly based on the design of the Holy House at Loreto,[9] but the simplicity and almost neo-classic character of the design contrasts with both its prototype and contemporary Roman architecture. It does recall, however, the background of Sacchi's *Miracle of St. Anthony of Padua* (Plate 61), where a very similar arrangement of niche enclosed in a rectangular moulding with Barberini bees in the upper corners and a flanking Corinthian order is used. They are columns, not pilasters, as befits the implied scale of the setting of St. Anthony's miracle, while the absence of decorative detail can be explained by the architecture's role as background. Two drawings at Windsor for the architectural setting and frame of an altarpiece[10] also show Sacchi working in a similar idiom—well-proportioned architectural forms of conservative, classical derivation, recalling early Renaissance designs but lacking their fragility and linear emphasis.

The frame of the 1637 inscription (Plate 79), the door frames in the sacristy (Plate 80) and the cupboards (Plate 82) and stucco decoration around the altar and fresco are treated very differently from the exterior of St. Catherine's room. In these areas, the freedom with which traditional motifs are distorted and blended with anthropomorphic forms recalls Pietro da Cortona or even Borromini. There is no need, however, to attribute the design of these details to another hand. Similar forms are found on the throne of Divine Wisdom in the Palazzo Barberini fresco (Plate 29) and in the painted and stucco frames surrounding it. Sacchi, like Bernini and Cortona, evidently used a more sober artistic vocabulary for the architecture of exteriors than for interior furniture and accessories. His drawing at Windsor of the Dominicans' punning symbol, a dog holding a flaming torch, in a cartouche, is also evidence of his concern with the decoration of this Dominican commission.

Although Sacchi was paid for his work in S. Maria sopra Minerva in June, 1639, work continued there until 1644. Sacchi began the plans for S. Giovanni in Fonte in May, 1639. It must have prevented him from supervising at all closely the remaining work in the Minerva, for the gold and grisaille decoration of the vaulting surrounding Bastoro's fresco, apparently executed at this time, is of disappointing quality. It has so little to do with Sacchi stylistically that it seems improbable that he did more than provide rough drawings for it.

The arguments in favour of an attribution to Sacchi of the architectural alterations to the sacristy of S. Maria sopra Minerva after the installation of St. Catherine's room and its subsequent decoration are not conclusive, but this hypothesis accounts for the known circumstances of the commission, for Sacchi's description in Cardinal Antonio's household from 1637 onwards as architect as well as painter, for the 1000 scudi payment made to Sacchi by Cardinal Antonio in 1639 and for Bellori's account of Sacchi's role in the Minerva. Stylistic analysis supports rather than contradicts this conclusion. The attribution to Sacchi of the sacristy altarpiece has never been doubted.[11] The fresco above it has sometimes been called assistant's work, but there is no reason to think that Sacchi did not paint it himself.[12]

1. CARDINALIS ANTONIUS BARBERINUS / ORDINIS PRAEDICATORUM PROTECTOR / OB SINGULAREM / IN SANCTAM CATHARINAM VIRGINEM / SENENSEM EIUSDEM ORDINIS / PIETATEM / CUBICULUM / UBI SERAPHICA VIRGO / SPONSUM NUNQUAM OCCIDENTEM SOLEM EXCEPIT / UNDE / AD SEMPER ORIENTIS THALAMUM EVOLAVIT / AB ANTIQUIS AEDIBUS SEIUNXIT / ET IN HOC SACRARIO AD MAIOREM EIUS CULTUM / COLLOCAVIT / ANNO DOMINI MDCXXXVII. This inscription was missed by Forcella.

2. Some work in the sacristy had been carried out earlier. It has a rectangular ceiling fresco by Giuseppe Puglia ('Il Bastoro', d. 1636) showing the apotheosis of St. Dominic, probably executed in the mid-twenties when he and some other third-rate Mannerists were working in the cloister nearby (Baglione, 1642, pp. 310, 351, 354, 361 and 376). The wooden cupboards in the main body of the sacristy, which differ in design from those in the altar recess here attributed to Sacchi, could also be of this date. The date of G. B. Speranza's overdoor fresco of the Conclave of 1431 is not known, but it may have been painted around 1631 to commemorate the bicentenary of that event. For the earlier history of the sacristy, see Baglione, 1642, p. 358; Passeri, p. 175; Berthier, p. 283 and Thieme-Becker, XXVII, p. 454.

3. According to Incisa della Rocchetta, *loc. cit.* Posse (1925, p. 71) says that Sacchi was paid 1045 scudi.

4. The sum is too large for a single altarpiece: only one of exceptional size and prestige, such as the largest altarpiece in St. Peter's, was so lavishly rewarded. It was not usual for an artist to be paid a large, lump sum for several, unconnected pieces of work. Payments for S. Giovanni in Fonte, which start in 1639, were all made through Angelo Giori, the Papal chamberlain. The only possible alternative explanation would be the decoration of the Gesù for the Jesuit Centenary celebrations in 1639, but as these took place in September and October, the 1000 scudi payment would have to be an advance, and it is improbably large for such a purpose.

5. For details of the interior of the room and its decoration, see A. Gottschewski. *Die Fresken . . . des Antoniazzo Romano im Sterbe-Zimmer der Heiligen Caterina von Siena zu S. Maria sopra Minerva in Rom,* Strassburg, 1904, and Armellini, 1942, p. 1362.

6. See note 2 above.

7. Wibiral (pp. 56–7) is the most recent writer to reject Bellori's statement. Piacentini (1940, pp. 29–30), quoting Bellori,

discusses the design of the convent as if it was by Sacchi but does so in such general terms that it is impossible to know which parts of the building he thinks are new and which old.

8. Posse, 1925, p. 6. Antonio Gerardi, in his description of the Jesuit Centenary celebrations published in 1639, calls Sacchi 'Architetto e Pittore', a point noted by Incisa della Rocchetta (p. 67). Sacchi is also called architect in the Stati d'Anime records of 1642 and 1644 (Hoogewerff, *art. cit. sub voce*). Maurizio Fagiolo dell'Arco has recently attributed the decoration here given to Sacchi to Borromini but without considering the evidence discussed here ('1638: una decorazione inedita', *Studi sul Borromini, Atti del Convegno promosso dall' Accademia Nazionale di San Luca*, 1967, Rome, 1972, II, 201–5).

9. This parallel was brought to my attention by Sir Anthony Blunt.

10. Blunt and Cooke, nos. 784 and 785 and fig. 75.

11. The only exception is Berthier, whose judgement ('...d'Andrea Sacchi ou de son école', p. 283) was perhaps prejudiced by the condition of the picture.

12. The fresco is not mentioned by Passeri and is ignored by most of the guide books of the seventeenth and eighteenth centuries. Posse thought it was by assistants, but Waterhouse and Refice thought it was autograph. Waterhouse identified the objects carried by the putti wrongly as instruments of Christ's Passion.

Bibliography: Where an author refers only to one or two of the three parts of the Minerva commission, this is specified by the following abbreviations in parenthesis: s—the decoration of the sacristy; a—the altarpiece; f—the fresco. Totti, 1637, p. 61 (s); Totti, 1638, p. 382 (s); Baglione, 1642, p. 171 (s, a); Martinelli, 1658, pp. 239–40 (s); Bellori, 1672–96, p. 58; Titi, 1674, p. 180 (s, a; and all later editions incl. 1763, p. 162); Pascoli, 1730, I, p. 16; Rossini, 1750, p. 184 (and 1776, II, p. 370); Pistolesi, 1841, p. 414 (1846, *ibid.*); Berthier, 1910, p. 283; Incisa della Rocchetta, 1924, p. 66; Posse, 1925, p. 71 f.; Posse, 1935, p. 290; Waterhouse, 1937, p. 92; Piacentini, 1940, pp. 29–30 (s); Refice, 1950, pp. 216–17; (a, f); Wibiral, 1955, pp. 57–8 (s).

47. St. Catherine of Siena in Prayer. Dulwich College Picture Gallery, London   Plate 86
87.7 × 101.6 cm.

Condition: The canvas is rectangular but the picture has until recently been kept in a circular frame. The paint has darkened but a cleaning would improve visibility. The copy at Bamberg suggests that the Dulwich picture may have been cut down slightly at the sides.

Versions: 1661 A version probably of this composition was in the artist's house in 1661 (Appendix II, no. 322). It may have been bought by Maratta, who owned a version in 1712, *q.v.*

1712 No. 173 on Maratta's 1712 inventory reads 'Due Teste rappresentanti una S.ta Catterina e una Madonna piangente, in misura da testa con le sue cornici indorate, la Santa Caterina e di mano d'Andrea Sacchi, e la Madonna piangente viene da Titiano' (Galli, XXIII, p. 62). The Titian composition was probably based on the *Madonna Dolorosa* now in the Prado, which would make a suitable pendant composition to the Sacchi *St. Catherine*. This may be the picture now in Dulwich, although there is no way of proving it.

1909 Version now in the Gallery at Bamberg, catalogued as Italian seventeenth century in 1909 and identified by Posse as a copy of the Dulwich *St. Catherine* (1925, p. 77, note 1). It has a broader format than the Dulwich picture (73 × 111 cm.) and suggests that the latter may have been trimmed at the sides.

THE Dulwich *St. Catherine of Siena in Prayer* first appears in the 1813 catalogue of pictures left to Dulwich by Sir Francis Bourgeois,[1] although it is incorrectly identified there as a *Mater Dolorosa*, an error corrected in the 1880 catalogue. The similarity of the Dulwich saint to her counterpart in the Minerva sacristy altarpiece is obvious, and the presence in Sacchi's own collection of a picture of this subject with the right format also tends to support the attribution, which has always been accepted. It is even possible that the picture which belonged to Sacchi, and which was then acquired by Maratta, is the picture now at Dulwich, although this cannot be proved.

A date around the time of the Minerva altarpiece is probable, with the reservation that a different opinion might be possible after both works are cleaned. Perhaps the *St. Catherine* was painted for 'Padre Mostro', as Niccolò Riccardi, the Dominican Master of the Holy Apostolic Palace was known, and whose contact with Sacchi is documented by a lost portrait.[2]

1. It does not appear in the 1802 list of pictures left to Bourgeois in 1811 by Noel Desenfans, who had been assembling a picture collection for King Stanislas of Poland before his abdication in 1795.

2. See Cat. No. 52. Riccardi died on May 30, 1639, but his connection with the *St. Catherine* is too hypothetical for this date to be used as a *terminus ante quem*.

Bibliography: Britton, 1813, no. 269; Richter and Sparkes, 1880, pp. 69–70 (and all later editions of the Dulwich Gallery catalogues incl. 1905, pp. 69–70; 1914, p. 161; 1953, p. 252); Posse, 1925, p. 77.

48. Portrait of Ludovico Aurelio (died 1637). Formerly Palazzo Barberini, Rome
Recorded Versions: 1642 Teti mentions a portrait of the Jesuit historian, Ludovico Aurelio, by Sacchi in the Palazzo Barberini (*Aedes Barberinae*, p. 18). It may be identified with the unattributed portrait of Aurelio that appears in Cardinal Antonio Barberini's inventory of 1644, or it may be a version of the head of a Jesuit listed in Sacchi's inventory in 1661 (Appendix II, no. 43).

SACCHI's portrait of Ludovico Aurelio has not survived, nor has it been possible to trace a portrait of Aurelio by another artist. Venturi suggested that a portrait in a Bolognese private collection should be attributed to Sacchi and Incisa della Rocchetta then suggested that the sitter might be Aurelio. Posse, correctly in my opinion, rejected the attribution to Sacchi of the portrait in question. There is no way of knowing whether it represents Aurelio.

Bibliography: Teti, 1642, p. 18; Venturi in *L'Arte*, 1903, p. 344; Incisa della Rocchetta, 1924, p. 70; Posse, 1925, pp. 130–1.

49. Daedalus and Icarus. Galleria di Palazzo Rosso, Genoa
147 × 117 cm.   Plate 87
Condition: The present condition of the picture is sound although it would profit from the removal of discoloured varnish. The head and arms of Icarus are hard compared with those of Daedalus and may have been repainted.

Versions: 1661 A version almost certainly of this composition was in Sacchi's house in 1661 (Appendix II, no. 306). Its later history is not known, although it may be the version recorded in the Barberini collections after 1671, *q.v.*

1671 'Un quadro grande di p^{mi} 5 rappresentante Icaro, e Dedalo mezze figure grande al naturale' was in Cardinal Antonio Barberini's collection in 1671, when it was valued at 200 scudi (Lavin, no. 149) and is recorded in several later Barberini inventories (Cardinal Antonio, 1672, no. 262; Prince Maffeo, 1672–86, no. 210; Casa Barberini, 1686, no. 78; Palestrina inventory, 1738–9, no. 43 [Posse, 1925, p. 76]). It was also seen in the Palazzo Barberini by De Cotte around 1689 (p. 205) and by Bellori. It has disappeared since 1739, but may perhaps be the picture now in the Palazzo Rosso, which is first recorded in Genoa in 1766 (Ratti, p. 232).

1750 Version in the Palazzo Doria and probably first recorded in the Doria collections by Roisecco as by the school of Albani (I, p. 163). Tonci (1784, p. 196) first connected the Doria *Daedalus and Icarus* with Sacchi, describing it as a school work. It differs from the Genoa picture in minor details only—Icarus' head is larger and he has been given some flimsy drapery. It is probably a late seventeenth or early eighteenth century copy.[1]

1767 A version is recorded in the collection of Lord Tavistock in 1767 and at Woburn Abbey until 1951, when it was sold at Christie's (see Scharf, p. 371 and Christie's, Jan. 19, 1951, lot 62. It was sold for £47.5.– to Chandris). Although clearly a copy after Sacchi, the Woburn picture has been attributed to Van Dyck since the eighteenth century. For Van Dyck's treatment of this theme, see *Klassiker der Kunst*, 1931, pl. 268.

1783 A copy recorded in the Palazzo Colonna in 1783 (Colonna, 1783, II, p. 113) has since disappeared.

1790 'Una copia ben fatta di Dedalo che mette le ali ad Icaro e l'originale è di Andrea Sacchi' is recorded by Orsini (p. 105) in Ascoli-Piceno in the collection of Marchese Antonio Massei. Its later history is not known.

1921 A copy was sold in the Bentheim and Steinfurt sale, Bangel, Frankfort, on October 4, 1921 (lot 73, 131 × 97 cm.). It was attributed to Guercino.

ALTHOUGH a *Daedalus and Icarus* is recorded in the artist's house in 1661, the first time a composition of this subject is certainly attributed to him is in the 1671 inventory of Cardinal Antonio Barberini. It disappears from Barberini inventories after 1738–9, but may be identical with the version now in the Palazzo Rosso in Genoa, first recorded there in the Brignole collection in 1766. The latter is anyway the only known autograph version. A number of copies attest to the popularity of the composition in the seventeenth and eighteenth centuries, while their later attributions to other, better known artists—Albani, Guercino, Van Dyck— document the decline in Sacchi's reputation in the later eighteenth and nineteenth centuries.

It is an awkward picture to date, unique in a number of respects and consequently difficult to compare with dated works. Posse thought a date in the 1640s probable, and this may be correct. The head of Daedalus recalls the small *profil perdu* heads of Noah's sons in the Berlin picture, which contrast clearly with the large skulls and massive brows of Sacchi's male heads in the early 1630s. The concentration on the figures at the expense of any setting also recalls trends seen in the Fonte series of the life of the Baptist. A date before the fall of the Barberini in 1644–5 is probable.[2] The subject comes from Ovid (*Met.* VIII, 183; *De Arte Am.* II, 48).

1. See also Pistolesi, 1841 and 1846, p. 106; Mariotti, p. 114 and the 1961 catalogue of the Doria Gallery, no. 125.

2. Venturi (1882, p. 326) gives no evidence for his statement that the *Daedalus and Icarus* was painted for G. B. Ingoni, a Modenese patron, which—if true—would imply a date of 1635–6 while Sacchi was travelling in North Italy. Bellori says it was a Cardinal Antonio commission, but presumably only because he knew it was in his collection in the 1660s. Sacchi is however, likely to have produced such a personal interpretation of a mythological subject while he was a member of Cardinal Antonio's household, for he was Sacchi's only steady and sympathetic patron after the death of Cardinal del Monte. The absence of the *Daedalus and Icarus* from the 1644 inventory of Cardinal Antonio cannot be taken as evidence of a later date of execution; the *Hagar and Ishmael* of about 1630 is also missing from that inventory and included in later ones.

Bibliography: De Cotte, c. 1689, p. 205; Bellori, 1672–96, p. 67; Ratti, 1766, p. 232; Ratti, 1780, p. 255; Venturi, 1882, p. 326; Voss, 1924, p. 532; Posse, 1925, p. 76 f. and pl. XIV; Posse, 1935, p. 290; Waterhouse, 1937, p. 91; Martinelli, 1950, p. 100, note 1.

50. The Virgin and Child with St. Basil of Cappadocia. Casa del Vescovo, S. Maria del Priorato, Rome   Plate 88

Oil and size colour on canvas, about 180 × 180 cm.

Condition: Although recently cleaned, the picture has suffered from past neglect. The canvas is visible in many places and the paint has completely worn away in parts of the lower quarter, especially on the right. Pentimenti are visible around the head and right shoulder of the Virgin and the dove.

Drawings: Study of the Virgin's drapery, Düsseldorf (Harris and Schaar, no. 58); study for the Virgin's drapery, Düsseldorf (Harris and Schaar, no. 59); study for the left leg and drapery of St. Basil, Düsseldorf (Harris and Schaar, no. 60).

BELLORI is the only seventeenth-century source to record that Sacchi painted the high altarpiece of S. Maria del Priorato, the church on the Aventine that belonged to the Knights of Malta and of which Cardinal Antonio Barberini the Younger was made Grand Prior in 1632.[1] Bellori left a blank in the manuscript where the subject of the picture was to be inserted, and his omission suggests that he was not familiar with the original, and consequently that it was not easily accessible in the seventeenth century. The first printed reference to the altarpiece is found in the 1763 edition of Titi, but the author of the picture is not named. Waterhouse was the first modern scholar to draw attention to the work, and his attribution was confirmed when Bellori's manuscript was published a few years later.

Refice has suggested that the *Virgin and Child with St. Basil* is an early work. The three preparatory studies in Düsseldorf, which are certainly drawings of the 1630s, suggest a date before 1635.[2] The style of the painting itself, on the other hand, indicates a date after 1636, and possibly even in the early 1640s. The Virgin recalls her namesake in the *St. Bonaventure* altarpiece, finished in 1636, the putti with this heavy build are not seen until the fresco of 1637–9 in the sacristy of S. Maria sopra Minerva, while the increased scale of the figures and virtual exclusion of any setting can only be paralleled in the Fonte *Baptist* series of the 1640s. Perhaps the *St. Basil*[3] altarpiece was commissioned in 1632, when Cardinal Antonio became Grand Prior, the execution being delayed until after Sacchi's return from north Italy in 1636. An approximate date of 1636–40 can be suggested on stylistic grounds; further research into Cardinal Antonio's relations with the Knights of Malta might provide the information needed to date the picture more precisely.[4]

1. Ciacconius, IV, col. 564.

2. The closest parallels are provided by the studies for the *St. Anthony of Padua* and *St. Longinus* altarpieces.

3. Nibby identified him as St. John of Jerusalem, who wears the same robes, but the dove makes it certain that St. Basil of Cappadocia is represented (Réau, III, p. 185).

4. Research into printed sources and letters of enquiry to the Order concerning contemporary archive material have yielded no results.

Bibliography: Bellori, 1672–96, p. 65; Titi, 1763, p. 65; Nibby, 1839, p. 473; Waterhouse, 1937, p. 92; Refice, 1950, p. 219; Renzo V. Montini, *S. Maria del Priorato le Chiese di Roma Illustrate*, no. 53, Rome, 1959, p. 70 and fig. 19.

51. Portrait of the Singer Marc' Antonio Pasqualini. Althorp House, Northamptonshire, Earl Spencer.   Plate 89

280.7 × 190.5 cm.

Condition: The picture needs cleaning but to remove the distortions of a restorer rather than yellowed varnish and surface grime. About 15 cm. have been added to the top and 30 cm. below, perhaps to make the canvas more nearly the same size as the Guido Reni that hangs opposite. Apollo's drapery has been extended to cover his genitals. His body looks flat and has probably been repainted, and

other areas also betray the crude retouchings of an eighteenth- or nineteenth-century hand. There is no sign in the original of the plants visible on the bank in Strange's engraving and also in Maratta's drawn copy at Windsor. It appears therefore that there has been some loss of surface detail over most of the canvas.
Drawings: There are four studies for the drapery of Pasqualini's shoulder and right arm at Düsseldorf (Harris and Schaar, no. 63). A drawing of a standing male nude facing left in the Dahlem Museum, Berlin (No. K.d.K. 15303), which is probably the study connected with this composition by Posse (1925, p. 107), cannot be for this work since Apollo faces to the right. Posse, however, only knew the composition in reverse from Strange's engraving. The drawing should be connected rather with the figure of Joachim in the Prado *Birth of the Virgin*. A drawing of Apollo, first attributed to Sacchi in Mariette's collection in 1776 and now in the Louvre (Bean, 1959, p. 27), is by Giuseppe Passeri. There is a red chalk copy after the painting at Windsor by Maratta (Blunt and Cooke, no. 495).
Versions: 1730 Copy by Pietro de' Pietri recorded by Wright without naming the owner. It may be one of the copies recorded in later English sales, *q.v.* below.
1739 Version in Mr. Jarvis' sale of pictures in London, March 25, lot 107, 'Apollo Crowning a Musician, after . . . And. Sacchi'. The price and buyer are not recorded.
1755 A version is recorded in the Palazzo Farnese in 1755 by an anonymous engraver (example in G.N.D.S., Rome). It is recorded there again in an engraving of 1771, dedicated to Sig. Conte Enea Arnaldi by Cristoforo dell'Aqua (G.N.D.S. 120188), but has since disappeared.
1756 Version sold in London on April 1, 1756, lot 2. It came from the collection of Mr. de Pester and was bought by Sir Thomas Sheffield for two guineas. Its later history is not known.
1783 A copy recorded in the Palazzo Colonna in 1783 ('Un Quadro di Testa per alto—Apollo che corona un Suonatore, e Marzia legato—copia d'Andrea Sacchi', Colonna pp. 117–18) is not recorded in later catalogues of the Colonna collection and is presumably lost.
Engravings: 1755 Engraving by Robert Strange of the painting now at Althorp but then in the collection of Henry Furnese, Esq. For the engravings of 1755 and 1771 after the version then in the Palazzo Farnese, see above under Versions.

THE HISTORY of this portrait, now in the collection of Earl Spencer at Althorp, can be traced back to the beginning of the eighteenth century, when it belonged to Marchese Niccolò Pallavicini (Rossini and Pascoli). When he died in 1714, the portrait was sold and went to England (Pascoli), where it is first recorded by Vertue in the collection of Henry Furnese some time between 1736 and 1741. It was bought from him by Lord Spencer and has remained with the family ever since.[1]
The age and career of the sitter offer some clues as to the picture's date. Marcantonio Pasqualini (1614–91) began his career as a castrato singer in the choir of S. Luigi dei Francesi in 1623. He was in Cardinal Antonio Barberini's service from 1630 to 1643, during which time he appeared in numerous operas and musical performances, taking the role of Fame, for example, in the Giostra in Piazza Navona in 1634. In 1646, he joined the Barberini in Paris, where they had been forced to flee after the death of Urban VIII in 1644. After singing in Luigi Rossi's *Orfeo* in 1647, Pasqualini returned to Rome where he remained, employed in the choir of the Sistine Chapel, until his death.[2] His age in the portrait is difficult to estimate,[3] but he looks young—maybe twenty, certainly not more than thirty. The portrait must therefore have been painted before his visit to Paris. It does not apparently commemorate a particular occasion, but rather flatters Pasqualini's talents generally—what Marsyas failed to do, Pasqualini achieved, namely to be crowned by the supreme musician, Apollo. Only a general date of 1634–44

can be deduced from the known circumstances of Pasqualini's career and possible contacts with Sacchi.
Stylistic analysis provides a little help with the date, although the unusual formal and iconographical content makes comparison with other works difficult. The landscape setting recalls works of the 1630s—the steep banks resemble those in *St. Francis Marrying Poverty*, the hills beyond those in *Adam and Abel* or the *Martyrdom of St. Longinus*. The Düsseldorf preparatory study also indicates a date in the 1630s; it is particularly close to the Holkham study of 1635–6 for the St. Bonaventure altarpiece. Maratta's drawn copy at Windsor, which is clearly a very early drawing,[4] also provides a clue as to the date, for he joined Sacchi's studio in 1636, and the Pasqualini portrait impressed Maratta sufficiently to leave its imprint on his first independent commission, the Monterotondo altarpiece of before 1645.[5] A date in the late 1630s would suit these historical and stylistic factors.
The history of the picture before 1700 is obscure. Pascoli says that Marchese Niccolò Pallavicini commissioned it, but since he was born in 1650, this is impossible. Cardinal Antonio Barberini's patronage can probably be excluded. Bellori does not include it among Cardinal Antonio's commissions, nor is there any record of the original, or even of a version, in the well-documented Barberini collections. The Marchese was an illegitimate son, a fact which complicates normal inheritance procedures and makes it difficult to reconstruct the history of his collection.[6] Speculation along those lines is unnecessary, however, for a third hypothesis is the most probable one, even though all the evidence is circumstantial. Giulio Rospigliosi (1600–69), who became a cardinal in 1657 and Pope Clement IX in 1667, was a close friend of the Barberini and wrote librettos in the 1630s and early 1640s for a number of operas produced in the Barberini theatre in which Pasqualini took leading roles.[7] The allegorical content of the portrait and the obvious formal allusions to classical art, both rare in Sacchi's work,[8] are also found in the works that Poussin painted for Giulio Rospigliosi in the late 1630s.[9] Moreover, the theme of Pasqualini's triumph, which the bound satyr indicates is the reward of those whose intellects control their passions, is in type like many of the themes of Rospigliosi's dramas, where faith or virtue triumphs over heresy or vice.[10] Maratta's friendship with various members of the Rospigliosi family, including Giulio when he was Pope, and with Marchese Niccolo, and Maratta's fondness for this particular work of Sacchi,[11] could explain how this particular work left the Rospigliosi collections after the death of Clement IX and was acquired by the Marchese. Confirmation of this hypothesis must await the discovery of an accurate, contemporary description of Giulio Rospigliosi's collection before his death.

1. See Waterhouse in the catalogue of the 1950–1 Royal Academy Winter Exhibition.
2. For Pasqualini, see C. Schmidl, *Dizionario Universale dei Musicisti*, Milan, 1929, II, p. 238; A. Cametti, *Musica d'Oggi*, Milan, 1921, III, pp. 67–71 and 79–99 and *Enciclopedia della Musica*, Milan, 1964, III, p. 386. Bellori (1672–96, p. 68) says that Sacchi and Pasqualini were close friends. This suggests that the Marcantonio Pasqualini who was put in charge of the immediate financial arrangements in the last codicil of Sacchi's will (see Appendix I) was the same man.
3. Pasqualini looks older in Strange's engraving and younger in Maratta's drawn copy than he appears in the painting.
4. Maratta's drawing is careful, accurate and sensitive, but the hatching betrays an immature understanding of form. Other drawings at Windsor in the same style, mainly copies after Raphael, are most probably early studies made while he was a student in Sacchi's studio in the late 1630s (see Bellori, 1672–1696, p. 75 f.).
5. Mezzetti, 1955, no. 78. The figure of St. Michael, especially the head, legs and feet with classical sandals, are based on the

figure of Apollo. Claude evidently knew Sacchi's portrait of Pasqualini, for he used the figure of Apollo in his painting of Apollo and the Cumaean Sibyl of 1646-7, now in the Hermitage (Röthlisberger, pl. 180).

6. Zeri, 1959, p. 16.

7. Haskell, 1963, pp. 56-7. See also note 2 above.

8. Only one of Sacchi's other portraits, known or recorded, has any allegorical content, his lost portrait of Cardinal Gaetano's poet secretary (Bellori, 1672-96, p. 68). His only other painting with an allegorical programme was a special commission, the *Divina Sapienza* ceiling in the Palazzo Barberini. Sacchi's preferred subject matter was much more straightforward. Apollo's pose, while close to those used for Christ in the lost *Pasce Oves Meas* or Joachim in the Prado *Birth of the Virgin*, is modelled more directly on classical prototypes. Two of the illustrations in *Le Gemme Antiche* by Sacchi's neighbour and friend, Leonardo Agostini (no. 9 in vol. II and no. 142 in vol. I of the 1685 Amsterdam edition) can be combined to provide the pose and crowning gesture of Apollo, but the pose is a common one, and Sacchi did not necessarily take it from these gems.

9. Poussin's *Dance to the Music of Time* in the Wallace Collection was painted for Rospigliosi, who also commissioned at least two other works with allegorical content from Poussin, a lost *Rest on the Flight into Egypt* with an elephant in the background and a lost *Time Saving Truth from Envy and Discord* (Blunt, 1967, text volume, pp. 153-4). Rospigliosi's literary tastes and fondness for allegory is also reflected to some extent in his patronage of Claude (see Röthlisberger, 1961, p. 213).

10. See Blunt and Röthlisberger, *loc. cit. supra* for a fuller discussion of Rospigliosi's career and writings.

11. On contacts between Maratta, the Rospigliosi family and Marchese Niccolo Pallavicini, see Mezzetti, 1955, pp. 314 and 345 and Zeri, 1959, p. 16. The composition and iconography of Maratta's double portrait of Pallavicini and himself, now at Stourhead, are indebted in a general way to Sacchi's portrait of Pasqualini.

Bibliography: Bellori 1672-96, p. 68; Rossini, 1700, p. 87; Wright, 1730, I, p. 295; Pascoli, 1730, I, p. 16; Vertue, 1736-41, IV, p. 164; Leeds Exhibition, 1868, no. 200; Graves, 1914, p. 1187; Posse, 1925, p. 106 f. and fig. 31; Royal Academy Winter Exhibition, 1950-1, no. 459; Blunt and Cooke, 1960, p. 67.

52. Portrait of Padre Niccolò Riccardi (1589-1639). Formerly Palazzo Barberini, Rome

Recorded Version: 1671 A portrait of Padre Niccolò Riccardi ('Padre Mostro') is recorded in Cardinal Antonio Barberini's inventory of 1671 (no. 74, 3½ palmi high, valued at 80 scudi) and in his inventory of 1672 (no. 12); in the Casa Barberini inventory of 1686 (p. 201); in Cardinal Carlo Barberini's inventory of 1692 (no. 277 as by Andrea del Sarto) and in his inventory of 1704 (p. 124); and finally in the Palestrina inventory of 1738. It has subsequently disappeared.

BELLORI mentions Sacchi's portrait of the Dominican scholar and preacher, Niccolò Riccardi, whose homely features inspired the nickname 'Padre Mostro',[1] as an example of how an artist should tactfully idealize the physical characteristics of a difficult sitter. According to Bellori, Sacchi chose a frontal view, which improved the proportions of Riccardi's nose in relation to the rest of his face. The portrait is recorded in Barberini collections between 1671 and 1738 but has subsequently disappeared.

If the portrait was originally a Barberini commission, which is by no means certain, it is unlikely to have been painted between 1631 and 1633, when Riccardi was out of favour with Urban VIII for granting an *imprimatur* to Galileo for his *Dialogue on the Great World Systems*.[2] If the picture was not commissioned shortly after

Riccardi's appointment as Master of the Holy Apostolic Palace in 1629, then it was probably painted in the later 1630s, when Sacchi was working for Cardinal Antonio on the sacristy of Riccardi's church, S. Maria sopra Minerva. It is tempting to identify as Riccardi the monk in the portrait drawing by Sacchi at Düsseldorf (Harris and Schaar, no. 102), for that sitter's long, thin nose has been skilfully obscured by foreshortening (Plate 85). There being no known record of Riccardi's appearance, however, the identification cannot be checked.

1. The name was also a pun on Riccardi's other title, 'Padre Maestro' (he was Master of the Holy Apostolic Palace from 1629 onwards). On Riccardi see G. Santillana, *The Crime of Galileo*, London, 1961, p. 170 and *The Catholic Encyclopedia*, New York, 1912, XIII, pp. 32-3.

2. F. Reusch, *Der Process Galilei's und die Jesuiten*, Bonn, 1879, pp. 195 and 357.

Bibliography: Bellori, 1672-96, pp. 67-8; Posse, 1925, pp. 130-1.

53-61. The Decoration of San Giovanni in Fonte. Rome (1639-49)

THIS catalogue entry has two sections. The first concerns the fresco decoration of the interior of the Lateran Baptistry, begun in 1639 under Sacchi's supervision. The second deals with the eight oil paintings illustrating the life of St. John the Baptist that Sacchi painted for the lantern above the font in the centre of the Baptistry. The bibliography will be found at the end of the second section.

53. The frescoed Decoration of the Lateran Baptistry

Plates 92-115

THE Lateran Baptistry is a centrally-planned octagonal structure, four of whose eight walls are pierced by doors of various sizes giving access to adjoining oratories (Plates 90, 91). A fifth wall is pierced by the entrance door. All eight walls have been divided horizontally at a point approximately two thirds of their height by a plain cornice that breaks forward to become the capitals of the paired pilasters that mark the eight angles where the walls meet. Each wall has a window, painted or real, in the centre of the section above the cornice. The decoration of these eight walls is described below in counter-clockwise order starting with the wall surrounding the main entrance. Above and below means above and below the cornice. There is a *trompe-l'oeil* bronze medallion in the centre of each of the upper section flanking the windows; the subjects shown in these medallions are listed from left to right.

1. Below, Carlo Maratta, *trompe-l'oeil* niches with bronze statues of the Emperor Constantine and of Pope Silvester I (Plates 103 104); above, Sacchi and studio, medallions with a profile portrait of Constantine and with the Chi Rho symbol flanked by Alpha and Omega, both medallions being partially obscured by large, *trompe-l'oeil* plum-red curtains.

2. Below, Giacinto Gimignani, *Constantine's Vision of the True Cross before the Battle of the Milvian Bridge* (Plate 94); above, Sacchi and studio, medallions of St. Peter's and St. John Lateran and putti playing with the standards of Constantine's army capped with a cross and with the Chi Rho symbol (this latter almost completely effaced) and with bound fasces, a helmet and an overflowing cornucopia (Plates 92, 93).

3. Below, Andrea Camassei, *Constantine Defeating Maxentius at the Battle of the Milvian Bridge* (Plate 97); above, Sacchi and studio, medallions of Constantine and of S. Paolo fuori le Mura and putti playing with broken spears, a suit of armour and the captured crown of Maxentius (Plates 95, 96).

4. Below, Andrea Camassei, *Constantine's Triumphal Entry into Rome after the Defeat of Maxentius* (Plate 100); above, Sacchi and

studio, medallions of Constantine and of S. Croce in Geru-salemme and putti playing with palms of victory, with Con-stantine's sceptre and with a sheathed sword and a helmet (Plates 98, 99).

5. Below, Carlo Maratta, *trompe-l'oeil* niches with bronze statues of St. John the Baptist and St. John the Evangelist (Plates 105, 106); above, Sacchi and studio, medallions of Urban VIII (Plate 101) and of Urban VIII receiving plans for the restored Baptistry from three men (Plate 102) (Bernini, Sacchi and Domenico Castelli?). The lower third of these two upper sections is occupied by an inscription of 1795 recording the restoration of the Baptistry undertaken then by Cardinal Rezzonico.

6. Below, Carlo Maratta, *Allegory in Honour of Innocent X Pamphili* (Plate 109); above, Sacchi and studio, medallions of Urban VIII and of S. Giovanni in Fonte before the pictorial decoration had been started and putti playing with the tools of the painters' and architects' professions (Plates 107, 108).

7. Below, Carlo Maratta using a cartoon by Sacchi, *Constantine Establishing the Christian Religion and Ordering the Destruction of Pagan Idols* (Plate 112); above, Sacchi and studio, medallions of Constantine and of S. Lorenzo fuori le Mura and putti playing with paschal candlesticks, a censer and other church ornaments (Plates 110, 111). A faint inscription, 'Andrea Sacchi Fecit 1647' is still visible on the book to the lower left of the left-hand section after later repainting was removed during the restora-tion campaign of 1967–8.

8. Below, Carlo Magnone using a Sacchi cartoon, *The Destruction of Pagan Writings at the Nicene Council* (Plate 115); above, Sacchi and studio, medallions of Constantine and of SS. Pietro e Marcellino and putti playing with ink wells, a scroll and a brazier into which they toss paper (Plates 113, 114).

Condition: These frescoes have been restored at least three times since 1700—by Christopher Unterberger in 1795, by S. Galimberti in 1928 and in 1967–8 by the Vatican under the direction of D. Redig de Campos.[1] After this last campaign, Sacchi's eight oil paintings were replaced in the cupola by copies. Photographs of the frescoes taken by the Archivio Fotografico Vaticano before and after the 1967–8 restoration show that most of the surfaces of the frescoes were obscured by lime efflorescence and also to some extent by Galimberti's retouchings. The only serious paint losses have occurred in the lower third of the fresco of St. John the Evangelist and in the lower left section of *The Destruction of Pagan Idols*. In general the frieze of putti and medallions is better pre-served than the main frescoes, the latter having lost more of their surface bloom.

Drawings: Sixteen drawings in the Royal Collection at Windsor Castle were catalogued by Blunt as for the *Destruction of Pagan Idols* fresco, namely no. 745 recto and nos. 746–59 and no. 763 verso. Three of these drawings (nos. 757–9) are now catalogued as for the Fabriano *Baptist in the Wilderness*. One study on the verso of no. 763 can be connected with the man in the foreground of the *Destruction of Pagan Idols*; all the other studies on the recto and verso of that sheet are for *The Martyrdom of St. Longinus and St. Andrew Adoring the Cross of his Martyrdom*, both painted 1633–4. The odd study should probably rather be catalogued as an alternative pose for St. Longinus, otherwise this sheet would be unique as an example of Sacchi's using the same sheet of paper for studies made at widely differing dates. Sacchi may, of course, have decided to use the rejected pose at a later date.

The majority of the drawings at Düsseldorf that can be associated with S. Giovanni in Fonte are also for *The Destruction of Pagan Idols* (Harris and Schaar, nos. 64–71; no. 69, tentatively linked with Magnone's fresco, is now catalogued as for the acolyte to the left in the Capuchins' *Miracle of St. Anthony of Padua*). There is also a lively study after one figure in this fresco at Düsseldorf (Harris and Schaar, no. 119).

Few studies relating to other parts of the fresco decoration have been traced. A few architectural notes on the verso of no. 67 in Düsseldorf may have something to do with the early planning of the work. A study of putti at Windsor (Blunt and Cooke, no. 760) appears to be an offset retouched by a very competent studio assistant (Maratta?), for the putti appear in the reverse sense to their counterparts in the Baptistry in the left field above Camassei's *Triumph of Constantine*. There is one autograph study at Windsor, however, for the putti in the left field above the *Pamphili Allegory* (Blunt and Cooke, no. 781; the foot in the lower left corner can be connected with the priest carrying the cross in *The Destruction of Pagan Idols*). A red chalk study of uncertain authorship in the Staedelsches Kunstinstitut in Frankfort (no. 579, 210 by 140 mm.; it has an old attribution to Bernini) combines a putto from the left field above Magnone's fresco with another from the right field above Gimignani's *Vision of Constantine*. A rough and much rubbed black chalk study of a putto on the verso of an autograph com-position study for *The Naming of the Baptist* in the Dahlem Museum, Berlin (K.d.Z. 23712), appears to be an early sketch for the putto carrying the tray of inkpots in the left field above Magnone's fresco. A small study of a putto on a sheet with other studies in Düsseldorf (Harris and Schaar, no. 98) comes close to the putto holding the broken spear in the right field above Camassei's *Battle of Constantine*.

A drawing exhibited in Florence in 1737 was said to be a study by Sacchi for the Lateran Baptistry (*Nota de' Quadri e Opere di Scultura esposti per la Festa di S. Luca dagli Accademici del Disegno*, Florence, 1737, p. 47, 'Disegno a lapis nero d'Andrea Sacchi dipinto da esso nel Battistero di San Gio. Laterano dell'Illustr. Sig. L.T.').

The only drawings so far identified by one of the other artists involved in this project are two by Giacinto Gimignani for *The Vision of Constantine* (Harris and Schaar, p. 46 and Bean, 1959, pp. 32–3, no. 45; on the latter see also Vitzthum in the *Burl. Mag.*, 1968, p. 362). The oil sketch in the collection of Professor Giuseppe Noferi that Roberto Longhi suggested might be a rejected idea for a fresco in the Lateran Baptistry by Camassei (*Tesori Segreti in Case Fiorentine*, catalogue by Mina Gregori, Florence, 1960, no. 83, pl. 65) is in fact a sketch by Guidobaldo Abbatini for his fresco of *St. Sylvester Baptizing Constantine* in the Vatican (Gemma di Domenico Cortese, 'La vicenda artistica di Andrea Camassei', *Commentari*, XIX, 1968, p. 294; see also Harris, 'A Contribution to Andrea Camassei', *Art Bulletin*, 1970, pp. 62–3)

Documents: See Pollak, I, pp. 142–3 and the discussion below.

THE LATERAN BAPTISTRY, known as San Giovanni in Fonte, which stands on the north-west corner of the complex of build-ings surrounding St. John Lateran, is revered as the place where Constantine was baptized by Pope Sylvester I, and while the legend is not true,[2] the building itself dates back to the fourth century and its antiquity and traditional associations have resulted in its centrally planned octagonal design becoming the model of many later baptistries.[3] A brief account of its later structural history is necessary here. The cupola was damaged during the Sack of Rome in 1527 and Paul III (1534–55) replaced the original vaulted structure with a flat roof. Other partial reconstructions and redecorations undertaken in the later sixteenth century include the door that opens into the main piazza, installed by Gregory XIII for the Jubilee of 1575,[4] and the redecoration of the Oratory of St. John the Baptist, undertaken by Clement VIII for the Jubilee of 1600.

Despite the attentions of three sixteenth-century Popes, the fabric of the Baptistry must have been in a poor state of repair when Maffeo Barberini became Pope in 1623, for he and the Canons of St. John Lateran had spent 5,640 scudi on the building by October, 1625.[5] A more thorough reconstruction was begun in 1629, when it was decided to replace four of the antique capitals of the eight central porphyry columns that support the octagonal lantern, to repair the bases of all the columns of the second order, to re-construct the carved and gilded ceiling and to redesign the lantern.[6] The architect in charge was Domenico Castelli but Bernini provided the designs. The ceiling was finished by 1635[7] and the entire reconstruction of the fabric must have been complete by 1637, when a medal was cast to commemorate the work.[8] It is thus virtually certain that all the architectural work had been completed when Sacchi took over from Bernini and Castelli in 1639.[9] It is important to establish this since Bellori states that Sacchi directed the architectural reconstruction as well as the pictorial decoration which followed.[10] It is odd that Bellori should have been misinformed about any aspect of this project, particularly since Maratta was involved and must have known the limited nature of Sacchi's responsibility for the final appearance of the Baptistry. Bellori may simply have been confused and, knowing that Sacchi worked for the Barberini as both painter and architect, assumed that the whole campaign of restoration was carried out under Sacchi's aegis[11]

The payments published by Pollak for the pictorial decoration of the Lateran Baptistry are incomplete.[12] There are no published payments to Giacinto Gimignani, only one to Andrea Camassei, and none to Sacchi after 1645 although it is known from other sources that he only received his final payments late in 1649.[13] A rough chronology of the ten-year campaign can nevertheless be pieced together from the published payments, from inscriptions in the Baptistry and from other contemporary sources. On May 10, 1639 Sacchi was paid 400 scudi 'a conto delle pitture á fresco da farsi da lui in S. Gio. in fonte' (Pollak). At this date therefore the frescoes had not been started, and it would seem that Sacchi himself was planning to execute them, a hypothesis supported by the wording of the payments for materials '(che) servono per li ponti del Pittore in detto luogo' in July, October and December, 1639, in June 1640 and in January 1641 (ibid.). The next payment to Sacchi himself was made in June 1640, when he was given 50 scudi for gold to be used for the eight paintings in the octagon (ibid.). Since no real gold was used in these paintings, it must have been for the frames, which were apparently made before work on the pictures themselves had started.[14]

The only recorded payment to an artist other than Sacchi was one of 25 scudi to Camassei made in June 1644 for services rendered up to that time (ibid.). The amount paid is relatively small and other payments are obviously missing but it does at least show when work on one of his two frescoes was in progress.[15] One of Camassei's two frescoes was originally assigned to Romanelli.[16] It was probably only given to Camassei in or after 1646, when Romanelli left Rome to join the Barberini family in Paris. We can probably assume therefore that it was Camassei's first fresco that was in progress in 1644 and that his second, begun in 1646, was ready in 1648 when both he and Giacinto Gimignani were busy working for the Pamphili.[17] It is possible that Romanelli, rather than Camassei, was given preference as the Barberini favourite, that the larger of the two frescoes, *The Triumph of Constantine*, was to be his, and that this is the later of Camassei's two compositions. It is certainly the more accomplished.[18]

An inscription above Maratta's *Pamphili Allegory* records the completion of the decoration in 1648. This can only refer to the frescoes because Sacchi's eight oil paintings were not ready until late the following year. Moreover, Maratta's fresco can only have been planned after Innocent x became Pope in 1644, the space presumably being reserved originally for a similar allegory honouring Urban VIII. Another inscription, 'Andrea Sacchi Fecit 1647', in the frieze above *The Destruction of Pagan Idols* also suggests that work on this side of the Baptistry was delayed until the later 1640s, presumably because Sacchi still hoped to execute some of the larger frescoes himself. As Maratta matured and demonstrated his ability to work independently, Sacchi handed over the task of completing the frescoes to him—providing a cartoon for the *Pagan*

Idols fresco but no direct assistance for the *Pamphili Allegory* or four niche figures. Carlo Magnone, on the other hand, after completing the *Nicene Council* fresco in 1646-7, seems to drop out of the picture.[19] To what extent he was responsible for the frieze of putti and bronze medallions is impossible to determine. The 1647 inscription indicates that Sacchi's personal contribution to that frieze is greater than has often been supposed[20] and on grounds of quality alone it seems unlikely that assistants had much to do with it. Possibly Magnone painted the medallions and Sacchi the rest.[21] The documentary and stylistic evidence in general supports the accounts of Passeri and Bellori, who state that Sacchi originally planned to decorate the entire building himself and gradually handed over the work to others, reserving finally for himself only the execution of the eight oil paintings in the cupola. Exactly when and why this decision was made is not known. Up to 1641, Sacchi was apparently working on the frescoes himself. By 1644 he had given some of the work to three other Barberini protégés—Camassei, Gimignani and Romanelli. Serious work on the left side of the Baptistry was however delayed until 1646, but even with the major responsibility for the frescoes shifted to Maratta, Sacchi only completed his eight oil paintings late in 1649. The chronology of the decoration of the Baptistry indicates that by the mid-1640s at least Sacchi's lack of self-confidence and tendency to procrastinate was a serious handicap.

It can be assumed that a general plan for the decoration had been worked out by the time that Camassei, Gimignani and Romanelli appeared on the scene. Sacchi had probably also painted the friezes above the narrative frescoes they were to execute.[22] The style of both Camassei's and Gimignani's frescoes is characteristic of both artists and there is no reason to think that Sacchi intervened beyond assigning subjects to those three wall spaces. The three frescoes do however seem to have been planned after some mutual agreement about the general lines of their compositions. The heaviest vertical emphasis in each of the larger compositions is on the side adjacent to the central fresco and each lateral composition reads away from the central one.[23] The fact that all the narrative frescoes are based on the frescoes by Raphael and his school in the Vatican suggests that Sacchi also provided his collaborators with some general advice before they started work.[24]

The iconographical programme of the pictorial decoration of S. Giovanni in Fonte is straightforward and was dictated by its function and dedication to the Baptist and by its traditional associations with Constantine. The five narrative frescoes, arranged in chronological order starting from the right of the main entrance, are devoted to events in the life of the first Christian Emperor who, after his conversion, established Christianity as the official religion of the Empire.[25] The sixth and smallest wall space was used for an allegory in honour of the Pope in whose reign the work was completed. The choice of figures for the four niches beside the entrance door needs no explanation except in the case of St. John the Evangelist; he appears because one of the small oratories attached to the Baptistry is dedicated to him. The iconography of the frieze above the main frescoes is also mainly straightforward. Churches founded by Constantine are shown and Urban VIII is linked with these foundations by reason of his restoration of the Lateran Baptistry. Putti play in front of the bronze medallions with various objects obviously associated with the subjects of the frescoes beneath them.[26]

1. For details, see the sources quoted in note 3. Galimberti's signature and date appear on the plain frieze above the fresco of Constantine's vision of the True Cross.

2. Constantine was baptized in Nicomedia in 337 by Eusebius, the local bishop (A. H. M. Jones, *Constantine and the Conversion of Europe*, New York, 1962, p. 195).

3. For a general history of the Baptistry from 1527 to 1649 as

well as before and after this period, see Giovenale; Ortolani, p. 103 f.; and Armellini, 1942, I, p. 133 f.

4. The door opposite leading to the chapel of SS. Secunda and Rufina, whose design is identical, may also have been built by Gregory XIII although it carries a 1625 Jubilee inscription. The door leading to the chapel of St. Venantius below Maratta's *Pamphili Allegory* is of a slightly different design but that design is stylistically close to that of the door installed by Gregory XIII and may also have been built at that time.

5. Pollak, I, p. 133. The 1625 Jubilee inscription presumably refers to this work.

6. The four new capitals, marked by a Barberini bee, have a flatter, Ionic design in contrast to the taller, Corinthian capitals of the other four columns.

7. The date appears twice in the ceiling; a final payment for gilding was made in August, 1635 (Pollak, *loc. cit.*).

8. Ciacconius, IV, p. 524.

9. Pollak, I, p. 141 and Posse, 1925, p. 80.

10. Bellori, 1672–96, p. 64; see also Passeri, p. 299.

11. Bellori was confused also about Sacchi's contribution as an architect to the restoration of the sacristy of S. Maria sopra Minerva and evidently paid little attention to Sacchi except as a painter. Baglione noted (1642, p. 180) that Domenico Castelli was responsible for the architectural restoration of the Baptistry.

12. The published payments were extracted from one account book that presumably contained other irrelevant material. I have not checked it nor have I looked for other missing payments in other Vatican documents.

13. See the correspondence between the Papal chamberlain, Cardinal Angelo Giori, and Cardinal Antonio Barberini published by Pollak (*Jahrb. k. pr. Ksts.*, 1913, no. 34, p. 61).

14. Simone Lagi was paid for gilding the lantern in June and July, 1640 (Pollak, I, p. 142). Presumably the spaces for the paintings had been measured so that the latter only needed to be installed to complete the decoration of the lantern.

15. The attributions given by Passeri (pp. 299–300), Titi (1675, pp. 230–1) and Pascoli (I, pp. 16, 40, 137 and 300) are supported by the documents (i.e. one payment to Camassei) and by stylistic evidence (i.e. the two drawings by Giacinto Gimignani for his fresco). See also Mezzetti, 1955, no. 79 and Harris, 'A Contribution to Andrea Camassei', *Art Bulletin*, 1970, p. 62.

16. See Passeri, p. 172; Hess, 1934, p. 310, no. 5; and Posse, 1925, p. 81.

17. Hess, 1934, p. 173, note 1.

18. See Harris, *art. cit.*, p. 62.

19. It is difficult to imagine that Sacchi would not have had Maratta execute this cartoon as well had it not been under way by the time the *Pagan Idols* fresco was completed in 1647. Magnone is not known to have worked for Sacchi in any capacity other than that of copyist. He is not recorded in Sacchi's house after 1647 and is not known to have executed any independent work before his death in 1653 at the age of 30. It appears therefore that he was an artist of meagre abilities who was replaced by Maratta as soon as the younger man was able to work as Sacchi's assistant (on Magnone see Hoogewerff, 1947; Thieme-Becker, *sub voce* and Hess, 1934, p. 300, note 2).

20. Passeri (p. 300) says that they were 'parte di sua (Sacchi's) mano, et alcuni delli suoi giovani, tutti fatti con suo disegno'. Bellori (1672–96, p. 65) does not attribute them to the studio. The only recent scholar to attribute even part of them to Sacchi himself was Refice (1950, p. 220). She was particularly impressed by the bronze medallions.

21. The repetitive chore of painting Constantine's profile and the equally straightforward task of drawing small pictures of the various churches, presumably using engravings as models,

could easily have been delegated to assistants. The types of the putti are characteristic of Sacchi and should be compared with those in the fresco in the sacristy chapel of S. Maria sopra Minerva.

22. The early payments to Sacchi for frescoes can be associated with these friezes.

23. The same is not true of the three frescoes in the equivalent spaces on the opposite side, probably because they do not form a symmetrical unit.

24. See the stylistic discussion in the main text.

25. The following inscriptions appear above the five narrative frescoes: Constantino Profectionem In Maxentium Agitanti Certam Victoriam Promittit Aspecta In Caelo Crux His Verbis Inscripta In Hoc Signo Vinces; Comissa Acie Ad Pontem Milvium Fusisque Hostibus Maxentioque In Tiberim Acto Victoria Potitur; Urbem Ad Triumphum Ingresso Arcus Ad Radices Palatii Erigitur; Simulacris Deorum Dirutis Aris Eversis Crucem Locari Iubet; In Concilio Nicaeno Ex Primis Residens Libellos In Episcopos Conburit Et Inflicta Martiribus Vulnera Deosculatur.

26. The only puzzling iconographical detail is the piece of paper held by a putto above the scene of Constantine's vision of the True Cross. It appears to have astrological symbols on it. Perhaps it is the horoscope of the date of the Battle of the Milvian Bridge.

54–61. Eight Events in the Life of St. John the Baptist. Eight oil paintings for the lantern of S. Giovanni in Fonte, now Lateran Palace, Rome 1641–9   Plates 116–23; Col. Plates I, II.

54. The Annunciation to Zacharias. 310 × 250 cm.   Plate 116
Condition: Bellori was the first person to report that the condition of these eight pictures was poor ('. . . ch'è gran peccato si consumino', 1672–96, p. 64). They may have been restored at the end of the eighteenth century by Christopher Unterberger; they were all restored in 1925 by De Prai and Buttinelli[1] and their condition both before and afterwards recorded in a series of photographs now in the Archivio Fotografico Vaticano. Comparison of these photographs with the preparatory studies so far traced and with Bombelli's engravings of these paintings in 1769 show that this series has suffered much from damp and neglect. Most of their surface finish and glazing have been removed and large areas of many of them are little more than repaint over underpaint. Another restoration was undertaken between 1964 and 1968; the originals were replaced in the Baptistry by copies and are now kept in a corridor of the Lateran Palace that is unfortunately not normally accessible to the public. This most recent restoration showed that the colour of even the most damaged paintings in the series was better preserved, and far stronger, than seemed to be the case before treatment in 1964. The *Annunciation* is one of the best preserved works in the series but even here there is evidence of loss of surface finish. The censer, for example, is a flat white but must once have been shaded with grey or gold.
Engravings: 1769 Engraving by Desiderio de Angelis and P. L. Bombelli dedicated to the Archduke of Austria, Pietro Leopoldo, Grand Duke of Tuscany (*Vita di S. Giovanni Battista dipinta in otto tavole da Andrea Sacchi Romano nel Battistero Lateranese*, Rome, 1769).
Documents: The first payment to Sacchi specifically connected with the eight oil paintings in the cupola was one of 50 scudi made in June, 1640 'a conto dell'oro che va per servitio delle pitture che si fanno nelli quadri dell'ottangolo' (Pollak, I, p. 142). The final payment to Simone Lagi for gilding the lantern is dated July 17, 1640. On November 18, 1641 Sacchi was given another 200 scudi 'a conto dell'opera sua delle Pitture fatte e da farsi et altro nell'ottangolo in detto loco' (*ibid.*). On May 2, 1644 he received another 100 scudi and on June 20, 1645 a further 100 scudi (*op. cit.* pp. 142–3). The remaining payments have not been traced, but correspondence

between Cardinal Angelo Giori, Urban VIII's chamberlain, and Cardinal Antonio Barberini reveals that by September 8, 1649, six of the eight paintings were finished and the remaining two were almost ready; all eight were ready by the end of the month (see Pollak, 1913, p. 61). The order in which the eight paintings were made is discussed below.

1. See Biagio Biagetti in *Rendiconti della Pontificia Accademia Romana di Architettura*, III, 1925, pp. 484–5 and 486–7. See also E. Steinmann, 'Gemälderestaurationen im Vatican', *Der Cicerone*, XVII, 1925, pp. 943–9.

55. The Visitation. 310 × 250 cm.   Plate 117
Condition: A general account of the condition of all eight pictures is given above under *The Annunciation to Zacharias*. This canvas has suffered particularly badly. Mice ate two holes just below the Virgin's shoulder: these were repaired in 1925. Comparison of the recently restored canvas with Bombelli's engraving shows that much detail has been lost, particularly from the lower parts of the two men on the left and the robes of the two women on the right as well as background detail.
Drawings: A drapery study on a sheet of studies at Düsseldorf for *The Destruction of Pagan Idols* fits the drapery around the shoulders of Elizabeth (Harris and Schaar, no. 67). Posse (1925, p. 95, note 1) connected a drawing in the Uffizi with this composition, but the drawing is a sixteenth-century production and has nothing to do with Sacchi.
Versions: 1661   There was a canvas in the artist's house in 1661 'con un sbozzo di un Somaro' (Appendix II, no. 241) which later apparently belonged to Maratta (Galli, XXIII, 1928, p. 68). Since the only donkey that Sacchi is known to have painted appears in the *Visitation*, the sketch may have been made in connection with this composition.
Engravings: 1769   Engraving by Desiderio de Angelis and P. L. Bombelli (details under *The Annunciation to Zacharias* above).

56. The Birth of the Baptist. 310 × 250 cm.   Plate 118
Condition: See above under *The Annunciation to Zacharias*. The preparatory studies at Düsseldorf for this composition give an idea of the original finish of this composition. In particular, they record the appearance of the woman to the left of the group attending Elizabeth who is now reduced to ghostly underpaint. Some colour areas now seem raw, others faded; the composition lacks balance as a result.
Drawings: Two drapery studies for the figure of Zacharias, Düsseldorf (Harris and Schaar, no. 72); two drapery studies and a study for the feet of Zacharias, Düsseldorf (Harris and Schaar, no. 73); studies for the woman in the left background attending Elizabeth, Düsseldorf (Harris and Schaar, no. 74); further studies for the same woman, Düsseldorf (Harris and Schaar, no. 75); two studies for the head of Zacharias, Copenhagen (Inventory no. Tu 17.3 recto, red chalk on buff paper, 225 by 352 mm.; Plate 125. For the verso, see *The Death of St. Anne*). Another drapery study at Düsseldorf may be connected with the drapery of the girl in the right foreground (Harris and Schaar, no. 96). There is a study in the Musée de Rennes (C. 67·1, 407 × 285 mm., red chalk on cream paper) for the heads of the standing woman at the right and of the woman who turns to look at her, and of the hands of the former.
Versions: 1661   Version of this composition recorded in Sacchi's house in 1661 (Appendix II, no. 205); its later history is not known. For another, earlier version of this subject by Sacchi, see *The Birth of the Virgin* in the Prado (No. 14).
Engraving: 1769   Engraving by Desiderio de Angelis and P. L. Bombelli (details under *The Annunciation to Zacharias* above).

57. The Naming of the Baptist. 310 × 250 cm.   Plate 119
Condition: See above under *The Annunciation to Zacharias*. This picture was cleaned for the 1962 *Ideale Classico* exhibition in

Bologna and again during the restoration campaign of 1964–8. The paint is very thin in a number of places, for example the left foot of the man in the left foreground and his undergarment, the drapery of Zacharias, the steps and the box on which Zacharias is seated. The colour is also paler than that of any of the other canvases, and while this is to some extent due to the choice of a grey-white-blue colour scheme, it is also due to surface wear and damage.
Drawings: Composition study, Berlin (K.d.Z. 23712, sepia wash with white body colour on white paper, 282 × 207 mm.; Plate 126. A study of a putto on the verso can be connected with the fresco frieze in the Baptistry. The drawing is currently catalogued among the unknowns. The composition is not close to that of the painting in the Baptistry, but since Sacchi is not known to have painted this subject on any other occasion, it seems reasonable to think that the drawing may have been an early, rejected idea for this canvas); studies for spectators, Düsseldorf (Harris and Schaar, no. 76); studies for spectators, Düsseldorf (Harris and Schaar, no. 77).
Engraving: 1769   Engraving by Desiderio de Angelis and P. L. Bombelli (see above under *The Annunciation to Zacharias* for details).

58. The Blessing of the Baptist before his Departure to the Wilderness. 310 × 250 cm.   Plate 120
Condition: See above under *The Annunciation to Zacharias*. Most of the paint loss or wear seems to have affected the two women in the doorway, although the preparatory studies at Düsseldorf suggest that Elizabeth and Zacharias have also been affected.
Drawings: Two studies for the drapery of Elizabeth and one for the drapery of Zacharias, Düsseldorf (Harris and Schaar, no. 78; Plate 124; the verso has studies for the head and hands of Elizabeth).
Engraving: 1769   Desiderio de Angelis and P. L. Bombelli (for details, see above under *The Annunciation to Zacharias*).

59. The Baptism of Christ. 310 × 250 cm.   Plate 121
Condition: See above under *The Annunciation to Zacharias*. God's head is now hardly visible, proof that the surface is badly worn. The sky and background landscape in general are badly rubbed and the lower right corner is also very worn.
Drawings: Studies for the angel on the left, Düsseldorf (Harris and Schaar, no. 80); studies for the figure of the Baptist and for the spectators in the right background, Düsseldorf (Harris and Schaar, no. 79). There is an early eighteenth-century copy after the composition in Düsseldorf (Harris and Schaar, no. 120).
Versions: 1644   'Un quadro per sopraporto con Cristo battezato nel Giordano da S. Gio. ta di mano del Sacchi' was in the collection of Cardinal Antonio Barberini in April, 1644 (Incisa della Rocchetta, 1924, p. 72). Bellori (1672–96, p. 67) also mentions a small version of the Fonte *Baptism of Christ* in the Palazzo Barberini, as do numerous guide books of the seventeenth and eighteenth centuries.[1] This version, which measured $5\frac{1}{2}$ palmi 'per ogni verso', appears in the 1671 inventory of Cardinal Antonio (no. 326, valued at 500 scudi), in the 1672–86 inventory of Maffeo Barberini (no.184), in a Casa Barberini inventory of 1686 (no. 170), in Carlo Barberini's inventory of 1692 (no. 76a), in Carlo Barberini's inventory of 1704, (p. 108), in the Palestrina Inventory of 1738, in the Colonna di Sciarra collection in 1818 (no. 155; see Mariotti, p. 134) and again in 1844 (no. 463) and 1850 (Mariotti, *loc. cit.*). For a larger version also recorded in the Barberini collections, see below under 1730. The present location of the smaller version is unknown.
1661   Version recorded in the inventory of Cardinal Mazarin made shortly after his death, on March 3, 1661 (no. 1128, 'Un auctre faict par André Xavier [*sic*], sur toille, représentant sainct Jean-Baptiste qui baptise Nostre-Seigneur, hault de dix poulces et large de huict, garny de sa bordure d'ébène profilé d'estain, prisé la somme de cent livres' (Cosnac, p. 324). Its later history is not known.
1661   Four versions are recorded in the artist's house in June,

1661 (Appendix II, nos. 40, 173, 219 and 301). Their later history is not known. Possibly one of them was sold by Sacchi's heirs to the Barberini, and was the larger version recorded in their inventories of 1730 and 1738.

1730 A version of this subject by Sacchi measuring 12 × 8 palmi was in the Barberini inventory of Aug. 4, 1730 (no. 3534, valued at 2000 scudi!) and again in the 1738 Palestrina Inventory. Its later history is not known.

1747 Version possibly of this composition which passed through a London sale room on July 1, 1747 (lot 2 in the sale of Mr. Josiah Burchett, 'Our Saviour, and St. John . . . A. Sacchi'; the price and buyer are not recorded).

1758 'St. John baptizing Christ . . . And. Sacchi' was in the sale of Henry Furnese on Feb. 4, 1758. Bought by Lord Ashburnham for £27.6.–, it appeared at Christie's on July 20, 1850. It cannot be associated definitely with any earlier or later version. I owe these last two references to Mr. Frank Simpson.

1960 A version first recorded in the collection of Signora Alice d'Ancona (*Tesori Segreti in Case Fiorentine*, Florence, 1960, no. 82) is now owned by Mr. Joseph McCrindle, who has lent it to the Minneapolis Institute of Arts. The tonal and spatial balance of this work have been affected by damage and restoration, and this makes its quality difficult to assess. It seems nevertheless to be a copy; the colour above all is much rawer than the original, even making allowances for condition. It is probably a late seventeenth- or early eighteenth-century production.

1962 A version with the main figures reversed and shown half-length is in the art collection of Notre Dame University (Dwight Miller, *Seventeenth and Eighteenth Century Paintings from the University of Notre Dame*, an exhibition held at the Krannert Art Gallery, Urbana, 1962, no. 28). It is not by Sacchi; an attribution to J. C. Loth has been suggested by Francis Dowley and E. K. Waterhouse.

1972 A small version with half-length figures was acquired from Colnaghi's recently by Denis Mahon (oval oil on panel, 30 × 40 cm.). The panel has almost certainly been trimmed in the eighteenth century from its original rectangular or square format. None of the early recorded versions attributed to Sacchi was said to be on panel and it is a support that Sacchi is known to have chosen on only one other occasion. The Mahon picture is a work of high quality, but an attribution to the young Maratta, who did adapt compositions by Sacchi during the later 1640s and 1650s and who did like the smoother working surfaces of panel and copper (e.g. *St. Andrew Adoring his Cross*, Corsini Gallery, Rome), should be considered.

Engraving: 1769 Engraving by Desiderio de Angelis and P. L. Bombelli (see under *The Annunciation to Zacharias* for details).

1. e.g. De Cotte, c. 1689, p. 205; Rossini, 1693, p. 57 and many later editions; Pinarolo, 1700, p. 175 and later editions; Panciroli, 1719, II, p. 362.

60. The Preaching of the Baptist. 310 × 250 cm.   Plate 122
Condition: For details, see above under *The Annunciation to Zacharias*. The photograph taken of this work before the 1925 restoration shows that it had had rain running down the centre of the canvas for some time. The damage in this area is consequently more serious than in the case of some of the other canvases.
Drawings: Studies of spectators, Düsseldorf (Harris and Schaar, no. 81); two studies of the woman in the lower, right corner with her back turned. Düsseldorf (Harris and Schaar, no. 82; the verso of this sheet has a slight sketch for the head of the Baptist and two studies for the drapery of the man seated in the foreground). A composition study published by Grassi (*Storia del Disegno*, Rome, 1947, p. 145 and pl. LXVII) is a later copy after the painting, as is a slight red chalk study in the Louvre (Inv. no. 16829, 227 × 197 mm.).
Engraving: 1769 Engraving by Desiderio de Angelis and P. L. Bombelli (details under *The Annunciation to Zacharias*).

61. The Beheading of the Baptist. 310 × 250 cm.   Plate 123
Condition: See above under *The Annunciation to Zacharias* for details. The *Beheading* is probably the best preserved of all eight canvases.
Version: 1661 A version of this subject was in Sacchi's house in 1661 (Appendix II, no. 209). It may have been a *modello* or sketch although it is not described as such. Its later history is not known.
Engraving: 1769 Engraving by Desiderio de Angelis and P. L. Bombelli (details above under *The Annunciation to Zacharias*).

THE EIGHT CANVASES illustrating events in the life of St. John the Baptist are the only part of the decoration of the Lateran Baptistry that Sacchi executed alone.[1] The order in which these important compositions was made can unfortunately be established only partially. The wording of a payment made to Sacchi in November, 1641, shows that work had started on the series by then.[2] Other smaller payments follow in May, 1644 and June, 1645. A small version of the *Baptism* was in the collection of Cardinal Antonio Barberini by April, 1644, a fact suggesting that the *Baptism* was one of the earlier canvases completed. The *Visitation* can tentatively be dated 1646–7, since a final study for the drapery of St. Elizabeth appears on a sheet of early figure studies for the *Destruction of Pagan Idols*, finished in 1647. It is also possible that the *Birth of the Baptist* was one of the last two canvases to be completed since the preparatory study in Copenhagen for the head of Zacharias is on the verso of a study for Joseph in the *Death of the Virgin* in S. Carlo ai Catinari, a work that was ready in November, 1649. Six of the eight canvases were ready on September 8, 1649; all eight were ready by the end of the month.
Only three therefore of the eight compositions can be dated even approximately in the decade during which Sacchi was engaged on this project. Nor does a stylistic analysis of these three compositions and of their relationships to other dated works of the late 1630s, 1640s or early 1650s suggest an obvious stylistic trend that would enable us to date the other five canvases. On the contrary, the special circumstances of the commission means that these eight works have more in common with each other than with any other works by Sacchi, even those on a similar scale. The unequal state of preservation of the eight Fonte canvases also makes detailed analysis of their colour, for example, unprofitable.

1. Biagetti (*loc. cit.*) suggested that *The Naming of the Baptist* and *The Blessing of the Baptist* were partly by assistants. The only part of autograph works that Sacchi ever delegated is the architectural background. The settings in the Fonte series are extremely simple and it seems highly unlikely that assistants intervened, nor is the quality of the two compositions named by Biagetti different in any obvious way from that of the other six compositions.

2. See the documents quoted for *The Annunciation to Zacharias* for this and all other references to precise dates in this section.

Bibliography: Caesare Rasponio, *De Basilica et Patriarcho Lateranensi*, Rome, 1656, p. 212; Mola, 1663, p. 115; Bellori, 1672–96, pp. 64–5; Titi, 1674, pp. 230–1 and all later editions including 1763, p. 209; Passeri, by 1679, pp. 299–300; Rossini, 1693, p. 152 (1700 and 1704, p. 172; 1750, p. 117; 1776, II, p. 20); Bonanni, 1696, p. 579; Pinarolo, 1700, II, p. 210 (1703, *ibid.*; 1713, II, p. 217; 1725, III, p. 298 and later editions); Panciroli, 1719, II, p. 607; Pascoli, 1730, I, p. 16; Roisecco, 1750, III, pp. 423–5; Vasi, 1765 (1770), p. 209; Nibby, 1839–41, III (1), p. 573; Pistolesi, 1841, p. 255 (1843 ed., *ibid.*); Pollak, 1913, p. 61; Voss, 1924, pp. 533 and 601; Posse, 1925, p. 79 f. and *passim*; Giovenale, 1929, pp. 106–7 and 120; S. Ortolani, *S. Giovanni in Laterano*, Rome, n.d., p. 103; Hess, 1934, p. 300, note 3; Posse, 1935, p. 290; J. Hess, 'Elementi plastici nello stile del pittore Andrea Sacchi', *Illustrazione Vaticana*, VII, 1936, pp. 374–6; Waterhouse, 1937, pp. 24–5 and 92; Armellini, 1942, I, p. 133 f.; Refice, 1950, p. 220; Wittkower, 1958, p. 170; Briganti, 1962, p. 91; Emiliani, 1962, pp. 334–7; Waterhouse, 1963, p. 59.

62. St. Francis of Sales and St. Francis of Paula. S. Maria in Via, Camerino   Plate 127
200 × 115 cm.

Condition: The general condition is good for a picture which seems to have had no attention since its installation. The canvas, which contains a few holes and is being weakened by a stretcher on the lower right, needs relining, and a cleaning is also necessary to remove surface grime, but not varnish, which never seems to have been applied. The landscape and the brown robes of St. Francis of Paula have darkened.

BELLORI is the only *seicento* source to mention this altarpiece, yet long before his life of Sacchi was published, local historians had connected it with Sacchi, and the attribution, which is convincing, has generally been accepted.[1] The left-hand saint recalls St. Bonaventure in the Capuchins' altarpiece, the right hand saint the St. Anthony Abbot in the Prado picture or St. Romuald. Both saints in the Camerino picture also resemble the Dominican saints in the Minerva sacristy picture. The simplicity of the iconography and the composition also are characteristic of Sacchi.[2] The comparisons cited suggest a date in the 1630s, but the picture can hardly have been commissioned before 1639, when the rebuilding of the church for which it was made was begun.[3] Unlike all the other altarpieces in the church, however, Sacchi's was not designed to fit its frame, which indicates that it was commissioned and executed before the interior decoration with uniform frames for all the altarpieces had been planned in detail.[4] This was presumably done after the building was completed in 1643, but the completed and decorated church was only dedicated eleven years later.[5] A date in the early 1640s when the patron, Cardinal Giori, still had access to Barberini money[6] and before Sacchi was too involved in the decoration of the Lateran Baptistry is indicated.

1. Sacchi is also frequently credited with a painting of *St. Ansovinus Distributing Alms* in the cathedral of Camerino. If I identified the picture correctly, it has nothing to do with Sacchi at all.
2. The iconography presumably depends on the chapel dedication to the two saints, who lived in different centuries and are not traditionally associated with each other.
3. Santoni, p. 37. For a discussion of Sacchi's authorship of this church, see p. 66, note 90 and no. 66, note 2.
4. A strip has been added to the top to fit the canvas into the long frame with the upper corners cut off; the canvases on the other altars also fit into the two small extensions of the frame below the two lower corners indicated by the bent beaded moulding.
5. Santoni, *loc. cit.*
6. Giori was Urban VIII's chamberlain, and was presumably not so well off after the death of Urban VIII and the fall of the Barberini. This is also presumably why it took him twice as long to decorate S. Maria in Via as to build it, and why he had to use local artists, except for the Sacchi altarpiece.

Bibliography: Bellori, 1672–96, p. 66; C. M. Santoni, *Di Santa Maria in Via di Camerino, Cenni Storico-Critici*, Camerino, 1866, p. 37; A. Conti, *Camerino e i Suoi Dintorni Descritti ed Illustrati*, Camerino, 1872, p. 20; Voss, 1924, p. 53; R. Romani, *Guida Storico-Artistica di Camerino e Dintorni*, Terni, 1927, pp. 20 and 171; Hess, 1934, p. 304, note 6; Posse, 1935, p. 290.

63. Urban VIII Visiting the Gesù on October 2, 1639 during the Centenary Celebrations of the Jesuit Order. Galleria Nazionale d'Arte Antica, Rome   Plates 130, 133
336 × 247 cm.

Condition: Apart from minor areas of paint loss, for example between the legs of the blond horse in the central foreground, the picture is in excellent condition.

Versions: 1642 Copy made under Sacchi's supervision between April and November, 1642 (Incisa della Rocchetta, 1924, p. 66).

This is presumably the second version recorded in the 1672 inventory of Cardinal Antonio Barberini. It is not listed in later Barberini inventories.

Engravings: 1640 Engraving by Antonio Gerardi based on a drawing by Sacchi and dated January 30, 1640. It is dedicated to two of Urban VIII's sisters, Innocenza and Maria Gratiani, who were Carmelite nuns (*Ritratti Italiani della Raccolta Cicognara-Morbio:* Rome, after 1881 and Incisa della Rocchetta, 1924, p. 69).

Documents: Sacchi was paid 100 scudi 'a buon c(on)to della spesa de quadro che rappresenta la festa del Gesù p(er) il centesimo de P(ad)ri Gesuiti' on November 8, 1641 (Incisa della Rocchetta, 1924, p. 66). No more payments for the original are recorded; a copy was in hand by April, 1642 (see Versions).

THE CHURCH is shown without its façade and with the street in the foreground filled with horses, carriages and spectators. A break in the crowd in the centre permits a clear view of the Pope and his entourage, among whom can be identified Cardinal Antonio Barberini to the Pope's left, Cardinal Francesco Barberini to the Pope's right, and Angelo Giori, the papal chamberlain, in blue immediately to the right of the cardinal with his back turned, who is presenting a group of Jesuits to Urban VIII. The child prominently placed on the steps in the foreground is probably Maffeo, the son of Taddeo Barberini, who can be seen wearing black, to the right of Giori. Cardinal Antonio the Elder is just behind the Pope.

The date of the painting is not in doubt. Sacchi was paid for the expenses it incurred in November, 1641, and a copy was in hand by April of the following year. What is in doubt is the extent of Sacchi's contribution to the execution of the picture, which in the 1671 inventory of Cardinal Antonio Barberini is said to be limited to the main figures, the 'prospettiva' being by Filippo Gagliardi and 'il restante' by Jan Miel.[1] This division of labour is convincing on practical and stylistic grounds. A hundred scudi would be too small a fee for Sacchi to have painted the whole work himself; the fact that the copy which Sacchi 'had made' cost the same also points to this conclusion. Neither Gagliardi nor Miel were then in a position to command such high fees.[2] Gagliardi, a specialist in architectural backgrounds, had already worked with Sacchi on two Barberini commissions,[3] and the pedantic accuracy of the interior of the Gesù and the layout of the interior compare well with Gagliardi's interior of St. Peter's in the Prado.[4] On stylistic grounds, the genre figures and the horses and carriages in the foreground must be Miel's contribution,[5] the background figures being filled in by Gagliardi. Miel's contribution in fact documents his brief apprenticeship with Sacchi, which ended when Sacchi told him that he was too old to learn to paint properly.[6] Sacchi was responsible, it seems, for planning the design, supervising the work of Gagliardi[7] and Miel, and for the principal figures whose portrait likenesses can be identified. To those mentioned above may perhaps be added the two men in black to the left of the papal entourage, who look out at the audience. The left-hand one of these resembles Sacchi as he appears in the much later portrait by Maratta in the Prado. Perhaps the man behind him is Gagliardi. Neither man can have been so prominently placed during the actual ceremonies, however, and for this reason the identifications must be tentative.[8]

1. 'Un quadro grande . . . rappresentante il Centesimo de' Gesuiti, prospettiva mano di Filippo Gagliardi, le principal(i) figure del fu Sr Andrea Sacchi, il restante di Gio(vanni) Miele' (no. 1, valued at 600 scudi). Jan Miel is only mentioned in this inventory. In 1672, when Cardinal Antonio's collection was divided, the Jesuit Centenary picture went to Cardinal Francesco. It appears next in the inventory of Prince Maffeo made between 1672 and 1686 (no. 105) and then in the 1686 Casa Barberini inventory (no. 25). In the Palestrina inventory of 1738–9, the figures are given to Sacchi, the setting to 'Andrea' [*sic*]

Gagliardi (Posse, 1925, p. 10). The double attribution may have been written on the frame, for Pistolesi, who records the picture in the Sciarra collection, attributed the setting to 'Galiasso', evidently a misreading for Gagliardi, whose name is correctly recorded with that of Sacchi in the 1818 Fidecommesso inventory of the Sciarra collection (Mariotti, p. 135). The picture was bought from the Sciarra collection by the State and kept in a room off the sacristy of the Gesù until 1950 at least (see Waterhouse and Refice).

2. The Prior of S. Martino ai Monti some eight to ten years later paid Gagliardi 10 and 12 scudi for frescoed views of Old St. Peter's and St. John Lateran, and Miel 25 scudi for another fresco in the same church (see Sutherland, 'The Decoration of S. Martino ai Monti', I and II, *ad vocem*).

3. See the entries for the *Giostra in Piazza Navona* and the *St. Bonaventure* altarpiece in the Capuchins' church (nos. 40 and 45).

4. On the accuracy of this record of the Gesù interior, see Sutherland, 'Pier Francesco Mola', p. 367 and figs. 12 and 13.

5. Miel's name has already been connected with the foreground figures on stylistic grounds by Refice and Briganti. Baldinucci (IV, p. 367) says that Miel helped Sacchi with a large picture kept on the ground floor of the Palazzo Barberini, and it is presumably to the Jesuit Centenary picture that he is referring.

6. Baldinucci, IV, p. 367.

7. The bands of light and shade in the Gesù's interior, like the similarly varied lighting of the Piazza Navona *Giostra* picture, seem to have been suggested by Sacchi, for they are not found in Gagliardi's independent works whereas Sacchi's sensitivity to tonal values is well known.

8. Gagliardi's appearance is not known, so his portrait identification cannot be checked. For a full description of the event, see Gerardi, 1639, *passim*; Bonanni, II, p. 68 and Incisa della Rocchetta, *loc. cit.*

Bibliography: Teti, 1642, p. 163 f.; Panciroli, 1719, II, p. 363; Pistolesi, 1841, and 1846, p. 93; Mariotti, 1892, p. 135; Incisa della Rocchetta, 1924, pp. 66–9; Voss, 1924, pp. 532–3; Posse, 1925, pp. 7–10 and *passim* and plates III and IV; *Mostra di Roma Seicentesca*, Rome, 1930, no. 13; Posse, 1935, p. 290; Waterhouse, 1937, p. 91; Refice, 1950, p. 220; Briganti, 1950, p. 32.

64. The Guardian Angel. Duomo, Rieti   Plate 128
242 × 149 cm.

Condition: It was cleaned for the 1957 Rieti exhibition and its present condition is therefore reasonable. Comparison with Iacoboni's mid-eighteenth-century engraving suggests that the *Guardian Angel* has been cut down on all sides and that parts of the background have been repainted.

Drawings: No autograph preparatory studies are known, the three drawings of this subject at Düsseldorf attributed to Sacchi being Maratta school drawings (see Harris and Schaar, nos. 116 to 118).

Versions: 1661 A small picture of this subject in Sacchi's house in 1661 (Appendix II, no. 122) may have been a sketch for, or a small version of, the Rieti altarpiece.

1950 Refice (p. 218) records a small version in the Palazzo Spada, but it does not appear in Zeri's catalogue and cannot now be traced.

Engravings: Eighteenth Century Engraving by G. B. Iacoboni dedicated to Ascanio Varese, the Abbot General of the Congregation of St. Salvator of Canons Regular of St. John Lateran; Plate 129. Iacoboni was active between 1750 and 1770 (Thieme-Becker, *sub voce*). If the engraving is accurate—and it records the figures faithfully—the painting has been cut down, particularly on the sides, and trees and foliage eliminated from the left foreground and right background.

BELLORI describes the *Guardian Angel* without giving its location. Since he wrongly attributes another picture in Rieti to Sacchi,[1] it would appear that he had not been there himself and depended instead on an unidentified local source for information. The *Guardian Angel* is first mentioned in the cathedral archives in 1777, when it was attributed to Sacchi,[2] as it was by the engraver Iacoboni, whose print was probably made before this date. The attribution is reasonable and has been accepted by all later authorities who have discussed the picture.

Palmegiani cites unpublished documents in the archives of Rieti cathedral that, he asserts, date the *Guardian Angel* 1635, but caution is necessary since, according to the catalogue of the 1957 Rieti exhibition, the picture itself is not mentioned in these archives before 1777. Moreover, it is not cited in Pompeo Angelotti's *Descrizione della Città di Rieti*, published in Rome in 1635. In addition, the period before Sacchi's journey to north Italy in 1635–6 was an exceptionally busy one for the artist, who had to leave at least two major Barberini commissions incomplete when he left for Bologna in June, 1635. It seems improbable that he completed a provincial commission at a time when he had contract obligations to his most powerful and important patrons. On practical grounds, therefore, a date in the later 1630s is far more probable:[3] such a date is also suitable on stylistic grounds. The child who symbolizes the Christian soul has the heavier build of Sacchi's children after 1636. The angel's classically idealized figure recalls the figure of Apollo in the Pasqualini portrait of the late 1630s and the devil recalls the bound figure of Marsyas in the same work. The condition of the Rieti picture makes a more detailed stylistic analysis impractical[4] and also makes it difficult to tell whether its disappointing appearance is the result of damage and repaint or studio intervention. It is possible that Sacchi delegated some of the work to Carlo Magnone, who is documented carrying out some of Sacchi's designs in the early 1640s, and that Magnone is responsible for the stiffness of the angel, for example. The evidence available only allows an approximate date of about 1640 to be suggested; further research into the cathedral archives may eventually produce a more precise date and some information about the patron who commissioned it.

1. See *The Martyrdom of St. Andrew*, S. Scholastica, Rieti, in the section on rejected attributions.

2. See the catalogue entry for no. 38 in the 1957 Rieti exhibition.

3. Refice believed that the *Guardian Angel* was an early work, on what grounds she does not state.

4. If the present bare landscape setting is autograph, a date after 1640 is possible. If the picture originally had the trees and bushes seen in Iacoboni's engraving, a date in the late 1630s is more probable.

Bibliography: Bellori, 1672–96, p. 58; Palmegiani, 1932, pp. 189 and 204; Refice, 1950, p. 218; *Mostra di Rieti*, Rieti, 1957, no. 38.

65. Portrait of Giovanni Cristofano. Location unknown
Recorded Version: 1672–96 Bellori reports that Sacchi painted a portrait of the poet, Giovanni Cristofano, 'onde finse in mezza figura la Pittura, che avendo dipinto il Retratto, in un Ovato con una mano l'addita, e con l'altra lo regge e vi tien sopra la tavoletta, ed i pennelli'. Bellori does not say to whom the portrait then belonged. It is not recorded elsewhere.

ACCORDING to Bellori, the 'insigne poeta' Giovanni Cristofano was the secretary of Cardinal Luigi Gaetano (Cardinal, 1631; died 1642) and a close friend of Sacchi. The artist's portrait of the poet alluded to their relationship in allegorical terms by showing the sitter in a *trompe-l'oeil* oval held by a figure representing Painting, a conceit similar to that of Pietro Testa in his etched *Triumph of Painting*, where Painting is shown holding the just-completed picture of the coat of arms of Testa's patron, Cardinal Girolamo Buonvisi.[1] Sacchi's allegory also recalls that of Poussin in his *Self-Portrait* for Chantelou.[2] Allegorical paintings by Sacchi are rare, but one of his other examples was also a portrait, that of the singer Pasqualini.

There seems to be no other printed reference to Cristofano. The literary bent of his patron, Cardinal Gaetano, is frequently noted in seventeenth-century sources,[3] although the talents of his secretary are not mentioned. It is not surprising to learn that Sacchi was friendly with a poet, however, for Sacchi's interest in lyric poetry is amply documented by the contents of his own library.

1. See Ann Sutherland Harris and Carla Lord, 'Pietro Testa and Parnassus', *Burl. Mag.*, CXII, 1970, pp. 15–21, esp. fig. 18.
2. Donald Posner, 'The Picture of Painting in Poussin's *Self-Portrait*', *Essays in the History of Art Presented to Rudolf Wittkower*, London, 1967, pp. 200–3.
3. See, for example, Barozzi and Berchet, I, p. 171.

Bibliography: Bellori, 1672–96, p. 68.

66. Portrait of Cardinal Angelo Giori. Present location unknown

135 × 105 cm.   Plate 135
Condition: Judging from the photograph taken in 1906, the condition then was good, the figure area being well-preserved even if the background had darkened.
Versions: The relationship of the *Portrait of a Cardinal* in Ottawa to the portrait of Giori is discussed below. The portrait of Giori in the sacristy of S. Maria in Via in Camerino, which he requested in his will be placed there (Feliciangeli, p. 12), has nothing to do with the portrait under discussion.
Engravings: 1658 Engraving by Hubert Clouet for *Effigies Nomina et Cognomina S.D.N. Alexandri Papae VII et RR. DD. S.R.E. Card. nunc viventium*, Rome, 1658, p. 7. It is in the reverse sense and shows only the head and shoulders in an oval frame. The artist responsible is not named.

THE SITTER'S IDENTITY is recorded on the letter he holds, which is inscribed 'Al Emin.mo Cardinale Giorie Per A. S ...'. His coat of arms is also just visible on the back of his chair.[1] Giori's features match those shown in the engraved portrait in the *Effigies Nomina ...*, probably based on this picture, and they can also be compared with those recorded by the very primitive portrait he left to the church of S. Maria in Via in Camerino. Only one detail raises some doubt. His right hand seems to be perfectly normal, but according to Cardella (VII, p. 40 f.), Giori lost his right thumb and index finger in a hunting accident and had a special papal dispensation allowing him to elevate the host in his third and fourth fingers. Perhaps the accident occurred after the portrait was made, or perhaps the artist was asked to omit this deformity. Although Sacchi's relations with Giori are well documented,[2] there is no record in any *seicento* source of a portrait by Sacchi of Giori.[3] Moreover, since the portrait has disappeared after being sold in Vienna in 1906,[4] its appearance being recorded only by a photograph taken at that time, it is difficult to assess its quality and style. The direct gaze of the sitter is found in all of Sacchi's other portraits, but is hardly an exclusive characteristic. The odd fold forms of the surplice around the chair arm are more distinctive, and can be paralleled in Sacchi's work elsewhere, as can the shadowed triangular shade patterns on the Cardinal's cape.[5] The principal evidence for connecting Sacchi's name with the Giori portrait is, however, its similarity to the Ottawa *Portrait of a Cardinal*, an earlier, unfinished picture which was almost certainly in the artist's possession until his death (No. 21 above). Why Sacchi chose to base Giori's portrait on the Ottawa picture can only be guessed. It is true that the compositions of seated portraits of Popes and cardinals vary little, but the borrowing on this occasion is a very direct one, down to the gestures and arrangement of the drapery. Perhaps Giori knew the earlier work, admired it and asked Sacchi to use the same design. More probably the borrowing is an indication of Sacchi's growing psychological problems and decreasing rate of production and of the strains the decoration of the Lateran Baptistry was exerting on his creative

energies. Copying the Ottawa picture meant that Sacchi only had to study Giori's head and alter the proportions of the body, for Giori was a much slighter man than the subject of the earlier work. Giori was made a cardinal in 1643; his portrait can only have been commissioned after this date, but may well have been commissioned to commemorate the occasion.

1. His crest has the three Barberini bees enclosed in two entwined branches of laurel set above three mountains. Only the lower part can be seen clearly in the photograph of the portrait.
2. Giori (1585–1662) was Urban VIII's 'Maestro di Camera' from 1632 and papal chamberlain from 1639 (Cardella, *loc. cit.*). Sacchi probably knew him after he started working regularly for the Barberini even though contact is not documented before the early summer of 1639, when Giori made the first payments to Sacchi for the Lateran Baptistry decoration (Pollak, I, p. 142). The portrait of Giori in the crowd attending the Jesuit Centenary celebrations is one of the most carefully executed of all the men near the Pope, which suggests that Sacchi and Giori were on good terms by 1641, when the Centenary picture was painted. Sacchi provided an altarpiece for S. Maria in Via in Camerino, the church built in Giori's home town at his own expense between 1639 and 1643, and possibly provided the plans for the church as well. Contacts were maintained long after the fall of the Barberini, for in his will of September, 1658 Giori asked that Sacchi value his pictures in the event of his death (Feliciangeli, p. 14).
3. None of the portraits listed in the 1658 or later Giori family inventories are attributed to Sacchi (Feliciangeli, *passim*).
4. At the Dorotheum, Nov. 19–20, 1906, lot 1256. The inscription on the paper held by Giori is quoted in the catalogue. Voss records the Giori portrait in the collection of Graf Pöttlich von Petterig in 1924. The photograph of the Ottawa portrait in the Witt collection, London, is inscribed 'Trotti Sale, Paris, 1927'. However, the Ottawa portrait was in Canada by this date. Perhaps the portrait in the Trotti sale was the Giori picture. It has not been possible to trace a catalogue or further information about this sale.
5. Compare the figures of St. Ignatius in the Collegio Romano fresco and the acolyte to the left in the Capuchins' *Miracle of St. Anthony of Padua* for the surplice drapery; compare Zacharias in the *Naming of the Baptist* in the Fonte series for the triangular shading patterns, which are mainly found in Sacchi's later work.

Bibliography: Dorotheum catalogue, Vienna, Nov. 19–20, 1906, lot 1256; Voss, 1924, p. 532; Posse, 1935, p. 290.

67. Portraits of Members of the Barberini Family
cf. Plates 131–133, 136–141
Drawings, engravings and inventory entries indicate that Sacchi painted portraits of Don Taddeo, Cardinal Antonio the Elder, Cardinal Antonio the Younger and Cardinal Francesco Barberini, although only one of these portraits survives. The evidence for portraits of each sitter is discussed in separate entries.

67–1. Don Taddeo Barberini (1603–1647)
Versions: 1661 A portrait of Don Taddeo Barberini was in Sacchi's house at the time of his death (Appendix II, no. 10). It was a head and shoulders portrait.
1672–86 'Un Ritratto dell'Ecc.mo Sig.r Don Taddeo in habito da Prefetto in Piedi' measuring 10 by 7 palmi and attributed to Sacchi was in the inventory of Maffeo Barberini prepared between 1672 and 1686 (no. 394).
1693 From this date on, portraits of Don Taddeo by Sacchi are recorded in a number of guide books (see bibliography) as in the Palazzo Barberini. It is not specified whether they are bust or full-length portraits.
1818 A portrait of Don Taddeo attributed to Sacchi appears in

the 1818 and 1850 Colonna di Sciarra inventories (Mariotti, p. 134 f.).

Engraving: 1642   An engraving by Cornelius Bloemaert (Plate 141) said by Baldinucci (1686, p. 63) to be based on a drawing by Sacchi appears in the 1642 and 1647 editions of Teti's *Aedes Barberinae* etc. (p. 75).

SACCHI is said by Baldinucci to have provided the drawing used by Bloemaert for his engraved portrait of Don Taddeo in Teti's *Aedes Barberinae.* That engraving shows Don Taddeo without the hat and robes of the Prefect of Rome, an office he assumed on April 28, 1631 and to which the Barberini attached great importance.[1] The drawing on which the engraving was based can be dated before April, 1631 therefore. The engraving when compared with Ottavio Leoni's drawn portrait of Taddeo in Berlin of October, 1627,[2] which shows him without a beard or moustache, seems slightly later in date. Sacchi probably drew Taddeo in 1630 while working for him on the *Divina Sapienza* ceiling.

A bust-length portrait of Don Taddeo in the collection of Princess Henriette Barberini in Rome (G.F.N. E 13942) has been attributed to Maratta by Gamba and Waterhouse. It is close in all essential details to the Bloemaert engraving and would appear to be based on it with the costume of the Prefect's office added to it. Mezzetti rejected an attribution to Maratta himself and suggested that the portrait might be identified with one of Don Taddeo owned by Faustina, Maratta's daughter, that was said to be by Maratta's brother. Although it is not impossible that the portrait is an early work of Carlo Maratta, who was working for Don Taddeo before he left Rome for Paris in 1646,[3] an attribution to Sacchi can be excluded. The paint handling is too stiff and impasted and the resulting image has little psychological life, something which is not true of Sacchi's autograph portraits or of Bloemaert's sensitive engraving. Further investigation of this problem must also take into account Taddeo's patronage of Camassei, who is also recorded as having painted portraits of him.[4]

1. Haskell, 1963, p. 47.
2. Dahlem Museum, K. d.Z. 17093, black chalk on blue paper with white heightening, 237 × 165 mm.
3. Mezzetti, 1955, no. 78.
4. Sutherland Harris, 'Camassei Studies', 1970, p. 66, no. 11 and p. 69, no. 5.

Bibliography: Baldinucci, 1686, p. 63; De Cotte, *c.* 1689, p. 205; Rossini, 1693, p. 56 (1700 and 1704, p. 69; 1750, p. 80; Pinarolo, 1700, p. 167 (1703, p. 167; 1713, 11, p. 176); Panciroli, 1719, 11, pp. 360–2; Gamba, 1927, pp. 24–5; Waterhouse, 1937, p. 81; Mezzetti, 1955, pp. 351–2.

67–2. Cardinal Antonio Barberini (1608–1671)

Drawings: Study of the head of Cardinal Antonio, Düsseldorf (Plate 138; Harris and Schaar, no. 32, as of Cardinal Francesco); study for the torso of a cardinal, Düsseldorf (Harris and Schaar, no. 33 verso, as probably for a portrait of Cardinal Francesco). A careful red chalk drawing in the Metropolitan Museum in New York (Rogers Fund, 1966.51, 129 × 102 mm.) has an old attribution to Sacchi but is not by him. It seems to be based on the portrait engraving in Teti's *Aedes Barberinae.*

Versions: 1661   Two portraits of Cardinal Antonio are recorded in Sacchi's house at the time of his death (Appendix 11, nos. 9 and 153).

1671   A portrait of Cardinal Antonio attributed to Sacchi was recorded in the Palazzo Barberini in 1671 in an inventory of Cardinal Antonio's collection (p. 550, no. 583). It is recorded there in 1673 by Silos and in several seventeenth and eighteenth-century guidebooks (see bibliography). The last record in Barberini collections of this work is in the 1812 inventory of the Colonna di Sciarra inventories (2nd class, no. 40), although a copy appears in

an inventory of 1849 of the Casa Barberini (no. 932, 5 × 4 palmi.) Panciroli (1719, 11, p. 360) actually records two portraits of the Cardinal by Sacchi, one of which showed the sitter 'all'ora giovane'. 1724   A profile portrait of Cardinal Antonio by Sacchi was in Maratta's collection in 1724 (Galli, XXIII, no. 310).

Engravings: 1642   The engraved portrait of Cardinal Antonio in Teti's *Aedes Barberinae* of 1642 (p. 73), Plate 139, is said by Baldinucci to have been based on a drawing by Sacchi (1686, p. 63).

ALTHOUGH no painted portraits of Cardinal Antonio that can be attributed to Sacchi are known,[1] seventeenth- and eighteenth-century inventories record four portraits of the Cardinal attributed to or associated with Sacchi. The engraving by Bloemaert in Teti's *Aedes Barberinae* is very probably based on a lost drawing by Sacchi and so preserves some record of Sacchi's portraits of his most important patron, as does a brief sketch in Düsseldorf. Two other sketches of a seated cardinal at Düsseldorf on a sheet with a study for a work commissioned by Cardinal Antonio may also have been made in connection with these lost portraits.

1. A photograph in the Witt collection in London records a portrait of Cardinal Antonio in the C. Brunner collection in Paris (65 × 51 cm.) attributed to Sacchi. The attribution is not impossible, but is difficult to settle on the basis of the only photograph available.

Bibliography: Silos, 1673, p. 163. For other guide books, see above under Taddeo.

67–3. Cardinal Francesco Barberini (1597–1679)

Drawings: Study of a seated cardinal, Düsseldorf (Harris and Schaar, no. 33 recto); red chalk study for the engraved portrait of Cardinal Francesco in Teti's *Aedes Barberinae,* Berlin (K.d.Z. 25044, See Karl Noehles, *La Chiesa dei SS. Luca e Martina nell'Opera di Pietro da Cortona,* Rome, 1970, pp. 89–90 and fig. 73).

Versions: 1661   A portrait of Cardinal Francesco on a 'tela da testa' was in Sacchi's own collection in 1661 (Appendix 11, no. 16). There are no portraits of Cardinal Francesco attributed to Sacchi in any later inventories, although several seventeenth- and eighteenth century guide books mention portraits of 'all the Barberini' by Sacchi in the Palazzo Barberini (see bibliography above under Taddeo).

1930   An oval portrait of Cardinal Francesco Barberini (oil on canvas, 129 × 95·5 cm.) attributed to Carlo Maratta was in the Schloss Schönbrunn sale of February 24, 1930, lot 36. It is now in the Wallraf-Richartz-Museum, Cologne (Plate 137).[1] Dr Brigitte Klesse of the museum recently drew my attention to this work, which I knew only from an old photograph, and suggested that it be attributed to Sacchi instead. This attribution, which seems correct, is discussed below.

Engravings: 1642   The engraved portrait of Cardinal Francesco Barberini in Teti's *Aedes Barberinae* (p. 71); Plate 132, by Cornelius Bloemaert is said by Baldinucci to be based on a drawing by Sacchi (1686, p. 63), a statement confirmed by Noehles' recent discovery of the drawing in question in Berlin (see above).

ONLY one painted portrait of Cardinal Francesco Barberini that can plausibly be associated with Sacchi is recorded in a seventeenth-century source, namely that in the artist's own collection in 1661, though it is highly likely that the Barberini owned at least one portrait of Francesco by Sacchi, as the guide books imply. The portrait of Francesco now in the Wallraf-Richartz-Museum in Cologne (Plate 137), which has clearly been cut down from a rectangular format to its present oval shape, would have been too large originally to qualify as a 'tela da testa', and is thus unlikely to have been the picture owned by Sacchi in 1661. The scale and quality indicate that the Cologne picture was an official commission, made either for the Barberini themselves or for presentation to a political ally. The existence of a preparatory study by Sacchi in Düsseldorf (Plate 136), that agrees with the composition of the Cologne picture (Harris and Schaar, no. 33 recto) supports the attribution of this portrait to Sacchi, as do numerous stylistic parallels with accepted portraits. The alert, arrested gaze of the sensitively drawn face recalls the portraits of Clemente Merlini and Francesco Albani. The plump, beautifully-drawn left hand also recalls that of Clemente Merlini. Compositional similarities with other portraits of seated clerics mean little in a genre that varied little throughout the sixteenth and seventeenth centuries. More significant is Sacchi's attempt to vary the formula by subtle differences of placement. The Ottawa cardinal is seen slightly from below, Merlini from a viewpoint roughly level with the arm of his chair, and Cardinal Francesco from a level above the arm of his chair. Merlini and the Ottawa cardinal look directly at the spectator; Cardinal Francesco looks to his left, away from the direction of his body, an unusual device that enlivens the portrait by drawing in the spectator on both sides. The Cologne picture appears rubbed in the head and cape areas, but the handling throughout is consistent with Sacchi's work in the 1630s and early 1640s. The sitter appears to be in his late thirties or early forties; a date between 1635 and 1640 is therefore indicated. It should be noted in addition that the discovery of Sacchi's portrait drawing (Plate 131) for the engraved portrait of Cardinal Francesco by Bloemaert in Teti's *Aedes Barberinae* confirms Baldinucci's statement that all four portraits of the Barberini in that volume are by Sacchi.

1. The picture is first recorded in the possession of the Galerie Ehrhardt, Berlin, in 1927 when it was attributed to Maratta. Before then it may have been in an English private collection, according to Hermann Voss. In 1928 it was exhibited at Schloss Schönbrunn (Schlesien), again as Maratta. From 1944 it was in the collections of the German state. Since 1968 it has been on loan from the Bundesrepublik Deutschland to the Wallraf-Richartz-Museum, Cologne.

Bibliography: See under Taddeo Barberini above. B. Klesse, *Katalog der Italienischen, Französischen und Spanischen Gemälde bis 1800 im Wallraf-Richartz-Museum*, Cologne, 1973, pp. 113–15.

67–4. Cardinal Antonio Barberini the Elder (1569–1646)
Versions: 1661 A portrait of Cardinal Antonio 'chiamato di Sant' Onofrio' was in Sacchi's collection at the time of his death (Appendix II, no. 3). It does not survive.
1693 A portrait of the elder Cardinal Antonio attributed to Sacchi is recorded in the Palazzo Barberini by Rossini (1693, p. 56 and later editions) and Panciroli (1719, II, p. 362) but it does not appear in any Barberini inventories.
Engravings: 1642 An engraved portrait of the elder Cardinal Antonio by Cornelius Bloemaert based on a drawing by Sacchi appears in Teti's *Aedes Barberinae* (p. 67); Plate 140. The frescoed portrait of the elder Cardinal Antonio in the Capuchins' monastery on the Via Veneto is clearly based on this print.
Bibliography: See under Taddeo above, especially Rossini and Panciroli.

67–5. Don Carlo Barberini (1630–1704)
Versions: 1704 The inventory of Carlo Barberini (who was made a Cardinal in 1652) made after his death in 1704 included a 'ritratto del Sr D. Carlo con collaro all'antica tela da testa' attributed to Sacchi (p. 131, no. 384). It does not appear in any later Barberini inventories. It is possible that the sitter was not the son of Taddeo Barberini but was the older Carlo Barberini, a brother of Urban VIII who died in 1630. However, Sacchi was not patronized

regularly by the Barberini until the 1630s, and it seems more probable that the sitter was the younger man, to whom it belonged.
Bibliography: Posse, 1925, p. 123.

68. Portrait of Prince Radziwill. Formerly Palazzo Barberini, Rome
Recorded Version: 1692 The inventory of Cardinal Carlo Barberini made in 1692 and his later inventory of 1704 both include a portrait of Prince Radziwill, the Polish Ambassador to the court of Urban VIII (1692, no. 256; 1704, p. 122 verso). It is also recorded by Rossini in 1693, 1700, 1704 and 1750. It is not mentioned in the edition of 1776. The Barberini inventory gives the picture's size as ten by six palmi, indicating a full-length portrait. Its later history is not recorded.

THE PORTRAIT of the Polish Ambassador, Prince Radziwill, is one of a number of portraits in the Palazzo Barberini associated with Sacchi. Others of the French King and Queen (presumably Louis XIII and Anne of Austria), the Dauphin and Cardinal Richelieu were painted by Carlo Magnone under Sacchi's supervision (Incisa della Rocchetta).

Bibliography: Rossini, 1693, p. 53 (1700 and 1704, p. 66; 1750, p. 76); Incisa della Rocchetta, 1924, p. 70; Posse, 1925, pp. 130–1.

69. Portrait of Francesco Bracciolini. Formerly Palazzo Barberini, Rome
Recorded Versions: 1671 A portrait, tentatively identified as of Francesco Bracciolini, by Sacchi appears in Cardinal Antonio Barberini's inventory of 1671 (p. 550, no. 583–2; 'e l'altro d'un poeta con libro serrato in mano, si crede essere il Bracciolini'). It is not recorded in any later Barberini inventories. A possible alternate identification is the poet Giovanni Cristofano, of whom Sacchi painted a portrait (No. 65), q.v. for details.
1712 Maratta owned a portrait of Francesco Bracciolini by Sacchi (Galli, XXIII, no. 216), which may have been the picture owned by Cardinal Antonio Barberini in 1671 and possibly sold after his death in 1672.

ALTHOUGH Sacchi's portrait of the poet, Francesco Bracciolini (1566–1645), does not survive, it is interesting to know that he did paint the man responsible for the iconography of Pietro da Cortona's famous ceiling of *Divine Providence* in the Palazzo Barberini.

70. Aurora. Formerly Palazzo Barberini, Rome
Drawings: Two studies for the figure of Aurora, Windsor; Plate 142 (Blunt and Cooke, no. 741); study for the figure of Aurora and putti, Windsor (Blunt and Cooke, no. 742); composition study, Dahlem Museum, Berlin (No. 21707, black chalk on greenish-grey paper, 198 × 258 mm. The drawing, which is squared for transfer, is damaged and rubbed). A copy after the lost picture was one of a number of drawings in an album sold at Sotheby's on July 10, 1963; Plate 143. A drawing at Düsseldorf of Aurora seated on clouds and surrounded by putti attributed to Sacchi by Budde (p. 17) is by Giuseppe Passeri (Harris and Schaar, no. 146).
Versions: 1644 A version painted by Carlo Magnone on Sacchi's instructions for the 'appartam(ent)o nuovo' of Cardinal Antonio Barberini was ready by December 31, 1644 (Incisa della Rocchetta, p. 70). It was 'a guazzo con l'aurora in ovato'. It is not recorded in any later Barberini inventories, nor is it mentioned by any of Sacchi's biographers.
1661 A version in the artist's house in 1661 (Appendix II, no. 220), described as an octagon three palmi wide, is not certainly recorded in any later sources. It might be the *Aurora* that later passed from a Milanese collection into that of the Liechtenstein family in Vienna, q.v.

1692   A version bought from the collection of Count Berka in Milan in 1692 for the Liechtenstein collection for 250 florins is not subsequently recorded in any later collections (Posse, 1925, p. 104).

THE COMPOSITION of this lost work is recorded by three preparatory studies for it and one drawing apparently based on a painting. It was ready by late December, 1644, when Carlo Magnone painted an *Aurora* on Sacchi's instructions for Cardinal Antonio Barberini. The style of the preparatory studies at Windsor suggests that the composition was prepared in the 1630s.[1] It would be surprising for Magnone to have painted a version for Cardinal Antonio Barberini if a version by Sacchi himself was available. Therefore it seems probable that the *Aurora* recorded in Sacchi's house in 1661 was only painted after 1644 and after his assistant had produced that 'guazzo . . . in ovato' using Sacchi's preparatory studies. It is also possible that a version painted in the 1630s by Sacchi himself for a patron other than Cardinal Antonio was then to be seen in a Roman private collection.

Blunt did not note the possible connection between Magnone's commission to paint *Aurora* and the drawings at Windsor and suggested instead that they were used by Maratta when preparing his *Aurora* formerly at Osterley. Maratta almost certainly knew both Sacchi's drawings and the finished composition, but the actual relationship between the compositions is not closer than the relationship between both Sacchi's and Maratta's *Auroras* and those by Guido Reni in the Casino Rospigliosi and by Francesco Albani in the Palazzo Verospi.

1. The Berlin drawing is too damaged to permit a proper analysis of its date.

Bibliography: Incisa della Rocchetta, 1924, p. 70; Posse, 1925, pp. 32 and 104; Blunt and Cooke, 1960, p. 93.

71. Portrait of an Officer. Staatliche Museen, East Berlin

72 × 60 cm.   Plate 134
Condition: It is good apart from signs of rubbing and wear on the forehead and bridge of the nose.

THIS PORTRAIT, acquired in Rome in 1841–2, was attributed to Bernardo Strozzi in 1904 in the catalogue of the Gemäldegalerie. This attribution was maintained by the museum in subsequent catalogues until 1930, when the portrait was described simply as Italian seventeenth-century. Luisa Mortari revived the Strozzi attribution in 1955 and repeated it in her monograph on Strozzi in 1966, but the attribution was challenged in a review by Matteucci. An attribution to Sacchi has not been suggested previously.

The portraits by Sacchi with which the Berlin *Officer* has most in common are those of Francesco Albani in the Prado, of a cardinal in Ottawa and of Clemente Merlini in the Borghese Gallery in Rome. The sitters in all four portraits have the same direct gaze with the head positioned in a similar way—not quite frontal and not quite three-quarter view. All four works are close technically in details such as the drawing of the eyes, hair and beard and in general qualities such as the understated paint handling and subtle tonal gradations. The treatment of costume details should be compared with similar passages in the Fonte series, for example the priest in the *Annunciation to Zacharias*.

The identification of the Berlin *Officer* remains to be discovered. He was presumably associated with the Barberini circle, as were most of Sacchi's sitters. Possible candidates would be men such as Pirro Gaetano, Vincenzo della Marra and Federico Savelli, all of whom directed Papal forces either in the Valtelline dispute or during the war against Castro.[1] A date around 1640 is indicated by the paint handling, which is more controlled than in portraits of an earlier date.

1. Aldo Valori, *Condottieri e Generali del Seicento*, Rome, 1943, *sub voce.*
Bibliography: Staatliche Museen zu Berlin, Gemäldegalerie—catalogues of 1904, 1906, 1909, 1921 and 1930; L. Mortari, 'Su Bernardo Strozzi', *Bollettino d'Arte*, 1955, p. 311 f.; L. Mortari, *Bernardo Strozzi*, Rome, 1966, p. 92 and fig. 296; A. M. Matteucci in *Arte Veneta*, 1966, XX, p. 297.

72. The Drunkenness of Noah. Various locations

Drawings: Composition study, Düsseldorf (Harris and Schaar, no. 83); study for the figures of Noah and Ham, Windsor; Plate 144 (Blunt and Cooke, no. 745). A final composition study in the Metropolitan Museum of Art, New York (red chalk on cream paper, 187 × 260 mm.; no. 1976.77, The Harry G. Sperling Fund) matches the final composition with only minor variants. A copy of this drawing was with J. Petit-Horry in Paris until 1972 (red chalk on white paper, 185 × 250 mm.). A slight sketch at Düsseldorf of a male nude (Harris and Schaar, no. 104) comes close to the pose of Ham in the Düsseldorf composition study and may be a preliminary study made for this figure before the pose was rejected. A brush drawing on blue paper said to be connected with Sacchi's *Noah* was sold from the Skippe collection at Christie's in 1958 (Nov. 20–21, lot 191). It was not photographed and I have not traced the present owner. Sacchi almost never used blue paper but the drawing might nevertheless have been autograph. There are drawn copies based on the final design at Windsor (Blunt and Cooke, nos. 738 and 739), in the Uffizi (Refice, 1950, p. 219 as an autograph drawing) and at Düsseldorf (Harris and Schaar, nos. 121–4).

Versions: 1648   Version painted for Marchese Antonio Ruffo, which reached Messina on April 2, 1648 (Ruffo, XIII, 1919, p. 44), for which Sacchi was paid 200 scudi. It is recorded in the Ruffo collections until 1818 (Ruffo, *art. cit.*, p. 45) but its later history is unknown. Posse (1925, p. 103, note 4) identified it with the version that went from the Sciarra collection in Rome to that of Senator Chimirri in Catanzaro, as did Ruffo (*loc. cit.*), but since the Sciarra picture is recorded in their collection in 1812 (see below under 1671), Posse cannot be right.

1658   A version of or an academy based on the *Noah* is recorded in the 1658 inventory of Cardinal Angelo Giori's collection (Feliciangeli, p. 31) where it is recorded as 'Un Noè nudo intiero fatto dal sig. Andrea Sacchi'. It is not mentioned in the extracts from later inventories of the family published by Feliciangeli and its later history is not known.

1659   A version now in the Kunsthistorisches Museum, Vienna (Plate 146), is first recorded in the 1659 inventory of Prince Leopold Wilhelm (Engerth, p. 286, no. 402). It has been catalogued as a copy since 1912 but it differs in a number of ways from the Berlin and Catanzaro compositions, principally in the relationship of Ham to the other three figures. He is set further back, a change that makes the cloak held by his brothers more prominent. The composition is also extended on all four sides. The foreground plants also differ from those in the Berlin and Catanzaro versions. I have not so far been able to study the original, but from photographs the quality appears to be good and may be partly autograph.

A version is recorded in the inventory of Cardinal Mazarin's collection made after his death on March 5, 1661 (No. 1253, 'Un autre tableau faict par André Sacqui, sur toile, raprasentant Noé couché nud soulz une treille, et ses enfans; figures grandes au naturel, la somme de six cens livres, cy . . . 600' [Cosnac, p. 340 and Aumale, p. 347]). Mazarin probably acquired the picture after 1656 since it does not appear in the inventory made of his collection in that year. Its later history is obscure although it may be the version bought by Rendorp in 1765, *q.v.*

1661   A version was bought from Sacchi's heirs on June 10, 1661 which was said to have been painted for 'Abbate Rospigliosi'

(Incisa della Rocchetta, 1924, p. 74). Sacchi's heirs were paid on June 30, 1661. The picture can probably be identified with the version still in Sacchi's house at the time of his death (Appendix II, no. 28). Giulio Rospigliosi was a cardinal by this date. His nephew Felice may have been an abbot by this date, although published documents only record him receiving the income from two abbeys six years later (Pastor, XXXI, p. 476). The later history of this version is not known; it may however be the picture first recorded in the Pallavicini collection in 1713, q.v.

1671 'Un quadro di Noè inebriato ... et altre tre figure ... di p(al)mi 8½ in c(irc)a per ogni verso' was in Cardinal Antonio Barberini's collection in 1671 (no. 161), when it was given the extremely high valuation of 900 scudi. In 1672 it passed to Cardinal Francesco Barberini (no. 64); in 1692, it is recorded in the collection of Cardinal Carlo Barberini (no. 421), as it was again in 1704 (Incisa della Rocchetta, p. 74). It appears also in the Palestrina Inventory of 1738–9. De Cotte (Actes II, p. 205) saw it in the Palazzo Barberini in about 1689 and it is recorded there also by Bellori and by many late *seicento* and *settecento* guide books (see bibliography). In 1812 the Barberini inheritance was divided between the heirs of Cornelia Costanza Barberini (1716–97) and her husband Giulio Cesare Colonna di Sciarra (d. 1796), the *Noah* going to the Colonna di Sciarra branch (Colonna di Sciarra inventory, 3rd class no. 39, 300 scudi), in whose collection it is next recorded in July, 1816 (Mariotti, p. 135, no. 42; see also Visconti, 1847, II, p. 660). It is next recorded in the collection of Senator Bruno Chimirri of Catanzaro (Ruffo, XIII, 1919, p. 45; Schlösser, 1931, pp. 420–1), who, according to Avvocato Antonio Pelaggi, the present director of the Museo Provinciale of Catanzaro, obtained it as a gift from Count H. M. von Bülow, the German Ambassador. Chimirri gave the picture to the Museo Provinciale. At present it is kept in the Salone Vecchio of the Prefettura (Plate 147).

1678 Version recorded by Passeri in the collection of the Contestabile Colonna (p. 304) and presumably identical with the copy recorded in the Palazzo Colonna in 1783 (Colonna, 1783, no. 112). Its later history is not recorded.

1713 'Un quadro in tela di p(almi) 12 e 9 ... rappresenta Noè che dorme con tre figlioli che uno lo deride—opera di Andrea Sacchi' was in the collection of Prince Niccolò Pallavicini on October 2, 1713 (Zeri, 1959, p. 306, no. 207). It is possible that this was the version bought by Cardinal Antonio Barberini for 'Abbate Rospigliosi' in 1661 (q.v. above) because the Rospigliosi and Pallavicini families were later related by marriage. It is presumably the same picture recorded in the Galleria Rospigliosi in an inventory of May 1, 1833 (Mariotti, p. 172, no. 177). No version now belongs to the Rospigliosi-Pallavicini family, although a version hangs in a wing of the Palazzo Rospigliosi now owned by the Federazione di Consorzi Agrari (G.F.N. E 38493). This is a less sensitive version than that now in Vienna; it is probably entirely the work of Sacchi's studio.

1740 Version sold in London from the collection of Lord Halifax (lot 80, 'Noah and his sons'). It went to an unknown buyer for £16 (Victoria and Albert Museum, manuscript sale catalogues, 1711–59)

1746 Version bought in Rome by Matthew Brettingham for the Earl of Leicester and described as a copy after Sacchi by Carlo Maratta (Holkham MS 744, p. 108). It is no longer in the family collections, nor is it known when or how it left Holkham.

1765 Version bought by Rendorp in Amsterdam for Frederick II of Prussia at the sale of pictures from Schloss Hubertusberg; they came from the collection of Frederick Augustus II, Elector of Saxony, who had died two years earlier. Rendorp paid 1175 guilders for the *Noah*. This version is now in the Staatliche Museen, East Berlin (oil on canvas, 208 × 256 cm.); Plate 145. Its earlier history is discussed below; for the information given here, see Schlösser, 1931, pp. 140–1, no. 422.

TWO OF the eleven recorded versions of Sacchi's composition of *The Drunkenness of Noah* can be dated 1644–8 from documentary, historical and stylistic evidence. Bellori includes a *Noah* among the pictures Sacchi painted for Cardinal Antonio Barberini and one version is first recorded in the Cardinal's inventory of 1671. It does not appear in the Cardinal's inventory of 1644, but its absence is not conclusive evidence for a *terminus post quem*.[1] It must have been commissioned shortly after 1644 at the latest, however, for Cardinal Antonio left Rome for exile in Paris on September 28, 1645, and could not, for political reasons, send commissions to Sacchi during the first years of his exile. Sacchi completed little work after the Cardinal's return to Rome in 1652. Therefore it seems probable that the Cardinal's version was commissioned and under way by 1644–5. The version completed and sent to Marchese Ruffo in Messina by April, 1648, provides a firm *terminus ante quem* for the composition. The existence of studies for the *Drunkenness of Noah* (Plate 144) on the recto of a sheet of studies for the fresco of *The Destruction of Pagan Idols* of 1645–7 in the Lateran Baptistry also indicates a date in the mid-1640s for the *Noah*.

Four of the eleven versions recorded in *seicento* and *settecento* sources can be traced today; the best of these are the pictures now in Berlin and Catanzaro[2] (Plates 145, 147). The Catanzaro picture is the version made for Cardinal Antonio Barberini. Ruffo's *Noah*, the earliest recorded version, cannot be identified with the Berlin picture, for the former was still in Sicily in 1818 while the Berlin picture was bought in Amsterdam in 1765. Prince Leopold Wilhelm's version is still in Vienna; the Rospigliosi version is probably that still in the Palazzo Rospigliosi; the Colonna version was in Rome still in 1783. This leaves Cardinal Mazarin's version, whose history after 1661 is not recorded, as the only plausible candidate for identification with the Berlin picture. The French connections of the Barberini family explain how Mazarin came to acquire a version of such high quality, which Cardinal Antonio may even have brought with him when he went to France in 1645.[3] Both the Berlin and the Catanzaro versions are in need of cleaning and restoration, the Berlin picture urgently so. Until this work has been carried out, a full analysis of their quality and character must wait.

1. The *Hagar and Ishmael* (No. 22) is not recorded in Cardinal Antonio's 1644 inventory either but on stylistic grounds it can be dated in the early 1630s.

2. When seen in June, 1968, the condition of the Berlin version (208 × 256 cm.) was precarious. The paint surface was separating from its coarse canvas support and was flaking off in neat squares, in particular along a central horizontal fold line. There were also small holes and tears, for example in Ham's left leg. A photograph taken before 1939 shows that the picture was in good condition then. Its present state is the result of unsuitable storage conditions during and after World War II. The authorities are aware of the urgent need to restore this picture but their limited facilities have so far prevented anything being done. The Catanzaro version is in a much healthier state than the Berlin picture. The surface is obscured by dust and old varnish to some extent. There are areas of paint loss from flaking on the lower left near the grapes and near the bowl held by Noah. Noah's right hand has been restored and vine leaves have been added relatively recently to cover his pudenda.

3. The Elector of Saxony bought pictures from the Palazzo Barberini in the 1750s, but the Barberini inventories of the eighteenth and nineteenth centuries, which Dr Frances Vivian has carefully rechecked for me, prove that their *Noah* did not leave Rome until the nineteenth century. I wish to thank Dr Annelise Mayer-Meintschel for going to a great deal of trouble on my behalf in order to answer my enquiries about Barberini purchases by the Elector of Saxony. She traced notes made by Hans Posse from eighteenth-century archives of the Gemälde-

galerie, now destroyed, which showed that on April 6, 1754, a certain Garini was writing from Florence to Rome on behalf of Count Brühl, the Elector's artistic adviser, 'wegen eines Andrea Sacchi'.

Bibliography: Bellori, 1672–96, p. 67; Passeri, 1679, p. 304; De Cotte, 1689, p. 205; Rossini, 1693, p. 53 (1700 and 1704, p. 66; 1750, p. 76; 1760, I, p. 94; 1771, I, p. 94; 1776, II, p. 188); Pinarolo, 1700, p. 171 (1703, p. 171; 1713, II, p. 179); Panciroli, 1719, II, p. 361; Pascoli, 1730, I, p. 16; Roisecco, 1750, II, p. 298; Chiusole, 1782, p. 49; Ruffo, 1916, pp. 30, 34, 42, 318 and 387; 1919, pp. 44–5; Florence, 1922, no. 872; Incisa della Rocchetta, 1924, p. 74; Voss, 1924, p. 531; Posse, 1925, p. 103 f. and *passim*; Schlösser, 1931, pp. 420–1.

73. Venus and Cupid. Formerly Villa Doria Pamphili, Rome
Versions: 1661   Six paintings of Venus are recorded in the artist's house in 1661. One depicted Venus and Cupid, another showed Venus, Cupid and an old woman. The rest were unfinished sketches of Venus alone, one of them on copper (Appendix II, nos. 116, 117, 118, 234, 243 and 294).
1776   A version possibly of the Pamphili picture was in the Palazzo Colonna in 1776 (Rossini, II, p. 207). The subject was described in 1783 as 'Venere (che) colca con Cupido' and was painted on an imperial-size canvas (Colonna, 1783, p. 29, no. 176).
1855   A *Venus and Cupid* attributed to Sacchi was sold from the Collot collection in 1855 for 325 francs (Mireur, VI, p. 388).

ONLY Passeri of Sacchi's biographers discusses this work. He says that it was commissioned by Prince Camillo Pamphili for his new villa on the Janiculum, 'Il Belrespiro', but there are no later references to the *Venus and Cupid* in later Pamphili inventories or records. Perhaps it was sold after the death in 1709 of Prince Giovanni Battista Pamphili, in whose collection Passeri saw it. It does not seem possible to identify the Pamphili picture with the version recorded later in the Colonna collections, for the latter was apparently a slightly smaller work.
The Pamphili picture showed Venus on a bed with putti aiming flowers and arrows at her, the flowers having been painted by another artist.[1] The figures must have been close to life size, for the canvas measured eight by ten palmi. No drawings certainly connected with this work survive. However, a careful red chalk study at Chatsworth of Venus seated in a landscape and crowned with garlands by flying putti while other putti play with her drapery may record a similar composition.[2] The Chatsworth drawing was made in the early 1630s however, whereas the Pamphili *Venus* must have been painted around 1648.[3]

1. The artist in question may have been Mario de' Fiori, who was living near Sacchi in 1647 and 1648 (Stati d'Anime, S. Nicola in Arcione, 1647, p. 27 verso and 1648, p. 69, in the Archivio del Vicariato di Roma). Mario certainly worked with Maratta later.
2. No. 536, red chalk on cream paper, 245 × 184 mm. The drawing is discussed more fully in *Master Drawings*, 1971, no. 4, p. 388 and pl. 28a.
3. Camillo, who resigned his cardinalate in order to marry Donna Olimpia Aldobrandini in February, 1647, was exiled from Rome by the Pope until late that year. Construction of the villa for which the picture was commissioned was complete by the spring of 1648 (O. Pollak, *Zeitschrift für Geschichte der Architektur*, IV, 1910–11, Heft 3–4). Passeri was friendly with both Algardi and Grimaldi, who were working on the Villa Belrespiro, so his information about the picture is likely to be correct.

Bibliography: Scannelli, 1657, pp. 207–8; Passeri, 1679, pp. 300–1 and 304; Posse, 1925, p. 106; Hess, 1934, p. 304, note 2.

74. Innocent X (Giovanni Battista Pamphili, 1572–1655). Present location unknown

Recorded Version: 1747   A portrait of the Pamphili Pope attributed to Sacchi was sold from the collection of Jonathan Richardson in 1747 (March 3, lot 36; sold to Sir Paul Methuen for £1.7.–). It is not recorded by any later sources. I owe this reference to Frank Simpson.

SIGNIFICANTLY, there were no portraits of Innocent X or other members of the Pamphili family in the collection of Sacchi, which included portraits of all his other major patrons. This fact does not prove that Sacchi never painted Innocent X, but his relations with the Pamphili family were not extensive, although he did work for them on at least two recorded occasions.[1] This one reference to a lost work is hardly sufficient evidence however to prove that Sacchi did paint Innocent X.

1. See the entry for the lost Pamphili *Venus*. Sacchi is also documented as painting frescoes in a chapel, now destroyed, in the Palazzo Pamphili in Piazza Navona (Jörg Garms, *Quellen aus dem Archiv Doria-Pamphili in Rom unter Innocenz X*, Rome and Vienna, 1972, Document 459, p. 107). The artist's name is given as 'C. Sacchi', evidently a misprint.

75. The Death of St. Anne. S. Carlo ai Catinari, Rome
430 × 230 cm.   Plates 150, 151
Condition: The paint surface is sound beneath a layer of yellowed varnish. The picture was last restored in 1839 by Camuccini (*Memorie di SS. Biagio e Carlo*, p. 109).
Drawings: Composition study, Windsor (Blunt and Cooke, no. 744); studies for the kneeling woman on the left, Düsseldorf (Harris and Schaar, no. 84); study for the figure of Joachim with separate studies of his hands and arms, Copenhagen (Inventory no. Tu 17.3 verso, red chalk with a little white heightening, 225 × 352 mm. Plate 148. For the recto, see cat. no. 57. This drawing is recorded in the Gaburri collection in Florence by Campori.[1] It was sold from it in 1742 and reputedly entered an English collection; in fact it has the marks of N. Hone (Lugt 2793) and Charles Rogers (Lugt 625) but its subsequent owners prior to its acquisition by the museum are not known. It was brought to my attention by Jacob Bean); two drapery studies for the lap of Joachim, Düsseldorf (Harris and Schaar, no. 85; it is incorrectly said to be for the figure of Joseph; Plate 149); two studies of a figure seen from behind, Düsseldorf (Harris and Schaar, no. 86; it seems to be a life study related to the kneeling woman holding a cloth on the left).
There is a copy after the Windsor composition study in the British Museum (No. D 24462, red chalk on buff paper, 252 × 304 mm.) and a Marattesque red chalk drawing after the painting in Leipzig (Museum der Bildenden Kunst, Renzi collection, book 89, p. 81). An autograph study by Maratta after the painting is in Düsseldorf (Harris and Schaar, no. 589). A composition study of this subject attributed to Sacchi in the Staedel Institute in Frankfort (no. 474) is not by him. There was a pen and wash composition study for the *St. Anne* in the Julienne collection in 1767 (Mireur, IV, p. 388). Another composition drawing described as 'The first Design for the death of St. Anne ... A. Sacchi' was sold in London in 1754 for 17 gns. (Victoria and Albert Museum, London, Manuscript Sale Catalogues, 1711–59, Mr. Blackwood's sale, 2nd day, lot 17).
Versions: 1661   Canvas recorded in the artist's house at the time of his death (Appendix II, no. 224). Its later history is not recorded.
1712   'Un abozzo del Transito di Sant'Anna, mano d'Andrea Sacchi, con cornice bianca' was in Maratta's possession in 1712 (Galli, XXIII, p. 72, no. 317). It may have been the picture in Sacchi's house in 1661 although that picture is not described as a sketch. Maratta also owned a drawing after the painting by himself (*op. cit.*, p. 235, no. 56), but since this was presumably a finished study of the whole work, it does not seem right to identify it with the sheet of studies based on the painting by him at Düsseldorf mentioned above.

1963   A copy of the *St. Anne* on the Paris art market in this year (oil on canvas, 60 × 36 cm.) was brought to my attention by Pierre Rosenberg. Its present location is not known. A second copy, possibly *seicento* but not of high quality, is currently (1969) on the Roman art market.

Engravings: There are *seicento* engravings by Cesare Fantetti and François Collignon. An engraving by Jacob Frey is dated 1726.

Documents: Payments to the artist, if recorded in the church archives, were destroyed in a nineteenth-century fire, but the date when the picture was installed—November, 1649—is recorded in an eighteenth-century summary of the church's history (*Memorie di SS. Biagio e Carlo*, p. 34).

The Death of St. Anne, which Bellori says was one of Sacchi's last works, was installed in S. Carlo ai Catinari in November, 1649, but was probably commissioned several years previously.[2] The Copenhagen drawing with studies on the verso for *The Birth of the Baptist* suggests, as might be expected, that Sacchi began working on the *St.. Anne* as the Fonte series neared completion in the late 1640s. It is his largest canvas and best preserved work of that decade.

1. p. 533, no. 113. The same collection also had a drawing attributed to Sacchi with a study for Joachim on the verso and a composition study and a study of Zacharias on the recto (p. 540, no. 177). It was this drawing that went to England in 1742, according to Campori, but the collectors' marks on the Copenhagen drawing indicate that it did too. The former is still lost.
2. Romanelli, Giacinto Gimignani, Mattia Preti, Pietro da Cortona and Lanfranco were all working for the Barnabites in S. Carlo ai Catinari during the 1640s, mostly before 1648–9. Sacchi was probably prevented from working on the *St. Anne* until the Fonte decorations were complete. For S. Carlo, see Waterhouse, 1937, *sub voce*.

Bibliography: Scannelli, 1657, pp. 207–8; Bellori, 1672–96, pp. 57–8; Silos, 1673, p. 38; Titi, 1674, p. 106 (and all later editions incl. 1763, p. 97); Sebastiani, 1689, p. 72; Panciroli, 1719, II, p. 239; Pascoli, 1730, I, p. 16; Roisecco, 1750, I, p. 583; Rossini, 1750, II, p. 155 (1776 ed., II, p. 398); Vasi, 1770 (1765), p. 539; *Memorie di SS. Biagio e Carlo*, 1861, pp. 34, n. 2 and 109; Voss, 1924, p. 530; Posse, 1925, pp. 95f. and *passim*; Hess, 1934 y. 304,, n. 6; Posse, 1935 p., 290; Waterhouse, 1937, p. 91; Wittkower, 1958, p. 355; Francis H. Dowley, 'Carlo Maratti, Carlo Fontana, and the Baptismal Chapel in Saint Peter's', *Art Bulletin*, 1965, pp. 76–7.

76. St. John the Baptist in the Wilderness. S. Niccolò, Fabriano
284 × 190 cm.   Plate 152

Condition: The surface is blotchy, as if it has been covered with water that was allowed to dry. There is a good deal of discoloured varnish and surface dirt. The greens and browns in the landscape have darkened. There seems to be no serious surface damage, however, and the condition may prove to be reasonable when the picture is cleaned.

Drawings: Studies for the Baptist's right arm, Windsor (Blunt and Cooke, no. 757; they are connected with *The Destruction of Pagan Idols* fresco in S. Giovanni in Fonte); studies for the Baptist's right hand and left leg, Windsor (Blunt and Cooke, no. 759; catalogued as no. 757); studies for the right arm and hand of the Baptist, Windsor (Blunt and Cooke, no. 758; catalogued as nos. 757 and 759); studies for the drapery and right leg of the Baptist, Düsseldorf (Harris and Schaar, no. 87); studies for the figure of Christ, Windsor (Blunt and Cooke, no. 782; catalogued as not connected with a known composition); studies for the drapery of Christ, Düsseldorf (Harris and Schaar, no. 88).

Versions: 1661   A *St. John the Baptist*, possibly a version of this composition, was in Sacchi's house at the time of his death (Appendix II, no. 4). Its later history is not known.

1670   A smaller version (190 × 150 cm.) of the Fabriano canvas

is in S. Maria dei Teatini in Ferrara, where it is first recorded by Borsetti. Its history and relationship to the Fabriano version are discussed below. No photograph is at present available.

THERE ARE two versions of Sacchi's *St. John the Baptist in the Wilderness*, one in a Camaldolese church in Fabriano and one in a Theatine church in Ferrara. Neither is documented or recorded by the artist's biographers, while the quality of both is obscured by their poor condition. However, some information about the Ferrara version is recorded by a local *seicento* historian, while the subject matter, style and preparatory studies provide other clues as to the date of this composition.

The Fabriano version is the larger and better preserved of the two, and may also be the better painted,[1] but nothing is known of its early history. S. Niccolò was rebuilt in 1626 and contains a Guercino of 1644 and a Giacinto Brandi of 1653,[2] but these two pictures are not part of a coordinated scheme of decoration and the Sacchi was not necessarily painted at the same time. A cardinal's coat of arms in the apparently original seventeenth-century setting would seem to be the clue necessary to identify the patron, but no seventeenth- or eighteenth-century cardinal used the crest shown.[3] Presumably the patron was, like Guercino's,[4] a local man, who on this occasion was perhaps encouraged to patronize Sacchi by the Camaldolese monks familiar with his high altarpiece in their Roman church.

The Theatine church in Ferrara was built between 1618 and 1653.[5] Borsetti records that the altar of San Giovanni was paid for by a certain Alessandro Scanaroli, whose recorded art patronage, with the exception of a commission from Guercino, was exclusively local.[6] Other members of the Scanaroli family had connections with Rome and the Barberini family, and this perhaps explains how Alessandro came to patronize Sacchi.[7] Guercino's *Presentation at the Temple* in the same church was under way in 1654 and was completed early in 1655.[8] Sacchi's altarpiece must also have been commissioned shortly after the church's structure was completed, if only because he apparently completed no commissioned works after 1655.

The subject and its treatment are clearly related to the *Life of the Baptist* series for S. Giovanni in Fonte and in particular to the scene of the Baptist preaching. Possibly Sacchi had planned a scene of the Baptist pointing to the coming Saviour as an alternative to one of the eight incidents finally chosen, and offered the design to his patrons in Fabriano and Ferrara afterwards. The Fonte series may, however, simply have attracted the attention of patrons wanting pictures of the Baptist. The related drawings are all in roughly handled black chalk, recalling similar preparatory studies for the *St. Romuald* and Forlì *St. Peter*, both works of the early 1630s. The *Baptist* studies differ from those earlier drawings in being close to the executed design instead of being early preliminary studies, and in having that emphasized *sfumato* found in other late drawings, notably the Düsseldorf studies for Joachim in *The Death of St. Anne* and for the Virgin in *The Dream of St. Joseph*. A date in the early 1650s fits the known circumstances of the Ferrara commission and the stylistic evidence. Whether either or both versions are wholly or partially the work of studio assistants will only be known after both have been cleaned.

1. The condition of both works at present makes any assessment of quality unwise.
2. *Inventario degli Oggetti*, p. 94 and Marcoaldi, *loc. cit.*
3. The *stemma* has three gold stars arranged to make an inverted triangle on a blue ground. A horizontal red band in the centre is decorated with a gold snake. This is the coat of arms of the Giampè family that lived in Bevagna, Fabriano, Assisi and Carrara (Spreti, III, p. 434), but no seventeenth- or eighteenth-century cardinal had that name. The meagre local historical literature provides no information about seventeenth-century members of the family. The parish priest informed me in 1963

that the chapel had belonged to the Giampè and Zonghi-Lotti families, but at what dates was unclear.

4. Malvasia, 1848, II, p. 324.
5. Scalabrini, pp. 145–6. Other writers (Cittadella, Frizzi) give 1629 as the starting date; all sources agree on 1653 for the completion of the structure.
6. The Guercino was also a *St. John the Baptist*, commissioned as a gift for the Emperor (Malvasia, 1848, II, p. 322). For his local activities, see Borsetti, pp. 136 and 231. I have been unable to trace his birth or death dates.
7. Cavaliere Camillo Scanaroli (d. 1648) and Giovanni Battista Scanaroli (d. 1664 in Rome as a bishop; buried in S. Giovanni Laterano) were both pages to Don Taddeo Barberini during the procession celebrating his election to the post of Prefetto of Rome (Borsetti, pp. 93–5).
8. Malvasia, 1848, II, pp. 335 and 336.

Bibliography: Borsetti, 1670, p. 127; Brisighella, 1704–35, p. 28; Barotti, 1770, p. 45; Scalabrini, 1773, p. 147; Frizzi, 1787, p. 48; Avventi, 1838, p. 96; Ramelli, 1852, no. 49; Marcoaldi, 1873, p. 161; Benigni, 1924, p. 97; Voss, 1924, p. 53; Medri, *Ferrara*, 1933, p. 156; Hess, 1934, p. 304, note 6; Posse, 1935, p. 290; Molajoli, 1936, p. 143; *Inventario degli Oggetti*, VII, 1936, p. 94. All the local literature refers only to the version in that town; the remaining authors mention both works.

77. St. Philip Neri's Vision of St. John the Baptist. Formerly in the Oratory of St. Philip Neri, S. Maria della Vittoria, Valletta
Size not recorded.   Plate 153
Condition: Judging from a photograph published in 1930, the condition of the picture then was not good. The varnish had bloomed and the picture needed cleaning.
Version: 1661 There was a picture in Sacchi's house in 1661 of 'S. Filippo, e S. Gio. Batt(ist)a' (Appendix II, no. 206). Its later history is unrecorded. It was probably a version of the Malta picture.

BELLORI records a picture by Sacchi of St. Philip Neri's vision of the Baptist in the church of the Oratorian Fathers in Malta. Only one descriptive guide to the city of Valletta, namely Roberto Paribene's *Malta*, makes any reference to the picture in question. He illustrates the picture which was then in the Oratory of St. Philip Neri attached to S. Maria della Vittoria, but identifies it only in the index of plates as a work by 'Filippo [sic] Sacchi'.[1] Sacchi's picture was destroyed when the church was bombed in World War II.[2]
Bellori's attribution seems to be right. The types in the altarpiece are Sacchi's and the composition can be paralleled in his other work. The pose of the Baptist recalls that used by Sacchi for God the Father in the altarpiece in S. Carlo al Corso executed by Luini with assistance from Sacchi. The putto recalls one of those on the lower right in the Capuchins' altarpiece, *The Vision of St. Bonaventure*, while St. Philip Neri's pose is that of St. Bonaventure reversed. Such extensive borrowings from his own work suggest that the Malta picture was painted in the 1640s, when Sacchi reused his own earlier ideas and depended on the works of his contemporaries to a greater extent than previously. He also executed two other commissions for the Oratorian Fathers in this decade, namely the *Visitation* in Perugia and the *Immaculate Conception* in Foligno. The Fathers evidently appreciated Sacchi's work, which explains how Sacchi's picture came to their chapel in Valletta. The recent loss of this work is regrettable, the 1640s being the most poorly documented decade of Sacchi's activity.

1. R. Paribene, *Malta*, Bergamo, 1930, pp. 64 and 103.
2. I am indebted to Dr. J. A. Cauchi of the National Museum in Valletta for this information and for the photograph of the destroyed picture. According to Ferres, a certain Reverend Giuseppe Ebejer brought Sacchi's picture from Rome.

Bibliography: Bellori, 1672–96, p. 66; Achille Ferres, *Descrizione storica delle Chiese di Malta*, Gozo (Malta), 1866; R. Paribene, *Malta*, Bergamo, 1930, pp. 64 and 103.

78. The Presentation of Christ in the Temple. Galleria Nazionale dell'Umbria, Perugia   Plate 154
244 × 163 cm.
Condition: This picture was cleaned and restored for the first time in 1965. The canvas, which had never been lined, had become very thin and was torn in places, the varnish and some of the paint had oxydized and had sunk into the canvas, and there were areas of paint loss from flaking. The cleaning arrested the decay, but the picture had become too fragile to be cleaned properly, and a small accumulation of dirt and oxydized paint remains, obscuring the colour to some extent. The cleaning is described in the catalogue of the exhibition of cleaned pictures held at the Galleria Nazionale in 1966 (p. 16).
Drawings: Composition study, Louvre (Inventory no. 14475, red chalk with sepia wash and pen on cream paper, 270 × 186 mm.; Plate 155. The drawing, formerly described as anonymous, was correctly identified independently by Philip Pouncey, Walter Vitzthum and myself. Vitzthum recently published it (*Burl. Mag.*, CX, 1968, p. 382 and fig. 54), identifying the subject as the Circumcision. Its relationship to the Perugia altarpiece is discussed below; study for the two men in the left foreground, Düsseldorf (Harris and Schaar, no. 89); study for the arms of the second angel from the left, Düsseldorf (Harris and Schaar, no. 70 as for *The Destruction of Pagan Idols* fresco).
Documents: Guardabassi records that the artist was paid 300 scudi for the picture in 1651. Posse reported that a manuscript history of San Filippo Neri, the church for which the picture was made, in the Archivio Comunale, records the arrival of the picture from Rome on July 3, 1651.

TWO DOCUMENTS records the completion of the *Presentation of Christ at the Temple* for San Filippo Neri in Perugia in 1651, making it the last major altarpiece by Sacchi to survive in reasonable condition.[1] It was kept in the second chapel on the right in San Filippo Neri until some time after 1872, when it was moved to the museum.[2] It is at present in store, awaiting the construction of new rooms that will house the late sixteenth- and seventeenth-century pictures of the Galleria Nazionale dell'Umbria.
The subject is said to be *The Presentation of the Virgin* in the chronicle that records the picture's arrival from Rome, but it is clearly Christ who is being brought to the temple by his parents. The young boy with the ritual doves, the old high priest Simeon and the priestess Anna in the right background also fit the text, Luke II, 22–38. The Louvre composition study is a little puzzling as Joseph seems to be carrying a knife and not a candle, but it would be most unusual for him and not an acolyte to carry the much smaller type of knife used for circumcision. The main elements of the final design are already present, most of the changes concerning the arrangement of the spectators and their roles. For example, in the drawing a woman on the left carries the cage of doves which in the painting has become a basket carried on the right by a youth, while the angels shown on the left in the painting do not appear in the drawing.

1. The dating of the Fabriano and Ferrara *Baptist* altarpieces is uncertain, although the Ferrara picture may well follow the Perugia altarpiece. Their condition is poorer than that of the Perugia picture, while the later frescoed altarpiece in San Giuseppe a Capo le Case in Rome is mostly repaint.
2. It is recorded in the church by Guardabassi in 1872 but was in the Pinacoteca by 1885 (see catalogues in bibliography).

Bibliography: Bellori, 1672–96, p. 65; Orsini, 1683, p. 36; Pascoli, 1730, I, p. 17; C. Costantini, *Guida al Forastiere per l'Augusta Città di Perugia*, Perugia, 1784, pp. 279–80; Siepi, 1822, II, p. 859;

Guardabassi, 1872, p. 180; *La Pinacoteca Vannucci—Catalogo*, Perugia, 1885, no. 31 and 1904 ed., p. 57; Gnoli, after 1918, p. 20; Voss, 1924, p. 532; Posse, 1925, p. 109 f.; Cecchini, 1932, p. 217; Posse, 1935, p. 290. 'Notiziario', *Boll. d'Arte*, 1967, p. 58 and fig. 59.

79. The Immaculate Conception. Formerly Oratorio del Buon Gesù, Foligno

BELLORI records an *Immaculate Conception* by Sacchi 'in the church of the fathers of the Oratory' in Foligno, and such a picture is recorded in the Oratory by Bragazzi in 1864 and by Pulignani in 1909. The Oratory and its contents were destroyed during a bombing raid on May 16, 1944. Sacchi's altarpiece was never apparently photographed. The only record of its appearance is a small copy rescued from the ruins of the Oratory after the bombing by Cavaliere Emilio de Pasquale, who in 1944 lived next to the church. He says that the copy records the design of the original faithfully except for the crown added after the Madonna in the painting moved her eyes miraculously on July 15, 1771. It has not been possible to learn from local guide books and descriptions of the city when the Oratory was founded and so to pinpoint the date of Sacchi's *Immaculate Conception*. A date in the late 1640s or early 1650s, when he executed several other commissions for provincial patrons in the same area—Perugia, Fabriano—is probable. The simplicity of the composition also indicates a late date.

Bibliography: Bellori, 1672–96, p. 65; G. Bragazzi, *La Rosa dell'Umbria Ossia Piccola Guida Storico-Artistico di Foligno e Città-Contermine*, Foligno, 1864, p. 49; D. M. Faloci Pulignani, *Guida Illustrata di Foligno e Dintorni*, Foligno, 1909, p. 26.

80. The Dream of St. Joseph. S. Giuseppe a Capo le Case, Rome

Fresco, approximately 180 × 150 cm.   Plate 157

Condition: Bellori reports that this fresco was restored by Maratta, indicating that it had begun to deteriorate in the late seventeenth century. The present surface is mostly repaint, but judging from Sacchi's own preparatory study, from copies and from Westerhout's engraving, Maratta and later restorers have preserved the composition while altering details such as facial types.
Drawings: Study for the figure of the Virgin, Düsseldorf (Harris and Schaar, no. 90); two composition studies based on the fresco by followers, Düsseldorf (Harris and Schaar, nos. 125 and 126); study after the figure of Joseph, Stockholm (N.M.H. 523/1863). A composition study of this subject in the British Museum attributed to Sacchi (no. 1946.7.13.720) is by Mola, as is no. FP 575 verso in Düsseldorf. A study at Nantes of an old man sleeping which Refice related to Joseph in this fresco has nothing to do with the pose of Joseph, nor with the technique of Sacchi drawings (p. 217 and fig. 217). It appears to be a study of a sleeping apostle in an unknown *Transfiguration* composition. There is another version of the final design in reverse in the Uffizi (no. 1428 F; see Gernsheim no. G 21027).
Versions: 1661 There seem to have been six versions of this subject in Sacchi's house in June, 1661 (Appendix II, nos. 44, 207, 211 and 232), although one may only have been a *Holy Family* (no. 207). One of the two versions on copper may be that later recorded in the Colonna collection, *q.v.*
1783 'Un Quadro in Rame di 2 per alto Il Sogno di S. Giuseppe Bozzetto di Andrea Sacchi' was in the Palazzo Colonna in 1783 (Colonna, p. 44, no. 310). Its later history is not known.
Engravings: c. 1700 Engraving in reverse by Arnold van Westerhout (1666–1725); Plate 156. It is of mediocre quality.

SCHOLARS have accepted Passeri's and Pascoli's word that *The Dream of St. Joseph* on the high altar of S. Giuseppe a Capo le Case was Sacchi's last public commission. In addition the fresco has been connected by Hess and Posse with an inscription of May, 1652, set up by the monks to commemorate Cardinal Marcello

Lante, a generous benefactor of the church who died that year and who was buried without any memorial, at his own request, in S. Niccolò dei Tolentini.[1] Lante had paid for the rebuilding of the convent of S. Giuseppe in 1628.[2] The 1652 inscription records that fact and the Cardinal's continued generosity, but it does not mention decorating the high altar and is placed on the entrance wall of the church. Lante may have paid for Sacchi's fresco, but the inscription does not prove it and is not sufficient evidence for a date of 1652.[3] There is other evidence, however, to support that date. In 1653, Sacchi's former patron, Cardinal Antonio Barberini, returned to Rome from Paris and immediately gave the artist a number of important commissions, none of which were ever completed. These developments make a date in or before 1653 probable for the S. Giuseppe fresco. The one autograph preparatory study has the stronger *sfumato* found in a few other late black chalk drawings,[4] while the functional simplicity of the composition fits well with Sacchi's other work after 1645.

1. Ciacconius, IV, col. 408; Cardella, VI, pp. 132–3; Forcella, X, no. 285.
2. Forcella, X, no. 284.
3. The remains of the church's archives in the Archivio di Stato contain nothing from the seventeenth century except one account book for domestic expenses in 1660.
4. Harris and Schaar, nos. 85 and 89; Blunt and Cooke, nos. 810 and 811.

Bibliography: Bellori, 1672–96, p. 57; Titi, 1674, p. 370 (and all later ed. incl. 1763); Passeri, 1675–8, p. 304; Sebastiani, 1683, p. 126; Panciroli, 1719, II, p. 419; Pascoli, 1730, I, p. 17; Roisecco, 1750 II, p. 224; Vasi, 1770 (1765), p. 116; Rossini, 1776, II, p. 358; Pistolesi, 1841 and 1846, p. 370; Voss, 1924, p. 532; Posse, 1925, p. 113 f. and fig. 32; Hess, 1934, p. 304; Posse, 1935, p. 290; Waterhouse, 1937, p. 93; Refice, 1950, p. 216.

81. The Decoration of San Luigi dei Francesi. Rome (1653–60)
cf. Plates 158–164

Drawings: Thirty-one studies for a decorative scheme with herms and bound slaves, Windsor (Blunt and Cooke, nos. 789–819 and no. 849; 803 has studies on the verso as well; Plates 159–64); study of a male nude seated with legs crossed and facing to the right, Academia de San Fernando, Madrid (Tome 8, no. 1621, red chalk on grey-green paper, 240 × 200 mm.; Plate 158). The drawings are discussed in greater detail below.

BELLORI says (1672–96, p. 61) that the entire length of the vault of San Luigi dei Francesi in Rome was to be decorated with frescoes by Sacchi. The ceiling was to be divided by bands, painted to resemble gilded stucco, which lined up with the pilasters below. There would be various ornamental friezes divided up by groups of putti, herms and ignudi. A large picture of St. Louis in glory was planned for the centre of the ceiling, with smaller, oval frescoes at each end depicting a naval and a terrestrial battle in which St. Louis was victorious. Along the main cornice and above each pilaster there were to be figures of the most celebrated French kings accompanied by trophies and slaves.
The commission was given to Sacchi by Cardinal Antonio Barberini shortly after the latter's return to Rome from Paris in 1653. Bellori reports that Sacchi made preparatory studies and even cartoons, that scaffolding was erected and that work was started near the entrance door, where Sacchi painted a few grisaille figures. However, a combination of psychological and physical handicaps delayed completion of the work. When Sacchi's gout became serious enough to confine him to bed, he gave the drawings, cartoons and the keys to the scaffolding to Maratta, a move of which Cardinal Antonio reportedly approved. After Sacchi's death, it seems that Cardinal Antonio lost interest in the commission, for it was not completed by Maratta. The few ignudi that

had been painted were destroyed—if indeed they were still visible—between 1756 and 1764, when the ceiling was finally decorated by Dériset.[1]

A group of thirty-one drawings at Windsor and an additional drawing in the Academia de San Fernando in Madrid can be connected with this lost, unfinished project. Bellori's account of the preparatory studies being given to Maratta by Sacchi is confirmed both by the record of one such study in Maratta's collection in 1712[2] and by the survival of studies for this commission in two collections known to have come from Maratta himself.[3] The decorative scheme indicated by this group of drawings agrees with details recorded by Bellori, while the window frames that appear in a few of the sheets resemble the window frames in S. Luigi dei Francesi. The handling of the drawings also suggests a date late in the artist's career.[4] Finally, the drawings fit no other project with which Sacchi is known to have been concerned.

Some of the Windsor drawings are composition studies for a decorative scheme surrounding a window. Others show studies for individual herms or seated and standing figures similar to or identical with those figures shown in the composition studies. The drawings can be sorted into two groups relating to two schemes for window bays, each window being framed by a herm with a bound, seated figure in front of him.[5] The final poses for the eight figures concerned are not clear in all cases, but the drawings permit an approximate reconstruction at least of one bay of the aisle. From two of the composition studies it appears that between each window bay was a standing male figure, presumably one of the French kings to whom Bellori refers. No drawings survive for the narrative scenes in the centre of the ceiling.[6]

Sacchi's failure to carry out the scheme, which seems to have been fully planned although probably not entirely executed as far as the cartoon stage, is discussed elsewhere. Bellori tactfully emphasizes the artist's physical disabilities. Passeri openly accuses Sacchi of the sin of sloth. Whatever the explanation for Sacchi's inactivity in the 1650s, his inability either to complete this important commission or to direct a workshop to complete it for him was regarded by his contemporaries as a humiliating finish to an important career.

1. Thieme-Becker, *sub voce*.
2. 'Altro foglio simile con tre disegni study d'Andrea Sacchi rappresentante certi termini per San Luigi de Francesi' (Galli, XXII, p. 236, no. 79). Sir Anthony Blunt drew my attention to this reference.
3. For the history of the Windsor collection, see Blunt and Cooke, p. 7 and for the Madrid drawings, Alcaide, p. 3.
4. The blurred *sfumato* of Windsor nos. 810 and 811 is found only in a few other late drawings such as the Düsseldorf study for the Virgin in the *Dream of St. Joseph* of 1652 or the drapery study at Düsseldorf for Joachim in the *Death of St. Anne* of 1649.
5. Scheme 1: study for whole window bay, 789; study for left side, 790; studies for right side, 804, 805, 807; studies for upper left herm, 791, 792; studies for lower left seated figure, 803 (recto and verso), 797, 796, 798, 793, 795, 795; studies for upper right herm, 808, 909; studies for lower right seated figure, 814, 817, 181. Scheme 2: study for left side of window, 799; study for right side of window, 806; studies for upper right herm, 810, 811; studies for lower left seated figure, 801, 800, 802; studies for lower right seated figure, 812, 816, 813, 819, 815, 849 and the Madrid drawing.
6. The relationship between the San Luigi project and the illustrations that Sacchi provided for Pierre Le Moyne's *Saint Louis ou La Sainte Couronne Reconquise* is discussed in the catalogue entry dealing with the latter (No. 88).

Bibliography: Bellori, 1672–96, pp. 61–2; Passeri, 1679, pp. 301 and 304; Posse, 1925, p. 89 f., 108 and 112, note 2; Posse, 1935, p. 290; Blunt and Cooke, 1960, pp. 92 and 98–9.

82. Portrait of Alexander VII. Formerly Casa Sacchi, Rome
Recorded Versions: 1661 Two portraits of Alexander VII are recorded in Sacchi's house in 1661 (Appendix II, nos. 1 and 184). There is no later reference to them.

Two portraits of Alexander VII (Fabio Chigi, 1599–1667) are recorded in Sacchi's collection at the time of his death and were almost certainly by Sacchi himself. They were presumably painted shortly after the Pope's election (1655), when Sacchi tried to gain the Pope's favour, according to Pascoli, failing when he presented the Pope with copies of two existing works instead of new compositions.[1] Sacchi was given at least one commission nevertheless by Alexander VII, namely the design for the Acqua Acetosa (Wibiral, 1955).

A circular drawing carefully executed in red and black chalk with a profile portrait of Alexander VII has been attributed to Sacchi.[2] The handling is a touch dry for him at this date but it may be autograph. The format suggests a medal design, though none of this Pope show him bareheaded.

1. See Versions, 1658, of both the *Divina Sapienza* ceiling and *The Vision of St. Romuald* for the pictures mentioned by Passeri (pp. 300–1).
2. Joseph McCrindle Collection, New York (exhibited P. and D. Colnaghi, 1961, no. 3, 128 mm. diameter).

ENGRAVINGS BASED ON DRAWINGS BY SACCHI

83. Limax and Brucas Transformed by Flora. Engraving by Cornelius Bloemaert for G. B. Ferrari's *Flora, seu De Florum Cultura*, Rome, 1633, p. 55.   Plate 166
196 × 141 mm.
Drawings: Composition study, British Museum (Fenwick Collection, 1946–7.13.803, red chalk on cream paper, 193 × 133 mm.; Plate 165. See Popham, 1935, p. 162). There is a drawing based on the engraving in the Ashmolean Museum, Oxford, that Philip Pouncey has attributed to Sacchi himself. A good red chalk copy in a Sacchiesque technique but based on the print is in the Philadelphia Museum of Art (Charles M. Lea Collection, 28–42–4043). It was brought to my attention by Ann Percy.

THE SCENE takes place in the grounds of a palace whose architecture is reminiscent of the Palazzo Barberini's east front.[1] Flora's lazy gardener, Limax, is being transformed into a snail and the flower thief, Brucus, into a caterpillar by Flora, who has just struck them with 'un fiore pellegrino, che per avventura teneva in mano'.[2] Ferrari's elaborate monograph on the art of gardening, first published in 1633, contains a number of such myths with illustrations provided by Pietro da Cortona and Guido Reni as well. Many of the myths seem to have been invented by Ferrari.[3] A payment of January 31, 1631,[4] to the engraver Greuter in connection with the Flora and an *imprimatur* of September 6, 1632 indicate that Sacchi's drawing should be dated 1632 or shortly before that date.

1. The similarity was noted by Blunt (1958, p. 265, note 24). The Palazzo Barberini also appears in the right background of Cortona's illustration opposite page 518.
2. Quoted from the Italian edition published in 1638, p. 52. Sacchi owned a copy of this and not of the first edition (see Appendix III, no. 59).
3. Bean, 1959, p. 27. For preparatory studies by Cortona, see Blunt and Cooke, p. 76 and fig. 57 and Bean and Stampfle, no. 57.
4. Pollak, I, p. 338.

84. An Allegory on the Birth of Urban VIII. Engraving by Charles Audran after Sacchi   Plate 167
310 × 405 mm.

Drawings: Final preparatory study for the print, Mathias Pola-
kowitz collection, Paris: red chalk on cream paper, squared for
transfer in black chalk (only dimly visible), 297 × 400 mm. A *P* in
pencil on the verso was almost certainly written by the dealer who
bought the drawing from the Paignon Dijonval sale in 1810
(Bénard, p. 20, no. 266, described as red chalk on white paper,
11″ × 15″). It can be further identified with the preparatory study
in the Crozat collection recorded by Mariette in 1741 (Blanc, I, p.
24). The drawing does not show the eagle of Zeus or the coats of
arms but otherwise follows the executed design closely.

A drawing at Windsor (Blunt and Cooke, 1960, no. 775) was
attributed to Sacchi by Posse (1925, pp. 33–4) on the grounds of its
similarity in style and subject to this print, but it can be identified
as a study by Andrea de Leone for his painting, *Elephants in a
Roman Amphitheatre* (Madrid, Prado). A drawing in the Louvre
(Inv. no. 14132, 223 × 321 mm.) inscribed 'dal Signor bartolomeo
Postilione alievo di Andrea Sacchi' and showing Latona and the
shepherds transformed into frogs is a pastiche of poses borrowed
from this engraving and from a drawing by Sacchi at Windsor
(Blunt and Cooke, no. 773). A painting of this composition by a
close imitator of Sacchi (Postiglione?) is in a private collection in
Berlin.

Versions: An undated version in the Bibliothèque Nationale, Paris
(Audran no. 154) shows the coat of arms of the Spinola family in
the lower right corner. The shield is broken in half and has a crown
above it. This may refer to Carlo Spinola, a Jesuit priest martyred
in Japan in 1622 (see M. Deza, *Istoria della Famiglia Spinola*,
Piacenza, 1694, p. 307; for Urban VIII's interest in this mission, see
A. Dunbar, *A Dictionary of Saintly Women*, London, 1904, p. 474).
An undated version in the British Museum has the arms of the
Rossetti family in the lower right corner and the arms of Cardinal
Francesco Barberini carried by a putto in the sky on the right.

THE SUBJECT of this engraving is an allegory based on the birth
of Urban VIII, which is compared to that of Zeus, nursed by the
nymphs Adrasteia and Io, and that of the poet Pindar (Philostratus,
Imag., II, 12), allusions to Urban's powers as Pope and his great
interest in poetry. The engraving has been dated around 1630
because of its formal and iconographical parallels with the *Flora* of
1631–2 and the *Sacrifice to Pan* at Castelfusano of 1628. The stocky
build of the male figures suggests a slightly later date, as does the
sponsorship of Cardinal Antonio Barberini, say around 1634–5.

The identification of the coat of arms on the ground in the version
of the print in the British Museum is uncertain. Cardinal Carlo
Rossetti (1605–81) used these arms but quartered.[1] Presumably
some other member of the family thought it wise to flatter Urban
VIII and Cardinal Francesco Barberini by sponsoring another
edition of this print. The arms of Cardinal Antonio Barberini
appear in the sky in the state preserved in the Bibliothèque
Nationale.

1. Ciacconius, IV, col. 623 and Cardella, VI, pp. 32–5. He was
   Papal legate in England between 1639 and 1643 and was made
   a cardinal on his return. He was a good friend of the Barberini
   circle.

Bibliography: Nagler, 1835–52, I, p. 185 (as by Gérard Audran) and
XV, p. 541; Posse, 1925, pp. 33–4; Posse, 1935, p. 290; Blunt and
Cooke, 1960, p. 96.

85. Romulus Decorating the Sacred Oak Tree on the Capitol.
Engraving by Charles Audran after Sacchi, Paris, Bibliothèque
Nationale   Plate 171
264 × 352 mm.
Drawings: Study for the left-hand side of the print, Louvre (no.
14146, red chalk with brown wash and pen and ink on buff paper,
260 × 233 mm., Plate 170. The correct identification was noted
independently by Jacob Bean and Walter Vitzthum [see Vitzthum,
Burl. Mag., CX, 1968, p. 362 and fig. 53]); study for the right-hand

side of the print, Metropolitan Museum, New York (no. 69.21,
brown ink, pen and wash over red chalk on buff paper, 239 × 150
mm., Plate 169. The drawing was first attributed to Sacchi by
Jacob Bean); study for the whole composition, Witt Collection,
London (no. 4213, red chalk with white heightening on light
brown paper, 269 × 356 mm.), Plate 168.

THE ENGRAVING of Romulus decorating a sacred oak tree with
the captured spoils of a slain Sabine king (Livy, I, ch. 10), of which
only one example has been traced, is attributed to Andrea Camassei
by Le Blanc. The print itself is inscribed only 'C. Audran sculp.'
The three drawings amply document Sacchi's responsibility for
the design.

The subject is rare but not unique in *seicento* Rome. The same
incident appears in Giacinto Gimignani's frieze in the Palazzo
Doria Pamphili in Piazza Navona. The story of one king dedicating
his triumph over another to the gods was presumably taken by
Roman patrician families as justifying their inherited wealth and
power. The patron for whom Sacchi's design was made is not
known. The shield behind Romulus in the Witt drawing displays
the Barberini bees and sun; in the print, the sun alone appears,
perhaps an allusion to Louis XIV. It has not been possible to identify the coat of arms in the print with the motto, 'Pomis Sua
Nomina Servant'.[1] The Barberini arms suggests that Sacchi must
have designed the print by 1644, even if it was only issued later in a
different form.

1. The same motto appears on several other prints in the same
   album in the Bibliothèque Nationale but with different coats of
   arms, suggesting that it is not the motto of the family with the
   arms shown in Sacchi's print. Weigert (I, p. 160) suggests that it
   is the crest of the Giustiniani family, but this is not correct, nor
   does it appear in Litta or Spreti. Arms with eagles and fleur-de-
   lys indexed by Renesse from the huge collection of arms in
   Crollanza and Rietstap have been checked without success.
   Weigert (1939, I, p. 187, no. 176) records another print after
   Sacchi by Audran showing the Barberini coat of arms held by a
   flying genius. I have not been able to trace an example of it.

Bibliography: Le Blanc, 1854, I, p. 324.

86. Harmonillus Transformed into a Lime Tree. Engraving by
Cornelius Bloemaert for G. B. de' Ferrari, *Hesperides sive de malorum
aureorum cultura et usu*, Rome, 1646, p. 89.   Plate 172
308 × 200 mm.
Drawings: Study for the whole composition, Louvre (Cabinet des
Dessins, no. 3821, pen and ink with brown wash over red chalk
with some white body colour, 300 × 200 mm. It was in the collection of P. J. Mariette. See Bean, pp. 26–7). There is a copy after
a lost study for the background in Bartolomeo Altomonte's sketch-
book of 1718 in the Albertina (folio 7, no. 26879. See Brigitte
Heinzl, *Bartolomeo Altomonte*, Vienna, 1964, p. 69).

THE DATE of Sacchi's drawing in the Louvre, which was probably
that used by Cornelius Bloemaert when engraving the design after
Sacchi for Ferrari's *Hesperides*, was recently shown to be around
1640 by Jacob Bean. He pointed out that the Hesperides has an
imprimatur of 1644, and may even have been ready two years
earlier, since Poussin during his visit to Paris was negotiating on
the author's behalf for a dedication to Louis XIII.

The mixed-media technique of the Louvre drawing differs from
the precise, red chalk study for the *Flora* engraving of 1631–2 and
from the similar red chalk studies in Darmstadt and Madrid for the
Sacrifice to Pan (No. 13). Perhaps Bloemaert worked from such a
drawing, now lost, and the Louvre drawing is the final preparatory
study on which the engraver's model was based. A number of
details, particularly of the setting, remain to be worked out in the
Louvre study. The Altomonte copy indicates that other preparatory studies closer to the executed design in certain details existed.
If Bloemaert did not have a complete, final design, he could no

doubt have made the engraving using several preparatory studies and selecting from them on the advice of Sacchi.

Gisela Bergsträsser has linked a beautiful red chalk study in Darmstadt with this print (*Dessins du Musée de Darmstadt Hessisches Landesmuseum*, XLVIIᵉ Exposition du Cabinet des Dessins, Musée du Louvre, Paris, 1971, no. 17), pointing out that I accepted it as an autograph drawing by Sacchi in a footnote to my catalogue of the Sacchi drawings at Düsseldorf. This drawing should, however, be attributed to Guglielmo Cortese.

There is no known classical source for the story of Harmonillus, and Bean is surely correct in thinking that Ferrari invented this and many of the other myths in the *Hesperides* himself.

Bibliography: Ferrari, 1646, p. 89; Basan, 1775, p. 105; Nagler, 1835–52, XV, p. 541; Posse, 1925, p. 78; Bean, 1959, pp. 26–7; W. Vitzthum in *Burl. Mag.*, 1960, p. 75 and fig. 32; *Le Cabinet d'un Grand Amateur P. J. Mariette*, Paris, 1967, no. 130; R. Bacou, *Drawings from the Louvre: The Italian Drawings*, London, 1968, no. 88.

87. An Allegory of the Catholic Church Triumphant over Heresy. Frontispiece engraved by Cornelius Bloemaert for Guido Bentivoglio's *Historia di Fiandra*, Venice, 1645. Plate 174
210 × 160 mm.

Drawings: Study for the whole composition, Leningrad (No. 21942, red chalk on cream paper, 215 × 165 mm.; Plate 173. It came to the State Hermitage Museum in 1925 from the Jussupov collection. See the *Catalogue of the Drawings in the State Hermitage Museum*, Leningrad, 1961, II, no. 1363).

ONLY the 1645 Venice edition of Cardinal Bentivoglio's *Historia di Fiandra* contains Bloemaert's engraved frontispiece based on a drawing by Sacchi.[1] As an edition appeared in Venice the previous year, it seems probable that Sacchi's drawing was only ready for the engraver in 1644 or early in 1645. The red chalk study in Leningrad follows the engraving closely,[2] unlike Sacchi's similar red chalk studies for the *Flora* print of about 1632 or the *Triumph of Pan* drawings in Madrid and Darmstadt, none of which follow the final design so precisely. This fact plus the disappointing quality of the Leningrad study in certain areas[3] suggests that it may be a studio drawing. Technically, an attribution to the young Maratta is possible.[4]

The composition shows Clio, the muse of history, on the left, preparing to record the story of Flanders after engraving the first scroll with the title of the work. The other end of the scroll is held by the trumpeting figure of Fame. To the right stands a young woman whose armour is marked with the cross of the Church. She places her right foot on the back of Heresy, a prostrate male figure who tears at the writhing snakes which form his hair. A battle and a town (Antwerp?) can be made out in the distance.

1. The first edition was published in Cologne in 1632 with a portrait of the author drawn and engraved by Claude Mellan as the frontispiece. A portrait of Philip II was added to the 1634 edition and Van Dyck's portrait of the author substituted for that of Mellan. There are many later editions, e.g. Cologne— 1633, 1635, 1636 and 1639; Paris—1645, 1649 and 1650; London—1654 and 1678 etc.

2. There is a pentimento in the drawing around the projecting base of the archway seen below the scroll. The relief on the inside wall of the archway to the left has been toned down in the engraving and the details of the town and battle in the distance sharpened up. All these changes could have been made by Bloemaert using the Leningrad drawing or the original on which it is based.

3. Particularly weak are the left arm of Fame, the left foot of the Church Militant and the right foot of Clio.

4. The Leningrad drawing may be compared with early studies by Maratta in Düsseldorf (Harris and Schaar, no. 183) and Berlin (Dreyer, nos. 108 and 109). Maratta began his career, according

to Bellori, making designs for engravings and it would have been an obvious way for him to assist Sacchi as soon as he was competent to do so. The linear and tonal control in the Leningrad drawing is not as good as in Maratta's dated drawings of a few years later (e.g. those cited here).

Bibliography: Bénard, 1810, p. 18, no. 688; *Catalogue of the State Hermitage Museum*, Leningrad, 1958, II, no. 21942 (the 1645 edition of Bentivoglio's book is not specified as the one edition which used Sacchi's design as a frontispiece).

88. Illustrations for Pierre Le Moyne's 'Saint Louis ou La Sainte Couronne Reconquise'. Paris, 1657
Drawings: St. Louis received into heaven, Albertina, Vienna, Plate 176 (F. Wickhoff, *Jahrbuch der Kunsthistorischen Sammlungen in Wien*, 1892, CCXLV, Roman drawings no. 1118, as Romanelli; St. Louis preparing to set out on the crusade to capture the crown of thorns, Albertina, Vienna, Plate 175 (Wickhoff, *art. cit.*, Roman Drawings no. 1117, as Romanelli).

SIX ENGRAVED ILLUSTRATIONS of scenes in chapters 8, 12, 13 and 15 of Pierre le Moyne's heroic poem, *Saint Louis ou la Sainte Couronne Reconquise*, first published in Paris in 1657, have been associated with Sacchi, although the evidence for the attributions is not conclusive.[1] In addition, two drawings in the Albertina illustrating scenes from chapters 1 and 8 of the poem can be associated with Sacchi's studio on stylistic grounds. Engravings based on these two drawings have not so far been traced.[2] None of the published editions of the poem contains the six engravings cited above. Nevertheless it is clear that all the illustrators worked from a uniform set of instructions since the illustrations for all the same chapters in all the editions of the poem traced in Paris, London and New York show the same incidents as those in the six engravings and the two drawings. It seems that Sacchi was commissioned to provide a set of illustrations for le Moyne's poem but failed to complete the set, the commission then going to François Chaveau (1613–76).[3] Sacchi's patron, Cardinal Antonio Barberini, was presumably responsible for obtaining the commission for Sacchi and probably arranged it either during his exile in Paris in the late 1640s or shortly after his return to Rome in 1652. The 1658 edition of the poem has four *imprimatur* dates— April 22, 1651; April 9, 1653; November 20, 1657 and August 27, 1658. These widely spaced dates could be explained by the delays caused by Sacchi's failure to carry out the commission and the time needed to find a substitute artist. None of Chaveau's designs are stylistically indebted to Sacchi but those of Sacchi that were engraved seem to have been used as the basis of Chaveau's compositions for the same scenes.

Two of the six engravings, namely those by Guillaume Chasteau for chapters 12 and 13 (Plate 177), have inscriptions attributing to Sacchi the drawing on which the engraving was based.[4] Both designs were used by Gérard Audran but without an engraved acknowledgement of the source; Plates 178–9.[5] Chasteau's dates are 1635 to 1683; Audran's are 1640 to 1703.[6] Chasteau was in Rome between 1655 and 1659, at which time he was in contact with Cornelius Bloemaert and Frederic Greuter, both of whom had made a number of engravings after drawings by Sacchi. Gérard Audran was only in Rome briefly in 1666, five years after Sacchi's death; otherwise he worked mainly in Paris. It seems probable that only Chasteau's prints were made in the 1650s and that Audran's prints were made at a later date, perhaps on the initiative of Maratta, who on stylistic grounds can be associated with the six engravings and the two Albertina drawings.[7] The drawings in particular are technically unlike any of Sacchi's other preparatory studies for engravings and cannot be attributed to Sacchi himself.[8] Nevertheless, the compositions and types are closely related to both Sacchi and the young Maratta. In my opinion, Sacchi collaborated with Maratta on the designs, their relationship being similar to that for the Lateran fresco, *The Destruction of Pagan Idols*. Then as Maratta established himself in the 1650s, he no doubt became reluctant to continue with a project that cast him in a dependent role. Sacchi meanwhile became increasingly less willing or able to finish any projects and the commission had to be abandoned.[9] After Sacchi's death, Maratta may have tried to salvage what had been completed of the project by getting Audran to engrave a few more of the completed designs, planning perhaps to sell them as single prints, the popularity of Pierre le Moyne's poem being sufficient to ensure a market for them.

This reconstruction of the commission and of Sacchi's share in it is speculative, the extant documentary and stylistic evidence being insufficient to permit a more definitive solution to the problem. In particular the evolution of Maratta's style from the time he joined Sacchi's studio in 1636 until he became a fully independent artistic personality in the early 1660s deserves more detailed study than it has received so far and than it can be given here. The connection between the commission to illustrate le Moyne's poem about St. Louis and the commission to decorate the ceiling of San Luigi dei Francesi in Rome might also be investigated. It is possible, for example, that the Vienna study of St. Louis received into heaven reflects Sacchi's plans for the central scene of the ceiling, which was to show the apotheosis of St. Louis.

1. One of the two engravings by Chasteau is listed in R.-A. Weigert, *Inventaire du Fonds Français, Graveurs du XVIIe Siècle*, Paris, 1939–54, II, p. 299, no. 74 (for chapter 12). There is an example of Chasteau's engraving for chapter 13 in the Kunstmuseum, Düsseldorf (no. 7573); Plate 177. For the three engravings by Audran, see Weigert, *op. cit.*, I, pp. 130–1, nos. 38–40 (for chapters 12, 13 and 15) and Plates 178–9. Posse (1925, p. 112, note 2) notes a print by Charles Simonneau of St. Louis receiving the crown of thorns in heaven, the subject chosen for the illustration to chapter 8, but according to Mireur (VII, p. 34), the design was attributed to Coypel, not to Sacchi. I have not traced an example of Simonneau's print. Chasteau's two prints are inscribed 'And. Sacchi Roma del. G. Chasteau ex. C.P.R.'. Examples of two of Audran's three prints have ink inscriptions attributing the designs to Sacchi; those for chapters 12 and 13 appear to be reissues of Chasteau's prints.
2. For the Simonneau print of the same subject as the first Vienna drawing, see note 1.
3. He inscribed eleven of the illustrations in the 1657 edition and

all the plates in the 1658 edition 'in. et fec.' See Weigert, *op. cit.*, II, p. 461, nos. 608–25.
4. See note 1.
5. See note 1. Audran's engraving after Romanelli's *Sacrifice of Iphigenia* (Weigert, *op. cit.*, I, p. 143, no. 142) was also made to illustrate le Moyne's poem according to Mariette (*Abécédario*, V, p. 151) but none of Chaveau's illustrations show a sacrifice scene with which Romanelli's design might be confused.
6. Thieme-Becker, *sub voce*.
7. The style of the drapery, which clings to the bodies beneath, leaving ridged, convoluted fold forms on the surface (e.g. in Chasteau's illustration for chapter 13), is common in Maratta's early work (e.g. Harris and Schaar, nos. 182 and 183; Dreyer, *Römische Barockzeichnungen*, nos. 107, 137, 134, 132 and 138). The types and poses of all the figures exhibit that mixture of Sacchi and Maratta found in the latter's early work (e.g. the *Adoration of the Shepherds* in S. Giuseppe ai Falegnami of 1650, *St. Andrew Adoring his Cross of Martyrdom* in the Galleria Nazionale d'Arte Antica, Rome and the Chatsworth *Sacrifice of Noah*). The same mixture, although based on Maratta drawings of a few years later, is seen in two slightly later engravings by Chasteau after Maratta in the Bibliothèque Nationale (Ed. 51.a., p. 8 and Ed. 51.a., p. 17). Sacchi's drapery style is fuller and simpler than Maratta's while his women have less obviously classical features than those, for example, of Lisamante in the scene from chapter 13.
8. The drawings were first carefully worked up with brown ink washes using only a brush. The contours were then sharpened with delicate pen lines and the tonal range extended by the addition of white body colour. The technique can not be paralleled in either Sacchi's or Maratta's extant drawings and may perhaps be that of the engraver. I have not been able to trace drawings by Chasteau or Audran.
9. Mariette (*Abécédario*, V, pp. 150–1) commenting on Audran's three prints stated that they 'avoient été faites pour estre mises dans le poëme de St. Louis, du père Lemoyne, mais la suite n'en ayant pas este finie, on s'est servy du celles qu'avoient gravées J. Le Pautre'. I have traced no printed references to such engravings by Le Pautre.

Bibliography: Florent Le Comte, *Cabinet des singularitez . . .*, Paris, 1699–1700, III, pp. 184–7; Mariette, *Abécédario*, 1851–60, V, pp. 150–1; Nagler, 1835–52, XVI, pp. 132–3; Posse, 1925, p. 112, note 2; R.-A. Weigert, *Inventaire du Fonds Français, Graveurs du XVIIe Siècle*, 1939–51, I, pp. 130–1 and 143; II, pp. 298–9 and p. 461.

LOST WORKS

The main catalogue includes a number of important lost works for which documentation and/or visual material (drawings, engravings, copies) survives. This section contains other lost works recorded in seventeenth- and early eighteenth-century documents. No works are mentioned here if they are recorded elsewhere as lost versions of surviving works. Also omitted are a small number of references in guide books or sale records to works attributed to Sacchi but unrelated to better documented references, since the reliability of such attributions is questionable.

LOST DOCUMENTED WORKS FOR THE BARBERINI FAMILY

L 1. Two Apostles
Sacchi was paid ten scudi by Cardinal Francesco Barberini on June 16, 1627 for 'un quadro, con due teste d'Apostoli' (Incisa della Rocchetta, 1924, p. 63). This is the first time that Sacchi is known to have worked for the Barberini. No work answering to this description appears in later Barberini inventories until 1692, when a picture of two apostles appears in Cardinal Carlo Barberini's inventory (no. 294).

L 2. Four Pictures for Bagnaia
On November 4, 1633 Sacchi was paid 34 scudi for 'quattro quadri havuti da lui per mandare a Bagnaia' (Incisa della Rocchetta, 1924, p. 65). The pictures were presumably intended for the present Villa Lante, which was acquired by Cardinal Antonio the Younger in 1632 after the death of Cardinal Ludovico Ludovisi. This payment is the first made to Sacchi by his most important regular patron from this date onwards, Cardinal Antonio, although he was

acting on Sacchi's behalf in 1631 over the commission for a second mosaic cartoon (Pollak, II, p. 575). Nothing more is known about these four pictures, although it is just possible that they were modellos of the four altarpieces which Sacchi was then painting for the crypt of St. Peter's.

L 3. Paintings for S. Agata dei Goti
Sacchi was paid 200 scudi on May 4, 1641 'per le pitture che fa a S. Agata d'ord(in)e di S(ua) Em(inen)za (Cardinal Antonio)' (Incisa della Rocchetta, 1924, p. 66). Cardinal Antonio succeeded Cardinal Francesco Barberini in 1632 as Protector of S. Agata and carried on the restoration work then in progress. Sacchi is documented as supervising this work between 1637 and 1641.[1] The paintings mentioned in the payment of 1641 must have been executed by others, for there are no pictures by Sacchi in the church today and none by him are recorded in seventeenth- or eighteenth-century descriptions of the church.[2]

L 4. A 'Virgin and Child' for the Chapel of the Palazzo Barberini at Segni
A 'Madonna S(antissi)ma col Bambino in braccio; fatto per la Cappella del Palazzo di Segni' was painted by Sacchi's assistant, Carlo Magnone, by May 19, 1643 (Incisa della Rocchetta, 1924, p. 70). Masons were working in the chapel in 1641.[3] Sacchi was almost certainly responsible for the design of the altarpiece painted by Magnone, which may even be recorded faintly by a drawing at Windsor for an altar which shows what could be figures of the Virgin and Child sketched in lightly in the space for the altarpiece (Blunt and Cooke, no. 784). It has not been possible so far to inspect the interior of the former Palazzo Barberini in Segni to see whether the chapel and its fittings still survive.

L 5. Paintings for the Capuchin Fathers at Pertuis in Provence

On July 10, 1645, and March 20, 1649, while Cardinal Antonio was in France, Sacchi was paid for pictures 'p(er) li P(ad)ri Capuccini di Portuis in Provenza' (Incisa della Rocchetta, 1924, p. 73). According to the 1958 Guide Bleu to Provence, the last chapel on the south side of the church of St. Nicolas in Pertuis contains two marble statues of the Virgin appearing to St. Anthony Bottà near Savona, which were given to the church in 1653 by 'le cardinal Barberini' (i.e. Francesco). It has not been possible to learn from enquiries whether the church contains any paintings by Sacchi, nor have I been able to visit Pertuis myself.

L 6. Copies after Dosso Dossi's 'Bacchanals' in the Castello Estense, Ferrara
On May 16, 1654 Sacchi was reimbursed for the expenses he incurred when he arranged for copies to be made of Dosso Dossi's Bacchanals in Ferrara (Incisa della Rocchetta, 1924, p. 74). Two copies of Bacchanals attributed to Carlo Magnone appear in Cardinal Antonio's inventory of 1671 (no. 15) and of 1672 (no. 390), but since Magnone died in 1653, he could only have carried out this commission for Sacchi if we assume that Sacchi was reimbursed a year after Magnone painted the Bacchanals. It seems possible therefore that another artist was responsible.

L 7. Silver Cups Designed by Sacchi
The inventory of Don Carlo Francesco Barberini made on October 2, 1687 includes 'Una sottocoppa di disegno di Andrea Sacchi No. 1 in peso libre due, et oncie tre di argento, con lettere che dicono Vino, et Venere dulcescit animus—Altre Simile No. 2—in peso l(i)b(r)e due, e oncie quattro et il disegno dimostra Noé che dorme, e viene scoperto da Cam suo figlio'. This document is the only evidence that Sacchi made designs for silver. It was kindly given to me by Marilyn Aronberg Lavin and will be published in her forthcoming book on the Barberini seicento archives.

WORKS RECORDED IN THE COLLECTION OF CARDINAL MAZARIN IN 1653

L 8. St. Andrew Holding a Fish and a Book
The inventory made of Cardinal Mazarin's pictures in 1653 included a 'St. André tenant en ses mains un livre et un poisson, envyron demy figure, avec sa bordure couleur de noix et or' attributed to Sacchi (Aumale, p. 311). It is recorded in Mazarin's collection again in 1661 (Cosnac, p. 300), when it was valued at 300 livres, but there are no later references to it. The attribution was first recorded while Sacchi's most important patron, Cardinal Antonio Barberini, was in Paris and is therefore probably reliable. Moreover, we know that Sacchi was in contact with Cardinal Mazarin because there was a miniature portrait of the Cardinal in Sacchi's collection in 1661 (Appendix II, no. 48). Mazarin also owned a Venus attributed to Sacchi (see below) and a version of Sacchi's Drunkenness of Noah, q.v.

L 9. Venus with a Chariot
Cardinal Mazarin's inventory of 1653 also includes 'Une Vénus nue, grande au naturel, ayant un chariot à coste d'elle et quantité de fleurs et un feston dans sa main, Andrea Sacchi' (Aumale, p. 326, no. 282). In Mazarin's inventory of 1661 the picture was valued at 600 livres (Cosnac, p. 320). From the description given, Mazarin's Venus sounds very much like a larger version of the Venus in a Landscape in the Hermitage attributed to Sacchi since 1775 (q.v. under Rejected Attributions). That picture should, however, in my opinion be attributed to G. F. Grimaldi. Grimaldi may have borrowed his figure staffage from Sacchi's composition, but without further evidence, for example drawings by Sacchi for the figure of Venus, we cannot know whether Grimaldi's picture does partially record Mazarin's lost picture. For other Venus pictures by Sacchi, see the entry for the lost Pamphili Venus (no. 73).

WORKS RECORDED IN SACCHI'S INVENTORY IN 1661

Most of the works listed in Sacchi's inventory are cited in the main catalogue of known works, the majority as lost versions of surviving compositions. The works discussed in this section are those for which additional evidence in support of an attribution to Sacchi—drawings, references in sources, guide books or early sale records—is available. The only works in Sacchi's house which were stated not to be by him were a Still Life by Cerquozzi, a Bamboccio and a Magnone Nativity. Of the rest, probably only the other Still Lifes and a few small landscape paintings in oval or round frames sound as if they might have been by other artists.

L 10. The Assumption of the Virgin with St. Nicholas of Bari and St. Francis
A large, unframed picture of this subject was kept in the front room along with the portraits of Sacchi's most important patrons. The whole display seems calculated to impress and we can assume therefore that this lost work was one to which Sacchi attached some importance (Appendix II, no. 8). Apart from a 'Madonnina Assunta' in another room (no. 170), there is no other record of Sacchi ever painting the Virgin's assumption, but one drawing at Düsseldorf (Harris and Schaar, no. 93) does show him considering

several poses for a Virgin (or saint) ascending heavenwards. Here it should also be noted that an *Assumption of the Virgin* with four saints attributed to Sacchi was sold from the Northwick collection on August 18, 1859 (lot. 1510) for £210 to Erle-Drax, who sold it at Christie's on Feb. 19, 1910 (lot 51) for 32 guineas to Higgins.[4] Its present location is not known. A nineteenth-century attribution to Sacchi should be treated with caution.

L 11. St. Sebastian
Besides the *St. Sebastian* in Sacchi's collection (no. 22), a copy after a picture of this subject attributed to Sacchi was in the Palazzo Colonna in 1783 (p. 117, no. 888) and 1848 (Mariotti, p. 151). The *St. Sebastian* in the Pitti formerly attributed to Sacchi (Posse, 1925, p. 110) is now simply labelled Bolognese School (Cipriani, p. 242, no. 271).

L 12. The Head of Christ
An 'effigie del S(antissi)mo Salvatore' is recorded in Sacchi's bedroom (no. 38) and three other pictures of Christ are recorded in other rooms (nos. 157, 198 and 307). It has not been possible to trace an example of Guillaume Vallet's print of a *Christ* based on a design by Sacchi (Posse, 1925, p. 110). There was 'Un quadretto in rame e grandezza di p(al)mi 2 per ogni verso rappresentante la Pietà con sua fodera e Cornice d'argento' attributed to Sacchi in Cardinal Antonio Barberini's inventory of 1671 (no. 425, valued at 220 scudi). A picture of 'Our Saviour's Head', attributed to Sacchi, was bought by Howard from Pond in 1759 for nineteen shillings (lot 53; Victoria and Albert Manuscript Sale Catalogues).

L 13. The Holy Family with St. John
Madonnas and *Holy Families* were subjects that Sacchi rarely, if ever, tackled although his most gifted student, Maratta, painted a good many examples of this genre. Sacchi's inventory includes one *Madonna* (no. 128) and this *Holy Family* (no. 121). The only recorded reference elsewhere to a work of this kind by Sacchi is a copy of a *Virgin and Child with St. John* in the collection of Duca G. B. Rospigliosi (Zeri, 1959, p. 319). Its later history is not known.

L 14. St. Anthony of Padua with Angels
The *St. Anthony* in Sacchi's collection (no. 152) may have had something to do with the *St. Anthony* altarpiece in Sacchi's parish church, S. Nicola in Arcione, which according to Titi (1721, p. 355) was by 'un allievo d'Andrea Sacchi'. The church was pulled down early in this century and there is no record of the appearance of any of the altarpieces then extant. There are also two engravings after drawings of miracles of St. Anthony attributed to Sacchi (C. Rogers, *Imitation of Drawings*, London, 1778). One of the two drawings on which Rogers based his print is now in the Pierpont Morgan Library in New York (no. IV, 27 F); it is not by Sacchi.

L 15. The Last Communion of St. Jerome
Sacchi owned both a drawing (no. 191) and a painting (no. 162) of St. Jerome in 1661, although only the latter is stated to show the saint receiving communion. Sacchi finally decided in a codicil to his will to leave the picture to Cardinal Antonio, and in fact a *St. Jerome* attributed to Sacchi appears in Cardinal Antonio's inventories of 1671 and 1672 (nos. 328 and 311 respectively) and in Prince Maffeo's inventory of 1672–86 (no. 188) and a Casa Barberini inventory of 1686 (no. 200 with an attribution to Agostino Carracci). The Barberini inventories also state that Sacchi's picture showed two angels in the sky, as does Agostino Carracci's *Last Communion of St. Jerome* in Bologna; one inventory ascribes the picture to Agostino. Malvasia and Bellori both report that Sacchi made a small copy of Agostino's picture. It is possible therefore that the *St. Jerome* in Sacchi's inventory was based on Agostino's composition. A *Head of St. Jerome with a*

Crucifix attributed to Sacchi is recorded in later Barberini inventories (Incisa della Rocchetta, 1924, p. 75).

L 16. The Magdalene
Sacchi's inventory mentions one painting of the *Magdalene* (no. 168). Drawings of a *Noli Me Tangere* composition have been ascribed to Sacchi in three different collections (see Harris and Schaar, nos. 132 and 133), and while none of those drawings is by Sacchi, they may indicate a tradition linking his name with this subject. Indeed, the subject with its intense spiritual dialogue between two protagonists would seem to be ideal for Sacchi.

L 17. Bacchus and Ariadne
One reference in an early eighteenth-century guide book to an *Ariadne* by Sacchi in the Palazzo Gaetani suggests that the three paintings and drawings of this subject in Sacchi's house (nos. 213, 225 and 226) were by Sacchi himself and were not copies after Titian or Guido Reni (see Rossini, 1750, p. 85). They may have been the 'Due Baccanali sopraporti e grandezza di p(al)mi 5, Una de' quali rappresenta una Vendemmia' in Cardinal Antonio's inventories of 1671 and 1672 (nos. 213 and 278 respectively), which should not be confused with the copies after (Titian's ?) *Bacchanals* listed separately in the Cardinal's inventories and attributed to Carlo Magnone (nos. 15 and 390). These in turn are probably not the copies after Dosso Dossi's *Bacchanals* in Ferrara which Sacchi had made (Incisa della Rocchetta, 1924, p. 74) because Sacchi was reimbursed in 1654 and Magnone died in 1653 (Thieme-Becker, *sub voce*).

L 18. Cato
Since Maratta owned a 'Mezza figure grande al naturale non terminata, rappresentante "Catone" ... mano d'Andrea Sacchi' (Galli, XXIII, p. 72, no. 321), it is probable that the two pictures of Cato in Sacchi's inventory were by him (no. 221). The actual subject may have been the death of Cato the Younger, which was the one event in his life usually singled out by artists and which Sacchi could have checked in his own Italian translation of Plutarch's *Lives*. (Appendix III, no. 81.)

L 19. Apollo and Vulcan
Apart from the picture in Sacchi's house (no. 222), only one other reference to a picture by Sacchi of this subject has been traced, namely a picture in the Palazzo Colonna in 1783 (p. 72, no. 511). It may have been an easel version of one of the narrative scenes in the lost Casino of Cardinal del Monte, *q.v.*

L 20. St. Paul
This large canvas with a design of St. Paul sketched out on it (no. 240) may have been intended to be part of the series of apostles for the Barberini to which Sacchi contributed a *St. Peter*. A half-length *St. Paul* attributed to Sacchi was recorded in the Oddi collection in Perugia in 1784 (*Guida al Forastiere di Perugia*, Perugia, 1784, p. 288: 'S. Paolo a mezza figura con attitudine magistrale, accomodata alla forma del quadro che è per traverso; onde ha in se opportuni accidenti di chiaroscuro') and again in 1822 (Siepi, II, p. 837). Its present location is not known.

L 21. Miscellaneous Items
Sacchi's inventory includes a fair number of heads of men and women variously described—some sketches, some unfinished portraits, some studies of allegorical figures. There are also heads attributed to Sacchi in Barberini inventories (Incisa della Rocchetta, 1924, p. 75 and Posse, 1925, p. 109, note 2), in Maratta's inventory in 1712 (Galli, XXIII, nos. 253 and 271) and in sale records (Mireur, IV, p. 388). It was common practice in the seventeenth century in Italy and elsewhere to make sketches of heads for use later in finished compositions as saints or other recurring types and Sacchi

clearly did this too. One of the examples in Maratta's collection went to Spain and may be identified with a picture now in the Prado, q.v.

There are a few puzzling items in Sacchi's inventory which research has failed to clarify. The 'Portrait of S. Maria Maggiore' (no. 151) may have been commissioned because it was the most important church for which Cardinal Antonio Barberini was responsible. It has not been possible to learn anything about the Bottugli family of Pavia (no. 230). The 'Testa di un Agonizante' (no. 45) may have been a picture of a member of the Confraternità degli Agonizzanti, which was attached to the church of the Nativity in the Piazza del Pasquaino (Silvio Valenti, *Roma Antica e Moderna*, 1750, II, p. 10).

WORKS ATTRIBUTED TO SACCHI IN BARBERINI INVENTORIES

L 22. A Dog on a Cushion with a Rattle
A picture of 'una cagna detta tigre sopra un' cuscino, con una sonagliera' attributed to Sacchi appears in Cardinal Antonio's inventory of 1644 only (Incisa della Rocchetta, 1924, p. 73). A drawing by Sacchi at Düsseldorf showing various studies of a small dog on a cushion, two for a composition in an oval frame, should probably be associated with this lost picture (Harris and Schaar, no. 94).

L 23. Portrait of a Bishop
The inventory made in 1692 of Cardinal Carlo Barberini's collection includes 'Un ritratto di un Vescovo coll'abito de' P(adri) di S(anti) Apostoli in tela di testa cornice dorata di Andrea Sacchi' (no. 276). It is recorded again in his inventory of 1704 (Posse, 1925, p. 132) but has since disappeared.

L 24. Miscellaneous
The inventory of Prince Maffeo's collection made between 1672 and 1686 includes 'Un ritratto di homo quadrato 1½ p(er) ogni verso' (no. 460). Cardinal Antonio's inventories of 1671 and 1672 include 'Un ritratto di un Huomo senza beretta in testa, manto di colore' (1671, no. 52; 1672, no. 11). Cardinal Francesco's inventory of 1679–80 includes 'Due quadri compagni rappresentano due teste con barba rossa di tela di mezza testa' (p. 82, no. 197). A Barberini inventory made on August 4, 1730 lists 'Due Ottangoli uno dei quali rappresenta un Santo Vescovo che tiene un Calice in mano guardando il Cielo alto p(al)mi 3 incirca, largo p(al)mi 2 incirca, l'altro una Santa, che tiene la testa alzata al Cielo, e le mani al petto, alto p(al)mi 3, e largo p(al)mi 2 incirca con cornice liscia d'ambedue, e dorate, mano di Andrea Sacchi' (p. 23, no. 3619; also Cardinal Carlo Barberini, 1704, p. 124; Palestrina Inventory, 1738–9, p. 36 verso).

WORKS ATTRIBUTED TO SACCHI IN THE INVENTORY OF CARDINAL FLAVIO CHIGI MADE IN 1692

L 25.
The Cardinal's inventory includes, besides works attributed to Sacchi that survive or are connected with known works, two items. One was 'Un quadro in tela da testa, cornice tutta dorata, con una Madonna, S. Matteo et un angelo', the other 'Un quadro tela di palmi 4 e 3, in forma ovata, cornice tutta dorata angolata, con una mezza figura d'una donna a giacere, che tiene una palla nelle mani'. I owe both references to Dr. Giovanni Incisa della Rocchetta. Neither picture can now be traced.

WORKS RECORDED BY G. P. BELLORI

L 26. St. Mark and St. Peter
Bellori reports (p. 84) that Sacchi was commissioned to paint an altarpiece of this subject for S. Marco, the Venetian nationals' church in Rome, which was restored by the Venetian Ambassador, Niccolò Sagredo, in the 1650s (Hess, 1934, p. 369, note 1). It was intended for the first chapel to the left, but Sacchi never completed it, nor do any drawings survive that can definitely be associated with this project.

L 27. The Virgin and Child with SS. Anthony, Francis, Peter and Anthony Abbot
Bellori says that a picture of this subject was painted by Sacchi for the Capuchin church in Reims (p. 66), and since he owned the preparatory sketch, it can be assumed both that his description of the composition, which is a detailed one, is correct and that he was accurately informed about the destination of the work itself. The head of St. Anthony, which was in profile facing to the left, was 'ritratta . . . alla similitudine di Papa Urbano Ottavo'. Cardinal Antonio Barberini was made archbishop of Reims in 1657, but this is a very late date for Sacchi to have begun and completed a major work. Other commissions, awarded in 1653, were never completed. The picture in question was not commissioned for the cathedral, and it seems probable that it was commissioned and painted some years earlier while Cardinal Antonio was in France (1645–53).

The Capuchins' church in Reims no longer survives and it seems highly probable that Sacchi's picture was destroyed, perhaps with the church during the Revolution.[5] The only work attributed to Sacchi which might have been identified with the lost Reims picture was the *Assumption with Four Saints* in the Northwick Collection in 1859 but the saints in that work—John, Paul the Hermit, Jerome and Peter—were not the same as those listed by Bellori, nor was the Reims picture said to be an Assumption (for the Northwick picture, see above, L 10).

WORKS ATTRIBUTED TO SACCHI IN THE INVENTORY OF CARLO MARATTA OF 1712

L 28. An Annunciation with Angels
Maratta owned a sketch by Sacchi of this subject measuring 4 palmi, 2½ oncie by 3 palmi, 10 oncie (Galli, XXIII, no. 302). It was hung with a sketch of the Magdalene by Domenichino.

L 29. Adam and Eve
An unfinished Adam and Eve by Sacchi also belonged to Maratta (Galli, XXIII, no. 315). Bellori says that Sacchi won a drawing contest at the age of fourteen at the Academy of St. Luke with a study of Adam and Eve (1672–96, p. 44), but Maratta owned a painting not a drawing, although the design of the former may have been related to the latter.

NOTES TO LOST WORKS

1. Archivio di Stato, Compagnie Religiose, S. Andrea della Valle, Busta 2162, no. 202, pp. 8–9. Professor Howard Hibbard kindly told me about these documents.
2. See for example G. Laurenti, *Storia della Diaconia Cardinalizia e Monasterio Abaziale di S. Agata alla Suburra,* Rome, 1797. Titi (1763, p. 272) attributes the high altarpiece and nave paintings to Paolo Perugino (Gismondi, *c.* 1612–*c.* 1685), an attribution supported by Longhi (*L'Arte,* 1924, pp. 224–5) and Waterhouse (1937, pp. 72–3). If—as seems to be the case—Gismondi, a Cortona follower, was the artist working for Sacchi in S. Agata (the documents mention the erection of scaffolding 'p(er) li Pitori' between 1637 and 1641 'di ordine dello Sig(no)r(e)

Andrea Sacchi'), then Sacchi was willing to give work to a representative of Cortona's aesthetic viewpoint after the debate in the Academy of St. Luke when Sacchi is supposed to have opposed Cortona's ideas.
3. No. 226 in the same Busta of documents cited in note 1 above mentions work in Segni, including the chapel of the Palazzo Barberini, in 1643.
4. I owe this reference to Frank Simpson.
5. The Capuchins' church was consecrated in 1620 and destroyed in 1790 (Prosper Tarbé, *Reims—Essais Historiques sur ses Rues et ses Monuments,* Reims, 1844, pp. 46–7).

REJECTED ATTRIBUTIONS

Works regularly but incorrectly attributed to Sacchi in the literature are discussed here in alphabetical order by location. Comparison of these attributed works with authentic pictures is in most cases sufficient to justify their exclusion without a lengthy analysis. Alternative attributions have been suggested when possible.

R 1. Ascoli Piceno, *Holy Family,* **Pinacoteca Comunale**
Luigi Serra first attributed this work to Sacchi, followed by Ludwig Schudt, who thought however it was only a studio copy of a lost composition. Refice also thought it was a school work, except possibly for the figure of Joseph. The poor quality of the execution certainly excludes the picture from Sacchi's autograph works. Possibly, his pupil from Ascoli, Lodovico Trasi (1634–94) was responsible.
Bibliography: L. Serra, *Le Gallerie Comunali delle Marche,* Rome, 1925, p. 82, no. 141); L. Schudt in *Jahrb. KWS.,* 1930, pp. 104–5; Refice, 1950, p. 220. On Trasi, see Posse, 1925, p. 149, note 2.

R 2. Bari, *Portrait of a Man,* **Pinacoteca Provinciale**
The portrait of a man, formerly on loan to the Pinacoteca Provinciale in Bari from the Galleria Nazionale d'Arte Antica (Palazzo Corsini) in Rome and now back in Rome, which has been attributed to Sacchi, should be attributed instead to Carlo Maratta.

R 3. Berlin, *Portrait of Alessandro dal Borro,* **Dahlem Museum**
This striking picture is one of the most puzzling unattributed works of the seventeenth century. It came to Berlin in the 1870s, having been acquired in 1823 from the Villa Passerini near Cortona where it was already identified as a portrait of Alessandro dal Borro (1600–56). It has been attributed to artists as diverse as Velazquez, Bernini, Tiarini, Pietro da Cortona, Tiberio Tinelli, Tiepolo and Luca Giordano, as well as to Sacchi, to whom it is currently ascribed in catalogues of the Dahlem Museum.
The identification of the sitter as Borro was challenged by Bombe, who drew attention to a portrait of Borro in the town hall of Arezzo and to a portrait by Sustermans in a private collection in Leningrad that he also identified as of Borro. The Arezzo picture is a crude, provincial work in poor condition and the sitter's features are difficult to read. The sitter in the Sustermans portrait has the same plump features, the same full head of hair with a quiff over the forehead, the same small moustache and goatee beard and the same broad nose and widely-spaced eyes as the man in the Berlin picture. These features are seen again in the engraved portrait of Borro in Crasso's *Elogii di Capitani Illustri* (Venice, 1683, p. 294). It needs to be remembered that the low viewpoint and low light source used by the artist of the Berlin picture to dramatize his subject distort the sitter's features somewhat, especially the nose and eyes, which are squinted against the light.
It is important to decide whether the Berlin picture represents

Borro or not because Borro fought against and defeated the Papal forces in 1643 during the War of Castro, and so is unlikely to have been painted by any artist who remained loyal to the Barberini, as Sacchi did even after their fall following the death of Urban VIII. Moreover, Sacchi never left Rome and Borro was never in Rome as far as is known in the 1640s or 1650s. The man who depicted Borro spurning the bee-laden flag of the Barberini probably worked in Florence, for Borro, who came from Arezzo, fought under the aegis of Prince Mattias de' Medici. The provenance of the picture from the countryside near Cortona not far from the land given to Borro by Prince Mattias, is also circumstantial evidence in favour of the Borro identification and in favour of a Tuscan origin for the artist concerned. Joan Nissman has pointed out to me that Baldinucci (VI, pp. 76–7) mentions a series of portraits of generals, including Borro, painted by Orazio Fidani, but an attribution of the Borro picture to him is not convincing. More recently Maurizio Fagiolo dell'Arco has suggested an attribution to Volterrano and a date in the 1640s, certainly the most plausible solution so far proposed.
Bibliography: On Borro see also Valori, *Condottieri e Generali del Seicento,* Rome, 1943, pp. 50–1. Bombe, *L'Arte,* 1909, pp. 374–6; H. Voss, *Monatsheft für Kunstgeschichte,* 1910, pp. 18–24; Gamba, 1927, p. 31; Pastor, 1938, XXIX, pp. 399–400, note 4; Refice, 1950, p. 221; L. Grassi, *Gian Lorenzo Bernini,* Rome, 1962, pp. 176–8; M. Fagiolo dell'Arco, *Storia dell' Arte,* nos. 7/8, 1970, p. 342 and catalogues of the Berlin Museum.

R 4. Burghley House, Northamptonshire
The Last Supper, The Marriage at Cana, The Way to Calvary and *An Allegory of the Church* in the collection of the Marquess of Exeter at Burghley House are attributed to Sacchi. They are in my opinion by Pasqualino de' Rossi. The *St. Gregory* in the same collection, which has been attributed to Sacchi, is by Carlo Saraceni.
Bibliography: A. Ottania Cavina, *Carlo Saraceni,* Milan, 1968, p. 97.

R 5. Camerino, *St. Ansovinus Distributing Alms,* **Duomo**
This picture is certainly not by Sacchi and would not appear even to be by a pupil working from drawings supplied by him. An attribution to Emilio Savonanzi, who worked with Sacchi before moving to Camerino around 1640, is possible.
Bibliography: On Savonanzi, see E. Schleier, 'Emilio Savonanzi: Inediti del Periodo Romano', *Antichità Viva,* 1969, no. 4, with further bibliography, especially the article by Vera Fortunati.

R 6. Chatsworth, Derbyshire, *The Sacrifice of Noah,* Collection the Duke of Devonshire
The attribution of this picture to Sacchi goes back to 1767 only when it was engraved by Liart for Boydell. Posse accepted it as a work of the 1640s. Spear left open the question of an attribution to either Sacchi or Maratta. It is in my opinion an early work by Maratta.
Bibliography: Posse, 1925, p. 84; R. Spear, 'The Source of an Early Falsification of Poussin', *Burl. Mag.,* 1964, p. 234 and figs. 59 and 61.

R. 7. Chiuduno, *The Assumption of the Virgin with Saints,* Chiesa Parrocchiale
A letter published by Bottari and Ticozzi, dated November 28, 1652, and purporting to be addressed to the parish priest of Chiuduno from his cousin in Rome, states that the 'Madonna' ordered from Sacchi for Chiuduno is almost ready. The document is puzzling because the altarpiece in the church is the work of a Caravaggesque artist such as Stomer and has nothing whatsoever to do with Sacchi, as both Posse and Refice noted. Perhaps the letter is a forgery.
Bibliography: Bottari and Ticozzi, 1822, v, p. 315; Posse, 1925, p. 110 f.; Refice, 1950, p. 220.

R 8. Dresden, *The Rest on the Flight into Egypt,* Gemäldegalerie
For the reattribution of this small copper to Andrea Camassei, see Sutherland Harris, 'Camassei Studies', pp. 64–5.

R 9. Greenville, S. C., *St. Gregory,* Bob Jones University Art Gallery
The *St. Gregory* recently acquired by the Bob Jones University collection (*Art, Quarterly* 1967, pp. 273 and 278) with an attribution to Sacchi is not by him.

R 10. Leningrad, *Landscape with Venus Resting,* Hermitage Museum
This work was first attributed to Sacchi in 1747 when Horace Walpole published it in his *Aedes Walpolianae.* It was bought for Catherine the Great of Russia in 1779 and has remained at the Hermitage since then. Posse thought that it was an early work of Sacchi, as did Voss, but the Hermitage catalogues of 1912 and 1958 attributed it tentatively to Domenichino while Refice thought that it was an early *seicento* Bolognese picture. In my opinion, the artist responsible was G. F. Grimaldi, although it is possible that the figure staffage records a lost *Venus* by Sacchi formerly in the collection of Cardinal Mazarin, *q.v.* The Hermitage picture may be compared with the four exquisitely finished copper landscapes by Grimaldi in the Borghese Gallery in Rome.
Bibliography: H. Walpole, *Aedes Walpolianae,* 1747 (cited in *The Works of Horace Walpole,* London, 1798, II, p. 243); Thomas Ripley, *The Plans, Elevations and Sections . . . of Houghton in Norfolk,* London, 1760, p. 2; Waagen, 1864, p. 81; Hermitage Catalogue, 1912, no. 210 and pl. 75; Voss, 1924, p. 690; Posse, 1925, p. 17 f. and pl. 2; Posse, 1935, p. 290; Refice, 1950, p. 220; *Catalogue of the State Hermitage Museum,* Leningrad and Moscow, 1958, I, p. 95, no. 217.

R 11. Madrid, *A Lupercal,* Prado Museum
For the reattribution of this work to Andrea Camassei, see Sutherland Harris, 'Camassei Studies', pp. 63–4.

R 12. Madrid, Miscellaneous Attributions
Pérez Sánchez included a number of works attributed to Sacchi in his recent survey of Italian *seicento* painting in Spain. Those not discussed elsewhere as originals or copies of originals may be presumed to be rejected attributions. The *St. Peter and St. Paul* (pl. 95) should be attributed rather to Romanelli. The *Crucifixion* in Palma

de Mallorca is not by Sacchi although I can suggest no convincing alternative label.
Bibliography: Pérez Sánchez, 1965, pp. 326–7. Pérez Sánchez, *Pintura Italiana del Siglo XVII,* Exposicion, Cason del Buen Retiro, Madrid, 1970, no. 163.

R 13. Montreal, *The Rape of Europa,* Museum of Fine Arts
Currently attributed to Sacchi, this painting is by a late seventeenth-century follower of Maratta, perhaps Benedetto Luti.

R 14. Nancy, *Pope Alexander VII Carried in Procession,* Musée des Beaux-Arts
This portrait of the Chigi Pope with his bearers was tentatively attributed to Sacchi in the museum catalogue of 1897. It is not by Sacchi and nor is the *Trinity* in the same collection.
Bibliography: *Musée de Nancy: Tableaux* etc., Nancy, 1897, pp. 34–5.

R 15. Oldenburg, *The Blind Belisarius,* Gemäldegalerie
Hermann Voss tentatively suggested Sacchi for this strange picture, acquired from the Doria Collection in Rome for the collection in 1803 by Tischbein. The traditional attribution was Salvator Rosa. There are many parallels with the work of Giulio Carpioni (cf. G. M. Pilo, *Carpioni,* Venice, 1961, pls. 25, 36, 106 and 115).
Bibliography: H. W. Keiser, *Gemäldegalerie Oldenburg,* Munich, 1967, p. 63.

R 16. Orleans, *The Raising of Lazarus,* Musée des Beaux-Arts
This work has been attributed to Sacchi since 1827 when it was acquired by the museum. It is clearly the work of a Neapolitan artist close to Massimo Stanzione.
Bibliography: *Inventaire des Richesses d'Art de la France,* Province I, Paris, 1878, p. 120.

R 17. Pommersfelden, *The Flight into Egypt,* Schönborn Collection. Longhi suggested in 1950 that this work might be by Sacchi although 'non al suo meglio'. It would appear to be a late seventeenth-century derivation of Maratta's treatment of this theme formerly in the Alaleona chapel in S. Isidoro in Rome.
Bibliography: R. Longhi, *Scritti Giovanili,* Florence, 1961, p. 487.

R 18. Rieti, *The Vision of St. Andrew,* S. Agnese
Palmegiani first gave this picture to Sacchi, presumably by linking it with Sacchi's *St. Andrew* in St. Peter's and with his lost *St. Francis Marrying Poverty.* The Rieti picture is an impressive work but neither the physiognomy nor the drapery forms are those of Sacchi. It is close in style to a picture by an anonymous Caravaggesque illustrated by Voss (1924, pl. 106) and also to the portrait of J. D. de la Barrière in S. Bernardino alle Terme, a work also formerly attributed to Sacchi (see R 24, below).
Bibliography: Palmegiani, 1932, p. 287.

R 19. Rieti, *The Martyrdom of St. Andrew,* S. Scholastica
The attribution of this altarpiece to Sacchi goes back to Bellori, a usually reliable source for works outside as well as in Rome. Perhaps he depended on a local informant who made a mistake. The picture should be attributed to Antonio Gherardi (1644–1702), who painted at least one other work in Rieti (Waterhouse, 1937, p. 69).
Bibliography: Bellori, 1672–96, p. 67; Palmegiani, 1932, p. 283.

R 20. Rome, *Portrait of a Cleric,* Palazzo Barberini
A picture of a cleric, maybe a cardinal, with his eyes raised to heaven is attributed to Sacchi in current inventories of the Galleria Nazionale d'Arte Antica (no. 834). It might be an early work, but the present condition of the surface makes any final judgement impossible. Dr. Italo Faldi kindly drew my attention to this work.

R 21. Rome, *Head of an Old Woman,* Palazzo Barberini (Galleria Nazionale d'Arte Antica)
Posse (1925, p. 124 f. and pl. XXII) gave this work to Sacchi, but it is now generally accepted as a work of P. F. Mola (e.g. Arslan 'Opere Romane di P. F. Mola', *Boll. d'Arte*, 1928, p. 55 f. and Voss in Thieme-Becker, *sub voce*).

R 22. Rome, *Portrait of a Cardinal,* Museo di Roma
This portrait of a prelate, tentatively identified as Cardinal Domenico Ginnasi, is attributed to Sacchi in the latest brief guide to the museum. The plump hands of the sitter and the simple, unaffected presentation of the sitter recall the Merlini portrait in the Borghese Gallery but the portrait in the Palazzo Braschi is hardly a work of that calibre. If the sitter is indeed Cardinal Ginnasi, then an attribution to his painter-niece, Caterina Ginnasi, would be worth investigating.
Bibliography: Museo di Roma, Itinerario, Rome, 1963, p. 30.

R 23. Rome, *The Scourging of Job,* Federazione di Consorzi Agrari, Palazzo Rospigliosi-Pallavicini
Zeri noted that a picture of Job described in a Pallavicini inventory of 1713 and attributed to Sacchi was still in the Palazzo (G.F.N. E 32303). It is much too crude in characterization and handling to be by Sacchi. An attribution to Daniele Seiter (cf. Voss, 1924, pl. 331) is possible.
Bibliography: Mariotti, 1892, p. 165; Zeri, 1959, pp. 324 and 330.

R 24. Rome, *Portrait of the Blessed Jean Dominique de la Barrière,* S. Bernardino alle Terme
The attribution of this tomb portrait to Sacchi, first made in an eighteenth-century manuscript, was revived by Ortolani in his monograph on the church. He compared the portrait in particular with the *St. Andrew* in S. Agnese in Rieti, which he also thought was by Sacchi (*q.v.* above). Voss, Posse, Waterhouse and Refice all accepted the attribution.
The sitter died in 1600 but the monument was only set up in 1626 according to Ortolani. This means that the portrait is contemporary with Sacchi's *Miracle of St. Gregory the Great* and would be an early work. In my opinion, neither the physiognomy of the sitter nor the technique of the painting have anything to do with Sacchi, although it is a good work in its own right. It may indeed be by the same hand as the Rieti picture, R 18.
Bibliography: S. Ortolani, *San Bernardino alle Terme,* Le Chiese di Roma Illustrate 8, Rome, n.d., pp. 25 and 43; Voss, 1924, p. 532; Posse, 1935, p. 290; Waterhouse, 1937, p. 91; Refice, 1950, p. 220.

R 25. Rome, *Virgin and Child with San Biagio (?),* S. Biagio alla Pagnotta
This small fresco, much of which has flaked off and been lost, is first noticed in guide books of the later eighteenth century when it was attributed—always with hesitation—to Francesco Albani, Guido Reni, Camassei and Sacchi. Although its present condition precludes making any attributions at all, the very uncertainty of the guide books suggests that the authors had no definite tradition to report. None of Sacchi's biographers mention it and for this reason the attribution to him seems unlikely to be correct.
Bibliography: Roisecco, 1750, II, p. 56 (Camassei); Titi, 1763, p. 421 ('si crede, o d'Andrea Sacchi, o dell'Albano'); Vasi, 1770 (1765), p. 310 ('si crede opera di Guido Reni, o dell'Albani'); Rossini, 1776, II, p. 466 ('si crede di Andrea Sacchi, o dell'Albano'); Pistolesi, 1841 and 1846, p. 551 ('quello di fuori è del Camassei').

R 26. Rome, *The Canonization of St. Philip Neri,* Pinacoteca Vaticana
The attribution of this picture to Sacchi, first made in 1922, was recently supported by Refice. While recognizing that it was not a work of high quality, she found in it hints of Venetian colour and handling which she believed to be typical of Sacchi's later style. The picture must have been made shortly after the canonization ceremonies took place in 1622. This means that the picture would be an early work of Sacchi, contemporary with the *St. Isidore,* which, although a very different work in scale and composition, shows that a high level of competence is to be expected by this date. On grounds of poor quality, the attribution of the Vatican picture to Sacchi seems dubious therefore. In addition, the figure on the right, presumably a self-portrait of the artist, neither looks like Sacchi nor like a man of 23. Sacchi directed the execution of two commemorative pictures of this kind—the *Festa in Piazza Navona* and the *Centenary Celebrations in the Gesù*—which is presumably why the Vatican picture was associated with him, but other artists than Sacchi and Filippo Gagliardi, Sacchi's assistant for the two works named, produced pictures of this kind and there is no good stylistic reason for associating Sacchi's name with this particular example.
Bibliography: Mostra della Pittura Italiana del Sei e Settecento in Palazzo Pitti, Florence, 1922, no. 869; *Mostra di Roma Seicentesca,* Rome, 1930, no. 20; Refice, 1950, pp. 218–19; Hess, *Kunstgeschichtliche Studien,* Rome, 1967, p. 358, note 9.

R 27. Schleissheim, *The Rape of Europa,* Staatsgalerie
Attributed to a follower of Albano in 1914, to Pier Francesco Mola by Voss, to Sacchi by Posse and to Maratta by Refice, Emiliani recently supported the attribution to Mola, which is in my opinion correct. The *Europa* may be compared with other presumably early works such as the *Narcissus* in the Ashmolean in Oxford, but not, as Emiliani suggested, with the *Assunta* in the Rospigliosi-Pallavicini collection, which Zeri—wrongly in my opinion—attributed to Pier Francesco Mola.
Bibliography: Katalog der Kgl. Gemäldegalerie zu Schleissheim, 1914, p. 2; Voss, 1924, pp. 262 and 560; Posse, 1925, pp. 17–18; Refice, 1950, p. 220; Emiliani, 1962, p. 340.

R 28. Versailles, *St. Bernard,* Musée de Versailles et des Trianons
A picture of *St. Bernard* at Versailles (Inventory no. MV 3022) carries an old attribution to Sacchi. Stylistically it is closer to Alessandro Turchi.

R 29. Vienna, *The Dying Mother of Aristides,* Kunsthistorisches Museum
According to Wickhoff, this picture was in the 1659 inventory of Prince Leopold Wilhelm of the Netherlands as 'del Andrea original'. Wickhoff identified Andrea as Sacchi, but this attribution is not possible. An attribution to Artemisia Gentileschi should be considered (cf. R. Ward Bissell, 'Artemisia Gentileschi—A New Documented Chronology', *Art Bulletin,* 1968, pp. 153–68, esp. fig. 7).
Bibliography: F. Wickhoff, 'Andrea Sacchi's Restauration der sterbenden Mutter des Aristides', *J.K.A.K.,* 1878, XIX, p. 344 f.

R 30. Wilton House, *Job with his Wife and Friends,* Collection of the Earl of Pembroke
Acquired by the family by 1730, this picture has always been attributed to Sacchi but is not by him. It appears to date from later in the seventeenth century.
Bibliography: Posse, 1925, p. 109, note 2; Sidney, sixteenth Earl of Pembroke, *A Catalogue of the Paintings and Drawings in the Collection at Wilton House,* London, 1968, p. 82 and pl. 101.

APPENDIXES

AND

BIBLIOGRAPHY

Preface to the Appendixes

The three appendixes contain transcripts of two unpublished documents, namely Andrea Sacchi's will and the inventory made of the contents of his house after his death. The first appendix concerns the will, which was drawn up on June 8, 1661, and to which codicils were added on June 17 and 19. Sacchi died on June 21. The will has been transcribed complete so far as this is possible. Besides the occasional difficulties of reading the handwriting, some words are concealed by the binding while others were lost when the ink ate through the paper, which then crumbled away. The last pages of the will and the codicils were bound at the back of the volume concerned, but as the hand-writing matches and the text continues logically, the identification of the final pages is not in doubt. My transcripts of the will and the inventory were checked by Dr Gino Corti, who caught many errors and unravelled many difficult passages.

In transcribing the will, abbreviations have been expanded in brackets. An abbreviated translation of the will and its codicils is also provided. Each paragraph of the will has been given a letter of the alphabet and some proper names have been italicized the first time they appear. This has been done in order to facilitate reference to the index of proper names that follows the will. The index has been substituted for footnotes because it enables all the information concerning one person, who may be mentioned in a number of places, to be discussed together. Proper names that have not been italicized have been omitted from the index because nothing more could be learnt about that individual. This is true of most of the witnesses.

The second and third appendixes concern the inventory. This has not been transcribed complete because it is extremely long—it lists every item in the house down to the broken sack of flour in the attic—and the descriptions of furniture, linen, clothing, crockery, and so on, are interesting only for what they can tell us about Sacchi's standard of living. He was evidently fairly well off because his house was large and quite well furnished. He had invested some of his money in jewellery, and owned a certain amount of property. However, we know from his will that he was some 400 scudi in debt at the time of his death. This information, added to the knowledge that many of the items in his house were old, broken or damaged, suggests that in recent years Sacchi's standard of living had declined somewhat. When we consider how little he painted after 1653 and how many children he had to support, this is hardly surprising.

The second appendix is therefore limited to items of immediate art historical interest—paintings, frames, canvases, painting materials, casts and drawings. These have been listed in the order in which they appear in the original document together with an indication of the room in which they were found. In a few cases this information is of particular interest. The first room, for example, which seems to have been the main entrance and reception room, contained portraits of most of the Barberini together with some of other important patrons, and other pictures—landscapes, subject pictures, studies of heads—which seem to have been arranged symmetrically. Both content and arrangement seem to have been designed to impress. This was not true of most of the other rooms, where the arrangement does not seem to have had any particular significance, although the presence of Cardinal Biscia's portrait in the same room as a version of the *St. Romuald*, an altarpiece which he commissioned, has some point. The drawings were found in a box in the artist's bedroom. We do not know, of course, how long they had been kept there, but it suggests at least that Sacchi valued them and looked after them, and that they were not available for casual use in the studio.

The pictures were listed by subject only, with a few exceptions. We are told that the *Galatea* (no. 15) was a copy after Raphael, that no. 164 was by Bamboccio,[1] and that no. 283, a *Nativity* ('una Notte') was by Carlo Magnone.[2] The attribution of the *Still Life* in Sacchi's bedroom to Cerquozzi is only given in the will. This suggests that a blanket attribution of every other painting in the house of Sacchi or his studio is not possible. It was not customary in the seventeenth century to inventory pictures in greater detail than was done here—subject, approximate size, material if unusual (e.g. on copper), and a brief description of the frame. In the case of the Bamboccio and the Raphael, to give the artist's name was probably the easiest way of identifying the picture in question.

The pictures can be divided into two groups—those of subjects which Sacchi is known to have painted, and those which he is not hitherto known to have painted. The first group includes pictures such as 'Un Quadro In

Ottangolo con Agar Hismaele e l'Angelo', 'Un Quadro Rapresentante Noè Inebriato . . . con tre Figure', 'Un quadro senza cornice con San Francesco che sposa la Carità', 'Un quadro senza cornice con San Ramualdo et altri frati', 'Caino et Abelle', 'Il transito di S. Anna' and 'Un quadro con una Divina Sapienza Teladi 7 palmi In circa'.[3] Although it is just conceivable that these were compositions by other seventeenth-century painters working in Rome, given the location the pictures in question were almost certainly either by Sacchi himself or were copies after his work by pupils. It has therefore been assumed throughout that a picture the subject of which Sacchi is known to have painted was in fact by him, and all these pictures have been discussed under 'Versions' in the relative catalogue entry. Very few can be traced with any certainty today, the *Portrait of Francesco Albano* (no. 210) in the Prado being almost unique in this respect.

The other group of pictures—those whose subjects Sacchi is not known to have painted—can be further divided into two groups: subjects which Sacchi is unlikely ever to have painted; subjects which Sacchi may possibly have painted. In the second group belong all the religious and mythological compositions such as *St. Peter Escaping from Prison, Cato, The Story of Actaeon, The Holy Family, The Holy Family with St. John,* and so on. All these have been included in the catalogue of lost works although here the possibility that another artist was responsible is much greater. However, given the fact that the majority of pictures do seem to have been his own, the chances that other unidentified subjects were also his seems fairly good.

The first group includes all the landscapes, seascapes, still lifes and genre subjects. Since Sacchi is not recorded elsewhere as a painter of pure landscape or genre or still life and since we know he owned a Bamboccio and a Cerquozzi, it seems reasonable to assume that the majority of these paintings were not by him. The only possible exceptions are the landscapes. Some of these—small, on panel, some with a tondo format, others hung in pairs—sound very much like the decorative landscapes of late sixteenth- or early seventeenth-century followers of Brill. The 'Quadro con una Ghirlanda de Fiori' or the 'Quadro con un Vaso di Fiori' might have been by Mario de' Fiori, a neighbour in 1647 and 1648 and possibly also a collaborator.[4] Others may however have been by Sacchi himself, for the landscape backgrounds of his own work, particularly that of the 1620s and 1630s, are outstanding, and he must have made landscape drawings and small landscape paintings, even though none are recorded.[5]

All the entries in the inventory which can be matched to references to Sacchi's authentic works, surviving or lost but recorded in reliable sources, have been listed again in the appropriate catalogue entry. The other 'serious' subjects have been tentatively included in the section of Lost Works. The remainder—landscapes, still lifes and genre subjects, altogether some thirty pictures—have not been discussed in greater detail than appears here and in the introduction.

The books have been given a separate appendix, although the place where they appear in the main inventory has been noted in Appendix II. When it has been possible to identify the book, the title, author and date of first publication, or a later date if relevant, have been given with each entry. Identification of the few items which it has not been possible to trace would not alter the total picture of Sacchi's library since their subject is known from the description given. The puzzling 'Anfolito Vigliega' is a religious work, and the 'Lacrime del Tevere' is probably another collection of lyric poetry. The contents of the library are discussed in more general terms in the introduction.

NOTES

1. Despite the eccentric spelling, there can be little doubt that Pieter van Laer, 'Il Bamboccio', is the artist intended.
2. For Magnone, see note 19 in the catalogue entry for *The Decoration of S. Giovanni in Fonte* (No. 53).
3. Nos. 23, 28, 131, 148, 223, 224 and 297.
4. See the catalogue entry for the lost Pamphili *Venus* for another possible connection between Sacchi and Mario de' Fiori.
5. A landscape drawing in the Louvre attributed to Sacchi by Mariette (Bean, 1959, no. 31) is by Herman van Swanevelt.

Appendix I

TRANSCRIPT OF SACCHI'S WILL AND CODICILS

Archivio di Stato, 30 Notaii Capitolini, Ufficio 9, 1659–66, pp. 279–87, 291–2 and 303–8.

Testam(en)tum Perill(ustris) D(omini) Andreae Sacchi de Pellegrinis Die octava Mensis Junij 1661 hora vi: gesima quarta cum septem luminibus accensis

A Presente e p(er)sonalm(en)te esistente alla p(resen)za di me Not(ai)o et delli Infr(ascritt)i Testimonij il Molto Ill(ustr)e Sig(no)re Andrea Sacchi e de Pellegrini Romano Pittore insigne figliolo del q(uondam) Sig(no)re *Nicola Pellegrini da Fermo* da me Not(ai)o cognosciuto il quale sano p(er) la Dio gratia di Mente Senso loquela vista Intelletto benchè Indisposto di corpo giacendo in letto gravato di male ritornandogli a memoria che lui è mortale et ha da morire di certo e senza dubbio alcuno e non sa quando p(er) il che gli bisogna stare apparecchiato e aspettarla da un momento all'altro essendo che al Mondo non vi si trovi cosa più certa della morte e più Incerta dell'hora e punto di essa; et volendo p(er)ciò come prudente quella prevenire con il maggior apparecchio sia possibile mentre lui stà ne' suoi sensi e il suo animo regge la mente con il provedere // alla salute dell'Anima sua, ha pensato et con animo deliberato fermato e stabilito di disporre delle sue facoltà e beni che Iddio Benedetto p(er) sua Infinita Bontà e Misericordia si è degnato concederli, e come prudente levare et p(er) quanto puole troncare ogni lite differenzie e controversie che potessero nascere p(er) causa et occasione della sua heredità e beni, con fare il p(rese)nte Testam(en)to che la ragione civile lo chiama nuncupativo senza scritti sì come chiamato il Divino aiuto et In Nome della S(antissi)ma Trinità Padre figliolo e Sp(irit)o Santo Spontaneam(en)te e di sua spontanea libera et assoluta volontà, certa et Indubitate scienza, et non p(er) forza, timore o errore alcuno et In ogni altro meglior' modo etc. Fà et con quello dispone nel modo e forma che segue cioè

B Ma p(er)chè si deve cominciare prima dalla cosa più degna p(er)ciò l'Anima Sua come più degna del corpo e di qualunque altra cosa di questo mondo, quella con tutto l'affetto del cuore e maggior humiltà e devot(io)ne possibile // gli si concede, raccomanda all'Omnipresente Iddio, alla S(antissi)ma e Gloriosissima Maria Sempre Vergine Madre del N(ost)ro Redentore Giesù Christo Avocato de'Peccatori, et a tutti li Santi e Spiriti Beati della Celeste e Trionfante Corte del Paradiso pregandoli Riverentem(en)te che p(er) li meriti della Passione di N(ostro) S(ignore) Giesù Christo voglino degnare appresso quello Intercedere p(er) la remissione e total p(er)dono delli peccati e colpe con le quali esso Sig(no)re Andrea Testatore havessi possuto p(er) il passato o potesse p(er) l'avenire sino alla sua morte offendere Sua Divina Maestà acciò quell'ottenuto, quando l'Anima sua p(er) volontà di Dio sarà separata dal Corpo possi in eterno essergli consocia in paradiso e participante della Divina Gloria

C Il Corpo però suo terrineo et che ha da tornare in quella doppo che sarà restato priva dell'Anima e ridotto In Cadavero, vuole ordina e commanda che sia seppelito in modo di deposito nella Chiesa Parocchiale di *San Nicola In arcionibus* con quel funerale che parerà all'Em(inentissi)mo e // Rev(erendissi)mo Sig(no)re Card(ina)l *Antonio Barberini* suo sing(ularissi)mo Padrone, desiderando però mediante li favori et authorità di d(ett)o Em(inentissi)mo Sig(no)re Card(ina)le che il suo Cadavero e sue Ossa e Cenneri siano trasferiti nella Basilica di *San Gioanni In Laterano* e posto In loco proportionato vicino al sepolcro del *Cavaliere d'Arpino*, volendo che il deposito di d(etta) sepultura in San Gioanni sia fatta a disegno del Sig(no)re *Cavalier Bernini* et opera del Sig(no)re *Paolo Nardini* [*sic*] a spese della sua heredità con spendervi la somma di scudi ducento al più.

D Item vuole che il giorno il suo corpo starà esposto In d(ett)a Chiesa di San Nicola si distribuischino fra li poveri che vi saranno, Incominciando dalla speciaria del Paolucci alla Fontana di Trevi sino a Capo di strada Rosella, nella quale esso Sig(no)re Testatore habita, dall'una al'altra parte scudi dieci m(one)ta, Che si distribuisca un giulio p(er) ciascuno p(er) carità et la Cura di d(ett)a distribut(io)ne lascia che si contenti haverla il Sig(no)re *Prospero Fidanza* suo amorevole, ad arbitrio del quale rimette d(ett)a distribut(io)ne.

E Item vuole p(er) salute dell'Anima sua che li siano celebrate le solite Messe di San Gregorio nella sua chiesa, Una Messa in San Lorenzo fuor delle Mura, Un'altra alla Colonna di N(ost)ro Signore In Santa Presede e Un'altra a S(an)ta Liberatrice a Campo Vacino.

F Item p(er) raggione di legato e titolo di carità rimette e rilassa a *Margharita Todesca,* Pigionante di una Stanza sotto la Casa di esso Sig(no)re Testatore, delle pigioni che lei ha da dare la somma di scudi sei—

G Item p(er) raggione di legato e p(er) salute dell'Anima sua lascia a P(ad)re *Filippo* in San' Carlo alle quattro fontane suo Confessore scudi dieci acciò celebri p(er) l'anima sua quelle Messe che li parerà

H Item p(er) raggion di legatore e recognit(io)ne della bona servitù che gli ha fatta e che spera li farà, lascia a Dom(eni)co Basso da Crema suo servitore scudi venticinque m(one)ta p(er) una sol volta dimodo che non possa pretendere altro p(er) sua Mercede e salario

I Item p(er) raggione di legato et in ogni altro meglior modo e titolo lascia a *Marcantonio Manucci* Figliolo di *Margharita Gaburri* la sua Casa che ha in Roma posta incontro la // d(ett)a Chiesa di San Nicola in Arcione che fà cantonata con il suo sito che ultimam(en)te ha comprato e circondato di Muraglia con il Peso del Canone, quale Marcantonio desidera che pigli il Cognome di Casa Sacchi, Volendo ancora che sino che esso Marcantonio starà Insieme con d(ett)a Margharita sua Madre d(ett)a Margharita sia Amministratrice delle piggioni di d(ett)a Casa con alimentarci d(ett)o Marcantonio e questa Amministrat(io)ne cessi caso che lei rimaritasse

J. Item vuole che siano venduti tutti li suoi argenti, mobili, supelletili e Massaritie di qualsivoglia sorte, eccetto una Tazza di argento Indorata la quale debbia restare p(er) l'Infra(scritto) suo herede, e le altre cose delle quali esso Testatore dispone nel p(rese)nte Test(ament)o o disporrà; e del prezzo di essi vole che prima si sodisfacino li debiti di esso Sig(no)re Testatore che asserisce essere di scudi quattrocento incirca, et anco le spese del sudetto deposito e delle Messe et elemosine come s(opr)a lasciate e altre spese che occoreranno In d(ett)a sua heredità, et anco si riscotino li pegni e poi quelli si vendino e del restante del prezzo di essi mobili e pegni vuole che si rinvesti In luoghi de'Mon- // ti in faccia et a favore di *Eufrasia Manucci* figliola della d(ett)a Margharita, et che li frutti di essi sino alla somma di scudi otto il Mese se vi ariveranno debbiano servire p(er) suoi alimenti sin tanto che d(ett)a Eufrasia si farà Monaca, e quando si farà Monaca vole che il Capitale di d(ett)o Investim(en)to sino alla somma di scudi mille cinquecento se vi ariverà debbia servire p(er) dote da darsi al Monasterio dove essa si farà Monaca e quello che sopravanzerà, si come anche il d(ett)o Capitale di scudi millecinquecento se d(ett)a Eufrasia morisse avanti che si facci Monaca e professione, vuole che vadi p(er) Egual portione al d(ett)o Marcantonio e alli Infra(scritti) Fran(ces)co e Gio(vanni) Bat(tis)ta—

K Item p(er) raggion di legato et In ogni'altro meglior modo e titolo lascia a *Gio(vanni) Bat(tis)ta* e *Fran(ces)co* fratelli, figlioli della q(uondam) *Vittoria lutij* o siano d'altra Madre che hora stanno In educat(io)ne appresso il Sig(no)re Pietro Paolo Frangi e Sig(no)ra Lavinia sua Madre, desiderando che piglino il cognome de'Sacchi, la Casa dove esso Sig(no)re Testatore habbita, posta in strada Rosella, con tutti li suoi membri e raggioni di essa e con il peso del suo Canone e con peso che // delli frutti o pigioni di d(ett)a Casa debbiano pagare scudi venticinque l'Anno a Pietro Paolo Manucci, altro figliolo della sud(ett)a Margharita, sinchè d(ett)o Pietro Paolo viverà, di tre in tre Mesi la rata parte, e morto che sarà d(ett)o Pietro Paolo, cessi il d(ett)o Peso e sin tanto che d(ett)o Gio(vanni) Bat(tis)ta e Fran(ces)co saranno maggiori di Anni venti vuole che l'amministrat(io)ne di d(ett)a Casa e riscossioni delle piggioni di essa si faccia dalli S(ignori) Gioseppe Giamberti e Prospero Fidanza et il d(ett)o Sig(no)re Pietro Paolo Frangi, con facoltà che dui di essi possino eseguire il tutto come fussero tutti tre e che li frutti o pigioni di d(ett)a Casa servino p(er) alimenti e mantenim(en)to di d(ett)i Gio(vanni) Bat(tis)ta e Fran(ces)co a ragione di scudi otto il Mese p(er) ciascuno se vi ariveranno, et se vi avanzeranno si rinvestino a loro favore, e morendo tanto d(ett)i Gio(vanni) Bat(tis)ta e Fran(ces)co quanto il sud(ett)o Marcantonio e senza Fig(lio)li leg(itti)mi e na(tura)li succedino gli altri sopraviventi nella portione del morto e morendo tutti senza figlioli vole che in d(ett)i beni succeda Il Collegio degli Orfanelli di Roma //

L Item p(er) raggione di legato et In ogn'altro meglior modo lascia al Sig(no)re *Gio(vanni) Alberti* suo Medico p(er) gratitudine di tante fattighe fatte nella sua Infermità e de medicam(en)ti dati, un quadro di frutti di mano di *Michel Angelo delle Battaglie* con la sua Cornice, che sta In Cam(er)a di esso Sig(no)re Testatore

M In tutti poi e singoli e qualsivoglia altri beni e facoltà, tanto stabili quanto mobili semoventi raggioni attioni e nomi de debitori p(rese)nti e futuri in qualsivoglia luogho posti et essistenti, che ad esso Sig(no)re Andrea p(er) qualsivoglia nome titolo e Causa spettano e spetteranno p(er) l'avenire, fa Instituisce lascia vuole che sia e con la sua propria bocca nomina suo herede Un(ivers)ale l'Ill(ustrissi)mo e Rev(erendissi)mo Sig(no)re Abbate *Don Carlo Vaini*, al quale p(er) titolo d'Institut(io)ne et In ogni meglior modo lascia il restante della sua heredità

E p(er)chè d(ett)o Sig(no)re Testatore desidera et vole che il Np(rese)nte suo ultimo Testam(en)to e volontà et le cose in esso disposte lasciate et ordinate s'habbino da esseguire, p(er)ciò con-// fidato nel Sig(no)re Abbate Bracese, Sig(no)re Fausto Tursi e *Sig(no)r Gasparo Marcaccioni* essi in Solidum fa lascia e deputa suoi Essecutori Testamentarij con tutte quelle facoltà necessarie et opp(ortu)ne et che in ciò si ricercano e sogliono darsi a simili Essecutori Testamentarij pregandoli Instantissimam(en)te a non voler sdegnarsi In accettare simil peso

O Et questo il d(ett)o Sig(no)re Testatore dice et asserisce essere et voler che sia il suo ultimo nuncupativo Testam(en)to et Sua ultima volontà e disposit(io)ne, quale vuole che vagli p(er) raggione di Testam(en)to et se p(er) tal raggione non valesse, vuole che vagli p(er) raggione di Codicilli, donat(io)ne p(er) Causa di Morte e di qualsivoglia altra sua disposit(io)ne e volontà, Cassando Irritando annullando et Invalidando qualsivoglia altro Testam(en)to et ultima volontà et disposit(io)ne Forse da lui fatte e fatti sino al p(rese)nte giorno con qualsivoglia parole ample et amplissime et derogatorie et derogatorie alla derogatorie, e rogati da qualsivoglia Not(at)o. Volendo che il p(rese)nte Testam(en)to sia derogatorio // a tutti li altri et a quelli si debbia onninam(en)te anteporre e preferire et habbia sortire il suo dovuto fine et effetto, et questo non solo nel modo e forma come sop(r)a ma In ogni altro meglior modo. Sup(er) quibus etc.

P Actum Romae Domi solitae habit(atio)nis d(icti) D(omini) Andreae Testatoris posita in Via Rasella Regionis Trivij presentibus etc. infras(criptis) v(idelic)et.
1. Ill(ustri) et adm(odu)m R(everendo) D(omino) Marco Antonio Joannino, fil(io) q(uondam) Attili de Castro Cinthiani seu Genzani Albanens(is) Dioc(esi)s
2. D(omino) Jo(hanno) bap(tis)ta Gilio, fil(io) q(uondam) Jacobi Januens(is)
3. Adm(odu)m R(everendo) D(omino) Vincentio de Rotundis, fil(io) q(uondam) Joh(anni)s de d(icto) Castro Cinthianis Albanens(is) Dioc(esi)s
4. D(omino) Francisco Carminato, fil(io) D(omini) Thomae, Rom(ano)
5. D(omino) Camillo Restorio, fil(io) q(uondam) Ludovici Rom(ano)
6. D(omino) Paulo Vercario, fil(io) q(uondam) Dom(inici), Rom(ano)
7. D(omino) Constantio Paris, fil(io) q(uondam) Petri, Pedemontano testibus etc.
Ab(sen)t(ibus) //
die 19 decembris 1661
Collat(um) in Arch(ivi)o g(e)n(era)li Urbano Alme Urbis Concordat salva semp(er) etc. In fidem etc.
Pro D(omino) Ant(oni)o de Nobilib(us)
Rodulphus Florellus

Codicilli
Die 17 Junij 1661

Q Ill(ustris) D(ominus) Andreas Sacchus de Pellgrinis Rom(anu)s, filius q(uon)d(am) D(omini) Nicolai Pellegrini de Firmo, mihi Not(ari)o bene cog(nitu)s, sanus Dei gratia mente sensu loquela visù et Intellectu, licet corpore Infirmus et In lecto Jacens, qui sub die 8ª Currentis Mensis Condidit eius Testam(en)tum p(er) acta mei etc. rog(atu)m, Volens aliquid In eo addere et reformare sponte etc. ac omni meliori modo etc. fecit hos p(rese)ntes Codicillos ut Infra v(ide)l(ic)et.

R In p(ri)ma Codicillando et in ogni altro meglior modo, p(er) la memoria che conserva e devot(io)ne che professa all'Em(inentis)si-mo Sig(no)re Card(ina)le Antonio Barberini suo singolariss(i)-mo Padrone, lascia p(er) raggione di legato e in ogni meglior modo al d(ett)o Em(inentiss)imo Sig(no)re Card(ina)le li desegni di accademia che esso Sig(no)re Andrea fece nel tempo che stava in lombardia, de' quali disse esserne informato il Sig(no)re *Carlo Maratti* da sceglersi dal d(ett)o Sig(no)re Carlo e consegnarsi dal med(esim)o etiam non de manu heredis al d(ett)o Em(inentiss)imo Sig(no)re Card(ina)le.

S Item lascia al med(esim)o Em(inentiss)imo Sig(no)re Card(ina)le Una tazza di argento dorata di // beliss(i)mo modello, che haveva destinato restasse all'Ill(ustrissi)mo Sig(no)re Abbate Vaini suo herede conforme nel suo d(ett)o Testam(en)to da consegnarseli et(iam) non de manu heredis come s(opr)a

T Item p(er) raggione di prelegato et in ogni altro meglior modo etc. lascia al sud(ett)o Ill(ustrissi)mo Sig(no)re Abbate Vaini Un Quadro con l'effigie di San Girolamo che si communica, con la sua cornice.

U Item lascia al sud(ett)o Sig(no)re Carlo Maratti sei pezzi di gessi di pittura a sua elettione, et al Sig(no)re Prospero Fidanza e Sig(no)re *Bartholomeo Postiglioni* sei disegni di Accademia p(er) ciascuno a loro elettione, da consegnarseli etiam non de manu heredis, et al Sig(no)r Dom(eni)co Bassi altri sei disegni di Accademia ad elettione del sud(ett)o Sig(no)re Carlo.

V Item vuole che il restante delli disegni et gessi sia di *Pietro Paolo Mannucci* sicome gli li lascia p(er) titolo di legato et in ogni altro meglior modo, ogni volta però che esso si applichi et attendi alla professione, et Intanto vole che quelli restino appresso al sud(ett)o Sig(no)re Carlo Maratti il quale gli debbia consegnare al d(ett)o Pietro Paolo in tutto o in parte, conforme gli parerà et sarà espediente p(er) d(ett)o Pietro // Paolo, il quale non li possi vendere ma servirsene p(er) suo studio in d(ett)a professione, et caso che d(ett)o Pietro Paolo non applicasse et attendesse a d(ett)a professione, vuole che quelli si vendino conforme l'altre sue robbe, et il prezzo si rinvesti a beneficio di Eufrasia sua sorella, conforme esse Sig(no)re Codicillante ha disposto nel sud(ett)o suo Testam(en)to, et questo vuole che si esseguischi anco doppo che gli fussero consegnati, caso che non attendesse, e proseguisse d(ett)a professione. Rimettendo il Tutto et l'essecut(io)ne del p(rese)nte legato al sud(ett)o Sig(no)re Carlo Maratti in ogni meglior modo etc.

W Item lascia al Sig(no)re Paolo Naldini scultore dui disegni di accademia ad elettione del sud(ett)o Sig(no)re Carlo Maratti.

X Item vuole che si faccia, seguita la sua morte, l'Inventario di tutta la sua robba, et se il sud(ett)o Ill(ustrissi)mo Sig(no)re Abbate Vaini suo herede fossi fuori di Roma nel tempo della sua morte, vuole che d(ett)o Inventario si faccia dalli suoi Essecutori Testamentarij, et che d(ett)e robbe et quello che si ritrovarà nella sua casa si consegnino al sud(ett)o Sig(no)re Prospero Fidanza et al Sig(no)re Pietro Paolo Franci suo amorevole, apresso de' quali dovranno restare finchè se ne farà // esito dal sud(ett)o Sig(no)re Abbate suo herede e di suo ordine, conforme al sud(ett)o suo Testam(en)to al quale etc.

Y In Reliquis confirmavit precedens eius testam(en)tum omni etc. Et has dixit esse ultimos eius Codicillos, quos valere voluit iure Codicillorum et si tali iure non valerent, valere voluit iure donat(io)nis causa mortis et alt(erius) cuiuscumque ultimae voluntatis et disposit(io)nis et alias omni etc. Et hoc non solum etc. sed omni etc. super quibus etc.

Z Actum Romae domi solitae habitat(io)nis d(icti) D(omini) Codicillantis, positae In Via Rosella Reg(io)nis Trivij, presentibus D(omino) Antonio Panico fil(io) q(uondam) Anibalis Rom(an)o, Perill(ustri) D(omino) Equite Laureto Victorio fil(io) q(uondam) Vincentij de Spoleto, D(omino) Nicolao fil(io) D(omini) Lud(uvi)ci de Ulixis Maceraten(sis), D(omino) *Ambrogio Coraggioso* fil(io) q(uondam) Io(hann)is Pauli Taurinens(is) et Perill(ustrissi)mo et Adm(odu)m R(everen)do D(omino) Hiacinto dell'Acciaia [*sic*; della Ciaja] fil(io) q(uon)d(am) Fulvii Sen(ensis) Testibus etc. Ab(sen)t(ibus) etc. //

Codicilli
Die 19 Junij 1661

AA Ill(ustris) D(ominus) Andreas Sacchus de Pellgrinus Rom(anus) fil(ius) q(uon)d(am) Nicolai Pellegrini de Firmo, mihi Not(ari)o bene cog(nitu)s, sanus Dei gratia mente sensu loquela visu et Intellectu, licet corpore Infermus et In letto Jacens, qui sub die octava currentis Mensis condidit eius Testam(en)tum p(er) acta mei etc. rog(atu)m et sub die 17 eiusd(em) fecit nunullos eius Codicillos p(rou)t in eisd(em) actis mei etc. ad quos etc.; et quia mens hominum est deambulatoria usq(ue) ad mortem, statuit condere et facere Infra(scri)ptos alios Codicillos p(rou)t sponte etc. ac omni melior modo etc. fecit ut Infra, v(ide)l(ice)t.

BB In p(ri)ma Codicillando et in ogni altro miglior modo disporre et vole che la tazza di argento dorata lasciata nelli suoi suoi Codicilli all' Em(inentiss)imo Sig(no)re Card(ina)le Antonio Barberini resti all'Ill(ustrissi)mo Sig(no)re Abbate Carlo Vaini suo herede, Revocando il legato fattone al d(ett)o Sig(no)re Card(ina)le.

CC Item disporre e vuole che il quadro di San Girolamo che si communica, lasciato nelli suoi Codicilli ad Sud(ett)o Sig(no)re Abbate // sia del Sud(ett)o Em(inentiss)imo Sig(no)re Card(ina)le Antonio, al quale glielo lascia p(er) raggione di legato et in ogni meglior modo volendo che gli ha consegnato etia(m) non de manu heredis, Revocando il prelegato fattone al Sig(no)re Abbate Vaini.

DD Item vuole e dispone che sin tanto che si venderanno li suoi mobili, si farà il rinvestim(en)to se la Casa dove esso habbita non sarà appiggionata, sicome anche l'altra a San Nicola, p(er) gli alim(ent)i necessarij di Marcantonio di Eufrasia Mannucci e di Fran(ces)co e di Gio(vanni) Batt(ist)a della q(uondam) Vittoria, e p(er) supplim(en)ti di essi si possi vendere quella quantità di d(ett)i mobili che sarà necessaria e come meglio parerà al *Sig(no)re Marcantonio Pasqualini* che a questo effetto deputa speciale Essecutore della pr(esen)te disposit(io)ne, con tutte quelle facoltà che saranno necessarij, et il simile s'intenda anco doppo fatto l'Investim(ent)o di d(ett)o prezzo, se farà bisogno, alfinchè li sud(ett)i habbino proportionabilm(en)te gli alim(en)ti necessarij rimettendo il tutto in piena facoltà di d(ett)o Sig(no)re Marcantonio in ogni meglior modo etc., dichiarando che li frutti di d(ett)o Investim(en)to debbiano servire p(er) tutti se le Case non fussero appigionate o le piggioni in qualunque modo fussero Impedite. //

EE Item vuole che a Piero Paulo Manucci se attendera alla professione come si e detto nelli altri suoi codicilli sud(ett)i oltre lo studio lasciatoli in essi se gli dia anco il Cimbalo di esso Sig(no)re Codicillante c(on) questo che non lo possa in alcun modo vendere ne distrarre et n(on) attendendo ne proseguendo allo studio si debba vendere e il prezzo rinvestire come si e detto delli altri mobili e se attendera o n(on) attenderà si stia alla dichiaratione che ne farà il Sig(nore) Carlo Maratti nel un libero arbitrio rimette il tutto nelli modi e forme che ha anco disposto nelli altri suoi Codicilli.

FF In reliquis confirmavit tam precedens eius testam(en)tum quam

predictos eius Codicillos omnis altros dixit esse ultimos eius
Codicillos quos valere valuit Jure donationis Causa mortis et
alterius cuiuscumque ultimae voluntatis et dispositionis et alias
omnis et hoc n(on) solum p(er) Jure et p(er) sup(er) quibusque

GG Actum Romae domi solitae habitationis d(icti) D(omini)
    Codicillantis, positae
    In Via Rasella Regionis Trivij presentibus
    Ill(ustre) D(omine) D(on) Domenico Legrenda fil(io) q(uondam)
    michaelis

Rom(an)o
D(omi)ne Prospero fidanza filio q(uondam) Jo(hanne)s Bap(tis)ta
de Genazzano testimone
D(omi)ne Paolo naldino filio q(uondam) Jo(hann)es Bap(tis)ta
Romano
D(omi)ne Bartholomeo Postigliano filio D(omine) nicolai
ablacer(is) (?)
Test(imo)nis
Pietro Paulo frangi filio Jo(hann)es fran(ces)co Romano
Absentibus

SUMMARY OF CONTENTS OF ANDREA SACCHI'S WILL

June 8, 1661.
Andrea Sacchi and Pellegrini, the distinguished Roman painter
and the son of the late Nicola Pellegrini from Fermo, being of
sound mind etc. although confined to bed by illness etc. . . . wishes
to dispose of his property in the following manner in order to
avoid any future litigation etc.

He recommends his soul to God, to the Virgin, Mother of Christ
etc. and hopes that his sins will be forgiven etc.

He wishes to be buried in the Parish church of S. Nicola in Arcione
with such ceremony as seems fitting to Cardinal Antonio Barberini, his distinguished protector; and hopes that he will also
make arrangements for his ashes to be moved to a suitable tomb in
S. Giovanni Laterano near that of Cavaliere Gioseppe d'Arpino,
to be made by Paolo Naldini from a design by the Cavalier Bernini
at a cost of 200 scudi.

His great friend Prospero Fidanza is to be in charge of a distribution of money to the poor in the Parish on the day of his death.

He wishes Masses (according to St. Gregory) to be said for his soul
in S. Lorenzo fuori le Mura, in the chapel of the column in S.
Prassede, and in Santa Liberatrice in the Campo Vaccino.

He remits the rent of 6 scudi owed to him by Margarita Todesca
for the room she occupies beneath his house.

He leaves 10 scudi to his confessor, Padre Filippo of S. Carlo alle
Quattro Fontane, so that he can celebrate those Masses which seem
suitable to him.

He leaves 25 scudi to his servant, Domenico Basso, for services
rendered and to be rendered, and this is the last payment of salary
he will get.

He leaves to Marcantonio Manucci, the son of Margharita Gaburri,
some recently acquired property near S. Nicola in Arcione; the
said Marcantonio is to take the surname Sacchi, and as long as he
lives with her, she is responsible for the rent and for his keep.

All silver, furniture and valuables are to be sold, except a silver
gilded cup which is to go to his chief heir; the value of the rest of
these goods is to be used first to settle outstanding debts, which
come to about 400 scudi; then for the expenses of the tomb, and
the above-named charity donations and any other expenses; the
remainder is to be invested in 'luoghi di monti' for Eufrasia, the
daughter of Margharita, and she has the use of the interest until
such time as she decides to become a nun; in that case, capital up
to 1500 scudi is to be used for her dowry to the nunnery, while the
remainder is to be divided equally between Marcantonio, and
Francesco and Giovanni Battista.

Giovanni Battista and Francesco, the sons of Vittoria Luti, or
whoever their mother is, who are now being educated by Pietro
Paolo Frangi and his mother Lavinia, are to take the surname
Sacchi. Sacchi leaves his house and the above-mentioned bit of
property to them. They are to pay Pietro Paolo Manucci, the other
son of Margharita, 25 scudi every year until his death. Giuseppe
Giamberti, Prospero Fidanza and Pietro Paolo Frangi are to look
after the financial arrangements made on behalf of Marc Antonio
and Eufrasia Manucci until they reach the age of 21. The rent is to
be used for their keep, that is 8 scudi a month each. Any left-over

money is to be invested in their names. If there are no heirs, this
property is to go to the Collegio degli Orfanelli.

As a token of gratitude for services rendered and medicines given,
he leaves a picture of fruit by Michelangelo Cerquozzi to his doctor,
Giovanni Alberti.

He appoints Abbate Carlo Vaini as his chief executor, responsible
for the correct execution of all these instructions, with the
assistance of Abbate Bracese, Fausto Tursi and Gaspar Marcaccioni
All other wills and codicils are invalidated.
Witnessed etc.

Codicil, dated June 17, 1661.
He leaves the Academy drawings that he made in Lombardy to
Cardinal Antonio Barberini, and puts Carlo Maratti in charge of
selecting them and handing them over.

He also leaves to Cardinal Antonio the above-named gilded silver
cup which was left to his heir.

He leaves Abbate Vaini a picture of *The Last Communion of St.
Jerome*

To Carlo Maratti he leaves the gesso casts used for painting, the
choice being left to him, and to Prospero Fidanza and Bartholomeo
Postiglioni some Academy drawings to be chosen by themselves,
and six more Academies to Domenico Bassi, to be selected by
Maratti.

The remainder of the casts and drawings are left to Pietro Paolo
Manucci on condition that he become a painter. Carlo Maratti is
made the guardian of this property, and he is to give Pietro whatever seems appropriate to his work. Nothing can be sold until such
time as Pietro decides not to become a painter. If the studio contents
are sold, the proceeds are to be invested in Eufrasia's name.

To Paolo Naldini, the sculptor, he leaves two Academies, to be
chosen by Carlo Maratti.

An inventory of all his goods is to be made, and this is to be
supervised by Abbate Vaini; should he be away from Rome,
Prospero Fidanza and Pietro Paolo Franci(Frangi) are put in
charge.
Witnessed etc.

Codicil, dated 19 June, 1661.
The gilded silver cup left in the codicil above to Cardinal Antonio
is to be left instead to Abbate Vaini. The picture of *St. Jerome*
mentioned above is to be left to Cardinal Antonio, and not to
Abbate Vaini, as said above.

Until all the property has been sold, enough should be sold immediately in order to maintain the various above-mentioned heirs, to
pay the church, and so on; Marcantonio Pasqualini is put in charge
of this, and is to judge what amount is necessary.

Pietro Paolo Manucci is to become a painter; to him is also left the
harpsichord on the same conditions as the contents of the studio;
if he does not learn to play it, it can be sold, and the proceeds
invested in Eufrasia's name. Maratti is also responsible for the
execution of this request.
Witnessed etc.

Appendix II

TRANSCRIPT OF THE INVENTORY OF CONTENTS OF SACCHI'S HOUSE IN JUNE 1661

Archivio di Stato, Trenta Notaii Capitolini, Testamenti, Ufficio 9 (Abinante), 1659–66, pp. 577–601 verso.

(Only items of art historical interest have been transcribed. Paintings, painting materials, drawings and casts have been listed in the order they appear; books are listed in a separate appendix.)

Inventarium bonor(um) Her(edum) q(uondam) D(omine) Andrea Sacchi p. 577
Die 21 Junij 1661
Hoc est Inventarium bonorum hereditariorum bo(nae) me(moriae) D(omine) Andreae Sacchi de Pellegrinis hodie et nu(per) defuncti, existentium et repertorum In domo suae solitae habitat(io)nis posita In Via Rosella nuncupata, factum ad Inst(anti)am Perill-(ustris) D(omini) Gasparis Marcaccioni Unius ex Exequutoribus Testamentarijs deputati In Test(ament)o d(icti) q(uondam) D(omini) Andreae In actis meis rogatum sub die octava huius ob absentiam ab Urbe Ill(ustrissi)mi et Rev(erendissi)mi D(omini) Abbatis Caroli Vayni heredis Testamentarij et cum assistentia D(ominorum) Prosperi Fidantiae et Petri Pauli Frangi de Frangis, deputatorum ad Curam et retentionem hu(ius)mo(d)i bonorum p(rou)t In Codicillis p(er) acta mei etc. rog(at)is sub die 17 eiusd(em) Currentis Mensis, p(rou)t Infra Videlicet
In p(ri)ma: Nella Sala li Infr(ascritt)i Quadri attaccate [sic] nelle muraglie In una facciata s(opr)a il Camino

(1) Un Ritratto di N(ost)ro Sig(no)re Papa Alesandro Settimo senza Cornice In Tela da testa
(2) Un Ritratto della fel(ice) me(moria) di Papa Urbano Ottavo Tela da testa con cornice nera con filetti di oro
(3) Un Ritratto della bo(na) me(moria) del Sig(no)re Card(ina)le v Frate Antonio Barberini chiamata di Sant'Onofrio Tela da testa con Cornice nera e filetti d'oro   p. 577
(4) Un Quadro con San Gio(vanni) Batt(ist)a tela da testa con Cornice dorata
(5) Un Quadro con una figura di testa di Donna con Cornice dorata
(6) Un Quadro con dui teste de vecchi tela da testa con cornice ordinaria con doi filetti d'oro
(7) Un altro quadro di altre teste di homini con cornice simile
          Nell'altra facciata a mano dritta
(8) Un Quadro Grande senza Cornice con la Madonna Assunta con Santo Nicolò Vescovo e San Fran(cesco) d'Assisi figure grande al Naturale
(9) Un Ritratto dell'Em(inentissi)mo Sig(no)re Card(ina)l Antonio Barberini tela da testa con cornice con dui filetti d'oro
(10) Un Ritratto della bo(na) me(moria) Sig(no)re P(ri)n(ci)pe Prefetto Don Tadeo Barberini con tela da testa con cornice simile
(11) Un Quadro con l'effigie di San Pietro Tela da testa con cornice simile
(12) Un altro quadro con testa da Vecchio e con cornice simile
(13) Un Quadro con Tempesta di Mare tela da Imperatore con sua Cornice
(14) Un'altro dell'Istessa grandezza con Paese e cornice simile facciata a mano manca
(15) Un Quadro Grande senza Cornice con figure chiamate Galatea copiata dal Originale da Rafaele   p. 578
(16) Un Ritratto dell'Em(inentissi)mo Sig(no)re Card(ina)l Fran(cesco) Barberini tela da testa con cornice con filetti di oro
(17) Un Ritratto del Card(ina)l del Monte di bo(na) me(moria) con Cornice simile
(18) Un Quadro con una testa di Vecchio che legge con Cornice con filetti di oro
(19) Un Quadro con un'altra testa di Vecchio con Cornice simile
(20) Un Quadro con Paesi e prospettiva tela da Imperatore con cornice con filetto giallo
(21) Un Quadro dell'Istessa grandezza e Cornice simile con Paesi con filetto giallo
          Nell'altra facciata verso la Porta
(22) Un Quadro con San sebastiano tela da Imperatore con Cornice dorata
(23) Un Quadro In ottangolo con Agar Hismaele e l'Angelo cornice
(24) Una Cornice In Ottangolo vota
(25) Un Quadro con Paesi tela da testa con cornice nera e filetto d'oro
(26) Un'altro con Paesi e Cornice simile
(27) Un altro con frutti e Cornice nera con filetto d'oro
          Quadri appoggiati al Muro In terra   p. 578 v
(28) Un Quadro Rappresentant Noè Inebriato In tela d'Imperatore con tre figure senza Cornice
(29) Un'altro Quadro In tela simile Vecchia con tre figure di homini che dimostra essere Gioseppe In pregion'che Interpretava il sogno al Fornaro e al Coppiere senza Cornice qual quadro si dice essere del decano de'Palafrenieri dell'Em(inentissi)ma Sig(no)ra Prencipessa di Palestrina ritenuto per Cauthela della pigione dovuta dal d(ett)o Palafreniere nel tempo che ha habitato sotto la Casa di d(ett)o q(uondam) Sig(no)re Andrea
(30) Una tela da Imperatore senza alcuna figura
(31) dui teste di gesso di homini
          Nella Camera dove d(ett)o q(uondam) Adrea dormiva p. 579
(32) Un Quadro con una Ghirlanda de fiori con Cornice con filetti d'oro
(33) Un altro Quadro da testa con un Vaso di fiori con cornice tutta dorata
(34) Un'altro Quadro con un altro vaso di fiori simile in tela da testa con cornice dorata
(35) Un'altro Quadro di fiori con cornice dorata
(36) Un'altro Quadro con frutti e Cornice con filetti di oro che è quello lasciato nel Testam(en)to al Sig(no)re Gio(vanni) Alberti Medico
(37) Una Cornice bianca con tela semplice
(38) Un Quadro con l'effigie del S(antissi)mo Salvatore con tela da testa con cornice con filetti di oro
(39) Un'altro Quadro con l'effi(gi)e di San Filippo Neri con Cornice nera e filetti di oro
(40) Un Quadretto ovato con San Gio(vanni) Batt(ist)a e Giesù Christo che si battezza
(41) Un altro storiato cornice dorata con Cristallo   p. 580

(42) Un Quadretto con la Madonna con il figliolino in braccio con Cornice con filetti di oro

(43) Una tela da testa dove vi è abozzato una Testa di un Gesuito

(44) dui Quadretti con San Giuseppe la Madonna e Christarello con l'Angelo, l'uno in tela e l'altro In Rame

(45) Un Quadretto piccolo con una Testa di un Agonizante con cornice nera

(46) Una Medaglia di Oro grande quanto una Piastra In una parte vi è una Croce e sotto vi stà Un leone e un altro Animale e dall'altra parte l'effigie di leopoldo Guilelmo Arciduca d'Austria (one of several items such as rings and coins in a small ebony chest)

(47) Una Tazza d'argento dorata fatta a Navicella con la sua Cassa coperta di Corame   p. 581

Cassato perchè fu detto essere proprio del Sig.r Card(ina)l Antonio

(48) Un Retrattino della b(u)o(na) me(moria) del Sig(nor)e Card(inale) Mazzarino fatto s(opr)a oro con un Cristaletto s(opr)a ovato della grandezza quasi di un giulio

(49) Un Bulettino del Monte della Pietà al p(ri)mo Custode sotto nome di Giorgio p(er) pauli trecento sotto sotto li 18 Ottobre 1660 no. 27461
Un altro del p(ri)ma detto Custode sotto nome di Giorgio p(er) pauli 300 li 20 (dece)mbre 1660 no. 3313
Un altro del (second)o Custode sotto nome di Pietro Paulo p(er) pauli 220 li 18 Genn(ai)o 1661 no. 1802
Un altro del (second)o Custode sotto nome di Pietro Paulo p(er) pauli 190 li 24 Gennaro 1661 no. 2825   p. 582 v

(50) Dieci Medaglie antiche

(51) Dui Puttini di Creta

(52) Un Puttino di creta rotto

(53) Quattuordici penelli di setole tra grossi e piccoli

(54) Una Carta con pezzetti di Colore di lacca fina
Nel pezzo di sotto di d(ett)o Studiolo

(55) Diversi disegni quali furono Consegnati al Sig(no)r Carlo Maratti per dover ricognoscere e distinguere quelli che sono stati lasciati all'Em(inentissi)mo Sig(no)r Card(ina)l Antonio Barberini (see no. 178)
Nella medema Stanza   p. 583
(For nos. 56–115 see Appendix III)

(116) Un rametto con un sbozzo d'una Venere   p. 586
Nella stanza a mano dritta della sala che risponde nella loggia
p. 587

(117) Un quadro In tela da Imperatore con una Venere e cupido con cornice con filetti d'oro

(118) Un quadro senza cornice con una altra Venere con un putto et una vecchia

(119) Un'altro quadro senza cornice Tela d'Imperatore con Paesi

(120) Un quadro tela di testa con una Testa di donna con cornice fiorata d'oro

(121) Una Madonnina con il Christarello, San Gioseppe e San Giovannino con cornice con filetti d'oro

(122) Un quadretto senza cornice con l'Angelo Custode

(123) Un'altro quadretto con la Madonna abbozzata con doi Santi

(124) Una cornice nera con filetto d'oro con disegno

(125) Un quadro senza cornice con ritratto con il Card(ina)le Biscia

(126) Un quadro senza cornice con Santa Teresia et altre Sante

(127) Un quadretto con sbozzetto di Christo e S. Pietro senza cornice

(128) Un altro con un sbozzo d'una Madonnina

(129) Un'altro con un sbozzo d'un giovane

(130) Un'altro con una Testa d'una Donna

(131) Un quadro senza cornice con San Francesco che sposa la Carità

(132) Un quadro senza cornice con un sbozzo di Agarre l'Angelo, et Ismaele

(133) Un quadro con cornice dorata con una testa d'un vecchio

(134) Un quadretto senza cornice con la Madonna, et alcuni Santi
p. 588

(135) Doi quadretti tondi con Paesi

(136) Un quadretto con uno sbozzo di S. Andrea che va al Martirio

(137) Un altro simile che N(ost)ro Sig(no)re và al Calvario

(138) Un quadretto tondo con un Vascello

(139) Un quadretto longo con certi puttini

(140) Un quadretto piccolo con Paesi

(141) Un quadro senza cornice con doi teste

(142) Un quadretto con doi Ucelli con cornice dorata

(143) Un quadretto con il ritratto di Urbano Ottavo con cornice

(144) Un quadro senza cornice con il ritratto del Duca Cesarini Vecchio

(145) Un quadro con cornice con un disegno

(146) Un quadro con un ritratto [d'] huomo con cornice, con filetti et rose d'oro

(147) Doi quadretti di tela da testa con paesi, con cornice con filetti d'oro

(148) Un quadro senza cornice con San Romualdo, et altri frati

(149) Un quadretto, con doi figure, cio è Teste di Dame con cornice dorata rabescata

(150) Un quadro senza cornice con l'effigie d'Urbano Ottavo

(151) Un'altro senza cornice con il ritratto di Sta. Maria Maggiore
Nell'Antrone avanti che s'entri in Sala   p. 589

(152) Una tela da Imperadore con S. Antonio di Padova et Angeli

(153) Un'altra tela d'Imperatore con il ritratto dell'Em(minentissi)mo
p. 589 v
Sig(no)r Cardinal Antonio Barberini

(154) Un'altra tela più grande da Imperatore con schezzo di gesso

(155) Un'altra tela d'Imperatore liscia

(156) Un'altra tela un poco più grande liscia

(157) Un'altra tela da testa con un sbozzo, che vi è incominciato un Christo, e un Puttino

(158) Un'altra tela da testa con un schezzo d'una fontana

(159) Doi gambe di gesso
Nella stanza a mano manca nella sala che risponde In strada
p. 590

(160) Una spinetta con suoi piedi

(161) Un cimbalo con suoi piedi fatti con tre Arpie

(162) Un quadro con S. Girolamo, che si comunica con cornice con filetti d'oro

(163) Un quadretto con San Pietro, e l'Angelo quando esce di carcere con cornice con filetti d'oro

(164) Un quadro che è del Panbocci con cornice con filetti d'oro

(165) Un quadro tela d'Imperatore con Caino che ha occiso Abelle con Cornice gialla

(166) Un quadretto con Arme Barberina con cornice negra

(167) Un quadro d'una Natività del Sig(no)re con sua cornice con filetti d'oro

(168) Un quadretto senza cornice con la Madalena

(169) Un quadretto ovato con la favola d'Adone con cornice dorata

(170) Una Madonnina assunta senza cornice

(171) Una cornice di legno semplice vota

(172) Un'altra cornice vota simile   p. 590 v

(173) Un quadretto con San Gio(vanni) Batt(ist)a, a Giesù Christo, che si battezza con cornice con filetti d'oro

(174) Una cornice dorata Intagliata vota con tela Imprimita
p. 591
First part of the inventory completed and witnessed by Ambrogio Coragioli [sic] and Paolo Naldini
Inventory begun again on June 26 under the supervision of Gaspare Marcaccioni, Prospero Fidanza and Pietro Paulo Franci.
Nell'ultima stanza   p. 592

(175) Due rametti di mezzo palmo In circa, uno con fiori l'altro

con frutti, et un bastone guarnito di madreperle con diverse
striscie d'argento ritrovati In camera, dove stava il defonto

(176) In una cassetta sotto il letto diverse cartuccie, con alcuni pezzi di libretti marescati

(177) Cinque pezzi di libri manoscritti di Teologia

(178) Desegni che furono ritrovati nella parte di sotto del Credenzone nella Camera del defonto conforme alla prima descrittione revisti e scelti dal sud(detto) Sig(no)r Carlo Maratti a sua relatione sono l'Infr(ascritt)i Trentasette disegni, che d(ett)o Sig(nore) Carlo ha scelto essere quelli

p. 592 v

che il Sig(no)re Andrea defonto fece In lombardia appresso il Coregio, e Paolo Veronese quali sono stati al med(esi)mo Sig(no)r Carlo p(er) diversi consegnare al'Em(inentissi)mo Sig(no)r Cardinal Antonio In conformità delli Codicilli del d(ett)o Sig(no)r Andrea.

E più disegni di Accademia parte abbozzati, parte finiti n(umer)o trecento

E più disegni diversi di studij diversi di opere fatte dal q(uondam) Sig(no)r Andrea no: 59 [sic] cinque cento novanta tre

E più altri disegni diversi no: 36

E più disegni d'accademia no: 9

E più di stampe diverse no: 24

E più sette putti di Creta Cotta rotti, sei de quali sono di mano del Sig(no)r Fran(ces)co Fiammenghi, quali restorono in potere, et In mano del d(ett)o Sig(no)r Carlo Maratti Deinde fuit aperta Janua ultimae stantiae versus viam rosellam, In qua fuerunt reperta bona Infr(ascritt)a v(ide)-l(ice)t

(179) Un quadro tondo con cornice di legno con S. Simeone, la Madonna, Christarello e S. Gioseppe

(180) Un quadro senza Cornice con Didone con la spada in petto

(181) Un quadro senza Cornice con S. Simeone senza testa

(182) Un quadro senza cornice con una figura di Donna rappresentante Racchelle In tela da testa   p. 593

(183) Una cornice dorata vota

(184) Un quadro senza Cornice con l'effigie di N(ostro) S(ignore) Papa Alesandro (setti)mo

(185) Un quadro senza Cornice con vecchio rappresentante l'Inverno

(186) Due tele dipinte à guazzo con due figure

(187) Una Cornice di legno vota d'altezza quattro palmi

(188) Un'altra da testa vota

(189) Un'altra più piccola negra col filetto d'oro vota

(190) Doi quadri tela da tre palmi con paesi senza cornice

(191) Un disegno di S. Girolamo con cornice negra filetto d'oro

(192) Una cornice grande Colore di noce con filetto d'oro Vota

(193) Un'altra cornice color di noce vota

(194) Un'altra negra con filetto d'oro vota

(195) Un'altra più piccola negra con filetto d'oro Vota

(196) Una Tela Imprimita con cornice dorata

(197) Un quadro con S(an)to Antonio di Padova, che risuscita un morto con altre figure con cornice negra e dorata

(198) Un quadro di un Ecce homo con cornice dorata   p. 593 v

(199) Una Tela imprimita con cornice negra rabescata

(200) Un'altra simile con cornice dorata

(201) Una cornice grande color di noce con filetti d'oro vota

(202) Una tela Imprimita con cornice dorata di quattro palmi incir(c)a

(203) Una cornice stretta vota con filetto d'oro

(204) Un'altra in ottancolo con filetti d'oro

(205) Un quadro senza cornice Tela da Imperatore con la Natività di di San Gio(vanni) Batt(ist)a

(206) Un quadro senza cornice con S. Filippo e S(an) Gio(vanni) Batt(ist)a

(207) Un quadro Tela di quattro palmi con la Madonna, Christo e S(an) Gioseppe con cornice dorata

(208) Due cornice vote una bianca e l'altra Color di noce

(209) Un quadro senza cornice con la decollatione di San Gio(vanni) Batt(ist)a Tela d'Imperatore

(210) Un ritratto di fran(ces)co Albano Pittor celebre con cornice color di noce e dorata

(211) Un quadretto In rame con S(an) Gioseppe dormiente con Angelo la Madonna, e Cristarello con cornice

(212) Un disegno di un Sacrificio con cornice negra filetto d'oro

(213) Un'altro disegno In carta con Arianda Cornice negra

p. 594

(214) Un Cornice d'ebbano vota

(215) Un ritratto d'una Testa d'huomo con una berretta In Testa con cornice negre, e filetti d'oro

(216) Tre cornicette vote

(217) Una Cornice dorata con una Tela imprimita di mezza testa

(218) Un quadro con due teste di S(an) fran(ces)co, e S(ant') Antonio con cornice negra rabbescata

(219) Un quadro grande con S(an) Gio(vanni) Batt(ist)a e Cristo che si battezza

(220) Un'ottangolo di tre palmi con l'aurora senza cornice

(221) Due tele Imperatori con la favola di Catone

(222) Un'altra simile con Appollo e Vulcano

(223) Un'altra più grande, con Caino et Abelle

(224) Una tela disegnata con il transito di S(ant') Anna

(225) Un quadro grande con Arianda e Bacco

(226) Un'altra con l'Istessi baccanali

(227) Un'altra più grande con un Sacrificio

(228) Un quadretto senza Cornice con una Testa del Salvatore

(229) Due cornicette vote

(230) Un quadro Tela d'Imperatore con l'Arbore della famiglia Bottugli da Pavia   p. 594 v

(231) Un paese In tela di tre palmi

(232) Due quadri di tela di quattro palmi In cir(c)a con Gioseppe che dorme, e l'Angelo

(233) Una tela d'Imperatore Imprimita con certi segni sopra

(234) Un'altra di tela d'Imperatore disegnata con una Venere di sopra

(235) Quattro Teste di gesso

Nella Stanza sud(ett)a di dietro

(236) Una Tela grande disegnata col gesso

(237) Un quadro con Caino et Abelle   p. 595

(238) Tela di sette palmi

(239) Due Tele grandi Imprimite p(al)mi 7 In circa

(240) Una Tela grande che vi à principiato un disegno di S(an) Paolo

(241) Un'altra tela d'Imperatore con un sbozzo di un Somaro

(242) Una Tela involtata con la Galatea

(243) Un'altra tela Involtata di una Venere sbozzata

(244) Un'altra tela grande In voltata con sbozzi di un Christo, che consegna le chiave à S(an) Pietro

(245) Una altra tela con l'historie di Moyse nel Deserto

(246) Due cavaletti d'alsare, et abbassare

(247) Nella loggia sei pezzi di quadri diversi rotti   p. 595 v

(248) Diversi gessi da scriversi in altra sessione (Pietro Paolo Frangi was present when the inventory was completed for that day. Work was resumed on July 3, 1661 with Abbot Giovanni Braccesi and Domenico del Colonello Vaini, brother of Abbot Carlo Vaini, Signori Carlo Maratti, Prospero Fidanza and Pietro Paolo Frangi present.   p. 596

(249) Otto pezzi di gesso formati alla Colonna Trogiana [sic]

(250) Sei pezzi di gesso di figure formati sopra à un p(ri)mo formate sul'Antico

(251) Tre pezzi di Gesso di Putti formati da fran(ces)co fiammenghi

(252) Dieci pezzi di gesso con teste puttini, leoni, et altre.

(253) Una testa del'Hercole di Farnese

(254) Una testa d'Appollo di belvedere
(255) Una Testa dell'Antino di belvedere
(256) Con tre altre Teste di grandezza simile
(257) Torso di belvedere
(258) Un torso di Una Venere formato su l'Antico
(259) Una gamba, e coscia del Gladiatore di Borghese
(260) Due piedi di gesso formati sul naturale
(261) Una Testa di Gesso di Alessandro Magno
(262) Due pezzi di Gesso di torso formati sul'Antico
(263) Due piedi di Gesso dell'Appollo di belvedere
(264) Una testa di gesso di un fauno
(265) Un braccio di gesso che vien da Michelangelo   p. 596 v
(266) Tre Teste di gesso con sui pieducci formati dall'Antico
(267) Una Testa di gesso rappresentante Roma
(268) Una testa di gesso Dell'Aoconte [sic] di belvedere
(269) Un'altra Testa con suo busto di gesso
(270) Altri sedici pezzi di teste diverse, che medem(amen)te vengono dall'Antico
(271) Due mani congiunte formate sul naturale
(272) Un'altro piede di un giovene formato sul naturale
(273) Altre cinque teste di Gesso diverse che vengono dall'Antico
(274) Un gruppo di due figure, che rappresentano dui Gladiatori rotti
(275) Un specchio in Triangolo con cornice d'oro
        Nella stanza da basso nell'Antrone vicina alla schala
(276) Il torso del Nilo di belvedere con la testa del med(esim)o separata rotta
(277) Un ritratto di gesso della fel(ice) me(moria) d'Urbano Ottavo
(278) Un torso formato al naturale grande sul'Antico
(279) Due altri torsi medem(amen)te formati sul'Antico più piccoli nel naturale
(280) Un'altro torso medemam(en)te formato rappresentante un Christo morto rotto   p. 597
(281) Una mano di gesso formata sopra à S(an) Andrea di mano del Sig(no)r fran(ces)co fiammenghi in S(an) Pietro
(282) Ventun'altri pezzi di gessi diversi della med(esim)a stanza
        Nella prima stanza a mano dritta nell'Entrare della Porta di strada
(283) Una tela grande dove è dipinto à guazzo una notte grande al naturale mano di Carlo Mangione
(284) Tre altre Tele liscie di palmi 9 In circa
(285) Una tela ovata impremita à guazzo grande dodeci palmi In circa   p. 598
        Nella stanza à mano dritta nel Cortile
(286) Un quadro senza cornice con un Donna che Zinna un putto et con un vecchio
(287) Due tele da Imperatore liscie
(288) Un'altra più grande liscia
(289) Un'altra simile liscia
(290) Due Telari de quadri
(291) Una cornice grande liscia
(292) Un quadro ottangolo con una Donna abbozzata
(293) Tre cornice due con filetti d'oro

        Nella stanza sopra alla sud(ett)a   p. 598 v
(294) Un quadro con una Venere abbozzato senza cornice
(295) Un quadro di sette palmi In circa
(296) Un'altro da testa è [sic] tre palmi con un sbozzo di un Santo
(297) Un quadro con una Divina Sapienza Tela di 7 palmi In circa
(298) Una Tela Impremita bislunga di palmi In circa
(299) Un ottangoletto ovato con paese
(300) Un quadro con figura di una donna sbozzata
(301) Un quadro tela d'Imperatore con S(an) Gio(vanni) Batt(ist)a, e Christo che si battezza
(302) Un quadro con un sbozzo di ritratto di donna
(303) Un quadruccio ovato con paese
(304) Un quadro senza cornice Tela di tre palmi con armatura
(305) Una tela d'Imperatore liscia
(306) Un quadro Tela d'Imperatore con la favola di Dedalo senza cornice
(307) Un altra cornice con l'Impresa della passione con un Christo morto
(308) Una cornice di sette palmi In circa con filetto à pater nostri   p. 599
        Nel Stantiolino Continguo alla sud(ett)a
(309) Una tela liscia tonda
(310) Un ritratto d'un Cardinale tela da Testa
(311) Un'altra teletta liscia
(312) Un'altra tele da testa liscia
(313) Un'altra tela disegnata con certi putti bislonga
(314) Una tela d'Imperatore liscia
(315) Un'altra tela di palmi tre
(316) Un'altra tela di palmi tre
(317) Un'altra tela di piccola Imprimita
(318) Una tela grande di palmi 7 Inc(irc)a liscia Imprimita
(319) Un'altra tela da testa
(320) Un'altra tela d'Imperatore con sbozzo di una Testa di Catone
(321) Due tele liscie di p(al)mi 7 In circa
(322) Un quadro bislongo con una S(an)ta Catarina
(323) Una Tela piccola rotta
(324) Un altra In ottangolo   p. 599 v
(325) Due altre tele
(326) Una cornice grande Intagliata
(327) Una tela Involtata con la sapienza rotta
(328) Un'altra con alcune figure tutta rotta
(329) Due altre tele Involtate liscie
(330) In due nicchi due Aquile di marmo
        Nel Giardino   p. 601
(331) Un vaso s(opr)a un piede di peperino rosso
(332) Una colonna alta più di un huomo
(333) Un vaso di peperino rotto
(334) Un pezzo di Colonna è s(opr)a una seppultura di pietra
(335) Quattro Colonelle In terra e una rotta s(opr)a Terra
(336) Due piedistalli di peperino   p. 601 v

The last section of the inventory was witnessed by Bartholomeo Rossiglione [sic] and Ambrogio Coragiolo [sic]

Appendix III

TRANSCRIPT OF THE LIST OF BOOKS FROM THE INVENTORY

For the archive reference, see Appendix II, especially no. 55.

Nella mede(si)ma stanza (i.e. Sacchi's bedroom) . . .   p. 583
Un Credenzino sopra detto Tavolino con sportelli ramati dentro il quale vi erano l'Infrascritti Libri

56. Un libro coperto di Carta pecora con filetti d'oro Intitolato le Gemme antiche figurate di leonardo Agostini senese
> *Le Gemme antiche figurate de L. Agostini Senese: Annotationi sopra le gemme antiche* etc. by G. P. Bellori, Rome, 1657. Sacchi is mentioned in the preface as 'mihi amicissimo'.
> Leonardo Agostini is recorded living in the same Parish as Sacchi in 1644 and 1645.

57. Un libretto coperto di Carta pecora con filetto d'oro e fettucie di Seta con diverse figure che comincia col nome di Giesù e seguita con diverse figurine di Giesù Bambino, e più Segue la vita di Sant'Ignatio Fondatore della Compag(ni)a di Giesù con altre figure
> It has not so far been possible to identify this book. Possibly it was a special presentation copy given to Sacchi by the Jesuits during the Centenary celebrations in 1639, when Sacchi was responsible for decorating the Gesù.

58. Un libro coperto di Carta pecora Intitolato Indici di sommi Pontefici degli Imperadori et de Consuli tratti da quelli del Card(ina)l(e) Baronio
> Although the catalogues of the British Museum and the Bibliothèque Nationale list a good many extracts, indexes and digests of Baronius' *Church Annals*, none of them fits the title of this book precisely.

59. Un'altro libro con Carta pecora con filetti d'oro con fetuccie Intitolato Flora overo cultura de Fiori del P(ad)re Gio: Bat(tis)ta Ferrari senese della Compagnia di Gies(u)
> *Flora, seu De Florum Cultura*, by Io. Bapt. Ferrarij, 4 volumes, Rome, 1633.
> From the inventory description it would appear that Sacchi owned a copy of the 1638 Italian edition and not the original Latin edition of 1633. Both editions contained one illustration based on a drawing by Sacchi now in the British Museum (see Catalogue No. 83).

60. Un libro intitolato Annali Eccl(esiast)ici tratti da quelli del Card(ina)le Baronio p(er) Oderico Rinaldi Triviggiano   p. 583 v
> *Annales ecclesiastici ab anno 1198, ubi descrivit Baronius*, auctore Oderico Raynaldo. 9 volumes published in Rome between 1646 and 1677; Baronius' *Annales Ecclesiastici* were first published in Rome between 1593 and 1607.

61. Un libro Intitolato Tesoro politico raccolto p(er) Comini Ventura da esemplari della accademia Italiana di Colonia
> *La Prima (-Seconda) parte del Thesoro Politico* (in cui si contengono relationi, instruttioni, trattati, and varii discorsi pertinenti alla perfetta intelligenza della ragion di stato) . . . *Raccolto per Comin Ventura da esemplari dell'Accademia Italiana di Colonia*. Two volumes, Milan, 1600.

62. Un libro Intitolato del vivere delli Romani o di Conservare la Sanità di Alesandro Petronio da Città Castellana
> *Del viver delli Romani et di conservar la sanità* (libri cinque . . . con dui libri appresso dell'istesso autore, del mantenere il ventre molle senza medecine, tradotti dalla lingua Latina dal . . . B. Paravicino). Rome, 1592, by Alexander Trajanus Petronius.

63. Un libro Intitolato Historia delle Guerre Civili di Francia di Enrico Caterino d'Avila.
> *Historia delle guerre civili di Francia* . . . (nella quale si contengono le operationi di quattro re, Francesco II, Carlo IX, Henrico III et Henrico IV . . . con l'indice delle cose più notabili). Enrico Catarino Davila, Venice, 1630.

64. Un libro Intitolato il Perfetto legendario della Vita e fatti di N(ost)ro Sig(nor)e Giesu Cristo e di tutti i Santi di Anfolito Vigliego.
> It has not been possible to identify this book. Possibly it has something to do with 'Il Vigliega de' Patriarchi e Profeti', which is one of the books listed by Scaramuccia in his chapter, 'Quanto sia l'utile al Pittore il dilettarsi di belle Lettere' (p. 195).

65. Un libro Intitolato Annali Eccl(esiast)ici tratti da quelli del Card(ina)le Baronio p(er) Odorico Rinaldi Trivignano
> See no. 60 above.

66. Un libro Intitolato le Bravure del Capitano Spavento di Fran(ces)co Andreini
> *Le Bravure del Capitano Spavento*, by Francesco Andreini, Venice, 1609.

67. Un libro coperto di Corame rosso con arme di Card(ina)le con alcune Figure di Medaglioni e con alcuni disegni e carte bianche
> Possibly drawings by Sacchi himself for a book.

68. Un libro Intitolato Orationi Militari di Remigio Fiorentino
> *Orationi Militari* (raccolte per M. Remigio Fiorentino, da tutti gli historici Greci et Latini, antiche e moderni. Con gli argomenti, che dichiarono l'occasione per le quali elle furono fatte. Con gli effetti, . . . chi elli i fecero negli animi di coloro che ascoltarono), by Nannini (Remigio) Fiorentino, Venice, 1560.

69. Un libro Intitolato continuat(io)ne del Tesoro politico di Ludovico Ricci   p. 584
> *Continuazione Del Tesoro Politico*, Ludovico Ricci, Venice, 1603.

70. Un libro Intitolato della Geneologia degli Dei di Gio. Boccaccia
> *Geneologia de gli Dei*, Giovanni Boccaccio, first published in Italian, Venice, 1547. Many later editions.

71. Un libro Intitolato gli Annali di Cornelio Tacito di Giorgio Dati Fiorentino
> *Gli Annali . . . di Cornelio Tacito*, translated by Giorgio Dati, Venice, 1563.

72. Un libro Intitolato Incomincia il Prologo del vulgarizzatore del Dialogo di Misere Santo Gregorio Papa
> *In comenza la tabula del primo libro del dialogo de Sa(n)cto Gregorio . . . Incomincia una opera molto devotissima laqual(e) e ditta el dialogo de sa(n)cto Gregorio tratto de latino i(n) vulgar(e)*. First published Modena, 1481. Many later editions.

73. Un libro Intitolato le Vite de S(an)ti Padri di Gio(vanni) Mario Verdizotti
> *Le Vite de' Santi Padri* (insieme col Prato Spirituale . . . by St. Jerome, St. Erhard and others), M. G. M. Verdizotti, Venice, 1586.

74. Un libro Intitolato il Vago e dilettevole giardino raccolto dal P(ad)re luigi Contarini
> *Il Vago e dilettevole giardino* etc., by Luigi Contarini, Vicenza, 1607.

75. Un libretto In carta pecora con fettucie Intitolato la perfettione del Cavallo di Fran(ces)co liberati Rom(an)o
La Perfettione del Cavallo (libri tre ... dove si tratta del mantenimento del Cavallo, e dell'osservationi circa la generatione, suoi mali, e cure di essi buon governo delle stalla, qualità delle razze antiche e moderne ... tradotto dal Greco nel nostro idioma Italiano), by Francesco Liberati, Rome, 1639. See Posse, 1925, p. 83, note 4.

76. Un libro Intitolato opere del Conte Ubaldo Bonarelli della Rovere
Opere del Co(nte) Guid. 'Ubaldo Bonarelli della Rovere, Rome, 1640
It is dedicated to Cardinal Antonio Barberini.

77. Un libro Intitolato Aedes Barberine ad Quirinale(m) a Comite Hieronijmo Decio [sic] Perusino descriptae
Aedes Barberinae ad Quirinalem a Comite Hieronymo Tetio Perusino Descriptae, Rome, 1642.
This book contains engravings after Sacchi's *Divina Sapienza* ceiling, and mentions some of his other works for the Barberini. According to Baldinucci (*Cominciamento e Progresso dell'Arte dell'Intagliatore in Rama* etc., Florence, 1681, p. 63), the engraved portraits of the three Barberini Cardinals and Don Taddeo Barberini by Cornelius Bloemaert were based on drawings by Sacchi.

78. Un libro Intitolato Martirologgio Rom(an)o
Presumably an Italian edition of a book such as *Martyrologium Romanum ... C. Baronii Notationibus illustratum*, Antwerp, 1613.

79. Un libretto Intitolato Hesperides sive malorum aureorum cultura et usu Gio(vanni) Bapt(ist)a Ferrarij Senensis
Hesperides, Sive de Malorum Aureorum Cultura et Usu, in 4 volumes, by Gio. Battista Ferrari, Rome, 1646.
Sacchi provided a drawing, now in the Louvre, for the story of Harmonillus transformed into a lime tree (see Catalogue No. 86).

80. Un libretto con alcuni disegni di Teste che vi è servito nella prima carta Jo. Pietro Stefanoni Romano
Presumably connected with Pietro Stefanoni's *Gemmae antiquitus sculptae, a Petro Stephanonio collectae et declarationibus illustratae*, Rome, 1627.

81. Un libro Intitolato vite di Plutarco Cheroneo degli huomini Illustri Grecie di Ludovico Domenichi
An Italian translation of Plutarch's *Lives* was published by Ludovico Domenichi in 1555.

82. Un libretto Intitolato la strage dell'Innocenti del Cavaliere Marino
La Strage degli'Innocenti, Cavaliere G. B. Marino, Venice, 1610 (?; 1st dated edition, Naples, 1632).

83. Un libretto Intitolato la sanpogna del Cavalier Marino p. 584 v
Cavalier Giovanni Battista Marino, *La Sampogna* (divisa in Idillij favolosi et pastorali), Paris, 1620.

84. Un altro della Poesie di Girolamo Preci
Girolamo Preti, *Poesie*, Rome and Bologna, 1631.
Preti, who was a member of Cardinal Francesco Barberini's circle, died in Spain in 1626. Among the poems is one entitled 'Ad un Pittore' (p. 36).

(The next part of the inventory was made on June 22, 1661, under the supervision of Carlo Maratta, Prospero Fidanza and Pietro Paolo Frangi.)

85. Un libretto Intitolato Opere Poetiche di Cesare Caporali p. 585
Rime piacevoli di Cesare Caporali (... et d'altri auttori. Accresciute ... di molto rime gravi, e burlesche del Sig. Torquato Tasso, del Sig. Annibal Caro, e di diversi nobilissimi ingegni). Ferrara, 1592; or *Rime di Cesare Caporali*, Venice, 1604.

86. Un'altro rime del sig(nore) Giuliano Cosellini
Rime, Giuliano Cosellini, Milan, 1592.

87. Un'altro Villa Borghese fuori di Porta Pinciana

Villa Borghese Fuori di Porta Pinciana descritta da Iacomo Marilli Romano Guardaroba di detta Villa, Rome, 1650.

88. Un'altro dittionario francese
Possibly the *Dittionario italiano e francese* by M. Filippo Venuti, Geneva, 1626.

89. Un'altro di carta Bianca con alcuni schizzi
See below, no. 178.

90. Un'altro delle guerre Civili de Romani d'Appiano Alesandrino
Delle guerre civili de' Romani, Appiano Alexandrino, translated by Alessandro Braccese, Florence, 1519. This is the first Italian edition of a work originally published in 1477.

91. Un'altro Arcadia del Sarazzano
Iacopo Sannazaro, *Libro Pastorale nominato Arcadio* [sic] etc., Venice, 1502.

92. Un'altro In lingua franzese di diversi habiti
Probably a French edition of a work such as Cesare Vecelli, *Habiti antiche et moderni di tutto il mondo*, Venice, 1598.

93. Un'altro Il Tesoro della Sanità di Castor durante
Il Tesoro della Sanità, Castore Durante, Venice, 1616.

94. Un'altro In foglio grande del modo Tenuto In trasferire l'obelisco Vaticano e delle fabriche fatte da Papa Sisto Quinto
Della trasportatione dell'Obelisco Vaticano, e delle fabriche di Nostro Signore Papa Sisto V, by Cav. Domenico Fontana, Rome, 1590.

95. Un'altro piccolo delle Guerre de Goti
It has not been possible to identify this.

96. Un'altro l'Immagine degli Dei degli Antichi
Vincenzo Cartari, *Imagini degli Dei delli Antichi*, Venice, 1566. Many later editions.

97. Un'altro stracciato Intitolato Goffredo, overo Gerusalemme Liberata, del Tasso
First published in Venice, 1580. A later edition whose title agrees quite closely with no. 97 was that published in Rome in 1607 with illustrations by Antonio Tempesta.

98. Comentarij di Anton(io) Fran(ces)co Cirni Cato
Antonfrancesco Cirni, *Commentarij nei quali si discrive la guerra ultima di Francia*, 1567.
This item was identified by Professor J. H. Whitfield for whose assistance I am grateful. Perhaps Sacchi owned a commentary on Cato, however, and not on the French Civil Wars.

99. Un libro In foglio di carta grossa con alcuni schezzi
See no. 178.

100. Un'altro dell'istessa qualità
See no. 178.

101. Un'altro con alcune stampe di caccie, animali, e figure
See no. 178.

102. Un'altro Intitolato agiunta al 2°. (secondo) libro di Don florisello   p. 585 v
Aggiunta al secondo libro di Don Florisello (chiamata libro delle prodezze di Don Florestano), Venice, 1594. The book to which this was an addendum was *L'historia et gran prodezze in Arme di Don Florisandro, Prencipe di Cantaria*, etc., Venice, 1550.

103. Un libretto Rime di Guglielmo Pagnino luchese
It has not been possible to trace an edition of *Rime* by Pagnino. A collection of his letters was published in 1658.

104. Un'altro Intitolato compendio Historico del vecchio e nove Testamento di Bartholomeo Dionigi da Fano
Compendio Historico del Vecchio e del Nuovo Testamento cavato dalla sacra Bibbia ... con la vita di Giesu Christo, by Bartollomeo Dionigi da Fano, Venice, 1588.

105. Doi libri di Musica
The inventory lists a 'spinetta' and a 'cimbalo' (see below, nos. 160 and 161), which Sacchi left to the same son who inherited the drawings and plaster casts.

106. Un libretto Intitolato corona d'Appollo

Della Corona di Apollo, Piergirolamo Gentile, Venice, 1610. I should like to thank Professor E. R. Vincent for identifying this title, and several others on this list.

107. Un libretto delle lacrime del Tevere
It has not been possible to identify this book.

108. Il maritaggio delle Muse di Gio(vanni) Giacomo Ricci
Il Maritaggio delle Muse, Giovanni Giacomo Ricci, Venice, 1633.

109. Le Rime del Cavalier Marino
Le Rime of Cavalier G. B. Marino were first published in Venice in 1602.

110. La Zampogna del Cavalier Marino
See above, no. 83.

111. Un libretto di manoscritti de ricordi, e note dell'Instr(ument)i

112. Un libro di diversi Instr(ument)i publici

113. Un'altro de ricordi

114. Un'altro Intitolato Il supplem(en)to delle Croniche del P(ad)re Giacomo Filippo da Bergamo
Sopplimento delle Croniche universali del Mondo, by F(ra) Giacomo Filippo da Bergamo (... nel quale si contenga tutte le cose avvenute nel mondo ... fino a quest'anno presente 1581 ... con due tavole), Venice, 1581.

115. Un libretto favole d'Issoppo
Favole d'Isopo (... e de molti altri tradotte nuovamente di Latino etc.), Venice, 1544. Many later editions.

Index

of Names and Places in Appendixes I and II

Abbreviations: I—Appendix I
Letters refer to paragraphs in the will and codicils.
II—Appendix II
Numbers refer to items in the inventory.

ALBERTI, Giovanni (I, L; II, 36)   Signore Giovanni Alberti was Sacchi's doctor and a neighbour throughout Sacchi's residence in Via Rasella. Alberti presumably looked after Sacchi during his last illness, which began with crippling attacks of gout in 1659. Sacchi gave his doctor a painting of fruit by Michelangelo Cerquozzi that hung in the artist's bedroom, where Alberti must have seen it and probably admired it as well.

ARPINO, Cesare d' (I, C)   Giuseppe Cesari, 'il Cavaliere d'Arpino', was one of Sacchi's teachers, according to Bellori. Sacchi's desire to be buried beside Cavaliere d'Arpino in San Giovanni Laterano suggests that he felt a real debt and sense of attachment to him. Their artistic relationship is discussed in the introduction.

BARBERINI, Cardinal Antonio (I, C, R, S, BB, CC; II, 55, 162, 178)   Sacchi's relations with Cardinal Antonio Barberini are discussed elsewhere. These documents show that, despite Sacchi's failure to complete any of the important commissions given to him after Cardinal Antonio's return to Rome from exile in 1652, the two men were on good terms at the end of Sacchi's life. Cardinal Antonio evidently granted the artist's request to be buried in S. Giovanni Laterano.[6] The bequest to Cardinal Antonio of drawings 'after Correggio, Veronese and others' made while Sacchi was travelling in North Italy at the Cardinal's expense is welcome confirmation that the trip, mentioned by both Bellori and Passeri, took place.[7] Sacchi's other bequest to his most important patron was an elaborate silver cup that was originally left to his chief executor, Abbot Carlo Vaini. In the first codicil, Sacchi changed his mind, giving the cup to the Cardinal and a picture of *The Last Communion of St. Jerome* to Vaini; in the last codicil these two bequests were switched once more. The explanation for this change may be Cardinal Antonio's desire to see the more valuable cup go to someone whose need was greater than his own. The picture of *St. Jerome* in Sacchi's inventory is not attributed to anyone nor said to be a copy after anyone. It is attributed to Sacchi, however, in Cardinal Antonio's inventory of 1671 (no. 328, 'Un quadro di grandezza de p(al)mi 3 e 2 rappresentante S. Girol(am)o che si comunica nel tempio, e due Angeletti in aria') and in two successive Barberini inventories (Cardinal Antonio, 1672, no. 311; Principe Maffeo, 1672–86, no. 188), but in the Case Barberini inventory of 1686, it is attributed to Agostino Carracci (no. 200). Since Sacchi did, according to Malvasia,[8] make a copy of Agostino's *Last Communion of St. Jerome* and since Cardinal Antonio's picture had two putti in the air above the figures, as does Agostino's composition, it is possible that the picture Sacchi gave the Cardinal was his own copy after Agostino's famous composition.

BERNINI, Gian Lorenzo (I, C)   Sacchi left 200 scudi towards the cost of his tomb in San Giovanni Laterano and asked that it be 'made from a design by Gian Lorenzo Bernini and executed by Signor Paolo Nardini [*sic*]'. Since relations between Sacchi and Bernini are thought to have been poor, Sacchi's request to have his tomb designed by the famous sculptor is a surprise. Their relationship is dicussed in the introduction. The tomb's design is pedestrian and would seem to be Naldini's in conception as well as in execution.

CERQUOZZI, Michelangelo (I, L)   Sacchi left a still life of fruit by Michelangelo Cerquozzi ('delle Battaglie') to his doctor, Giovanni Alberti. Passeri (p. 286) says that Cerquozzi only painted still lifes at the beginning of his career, a statement confirmed by the fact that only a small number of still lifes have ever been attributed to him.[9] Sacchi may have acquired it around 1630 when he and Cerquozzi were living in the same area of Rome near Sant'Andrea delle Fratte.[10] The other pictures in his collection in 1661 that were not apparently his own—paintings of fruits and flowers, some small landscapes—were also probably bought from friends when Sacchi was young, single and successful. After 1640 he seems to have invested his money in property. He also had mistresses and an increasing number of illegitimate children to support.

CORAGGIOSO, Ambrogio (I, Z; II, 171–2)   Ambrogio Coraggioso was a witness to the first codicil and was also present on June 22 when the unexamined rooms were sealed. His etching based on Sacchi's *Adam and Abel* is discussed in the catalogue entry for that painting.

FIDANZA, Prospero (I, D, K, X, GG; II, June 21, 22, 26 and July 3)   Prospero Fidanza, Sacchi's 'amorevole', is put in charge of the distribution of money to the poor of Sacchi's parish after the artist's death. His close relationship with Sacchi is also made clear by the other responsibilities he is to assume at that time. He was to look after the financial investments made on behalf of Giovanni Battista and Francesco Luti. He was also to deputize for the chief executor, Abbot Vaini, if the latter was not in Rome when the inventory was prepared. This proved to be the case and we find Fidanza present on all four days. Fidanza was also one of the few people allowed to select his own drawings from Sacchi's academies instead of accepting the choice made for them by Maratta. Apart from the fact that he joined the Virtuosi al Pantheon and the Academy of St. Luke in 1663,[11] nothing else is known about him.

FILIPPO, Padre (I, G)   Padre Filippo was Sacchi's confessor and a member of the Spanish Discalzed Trinitarians, for whom Borromini built San Carlo alle Quattro Fontane. The information is interesting only in that it shows Sacchi regularly visited Borromini's church, of which Bellori strongly disapproved. Presumably if the architecture offended Sacchi, he would have gone to confession elsewhere.

GABURRI, Margharita (I, I, J, K)   Margharita Gaburri, the mother of Pietro Paolo, Marc Antonio and Eufrasia Manucci, is first recorded living near Sacchi in 1658, when she was thirty-five, according to the Stati d'Anime. She is recorded as a local resident again in 1659. Her son is living with Sacchi as a 'nepote' in 1660 and 1661. Sacchi's relations with her and with the other two women mentioned in the will may have been perfectly proper, but Sacchi's concern for the welfare of these apparently unrelated families suggests otherwise. Moreover, Sacchi's fondness for women was well known to Passeri, who even attributes Sacchi's failure to finish any major works during the last years of his life to his emotional preoccupations.[12] Bellori generally prefers to gloss over such details in his *Vite*: that he omits any mention of Sacchi's illegitimate heirs should not be interpreted as proof that Sacchi's will was made in a spirit of pure charity rather than of belated moral obligation.

LUTIJ, G. B. and F. (1, K, DD) Giovanni Battista and Francesco Lutij were almost certainly Sacchi's sons by Vittoria Lutij, presumably a relative of the tailor, Francesco Lutij, who with his wife Caterina rented part of Sacchi's house between 1644 and 1650. Vittoria was said to be 38 years old in 1644 and to have seven children in 1646 (Stati d'Anime, S. Nicola in Arcione, Archivio del Vicariato, Rome). At the time of Sacchi's death, Giovanni Battista and Francesco were living with Pietro Paolo Frangi, who, with Prospero Fidanza and Gioseppe Giamberti, was put in charge of the money invested for their support.

MANUCCI, E., P. P. and M. A. (1, I, J, K, V, DD, EE) Sacchi's relationship with Margharita Gaburri (q.v.) seems to have required that he assume responsibility for her three children at the time of his death. Eufrasia Manucci was five in 1661, Pietro Paolo was fourteen and Marc Antonio was eight.[12a] Pietro Paolo, who in the 1661 Stati d'Anime record is called Sacchi's 'nepote', was encouraged to become a painter, all Sacchi's drawings and casts after sculpture being left to him on condition that he followed that profession. Maratta was, however, put in charge of this valuable property and was to allow Pietro Paolo access as necessary. If he did not become a painter, the drawings and casts were to be sold and the money invested for Eufrasia, presumably as additional inducement to Pietro to take up an artistic career. Since nothing is known of the artistic activities of a 'Pietro Paolo Sacchi' or 'Manucci', it seems possible that he did not become a painter and that the one thousand odd drawings in Sacchi's studio were therefore sold within ten years of his death.[13] Maratta, being in charge of the collection, was in a good position to select those he wanted, and the Sacchi drawings now at Windsor and Düsseldorf almost certainly reflect Maratta's personal choice to some extent.[14] The Sacchi drawings in those two collections amount to barely a fifth of the known total in 1661. The rarity of Sacchi drawings in other collections suggests that the remainder of the drawings were dispersed in small lots and thus for the most part lost.[15]

MARATTA, Carlo (1, R, U, V, W, EE; 11, 51a, 173 and June 22, 26 and July 3) Sacchi's only famous pupil and subsequently one of the most successful and influential of later seventeenth-century painters in Italy, Carlo Maratta's presence at Sacchi's death-bed is to be expected from the account of their friendship given by Bellori.[16] Maratta's name first occurs in the codicil of June 17 made nine days after the will. Within that time Sacchi seems to have given his artistic heritage a little more thought, almost certainly after discussions with Maratta. Sacchi arranged for various friends to choose academy studies or to be given studies selected for them by Maratta. Sacchi also arranged for his remaining casts and drawings to be held in trust by Maratta for the use of the son who was thinking of becoming a painter. Maratta was allowed to choose some casts for himself,[17] but he was not given any drawings. This bears out Bellori's report that Sacchi told Maratta that he would receive none of his teacher's drawings because others had greater need of them. Maratta was also responsible for selecting the studies after Correggio, Veronese and others that Sacchi had made in North Italy and for giving those drawings to Cardinal Antonio Barberini.

MARCACCIONI, Gaspare (1, N; 11, June 21) Gaspare Marcaccioni (1620–74) was Cardinal Antonio Barberini's treasurer; he later served the Altieri family in the same capacity. His wife, Helena dal Pozzo, survived him. His portrait was painted by Maratta and the family chapel in S. Maria del Suffragio was decorated by Paolo Naldini, Niccolò Berettoni and Giuseppe Chiari.[18] He and Carlo Vaini were two of Sacchi's chief executors. Marcaccioni's only other recorded connection with Sacchi is a payment he made to

Sacchi's heirs on June 30, 1661, for a copy of the *Drunkenness of Noah* (Incisa della Rocchetta, 1924, p. 74).

NALDINI, Pietro Paolo (1, C, W, GG; 11, June 26) The sculptor Pietro Paolo Naldini (1614–91) trained as a painter in Sacchi's studio at the same time as Maratta, according to Pascoli (11, pp. 463–4), but decided to become a sculptor when he realized that he could never compete with Maratta. Sacchi asked Naldini to carve his tomb and left him two academy drawings. Naldini was also present on one of the days when the inventory was prepared. Clearly the two men remained on good terms, despite the fact that Naldini on occasion worked for Bernini.[19]
Pascoli says that Sacchi encouraged Naldini by commissioning two marble putti from him but there is no trace of them in the 1661 inventory. Pascoli also says that Naldini was extremely upset by Sacchi's death and could only pull himself together and face work again after Maratta had comforted him. Perhaps Maratta lent Naldini the portrait of Sacchi that he made around this time as a model for the bust on the tomb.
Bellori, who noted that Naldini made Sacchi's tomb and indeed reported every detail of this part of the will accurately, omitted any mention of the request for a design by Bernini (1672–96, p. 63). Perhaps he knew that Bernini refused to honour his old rival's memory by giving Naldini a drawing, or perhaps Bellori preferred not to associate himself publicly with Bernini, Bellori having provided the inscription for the monument.

PASQUALINI, Marc Antonio (1, DD) Marc Antonio Pasqualini, the castrato singer, was, according to Bellori, a good friend of Sacchi. Their relationship is discussed in the catalogue entry for Sacchi's portrait of Pasqualini. He was to supervise the various financial arrangements made on behalf of Sacchi's children.

PELLEGRINI, Nicola (1, A, Q, AA) According to the opening statement in the will, Nicola Pellegrini from Fermo was Sacchi's father, a fact that flatly contradicts Passeri, Bellori and Pascoli, all of whom say that Sacchi's father was a certain Benedetto Sacchi. Moreover, Hoogewerff (p. 124) found Benedetto and Andrea Sacchi living together as father and son in the parish of S. Maria del Popolo in 1624. Passeri implies that Sacchi was illegitimate.[20] It would appear that Andrea was adopted by Benedetto Sacchi when he was apprenticed to him, a not uncommon practice.

POSTIGLIONE, Bartolomeo (1, U) Sacchi left six academy drawings to Bartolomeo Postiglione, which he was to select himself. A drawing in the Louvre labelled 'dal Signor bartolomeo Postilione alievo di Andrea Sacchi' (Inventory no. 14132 among the Anonymous Italian Drawings) shows the use he probably made of those drawings. It is a careful pen and ink composition study showing Latona and the shepherds, based on Sacchi's engraved allegory on the birth of Urban VIII and on one red chalk study of a man surprised now in the Royal Collection at Windsor (Blunt and Cooke, no. 773). The drawings used by Postiglione when composing the Louvre sheet were not necessarily those left to him by Sacchi, but that he was a pupil and weak pasticheur of his master's work there seems no doubt.

SAN NICOLA IN ARCIONE (1, C, D, I) San Nicola in Arcione was Sacchi's parish church. He was buried there until his tomb in S. Giovanni in Laterano was ready, according to his will, although Bellori says that his body was never transferred. The church, which was pulled down between 1907–8 to make way for the tunnel that now runs between Via Milano and the Largo del Tritone, contained paintings by Luigi Gentile, Cavaliere d'Arpino, Maratta and 'pupils of Sacchi' (Titi, 1674, p. 362; 1763, p. 331).

TODESCA, Margharita (1, F) Margharita Todesca is recorded in part of Sacchi's house from 1641 onwards. According to the Stati d'Anime she was 30 in 1644 and had three children in 1661, aged 18, 9 and 6. Sacchi absolves her of a six scudi debt for rent. Since

Sacchi did not assume responsibility for her children, it would appear that Sacchi was not their father, even though she is the only single woman recorded living in Sacchi's house regularly for over twenty years.

VAINI, Carlo (I, M, S, T, X, BB, CC) Abbate Carlo Vaini was Sacchi's chief executor, the task being shared with Gaspare Marcaccioni (*q.v.*) and two other unidentified men. For the history of the silver cup finally left to Vaini, the reader is referred to the entry on Cardinal Antonio Barberini. Vaini's chief duty was to supervise the preparation of the inventory, but this finally had to be done by others as he was away from Rome at the time of Sacchi's death.

Very little is known about Vaini. He was a member of the 'Squadriglia di Provenza' in the festivities in Piazza Navona in 1634, along with three other Roman gentlemen (Mascardi, 1635, pp. 57 and 62–3). He was a consul of Rome in 1653 (Forcella, I, p. 2, col. 2) and in 1662 accepted payment on behalf of Sacchi's heirs for the purchase of a copy of Sacchi's *Adam and Abel* (Incisa della Rocchetta, 1924, p. 74). He was presumably a minor cleric on the fringes of the Barberini circle who had befriended Sacchi.

NOTES

6. Clemente Merlini also had to ask for Cardinal Antonio to arrange for his monument to be set up in S. Maria Maggiore (Pollak, I, p. 175).
7. The drawings were hung in a small room in the Palazzo Barberini where they were seen by Richardson (1722, p. 165). Malvasia (I, pp. 351 and 381) also knew them and reported that drawings after Cavedone and Brizio were to be seen as well, although this may simply be a characteristic bit of Bolognese embroidery on his part. No eighteenth-century guide books mention the drawings but they are recorded in Cardinal Antonio's inventory of 1671 ('Disegni in Carta, Pezzi nº trenta-tre, cio è No. 5 di simil grandezza dipinti in carta, e Nº 28 disegnati di lapis rosso, mano di Andrea Sacchi copiati dall'opere del Correggio, Paolo Veronese, e Caraci . . . il maggior pezzo d'essi di grandezza di pᵐⁱ, 2 et un ½ in (cir)ca'; no. 499, valued 350 scudi) and again in his inventory of 1672 (no. 195).
8. II, p. 224. He reports that the *ricordo* made by Sacchi was on copper. Neither Sacchi's nor Cardinal Antonio's inventory state the kind of support on which his *St. Jerome* was painted, but a copper support was unusual and would probably have been recorded for identification purposes. Either Malvasia was mistaken or Sacchi made two copies of Agostino's *St. Jerome*.
9. See G. Briganti, 'Michelangelo Cerquozzi, Pittore di Nature Morte', *Paragone*, v, no. 53, 1954, pp. 47–52, esp. fig. 43.
10. Hoogewerff, p. 124.
11. Orbaan, 1914, p. 46 and Thieme-Becker, XI, p. 353.
12. 'Si lasciò trasportare dall'amore delle Donne, le quali, al solito stile, lo distoglievano dalla applicazione: ma si tratenne sempre imbarrazzato con alcune carogne con qualque suo pregiudizio, e discapito (p. 303).
12a. Stati d'Anime, S. Nicola in Arcione, 1659 (see Hoogewerff, 1947, p. 128).
13. The only Sacchi said to be a son of Andrea active as a painter was a certain 'P. Giuseppe', to whom an altarpiece in the sacristy of SS Apostoli was attributed by the 1763 edition of Titi (p. 316). No Giuseppe Sacchi is mentioned in any contemporary documents, nor in Andrea's will.
14. See Harris and Schaar, p. 18.
15. Passeri implies that Sacchi's sons did not appreciate their heritage. Discussing the artist's heirs, whom he describes as 'alcuni suoi figlioli nati così di balzo', Passeri says that they 'con poco buon genio furono per tener conto di quelle facultà lasciategli da lui' (p. 304).
16. Bellori is never mentioned in these documents, a fact that suggests that he was not a close friend of Sacchi and that he relied on Maratta for information about him. Bellori's account of Sacchi's death reads, however, as if Bellori was present (1672–96, pp. 62–3).
17. Several Duquesnoy putti and other figures said to have come from Sacchi are mentioned in Maratta's inventory of 1712 (Galli, XXIII, p. 60, nos. 39 and 153–9). One is described as 'Altro Puttino a sedere in terra terminata la schiena, che fu fatto per il Sig.r Andrea Sacchi . . . fatto dal fiamengo'.
18. For all this information, see Forcella, VIII, p. 442, no. 1040; Bellori, 1672–96, p. 100; Titi, 1674, p. 462 and Titi, 1763, p. 420.
19. Wittkower, 1955, p. 218.
20. 'Il Padre chiamossi Benedetto Sacchi Pittore; ma di mediocre levatura; hebbe figliolo; chi legge puo capire il come, basta, che da lui nacque Andrea naturalmente' (p. 291).

Bibliography

The bibliography includes all essential literature, together with a representative selection of references from guide books of the seventeenth, eighteenth and nineteenth centuries. All works have been cited in abbreviated form. Full titles are given below. The only exceptions are works which have been cited on one occasion only.

ACTES   *Actes du Colloque Nicolas Poussin*, 2 vols., Paris, 1960.

ADEMOLLO   Ademollo, A.: *Il Carnevale di Roma nei Secoli XVII e XVIII*, Rome, 1883.

ADRIANI   Adriani, Gert: *Anton van Dyck, Italienisches Skizzenbuch*, Vienna, 1940.

ALCAIDE   Alcaide, Victor Manuel Nieto: *Carlo Maratta, Cuarenta y Tres Dibujos de Tema Religioso*, Dibujos de la Real Academia de San Fernando, Madrid, 1965.

AMAYDEN   Amayden, Teodoro: *La Storia delle Famiglie Romane*, ed. C. A. Bertini, Roma, 1910–17.

ANGELI   Angeli, Diego: *Le Chiese di Roma*, Rome, n.d. (1903?).

ANGELI   Angeli, Paolo de: *Basilicae Veteris Vaticanae Descriptio*, Rome, 1646.

ARCANGELI   Arcangeli, Francesco: entries in the catalogue of the 1962 Bologna Exhibition, *L'Ideale Classico del Seicento in Italia e la Pittura del Paesaggio*, Bologna, 1962, pp. 256–89.

ARCHIVES   Arch. Acad. S. Luca: Archivio dell'Accademia di San Luca, Piazza dell'Accademia di S. Luca, Rome.

ARCHIVES   Arch. Stor. Capit.: Archivio Storico Capitolino, Corso Vittorio Emmanuele, Rome.

ARCHIVES   Arch. Stat.: Archivio di Stato, Corso del Rinascimento, Rome.

ARCHIVES   Arch. Vic. Roma: Archivio dell'Vicariato di Roma, Via dell'Amba Aradam, Rome.

ARFELLI   Arfelli, Adriana: *La Pinacoteca e i Musei Comunali di Forlì*, Rome, 1936.

ARMELLINI, 1891   Armellini, Mariano: *Le Chiese di Roma*, Rome, 1891.

ARMELLINI, 1942   Armellini, Mariano: *Le Chiese di Roma*, edited by Carlo Cecchelli, Rome, 1942.

AUMALE   Aumale, Le Duc d': *Inventaire de tous les meubles du Cardinal Mazarin*, London, 1861.

AVVENTI   Avventi, F.: *Il Servitore di Piazza, Guida per Ferrara*, Ferrara, 1838.

BAGLIONE, 1639   Baglione, Giovanni: *Le Nove Chiese di Roma*, Rome, 1639.

BAGLIONE, 1642   Baglione, G. *Le Vite de' Pittori, Scultori, Architetti . . . (1572–1642)*, Rome, 1642. (Ed. cit. pub. Rome, 1935).

BALDINUCCI   Baldinucci, Filippo: *Notizie de Professori del Disegno da Cimabue in qua*, Florence, 1680–1728.

BALDINUCCI   Baldinucci, F.: *Vocabolario Toscano dell' Arte del Disegno*, Florence, 1681.

BARI   Bari, Giacomo: *The Painters' Voyage of Italy*, London, 1679.

BAROTTI   Barotti, Cesare: *Pittura e Scolture Che Si Trovano nelle Chiese, Luoghi Pubblici e Sobborghi della Città di Ferrara*, Ferrara, 1770.

BAROZZI AND BERCHET Barozzi, Niccolò and Berchet, Guglielmo: *Relazioni degli Stati Europei lette al Senato dagli Ambasciatori Veneti del Secolo Decimosettimo, Serie III—Italia Relazioni di Roma*, 2 vols, Rome, 1877–8.

BARTSCH   Bartsch, Adam: *Le Peintre-Graveur*, Vienna, 1803–21.

BASAN   Basan, F.: *Catalogue Raisonné des differens objets de curiosites dans les sciences et arts . . . qui comptoient le Cabinet de feu Mr Mariette*, Paris, 1775.

BATTISTI   Battisti, Eugenio: 'Acquisti della Collezione Maratti: Postille documentarie su artisti italiani a Madrid e sulla collezione Maratta', *Arte Antica e Moderna*, 1960, pp. 86–88.

BEAN   Bean, Jacob: *Dessins Romains du XVIIe Siècle*, XXIIIe Exposition du Cabinet des Dessins, Musée du Louvre, Paris, 1959.

BEAN AND STAMPFLE   See Stampfle.

BELLORI, 1672   Bellori, Giovanni Pietro: *Le Vite de' Pittori, Scultori et Architetti moderni*, parte prima, Rome, 1672. (Ed. cit. pub. Rome, 1931).

BELLORI, 1672–96   Bellori, G. P.: *Le Vite Inedite (Guido Reni. Andrea Sacchi, Carlo Maratta)*. Ed. M. Piacentini, Rome, 1942.

BELLORI, 1695   Bellori, G. P.: *Descrizione delle Imagini dipinte da Raffaele d'Urbino*, Rome, 1695.

BELLORI(?)   *Nota delli Musei*, anonymous (G. P. Bellori?), Rome. 1664.

BÉNARD   Bénard, M.: *Cabinet de M. Paignon Dijonval*, Paris, 1810.

BENIGNI   Benigni, V.: *Compendioso Ragguaglio delle Cose più Notabili di Fabriano*, Fabriano, 1936, p. 143.

BENTIVOGLIO   *Historia di Fiandra del Cardinal Bentivoglio*, Cologne, 1632.

BERTHIER   Berthier, J. J.: *Chroniques du Monastère . . . de SS. Domenico e Sisto . . .*, Levanto, 1919–20.

BERTOLOTTI   Bertolotti, Antonio: *Artisti Subalpini in Roma nei Secoli XV, XVI e XVII*, Mantua, 1884.

BERTOLOTTI   Bertolotti, A.: *Artisti Lombardi a Roma nei Secoli XV, XVI e XVII*, Milan, 1881.

BEZZI,   Bezzi, G.: *Il Fuoco Trionfante*, Forlì, 1637.

BIARDI   Biardi, Luigi: *Notizie sulle antiche fabriche di Firenze non terminate*, Florence, 1824.

BIGAZZI   Bigazzi, Francesco: *Iscrizioni e memorie della Città di Firenze*, Florence, 1886.

BILDT   Bildt, Baron C. de: 'Queen Christina's pictures', *The Nineteenth Century*, LVI, 1904, pp. 989–1003.

BLANC   Blanc, Charles: *Manuel de l'amateur d'estampes*, Paris, 1850–6.

BLANC   Blanc, C.: *Le Trésor de la Curiosité*, Paris, 1857 and 1858.

BLUNT, 1958   Blunt, Anthony F.: 'The Palazzo Barberini: the contributions of Maderno, Bernini and Pietro da Cortona', *J.W.C.I.*, 1958, pp. 256–87.

BLUNT, 1969   Blunt, A. F.: *The Paintings of Nicolas Poussin*, London, 1969.

BLUNT AND COOKE   Blunt, Anthony, and Cooke, Hereward Lester: *Roman Drawings at Windsor Castle*, London, 1960.

BOMBELLI   Bombelli, Pietro Leone: *Vita di S. Giovanni Battista . . . nel Battistero Lateranese*, Rome, 1769.

BONANNI   Bonanni, Philippo: *Numismata Pontificum Romanorum*, Rome, 1699.

BORSETTI   Borsetti, Andrea: *Supplemento al Compendio Historico del Signor D. Marc'Antonio Guarini Ferrarese*, Ferrara, 1670.

BOSCHETTO   Boschetto, A.: 'Per la conoscenza di Francesco Albani pittore', *Proporzioni*, II, 1948, pp. 109–46.

BOTTARI   Bottari, Giovanni: *Dialoghi sopra le tre arti del disegno*, Lucca, 1754.

BOTTARI   Bottari, G.: *Vite de' Pittori, Scultori ed Architetti* by G. B. Passeri, ed. by G. Bottari, Rome, 1772.

BOTTARI AND TICOZZI   Bottari, Giovanni: *Raccolta di lettere sulla Pittura, Scultura et Architettura ... pubblicata da M. Gio. Bottari e continuata fino ai nostri giorni da Stefano Ticozzi*, Milan, 1822.

BOYDELL   Boydell, Jean: *Catalogue Raisonné d'un Recueil d'Estampes d'Après les Plus Beaux Tableaux qui Soient en Angleterre*, London, 1779.

BRAHAM   Braham, Alan: 'Bernini's design for the Bourbon Chapel', *Burl. Mag.*, 1960, pp. 443-7.

BRIGANTI, 1950   Briganti, Giuliano: *I Bamboccianti*, Rome, 1950.

BRIGANTI, 1960   Briganti, G.: 'L'Altare di Sant'Erasmo, Poussin e il Cortona', *Paragone*, 1960 (no. 123), pp. 16-20.

BRIGANTI, 1962   Briganti, G.: *Pietro da Cortona*, Florence, 1962.

BRIGANTI   Briganti, G.: *Il Palazzo del Quirinale*, Rome, 1962.

BRISIGHELLA   Brisighella, C.: *Descrizione delle pitture e sculture che adornano le chiese et oratori della Città di Ferrara*, ed. G. Baruffaldi and Gianandrea Barotti, manuscript, Biblioteca Comunale, Bologna.

BRITTON   Britton, John: *Catalogue of the Pictures Bequeathed to Dulwich College by Sir Francis Bourgeois*, London, 1813.

BROVELLI-SOFFREDINI   Brovelli-Soffredini, Giuseppe: *Neptunia*, Rome, 1923.

BUCHANAN   Buchanan, W.: *Memoirs of Paintings with a chronological history of the importation of pictures by the great masters into England since the French Revolution*, London, 1824.

BUDDE   Budde, Illa: *Beschreibender Katalog der Handzeichnungen in der Staatlichen Kunstakademie Düsseldorf*, Düsseldorf, 1930.

BUTLER   *Butler's Lives of the Saints*, ed. H. Thurston, S. T. and D. Attwater, London, 1956.

CACCIARI   Cacciari, M. L.: *Memorie intorno alla Chiese de' SS. Biagio e Carlo a' Catinari in Roma*, Rome, 1861.

CALZINI   Calzini, E. and Mazzatinta, G.: *Guida di Forlì*, Forlì, 1893.

CAMPORI   Campori, Giuseppe: *Raccolta di Cataloghi ed Inventari Inediti di Quadri, Statue, Disegni, Bronzi, Dorerie, Smalti, Medaglie, Avorii ecc.*, Modena, 1870.

CANTALMESSA   Cantalmessa, Giulio: 'Un Dipinto di Velazquez nella Galleria Borghese?', *Boll. d'Arte*, 1922-3, pp. 97-100.

CARDELLA   Cardella, Lorenzo: *Memorie Storiche de' Cardinali della Santa Romana Chiesa*, Rome, 1793.

CARTARI   Cartari, Vincenzo: *Imagini degli Dei delli Antichi*, Venice, 1566. (Ed. cit. pub. Padua, 1603).

CASALI   Casali, Matteo: *Iscrizioni nella Città di Forlì e Suoi Territorio dall'anno 1680 al 1800*, Forlì, 1849.

CAVALLI   Cavalli, Gian Carlo: *Mostra dei Carracci*, Bologna, 1956 (Ed. cit. pub. June 1958).

CECCHINI   Cecchini, Giovanni: *La Galleria Nazionale dell'Umbria in Perugia*, Rome, 1932.

CHATTARD   Chattard, Giovanni Pietro: *Nuova Descrizione del Vaticano*, Rome, 1762.

CHIUSOLE, 1781   Chiusole, Cav. Adamo: *De' Precetti della Pittura*, Vicenza, 1781.

CHIUSOLE, 1782   Chiusole, A.: *Le Pitture, Sculture ed Architetture più Rare di Roma*, Vicenza, 1782.

CHUDANT   Chudant, Adam: *Catalogue des Peintures et Dessins, Musées de Besançon*, Besançon, 1929.

CIACCONIUS   Ciacconius, A.: *Vitae et res gestae Pontificum Romanorum et S.R.E. Cardinalium*, Rome, 1677.

CINELLI   Cinelli, M. G.: *Le Bellezze di Firenze*, Florence, 1677.

CITTADELLA   Cittadella, N. L.: *Indice Manuale delle Cose più Rimarcabili in Pittura, Scultura, Architettura della Città di Ferrara*, Ferrara, 1844.

CLEARY   Cleary, Gregory: *Father Luke Wadding and St. Isidore's College*, Rome, 1925.

COLONNA   *Catalogo dei Quadri ... nel Palazzo ... Colonna*, Rome, 1783.

CORTI   Corti, G.: *Galleria Colonna*, Rome, 1937.

COSNAC   Cosnac, Le Comte Gabriel Jules de: *Les Richesses du Palais Mazarin*, Paris, 1885 (2nd ed. cit.).

COSTELLO   Costello, Jane: 'The Twelve Pictures 'ordered by Velazquez' and the Trial of Valguarnera', *J.W.C.I.*, 1950, p. 237 f.

CRELLY   Crelly, William R. *The Paintings of Simon Vouet*, New Haven, 1962.

CUMBERLAND   Cumberland, Richard: *An Account and Descriptive Catalogue of the ... Paintings in the Royal Collection (New Palace) at Madrid*, London, 1787.

D'ARGENVILLE   D'Argenville, A. J. Dézalliers: *Abrégé de la vie des plus fameux peintres*, Paris, (Ed. cit. 1762-70, I, pp. 33-6).

DENIS   Denis, Paul: *Nouvelles de Rome*, Paris, 1913.

DONAHUE   Donahue, Kenneth: 'The Ingenious Bellori—a biographical study', *Marsyas*, 1943-5.

DREYER   Dreyer, Peter: *Römische Barockzeichnungen aus dem Berliner Kupferstichkabinett*, Ausstellung, Berlin, 1969.

EFFIGIES   *Effigies Nomina et Cognomina S. D. N. Alexandri Papae VII et RR.DD.S.R.E. Card. nunc viventium*, Io Iacobo de Rubeis, Rome, 1658.

EMILIANI   Emiliani, Andrea: entries in the catalogue of the 1962 Bologna Exhibition, *L'Ideale Classico del Seicento in Italia e la Pittura di Paesaggio*, Bologna, 1962, esp. pp. 305-9 and 331-9.

ENGERTH   Engerth, Eduard v.v.: *Gemälde-Beschreibendes Verzeichnis*, Vienna, 1884.

FABRICZY   Fabriczy, C. de: 'Memorie sulla Chiesa di S. Maria Maddalena de'Pazzi a Firenze e sulla Badia di S. Salvatore a Settimo', *L'Arte*, IX, 1906, pp. 255-62.

FAGIOLO DELL'ARCO, Maurizio and Marcello: *Bernini: una introduzione al gran teatro barocco*, Rome, 1967.

FÉLIBIEN, 1679   Félibien, André: *Noms de Peintres les plus célèbres et les plus connus anciens et modernes*, Paris, 1679.

FÉLIBIEN, 1685-8   Félibien, A.: *Entretiens sur les vies et sur les ouvrages des plus excellens peintres anciens et modernes*, Paris, 1685-8. (Ed. cit. Paris, 1725).

FELICIANGELI   Feliciangeli, B.: *Il Cardinale Angelo Giori da Camerino e Gian Lorenzo Bernini*. Sanseverino-Marche, 1917.

FERRARI, 1633   Ferrari, G. B.: *Flora, seu De Florum Cultura*, Rome, 1633.

FERRARI, 1646   Ferrari, G. B.: *Hesperides, Sive de Malorum Aureorum Cultura et Usu*, Rome, 1646.

FLORENCE, 1922   *Mostra della pittura italiana del seicento e del settecento*, Florence, Palazzo Pitti, 1922.

FORCELLA   Forcella, Vincenzo: *Iscrizioni delle Chiese e d'altri edifici di Roma*, Rome, 1869-84.

FRANSOLET   Fransolet, Mariette: *François du Quesnoy, Sculpteur d'Urbain VIII, 1597-1643*, Brussels, 1942.

FRANZINI   Franzini, Gio. Dom.: *Descrizione di Roma antica e moderna ...*, Rome, 1643 (and 1653).

FRASCHETTI   Fraschetti, Stanislao: *Il Bernini*, Milan, 1900.

FRIZZI   Frizzi, Antonio: *Guida del Forastiere per la Città di Ferrara*, Ferrara, 1787.

FRUTAZ   Frutaz, Amato Pietro: *Le Piante di Roma*, Rome. 1962.

GALASSI PALUZZI   See Paluzzi.

GALLI   Galli, Romeo: 'I Tesori d'arte di un pittore del Seicento', *L'Archiginnasio*, XXII (1927), pp. 217-38 and XXIII (1928), pp. 59-78.

GAMBA   Gamba, Carlo *et al.*: *Il Ritratto Italiano dal Caravaggio al Tiepolo*, Bergamo, 1927.

GAMS   Gams, P. Pius Bonifacius: *Series Episcoporum Ecclesiae Catholicae*, Ratisbon, 1873.

GAUTHIER   Gauthier, Jules: 'La Musée Jean Gigoux à Besançon', *Réunion des Sociétés des Beaux-Arts*, Paris, 1898, pp. 282-90.

GIGLI   Gigli, Giacinto: *Diario Romano (1608-70)*, ed. Giuseppe Racciotti, Rome, 1958.

GIOVENALE Giovenale, Giovanno Battista: *Il Battistero Later-anese*, Rome, 1929.

GNOLI Gnoli, Umberto: *La Pinacoteca di Perugia*, Firenze, n.d.

GNUDI AND CAVALLI Gnudi, Cesare and Cavalli, G. C.: *Guido Reni*, Florence, 1955.

GRANBERG Granberg, Olof: *La Galerie de Tableaux de la Reine Christine de Suède*, Stockholm, 1897.

GRASSI Grassi, Luigi: *Bernini Pittore*, Rome, 1946.

GRAVES Graves, Algernon: *A Century of Loan Exhibitions, 1813-1912*, London, 1914.

GUALDO PRIORATO Gualdo Priorato, Galeazzo: *Scena di Huomini Illustri d'Italia*, Venice, 1659.

GUARDABASSI Guardabassi, Mariano: *Indice-Guida dei monumenti pagani e cristiani riguardanti la storia e l'arte cristiana nella provincia dell'Umbria*, Perugia, 1872.

GUARINI Guarini, Filippo: *Notizie Storiche e Descrittive della Pinacoteca di Forlì*, Forlì, 1874.

HAROLDO Haroldo, P. Francisco, O.F.M.: *Vita Fratris Lucae Waddingi*, Florence, 1931.

HARRIS AND SCHAAR Sutherland Harris, Ann, and Schaar, Eckhardt: *Die Handzeichnungen von Andrea Sacchi und Carlo Maratta*. Kataloge des Kunstmuseums Düsseldorf III, Hand-zeichnungen I, Düsseldorf, 1967.

HASKELL Haskell, Francis: *Patrons and Painters*, London, 1963.

HASKELL AND RINEHART Haskell, F., and Rinehart, Sheila Somers: 'The Dal Pozzo Collection, Some New Evidence', *Burl. Mag.*, 1960, pp. 318-26.

HEMPEL Hempel, Eberhard: *Francesco Borromini*, Vienna, 1924.

HESS Hess, Jacob: Notes to his edition of the *Vite* of G. B. Passeri (*q.v.*), Leipzig, 1934.

HOOGEWERFF Hoogewerff, G. J.: 'Andrea Sacchi en Carlo Maratti', *Mededeelingen van het Nederlandisch Historisch Instituut te Rome*, 3, v, 1947. pp. 123-35.

HYGINUS *Hyginus Mythographus: The Myths of Hyginus*, ed. by Mary L. Grant, Kansas City, 1960.

INCISA DELLA ROCCHETTA Incisa della Rocchetta, Giovanni: 'Notizie Inedite su Andrea Sacchi', *L'Arte*, 1924, pp. 60-76.

INCISA DELLA ROCCHETTA, 1959 Incisa della Rocchetta, G.: 'Tre Quadri Barberini Acquistati dal Museo di Roma', *Bollettino dei Musei Comunali di Roma*, VI, 1959, 1-4, pp. 20-37.

INVENTARIO *Inventario degli Oggetti d'Arte d'Italia*, VII, Rome, 1936.

ISNELLO Isnello, Domenico da: *Il Convento della Santissima Con-cezione de' Padri Cappucini*, Viterbo, 1923.

JAMESON Jameson, Mrs A. B. M.: *Legends of the Madonna*, London, 1864.

KAFTAL Kaftal, George: *Iconography of the Saints in Tuscan Painting*, Florence, 1952.

KURZ Kurz, Otto: *Bolognese Drawings at Windsor Castle*, London, 1955.

LAPRET Lapret, Paul: *Musée Jean Gigoux à Besançon, Catalogue des Peintures et Dessins*, Besançon, 1902.

LAVIN Lavin, Irving: *Bernini and the Crossing of Saint Peter's*, New York, 1968.

LITTA Litta, Pompeo: *Famigilie celebri d'Italia*, Milan and Turin, 1819-81.

LONGHI Longhi, Roberto: *Scritti Giovanili, 1912-22*, Florence, 1961.

LUGT Lugt, Frits: *Repertoire des Catalogues de Ventes Publiques, 1600-1825*, The Hague, 1938.

LUGT Lugt, F.: *Les Marques de Collections, de Dessins et d'Estampes*, The Hague, 1921 and 1956.

LUZIO Luzio, Alessandro: *La Galleria dei Gonzaga venduta all'Inghilterra nel 1627-8*, Milan, 1913.

MAGNIN Magnin, J.: *La Peinture et le Dessin au Musée de Besançon*, Dijon, 1919.

MAHON, 1947 Mahon, Denis: *Studies in Seicento Art and Theory*, London, 1947.

MAHON, 1962 Mahon, D.: 'Poussiniana' in *G.B.A.*, 1962, pp. 1-138.

MÂLE Mâle, Emile: *L'art religieux de la fin du XVIe siècle, du XVII siècle et du XVIIIe siècle: étude sur l'iconographie après le concile de Trente*, 2nd ed., Paris, 1951.

MALVASIA Malvasia, Carlo Cesare: *Felsina Pittrice, Vite de pittori bolognesi*, Bologna, 1678. (Ed. cit. pub. Bologna, 1841).

MANCINI Mancini, Giulio: *Considerazioni sulla Pittura*, ed. by Adriana Marucchi and Luigi Salerno, Rome, 1956.

MARATTA, 1724 'Nota delli Quadri che si ritrovano nella cassa de Maratti per la Maestà di Filippo Quinto', *Revista de Archivos Bibliotecas y Museos*, VI, 1876, pp. 128-9 and 143-5.

MARCOALDI Marcoaldi, Oreste: *Guida e Statistica della Città e Comune di Fabriano*, Fabriano, 1873.

MARIETTE Mariette, P. J.: *Abcédario et autres notes inédites de cet amateur sur les arts et les artistes . . .*, Paris, 1851-60.

MARIOTTI Mariotti, Filippo: *La Legislazione delle Belle Arti*, Rome, 1892.

MEDER Meder, Joseph: *Die Handzeichnung—Ihre Technik und Entwicklung*, Vienna, 1919.

MEZZETTI Mezzetti, Amalia: 'Contributi a Carlo Maratta', *Rivista del Istituto Nazionale d'Archeologia e Storia dell'Arte*, nuova series, anno IV, 1955, pp. 253-354.

MIREUR Mireur, H.: *Dictionnaire des Ventes d'Art*, Paris, 1912.

MISSIRINI Missirini, Melchior: *Memorie per servire alla storia della Romana Accademia di S. Luca*, Rome, 1823.

MOLA Mola, G. B.: *Roma l'anno 1633 di Giov. Batt. Mola*, ed. K. Noehles, Berlin, 1966.

MOLAJOLI Molajoli, Bruno: *Guida Artistica di Fabriano*, Fabriano, 1936.

MONTAGU Montagu, Jennifer, 'Painted Enigma and French Seventeenth Century Art', *J.W.C.I.*, XXXI, 1968, pp. 307-335.

MONTI Monti, Achille: 'Di Andrea Sacchi e della Sua Casa', *Il Buonarotti*, 1866, pp. 188-92.

MONTINI Montini, Reno. V. Montini: *Sta Maria del Priorato* (*Le Chiese di Roma Illustrate*, no. 53), Rome, 1959.

NAGLER Nagler, G. K.: *Künstlerlexicon*, Munich, 1835-52.

NOEHLES Noehles, K.: *La Chiesa di SS. Luca e Martina nell'Opera di Pietro da Cortona*, Rome, 1970.

ORBAAN, 1914 Orbaan, J. A. F.: 'Virtuosi al Pantheon', *Rep. K.W.S.*, XXXVII, 1914-15, pp. 17-52.

ORBAAN, 1920 Orbaan, J. A. F.: *Documenti sul Barocco a Roma*, Rome, 1920.

ORSINI, 1788 Orsini, Baldassare: *Abrégé della guida al forastiere per l'augusta città di Perugia*, Perugia, 1788.

ORSINI, 1790 Orsini, B.: *Descrizione delle Pitture, Sculture, Archi-tetture ed altre cose rare della Città di Ascoli nella Marca*, Perugia, 1790.

ORTOLANI Ortolani, Sergio: *S. Giovanni in Laterano* (*Le Chiese di Roma illustrate*, no. 13), Rome, n.d.

PAATZ Paatz, W. and E.: *Die Kirchen von Florenz*, Frankfort, 1952.

PAGÉS Pagés, Léon: *Histoire de la Religion Chrétienne au Japon (1598-1651)*, Paris, 1959.

PALMEGIANI Palmegiani, Francesco: *Rieti e la Regione Sabina*, Rome, 1932.

PANCIROLI See Rossi.

PARKER Parker, Karl T.: *A Catalogue of the Collection of Drawings in the Ashmolean Museum*, Vol. II, Italian Schools, Oxford, 1956.

PASCOLI Pascoli, Leone: *Vite de' pittori, scultori ed architetti moderni*, Rome, 1730 and 1736 (Ed. cit. pub. Rome, 1933).

PASSERI Passeri, Giovanni Battista: *Vite de' pittori, scultori ed architetti dall'anno 1641 sino all'anno 1673*, Rome, 1772 (Ed. cit. pub. Leipzig, 1934).

PASTOR Pastor, Ludwig Freiherr von: *The History of the Popes*, London, 1938.

PECCHIAI Pecchiai, Pio: *Il Gesù di Roma*, Rome, 1952.

PECCHIAI, 1959 Pecchiai, P.: *I Barberini* (*Archivi d'Italia Rassegna Internazionale degli Archivi*), Rome, 1959.

PEREZ SANCHEZ Pérez Sánchez, Alfonso: *Pintura italiana del siglo XVII en España*, Madrid, 1965.

PERIODICALS

Boll. d'Arte—Bollettino d'Arte

B.S.H.A.F.—Bulletin de la Société de l'Histoire de l'art français.

Burl. Mag.—Burlington Magazine

G.B.A.—Gazette des Beaux Arts

J.K.A.K.—Jahrbuch der Kunsthistorischen Sammlungen des Allerhöchsten Kaiserhauses

J.W.C.I.—Journal of the Warburg and Courtauld Institutes

Rep.K.W.S.—Repertorium für Kunstwissenschaft

Mitt. Sächs.KSG—Mitteilungen aus den Sächsischen Kunstsammlungen.

PHOTOGRAPHIC SOURCES

A.F.V.—Archivio Fotografico della Pinacoteca Vaticana, Rome

G.F.N.— Gabinetto Fotografico Nazionale, Rome.

PIACENTINI Piacentini, M.: 'Architetti Romani minori nel seicento', *Palladio*, IV, 1940, pp. 29–33.

PIGLER Pigler, A.: *Barockthemen*, Berlin, 1956.

PINAROLO Pinarolo, Giacomo: *Trattato delle cose più memorabili di Roma*, Rome, 1700 (Ed. of 1703, 1713 and 1725).

PISTOLESI Pistolesi, Erasmo: *Il Vaticano Descritto*, Rome, 1829.

PISTOLESI, 1841 Pistolesi, E.: *Descrizione di Roma e suoi dintorni*, Rome, 1841 (and ed. 1846).

POLLAK, 1913 Pollak, Oscar: 'Alessandro Algardi als Architekt', *Zeitschrift für Geschichte der Architektur*, 1910–11, IV, pp. 49–79.

POLLAK Pollak, Oscar: *Die Kunsttätigkeit unter Urban VIII*, Vienna, 1928 and 1931.

PONZ Ponz, Antonio: *Viaje de España*, Madrid, 1772–94.

POPE-HENNESSY Pope-Hennessy, John: *Domenichino Drawings in the Royal Library at Windsor Castle*, London, 1948.

POPHAM Popham, A. E.: *Catalogue of the T. Fitzroy Philipps Fenwick Collection of Drawings*, London, 1935.

POSNER Posner, Donald: 'The Early Development of Baroque Painting in Rome', *Essays in Honor of Walter Friedlander* (*Marsyas*), New York, 1965, pp. 135–46.

POSNER Posner, Donald: *Annibale Carracci*, London, 1971.

POSSE, 1912 Posse, Hans: 'Einige Gemälde des Römischen Malers Andrea Sacchi', in *Mitt. Sachs. KSG.*, III, 1912, p. 49 f.

POSSE, 1925 Posse, Hans: *Der Römische Maler Andrea Sacchi*, Leipzig, 1925.

POSSE, 1935 Posse, H.: 'Andrea Sacchi' in Thieme-Becker, 1935.

PRADO For a complete list of Prado catalogues, see the 1952 catalogue, bibliography.

PRESENZINI Presenzini, A.: *Vita ed Opera di Andrea Camassei*, Assisi, 1880.

QUINN Quinn, Hubert, O.F.M.: *St Isidore's Church and College of the Irish Franciscans*, Vatican City, 1950.

RAMELLI Ramelli, C.: *Indice degli Oggetti d'Arte in Fabriano*, Fabriano, 1852.

RATTI Ratti, Carlo Giuseppe: *Istruzione di Quanto può Vedersi di più Bello in Genoa*, Genoa, 1780.

RÉAU Réau, Louis, *L'Iconographie de l'art chrétien*, Paris, 1955–9.

REFICE Refice, Claudia: 'Andrea Sacchi, Disegnatore', *Commentari*, I, 1950, pp. 214–21.

REUSCH Reusch, F. H.: *Der Process Galilei's und die Jesuiten*, Bonn, 1879.

RICHA Richa, G.: *Notizie Istoriche delle Chiese Fiorentine*, Florence, 1754–62.

RICHARDSON Richardson, Jonathan: *An account of the statues, bas-reliefs, drawings and picures in Italy, France etc.*, London, 1722.

RICHTER Richter, Jean Paul, and Sparkes, J. C. L.: *Catalogue of the Pictures in the Dulwich College Gallery*, London, 1880.

RIPA Ripa, Cesare: *Iconologia, etc.* (Ed. cit. pub. Padua, 1611).

ROGERS Rogers, Samuel: *The Samuel Rogers Sale* (Saturday, May 3, 1856), Christie's, London, 1856.

ROISECCO Roisecco, Gregorio: *Roma Antica e Moderna*, Rome, 1725 (Ed. cit. pub. 1750).

ROME, 1930 *Mostra di Roma Seicentesca, a cura dell'Istituto di Studi Romani*, Rome, 1930.

ROSSI Rossi, Michelangelo and Panciroli, Pier Vincenzo: *Descrizione di Roma Moderna formata Nuovamente . . .*, Rome, 1697 (Ed. cit. pub. Rome, 1719).

ROSSINI Rossini, Pietro: *Il Mercurio Errante delle Grandezze di Roma . . .*, Rome, 1693 (Later ed. cit. pub. Rome, 1700, 1704, 1725, 1750, 1776).

RÖTHLISBERGER Röthlisberger, Marcel: *Claude Lorraine, The Paintings*, New Haven, 1961.

RUFFO Ruffo, Vincenzo: 'La Galleria Ruffo nel Secolo XVII in Messina', *Boll. d'Arte*, X, 1916 and f.

SALERNO Salerno, Luigi: entries for paintings in the catalogue of the exhibition, *Il Seicento Europeo*, Rome, 1956–7, esp. pp. 215–16.

SANDRART Sandrart, Joachim von: *Academie der Bau- Bild- und Mahlerey Künste von 1675*, ed A. R. Peltzer, Munich, 1925.

SAINTS *The Book of Saints*, London, 1947.

SCALABRINI Scalabrini, Giuseppe Antenore: *Memorie Istoriche delle Chiese di Ferrara e di' Suoi Borghi*, Ferrara, 1773.

SCANNELLI Scannelli, Francesco: *Il Microcosmo della Pittura*, 1657.

SCARAMUCCIA Scaramuccia, Luigi: *Le Finezze de' Pennelli Italiani*, Pavia, 1674.

SCHAAR Schaar, Eckhardt: *Italienische Handzeichnungen des Barock*, Exhibition Catalogue, Düsseldorf, 1964.

SCHLÖSSER Schlösser, K.: *Beschreibendes Verzeichnis der Gemälde im Kaiser-Friedrich-Museum*, Berlin, 1931.

SEBASTIANI Sebastiani, Pietro: *Viaggio Sagio e Curioso delle Chiese più principali di Roma*, Rome, 1689.

SIEPI Siepi, Serafino: *Descrizione Topologico-Istorica della Città di Perugia*, Perugia, 1822.

SILOS Silos, Ioanne Michaele: *Pinacotheca sive Romana Pictura et Sculptura*, Rome, 1673.

SOFFREDINI Soffredini, Calcedonio: *Storia di Anzio Astura e Nettuno*, Rome, 1879.

SPRETI Spreti, Vincenzo: *Enciclopedia Storico-Nobiliare Italiana*, Milan, 1928–43.

STAMPFLE AND BEAN Stampfle, Felice and Bean, Jacob: *Drawings from New York Collections: The 17th Century*, New York, 1967.

STEINMANN Steinmann, Ernst: 'Gemälderestaurationen im Vatikan', *Cicerone*, 1925, esp. p. 946.

SUTHERLAND Sutherland, Ann B.: 'The Decoration of San Martino ai Monti', *Burl. Mag.*, 1964, pp. 58–69 and 115–20.

SUTHERLAND Sutherland, A. B.: 'Pier Francesco Mola—His Visits to North Italy and His Residence in Rome', *Burl. Mag.*, 1964, pp. 363–8.

SUTHERLAND HARRIS Sutherland Harris, Ann B.: 'Notes on the Chronology and Death of Pietro Testa', *Paragone*, no. 213, 1967, pp. 35–60.

SUTHERLAND HARRIS Sutherland Harris, A. B.: 'Andrea Sacchi and Emilio Savonanzi in the Collegio Romano', *Burl. Mag.*, 1968, pp. 249–57.

SUTHERLAND HARRIS Sutherland Harris, A. B.: 'The date of Andrea Sacchi's *Vision of St. Romuald*', *Burl. Mag.*, 1968, pp. 489–94.

SUTHERLAND HARRIS Sutherland Harris, A. B.: 'A Contribution to Andrea Camassei Studies', *Art Bulletin*, 1970, LII, pp. 49–70.

SUTHERLAND HARRIS, 1969 'Andrea Sacchi's "Portrait of a Cardinal"', *Bulletin of the National Gallery of Canada*, XIV, 1969, pp. 9–15.

SUTHERLAND HARRIS, 1971 'Drawings by Andrea Sacchi: Additions and Problems', *Master Drawings*, IX, no. 4, pp. 384–91.

SUTHERLAND HARRIS, 1973 'Academy Drawings by Andrea Sacchi: Addenda', *Master Drawings,* XI, 1973, no. 2, pp. 160–1.

TERVARENT Tervarent, Guy de: *Attributs et symboles dans l'art profane, 1450–1600,* Geneva, 1959.

TETI Teti, Girolamo: *Aedes Barberinae ad Quirinalem,* Rome, 1642.

THIEME-BECKER Thieme-Becker: *Allgemeines Lexicon der Bildenden Künstler,* Leipzig, 1907 f.

TITI Titi, Abbate Filippo: *Studio di Pittura, Scoltura et Architettura,* Rome, 1674 (and ed. of 1675, 1684 and 1763).

TOTTI Totti, Pompilio: *Ristretto delle Grandezze di Roma,* Rome, 1637.

TOTTI, 1638 Totti, P.: *Ritratto di Roma Moderna,* Rome, 1638.

VALCANOVER Valcanover, Francesco: *Tutta La Pittura di Tiziano,* Milan, 1960.

VALENTI Valenti, Silvio: *Ritratto di Roma moderna,* Rome, 1750.

VASI Vasi, Giuseppe: *Indice Istorico del Gran Prospetto di Roma,* Naples, 1770 (Dedication dated 1765).

VERTUE Vertue, George: *Notebooks,* published in 6 vols., by the Walpole Society, London, 1930 and f.

VILLOSLADA Villoslada, Riccardo G., S.J.: *Storia del Collegio Romano,* Rome, 1954.

VISCONTI Visconti, Pietro Ercole: *Città e Famiglie Nobili e Celebri delle Stato Ponteficio: Dizionario Storico,* Rome, 1843–7.

VOLPE, 1962 Volpe, Carlo: entries for Francesco Albano in the catalogue of the 1962 Bologna Exhibition, *L'Ideale Classico del Seicento in Italia e la Pittura del Paesaggio,* pp. 125–49.

VOSS Voss, Hermann: *Die Malerei des Barock in Rom,* Berlin, 1924.

WAAGEN Waagen, G. F.: *Die Gemäldesammlungen in der Kaiserlichen Ermitage zu St. Petersburg,* Munich, 1864.

WAAGEN Waagen, G. F.: *Treasures of Art in Great Britain,* London, 1854–7.

WATERHOUSE, 1937 Waterhouse, Ellis K.: *Baroque Painting in Rome,* London, 1937.

WATERHOUSE, 1963 Waterhouse, Ellis K.: *Italian Baroque Painting,* London, 1963.

WEISBACH Weisbach, Werner: *Die Kunst des Barock in Italien, Frankreich, Deutschland und Spanien,* Berlin, 1924.

WIBIRAL Wibiral, Norbert: 'A Proposito di Andrea Sacchi Architetto', *Palladio,* 1955, pp. 56–65.

WICKHOFF Wickhoff, Franz: 'Die Italienischen Handzeichnungen'; Part II, *J.K.A.K.,* XIII, Vienna, 1898, nos. 103–40.

WITTKOWER, 1952 Wittkower, Rudolf: *Carracci Drawings in the Royal Library at Windsor Castle,* London, 1952.

WITTKOWER, 1955 Wittkower, R.: *The Sculptures of Gian Lorenzo Bernini,* London, 1955.

WITTKOWER, 1958 Wittkower, R.: *Art and Architecture in Italy, 1600–1750,* Harmondsworth, 1958.

WRIGHT Wright, E.: *Some Observations made in travelling through France, Italy . . .,* London, 1730.

ZERI Zeri, Federico: *La Galleria Spada in Roma,* Florence, 1953.

ZERI, 1959 Zeri, F.: *La Galleria Pallavicini in Roma, Catalogo dei Dipinti,* Florence, 1959.

Sources of Photographs

Albertina, Vienna, 175, 176
Alinari, Florence, 8, 41, 49, 90, 91
De Antonis, Rome, 15, 17, 19

Musée de Besançon, 50
Biblioteca Ambrosiana, Milan, 11, 12
Bibliothèque Nationale, Paris, 129, 167, 171, 178, 179
British Museum, London, 174

Comune de Genova, 87
The Cooper-Hewitt Museum of Design, New York, 27
Courtauld Institute of Art, London, Fig. 2, 10, 26, 53, 68, 135, 166, 168

Deutsche Fotothek Dresden, 45
Dulwich College Picture Gallery, London, 86

R. B. Fleming and Co. Ltd, London, 62, 69
Foto-Manso, Madrid, 158

Gabinetto Fotografico, Florence, 55
Gabinetto Fotografico Nazionale, Rome, 4, 24, 28, 29, 30, 31, 33, 34, 36, 44, 51, 52, 54, 57, 61, 75, 76, 77, 81, 83, 84, 88, 128, 130, 133, 150, 151

Hessisches Landesmuseum, Darmstadt, 16

Den Kongelige Kobberstik Samling, Copenhagen, 125, 148
Kunsthistorisches Museum, Vienna, 146

Landesbildstelle Rheinland, Düsseldorf, 2, 14, 18, 22, 23, 32, 56, 70, 71, 85, 124, 136, 138, 149, 177

Hermitage, Leningrad, 173

Giorgio Liverani, Forlì, 48
Louvre, Paris, 155, 169

National Gallery, London, 6
National Gallery of Canada, Ottawa, 46, 47
Nationalmuseum, Stockholm, 40
National Museum, Valletta, 153
National Museum of Wales, Cardiff, 42

R. J. Paté, Caen-Venoix, 58
Phaidon Press Archives, 9, 142
Museo del Prado, Madrid, 1, 20, 43, 59, 60, 74

Rheinisches Bildarchiv, Cologne, 137
F. Rigamonti, Rome, 5, 35, 37, 38, 39, 79, 80, 92, 93, 95, 96, 98, 99, 101, 102, 103, 104, 105, 106, 107, 108, 110, 111, 113, 114, 116, 117, 118, 119, 120, 121, 122, 123, 127, 152, 157
Royal Academy of Arts, London, 89

Oscar Savio, Rome, 67
Service de documentation photographique de la réunion des musées nationaux, Paris, 7
Soprintendenza ai Monumenti e alle Gallerie dell' Umbria, Perugia, 154
Staatliche Museen, East Berlin, 134, 145
Walter Steinkopf, Berlin-Dahlem, 126, 131

Vasari, Rome, 78
Archivio fotografico, Musei Vaticani, 63, 64, 65, 66, 94, 97, 100, 109, 112, 115

PLATES

INDEX

Index of Names

Abbatini, Guidobaldo, 85

Agostini, Leonardo, 36, 84, 123

Albani, Francesco, 1–2, 3, 4, 5, 17, 22, 26, 27, 29, 35–6, 38 (note 11), 39 (note 30), 45 (note 70), 49, 56, 62, 64, 73, 77–8, 82, 94, 95, 110; Plate 74

Albers, Josef, 40 (note 56)

Alberti, Giovanni, 118, 126

Alberti, Leon Battista, 26, 36

Aldobrandini, Olimpia, 97

Aldobrandini, Cardinal Pietro, 29, 43 (note 22)

Alexander VII, Pope (Fabio Chigi), 23, 42 (note 104), 57, 58, 61, 65, 68, 101, 107, 109

Alexander VIII, Pope, 57

Alessandrino, Appiano, 124

Algardi, Alessandro, 2, 26, 31, 32, 35, 36, 44 (notes 35, 45), 45 (notes 57, 67), 46 (note 77), 62, 79, 97

Aliamet, F., 54; Plate 18

Allegrini, Francesco, 31, 57

Almada, Francesco di, 72

Altieri family, 49, 127

Altomonte, Bartolomeo, 102

Anconio, Mario, 51

Andrea del Sarto, 2, 84

Andreini, Francesco, 123

Angeli, Filippo d', 2, 39 (note 27)

Angelis, Desiderio de, 72, 87, 88, 89

Angelotti, Pompeo, 91

Anne of Austria, 94

Antiveduto Grammatica, 2, 14, 41 (note 82)

Antonelli, Vincenzo, 72

Archibusieri, Rev. Clement Reginald, 61

Aristotle, 36

Arnaldi, Conte Enea, 83

Arpino, Cesare d', 1, 2, 3, 5, 15, 16, 26, 27, 29, 41 (notes 84, 85), 45 (note 68), 126, 127

Ashburnham, Lord, 89

Audran, Charles, 101–2; Plates 167, 171

Audran, Gérard, 103, 104; Plates 178, 179

Aurelio, Ludovico, 81

Avila, Enrico Caterino d', 123

Baldinucci, Filippo, 24, 44 (note 52), 52, 91, 93, 94, 108, 124

Balducci, Giovanni, 4, 39 (note 20)

Baglione, Giovanni, 2, 31, 43 (note 19), 44 (note 31), 51, 57, 67, 74, 80, 87

Bamboccianti, 26, 27, 28, 36

Il Bamboccio (Pieter van Laer), 28, 45 (note 70), 105, 113, 114

Barberini family, 5, 9, 11, 13, 18, 26, 30, 36, 41 (note 76), 45 (note 62), 51, 52, 58, 62, 66, 75, 76, 80, 83, 86, 89, 90, 92, 94, 96, 98, 104–5, 106, 108, 113

Barberini, Cardinal Antonio, 5, 13, 15, 23, 24, 32, 42 (note 105), 43 (note 116), 44 (note 44), 56, 59, 60, 63, 64, 65, 66, 68, 70, 71, 74, 75, 76, 78, 79, 80, 81, 82, 83, 84, 87, 88, 89, 90, 93, 94, 95, 96, 100, 102, 103, 104–5, 106, 107, 118, 124, 126, 127, 128; Plates 138, 139

Barberini, Cardinal Antonio the Elder, 90, 94; Plate 140

Barberini, Cardinal Antonio the Younger, 71, 82, 104

Barberini, Cardinal Carlo, 59, 65, 70, 84, 88, 94, 96, 104, 107, 124

Barberini, Carlo Francesco, 105

Barberini, Cornelia Costanza, 96

Barberini, Cardinal Francesco, 7, 18, 25, 39 (note 28), 45 (note 57), 63, 65, 70, 90, 93–4, 96, 102, 104, 105, 107, 124; Plates 131, 132, 136, 137

Barberini, Maffeo, see Urban VIII, Pope

Barberini, Prince Maffeo, 60, 75, 78, 90, 106, 107

Barberini, Taddeo, 39 (notes 27, 28), 58, 59, 90, 92–3, 99, 124; Plate 141

Barocci, Federico, 3, 4, 5, 31

Baronius, 123

Bassano, Francesco, 2, 29

Basso, Domenico, 118

Batoni, Pompeo, 67, 68

Battista, 43 (note 22)

Bellori, Giovanni Pietro, 1, 2, 3, 4, 5, 6, 8, 11, 14, 15, 17, 19, 21, 23, 25, 26, 27, 28, 29, 30, 36, 38 (notes 2, 8), 39 (notes 22, 32, 37), 40 (notes 46, 50), 41 (notes 73, 90), 42 (notes 102, 105, 110, 112), 43 (note 19), 44 (note 27), 45 (notes 66, 68–70), 49, 50, 53, 54, 56, 57, 58, 59, 63, 64, 65, 66, 68, 71, 76, 77–8, 79, 80–1, 82, 83, 84, 86, 87, 88, 90, 91, 96, 98, 99, 100, 101, 103, 106, 107, 109, 123, 126–7, 128

Benedetti, Elpidio, 42 (note 106)

Benedict XIV, Pope, 57

Bentivoglio, Cardinal Guido, 74, 103

Berettini, Luca, 54

Berettoni, Niccolò, 127

Bergamo, Fra Giacomo Filippo da, 125

Berka, Count, 63, 94

Bernini, Domenico, 52

Bernini, Gian Lorenzo, 2, 7, 8, 16, 19, 25, 26, 27, 30–3, 36, 39 (note 38), 43 (notes 24, 25), 44 (notes 26, 34–7, 44, 50, 52–4), 51–2, 57, 59–60, 74, 80, 85, 86, 108, 118, 126, 127

Biscia, Cardinal Lelio, 39 (note 28), 62, 113

Blanchet, Horace, 42 (note 106)

Blanchet, Thomas, 42 (note 106)

Bloemart, Cornelius, 93, 94, 101, 102–3, 124; Plates 132, 139, 140, 141, 166, 172, 174

Boccaccio, Giovanni, 36, 123

Bol, Hans, 76

Bolgi, 16, 74

Bombelli, P. L., 32, 72, 73, 87, 88, 89

Bonanni, 57, 74

Bonone, Carlo, 50

Bonvicino, Ambrogio, 31

Borghese, Cardinal Scipione, 29

Borro, Alessandro dal, 108

Borromini, Francesco, 26, 75, 80, 81, 126

Borrus, Cristoforo, 69

Bottari, Giovanni, 1, 51

Bottugli family, 107

Bourbon, Petit & Dambrun, 61

Boydell, 109

Braccese, Alessandro, 124

Bracciano, Duke of, 76

Bracciolini, Francesco, 94

Bracese, Abbate, 118

Bragge, Dr, 66

Brahe, Tycho, 12

Brandi, Giacinto, 42 (note 113), 69, 98

Brettingham, Matthew, 75, 96

Brill, 114

Brizio, Francesco, 2, 38 (note 4), 128

Brunelleschi, 26

Buontalenti, 69

Buonvisi, Cardinal Girolamo, 91

Burchett, Josiah, 89

Buti, F., 43 (note 116)

Calandra, G. B., 60, 61; Plates 35, 37–9

Camassei, Andrea, 6, 9, 26, 38 (note 7), 40 (note 45), 44 (notes 28, 29), 53, 57, 67, 84, 85, 86, 87, 93, 102, 109, 110; Plates 97, 100

Campanella, Angelo, 72

Campanella, Tommaso, 41 (note 76)

Campori, 97, 98

Caporali, Cesare, 124
Caporali, F., 43 (note 116)
Caracciolo, 2
Caravaggio, 5, 23, 26, 28, 29, 38 (notes 6–8), 43 (note 19), 62, 67
Carpi, Girolamo da, 43 (note 22)
Carpioni, Giulio, 109
Carracci family, 1, 2, 74
Carracci school, 3
Carracci, Agostino, 2, 5, 17, 45 (note 66), 106, 126, 128
Carracci, Annibale, 2, 4, 5, 19, 22, 23, 24, 26, 27, 28, 29, 35, 38 (notes 13, 15), 39 (notes 17, 26), 42 (note 111), 45 (note 68), 46 (note 77), 49
Carracci, Ludovico, 2, 4, 5, 38 (note 13), 39 (note 17), 41 (note 88), 49, 56
Cartari, Vincenzo, 36, 124
Casone, Antonio, 50
Castelli, Domenico, 85, 86, 87
Castiglione, Baldassare, 5
Catherine the Great, Empress of Russia, 63, 109
Cavedone, Giacomo, 2, 14, 41 (note 83), 128
Cerquozzi, Michelangelo, 45 (note 70), 105, 113, 114, 118, 126
Cerrini, Gian Domenico, 31
Chantelou, 40 (note 45), 91
Chasteau, Guillaume, 103, 104; Plate 177
Chaveau, François, 103, 104
Chiari, Giuseppe, 127
Chigi, Agostino, 58
Chigi, Fabio, see Alexander VII, Pope
Christina, Queen of Sweden, 75, 76
Ciampelli, Agostino, 2, 31, 39 (note 20), 44 (note 29), 57
Cigoli, Ludovico, 2, 5, 10, 15–16, 38 (notes 6, 8), 39 (note 20)
Cirni, Antonfrancesco, 124
Claude Lorrain, 40 (note 45), 84
Clement VIII, Pope, 85
Clement IX, Pope, see Rospigliosi, Giulio
Clement X, Pope, 44 (note 31), 57
Clement XIII, Pope, 57
Clouet, Hubert, 92
Coccapani, Sigismondo, 39 (note 20)
Colladus, Didacus, 69
Collaert, Abraham, 76
Collignon, François, 98
Colonna di Sciarra, Giulio Cesare, 96
Contarini, Luigi, 123
Conti, Prince de, 63
Copernicus, 12
Coraggioso, Ambrogio, 76, 126
Correggio, 17, 20, 28, 29, 40 (note 55), 41 (note 87), 73, 74, 126, 127
Cortese, Guglielmo, 72, 103
Cortona, Pietro da, 2, 4–5, 6, 8–9, 10, 13, 17–18, 19, 20, 21, 25, 26, 27–8, 29, 33, 34–5, 36, 38 (note 10), 39 (notes 27, 32–6), 40 (notes 43, 45, 64), 42 (notes 109, 112), 45, (notes 57, 58, 61, 62, 64, 68), 49, 54–5, 58, 59, 64, 80, 94, 98, 101, 108
Cosellini, Giuliano, 124
Coypel, 104

Cozza, 40 (note 63)
Crasso, 108
Cristofano, Giovanni, 91–2, 94
Crozat, Louis-Antoine, 54, 63

Da Fano, Bartollomeo Dionigi, 124
Dati, Giorgio, 123
De Cotte, 61, 69, 70, 75, 81, 96
Dell'Abbate, Niccolò, 43 (note 22)
Della Bella, Stefano, 39 (note 20)
Della Greca, Vincenzo, 45 (note 58)
Della Marra, Vincenzo, 95
Della Rovere, Guido Ubaldo Bonarelli, 124
Dell'Aqua, Cristoforo, 83
Del Monte, Cardinal Francesco Maria, 1, 2, 3, 4, 5, 12, 13, 14, 38 (notes 6–8), 39 (notes 16, 22), 41 (note 82), 49, 50, 51, 52, 53–4, 62, 82, 106
De Pester, Mr, 83
Dériset, 101
Dezailler d'Argenville, 37
Domenichi, Ludovico, 124
Domenichino, 5, 6, 7–8, 10, 17, 18, 19–20, 22, 23–4, 25, 26, 27, 28, 29, 35, 39 (notes 32, 34–6), 41 (note 89), 42 (note 110), 43 (note 15), 45 (notes 66, 68), 77, 107, 109
Dossi, Dosso, 43 (note 22), 105, 106
Du Bois, Jean Baptiste, 76
Dufresnoy, Alphonse, 40 (note 45)
Duquesnoy, Francesco, 5, 7, 8, 15, 16, 24, 26, 27, 31, 32, 33, 36, 39 (note 25), 40 (note 46), 43 (note 24), 44 (notes 35–7), 45 (note 64), 71, 74, 128
Durante, Castore, 124
Dürer, Albrecht, 2
Dyck, Sir Anthony van, 25, 82, 103

Eggenberg, Prince von, 58
Ensenada, Marquis de la, 55
Erithreus, 65
Este family, 32
Evelyn, John, 44 (note 37)

Falconieri, Paolo, 78
Fantetti, Cesare, 98
Farnese family, 42 (note 111), 45 (note 68)
Félibien, 40 (note 45)
Ferrari, G. B., 75, 101, 102, 103, 123, 124
Ferri, Ciro, 54
Fidani, Orazio, 108
Fidanza, Prospero, 118, 124, 126, 127
Filippini, Prior, 32, 44 (note 50)
Filippo, Padre, 118, 126
Fiorentino, Remigio, 123
Fiori, Mario de', 97, 114
Florisello, Don, 124
Fontana, Cav. Domenico, 124
Frangi, Lavinia, 118
Frangi, Pietro Paolo, 118, 124, 127
Frederick II, King of Prussia, 96
Frederick Augustus II, Elector of Saxony, 96
Frey, Jacob, 61, 98
Frezza, Girolamo, 77

Furini, Francesco, 39 (note 20)
Furnese, Henry, 83, 89

Gaburri, Margharita, 118, 126–7
Gaetano, Cardinal Luigi, 84, 91–2
Gaetano, Pirro, 95
Gagliardi, Filippo, 74, 75, 78–9, 90–1, 110
Galileo, 12, 39 (note 22), 84
Galimberti, S., 85, 86
Garofalo, 43 (note 22)
Garzi, Luigi, 42 (notes 106, 109), 43 (note 15)
Gaulli, G. B., 10, 25, 26, 40 (note 64), 62
Gentile, Luigi, 127
Gentile, Piergirolamo, 125
Gentileschi, Artemisia, 110
Gerardi, Antonio, 44 (note 44), 81, 90
Gerardini, Giovanni, 58
Gherardi, Antonio, 109
Giamberti, Giuseppe, 118
Giampè family, 98–9
Gianni, 62
Giaquinto, Corrado, 56
Gimignani, Giacinto, 21, 26, 84, 85, 86, 87, 98, 102; Plate 94
Ginnasi, Caterina, 63, 110
Ginnasi, Cardinal Domenico, 62–3, 110
Giordano, Luca, 108
Giorgetti, Antonio, 46 (note 77)
Giorgione, 43 (note 19)
Giori, Cardinal Angelo, 62, 63, 74, 80, 87, 88, 90, 92, 95; Plate 135
Giotto, 25
Girardon, 39 (note 25)
Gismondi, 108
Giulio Romano, 20
Giustiniani family, 29, 102
Gonzalez, B., 50
Granberg, 76
Gratiani, Innocenza, 90
Gratiani, Maria, 90
Gregory XIII, Pope, 85, 87
Gregory XV, Pope, 26
Greppi, G. B., 42 (note 109), 67, 68
Greuter, Frederic, 101, 103
Grimaldi, G. F., 36, 46 (note 77), 97, 105, 109
Guercino, 2, 3, 5, 26, 28, 39 (note 27), 40 (note 55), 43 (note 1), 57, 82, 98, 99
Guglieli, Paolo, 62
Guidotti, Paolo, 44 (note 29), 57

Halifax, Lord, 96
Hamilton, Captain, 72
Hortemels, Frederic, 75, 76; Plate 68
Howard, 106

Iacoboni, G. B., 91; Plate 129
Ingoni, G. B., 82
Innocent X, Pope, 26, 45 (note 62), 86, 97

Jarvis, Mr, 83

Kepler, Johann, 12

La Barrière, J. D. de, 109

Laer, Pieter van, *see* Il Bamboccio
Lagi, Simone, 79, 87
Lanfranco, 2, 3, 4, 5, 6, 7, 8, 10, 14, 17, 24, 26, 29, 38 (notes 10, 13), 39 (notes 27, 32, 34, 37, 38), 40 (notes 45, 55, 64), 41 (notes 80, 88), 42 (note 106), 45 (notes 66, 68), 55, 57, 60, 67, 71, 73, 98
Lante, Cardinal Marcello, 50, 100
Lanzi, 25
Lauri, Baldassare, 39 (note 24), 42 (note 109)
Lauri, Filippo, 5, 39 (note 24), 42 (note 109)
Lauri, Francesco, 24, 39 (note 24), 42 (note 109)
Le Blanc, 42 (note 106)
Le Dreux, M., 63
Leggeri, 60
Leicester, Earl of, 75, 96
Le Moyne, Pierre, 42 (note 105), 101, 103, 104
Lempereur, 54
Leonardo da Vinci, 2, 36
Leone, Andrea de, 67, 102
Leone, Corporal, 7, 40 (note 44)
Leoni, Ottavio, 2, 54, 62, 93
Leopold Wilhelm, Prince, 53, 95, 96, 110
Le Pautre, J., 104
Liart, 109
Liberati, Francesco, 124
Liechtenstein, Prince of, 63
Lincoln, Earl of, 54
Locatelli, Pietro, 61
Lomazzo, 36
Loth, J. C., 89
Louis XIII, King of France, 94, 102
Louis XIV, King of France, 102
Ludovisi family, 29
Ludovisi, Cardinal Ludovico, 104
Luini, Tommaso, 24, 42 (note 109), 55, 67, 99; Plate 51
Luti, Benedetto, 109
Luti, Caterina, 127
Luti, Francesco, 118, 126, 127
Luti, Giovanni Battista, 118, 126, 127
Luti, Vittoria, 118, 127

Magnone, Carlo, 20, 21, 65, 70, 76, 78, 85, 86, 87, 91, 94-5, 105, 106, 113; Plate 115
Malvasia, Carlo Cesare, 2, 28, 42 (note 112), 45 (note 70), 46 (note 77), 77, 106, 126, 128
Mancini, 39 (notes 27, 34)
Manfredi, 67
Manucci, Eufrasia, 118, 126, 127
Manucci, Marc Antonio, 118, 126, 127
Manucci, Pietro Paolo, 118, 126, 127
Maratta, Carlo, 20, 21, 23, 24, 25, 27, 32, 34, 35, 36-7, 38 (note 2), 40 (note 46), 41 (note 92), 42 (notes 102, 105, 108-10), 45 (notes 66, 70), 49, 51, 54, 59, 60, 64, 66, 68, 70, 72, 75, 76, 77, 78, 79, 81, 83, 84, 85, 86, 87, 88, 89, 90, 91, 93, 94, 95, 96, 97, 100-1, 103-4, 106-8, 109, 110, 118, 124, 126,

127, 128; Plates 103-6, 109, 112, 175, 176
Maratta, Faustina, 93
Marcaccioni family, 32
Marcaccioni, Gaspar, 44 (note 50), 118, 127, 128
Marchelli, Domenico, 62
Mariette, P. J., 83, 102, 104, 114
Marilli, Iacomo, 124
Marino, Cavaliere Giovanni Battista, 124, 125
Marucelli, Paolo, 80
Masaccio, 25
Mascardi, Vitale, 13, 74
Mascherino, 77
Mazarin, Cardinal, 42 (note 106), 61, 88, 95, 96, 105, 109
Mazzolino, 43 (note 22)
Medici, Prince Leopold de', 78
Medici, Prince Mattias de', 108
Mellan, Claude, 103
Méréville, Laforde de, 72
Merlini, Clemente, 12, 39 (note 28), 62, 64-5, 66, 94, 95, 110, 128; Plate 49
Methuen, Sir Paul, 97
Metzger, 62
Michelangelo, 2
Miel, Jan, 24, 60, 90, 91
Mignard, Nicolas, 40 (note 45)
Mocchi, 16, 74
Mola, Pier Francesco, 25, 42 (note 113), 100, 110
Moroni, 45 (note 57)
Muziano, Girolamo, 2, 14, 29, 43 (note 23), 69

Naldini, Pietro Paolo, 32, 44 (notes 45, 48, 50), 118, 126, 127
Napoletano, Filippo, 53
Natalis, Michael, 58
Neri, Pietro Martire, 45 (note 57)
Normand, C., 62

Oliva, Padre, 25
Omodei, Cardinal Luigi, 63
Orleans, Duke of, 71-2, 75
Orsini, 82
Ortolano, 43 (note 22)

Pagnino, 124
Palladio, Andrea, 20, 26
Pallavicini family, 96
Pallavicini, Cardinal Lazzaro, 65
Pallavicini, Prince Niccolò, 65, 83, 84, 96
Pallavicino, Sforza, 12-13
Palma Giovane, 29, 43, (note 23), 61
Pamphili family, 86, 97
Pamphili, Prince Camillo, 97
Pamphili, Prince Giovanni Battista, *see* Innocent X, Pope
Panciroli, 50, 93, 94
Pannini, G. P., 77
Pascoli, Leone, 24, 33, 42 (notes 106, 109), 43 (notes 15, 24), 44 (note 48), 50, 76, 83, 87, 100, 101, 127
Pasqualini, Marcantonio, 46 (note 73), 55, 82-4, 91, 118, 127; Plate 89

Passeri, Giovanni Battista, 1, 2, 5, 6, 7, 11, 17, 19, 23, 25, 27, 31, 38 (note 8), 40 (notes 50, 55), 41, (note 72), 42 (notes 102, 115), 44 (note 35), 49, 50, 53, 58, 61, 71, 73, 78, 81, 86, 87, 96, 97, 100, 101, 126, 128
Passeri, Giuseppe, 83, 94
Passignano, Domenico, 39 (note 20)
Paul III, Pope, 85
Pellegrini, Carlo, 59, 60
Pellegrini, Nicola, 1, 118, 127
Pernetti, 42 (note 106)
Perrier, 42 (note 106)
Perugino, Paolo, 108
Petronius, Alexander Trajanus, 123
Philip II, King of Spain, 103
Philip IV, King of Spain, 69
Philip V, King of Spain, 49, 64, 72, 77
Picart, Stephanus, 77
Piccione, 68
Pietri, Pietro de', 55, 77, 83
Pietro Leopoldo, Archduke of Austria, 87
Pilsen, Franz, 76-7; Plate 70
Pinarolo, 49
Pius VIII, Pope, 57
Pliny, 36
Plutarch, 36, 124
Po, Pietro del, 40 (note 49), 56
Polidoro da Caravaggio, 1, 2, 6, 42 (note 110), 45 (note 61)
Pomarancio, Antonio, 31, 44 (note 29), 57
Pond, Mr, 72, 106
Postiglioni, Bartolomeo, 102, 118, 127
Poussin, Nicolas, 2, 5, 6, 7-8, 15, 16, 18-19, 21, 22, 23, 24, 25, 26, 27, 28, 29, 35, 36, 39 (notes 27, 40), 40 (notes 43, 45, 46, 49, 55), 43 (note 15), 45 (notes 65, 68), 46 (note 75), 58, 83, 84, 91, 102
Pozzi, Francesco, 73
Pozzo, Cassiano dal, 6, 7, 21, 36, 39 (note 42), 45 (note 72)
Pozzo, Helena dal, 127
Preti, Girolamo, 124
Preti, Mattia, 31, 98
Puglia, Giuseppe ('Il Bastoro'), 80
Pulzone, Scipione, 2

Radziwill, Prince, 94
Raphael, 1, 2, 3, 4, 5, 6, 7, 8, 10, 19-20, 22, 24, 26, 27, 35, 39 (note 30), 40 (note 62), 42 (note 102), 43 (note 15), 45 (note 61), 49, 83, 86, 113
Raynaldo, Oderico, 123
Rembrandt, 41 (note 91)
Rendorp, 96
Reni, Guido, 2, 5, 21, 26, 31, 38 (notes 13, 14), 57, 63, 69, 82, 95, 101, 106, 110
Rezzonico, Cardinal, 85
Ribera, Giuseppe, 2, 25, 39 (note 21), 66
Riccardi, Niccolò ('Padre Mostro'), 81, 84
Ricci, Giovanni Giacomo, 125
Ricci, Ludovico, 123

Richardson, Jonathan, 58, 61, 97, 128
Richelieu, Cardinal, 40 (note 55), 58, 94
Ripa, Cesare, 11–12, 40 (notes 60, 65), 41 (notes 72, 73)
Roisecco, 82
Romanelli, Francesco, 14, 26, 39 (note 35), 45 (note 57), 57, 60, 70, 86, 98, 103, 104, 109
Rosa, Salvator, 109
Rospigliosi family, 84, 96
Rospigliosi, Felice, 96
Rospigliosi, Cardinal Giulio, 65, 83, 84, 95–6
Rosselli, Matteo, 39 (note 20)
Rossetti family, 102
Rossetti, Cardinal Carlo, 102
Rossi, Lorenzo Filippo de', 71
Rossi, Luigi, 83
Rossi, Pasqualino de', 108
Rossini, Pietro, 74, 94
Rubens, Peter Paul, 4, 46 (note 75)
Ruffo, Marchese Antonio, 42 (note 112), 71, 95, 96

Sacchetti family, 29, 39 (note 33), 54
Sacchi, Benedetto, 1, 38 (note 6), 127
Sacchi, Giuseppe, 38 (note 1), 42 (note 106), 128
Sagredo, Niccolò, 107
San Giovanni, Giovanni da, 39 (note 20)
Sannazaro, Iacopo, 124
Saraceni, Carlo, 2, 108
Sarbiewski, 41 (note 76)
Sassoferrato, 26
Savelli, Federico, 95
Savonanzi, Emilio, 57, 65, 108
Scanaroli family, 98
Scanaroli, Alessandro, 98
Scanaroli, Cavaliere Camillo, 99
Scanaroli, Giovanni Battista, 99
Scaramuccia, 36
Scarsellino, 43 (note 22)
Scilla, Agostino, 42 (note 106)
Sebastiano del Piombo, 41 (note 85)

Segneri, Fabio, 51
Segneri, Francesco, 51
Seignelay, Marquis de, 63
Seiter, Daniele, 110
Sheffield, Sir Thomas, 83
Silos, 93
Silvestre, Israel, 43 (note 116)
Simonneau, Charles, 104
Solimena, 56
Soria, 45 (note 57), 62
Spencer, Lord, 83
Speranza, G. B., 80
Spinola family, 102
Spinola, Carlo, 102
Stanislas, King of Poland, 81
Stanzione, Massimo, 109
Stefanoni, Pietro, 124
Stella, Claudine Bouzonnet, 46 (note 75)
Stella, Jacques, 2
Sus, Francesco, 74
Strange, Robert, 83
Strozzi, Bernardo, 25, 62, 95
Stomer, 109
Sustermans, 108

Tacitus, 36, 123
Tassi, 40 (note 55)
Tasso, Torquato, 36, 124
Tavistock, Lord, 82
Tempesta, Antonio, 2, 124
Testa, Pietro, 6, 7, 8, 24, 36, 39 (note 36), 40 (note 49), 42 (notes 98, 111), 91
Teti, Girolamo, 11, 58, 74, 75, 81, 93, 94, 124
Tiarini, 108
Tiepolo, Giovanni Battista, 108
Tinelli, Tiberio, 108
Tintoretto, 29, 64
Titi, Abbate Filippo, 42 (note 106), 44 (note 31), 67, 77, 82, 87, 106
Titian, 2–3, 4, 5, 6, 10, 28, 29, 31, 81, 106
Todesca, Margharita, 118, 127–8
Tonci, 82

Torelli, Iacopo, 43 (note 116)
Totti, 50, 79
Trasi, Lodovico, 108
Trevisani, Francesco, 56
Turchi, Alessandro, 2, 110
Tursi, Fausto, 118

Unterberger, Christopher, 85, 87
Urban VIII, Pope (Maffeo Barberini), 16, 20, 26, 32, 40 (note 43), 44 (note 53), 50, 51, 52, 56, 59–60, 68, 70, 83, 84, 85, 86, 88, 90–1, 92, 94, 102, 108, 127; Plates 56, 101, 102, 130

Vaini, Abbot Carlo, 118, 126, 127, 128
Valentin, 64
Valguarnera, 5, 45 (note 72), 57, 58, 59, 66, 71
Vallée, Simon, 72
Vallet, Guillaume, 106
Vanni, G. B., 74
Varese, Ascanio, 91
Vasari, Giorgio, 30, 36, 43 (note 19), 46 (note 77)
Vecelli, Cesare, 124
Velazquez, 46 (note 75), 108
Venuti, Filippo, 124
Verdizotti, M. G. M., 123
Veronese, 17, 20, 28, 29, 126, 127
Vertue, 83
Vitruvius, 36
Volterrano, 108
Vouet, Simon, 2, 4, 6, 36, 39 (note 19), 41 (note 82), 46 (note 75)

Wadding, Lucas, 50
Walpole, Horace, 109
Wasa, Prince Alexander, 74
Westerhout, Arnold van, 100; Plate 156
Westmacott, Sir Richard, 61

Zampa, G. B., 65
Zeggin, Paul, 53
Zonghi-Lotti family, 99
Zuccaro, Federico, 29, 34, 43 (note 19)

Index of Places

ALTHORP HOUSE, Northamptonshire, Earl Spencer
  Portrait of the Singer Marc' Antonio Pasqualini, 82–4 (Cat. No. 51); Plate 89
ASCOLI PICENO, Pinacoteca Comunale
  Holy Family, 108 (Cat. No. R 1)
AUCKLAND, City Art Gallery
  The Vision of St. Romuald, 61 (Cat. No. 20)
AYNHOE PARK, Northants., Cartwright Collection (formerly)
  Christ Carrying the Cross, and St. Veronica, 72 (Cat. No. 36)
BAMBERG, Gallery
  St. Catherine of Siena in Prayer, 81 (Cat. No. 47)
BARI, Pinacoteca Provinciale
  Portrait of a Man, 108 (Cat. No. R 2)
BERLIN-DAHLEM, Staatliche Museen
  Drawings, 55 (Cat. No. 14), 88 (Cat. No. 57), 94 (Cat. No. 70); Plate 126

Portrait of Alessandro dal Borro, 108 (Cat. No. R 3)
BERLIN (EAST), Staatliche Museen
  The Drunkenness of Noah, 96 (Cat. No. 72); Plate 145
  Portrait of an Officer, 25, 95 (Cat. No. 71); Plate 134
BESANÇON, Musée des Beaux-Arts
  Drawing, 61 (Cat. No. 20)
  St. Peter, 66 (Cat. No. 28); Plate 50
BURGHLEY HOUSE, Northants. Marquess of Exeter
  An Allegory of the Church, The Last Supper, The Marriage at Cana, The Way to Calvary, 108 (Cat. No. R 4)
CAEN, Musée des Beaux-Arts
  The Suicide of Dido, 18–19, 24, 69 (Cat. No. 31); Plate 58
CAMERINO, Duomo
  St. Ansovinus Distributing Alms, 108 (Cat. No. R 5)
CAMERINO, S. Maria in Via
  St. Francis of Sales and St. Francis of Paula, 90 (Cat. No. 62); Plate 127

CARDIFF, National Museum of Wales
    Hagar and Ishmael in the Wilderness, 63 (Cat. No. 22); Plate 42,
      Col. Plate III
CASTELFUSANO, Villa Chigi, 6
    Allegory of the Four Seasons, 4, 54 (Cat. No. 13); Plate 15
    Romulus among the Shepherds, 54 (Cat. No. 13); Plate 17
    Sacrifice to Pan, 5, 54–5 (Cat. No. 13); Plate 19
    The Story of Cincinnatus, 54–5 (Cat. No. 13)
CATANZARO, Museo Provinciale
    The Drunkenness of Noah, 96 (Cat. No. 72); Plate 147
CHATSWORTH, Collection the Duke of Devonshire
    The Madonna and Child with Saints, 57 (Cat. No. 16)
    The Sacrifice of Noah, 109 (Cat. No. R 6)
CHIUDUNO, Chiesa Parrocchiale
    Assumption of the Virgin with Saints, 109 (Cat. No. R 7)
COLOGNE, Wallraf-Richartz Museum
    Portrait of Cardinal Francesco Barberini, 25, 93–4 (Cat. No.
      67–3); Plate 137
COPENHAGEN, Kobberstiksamling
    Drawings, 88 (Cat. No. 56), 97, 98 (Cat. No. 75); Plates
      125, 148
DARMSTADT, Hessisches Landesmuseum
    Drawings, 54–5 (Cat. No. 13); Plate 16
DRESDEN, Gemäldegalerie
    Head of an Old Man, 64 (Cat. No. 25); Plate 45
    Rest on the Flight into Egypt, 109 (Cat. No. R 8)
DÜSSELDORF, Kunstmuseum
    Drawings, 9, 50 (Cat. No. 6), 52 (Cat. No. 9), 54 (Cat. No.
      13), 55 (Cat. No. 14), 56 (Cat. No. 15), 58 (Cat. No. 17),
      59 (Cat. No. 18), 60 (Cat. No. 19a, 19b), 61 (Cat. No. 20),
      63 (Cat. No. 22), 64 (Cat. No. 26), 67 (Cat. No. 30), 69
      (Cat. Nos. 32, 33), 70 (Cat. Nos. 34, 35), 73 (Cat. Nos. 38,
      39), 75 (Cat. No. 41), 76 (Cat. No. 42), 78 (Cat. No. 45), 82
      (Cat. No. 50), 83 (Cat. No. 51), 85 (Cat. No. 53), 88 (Cat.
      Nos. 55–9), 89 (Cat. No. 60), 93 (Cat. No. 67–2), 95 (Cat.
      No. 72), 97 (Cat. No. 75), 98 (Cat. No. 76), 99 (Cat. No.
      78), 100 (Cat. No. 80), 105–6 (Cat. No. L 10), 107 (Cat.
      No. L 22); Plates, 2, 14, 22, 23, 32, 56, 70, 71, 85, 124,
      136, 138, 149, 177
FABRIANO, S. Niccolò
    St. John the Baptist in the Wilderness, 22, 98–9 (Cat. No. 76);
      Plate 152
FERRARA, S. Maria dei Teatini
    St. John the Baptist in the Wilderness, 98 (Cat. No. 76)
FLORENCE, Convent of San Salvi
    The Three Magdalenes, 13, 16, 67–9 (Cat. No. 30); Plate 55
FLORENCE, formerly Corsini Collection
    St. Francis marrying Poverty, 18–19, 24, 70 (Cat. No. 34);
      Plate 57
FLORENCE, R. Longhi Collection
    Madonna and Child with Saints, 57 (Cat. No. 16)
FLORENCE, Uffizi, Drawings, 18, 56 (Cat. No. 15), 57 (Cat.
    No. 16), 61 (Cat. No. 20), 75 (Cat. No. 41), 77 (Cat. No. 43),
    95 (Cat. No. 72), 100 (Cat. No. 80); Plates 21, 72
FOLIGNO, formerly Oratorio del Buon Gesù
    The Immaculate Conception, 100 (Cat. No. 79)
FONTE AVELLANA, Camaldolese abbey
    The Vision of St. Romuald, 61 (Cat. No. 20)
FORLÌ, Pinacoteca Comunale
    St. Peter, 13, 14, 15 64–5 (Cat. No. 26); Plate 48
GENOA, Galleria di Palazzo Rosso
    Daedalus and Icarus, 18–19, 22, 24, 81–2 (Cat. No. 49); Plate
      87
GHENT, formerly Du Bois collection
    The Adoration of the Shepherds, 76–7 (Cat. No. 42)
GREENVILLE, Bob Jones University Art Gallery
    St. Gregory, 109 (Cat. No. R 9)

HOLKHAM HALL, Earl of Leicester, Drawings, 66–7 (Cat.
    No. 29), 78–9 (Cat. No. 45); Plate 53
LENINGRAD, Hermitage Museum
    Drawings, 103 (Cat. No. 87); Plate 173
    La Divina Sapienza, 58 (Cat. No. 17)
    Hagar and Ishmael in the Wilderness, 63 (Cat. No. 22)
    Landscape with Venus Resting, 109 (Cat. No. R 10)
LISBON, Museu Nacional de Arte Antiga, Drawing, 60
    (Cat. No. 19c)
LONDON, Brian Sewell
    *The Madonna and Child with Saints Ignatius of Loyola, Francis
      Xavier, Cosmas and Damian*, 57 (Cat. No. 16); Plate 26, Col.
      Plate IV
LONDON, British Museum
    Drawings, 4, 15, 18 (Cat. No. 43), 52 (Cat. No. 9), 53 (Cat.
      No. 11), 54 (Cat. No. 13), 61 (Cat. No. 20), 67 (Cat. No.
      29), 70 (Cat. No. 35), 73 (Cat. No. 38), 77 (Cat. No. 43), 101
      (Cat. No. 83); Plates 10, 73, 156, 165
    An Allegory on the Birth of Urban VIII, 102 (Cat. No. 84)
LONDON, Dulwich College Picture Gallery
    St. Catherine of Siena, 81 (Cat. No. 47); Plate 86
LONDON, Denis Mahon collection
    The Baptism of Christ, 89 (Cat. No. 59)
    St. Anthony of Padua reviving a Dead Man, 15–16, 70–1 (Cat.
      No. 35); Plate 62
LONDON, National Gallery
    St. Anthony Abbot and St. Francis, 5, 30, 33, 51–2 (Cat. No.
      8); Plate 6
LONDON, Witt Collection
    Drawing, 102 (Cat. No. 85); Plate 168
LOS ANGELES, County Museum of Art
    The Vision of St. Romuald, 61 (Cat. No. 20)
LULWORTH, Dorset, Colonel Sir Joseph Weld
    Christ Carrying the Cross, and St. Veronica, 72 (Cat. No. 36)
MADRID, Academia de San Fernando
    Drawings, 23, 54 (Cat. No. 13), 100, 101 (Cat. No. 81);
      Plate 158
MADRID, Biblioteca Nacional
    Drawing, 50 (Cat. No. 6); Plate 3
MADRID, Museo del Prado
    The Birth of the Virgin, 6, 7, 15, 22, 55–6 (Cat. No. 14);
      Plate 20
    Copy after Annibale Carracci's *Christ Crowned with Thorns*, 49
      (Cat. No. 2); Plate 1
    A Lupercal, 109 (Cat. No. R 11)
    Portrait of Francesco Albani, 17, 77–8 (Cat. No. 44), 114;
      Plate 74
    St. Paul the Hermit and St. Anthony Abbot, 69 (Cat. No. 32);
      Plate 60
    Santa Rosalia Sinibaldi of Palermo, 69–70 (Cat. No. 33);
      Plate 59
MALAGA, Museo
    Head of an Apostle with a Book, 64 (Cat. No. 24); Plate 43
MILAN, Ambrosiana
    Drawings, 53 (Cat. No. 11), 64 (Cat. No. 26); Plates 11,
      12
MINNEAPOLIS, Institute of Arts
    Adam grieving over the Dead Abel, 75 (Cat. No. 41); Plate 69
    The Baptism of Christ, 89 (Cat. No. 59)
MONTREAL, Museum of Fine Arts
    The Rape of Europa, 109 (Cat. No. R 13)
NANCY, Musée des Beaux-Arts
    Pope Alexander VII Carried in Procession, 109 (Cat. No. R 14)
NETTUNO, S. Francesco
    *The Madonna of Loreto with St. Bartholomew, St. Joseph, St.
      James of Compostela and St. Francis*, 1, 2, 3, 5, 51 (Cat. No.
      7); Plate 5

262] INDEX OF PLACES

NEW YORK, Cooper Hewitt Museum
Drawing, 9–10, 12, 58 (Cat. No. 17); Plate 27
NEW YORK, Metropolitan Museum
Drawing, 102 (Cat. No. 85); Plate 169
NOTRE DAME, University
The Baptism of Christ, 89 (Cat. No. 59)
OLDENBURG, Gemäldegalerie
The Blind Belisarius, 109 (Cat. No. R 15)
ORLEANS, Musée des Beaux-Arts
The Raising of Lazarus, 109 (Cat. No. R 16)
OTTAWA, National Gallery of Canada
Portrait of a Cardinal, 25, 62–3 (Cat. No. 21); Plates 46, 47
OXFORD, Ashmolean Museum
Drawing, 101 (Cat. No. 83)
PARIS, Bibliothèque Nationale
An Allegory on the Birth of Urban VIII, 102 (Cat. No. 84)
PARIS, École des Beaux-Arts
Drawing, 52 (Cat. No. 9); Plate 7
PARIS, Louvre
Drawings, 61 (Cat. No. 20), 99 (Cat. No. 78), 102 (Cat. Nos. 85, 86); Plates 155, 170
PARIS, St. Germain l'Auxerrois
St. Gregory and the Miracle of the Corporal, 52 (Cat. No. 9)
PERUGIA, Galleria Nazionale dell'Umbria
The Presentation of Christ in the Temple, 22, 99–100 (Cat. No. 78); Plate 154
POMMERSFELDEN, Schönborn Collection
The Flight into Egypt, 109 (Cat. No. R 17)
POUGHKEEPSIE (N.Y.), Vassar College Art Gallery
Christ Carrying the Cross, and St. Veronica, 72 (Cat. No. 36)
RENNES, Musée de Rennes, Drawing, 88 (Cat. No. 56)
RIETI, Duomo
The Guardian Angel, 91 (Cat. No. 64); Plate 128
RIETI, S. Agnese
The Vision of St. Andrew, 109 (Cat. No. R 18)
RIETI, S. Scholastica
The Martyrdom of St. Andrew, 109 (Cat. No. R 19)
ROME, Accademia di S. Luca
Portrait of Francesco Albani, 77 (Cat. No. 44)
ROME, formerly Casa Sacchi
Portrait of Alexander VII, 101 (Cat. No. 82)
Portrait of Cardinal Francesco Maria del Monte, 53–4 (Cat. No. 12)
ROME, formerly Casino of Cardinal del Monte, 4, 6, 53 (Cat. No. 11)
ROME, Collegio Romano
The Madonna and Child with Saints Ignatius of Loyola, Francis Xavier, Cosmas and Damian, 6, 7, 57 (Cat. No. 16); Plate 24
ROME, Don Augusto Barberini
St. Anthony of Padua reviving a Dead Man, 70 (Cat. No. 35)
ROME, Galleria Borghese
Portrait of Monsignore Clemente Merlini, 25, 65–6 (Cat. No. 27); Plate 49
ROME, Galleria Nazionale d'Arte Antica
La Divina Sapienza, 4, 6, 7, 8–13, 18, 23, 25, 57–9 (Cat. No. 17); Plates 28–31, 33
Head of an Old Woman, 110 (Cat. No. R 21)
Portrait of a Cleric, 109 (Cat. No. R 20)
St. Leo the Great, 14, 60 (Cat. No. 19c); Plate 36
St. Peter, 13, 66 (Cat. No. 28); Plate 52
St. Thomas Aquinas with St. Peter and St. Paul, 13, 14, 60 (Cat. No. 19a); Plate 34
The Three Magdalenes, 68 (Cat. No. 30); Plate 54
Urban VIII visiting the Gesù, 90–1 (Cat. No. 63); Plates 130, 133
ROME, Lateran Palace
The Annunciation to Zacharias, 20–1, 87–8 (Cat. No. 54); Plate 116, Col. Plate I
The Baptism of Christ, 20–2, 88–9 (Cat. No. 59); Plate 121
The Beheading of the Baptist, 20–2, 89 (Cat. No. 61); Plate 123
The Birth of the Baptist, 20–2, 88 (Cat. No. 56); Plate 118
The Blessing of the Baptist before his Departure to the Wilderness, 20–2, 88 (Cat. No. 58); Plate 120
The Naming of the Baptist, 20–2, 88 (Cat. No. 57); Plate 119
The Preaching of the Baptist, 20–2, 89 (Cat. No. 60); Plate 122, Col. Plate II
The Visitation, 20–2, 88 (Cat. No. 55); Plate 117
ROME, Marchese Giovanni Incisa della Rochetta
La Divina Sapienza, 58 (Cat. No. 17)
The Vision of St. Romuald, 61 (Cat. No. 20)
ROME, Museo di Roma
The Festa del Saraceno in Piazza Navona, 74–5 (Cat. No. 40); Plate 67
Portrait of a Cardinal, 110 (Cat. No. R 22)
ROME, Palazzo Altieri
Copy after Raphael's Galatea, 49 (Cat. No. 1), 113
ROME, formerly Palazzo Barberini
Aurora, 94–5 (Cat. No. 70)
Christ's Command to St. Peter, 'Feed My Sheep!', 56–7 (Cat. No. 15)
Portrait of Francesco Bracciolini, 94 (Cat. No. 69)
Portrait of Ludovico Aurelio, 81 (Cat. No. 48)
Portrait of Padre Niccolò Riccardi, 84 (Cat. No. 52)
Portrait of Prince Radziwill, 94 (Cat. No. 68)
ROME, Palazzo Corsini
St. Anthony of Padua reviving a Dead Man, 70–1 (Cat. No. 35)
ROME, Palazzo del Quirinale
Christ Crowned with Thorns and the Transfiguration, 18, 77 (Cat. No. 43)
ROME, Palazzo Doria
Daedalus and Icarus, 82 (Cat. No. 49)
ROME, Palazzo Rospigliosi-Pallavicini
The Drunkenness of Noah, 96 (Cat. No. 72)
Head of an Apostle, 63–4 (Cat. No. 23); Plate 44
Portrait of Monsignore Clemente Merlini, 65 (Cat. No. 27)
The Scourging of Job, 110 (Cat. No. R 23)
ROME, Pinacoteca Vaticana
The Canonization of St. Anne, 110 (Cat. No. R 26)
The Vision of St. Romuald, 13, 14–15, 23, 25, 33, 61–2 (Cat. No. 20); Plate 41
ROME, S. Bernardino alle Terme
Portrait of the Blessed Jean Dominique de la Barrière, 110 (Cat. No. R 24)
ROME, S. Biagio alla Pagnotta
Virgin and Child with San Biagio (?), 110 (Cat. No. R 25)
ROME, S. Carlo ai Catinari
The Death of St. Anne, 21, 22, 23, 97–8 (Cat. No. 75); Plate 150
ROME, formerly S. Chiara alla Ciambella
The Virgin and Child with St. Joseph, 49–50 (Cat. No. 3)
ROME, San Giovanni in Fonte
The frescoed decoration of the Lateran Baptistry, 17, 19–22, 25, 27, 84–7 (Cat. No. 53); Plates 90–115
ROME, S. Giuseppe a Capo le Case
The Dream of St. Joseph, 100 (Cat. No. 80); Plate 157
ROME, formerly S. Giuseppe a Capo le Case
St. Teresa in Ecstasy, 50 (Cat. No. 4)
ROME, S. Isidoro
The Vision of St. Isidore the Farmer, 1, 2–3, 5, 50–1 (Cat. No. 6); Plate 4
ROME, San Luigi dei Francesi, 100–1 (Cat. No. 81)
ROME, S. Maria del Priorato
The Virgin and Child with St. Basil of Cappadocia, 82 (Cat. No. 50); Plate 88

ROME, S. Maria della Concezione
St. Anthony of Padua reviving a Dead Man, 13, 15–17, 31, 70–1 (Cat. No. 35); Plate 61
The Vision of St. Bonaventure, 17, 78–9 (Cat. No. 45); Plate 76
ROME, S. Maria in Via
A Miracle of St. Philip Benizzi, 66–7 (Cat. No. 29); Plate 51
ROME, S. Maria sopra Minerva
Christ crucified with St. Dominic, St. Thomas Aquinas, St. Peter Martyr, an unidentified Dominican Saint and St. Catherine of Siena, 18, 79 (Cat. No. 46); Plates 75, 77
Six Putti and an Angel carrying the Attributes of five Dominican Saints, 9, 17, 79–81 (Cat. No. 46); Plate 78
Room of St. Catherine of Siena, 17–18, 79–80 (Cat. No. 46); Plates 79–84
ROME, St. Peter's
Christ carrying the Cross, and St. Veronica, 13, 15, 16, 71–2 (Cat. No. 36); Plate 63
The Martyrdom of St. Longinus, 15, 16, 72–3 (Cat. No. 38); Plate 65
St. Andrew adoring the Cross of his Martyrdom, 15, 16, 72 (Cat. No. 37); Plate 64
St. Denys the Areopagite, 60 (Cat. No. 19d); Plate 39
St. Gregory and the Miracle of the Corporal, 3–4, 52 (Cat. No. 9); Plate 8
St. Helen and the Miracle of the True Cross, 16–17, 73–4 (Cat. No. 39); Plate 66
St. John Damascene, 60 (Cat. No. 19b); Plate 38
St. Leo the Great, 60 (Cat. No. 19c); Plate 37
St. Thomas Aquinas with St. Peter and St. Paul, 60 (Cat. No. 19a); Plate 35
ROME, formerly S. Urbano
St. Urban with St. Chiara and St. Francis, 50 (Cat. No. 5)

ROME, formerly Villa Doria Pamphili
Venus and Cupid, 97 (Cat. No. 73)
SAN MARINO, Calif., Huntington Library
Drawing, 75 (Cat. No. 41)
SCHLEISSHEIM, Staatsgalerie
The Rape of Europa, 110 (Cat. No. R 27)
STOCKHOLM, National Museum
Drawings, 14, 61 (Cat. No. 20), 100 (Cat. No. 80); Plate 40
VALLETTA, S. Maria della Vittoria
St. Philip Neri's Vision of St. John the Baptist, 99 (Cat. No. 77); Plate 153
VERSAILLES, Musée de Versailles et des Trianons
St. Bernard, 110 (Cat. No. R 28)
VIENNA, Albertina
Drawings, 58 (Cat. No. 17), 103 (Cat. No. 88); Plates 175, 176
VIENNA, Kunsthistorisches Museum
La Divina Sapienza, 58 (Cat. No. 17)
The Drunkenness of Noah, 95 (Cat. No. 72); Plate 146
The Dying Mother of Aristides, 110 (Cat. No. R 29)
Juno in her Peacock Chariot, 52–3 (Cat. No. 10); Plate 13
WILTON HOUSE, Collection of the Earl of Pembroke
Job with his Wife and Friends, 110 (Cat. No. R 30)
WINDSOR CASTLE, Royal Library
Drawings, 23, 38 (note 7), 52 (Cat. No. 9), 56 (Cat. No. 15), 57 (Cat. No. 16), 61 (Cat. No. 20), 67 (Cat. No. 30), 70 (Cat. No. 35), 71 (Cat. No. 36), 72 (Cat. Nos. 37, 38), 74 (Cat. No. 40), 79, 80 (Cat. No. 46), 85 (Cat. No. 53), 94 (Cat. No. 70), 95 (Cat. No. 72), 97 (Cat. No. 75), 98 (Cat. No. 76), 100, 101 (Cat. No. 81), 127; Plates 9, 25, 142, 144, 159–64

Index of Works

a. BIBLICAL SUBJECTS
Adam and Eve, 107–8 (Cat. No. L 29)
Adam grieving over the dead Abel, 18–19, 75–6 (Cat. No. 41); Plate 69
The Adoration of the Shepherds, 76–7 (Cat. No. 42)
The Annunciation to Zacharias, 20–1, 87–8 (Cat. No. 54); Plate 116, Col. Plate I
An Annunciation with Angels, 107 (Cat. No. L 28)
The Baptism of Christ, 20–2, 88–9 (Cat. No. 59); Plate 121
The Beheading of the Baptist, 20–2, 89 (Cat. No. 61); Plate 123
The Birth of the Baptist, 20–2, 88 (Cat. No. 56); Plate 118
The Blessing of the Baptist before his Departure to the Wilderness, 20–2, 88 (Cat. No. 58); Plate 120
Christ carrying the Cross, and St. Veronica, 13, 15, 16, 71–2 (Cat. No. 36); Plate 63
Christ crowned with Thorns (after Annibale Carracci), 49 (Cat No. 2); Plate 1
Christ crowned with Thorns and the Transfiguration, 18, 77 (Cat. No. 43)
Christ crucified with St. Dominic, St. Thomas Aquinas, St. Peter Martyr, an Unidentified Dominican Saint and St. Catherine of Siena, 18, 79 (Cat. No. 46); Plates 75, 77
Christ's Command to St. Peter, 'Feed My Sheep!', 56–7 (Cat. No. 15)
The Dream of St. Joseph, 22, 100 (Cat. No. 80); Plate 157
The Drunkenness of Noah, 24, 25, 95–7 (Cat. No. 72); Plates 144, 145, 146, 147
The Flight into Egypt, 109 (Cat. No. R 17)
Hagar and Ishmael in the Wilderness, 63 (Cat. No. 22); Plate 42, Col. Plate III

Head of an Apostle, 63–4 (Cat. No. 23); Plate 44
Head of an Apostle with a Book, 64 (Cat. No. 24); Plate 43
The Head of Christ, 106 (Cat. No. L 12)
Holy Family, 108 (Cat. No. R 1)
The Holy Family with St. John, 106 (Cat. No. L 13)
Job with his Wife and Friends, 110 (Cat. No. R 30)
The Last Supper, 108 (Cat. No. R 4)
The Magdalene, 106 (Cat. No. L 16)
The Marriage at Cana, 108 (Cat. No. R 4)
The Naming of the Baptist, 20–2, 88 (Cat. No. 57); Plate 119
The Preaching of the Baptist, 20–2, 89 (Cat. No. 60); Plate 122, Col. Plate II
The Presentation of Christ in the Temple, 22, 99–100 (Cat. No. 78); Plate 154
The Raising of Lazarus, 109 (Cat. No. R 16)
Rest on the Flight into Egypt, 109 (Cat. No. R 8)
The Sacrifice of Noah, 109 (Cat. No. R 6)
St. John the Baptist in the Wilderness, 22, 98–9 (Cat. No. 76); Plate 152
The Scourging of Job, 110 (Cat. No. R 23)
Two Apostles, 104 (Cat. No. L 1)
The Visitation, 20–2, 88 (Cat. No. 55); Plate 117
The Way to Calvary, 108 (Cat. No. R 4)

b. OTHER RELIGIOUS SUBJECTS
An Allegory of the Church, 108 (Cat. No. R 4)
The Assumption of the Virgin with St. Nicholas and St. Francis, 105–6 (Cat. No. L 10)
Assumption of the Virgin with Saints, 109 (Cat. No. R 7)

St. Andrew adoring the Cross of his Martyrdom, 15, 16, 72 (Cat. No. 37); Plate 64

St. Andrew Holding a Fish and a Book, 105 (Cat. No. L 8)

The Martyrdom of St. Andrew, 109 (Cat. No. R 19)

The Vision of St. Andrew, 109 (Cat. No. R 18)

The Death of St. Anne, 21, 22, 23, 97–8 (Cat. No. 75); Plate 150

St. Ansovinus Distributing Alms, 108 (Cat. No. R 5)

St. Anthony Abbot and St. Francis, 5, 30, 33, 51–2 (Cat. No. 8); Plate 6

St. Anthony of Padua reviving a Dead Man, 13, 15–17, 31, 70–1 (Cat. No. 35); Plates 61, 62

St. Anthony of Padua with Angels, 106 (Cat. No. L 14)

St. Bernard, 110 (Cat. No. R 28)

The Birth of the Virgin, 6, 7, 15, 22, 55–6 (Cat. No. 14); Plate 20

The Vision of St. Bonaventure, 17, 78–9 (Cat. No. 45); Plate 76

St. Catherine of Siena, 81 (Cat. No. 47); Plate 86

St. Denys the Areopagite, 60 (Cat. No. 19d)

La Divina Sapienza, 4, 6, 7, 8–13, 18, 23, 25, 57–9 (Cat. No. 17); Plates 28–31, 33

St. Francis marrying Poverty, 18–19, 24, 70 (Cat. No. 34); Plate 57

St. Francis of Sales and St. Francis of Paula, 90 (Cat. No. 62); Plate 127

St. Gregory, 109 (Cat. No. R 9)

St. Gregory and the Miracle of the Corporal, 3–4, 52 (Cat. No. 9); Plate 8

The Guardian Angel, 91 (Cat. No. 64); Plate 128

St. Helen and the Miracle of the True Cross, 16–17, 73–4 (Cat. No. 39); Plate 66

The Immaculate Conception, 100 (Cat. No. 79)

The Vision of St. Isidore the Farmer, 5, 50–1 (Cat. No. 6); Plate 4

Portrait of the Blessed Jean Dominique de la Barrière, 110 (Cat. No. R 24)

The Last Communion of St. Jerome, 106 (Cat. No. L 15)

St. John Damascene, 60 (Cat. No. 19b)

St. Leo the Great, 14, 60 (Cat. No. 19c); Plate 36

The Martyrdom of St. Longinus, 15, 16, 72–3 (Cat. No. 38); Plate 65

The Madonna and Child with Saints Ignatius of Loyola, Francis Xavier, Cosmas and Damian, 6, 7, 57 (Cat. No. 16); Plates 24, 26, Col. Plate IV

The Madonna of Loreto with St. Bartholomew, St. Joseph, St. James of Compostela and St. Francis, 1, 51 (Cat. No. 7); Plate 5

The Three Magdalenes, 13, 16, 67–9 (Cat. No. 30); Plate 55

St. Mark and St. Peter, 107 (Cat. No. L 26)

St. Paul, 106 (Cat. No. L 20)

St. Paul the Hermit and St. Anthony Abbot, 69 (Cat. No. 32); Plate 60

St. Peter (c. 1631–2), 13, 14, 15, 64–5 (Cat. No. 26); Plate 48

St. Peter (c. 1632), 13, 66 (Cat. No. 28); Plate 52

A Miracle of St. Philip Benizzi, 66–7 (Cat. No. 29); Plate 51

St. Philip Neri's Vision of St. John the Baptist, 99 (Cat. No. 77); Plate 153

The Canonization of St. Philip Neri, 110 (Cat. No. R 26)

Santa Rosalia Sinibaldi of Palermo, 69–70 (Cat. No. 33); Plate 59

The Vision of St. Romuald, 13, 14–15, 23, 25, 33, 61–2 (Cat. No. 20); Plate 41

St. Sebastian, 106 (Cat. No. L 11)

St. Teresa in Ecstasy, 50 (Cat. No. 4)

St. Thomas Aquinas with St. Peter and St. Paul, 13, 14, 60 (Cat. No. 19a); Plate 34

St. Urban with St. Chiara and St. Francis, 50 (Cat. No. 5)

Urban VIII Visiting the Gesù, 90–1 (Cat. No. 63); Plates 130, 133

Six Putti and an Angel Carrying the Attributes of five Dominican Saints, 9, 17, 79–81 (Cat. No. 46); Plate 78

A 'Virgin and Child' for the Chapel of the Palazzo Barberini at Segno, 105 (Cat. No. L 4)

The Virgin and Child with SS. Anthony, Francis, Peter and Anthony Abbot, 107 (Cat. No. L 27)

The Virgin and Child with St. Basil of Cappadocia, 82 (Cat. No. 50); Plate 88

Virgin and Child with San Biagio (?), 110 (Cat. No. R 25)

The Virgin and Child with St. Joseph, 49–50 (Cat. No. 3)

Paintings for S. Agata dei Goti, 105 (Cat. No. L 3)

Paintings for the Capuchin Fathers at Pertuis 105 (Cat. No. L 5)

c. PORTRAITS

Francesco Albani, 17, 77–8 (Cat. No. 44), 114; Plate 74

Alexander VII, 101 (Cat. No. 82)

Pope Alexander VII Carried in Procession, 109 (Cat. No. R 14)

Ludovico Aurelio, 81 (Cat. No. 48)

Cardinal Antonio Barberini the Elder, 94 (Cat. No. 67–4)

Cardinal Antonio Barberini, 93 (Cat. No. 67–2)

Don Carlo Barberini, 94 (Cat. No. 67–5)

Cardinal Francesco Barberini, 25, 93–4 (Cat. No. 67–3); Plate 137

Don Taddeo Barberini, 92–3 (Cat. No. 67–1)

Alessandro dal Borro, 108 (Cat. No. R 3)

Francesco Bracciolini, 94 (Cat. No. 69)

Giovanni Cristofano, 91–2 (Cat. No. 65)

Cardinal Angelo Giori, 92 (Cat. No. 66); Plate 135

Innocent X, 97 (Cat. No. 74)

Monsignore Clemente Merlini, 25, 65–6 (Cat. No. 27); Plate 49

Cardinal Francesco Maria del Monte, 53–4 (Cat. No. 12)

Marc' Antonio Pasqualini, 82–4 (Cat. No. 51); Plate 89

Prince Radziwill, 94 (Cat. No. 68)

Padre Niccolò Riccardi, 84 (Cat. No. 52)

Urban VIII, 59–60 (Cat. No. 18)

A Bishop, 107 (Cat. No. L 23)

A Cardinal (Museo di Roma), 110 (Cat. No. R 22)

A Cardinal (Ottawa), 25, 62–3 (Cat. No. 21); Plates 46, 47

A Cleric, 109 (Cat. No. R 20)

A Man, 108 (Cat. No. R 2)

An Officer, 25, 95 (Cat. No. 71); Plate 134

d. MISCELLANEOUS SUBJECTS

Allegory of the Four Seasons, 4, 54 (Cat. No. 13); Plate 15

Apollo and Vulcan, 106 (Cat. No. L 19)

Aurora, 94–5 (Cat. No. 70)

Bacchanals (after Dosso Dossi), 105 (Cat. No. L 6)

Bacchus and Ariadne, 106 (Cat. No. L 17)

The Blind Belisarius, 109 (Cat. No. R 15)

Cato, 106 (Cat. No. L 18)

Daedalus and Icarus, 18–19, 22, 24, 81–2 (Cat. No. 49); Plate 87

A Dog on a Cushion with a Rattle, 107 (Cat. No. L 22)

The Dying Mother of Aristides, 110 (Cat. No. R 29)

The Festa del Saraceno in Piazza Navona, 74–5 (Cat. No. 40); Plate 67

Four Pictures for Bagnaia, 104–5 (Cat. No. L 2)

Galatea (after Raphael), 49 (Cat. No. 1), 113

Head of an Old Man, 64 (Cat. No. 25); Plate 45

Head of an Old Woman, 110 (Cat. No. R 21).

Juno in her Peacock Chariot, 52–3 (Cat. No. 10); Plate 13

Landscape with Venus Resting, 109 (Cat. No. R 10)

A Lupercal, 109 (Cat. No. R 11)

The Rape of Europa (Montreal), 109 (Cat. No. R 13)

The Rape of Europa (Schleissheim), 110 (Cat. No. R 27)

Romulus among the Shepherds, 54 (Cat. No. 13); Plate 17

Sacrifice to Pan, 5, 54–5 (Cat. No. 13); Plate 19

Silver Cups Designed by Sacchi, 105 (Cat. No. L 7)

The Story of Cincinnatus, 54–5 (Cat. No. 13)

The Suicide of Dido, 18–19, 24, 69 (Cat. No. 31); Plate 58

Venus and Cupid, 97 (Cat. No. 73)

Venus with a Chariot, 105 (Cat. No. L 9)

1. *Christ crowned with Thorns*. By 1618. Madrid, Museo del Prado. (Cat. No. 2)

3. Composition study for *The Vision of St. Isidore* (Plate 4). Madrid, Biblioteca Nacional

2. Composition study for *The Vision of St. Isidore* (Plate 4). Düsseldorf, Kunstmuseum

5. *The Madonna of Loreto with St. Bartholomew, St. Joseph, St. James of Compostela and St. Francis.* 1623–4. Nettuno, S. Francesco. (Cat. No. 7)

4. *The Vision of St. Isidore the Farmer.* 1621–2. Rome, S. Isidoro. (Cat. No. 6)

6. *St. Anthony Abbot and St. Francis.* 1623–4. London, National Gallery. (Cat. No. 8)

7. Composition study for *St. Gregory and the Miracle of the Corporal* (Plate 8). Paris, École des Beaux-Arts

8. *St. Gregory and the Miracle of the Corporal.* 1625–6. Rome, Chapter House of St. Peter's. (Cat. No. 9)

9. *Allegory of the Foundation of Rome*. Windsor Castle, Royal Library
(see p. 38, note 7)

10. *Bacchanal with Midas, Silenus and Bacchus*. Composition study for a lost fresco in the Casino of Cardinal del Monte.
By 1626. London, British Museum. (Cat. No. 11)

11. Copy after lost drawing of *Mercury, Argus and Io*. Milan, Ambrosiana. (See Cat. No. 11)

12. Copy after the British Museum study (Plate 10) for the *Bacchanal* fresco formerly in the Casino of Cardinal del Monte. Milan, Ambrosiana. (Cat. No. 11)

13. *Juno in her Peacock Chariot*. Vienna, Kunsthistorisches Museum. (Cat. No. 10)

14. Studies for the figures of Spring and Summer in the *Allegory of the Four Seasons* (Plate 15). Düsseldorf, Kunstmuseum

15. *Allegory of the Four Seasons. c.* 1628. Castelfusano, Upper Gallery, Villa Chigi (ex-Sacchetti). (Cat. No. 13)

16. Composition study for the *Sacrifice to Pan* (Plate 19). Darmstadt, Hessisches Landesmuseum

17. *Romulus among the Shepherds*. *c.* 1628. Castelfusano, Upper Gallery, Villa Chigi (ex-Sacchetti). (Cat. No. 13)

18. Engraving by F. Aliamet after the *Sacrifice to Pan* formerly in the collection of the Earl of Lincoln. Düsseldorf, Kunstmuseum. (See Cat. No. 13)

19. *A Sacrifice to Pan. c.* 1628. Castelfusano, Upper Gallery, Villa Chigi (ex-Sacchetti). (Cat. No. 13)

20. *The Birth of the Virgin. c.* 1628–9. Madrid, Museo del Prado. (Cat. No. 14)

21. Composition study for a fresco of *Christ's Command to St. Peter, 'Feed my sheep!'* 1628–9. Florence, Uffizi. (Cat. No. 15)

22. Study for the figure of Christ in *Pasce Oves Meas* (see Plate 21). Düsseldorf, Kunstmuseum

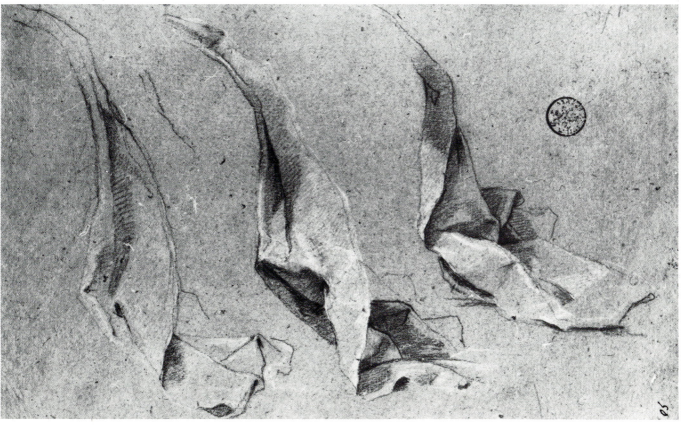

23. Study for the drapery of St. Peter in *Pasce Oves Meas* (see Plate 21). Düsseldorf, Kunstmuseum

24. *The Madonna and Child with SS. Ignatius of Loyola, Francis Xavier, Cosmas and Damian.*
(Considerably damaged.) 1629. Rome, Old Pharmacy of the Collegio Romano. (Cat. No. 16)

25. Study for the figure of St. Ignatius in the Collegio Romano fresco (Plate 24). Windsor Castle, Royal Library

26. Sketch for the Collegio Romano fresco (Plate 24).
London, Brian Sewell. (Cat. No. 16)

27. Composition study for the *Divina Sapienza* ceiling (Plate 28). New York, The Cooper-Hewitt Museum of Design

28. General view of the *Divina Sapienza* ceiling (See Plates 29–33)

29. Detail from Plate 28: Divine Wisdom, Holiness, Purity, Perspicacity

30. *La Divina Sapienza* (An Allegory of Divine Wisdom). 1629–31. Rome, Galleria Nazionale d'Arte Antica (Palazzo Barberini).
(Cat. No. 17)

31. Detail from Plate 28: Nobility, Justice, Eternity, Fortitude, Harmony, Divinity and Beneficence

32. Study for the figure of Divinity (cf. Plate 31).
Düsseldorf, Kunstmuseum

33. Detail from Plate 28: Beneficence with Harmony and Divinity behind

34. Cartoon for the mosaic pendentive of *St. Thomas Aquinas with St. Peter and St. Paul.* 1631.
Rome, Galleria Nazionale d'Arte Antica (Palazzo Barberini). (Cat. No. 19a)

35. G. B. Calandra after Sacchi: *St. Thomas Aquinas with St. Peter and St. Paul.* 1632.
Rome, St. Peter's, Cappella della Colonna. (Cat. No. 19a)

36. Cartoon for the mosaic pendentive of *St. Leo the Great*. 1638–9.
Rome, Galleria Nazionale d'Arte Antica (Palazzo Barberini). (Cat. No. 19c)

37. G. B. Calandra after Sacchi: *St. Leo the Great*. 1638–9. Rome, St. Peter's, Cappella di S. Michele Arcangelo. (Cat. No. 19c)

38. G. B. Calandra after Sacchi: *St. John Damascene*. 1634–6. Rome, St. Peter's, Cappella della Colonna. (Cat. No. 19b)

39. G. B. Calandra and assistants after Sacchi: *St. Denys the Areopagite*. 1639-47. Rome, St. Peter's, Cappella di S. Michele Arcangelo.
(Cat. No. 19d)

40. Composition study for *The Vision of St. Romuald* (Plate 41). Stockholm, National Museum

41. *The Vision of St. Romuald.* 1631. Rome, Pinacoteca Vaticana. (Cat. No. 20)

42. *Hagar and Ishmael in the Wilderness*. Cardiff, National Museum of Wales. (Cat. No. 22)

43. *Head of an Apostle with a Book.* Malaga, Museo.
(Cat. No. 24)

44. *Head of an Apostle* (Bartholomew?). Rome,
Rospigliosi-Pallavicini Collection. (Cat. No. 23)

45. *Head of an Old Man.* Dresden, Gemäldegalerie.
(Cat. No. 25)

46. *Portrait of a Cardinal* (Lelio Biscia?). *c.* 1630. Ottawa, National Gallery of Canada. (Cat. No. 21)

47. Detail from Plate 46

48. *St. Peter.* 1631–2. Forlì, Pinacoteca Comunale. (Cat. No. 26)

49. *Portrait of Monsignore Clemente Merlini.* 1631–2. Rome, Galleria Borghese. (Cat. No. 27)

50. Sketch for the *St. Peter* (Plate 52). Besançon,
Musée de Besançon

51. Tommaso Luini after Sacchi: *A Miracle of St. Philip Benizzi* 1630–2. Rome,
S. Maria in Via (Cat. No. 29)

52. *St. Peter. c.* 1632. Rome, Galleria Nazionale d'Arte Antica
(Palazzo Barberini). (Cat. No. 28)

53. Study for the head of a monk in the *Miracle of St. Philip Benizzi*
(Plate 51). Holkham Hall, Collection of the Earl of Leicester

54. Sketch for *The Three Magdalenes* (Plate 55). Rome, Galleria Nazionale d'Arte Antica (Palazzo Corsini)

55. *The Three Magdalenes.* 1632. Florence, Convent of S. Salvi (on deposit from the Uffizi). (Cat. No. 30)

56. Drapery study for a lost portrait of Urban VIII. Düsseldorf, Kunstmuseum. (Cat. No. 18)

57. *St. Francis marrying Poverty. c.* 1633. Formerly Florence,
Corsini Collection. (Cat. No. 34)

58. *The Suicide of Dido*. Caen, Musée des Beaux-Arts. (Cat. No. 31)

EGO ROSALIA
SINIBALDI

59. *Santa Rosalia Sinibaldi of Palermo. c.* 1633. Madrid, Museo del Prado. (Cat. No. 33)

60. *St. Paul the Hermit and St. Anthony Abbot. c.* 1633. Madrid, Museo del Prado. (Cat. No. 32)

61. *St. Anthony of Padua reviving a dead Man.* 1632–3. Rome, S. Maria della Concezione. (Cat. No. 35)

62. *St. Anthony of Padua reviving a dead Man*. London, Denis Mahon Collection. (See Cat. No. 35)

63. *Christ carrying the Cross, and St. Veronica.* 1633–4. Rome, Chapter House of St. Peter's. (Cat. No. 36)

64. *St. Andrew adoring the Cross of his Martyrdom.* 1633–4. Rome, Chapter House of St. Peter's. (Cat. No. 37)

65. *The Martyrdom of St. Longinus.* 1633–4. Rome, Chapter House of St. Peter's. (Cat. No. 38)

66. *St. Helen and the Miracle of the True Cross.* 1634–50. Rome, Chapter House of St. Peter's. (Cat. No. 39)

67. *The 'Festa del Saraceno' in Piazza Navona, February 25, 1634. 1634–5.* Rome, Museo di Roma. (Cat. No. 40)

68. Frederic Hortemels after Sacchi: *Adam grieving over the dead Abel*. London, British Museum. (See Cat. No. 41)

69. Studio of Sacchi: *Adam grieving over the dead Abel*. Minneapolis, Institute of Arts. (Cat. No. 41)

70. F. Pilsen after Sacchi: *The Adoration of the Shepherds*.
Düsseldorf, Kunstmuseum. (See Cat. No. 42)

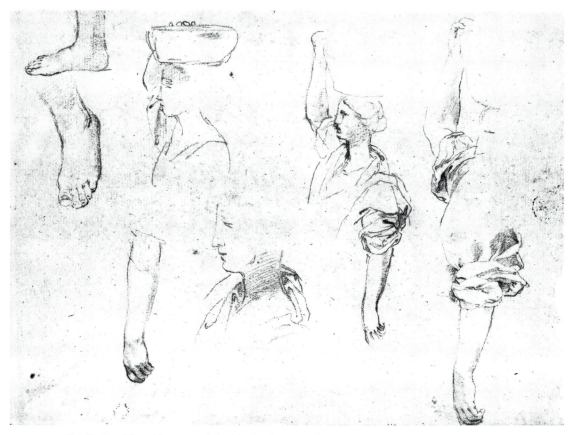

71. Study for *The Adoration of the Shepherds*. Düsseldorf, Kunstmuseum. (See Cat. No. 42)

72. Studies for the left soldier in the lost *Christ crowned with Thorns*, formerly in the Quirinale Palace. Florence, Uffizi. (See Cat. No. 43)

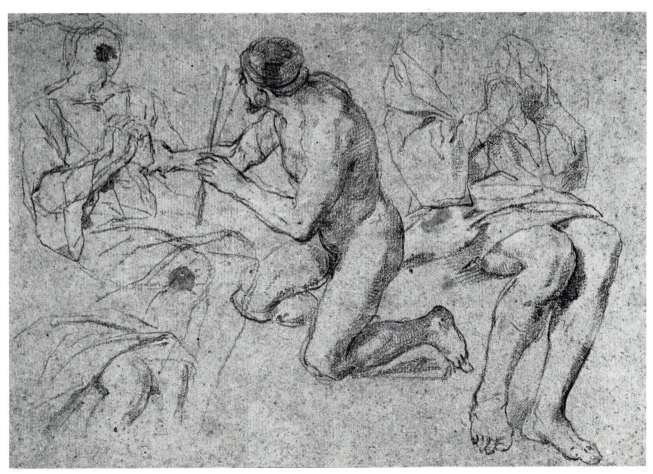

73. Studies for the figure of Christ and the right soldier in the lost *Christ crowned with Thorns*, formerly in the Quirinale Palace. 1635. London, British Museum. (See Cat. No. 43)

622.

74. *Portrait of Francesco Albani* (1578–1660). 1635. Madrid, Museo del Prado. (Cat. No. 44)

75. Detail from Plate 77: St. Dominic and St. Thomas Aquinas

76. *The Vision of St. Bonaventure.* 1635–6. Rome, S. Maria della Concezione. (Cat. No. 45)

77. *Christ crucified with St. Dominic, St. Thomas Aquinas, St. Peter Martyr, an unidentified Dominican saint and St. Catherine of Siena.* 1637–8. Rome, Sacristy of S. Maria sopra Minerva. (Cat. No. 46)

78. Six putti and an Angel carrying the Attributes of five Dominican Saints. 1637–8. Frescoed vault in the altar recess of the sacristy. Rome, S. Maria sopra Minerva. (Cat. No. 46)

CARDINALIS·ANTONIVS·BARBERINVS
ORDINIS·PRAEDICATORVM·PROTECTOR
OB·SINGVLAREM
IN·SANCTAM·CATHARINAM·VIRGINEM
SENENSEM·EIVSDEM·ORDINIS
PIETATEM
CVBICVLVM
VBI·SERAPHICA·VIRGO
SPONSVM·NVNQVAM·OCCIDENTEM·SOLEM·EXCEPIT
VNDE
AD·SEMPER·ORIENTIS·THALAMVM·EVOLAVIT
AB·ANTIQVIS·AEDIBVS·SEIVNXIT
ET·IN·HOC·SACRARIO·AD·MAIOREM·EIVS·CVLTVM
COLLOCAVIT
ANNO·DOMINI·MDCXXXVII

79. Inscription behind the altar wall of the sacristy. Rome, S. Maria sopra Minerva

80. The Sacristy of S. Maria sopra Minerva, Rome

81. The Chapel of St. Catherine of Siena. 1637–9. Rome, Sacristy of S. Maria sopra Minerva. (Cat. No. 46)

82. Cupboards in the altar recess of the sacristy.
Rome, S. Maria sopra Minerva

83. Cornice on the exterior of the Chapel of St. Catherine of Siena.
Rome, S. Maria sopra Minerva

84. Frieze on the exterior of the Chapel of St. Catherine of Siena. Rome, S. Maria sopra Minerva

85. *Portrait of a Monk* (Padre Niccolò Riccardi?).
Düsseldorf, Kunstmuseum. (See Cat. No. 52)

86. *St. Catherine of Siena in Prayer. c.* 1637–9. London, Dulwich College Picture Gallery. (Cat. No. 47)

87. *Daedalus and Icarus*. Genoa, Galleria di Palazzo Rosso. (Cat. No. 49)

88. *The Virgin and Child with St. Basil of Cappadocia.* Rome, Casa del Vescovo, S. Maria del Priorato. (Cat. No. 50)

89. *Portrait of the Singer Marc' Antonio Pasqualini*. 1636–40. Althorp House, Northamptonshire,
Collection of Earl Spencer. (Cat. No. 51)

90. The interior of S. Giovanni in Fonte, Rome. (Cat. No. 53)

91. The interior of S. Giovanni in Fonte, Rome

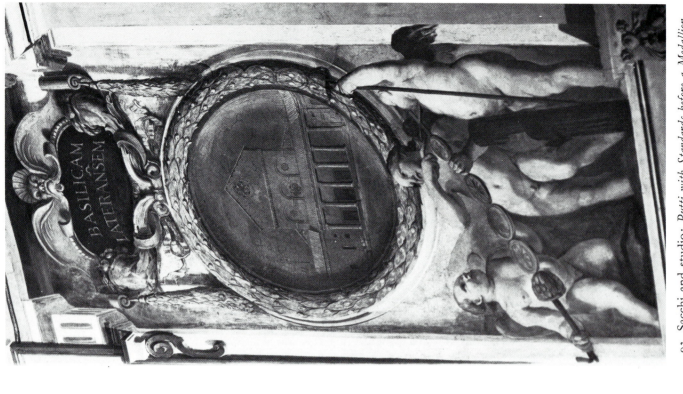

93. Sacchi and studio: *Putti with Standards before a Medallion depicting St. John Lateran.* By 1647. Rome, S. Giovanni in Fonte. (Cat. No. 53.2)

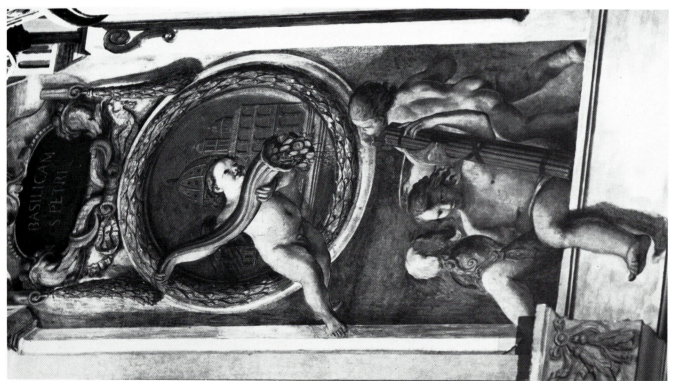

92. Sacchi and studio: *Putti holding a Cornucopia, a Dish, a Helmet and Fasces before a Medallion depicting St. Peter's.* By 1647. Rome, S. Giovanni in Fonte. (Cat. No. 53.2)

94. Giacinto Gimignani: *Constantine's Vision before the Battle of the Milvian Bridge.* Rome, S. Giovanni in Fonte. (Cat. No. 53.2)

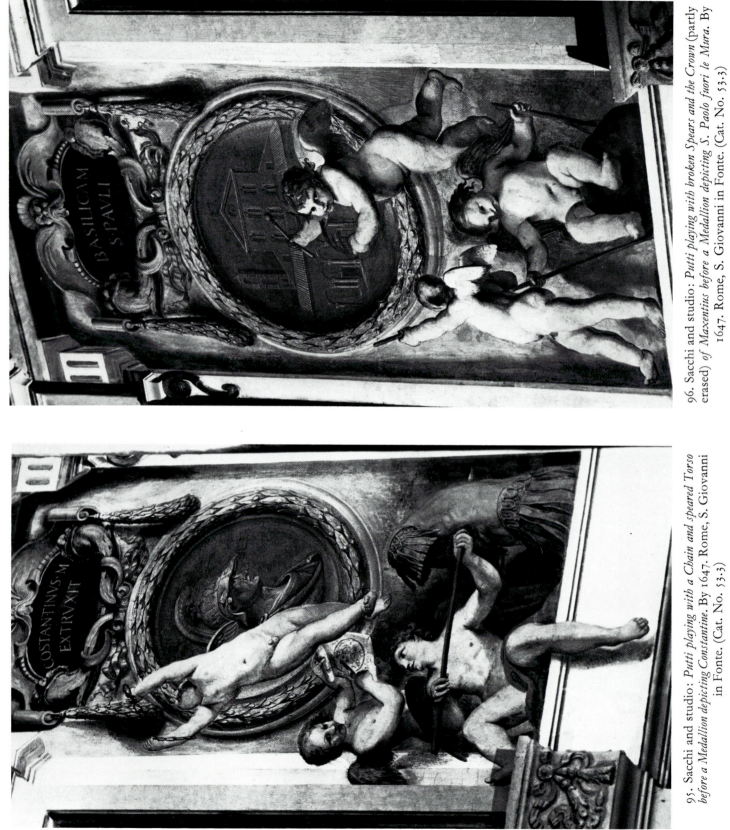

96. Sacchi and studio: *Putti playing with broken Spears and the Crown (partly erased) of Maxentius before a Medallion depicting S. Paolo fuori le Mura.* By 1647. Rome, S. Giovanni in Fonte. (Cat. No. 53.3)

95. Sacchi and studio: *Putti playing with a Chain and speared Torso before a Medallion depicting Constantine.* By 1647. Rome, S. Giovanni in Fonte. (Cat. No. 53.3)

97. Andrea Camassei: *Constantine defeating Maxentius at the Battle of the Milvian Bridge. c.* 1644. Rome, S. Giovanni in Fonte. (Cat. No. 53:3)

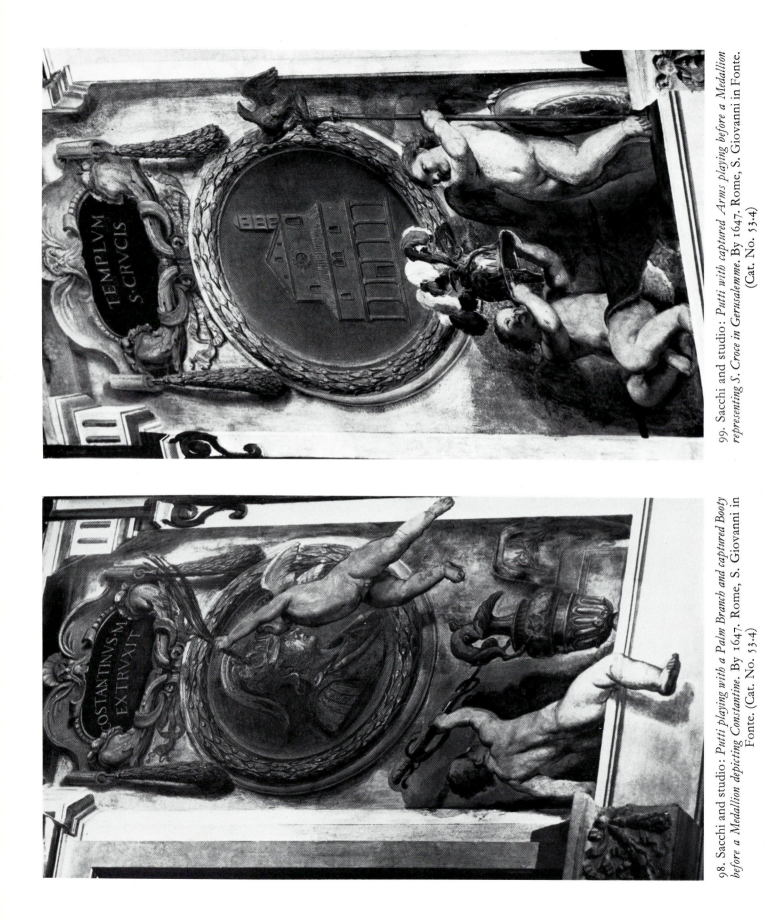

99. Sacchi and studio: *Putti with captured Arms playing before a Medallion representing S. Croce in Gerusalemme*. By 1647. Rome, S. Giovanni in Fonte. (Cat. No. 53·4)

98. Sacchi and studio: *Putti playing with a Palm Branch and captured Booty before a Medallion depicting Constantine*. By 1647. Rome, S. Giovanni in Fonte. (Cat. No. 53·4)

100. Andrea Camassei: *Constantine's triumphal Entry into Rome after the Defeat of Maxentius*. 1646–8. Rome, S. Giovanni in Fonte. (Cat. No. 53.4)

101. Sacchi and studio: *Medallion representing Pope Urban VIII.* By 1647. Rome, S. Giovanni in Fonte.
(Cat. No. 53.5)

102. Sacchi and studio: *Urban VIII receiving Plans for the Restoration of S. Giovanni in Fonte from three Men (Bernini, Sacchi and B. Castelli?)*. By 1647. Rome, S. Giovanni in Fonte. (Cat. No. 53.5)

103. Carlo Maratta: *The Emperor Constantine*. By 1648. Rome, S. Giovanni in Fonte. (Cat. No. 53.1)

104. Carlo Maratta: *Pope Silvester I*. By 1648. Rome, S. Giovanni in Fonte.
(Cat. No. 53.1)

105. Carlo Maratta: *St. John the Baptist*. By 1648. Rome, S. Giovanni in Fonte. (Cat. No. 53.5)

106. Carlo Maratta: *St. John the Evangelist*. By 1648. Rome, S. Giovanni in Fonte.
(Cat. No. 53.5)

107. Sacchi and studio: *Putti playing with the Tools of the Painters'
and Architects' Professions before a Medallion representing Urban
VIII*. By 1647. Rome, S. Giovanni in Fonte. (Cat. No. 53.6)

108. Sacchi and studio: *Putti playing with Architects' Tools before
a Medallion representing the Lateran Baptistery*. By 1647. Rome,
S. Giovanni in Fonte. (Cat. No. 53.6)

109. Carlo Maratta: *Allegory in Honour of Innocent X Pamphili*. 1648. Rome, S. Giovanni in Fonte. (Cat. No. 53.6)

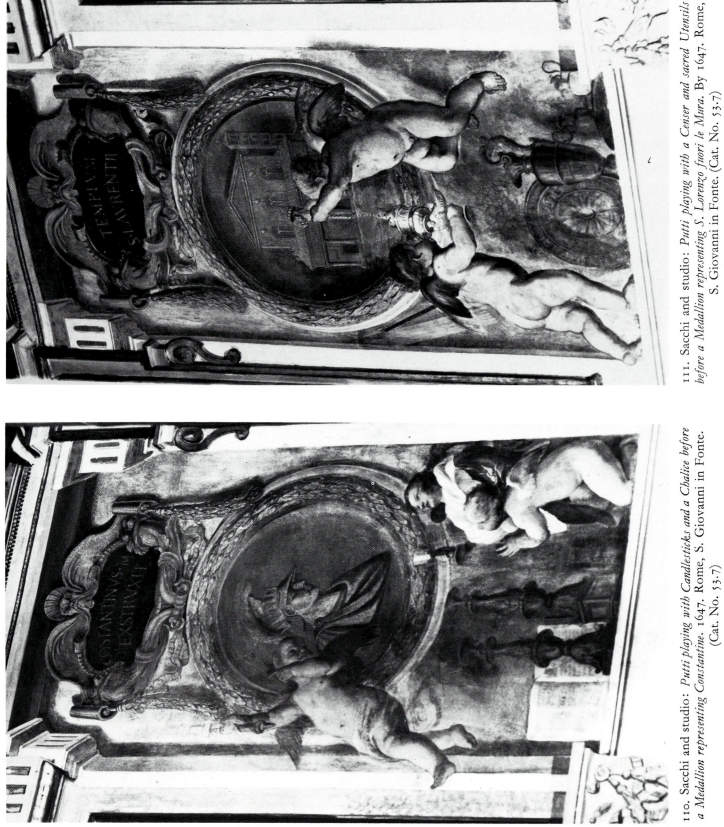

111. Sacchi and studio: *Putti playing with a Censer and sacred Utensils before a Medallion representing S. Lorenzo fuori le Mura.* By 1647. Rome, S. Giovanni in Fonte. (Cat. No. 53·7)

110. Sacchi and studio: *Putti playing with Candlesticks and a Chalice before a Medallion representing Constantine.* 1647. Rome, S. Giovanni in Fonte. (Cat. No. 53·7)

112. Carlo Maratta after Sacchi: *Constantine establishing the Christian Religion and ordering the Destruction of Pagan Idols.* By 1648. Rome, S. Giovanni in Fonte. (Cat. No. 53.7)

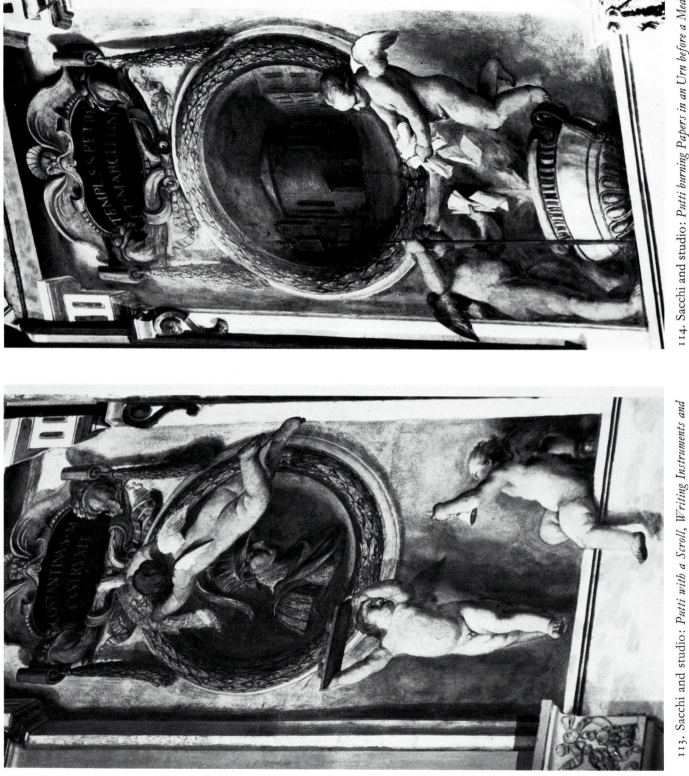

114. Sacchi and studio: *Putti burning Papers in an Urn before a Medallion representing SS. Pietro e Marcellino. 1647. Rome, S. Giovanni in Fonte.* (Cat. No. 53.8)

113. Sacchi and studio: *Putti with a Scroll, Writing Instruments and a Bell playing before a Medallion representing Constantine.* By 1647. Rome, S. Giovanni in Fonte. (Cat. No. 53.8)

115. Carlo Magnone after Sacchi: *The Destruction of Pagan Writings at the Nicene Council*. By 1648. Rome, S. Giovanni in Fonte. (Cat. No. 53.8)

116. *The Annunciation to Zacharias*. 1641–9. Rome, Lateran Palace. (Cat. No. 54)

117. *The Visitation.* 1646–7. Rome, Lateran Palace. (Cat. No. 55)

118. *The Birth of the Baptist*. 1648–9. Rome, Lateran Palace. (Cat. No. 56)

119. *The Naming of the Baptist.* 1641–9. Rome, Lateran Palace. (Cat. No. 57)

120. *The Blessing of the Baptist before his Departure to the Wilderness.* 1641–9. Rome, Lateran Palace. (Cat. No. 58)

121. *The Baptism of Christ*. 1641–4. Rome, Lateran Palace. (Cat. No. 59)

122. *The Preaching of the Baptist*. 1641–9. Rome, Lateran Palace. (Cat. No. 60)

123. *The Beheading of the Baptist.* 1641–9. Rome, Lateran Palace. (Cat. No. 61)

124. Studies for Elizabeth and Zacharias in *The Blessing of the Baptist* (Plate 120). Düsseldorf, Kunstmuseum

125. Studies for the head of Zacharias in *The Birth of the Baptist* (Plate 118). Copenhagen, Royal Museum

126. Rejected composition study for *The Naming of the Baptist*. Berlin–Dahlem, Staatliche Museen. (See Cat. No. 57)

127. *St. Francis of Sales and St. Francis of Paula. c.* 1640. Camerino, S. Maria in Via. (Cat. No. 62)

128. *The Guardian Angel*. Rieti, Duomo. (Cat. No. 64)

129. Engraving by G. B. Iacoboni after Sacchi's
Guardian Angel. (See Cat. No. 64)

130. *Urban VIII visiting the Gesù on October 2, 1639, during the Centenary Celebrations of the Jesuit Order.* 1641–2.
Rome, Galleria Nazionale d'Arte Antica (Palazzo Barberini). (Cat. No. 63)

131. Study for the engraved Portrait of Cardinal Francesco Barberini in Teti's *Aedes Barberinae*. Berlin–Dahlem, Staatliche Museen. (See Cat. No. 67.3)

132. C. Bloemaert after Sacchi: *Cardinal Francesco Barberini*, from Teti, *Aedes Barberinae ad Quirinalem*, Rome, 1642. (Cat. No. 67.3)

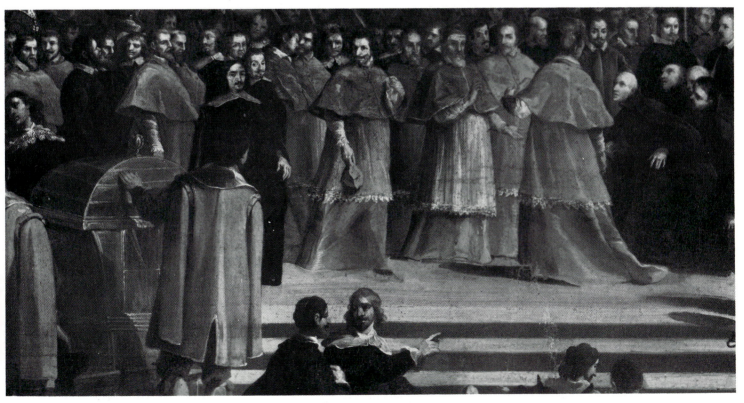

133. Detail from Plate 130

134. *Portrait of an Officer. c.* 1640. East Berlin,
Staatliche Museen. (Cat. No. 71)

135. *Portrait of Cardinal Angelo Giori. c.* 1643. Present location
unknown. (Cat. No. 66)

136. Study for the Portrait of Cardinal Francesco Barberini.
Düsseldorf, Kunstmuseum. (See Cat. No. 67.3)

137. *Portrait of Cardinal Francesco Barberini*. Cologne, Wallraf-Richartz Museum
(on loan from the West German Republic). (Cat. No. 67.3)

138. Study for the Portrait of Cardinal Antonio Barberini. Düsseldorf, Kunstmuseum. (See Cat. No. 67.2)

139. C. Bloemaert after Sacchi: *Cardinal Antonio Barberini*, from Teti, *Aedes Barberinae . . .*, Rome, 1642. (See Cat. No. 67.2)

140. C. Bloemaert after Sacchi: *Cardinal Antonio Barberini the Elder*, from Teti, *Aedes Barberinae . . .*, Rome, 1642. (See Cat. No. 67.4)

141. C. Bloemaert after Sacchi: *Don Taddeo Barberini*, from Teti, *Aedes Barberinae . . .*, Rome, 1642. (See Cat. No. 67.1)

142. Studies for the lost *Aurora*. Windsor Castle, Royal Library. (See Cat. No. 70)

143. Copy after the lost *Aurora*. Present location unknown. (See Cat. No. 70)

144. Studies for Noah and Ham in *The Drunkenness of Noah*. Windsor Castle, Royal Library. (Cat. No. 72)

145. *The Drunkenness of Noah*. East Berlin, Staatliche Museen (photograph taken before 1940). (Cat. No. 72)

146. Studio of Sacchi: *The Drunkenness of Noah*. Vienna, Kunsthistorisches Museum. (Cat. No. 72)

147. *The Drunkenness of Noah*. 1644–8. Catanzaro, Museo Provinciale. (Cat. No. 72)

148. Studies for Joachim in *The Death of St. Anne* (Plate 150). Copenhagen, Royal Museum

149. Studies for the drapery of Joachim in *The Death of St. Anne* (Plate 150). Düsseldorf, Kunstmuseum

150. *The Death of St. Anne.* 1648–9. Rome, S. Carlo ai Catinari. (Cat. No. 75)

151. Detail from *The Death of St. Anne* (Plate 150)

152. *St. John the Baptist in the Wilderness. c.* 1650.
Fabriano, S. Niccolò. (Cat. No. 76)

153. *St. Philip Neri's Vision of St. John the Baptist.*
c. 1650. Destroyed; formerly Oratory of St. Philip
Neri, S. Maria della Vittoria, Valletta. (Cat. No. 77)

154. *The Presentation of Christ in the Temple.* 1651. Perugia,
Galleria Nazionale dell' Umbria. (Cat. No. 78)

155. Composition study for *The Presentation of Christ in
the Temple* (Plate 154). Paris, Louvre

156. Arnold van Westerhout after Sacchi: *The Dream of St. Joseph*. London, British Museum. (See Cat. No. 80)

157. *The Dream of St. Joseph*. 1652. Rome, S. Giuseppe a Capo le Case. (Cat. No. 80)

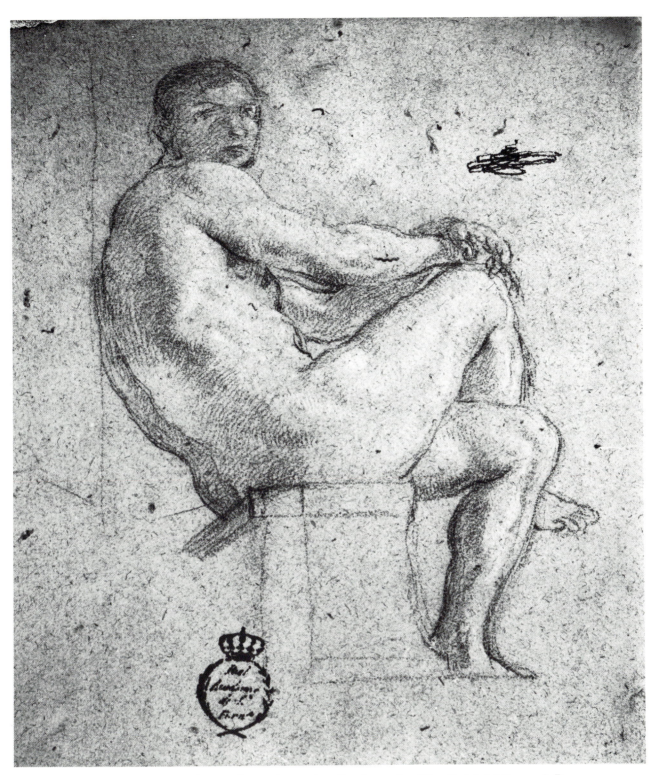

158. Study for an ignudo in a decorative project for the vault of San Luigi dei Francesi, Rome. Madrid, Academia de San Fernando. (See Cat. No. 81)

159–161. Three studies for figures in a decorative project for the vault of San Luigi dei Francesi, Rome. Windsor Castle, Royal Library. (See Cat. No. 81)

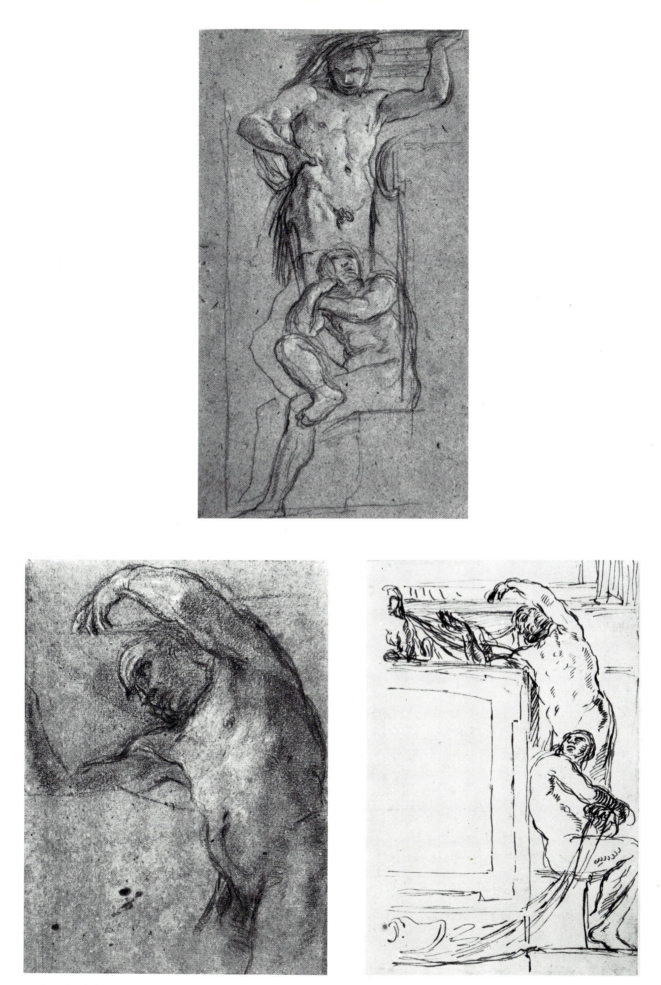

162–164. Three studies for an ignudo in a decorative project for the vault of San Luigi dei Francesi, Rome. Windsor Castle, Royal Library. (See Cat. No. 81)

166. C. Bloemaert after Sacchi: *Limax and Brucas transformed by Flora*, from G. B. Ferrari's *Flora seu de Florum Cultura*, Rome, 1633. (Cat. No. 83)

165. Study for *Limax and Brucas transformed by Flora*. London, British Museum. (Cat. No. 83)

167. C. Audran after Sacchi: *An Allegory on the Birth of Urban VIII.* Paris, Bibliothèque Nationale. (Cat. No. 84)

168. Composition study for the print of *Romulus decorating the Sacred Oak* (Plate 171). London, Courtauld Institute, Witt Collection.

169. Study for two figures on the right in Plate 171. New York, Metropolitan Museum of Art

170. Study for the left half of the print in Plate 171. Paris, Louvre

171. C. Audran after Sacchi: *Romulus decorating the Sacred Oak Tree on the Capitol.*
Paris, Bibliothèque Nationale. (Cat. No. 85)

172. C. Bloemaert after Sacchi: *Harmonillus transformed into a Lime Tree,*
from G. B. Ferrari, *Hesperides sive de malorum aureorum cultura et usu*, Rome, 1646. (Cat. No. 86)

174. C. Bloemaert after Sacchi: *An Allegory of the Catholic Church Triumphant over Heresy*, from G. Bentivoglio, *Historia di Fiandra*, Venice, 1645. (Cat. No. 87)

Aut. Sacchi Rom. pin:
C. Bloemaert sculp:

HISTORIA
DI FIANDRA
DEL
CARDINAL
BENTIVOGLIO

173. Composition study for *An Allegory of the Catholic Church Triumphant over Heresy* (Plate 174). 1645. Leningrad, State Hermitage Museum

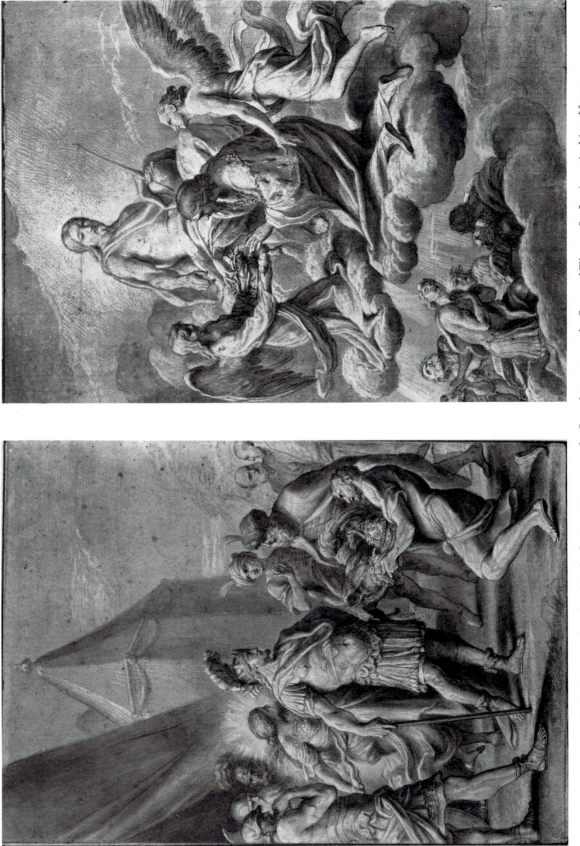

175–176. Carlo Maratta after Sacchi: *St. Louis setting out on the Crusade to capture the Crown of Thorns; St. Louis received into Heaven.* Vienna, Albertina. (Cat. No. 88)

177. G. Chasteau after Sacchi: *Lisamante slaying Meledin, the Saracen Leader*. Düsseldorf, Kunstmuseum. (Cat. No. 88)

178–179. G. Audran after Sacchi: *The shipwrecked Alphone rescues Lisamante from a Panther; Archambaut slays the Dragon.* Paris, Bibliothèque Nationale. (Cat. No. 88)